A Companion to the French Revolution

WILEY-BLACKWELL COMPANIONS TO HISTORY

This series provides sophisticated and authoritative overviews of the scholarship that has shaped our current understanding of the past. Defined by theme, period, and/or region, each volume comprises between twenty-five and forty concise essays written by individual scholars within their area of specialization. The aim of each contribution is to synthesize the current state of scholarship from a variety of historical perspectives and to provide a statement on where the field is heading. The essays are written in a clear, provocative, and lively manner, designed for an international audience of scholars, students, and general readers.

WILEY BLACKWELL COMPANIONS TO BRITISH HISTORY

A Companion to Roman Britain
Edited by Malcolm Todd

A Companion to Britain in the Later Middle Ages
Edited by S. H. Rigby

A Companion to Tudor Britain
Edited by Robert Tittler and Norman Jones

A Companion to Stuart Britain
Edited by Barry Coward

A Companion to Eighteenth-Century Britain
Edited by H. T. Dickinson

A Companion to Nineteenth-Century Britain
Edited by Chris Williams

A Companion to Early Twentieth-Century Britain
Edited by Chris Wrigley

A Companion to Contemporary Britain
Edited by Paul Addison and Harriet Jones

A Companion to the Early Middle Ages: Britain and Ireland c.500-c.1100
Edited by Pauline Stafford

WILEY BLACKWELL COMPANIONS TO EUROPEAN HISTORY

A Companion to Europe 1900–1945
Edited by Gordon Martel

A Companion to Eighteenth-Century Europe
Edited by Peter H. Wilson

A Companion to Nineteenth-Century Europe
Edited by Stefan Berger

A Companion to the Worlds of the Renaissance
Edited by Guido Ruggiero

A Companion to the Reformation World
Edited by R. Po-chia Hsia

A Companion to Europe Since 1945
Edited by Klaus Larres

A Companion to the Medieval World
Edited by Carol Lansing and Edward D. English

A Companion to the French Revolution
Edited by Peter McPhee

A Companion to Mediterranean History
Edited by Peregrine Horden and Sharon Kinoshita

WILEY BLACKWELL COMPANIONS TO WORLD HISTORY

A Companion to Western Historical Thought
Edited by Lloyd Kramer and Sarah Maza

A Companion to Gender History
Edited by Teresa A. Meade and Merry E. Wiesner-Hanks

A Companion to the History of the Middle East
Edited by Youssef M. Choueiri

A Companion to Japanese History
Edited by William M. Tsutsui

A Companion to International History 1900–2001
Edited by Gordon Martel

A Companion to Latin American History
Edited by Thomas Holloway

A Companion to Russian History
Edited by Abbott Gleason

A Companion to World War I
Edited by John Horne

A Companion to Mexican History and Culture
Edited by William H. Beezley

A Companion to World History
Edited by Douglas Northrop

A Companion to Global Environmental History
Edited by J. R. McNeill and Erin Stewart Mauldin

A Companion to World War II
Edited by Thomas W. Zeiler, with Daniel M. DuBois

A Companion to Global Historical Thought
Edited by Prasenjit Duara, Viren Murthy, and Andrew Sartori

A COMPANION TO THE FRENCH REVOLUTION

Edited by

Peter McPhee

WILEY Blackwell

This paperback edition first published 2015

Edition history: Blackwell Publishing Ltd (Hardback, 2013)

Registered Office
John Wiley & Sons, Ltd, The Atrium, Southern Gate, Chichester, West Sussex, PO19 8SQ, UK

Editorial Offices
350 Main Street, Malden, MA 02148-5020, USA
9600 Garsington Road, Oxford, OX4 2DQ, UK
The Atrium, Southern Gate, Chichester, West Sussex, PO19 8SQ, UK

For details of our global editorial offices, for customer services, and for information about how to apply for permission to reuse the copyright material in this book please see our website at www.wiley.com/wiley-blackwell.

Library of Congress Cataloging-in-Publication Data

A companion to the French Revolution / edited by Peter McPhee.
p. cm.
Includes bibliographical references and index.
ISBN 978-1-4443-3564-4 (cloth) ISBN 978-1-118-97752-1 (pbk.)
1. France–History–Revolution, 1789–1799–Historiography. 2. France–History–Revolution, 1789–1799. I. McPhee, Peter, 1948–
DC147.8.C75 2013
944.04–dc23

2012022352

A catalogue record for this book is available from the British Library.

Cover image: Paul Delaroche, *The Conquerors of the Bastille before the Hotel de Ville in 1789*, 1839 (oil on canvas). Musée de la Ville de Paris, Musée du Petit-Palais, France/ The Bridgeman Art Library

Set in 10/12pt Galliard by SPi Publisher Services, Pondicherry, India

1 2015

For Lynn Hunt

whose innovative research and generous scholarship pervade this collection

Contents

Notes on Contributors

Serge Aberdam is a researcher with the National Institute for Agronomic Research (INRA), Department of Social Sciences. He completed his doctoral thesis in 2001 under Michel Vovelle on "The Widening of the Right to Vote 1792–95," for which the statistical material is available online through the Société des Études Robespierristes. He has published on many aspects of popular participation in the French Revolution.

David Andress is Professor of Modern History at the University of Portsmouth, UK. His specialized research has focused on the history of Paris in the period 1789–91, and more recently on the place of melodramatic sentimentality in revolutionary language and perceptions. He has also written extensively on the wider history of the period, most notably *The Terror: Civil War in the French Revolution* (2004), and *1789: The Threshold of the Modern Age* (2008).

Howard G. Brown (D.Phil., Oxford) is Professor of History at Binghamton University (State University of New York). He has published several books, most notably *Ending the French Revolution: Violence, Justice, and Repression from the Terror to Napoleon* (2006), which received the Leo Gershoy Award from the American Historical Association.

Peter Campbell is Professor of Modern History in the Institute of Cultural Studies (IEC) at the University of Versailles Saint-Quentin. He has published widely on Louis XIV, the early modern state, the court, the Parlement of Paris, the political culture of the *ancien régime*, patriotic ideology and politics, and the origins of the Revolution.

Stephen Clay is a "Maître de Conférences" at Sciences Po, Paris. His research focuses on political conflict and violence during the French Revolution and Napoleonic periods, chiefly in the Midi, about which he has published numerous articles. He is the author of a forthcoming book on this subject, and is also the general editor of an international dictionary of the French Revolution to be published by Armand Colin.

Ian Coller is Lecturer in European History at La Trobe University in Melbourne, Australia. He is the author of *Arab France: Islam and the Making of Modern Europe, 1798–1831* (2011) and is currently working on a history of extraterritorial European spaces in the eighteenth-century Muslim world.

Suzanne Desan is Vilas Distinguished Professor of History at the University of Wisconsin-Madison. Her current research focuses on foreigners and international influences in revolutionary France. She is author of *Reclaiming the Sacred: Lay Religion and Popular Politics in Revolutionary France* (1990) and *The Family on Trial in Revolutionary France* (2004).

Pascal Dupuy is "Maître de Conférences" in Modern History at the University of Rouen. He teaches the history of the French Revolution and its memory using imagery, both fixed and moving, which he has made the object of his major studies. He has published several books, including *Caricatures anglaises: Face à la Révolution et l'Empire (1789–1815)* (2008); and *La Révolution française* (with Claude Mazauric, 2005).

Michael P. Fitzsimmons is Professor of History at Auburn University Montgomery. He is the author of *The Parisian Order of Barristers and the French Revolution* (1987), *The Remaking of France* (1994), *The Night the Old Regime Ended* (2003), and *From Artisan to Worker* (2010), as well as articles in various journals.

Alan Forrest is Professor of Modern History at the University of York. He has published widely on the history of the French Revolution and Napoleonic Empire, and on the history of modern warfare. Recent books include *The Legacy of the French Revolutionary Wars: The Nation-in-Arms in French Republican Memory* (2009) and *Napoleon* (2011).

Jean-Pierre Jessenne is Emeritus Professor at the University of Lille 3. He is a member of the Conseil d'Administration of the Société des Études Robespierristes. Among his recent publications are *Les Campagnes françaises entre mythe et histoire (XVIIIe–XXIe s.)* (2006); *Vers un ordre bourgeois? Révolution française et changement social* (edited, 2007); and "Une Révolution sans ou contre les paysans?", in Michel Biard (ed.), *La Révolution française, une histoire toujours vivante* (2009).

Peter M. Jones has written extensively on the French Revolution. He is Professor of French History in the University of Birmingham, UK. Among his books are *The French Revolution, 1787–1804* (revised edition, 2009); *Liberty and Locality in Revolutionary France, 1760–1820: Six Villages Compared, 1760–1820* (2003); and *Reform and Revolution in France: the Politics of Transition, 1774–1791* (1995).

Thomas E. Kaiser is Professor of History at the University of Arkansas at Little Rock. Author of more than twenty-five articles and book chapters on the *ancien régime* and the French Revolution, he is also co-author of *Europe, 1648–1815: From the Old Regime to the Age of Revolution* (2004), and co-editor of *Conspiracy in the French Revolution* (2007) and *From Deficit to Deluge: The Origins of the French Revolution* (2011). His current research project is a monograph entitled "Marie-Antoinette and the Austrian Plot, 1748–1794."

Marisa Linton is Reader in History at Kingston University, London. She is the author of *The Politics of Virtue in Enlightenment France* (2001) and a co-editor of *Conspiracy in the French Revolution* (2007). Other writings include the political ideas of Robespierre, friendship in Jacobin politics, Saint-Just and antiquity, and the intellectual origins of the French Revolution.

James Livesey works on the cultural history of the eighteenth-century Atlantic with an emphasis on the British Isles and France. Among his books, *Making Democracy in the French Revolution* (2001) established his position in the historiography of the French Revolution. A current project is on the origins of social change in the Languedoc, a new approach toward synthesizing European history.

Peter McPhee was appointed to a Personal Chair at the University of Melbourne in 1993 and was the university's provost in 2007–9. He has published widely on the history of modern France, most recently *Living the French Revolution* (2006) and *Robespierre: A Revolutionary Life* (2012). He is a Fellow of both the Australian Academy of the Humanities and the Academy of Social Sciences.

Jean-Clément Martin is Emeritus Professor at Paris-1 Panthéon-Sorbonne University, and former director of the Institut d'Histoire de la Révolution Française. He wrote his "Thèse d'État" on the War of the Vendée and its memory (Paris IV, 1989). His recent publications are *Violence et Révolution* (2006); *La Révolte brisée* (2008); *La Machine à fantasme* (2012); and the editing of *Dictionnaire de la Contre-Révolution* (2011).

Laura Mason is Senior Lecturer in History at Johns Hopkins University. The author of *Singing the French Revolution: Popular Culture and Politics* (1996) and co-author of *The French Revolution: A Document Collection* (1998), she is completing a book about the conspiracy trial of Gracchus Babeuf and the politics of the Directory.

Sarah Maza, Northwestern University, is a specialist in the social and cultural history of France from the eighteenth to the twentieth centuries. Her books include *Private Lives and Public Affairs: The Causes Célèbres of Pre-Revolutionary France* (1993); *The Myth of the French Bourgeoisie: An Essay on the Social Imaginary, 1750–1850* (2003); and *Violette Nozière: A Story of Murder in 1930s Paris* (2011).

Noelle Plack is Reader in French History at Newman University College, Birmingham. Her research interests concern the rural dimensions of the French Revolution as well as the social history of wine and drinking in Revolutionary and Napoleonic France. In addition to numerous articles and chapters, she is the author of *Common Land, Wine and the French Revolution* (2009).

Mike Rapport teaches European history at the University of Stirling in Scotland. Among his books are *Nationality and Citizenship in Revolutionary France: The Treatment of Foreigners, 1789–1799* (2000) and *Nineteenth-Century Europe, 1789–1914* (2005). His most recent book is *1848: Year of Revolution* (2008), but he remains mostly obsessed with the French Revolution and its wider impact.

Frédéric Régent is "Maître de Conférences" in Modern History at the University of Paris 1-Panthéon-Sorbonne in the Institut d'Histoire de la Révolution Française.

He is the author of *Esclavage, métissage, liberté: La Révolution française en Guadeloupe (1789–1802)* (2004) and *La France et ses esclaves, de la colonisation aux abolitions (1620–1848)* (2007).

Barry M. Shapiro is Professor of History at Allegheny College, Meadville, Pennsylvania. He is the author of *Revolutionary Justice in Paris, 1789–1790* (1993) and *Traumatic Politics: The Deputies and the King in the Early French Revolution* (2009), and of several articles on psychohistory, revolutionary justice, and early revolutionary politics. He is currently working on a study of the negotiation process that led to the end of apartheid in South Africa.

Miranda Spieler is an Associate Professor in the History Department at the University of Arizona. Her research focuses on the relationship between law and violence in France and the colonies during the eighteenth and nineteenth centuries. She is the author of *Empire and Underworld: Captivity in French Guiana* (2012).

Donald Sutherland studied at the University of Sussex and the University of London. He has taught in the United Kingdom, Canada, and, since 1986, at the University of Maryland. Among his published work is *The French Revolution and Empire: The Quest for a Civic Order* (2003). His latest book is *Murder in Aubagne: Lynching, Law and Justice in the French Revolution* (2009).

Dale Van Kley, Professor of Early Modern European History, Ohio State University, has published and edited several books and many articles. Among the books are *The Religious Origins of the French Revolution: From Calvin to the Civil Constitution of the Clergy, 1560–1791* (1996) and, with Tom Kaiser, *From Deficit to Deluge: The Origins of the French Revolution* (2011). Among his edited volumes is *The French Idea of Freedom: The Old Regime and the Declaration of Rights of 1789* (1994).

Anne Verjus has been a researcher at the Centre National de Recherches Scientifiques since 1998. She is currently working at the "Laboratoire Triangle" of the University of Lyon. She has published many books and articles on citizenship during the revolutionary period as well as a book, in collaboration with Denise Z. Davidson, on conjugal correspondence, *Le Roman conjugal: Chroniques de la vie familiale à l'époque de la Révolution et de l'Empire* (2011).

Edward J. Woell is an Associate Professor of History at Western Illinois University in Macomb and the author of *Small-Town Martyrs and Murderers: Religious Revolution and Counterrevolution in Western France, 1774–1914* (2006). Currently he is researching religion in the small towns of eight regions during the French Revolution.

Isser Woloch is the Moore Collegiate Professor of History Emeritus at Columbia University. His books include *The New Regime: Transformations of the French Civic Order, 1789–1820s* (1994); *Napoleon and his Collaborators: The Making of a Dictatorship* (2001); and, with Gregory S. Brown, *Eighteenth-Century Europe: Tradition and Progress, 1715–1789* (2nd edition, 2012).

Abbreviations

AHR	*American Historical Review*
AHRF	*Annales Historiques de la Révolution Française* (*AHRF* changed from volumes to individual issue numbers in 1977)
Annales	*Annales. Histoire, Sciences Sociales*
CNRS	Centre National de Recherches Scientifiques
CTHS	Comité des Travaux Historiques et Scientifiques
ÉHÉSS	École des Hautes Études en Sciences Sociales
EHR	*English Historical Review*
FH	*French History*
FHS	*French Historical Studies*
HJ	*Historical Journal*
JMH	*Journal of Modern History*
JSH	*Journal of Social History*
P&P	*Past and Present*
PUF	Presses Universitaires de France
RÉ	*Revue Économique*
RF	*Révolution Française*
RHMC	*Revue d'Histoire Moderne et Contemporaine*
SÉR	Société des Études Robespierristes

Introduction

Peter McPhee

In the years after 1789 French revolutionaries sought to remake their society on the basis of the principles of popular sovereignty and civic equality. This was an awesome challenge in a large, diverse kingdom hitherto structured on custom, corporate and provincial privileges, and exemptions. Others, both French and foreign, took up arms in an attempt to destroy a revolution seen to be inimical to established practices of social hierarchy, religious belief, and authority.

In June 1789 commoner deputies to the Estates-General in Versailles vowed to achieve constitutional government; on 14 July several thousand armed Parisians seized the Bastille fortress in eastern Paris. Ever since, people have debated the origins and meaning of what had happened. By the time of Napoleon Bonaparte's seizure of power in December 1799, the first historians of the Revolution had begun to outline their narratives of these years and their judgments about the consequences of revolutionary change. Why was there a Revolution in 1789? Why had it proved so difficult to stabilize a new regime based on representation and rights? Why did the Revolution take its particular course? What were the consequences of a decade of revolutionary change?

The drama, successes, and tragedies of the Revolution, and the scale of the attempts to arrest or reverse it, have attracted scholars to it for more than two centuries.[1] Historians, like those who lived through those years, have agreed on the unprecedented and momentous nature of these and other acts of revolution in the months between May and October 1789. They have never agreed, however, on why what came to be called the *ancien régime* was overthrown with such widespread support, nor on why the Revolution took its subsequent course or on its outcomes.

The bicentenary of the Revolution in 1989 coincided with a new wave of revolutions, this time against Soviet hegemony in eastern Europe. Celebrations of the bicentenary in Paris occurred in the aftermath of the crushing of student protests in Tiananmen Square in Beijing. Since the dominant historical interpretation of the French Revolution had been within a Marxist paradigm of explanation – that this was essentially a triumph for urban bourgeois and landholding peasants which accelerated the transition from feudalism to capitalism – historians and journalists hostile to the Revolution rushed to proclaim that the lesson of contemporary rebellion against communist regimes was that Marxism was "dead" both as a tool for historical understanding and as a guide to a better future. The French Revolution was "over."[2]

Such claims were no more than wishful thinking. The consequences of the events of 1789 were so complex and significant that reflection and debate on their origins and course show no signs of concluding. The Revolution continues to fascinate, perplex, and inspire. The two great waves of revolutionary change since the 1980s – the overthrow of regimes in eastern and southeastern Europe and the "Arab spring" – have served to revivify our interest in the world-changing upheavals of the late eighteenth century. In the decades since 1989, however, a more supple and critical use of materialist explanations has been paralleled – and challenged – by the insights of discursive analysis and other forms of cultural history and by more probing application of categories drawn from histories of gender and race, often within a trans-Atlantic or even global context.[3]

This *Companion* showcases the ways in which historians now respond to the most fundamental questions about the French Revolution. Why and how did an apparently stable regime collapse in 1789? Why did it prove to be so difficult to stabilize a new order? Did the political instability of these years disguise a more fundamental social and economic continuity? Was the French Revolution a major turning-point in French – even world – history, or instead a protracted period of violent upheaval and warfare which wrecked millions of lives? The collection draws on the expertise of many of those historians whose fresh approaches to the era of the French Revolution both exemplify the great richness of current historical writing on these questions and point the way to future directions in revolutionary historiography. The twenty-nine contributions – from France, the United Kingdom, the United States, and Australia – have all been written specifically for this volume.[4] Approaches vary from wide-ranging reflections about key concepts, such as rights, gender, and terror, to cutting-edge archive-based research. None of the authors would claim that theirs is the final word: like all fine historical writing, their chapters pose questions while advancing our understanding.

***

One of the most fundamental and difficult questions about the French Revolution has always been how to explain its origins. France was apparently the most stable kingdom in western Europe, so how might one best explain why and how revolution occurred in 1789? Historians have long debated whether there were deep-seated, long-term causes of the political friction which erupted in 1787, and whether there were clear lines of social antagonism. Some have insisted that political conflict was short-term and avoidable: the royal state may have been under critical financial pressure, but its collapse was the outcome of a contingent political process. In his very wide-ranging overview of the current debates on the causes, Peter Campbell argues that the origins of the collapse of the *ancien régime* and of the Revolution are not the same question. A revolution which was neither foreseen nor planned will never, he suggests, have a definitive, agreed cluster of causes.

Other historians have argued that the French Revolution was in large measure the work of a bourgeoisie determined to overthrow privilege and be accorded political and social recognition in accord with their economic importance. Urban and rural working people had their own reasons for responding collectively to the opportunities presented by the greater political liberties that accompanied the calling of the Estates-General of 1789. Jean-Pierre Jessenne provides both an overview of French society in the late eighteenth century and a powerful argument that a deep-seated and complex social and economic crisis could not be resolved within existing social relations nor by the monarchy. While recognizing the specificities of the political crisis that erupted in 1787–89, he demonstrates that this crisis was interdependent with socio-economic changes and grievances across the kingdom.

Others have identified different economic, social, and cultural shifts, best observed through an analysis of the material and political "cultures" of eighteenth-century France: that is, the objects and practices of economic life, and changing assumptions being made about legitimacy and opinion. Sarah Maza offers an elegant synthesis of this new research: the emergence of concepts such as "despotism," "patriotism," "public opinion," and "nation" paralleling the rise of a commercial and consumer culture which, if not a direct "cause" of the crisis, informed the political culture through which it was expressed.

This material culture was inextricably linked to an expanding Atlantic economy of trade in colonial produce, French manufactures and wine, and slaves. The involvement of French armed forces in the American War of Independence led to the ruinous expenditure which prompted the calling of the Estates-General in 1789. Like contemporaries, however, historians have long reflected on the intellectual and cultural similarities and differences in what has been called the age of the "Atlantic" revolution. Miranda Spieler's focus on the concept of "martial law," introduced in Paris in October 1789, illuminates the importance of practices across the Atlantic, including North America, and demonstrates the explosive uncertainty about whether the colonies were part of metropolitan jurisdiction.

As Michael Fitzsimmons elaborates, deputies did not arrive for the meeting of the Estates-General in Versailles in May 1789 with clearly formulated revolutionary or conservative agendas. He stresses that the renunciation of privileges at the session of 4 August was not only a dramatic response to the revolts in much of the countryside but was also the moment which galvanized deputies into far more coherent and sweeping reforms than most had as yet contemplated. This unanticipated boldness had its most resounding expression in the Declaration of the Rights of Man and of the Citizen voted on 27 August 1789. The Declaration asserted the essence of liberalism, that "liberty consists of the power to do whatever is not injurious to others." Accordingly, it guaranteed rights of free speech and association, of religion and opinion. This was to be a land in which all were to be equal in legal status, and subject to the same public responsibilities: it was an invitation to become citizens of a nation instead of subjects of a king. Some historians have instead highlighted an evidently bourgeois conception of property in the Assembly's subsequent economic legislation, mirrored in the inconsistency between the

Declaration's universalist proclamation of rights and its decision to limit formal politics to "active" citizens, property-owning white males.

Across the next two years the Assembly undertook the awesome task of remaking France in line with the Declaration's principles. The reconstruction of public space was based on a belief in the common identity of French citizens whatever their social, ethnic, or geographic origin. As Alan Forrest explains, this was a fundamental change in the relationship between the state, its provinces, and the citizenry. In every aspect of public life – administration, the judiciary, the armed forces, the church, policing – traditions of corporate rights, appointment, and hierarchy gave way to civil equality, uniformity, and elections within national structures. Forrest highlights as well the imperative felt by revolutionaries to remake symbolic space in public places and festivals hitherto redolent of seigneurial and ecclesiastical authority.

Attitudes to royal authority were more ambiguous, since basing the new order on constitutional monarchy sat uneasily with evidence of Louis' hesitation – and the outright opposition of members of his court – toward major revolutionary reform. Gendered attacks on the moral stature of the king and queen sapped the monarchy's symbolic standing; Louis' own incapacity to manage political upheaval further eroded popular goodwill. But was this apparent from the outset? Barry Shapiro's thought-provoking chapter applies theories of emotional trauma to evidence of the ways deputies responded to intense feelings of betrayal and fear induced as early as the summer of 1789 by interpretations of the behavior of the king and court. His argument poses a challenge to established understandings of the importance of Louis' image as the "restorer of French liberty" in the early period of the Revolution.

One of the most common themes in the *cahiers de doléances* of 1789 was the necessity of sweeping reform to the Catholic Church. There was no question of separating church and state: the public functions of the church were assumed to be integral to daily life, and the Assembly accepted that public revenues would financially support the church after the abolition of the tithe. It was argued that, like the monarchy before it, the government had the right to reform the church's temporal organization. Many historians have seen the Assembly's reforms – the Civil Constitution of the Clergy – as the moment which fatally fractured the Revolution, and have debated why the Assembly seemed unwilling to negotiate or compromise. Dale Van Kley offers original insights by considering the origins of the schism not only in terms of France's particular religious and political history but from the perspective of the papacy and Catholic Europe. A revolution which began with high hopes for the "regeneration" of the church spiraled into reciprocal antipathy, laying the ideological groundwork, argues Van Kley, for the hostility to Catholicism later embedded in terroristic practices during the Year II.

Ultimately, only a handful of bishops and perhaps half the parish clergy took the civic oath to enable them to continue to officiate as clergy. Many of the latter subsequently retracted when, in April 1791, the pope, also antagonized by the absorption of his lands in and around Avignon into the new nation, condemned the Civil Constitution and the Declaration of the Rights of Man as inimical to a Christian life. Edward Woell explores how the sharp regional contrasts in clerical preparedness to take the oath reflected not only individual choice or the influence of senior clergy, but also local ecclesiastical culture. As he demonstrates, the outcomes were to be fundamental to subsequent political choice and division at every level across the revolutionary decade.

Historians have agreed that, before 1789 and after 1791, issues of foreign policy and military strategy dominated the domestic reform agenda; they generally assume, too, that the two intervening years of sweeping revolutionary change, 1789–91, were a time when radical internal reform preoccupied the Assembly. Thomas Kaiser reveals instead that a major impulse for revolutionary reform was in fact the desire to "regenerate" as well France's capacity to act as the key military and commercial player in international politics. Extensive research has enabled him to identify both France's increasing diplomatic isolation and different narratives developed inside France to explain this. The narratives were to transform the course of the Revolution, for on 20 April 1792 the Legislative Assembly declared war on Austria. By early 1793 the nation would be surrounded by a hostile coalition.

By 1792 revolutionaries faced two fundamental questions: could the Revolution survive external military threat and increasing internal division; and in whose interests should the Revolution itself be concluded? The tension between the universalism of the Declaration of Rights and the exclusion of slaves and mulattoes was immediately apparent. Similarly, the contradiction between the inclusive promises of the Declaration and the exclusions enshrined in subsequent legislation was not lost on women activists. Finally, while religious liberty and civil equality were quickly granted to Protestants and the Sephardi Jews of Bordeaux and Avignon, it was only during the final sessions of the National Assembly in September 1791 that the Ashkenazi Jews of eastern France were granted full equality. In his challenging reflection, however, Serge Aberdam warns against an approach which measures the extensions of rights on a spectrum imposed by hindsight, arguing instead that contemporary understandings of "rights" about gender, race, and class were neither so fixed nor limited, and that the question of "whose" revolution this was is best answered by a close analysis of specific claims and struggles.

Some historians have argued that despite, or because of, the political challenge of radical women, the transition from absolutism – under which all were subjects of the king – to a republican fraternity of male citizens served to reinforce the subordinate political position of women. In contrast, others have stressed that the repeated strictures about "women's place" must be understood as a prescriptive reaction to women's political activism and the central importance of legislation on the family and citizenship rather than as a simple reflection of gendered actuality. Anne Verjus discusses incisively these and other approaches to gender and political culture, drawing as well on studies of English and American society to elaborate contemporary assumptions about the sovereignty of heads of households.

Battles over the limits to change were also played out in the countryside, where the flashpoints of continuing revolution concerned not only the incomplete abolition of seigneurial rights in August, but control of resources. From 1789 a plethora of reports poured in to Paris of seizures of land belonging to the state and to seigneurs, and of unchecked felling of trees in forests. Marginal, uncultivated land was seized and cleared by the rural poor, desperate for an arable plot. Noelle Plack surveys legislation seeking to resolve rural conflict and to protect the environment; while seigneurial dues were not finally abolished until July 1793, she stresses the differential impact across rural society of this legislation, the sale of national property, and attempts to regulate common land.

All revolutionaries have to come to terms with large-scale popular violence, both its successes and its excesses. Such violence made the Revolution possible, but from the outset its particular cruelty startled contemporaries. Two of the most notorious examples of revolutionary bloodshed erupted in Paris. The governor of the Bastille had been killed in horrific fashion after his surrender on 14 July 1789. A few days later, the royal governor of Paris and his father-in-law were battered to death and decapitated, their heads paraded through Paris. Then, in early September 1792, convinced that "counter-revolutionaries" (whether nobles, priests, or common-law criminals) in prisons were waiting to break out and welcome the foreign invaders once the volunteers had left Paris for the war-front, about 1,200 of the 2,700 prisoners were killed, many after being brought before hastily convened popular courts. Donald Sutherland's confronting chapter details the vindictiveness which horrified observers of these two episodes, noting that there were many other similar acts outside the capital. He uses these examples to question George Rudé's longstanding linking of crowd action to the price and availability of bread, insisting on the importance instead of beliefs about inequitable taxation and political manipulation of food supply.

Revolutionary governments also had to come to terms with a range of anti- and counter-revolutionary insurrection. The Convention responded to military crisis by ordering a levy of 300,000 conscripts in February 1793. In the west the levy provoked massive armed rebellion, known, like the region itself, as "the Vendée." Resulting in terrible loss of life, the civil war left permanent scars on French society and politics. Jean-Clément Martin's challenging, lucid reflection explores the insurrection and meanings attributed to what contemporaries described as the "war" in the Vendée and differentiates it from the "chouannerie" to the north, where the army engaged in protracted but sporadic repression of rebels.

The course of the French Revolution has commonly been understood as a response to armed counter-revolution and military invasion at a time of deep internal division about the objectives of the Revolution itself. More recently, historians have sought to restore greater personal agency, acknowledging that revolutionaries were choosing between alternative ways of saving the Republic, and emphasizing personal friendships and antipathies. Those who battled over the implementation of the revolutionary project worked within pre-existing or newly formed networks of friends and the like-minded. There were others they came to mistrust, even to hate. How did particular individuals seen to personify particular phases of the Revolution come to be so loved or demonized? Marisa Linton considers three men at various points powerful within the Jacobin Club – Barnave, Brissot, and Desmoulins – and whose relationships became venomous and fatal. Linton teases out the tension between friendship and civic virtue, where personal ties and loyalties could be seen as inimical to the public good.

At a local level, too, the Revolution was mediated through existing networks of exchange, family, and faith, all tested and changed by the Revolution of 1789. The radical decentralization of power after 1789 created a situation where revolutionary legislation from Paris was interpreted and adapted to local needs. In this process – the social history of administration – the one million or more men who were elected to local government, the judiciary, and administrative and national guard positions played the key role in the void that existed between the Assembly's national program and the exigencies of the local situation. Where particular legislation was unpopular, especially that concerning the redemption of seigneurial dues or religious reform, this was a commitment which could also earn them isolation and contempt. How might we go about explaining the physical and social geography of opinion? Peter Jones argues convincingly that the choices that individuals, families, and communities made were neither scripted from the outset of the Revolution nor were they fixed. Polarities of "patriots" and "aristocrats" disguised complexities among those who were resistant to the Revolution rather than opposing it outright and between those who acquiesced in change rather than supporting it.

Certainly, however, the great internal and external crises of these years left no family untouched by or undecided about the Revolution. This was particularly the case as the crisis of war and counter-revolution reached a peak in the summer of 1793. Most historians have seen the Revolution as based on sincere liberal beliefs in tolerance and judicial process until the National Convention was forced by the circumstances of violent counter-revolution to compromise some of its founding principles through a policy of "terror until the peace" – only after Robespierre's death in 1794 labeled "the Terror." Recently, however, other historians have argued that the *mentalité* of the Terror was present at the very outset of the Revolution in May 1789, when "patriots" began stigmatizing their opponents as enemies of the new order of things rather than simply adherents of contrary points of view, culminating in a preparedness to make a millenarian attempt to force "regeneration" on an unwilling populace. David Andress demonstrates in contrast that "the Terror" was not a monolith of repression imposed at a particular moment in 1792 or 1793. Instead, he argues that internal counter-revolution and external military threat pushed deputies toward increasingly draconian controls and, as perceived and actual conspiracy further undermined the unity and moral resolve of Jacobins, so these ordinary men caught in extraordinary circumstances became more likely to turn on each other, with deadly consequences.

The ending of "the Terror" in Thermidor II (July 1794) has commonly been seen also as the "end" of revolution, at least in the sense of the most radical politics and popular intervention. Laura Mason engages explicitly with the seminal work of Bronislaw Baczko, agreeing that the Thermidorians may have ended the Terror, but also managed to preserve the Republic. Mason argues, however, that this was at the expense of popular participation, a commitment to social welfare and even effective civil order. Their legacy was the Constitution of 1795, in its essentials a return to the provisions of the Constitution of 1791: while now a republic, France was again to be governed by representative, parliamentary government based on a property qualification and the safeguarding of economic and civil liberties. Gone now was the optimism of 1789–91, the belief that with the liberation of human creativity all could aspire to the "active" exercise of their capabilities. The men of 1795 now appended a declaration of "duties" to their constitution, exhorting respect for the law, the family, and property.

The years of the Directory, 1795–99, have thus commonly been seen as characterized by the increasingly unstable rule of a narrow elite of propertied conservatives who shunned popular participation in politics and embarked on territorial expansion, opening the way for military dictatorship. More recently, however, historians such as James Livesey have seen these years as an integral part of a revolutionary decade which further embedded the assumptions of a new "political culture" of popular sovereignty and citizenship. Livesey extends Laura Mason's argument about the Thermidorians, for example, by teasing out the ways in which new property relationships and markets became embedded in the countryside, a "commercial republicanism."

Such arguments have necessarily reopened debate on whether the foundation of the Directory in 1795 represented the "settlement" of the Revolution, or whether the years 1795–99 were an integral phase of a revolution which was only ended by Napoleon's *coup d'état* of 1799. Howard Brown places emphasis on the way in which the men of the Directory, by choosing territorial expansion over social welfare and democracy at home, created a new bureaucratic and military professionalism which Napoleon was to use to replace them. Brown makes a telling case about the way the regime became more proficient in dealing with deserters, crime, and political insurrection: a "new security state" ready for strong rule.

Much of the political violence with which the Directory had to deal drew its visceral hatreds from the years of intense sacrifice and division in 1792–94. Stephen Clay draws on research in the Midi, Provence, and the valley of the Rhône, showing in rich detail how the powerful image of polarity of Terror/White Terror in 1794–95 misses the complexity and durability of violent division and revenge. He, like Jones, Martin, Woell, and others, points to the way these experiences would remain etched on memories and political choices.

By the time Napoleon seized power in December 1799, France had been at war with much of Europe for more than seven years. On 20 April 1792 the Assembly had declared that the war was "the rightful defence of a free people against the unjust aggression of a king." By 1799 it was engaged in wars of national expansion that had abandoned any such defensive pretext, but the impact of the Revolution went well beyond military conquest, and challenged existing social structures and assumptions about power across the northern hemisphere. The concept of the Atlantic or democratic revolution – first articulated in the 1950s by Jacques Godechot and R.R. Palmer and long seen as sterile because of its perceived reflection of Cold War politics – has been revivified by recent histories of the republic of letters, of women's cultures, and above all of slavery and revolt in our own context of the globalizing world of the twenty-first century.

The new historiography includes studies of global politics, personal and intellectual networks, Caribbean slave societies, and wider European and Mediterranean links. In his remarkable overview essay, Mike Rapport identifies the revolutionary wars as a major element in international relations and the internal politics of affected nations. Nowhere was this more explosive than in the French colonies of the Caribbean, as Frédéric Régent notes in his detailed outline, far more important in the total slave and colonial trade than hitherto assumed. Régent highlights a central paradox of these years, that the French abolitionists who wrestled with the question of when and how to emancipate slaves should have hesitated, while the pragmatic Napoleon, who had no qualms about slavery, later agreed to a treaty which liberated forever the slaves of the main colony. The resolve of rebellious slaves explains the paradox. Like Miranda Spieler, Régent explores the tensions created by claims that the colonies should be governed within metropolitan jurisdiction. One of Rapport's key points is that the international impact of the Revolution cannot be confined to Europe and the societies across the Atlantic, and included south Asia and the Mediterranean. In his innovative and thought-provoking chapter, Ian Coller explores the complexities of the reception and responses to the Revolution in the Muslim world of the Mediterranean. This was indeed a revolution which had an impact – profound but diverse – across much of the northern hemisphere and ultimately the globe.

A revolution which had begun in 1789 with boundless hopes for a golden era of political liberty and social change had ended in 1799 with a military seizure of power. It had not proved possible to stabilize the Revolution after the initial overthrow of the *ancien régime*. Instead, French people had had to endure a decade of political instability, civil war, and armed conflict with the rest of Europe, at the cost of hundreds of thousands of French lives. How "revolutionary" had been their experience? Responses to this question go to the heart of important and often trenchant divisions among historians. Certainly, historians agree that French political life had been fundamentally transformed by examining the practice of power within the context of "political culture" and the "public sphere" to consider a fuller array of ways in which people thought about and acted out politics. This imaginative approach is exemplified in the fertile discussion by Isser Woloch, which ranges across elections, the press, and political associations. In the end, however, an extraordinary decade of activity and contestation was compromised by a failure to produce a stable constitutional settlement; the Revolution's legacy was innovative and profound but also unstable and deeply divisive. No less than the nature of local and national politics, the various genres of performance were cultural forms through which the Revolution was mediated but which were also necessarily implicated in the protracted process of revolution after 1789.[5] From journalism and the novel to theater, music, and painting, the Revolution was embedded in cultural performance. These years shattered the conventions and privileges of the *ancien régime*, but the political dimension of cultural production left the arts vulnerable thereafter to new state controls. These political and cultural outcomes – transformative, contentious, ambiguous – are paralleled in economic structures and broader patterns of social relationships, including the place of ethnic minorities. Peter McPhee demonstrates the profound impact of institutional and regulatory change, of the abolition of seigneurialism and the sales of national property, and battles over the control of natural resources. At the same time, there was a remarkable continuity in the power of large landowners and, in many areas, of longstanding agricultural practices. Reforms to family life and challenges to patterns of personal relationships were of fundamental importance, argues Suzanne Desan, as were the attempts to wind them back. As she argues in a seminal chapter, reforms to family law opened up opportunities for many women within the family, and changes to inheritance laws strengthened the focus on the conjugal couple and put pressure on families to change their lineage strategies.

It is not surprising that the Revolution engendered personal and collective memories of sacrifice and triumph, suffering and loss. To the powerful revolutionary tradition which informed French and European politics and culture across the nineteenth century corresponded a *légende noire*, of mass killings, desecration, and destruction of family life and the natural environment. Until the Third Republic became embedded in institutional politics, politics of right and left were imbued with revolutionary imagery, and often personal memory. Only in the second half of the twentieth century did commemoration as "public" or "official" memory start to take on a life of its own independent of the earlier collective memory of regions and social groups. In his wide-ranging concluding chapter, Pascal Dupuy discusses how contested memories were paralleled in polarized histories and the controversies of commemoration. But he ponders whether, as this volume exemplifies, we may be at a point where a scholarly consideration of a revolutionary decade may be less rancorous and more fruitful than before.

Notes

1 There are many surveys of the historiography of the Revolution, including William Doyle (1999). *Origins of the French Revolution*, 3rd edn. Oxford: Oxford University Press; Alan Forrest (1995). *The French Revolution*. Oxford: Oxford University Press; Gwynne Lewis (1993). *The French Revolution: Rethinking the Debate*. London and New York: Routledge; Paul R. Hanson (2009). *Contesting the French Revolution*. Oxford: Wiley-Blackwell; Peter J. Davies (2006). *The Debate on the French Revolution*. Manchester: Manchester University Press.

2 Steven Laurence Kaplan (1995). *Farewell Revolution: Disputed Legacies, France 1789/1989*; (1995). *Farewell Revolution: The Historians' Feud, France 1789/1989*. Ithaca, N.Y.: Cornell University Press.

3 Recent historiographical trends are charted and discussed in a special issue of *FHS*, 32 (2009). In 2011, the major journal devoted to the Revolution, the *AHRF*, devoted two special issues (363, 365) to the North and South American dimensions of "the age of revolutions."

4 The six chapters by French historians have been translated by Juliet Flesch and Peter McPhee. Dr. Flesch's contribution is warmly acknowledged.

5 These shifts are explored expertly by Carla Hesse (1991). *Publishing and Cultural Politics in Revolutionary Paris, 1789–1810*. Berkeley: University of California Press; (2001). *The Other Enlightenment: How French Women Became Modern*. Princeton, N.J.: Princeton University Press.

Part I

The Origins and Nature of the Crisis of 1789

Chapter One

Rethinking the Origins of the French Revolution

Peter Campbell

The origins of the Revolution have been a subject of debate and conjecture since the first year of the Revolution itself. After more than two centuries no one now believes it was primarily a "révolte de la misère," as Michelet suggested, the very spirit of justice a long time coming, nor a philosophic plot, as the abbé Barruel argued, nor a Jansenist conspiracy (Michelet 1847). It would appear that millions of savages were not in fact launched into revolt and revolution by the babblings of the *philosophes*, as Hippolyte Taine argued after the Paris Commune of 1871, not least because illiteracy was widespread, education limited, and books very expensive. Nor was it predominantly caused by the rise of a democratic republican ideology that neatly prepared the way for the Third Republic in France, as in Alphonse Aulard's interpretation a generation later (1910). Echoes of these can still be heard of course, for poor arguments never die, they just get recycled into novels and television. But one major early line of interpretation had a long posterity: the idea that the Revolution was caused by a rising bourgeoisie, harbingers of capitalism, eager for the political power from which the privileged *ancien régime* society excluded them. From the mid-nineteenth century onwards the notion of a bourgeois revolution was widely accepted; it was given an explicitly capitalist sense by Marx, then a socialist inflection by Jean Jaurès. For Albert Mathiez (1922), the Russian Revolution of 1917 seemed to confirm the diagnosis. The idea came to dominate scholarly work to such an extent that it could be called an orthodox view by the 1950s. As such, it was about to come under a sustained attack. This essay will consider what this view was and how it was undermined by two generations of work in social, cultural, economic, intellectual, and, finally political history.

A Companion to the French Revolution, First Edition. Edited by Peter McPhee.

Can We Explain the Origins?

Before moving ahead with this agenda let us pause for a moment to consider what it means to study the origins of something as shatteringly transformative of state and society as the French Revolution. Most historical arguments about the origins of the Revolution depend on a process of defining the Revolution first – itself a hugely controversial topic – and then reading back into the causes or origins of 1789 the elements that seemed to triumph later. Secondly, the occurrence of the Revolution is often assumed to have been an act of will by particular groups. This too is problematic, because if the notion of deliberate revolutionaries does fit some later revolutions and suits the process of constructing a new state and society by the various assemblies in and after 1789, it is much less clear that the process of the collapse of the *ancien régime* into revolution shows the same intentionality. The *ancien régime* collapsed and out of its crisis a revolution developed, but the origins of the collapse and the origins of the Revolution are not the same (Campbell 2006). The collapse should also be seen as a process in itself that fractured society (Cubells 1987), brought more groups into the public sphere, and, as interests became endangered, produced moments of choice for those involved. Even those who chose revolution did so rather late in the day in the early or mid-summer of 1789, for the most part. It is hard to discern bourgeois involvement in 1787 and before the autumn of 1788, while few would deny that the collapse of the state in 1789 opened the door to bourgeois participation in a new politics. Most historians have found a way around this problem of choice or intentionality by assuming that the collapse of state authority and local institutions was merely the occasion for a more intentional revolution, the precipitant of a revolution whose origins lay in impersonal factors like rising social tensions, economic transition, or cultural change. In short, they stress the long-term processes that go beyond the individual and the contingent.

In this way, the participants are seen to be in the grip of historical forces they were not aware of, but were nevertheless furthering. A classic example of this is Alexis de Tocqueville's *Old Regime and the Revolution* (1856), in which the Revolution is defined as a further stage in a process of centralization going back to Louis XIV (though it would be a grave injustice to imply that his study argued no more than this). The same could be said about the role of the bourgeois or artisanal "actors" in a revolution that was thought to be essentially about class struggle. It is unsurprising that this approach should continue to dominate historical analysis, because History has long been about meaningful generalization, about finding *patterns*, and about making sense of the past for the present. The very essence of History is a dialectic of challenge and debate. But caution is required, especially when we are dealing with the problem of motivation. On the one hand we have a revolution that can be conceived as being about what the people at the time thought it was about – and remember they themselves differed in their views – and on the other hand we have a rather different set of revolutions postulated by historians that embodied wider processes of which the participants were partly or largely unaware. The latter approach today looks for example at economic trends and conjunctures, cultural developments, at shifts in the way society and politics were conceptualized in the decades preceding the Revolution and during the Revolution itself. But there is also a return to the role of individuals, to their politics, their strategies, and their emotions. How might we bring the broader conditions together with the role of individuals? Explaining the origins was never going to be easy.

Any attempt to make sense of something as complex as the first major world-changing revolution must encounter major difficulties. Today there is no agreed interpretation of the "causes" (or indeed "origins") of the Revolution, just as there is no agreed definition of the Revolution itself. The various aspects of the Revolution discussed in this very volume all have different sets of origins. It was a phenomenon of such breadth, reach, and variety that attempts to make sense of it often fall prey to a tendency to oversimplification, or teleology (especially in the case of intellectual history), while any attempt to take into account all the variables would surely be immensely long and confusing. A short essay such as this one can never do justice to all the fine work produced by recent historians, nor can it be more than one scholar's view, with all the shortcomings that implies.

The Orthodox View

The divisive nature of the Revolution meant that the first generation of memoirists and early historians adopted a range of very different views. From about the 1840s, History was developing as a discipline based on archival sources, but in the nineteenth century the rigorous treatment of documents that we expect today was usually confined to such sources as memoirs, correspondence, pamphlets, and newspapers, which led to a very political and intellectual vision of events. Nevertheless, because the Revolution was so divisive, there was a vehement debate in the sense that different views were put forward, often highly politicized, which were then criticized and evaluated by other scholars. However, with few exceptions the question of the origins has taken second place to the debate over the nature of the Revolution as a whole. In fact, right up until the 1980s relatively few books dealt with just the origins, and most views were expressed in a chapter at the start of a larger book on the Revolution. Instead of there being an explicit field of study known as "the origins debate," the process seems to have been much more one of setting out positions about the nature of the Revolution, and inferring causes from its nature. For example, in this way Jules Michelet, Louis Blanc, Aulard, and Jaurès put forward influential views. In the century before the 1950s only Marx, Tocqueville, Taine, and Georges Lefebvre really focused on the problem of the origins of the Revolution. From the 1920s to the 1950s the prevailing view was that the Revolution was the product of class struggle.

This socialist viewpoint was expressed in a classic book published in 1939, *Quatre-vingt-neuf*, translated as *The Coming of the French Revolution*. In this popular book, Lefebvre, a towering scholar and a socialist, had the great merit of making sense of the complexities. Moreover, he integrated his own research on the peasantry into the more classic Marxist schema. Peasants were restored to conscious and proactive actors, not masters of their own fate but developing strategies in the face of pressures. The field has grown since then with classic studies by Pierre de

Saint-Jacob (1960) and John Markoff (1996). Thus the causes of the French Revolution lay in the development of capitalism, which had slowly been generating a rising bourgeois class and its concomitant, a declining nobility, which by its cultural values was less well adapted to capitalism. Nonetheless, the aristocratic opposition to royal reform in 1787 had to be fitted into the schema. Hence the appeal of the notion of a century-long aristocratic reaction by a nobility presumed to have been cut out of power by Louis XIV (which we no longer believe: Campbell 1993; Beik 2005; Chaline 2005). So a sort of last-gasp aristocratic reaction was postulated for the Assembly of Notables in 1787, during which the nobility not only blocked vital royal reforms but also revealed its hand by suggesting a greater role for the nobility in government, with the monitoring of royal policy through the dominance of the estates. The opposition of the noble magistrates in the *parlements* was interpreted as a part of the same aristocratic reaction (Ford 1953), along with increased exploitation of the vestiges of the feudal system in the countryside to extract more revenue from estates and seigneurial dues. However, the establishment of new representative provincial assemblies in 1788 and then the elections to the Estates-General in 1789 gave the bourgeoisie its opportunity. This rising class of commercial and liberal professions tried to seize the initiative (Kaplow 1965). The intransigence of the nobility in the Estates-General led to a clash with the determined bourgeoisie of the Third Estate, whose ideology was enlightened, liberal, and egalitarian. (And here we must note that the world of ideas, what Marxists call the ideological superstructure of society, was regarded as a product of the economic infrastructure.) The liberal revolution itself was made by the bourgeoisie, in a situation in which the artisans lent their support in a time of great economic distress. For Lefebvre, alongside this bourgeois revolution an autonomous peasant revolution took place; it destroyed feudalism in an act of will and as a consequence of the Great Fear. The bourgeoisie, henceforth in power, soon enacted the principles of liberty and equality that ultimately advanced the cause of capitalism. With the abolition of seigneurialism or "feudalism" the peasantry would have a partially successful revolution; the artisans would play a crucial role in the revolution but would not benefit in the long term. Thus the French Revolution in its origins and nature was a bourgeois revolution against feudalism in favor of capitalism.

This was a neat and elegantly put argument repeated in many a textbook and in standard works. But would it stand up to further research and critical analysis? In France it held sway until the 1970s partly because of the domination of French Revolution studies by historians on the left; many were members of the Communist Party, like Lefebvre's successor as Professor of the French Revolution at the Sorbonne, Albert Soboul. The attack was launched by British and American historians. For twenty years from the mid-1950s onwards this challenge took the form of the critical redefinition of a series of key terms. Instead of taking the reader through a blow-by-blow account of the evolution of this historiography, I will summarize the conclusions of the research by topic as seen from the perspective of today – at the risk of compressing into a single set of conclusions on each topic much longer processes of research that often took a generation. The word "revisionism" is often used to describe this historiography, but it has nothing to do with its original sense of a left-wing internal critique of Marxism; quite the contrary. Its heyday was the 1970s, and since then different perspectives on causality and history – as well as new research into new areas like political culture and cultural history – have led to a new phase of interpretation.

A Revolutionary Bourgeoisie?

If the Revolution was a bourgeois revolution, then who actually did participate in it, who were the deputies of the Third Estate? In a lecture of 1954 and a book a decade later, Alfred Cobban criticized the concept of the bourgeoisie as being far too elastic and imprecise, an unsuitable category of analysis. He showed that the deputies were in fact overwhelmingly representatives of the non-noble office-holders and legal professions. Such men were often on the way to acquiring nobility, and they were not involved in the commercial and industrial capitalism that the Revolution was supposed to have benefited. Their long-term patterns of investment were the purchase of land and office, and many richer members of the Third Estate held seigneuries just like nobles. Much other research on social mobility under the *ancien régime* since then has tended to confirm the assessment of these notables of local society as belonging to families that had initially risen through larger-scale commerce but then abandoned trade in favor of investments in land and office (especially in the judiciary and royal finances) that brought them closer to the noble lifestyle. From Cobban's tables, it is clear that hardly any representatives of manufacturing or capitalism were elected to the Third Estate in the Estates-General (Cobban 1971). Nearly one-third of the "bourgeois" deputies in 1789 were bailiwick judges well versed in local politics (Dawson 1972). This view was more recently confirmed by a more extensive analysis of the Third Estate: most had some political experience and many had published pamphlets (Tackett 1996). Cobban had postulated that such an office-holding class was struggling against a decline in office values during the eighteenth century, but this has since been disproved (Doyle 1995). Overall the "revolutionary bourgeoisie" has come to look not so much a class as a group of ambitious local notables without a particular class identity but with a fair amount of local or regional administrative and judicial experience.

Their aspirations tended toward the noble lifestyle, and if they were frustrated by the *ancien régime* it was argued that it was more because their social mobility was jeopardized by greater competition for access to the noble order (Lucas 1973). Such men were hardly candidates for the label "capitalists" in Marx's sense, and Cobban actually thought them anti-capitalist. However, we should note that they were also representatives of a "proprietary capitalism" and so did benefit enormously from the recycling of their investment in office into the purchase of church and *émigré* property whose sale was decreed by the early Revolution. The argument has turned on the characteristics of the deputies to the Third Estate (and who but the existing *ancien régime* elites would have been elected to the Estates-General?), and not on the members of the Third Estate in France as a whole, who did indeed play a much greater role in government once the Revolution had begun: as municipal officers, local government officials, and members of the Jacobin clubs. These new officials came from a more commercial or professional set of social groups in society, and some of these were even represented in the later national assemblies. It is highly likely that to understand this "middle-class" involvement we have to look not only at the economic conditions and practices in the context of which such groups thrived and expanded, but also at the rising notion of active and participatory citizenship that spread through the middling and upper reaches of society from mid-century onwards (Mornet 1933; Jones 1991). So the debate over the bourgeoisie was never conclusively concluded.

Eighteenth-Century Capitalism in Question

Further exploration of eighteenth-century capitalism was clearly necessary. Was the capitalism that the "bourgeois revolution" was supposed to have promoted actually around in the eighteenth century? For it to have constituted some kind of motivation for the Third Estate revolutionaries, it was implied that this capitalism ought logically to have comprised the commercial and entrepreneurial practices that we associate with the nineteenth-century styles of capitalism. In fact, as George Taylor showed in some key articles (1962, 1967), late *ancien régime* capitalism was a long way from conforming to such a model. He identified four types – merchant, court, industrial, proprietary – none of which was organized much like the forms later associated with a nineteenth-century definition of capitalism. The research would seem to complement Cobban's argument that, if the bourgeoisie made the Revolution, then this bourgeoisie was not progressively capitalist but a *rentier* class of lawyers and office-holders. (Here we have an example of the way debate progresses unsystematically in History. A crucial issue is whether any kind of capitalism, even proprietary, in practice generated a desire to remove remaining impediments to wealth accumulation as the Revolution did indeed do – but such a question has not been debated.) Moreover the pre-revolutionary noble involvement in manufacturing and investment in production did not survive the attack on the nobility in the Revolution, while the triumph of proprietary capitalism slowed later growth.

The reassessment of feudalism that Cobban had drawn upon had already shown that what the eighteenth century called "feudalism" was merely the vestiges of the practices of the Middle Ages that now served a very different purpose. In fact, the whole system of seigneurial dues and services had long been converted into property rights that could be traded and were certainly exploited for profit by estate owners – be they nobles, rising "bourgeois" *rentiers*, or even richer peasants – in a system that was becoming slowly more capitalist (though much depended on the region). Perhaps there was increased exploitation of such revenues (a "feudal reaction") but it hit not the bourgeoisie but the poorer peasantry, and explains their vehement and growing hostility to seigneurialism in all its forms. Evidence of this is to be found in increasing rural violence but was probably masked in the parish *cahiers* of 1789 by the dominance of the views of the richer peasants (Markoff 1996; Nicolas 2002). Pierre de Saint-Jacob (1960) showed exactly how the process worked in rural Burgundy. However, one of the major problems for systematic argument is that rural France was regionally very varied with different conditions prevailing, making generalizations hard to sustain.

The Nature of the Nobility

Alongside the redefinition of the bourgeoisie and capitalism came a re-evaluation of the nature and role of the nobility. The prevailing view had been that the nobility was a fairly closed caste, split between itself into robe and sword, which had been cut out of power by Louis XIV. It was supposed to have been making a comeback during the eighteenth century, with the parlementary robe magistrates (for whom Montesquieu was the ideologue) taking the lead (Ford 1953). But this took place in the context of an economy more favorable to a growing number of "bourgeois" entrepreneurs. It was time for a reassessment. The pioneer was Robert Forster, who initially studied the estate management practices of the nobility of Toulouse, then went on to consider other regions and a ducal family as well, the Sault-Tavannes (Forster 1960, 1963). He found the provincial nobles of Toulouse and other regions to be displaying attitudes to thrifty estate management and to the maximizing of landed revenue that Marxists claimed was a particular characteristic of the bourgeoisie rather than the nobility.

Suddenly the categories seemed blurred, for our bourgeois were looking very noble and the nobles were looking quite bourgeois! Further research in economic history, on the origins of nineteenth-century heavy industry, showed that in so far as it existed it owed a lot to the investment of some leading courtly families (though many remained traditionally aloof). And why not, for this could be considered the exploitation of landed estates for their resources, and it was done on a grand scale (Taylor 1962)? Half the forges in France belonged to nobles, as landed estates were the main source of wood for power and shipbuilding. Colonial trade attracted noble investment, as did the wine estates of the Bordelais for example (Poussou 1983). So the nobility was involved with many aspects of eighteenth-century-style capitalism. Even so, the prevailing values of this order were far from being modern capitalist. Court nobles could afford to flout the anti-trade conventions that many families still adhered to, but the newly ennobled or rural nobles were still afraid of *dérogeance*. Seigneurialism was not their main source of revenue, though it was in some regions an important one, and it mixed honorific rights that were held vital to the social distinction of the elite, with "useful" rights that brought in revenue. Mixed values or not, studies of social mobility and venality of office showed that this elite was far from being a beleaguered, closed caste destined for destruction (Figeac 2002). Half the nobility of perhaps 120,000 individuals could trace their titles back no further than the reign of Louis XIV.

On the other hand, let us not exaggerate the modernity of the nobility. Many provincial and courtly families remained wedded to traditional values and sources of income and there was a cleavage between more conservative provincial nobility and a more fashionable court and Parisian nobility (Chaussinand-Nogaret 1985). But everyone was associated with an increasingly consumerist society. Tea, coffee, sugar, spices, *patisserie*, mirrors, porcelain, and *toiles peintes* were all avidly consumed by the social elites, and distribution networks developed. So the nobility was more progressive than previously thought in terms of rural and industrial wealth creation, and more enlightened too. It also paid more in direct taxation as its privileges were eroded. But it still benefited from enormous social privileges that formed part of the very structure of the regime, and to which it was very attached.

The Enlightenment and the Revolution

The new research on the richer members of the Third Estate and the nobility tends to show that a relatively simple model of economic or social determinism was becoming harder to sustain. So, if economic and social motives were now decidedly blurred, and motivation therefore more complex, what did cause the elites of magistrates and notables in 1787–88 to oppose royal reforms; what precise concerns led the intervention of bourgeois militants in the crisis over the provincial estates in mid- to late 1788; what did motivate the deputies to the Estates-General of May 1789? Does the answer lie in the values of the Enlightenment? The progressive discrediting of a clear social and economic model of revolution returned the debate to the intellectual sphere. A key epistemological development also took place even among Marxists with the argument that ideologies or mentalities should not be regarded as simply a product of social and economic circumstances, but as a relatively autonomous sphere of human activity (Vovelle 1990). Clearly the Revolution, with its Declaration of the Rights of Man, constitutional representative government, civic liberty, religious toleration, educational reform, reform of the judicial system, and liberty of commerce, drew profoundly upon the movement of ideas in the eighteenth century. (Much less in view was the extent to which it also drew upon the classical world for key notions like patriotism and virtue.) In fact, a major redefinition of the Enlightenment in its various guises was taking place. There was a growing consensus among historians that the Enlightenment was not as radical as had sometimes been argued, that this "Party of Humanity" was not in favor of revolution but of reform led from above by enlightened rulers. The issue was broadened out by recasting questions about the role of the Enlightenment as questions about "intellectual origins." This concept is more open to the inclusion of religious motivations, classical republicanism, economic (largely physiocrat) thought, and key notions like virtue and citizenship, none of which was exclusively the product of "Enlightenment" (Linton 2001; Smith 2005a).

This kind of argument has something in common with another major new strand of Enlightenment studies, which stressed discourses and cultural practices rather than specific ideas. The practices of the Enlightenment transformed attitudes and values as much as did a set of specific social or political doctrines. The availability of periodicals, the spread of reading rooms, libraries, *sociétés de pensée*, and provincial academies helped sustain what has been termed a "reading revolution"; the famous art exhibitions in the Louvre from 1737 onwards, the parterre of the theatre, the critical subtexts to paintings and plays, the promenades with newsmongers, the clandestine pamphleteering – all were helping to create a public sphere in which critical discussion took place (Habermas 1989; Kaiser 2011). Religious controversies over Jansenism also led to a more politically aware Parisian bourgeoisie, and famous trials became a vehicle for public discussion of government and social injustice (Garrioch 1996; Maza 1993). Even Parisian artisans would have become familiar with the language of virtue and natural rights via their lawyers, employed to defend their *compagnon* clients against masters (Sonenscher 1989). When combined with notions of patriotism and citizenship, these cultural practices prepared sections of the population to make new choices when the opportunity arose in 1789. Thus living the Enlightenment prepared the way for a triumph of democratic sociability and a desire for participation and transparency that characterized the revolutionaries. A sense of virtuous citizenship promoted oppostion to any government action that could be called "despotic."

Alongside this research a field sketched out in the 1930s returned to prominence. Daniel Mornet's pioneering study of the intellectual origins of the French Revolution, a masterpiece never translated, was later buttressed by major studies of the notion of happiness, of progress, of equality. But from the mid-1960s Robert Darnton took up the challenge and made a major contribution with several new works on the diffusion of ideas. He was addressing a significant issue for historians: how far did enlightened ideas remain those of a narrow elite and how far did they percolate down the social scale to artisans and peasants (as Taine had thought)? The work on diffusion complemented work on the practices of the Enlightenment to answer this question. Who indeed was affected by the new ideas, methods, discourses, and practices of the Enlightenment? Even for Mornet the answer to the question could not be limited to the diffusion of texts like the *Social Contract*, the *Spirit of the Laws*, or the *Encyclopedia*, in other words to the corpus of major enlightened texts by its principal exponents, such as Locke, Fénelon, Voltaire, Rousseau, Montesquieu, Diderot, d'Holbach, the marquis de Mirabeau, and Buffon, to name but a few. Such texts were costly and were mainly available to the social elite who engaged in polite discussion in Academies (Roche 1998). The composition of private libraries could be analyzed from sale catalogues and inventories, the volume of publications of different sorts quantified (Chartier 1990). But it was found that the educated but less well-off readers also had access through the new reading rooms and might discuss ideas in bookshops and cafés. So the Enlightenment did resonate quite widely in educated society. Nevertheless, the "bourgeois ideology" of the Enlightenment soon came to look almost as noble as it was bourgeois. Both in terms of the contents of its libraries and the *cahiers* of 1789, the nobility as a social order was in many ways profoundly enlightened. The civility of the leading salons, and of the drawing rooms, required a familiarity with this world of ideas; and they were readily adopted, especially after the beginning of the American War of Independence, and even the higher clergy drew upon them (Lilti 2012). There was an anti-Enlightenment, and a Catholic Enlightenment, and these movements did create tensions in the elite, but in the main one has the impression that the elite, because it also profited from the *ancien régime* state, seemed to live in a state of ambiguity or a double-think in which the implications of the new ideas were not followed through (Burson 2010; McMahon 2001). It helped that the major ideas were reformist rather than revolutionary – and the reformist state itself began to embody them in its policies in some spheres, notably in economics, finance, and public works. There was even ministerial and courtly protection for the *Encyclopedia*, and for networks of economic thinkers (Skornicki 2011). But another problematic is the influence of ideas that do not strictly fit the definition of the Enlightenment. The civic humanism of the Renaissance, that is Pocock's "Machiavellian Moment," should obviously be extended to eighteenth-century France. Sixteenth-century ideas of the public good seem to have undergone a revival and transmutation in the eighteenth century, and classical republicanism had a great influence. Everyone read Cicero, Plutarch, and Tacitus quite as much as they read Sidney, Locke, Voltaire, Rousseau, and Montesquieu. The quarrels over Jansenism also fed into the pre-revolutionary mix in a potent way; so not all motivation was "enlightened" (Van Kley 1996). The two key discourses on virtue and *patrie* are typical of this range of influences (Bell 2001; Campbell 2007; Linton 2001, 2006).

But Darnton argued that a literary underground of writers excluded from the institutions of the high Enlightenment (membership of academies, posts as librarians) purveyed a much more radical form of enlightenment in pamphlets, minor works, and an especially desacralizing form of political pornography (Darnton 1982). These writings reached a much wider market than the 25,000 copies of the *Encyclopedia*. Darnton (1995, 1996) identified a whole new corpus of popular texts from clandestine literature that, for all their ephemeral nature and strange mixture of pornography and politics, were widely read and which were a vehicle for some enlightened notions as well as being massively subversive of the established order. For all the importance of this research, it is hard to agree that the culture of calumny and desacralization had a causal connection to the outbreak of revolution.

The fertile ground of Enlightenment studies also produced a major new perspective that combined philosophy with intellectual history. Its fundamental inspiration was the intellectual revolution produced by Michel Foucault. Both a historian and a linguistic philosopher, Foucault was interested in language and power. To vastly oversimplify his complex thought, he explored the way "discourses," that is historical streams of language and concepts, assembled and reassembled by succeeding generations (and which, in a major intellectual achievement, he identified or defined into existence), created and represented the environment and the issues. Discourses not only provide a conceptual toolbox, one used by actors to conceptualize what is going on, but they also actually mold or create the actors themselves. We are a bundle of discourses. Thus a certain idea of madness or criminality, or sexuality, once internalized, profoundly affects our historical choices and is often a function of power relations. Discourses are unstable, improvised, and can serve to marginalize or exclude "the other." So people that historians had been accustomed to interpret as individuals in groups were now transformed into vehicles for discourses – as Foucault showed in a key essay, "What Is an Author?" (1991). Such a perspective was brilliantly adapted by Keith Baker, who argued that the historical conjuncture that gave rise to the Revolution was the product of the competition between three discourses within the new public sphere. These he dubbed the discourses of justice, reason, and will. For a generation before the Revolution the operation of these discourses gave rise to a new politics of contestation, and may be presumed to have defined for the actors the possible and varied significances of the events of 1787–89 (Baker 1990). The argument broke the mold of causality or socio-economic determinism used by historians, and gave a great impetus to new research. François Furet (1981) also argued that the inherent contradictions in the – for him, *new* – discourses of 1789 were the very motor of the Revolution, leading almost inevitably to the Terror of 1793–94. (He was a major historian of the Revolution whose work dealt principally with its nature as a radical break and so his work is not discussed here.) Many empiricist historians, especially in England, rejected such a philosophical and intellectual approach out of hand, but the debate moved on without them, because the issues today are conceptual not empirical.

The rise of a Foucauldian approach opened the door for studies on broader notions like virtue, citizenship, nobility, sociability, natural law, republicanism, and patriotism – and on the way these discourses were employed in practice. These studies, however, show the actors actually manipulating the discourses more self-consciously and strategically than ought to have been possible had they merely been mouthpieces or actors speaking a script. This poses a problem for the Foucauldian approach, what is known as the problem of "agency." How can the actors be speaking a script already in existence and at the same time skillfully improvising one? How far do they exist as individuals, or must all individuals be "emblematic"? Moreover, there is a problem of the type of sources used, for is the discourse on politics seen through theoretical texts really the same as politics as studied through the texts generated by its practice, and what of context (Campbell 1989)?

"Enlightenment" has now become so capacious a concept that it is in danger of losing its role as an explanatory model for the birth of the French Revolution. The Enlightenment has merged into the new cultural history. In my opinion, like the Enlightenment, the cultural developments can be more easily linked to the choices revolutionaries made once the state had failed than to the process that brought about its failure. That is not to say there are no links, just that they still need exploring more precisely in their political context to isolate them from the general mass of cultural phenomena currently evoked. The notion of cultural origins is too vague; instead of saying that the Revolution was the product of the many cultural changes that were taking place, we need to know which cultural elements were important for precisely which choices. Roger Chartier (1990), having summarized in magisterial fashion much of the new cultural and intellectual history of the period, argued rather broadly that the Revolution was possible because it was thinkable. Even that view has been challenged.

Rethinking the Models of Revolution

George Taylor (1967) said that the Revolution was "essentially a political revolution with social consequences and not a social revolution with political consequences." This perspective raises the question of what model could replace the orthodox view. At this point in the debate, sociologists were doing much comparative work on the nature of revolution. But thanks to the influence of Marxism in this relatively new academic field, the Revolution was still assumed to be essentially social in origins. The first major attempt at reconceptualizing the origins and nature of the French Revolution was by the historians Robert Palmer and Jacques Godechot (Palmer 1959–64). Looking at the apparent wave of revolutions in Europe and America from the 1770s to 1800, they argued that a common denominator was the notion of democracy, starting in America and influencing subsequent revolutions. The theory was virtually ignored in France, but made an impact elsewhere and has become a renewed subject of discussion today (Jourdan 2008). To the extent that there was a common ideology, in my view it was surely patriotism, in its eighteenth-century civic guise, and not democracy that was the key idea. Attempts to re-put this kind of argument today in an age of globalization are problematic as far as origins are concerned. It is not that there are not influences, and a similar general context, but the whole educated culture of western Europe and the colonies already read the same books and had the same sort of classical education, so the notion of contagion or influence does not work as it is almost impossible to isolate and trace specific influences. It is a big step from the useful and necessary task of exploring these to showing, through the existence of rigorously traced networks, that the ideas and connections played a vital role in generating a revolution in France; and the argument presupposes "revolutionaries" before the revolution. In the present state of studies it is of course too early to know, but then, as with the Enlightenment, it may be that the ideas played a more significant role in the choices made and policies adopted to remodel France *after* the state had collapsed and a power and civic vacuum had to be filled than they did in the collapse of the *ancien régime*. In that process the internal contradictions of the regime, the nature of the crisis, failures of political management, and long-term fiscal and institutional problems played by far the greater role. In that sense the origins of the Revolution were specifically French. But what does it mean to say specifically French in an age of international commerce of goods and ideas? The "Atlantic revolution" theory is another unresolved area for debate.

A generation after Palmer wrote, sociologists, influenced by the rise of a notion of political culture and a comparative methodology, finally moved away from their essentially social view of revolution. In 1979 and 1991 two influential models were put forward. The first, by Theda Skocpol (1979), argued that three major revolutions, the French, the Russian, and the Chinese, were cases of state failure produced by international involvement that produced stresses of modernization (though for historians modernization, like globalization, is a very imprecise concept) for an agrarian bureaucracy. Her model (which few historians today, in a new stage of studies on the state, would recognize as valid) was also criticized for leaving out the intellectual sphere. Jack Goldstone (1991), in contrast, put the accent on the multiple pressures induced by demographic growth and the failure of the fiscal systems to gather resources from new types of wealth. What they lacked in understanding the specific complexities of France and its political culture – which historians were in the process of redefining at that time – they made up for in impressive and stimulating breadth of vision. They broke the mold of the old sociological model of revolution or "internal civil war," and have fed into the comparative analysis of the French Revolution. A lasting merit is the attempt to analyze "state failure." More recently there has been a renewal of sociological interest in the early modern states, particularly as multinational structures (Smith 2005b). More conceptual work needs to be done on the responses of states ill adapted to facing the costs of defending an international empire; and on the centrifugal strains in multinational states (as in 1848 in Austria-Hungary).

Redefining the State and Power

The most recent redefinition to be taking place is of the state and politics. If the Revolution was to be viewed as political (as it was for Taylor, Furet, and Doyle), what then was "politics"? For *ancien régime* politics was a world away from the modern politics that the Revolution was to invent. And how should we define the state in which this *ancien régime* style of politics took place? William Doyle (1981) put together the case against Lefebvre and substituted a political narrative of the fall of the *ancien régime*. Since then, with the rise of the notion of political culture and a great deal more work on the nature of the state, there has been a major shift in our view of the state (Collins 2009). But the whole question of political or state origins still needs reconceptualizing.

The orthodox view of the state was that the absolute monarchy was a centralized bureaucratic or administrative state by the eighteenth century (Tocqueville 1856; Antoine 1986). The central institutions and power of the more collaborative Renaissance monarchy were supposed to have been extended and transformed under Richelieu and Louis XIV, with the eighteenth century creating an "administrative monarchy." The argument had been adopted by Tocqueville and became the core of a belief in the development of "absolutism," a word to be avoided today for its anachronism and centralizing agenda. The rise of the state to pre-eminence over society (which did indeed take place) was thought to have led to the decline of provincial estates, the exclusion of the nobility from power, their domestication at a largely ornamental court, and the crushing of the *parlements* – hence their counter-offensive after the death of Louis XIV. Even by 1988 enough research had been done to show this was unconvincing in all respects (Campbell 1988). In so far as the origins of the Revolution were concerned, it should have been apparent that a powerful, centralized state should not have collapsed under the strains of war finance; if it was strong it should have been able to solve its fiscal problem by imposing fiscal reform. (The history of fiscal reform is actually one of erosion and compromise.) No one seemed to notice this paradox, perhaps because the origins of the Revolution were seen as essentially social. The crisis of the state was viewed as merely a precipitant. The Revolution was not viewed as a progressive process in which its crisis played a dynamic transformative role. Perhaps the metaphors of revolution as volcanic eruption, as an explosion of social change, as a tsunami, diverted historians from a more searching analysis.

Much of the empirical work for a reconceptualization of the nature of both the state and the regime focused on the seventeenth century, because it was the period that was supposed to have witnessed a profound transformation (Cossandey and Descimon 2002; Mettam 1988). My own work on defining power and politics, at court and in the Parlement of Paris, in the thirty years after Louis XIV, convinced me that if the system functioned as it did under Cardinal Fleury, then the supposed transformation under Louis XIV had not lasted – or even taken place (Campbell 1996). So the continuities with the more makeshift seventeenth century predominate. Institutional historians have tended to stress the official administrative structures and royal claims, but we should be skeptical of the image the state was careful to project. Much other work on the eighteenth century has since shed a different light on two more key aspects: *parlements* and estates. Beneath the official pronouncements, there lay a world of practical politics that characterized a regime with many tensions that needed to preserve delicate equilibriums. (One might almost view the monarchy as the apex of a corporative balancing act.) The *parlements* have emerged as more a part of government, a troublesome but vital set of judicial and administrative institutions (Campbell 2006; Chaline 1996; Swann 1995). They did use ideology to defend their corporate position and could be dragged into other controversies by appeals to or attacks on their interests, but as judges they were not spearheading an ideological opposition on behalf of the nobility (Stone 1986). Moreover their interrelationship with the courtly and ministerial environment meant that through patronage they could nevertheless be managed by the central government – if it remained cautious and united. Of course the ministry often failed to display unity, and crises arose, notably in 1770, which as in 1788 led to radical reform that looked despotic. Work on some of the provincial estates has added to older studies on Brittany and Languedoc in stressing their important and indeed increasing role in the government of their regions rather than an outright decline (Legay 2001). It also confirms the continued role of the higher nobility based at court, but vital for governance through compromise, the dominance of the provincial nobility within the institutions, and their importance for the system of royal credit (Potter and Rosenthal 1997; Swann 2009). It is true that many areas had no estates, but their existence in the frontier provinces limited and profoundly conditioned the development of the monarchy. Meanwhile, the *intendants* are now perceived to have been rather less the agents of centralization they were portrayed as, and more as authoritative intermediaries working with the local elites (Emmanuelli 1981).

Research on royal finances has revealed the taxation strategies, the complex credit mechanisms, and the money circuits involved (Bonney 1998; Félix 1999, 2006; Legay 2011). The finances of the absolute monarchy were always precarious back to the sixteenth century, and nearly catastrophically so under Louis XIV, who in 1715 left France twenty years of revenue in debt. All wars were paid for mostly by credit, with taxes increased during and immediately after wars. In the short term, funds would be raised from the Farmers General, whose profits from the indirect tax farms gave them wealth and credit. The French monarchy's fundamental problem was how to tax the rich, who tended to acquire exemptions. It partially solved this problem with new direct taxation (the *capitation*, the *dixièmes*, the *vingtièmes*) that targeted the nobility and, less successfully, the church, but the whole system was skewed toward landed wealth rather than the fast-increasing commercial wealth from, for example, the colonial trade. So with ever more expensive wars, and maritime wars at that, the system was under huge pressure (Riley 1986). The cost of credit rose, and during the American War Necker took out too many loans instead of tackling the difficult job of forcing the *parlements* and privileged to consent to higher taxes. And yet most European states, including Britain, were in a similar position, but although France was the most populous power for geopolitical reasons it had both land and maritime military commitments. The fundamental reason for the French failure to reform its finances was its political culture based on a court system with vested interests that made drastic reform too hazardous for ministers to undertake if they were to remain in power. A finance minister did not even have control of the expenditure by his ministerial colleagues. But if the problems were long term, and crises frequent, perhaps historians should ask not so much why royal finances failed, but how it was that the socio-politico-fiscal system of the absolute monarchy lasted so long. How did power work in the *ancien régime*?

Of course the answer is not that the state power simply worked through a centralized bureaucracy. Such a structure existed, with a council of state, *intendants*, *parlements*, tax authorities, provincial estates, and governors, but their coherence was limited and the whole structure's action was subject to many historically founded constraints. It was a pre-modern administration, a hybrid in terms of Weberian models, so the state was a particular early modern formation that has not really been recognized in historical models. This state formation developed a certain *habitus* and coherence in the later sixteenth century and survived the challenges of war and empire into the later eighteenth century (Campbell 2011). The General Farms were the most bureaucratic, and administrative change did begin to take some effect in the last two or three decades of the regime. But fundamentally the ethic was not of a modern bureaucracy, and the office-holders had a patrimonial conception of their functions. Social privilege, hierarchy, and a strong sense of the legitimacy of limits to royal interference remained so important that a proactive royal administration generated tensions. So rhetoric, representation, patronage and clientage, bluff, negotiation, and compromise remained fundamentally important, as in the seventeenth century. The more so as the theoretically absolute monarchy was based on a working compromise with the elites (Beik 2005). The *intendants* worked with the provinces, and the centralization was often more apparent than real as initiatives often stemmed from the localities and were confirmed by the royal council (Emmanuelli 1981). It could even be argued that the provincial elites were playing an ever greater role in government which only increased their resentment of attempts at centralization or, as they saw it, "royal despotism" (Legay and Baury 2009).

With an essentially bureaucratic conception of state power, historians and sociologists of the absolute monarchy long failed to consider three areas now regarded as fundamental for understanding the regime; the royal court, the royal decision-making structures, and the role of patronage and clientage in the political system (Fantoni 2012; Kettering 1986; Mettam 1988). Research has shown that the court was in fact the nerve center of the realm, the place from which the administration was run, but also the center of networks of patronage and clientage that were vital to effective government through their potential to manage conflict and prevent the potentially dangerous escalation of crises. Thus the exercise of royal authority was about political management of the constantly disruptive social and political tensions, and patronage networks were the key to this technique (Campbell 1996). Perhaps the key element for the survival – and potentially the failure – of the regime in the seventeenth and eighteenth centuries was indeed good political management by king and ministers. But if the court facilitated this as a theater of power and a space for negotiation, the dominance of the leading families (who defined politics as remaining influential at court) created coteries and factions without which ministers could not survive (Hardman 1995; Horowski 2003). Anything but very gradual reform was thus almost structurally impossible, doomed to failure as it became too risky. Decision-making required a proactive, experienced monarch who kept a firm grip on ministerial rivalries and court faction, but even then it took place in context of huge structural limitations on the exercise of royal power (Wick 1980). Faction was rife at the center, as several empirical studies have shown, and it could be described as a constant in the political culture (Gruder 2007; Hardman 1995, 2010; Price 1995). If we change our definition of the state and rethink its power processes and techniques of control, then new questions arise about the origins of the Revolution. We might for example develop a typology of crisis under the *ancien régime* in the seventeenth and eighteenth centuries, and compare that with the 1780s to understand the similarities and differences (Campbell 2012).

Crisis and Revolution

So we come back to our initial questions about the origins of the Revolution, but in a very different state of studies. What is a revolution? What stages does it go through in order to take place? Are revolutions produced by social, economic, ideological, or political (including fiscal) tensions? What is the relationship of crisis to revolution? Historians are always trying to take into account new research, without so far having produced a complete reconceptualization of the problem in the French case. Sociologists have various models, but my preferred inspiration is one of "state failure" applied in a more historically grounded fashion. Various elements lead to a crisis that is dynamic, transformative by its very nature. The crisis is far more than a precipitant of a revolution ready made in the minds of men. This crisis brings forth in response attempts at reform that then invite into politics new groups who find their interests threatened or advanced, but who at first are traditionally, not revolutionarily, motivated, because they do not expect the regime to fail. Most political systems are rather good at dealing with traditional problems, and a degree of tension is normal, but when the issues are new, or politics is under pressure conceptually, or simply the scale of the problems is too vast, existing strategies and techniques of government become over-stretched, ineffective. Thus it was with the baroque state in an age of international competition. So the crisis snowballs, as ineffectual attempts to resolve it (political mismanagement) bring in wider groups, like ripples made by a stone in a pool. The role of the public sphere is crucial in facilitating widening debate. (In the 1780s this is a major difference with previous crises.) Gradually, in some cases quite suddenly, and usually quite late in the day, people realize that something is changing, and begin to make new choices in defense of their interests. From the growing competition the crisis spreads, until governance becomes nearly impossible, and political collapse occurs. Into the vacuum step new contending groups, alarmed and empowered, having to decide how to replace the discredited regime. Some are more militantly and idealistically determined to remodel the system to serve their interests better. So, in this view of revolution as process, what needs to be explained is "state failure."

This means first investigating the nature of the state, its resources and political management, its inherent tensions and contradictions, its governing elite's ability to deal with crises. Then we must ask how the crisis develops to undermine confidence and pose virtually insurmountable problems for the regime. Finally, we must consider how and why new groups become involved, and try to understand their choices in 1788–89. Here intellectual and cultural history have a particularly important role to play, for their choices had complex motivations and were far from being mere political, social, or economic reflexes (Campbell forthcoming). So a state-centered perspective as the basis of an analytical narrative, actually restore the political (in a new, wider, definition) and bring in the other approaches. It does so not in general terms, but rather in terms of more specific questions about motives in the particular and ever-changing succession of situations as the crisis develops. Motives and perceptions change during a crisis, they evolve, and they must be studied in their precise context. The Revolution was not produced by cultural or social or economic change in general; it was produced by a developing crisis that involved various aspects of all of these elements, for politics broadly defined incorporates the defense of group interests and their perceptions of the nature of the issues. Not all social or cultural concerns or traits will be important at a given moment – and many of those that are important are not new ones but older attitudes and quarrels, sometimes expressed in a new language (Blaufarb 2006; Cubells 1987; Wick 1980). So the notion of strategy becomes important for the historian, and the actors regain the power of speech that Foucault took away. We do however need to work with an expanded definition of politics that is less related to state policy and more about how people get what they want. The challenge is to find new ways of talking about the motivation of individuals and groups in political situations, and then to situate these within the structures at all levels.

Currently there are only two collections dealing explicitly with the origins of the Revolution (Campbell 2006; Kaiser and Van Kley 2011). Both throw a good deal of new light on the problem of the origins, but neither even attempts to offer more than a provisional explanation any more than does the best survey article (Bossenga 2007). We must accept that in the current fragmented state of studies a convincing new model would be unlikely. On the other hand, it is extremely useful to take stock of an established view or a debate, to question where we have got to, in order to ask valid new questions in the light of new work. The journey may be unending, but that is no reason to ignore the changing scenery along the way.

References

Antoine, Michel (1986). *Le Dur métier de Roi.* Paris: PUF.

Aulard, François-Alphonse (1910). *The French Revolution, a Political History, 1789–1804.* London: Unwin.

Baker, K.M. (1990). *Inventing the French Revolution.* Cambridge: Cambridge University Press.

Beik, William (2005). "The Absolutism of Louis XIV as Social Collaboration." *P&P*, 188: 195–224.

Bell, David A. (2001). *The Cult of the Nation in France.* Cambridge, Mass.: Harvard University Press.

Blaufarb, Rafe (2006). "Noble Tax Exemption and the Long-Term Origins of the French Revolution: The Example of Provence, 1530s to 1789." In Jay M. Smith (ed.). *The French Nobility in the Eighteenth Century: Reassessments and New Approaches.* University Park: Pennsylvania State University Press.

Bonney, Richard (1998). "What's New About the New French Fiscal History?" *JMH*, 70: 639–667.

Bossenga, Gail (2007). "The Origins of the French Revolution." *History Compass*, 5: 1294–1337.

Burson, Jeffrey D. (2010). "The Catholic Enlightenment in France from the Fin-de-Siècle Crisis of Consciousness to the Revolution, 1650–1789." In Ulrich Lehner and Michael Printy (eds.). *Brill Companion to Catholic Enlightenment.* Leiden: Brill. 63–126.

Campbell, Peter R. (1988). *The Ancien Régime in France.* Oxford: Blackwell.

Campbell, Peter R. (1989). "Old Regime Politics and the New Interpretation of the French Revolution." *Renaissance and Modern Studies*, 33: 1–20.

Campbell, Peter R. (1993). *Louis XIV, 1661–1715.* London: Pearson.

Campbell, Peter R. (1996). *Power and Politics in Old Regime France, 1720–1745.* London and New York: Routledge.

Campbell, Peter R. (ed.) (2006). *The Origins of the French Revolution.* Basingstoke and New York: Palgrave.

Campbell, Peter R. (2007). "The Language of Patriotism in France, 1750–1770." *e-France, Journal of French Studies*, 1: 1–43, http://www.rdg.ac.uk/e-France/issues.htm.

Campbell, Peter R. (2011). "Absolute Monarchy." In William Doyle (ed.). *The Handbook of The Ancien Regime.* Oxford: Oxford University Press. 11–37.

Campbell, Peter R. (2012). "Crises "politiques" et parlements: Pour une micro-histoire des crises parlementaires au XVIIIe siècle." *Histoire, Économie, Société.*

Campbell, Peter R. (forthcoming). *Crisis and Revolution: State Failure and the Origins of the French Revolution.* Oxford: Oxford University Press.

Chaline, Olivier (1996). *Godart de Belbeuf: Le Parlement, le roi et les normands.* Luneray: Bertout.

Chaline, Olivier (2005). *Le Règne de Louis XIV.* Paris: Flammarion.

Chartier, Roger (1990). *Histoire de l'édition française*, vol. 2: *Le Livre triomphant.* Paris: Fayard.

Chartier, Roger (1991). *The Cultural Origins of the French Revolution.* Durham, N.C.: Duke University Press.

Chaussinand-Nogaret, Guy (1985). *The French Nobility in the Eighteenth Century*, trans. William Doyle. Cambridge: Cambridge University Press.

Cobban, Alfred (1971). *Aspects of the French Revolution.* London: Paladin.

Collins, James C. (2009). *The State in Early Modern France*, 2nd edn. Cambridge: Cambridge University Press.

Cossandey, Fanny and Robert Descimon (2002). *L'Absolutisme en France: Histoire et historiographie.* Paris: Le Seuil.

Cubells, Monique (1987). *Les Horizons de la liberté: La Naissance de la Révolution en Provence, 1787–1789.* Aix-en-Provence: Édisud.

Darnton, Robert (1982). *The Literary Underground of the Old Regime.* Cambridge, Mass.: Harvard University Press.

Darnton, Robert (1995). *The Corpus of Clandestine Literature in France, 1769–1789.* New York: Norton.

Darnton, Robert (1996). *The Forbidden Best-Sellers of Pre-Revolutionary France.* New York: Norton.

Dawson, Philip (1972). *Provincial Magistrates and Revolutionary Politics in France, 1789–1795.* Cambridge, Mass.: Harvard University Press.
Doyle, William (1981). *The Origins of the French Revolution*, Oxford: Oxford University Press.
Doyle, William (1995). *Officers, Nobles and Revolutionaries: Essays on Eighteenth-Century France.* London: Hambledon Press.
Emmanuelli, François-Xavier (1981). *Un Mythe de l'absolutisme bourbonien: L'Intendance du milieu du XVIIe siècle à la fin du XVIIIe siècle.* Aix-en-Provence: Université de Provence.
Fantoni, Marcello (ed.) (2012). *The Court in Europe.* Bulzoni: Rome.
Félix, Joël (1999). *Finances et politique au Siècle des Lumières: Le Ministère L'Averdy, 1763–1768.* Paris: Imprimerie Nationale.
Félix, Joël (2006). "The Financial Origins of the French Revolution." In Peter R. Campbell (ed.). *The Origins of the French Revolution.* Basingstoke and New York: Palgrave. 35–62.
Figeac, Michel (2002). *L'Automne des gentilshommes: Noblesse d'Aquitaine, noblesse française au siècle des lumières.* Paris: H. Champion.
Ford, Franklin (1953). *Robe and Sword: The Regrouping of the French Aristocracy after Louis XIV.* Cambridge, Mass.: Harvard University Press.
Forster, Robert (1960). *The Nobility of Toulouse in the Eighteenth Century: A Social and Economic Study.* Baltimore: Johns Hopkins University Press.
Forster, Robert (1963). "The Provincial Noble: A Reappraisal." *AHR*, 68, 681–691.
Foucault, Michel (1991). *The Foucault Reader*, ed. Paul Rabinow. London: Penguin Books.
Furet, François (1981). *Interpreting the French Revolution*, trans. Elborg Forster. Cambridge: Cambridge University Press.
Garrioch, David (1996). *The Formation of the Parisian Bourgeoisie.* Cambridge, Mass.: Harvard University Press.
Goldstone, Jack A. (1991). *Revolution and Rebellion in the Early Modern World.* Berkeley and London: University of California Press.
Gruder, Vivian (2007). *The Notables and the Nation: The Political Schooling of the French, 1787–1788.* Cambridge, Mass.: Harvard University Press.
Habermas, Jürgen (1989). *The Structural Transformation of the Public Sphere: An Enquiry into a Category of Bourgeois Society.* Cambridge, Mass.: Harvard University Press.
Hardman, John (1995). *French Politics, 1774–1789.* London and New York: Longman.
Hardman, John (2010). *Overture to Revolution: The Assembly of Notables and the Crisis of France's Old Regime.* Oxford: Oxford University Press.
Horowski , Leonhard (2003). "'Such a Great Advantage for My Son': Office-Holding and Career Mechanisms at the Court of France (1661 to 1789)." *The Court Historian*, 8: 125–175.
Jones, Colin (1991). "Bourgeois Revolution Revivified." In Colin Lucas (ed.). *Rewriting the French Revolution.* Oxford: Oxford University Press. 69–118.
Jourdan, Annie (2008). *La Révolution batave: Entre la France et l'Amérique (1795–1806).* Rennes: Presses Universitaires de Rennes.
Kaiser, Thomas E. (2011). "The Public Sphere." In William Doyle (ed.). *The Oxford Handbook of the Ancien Régime.* Oxford: Oxford University Press. 409–431.
Kaiser, Thomas E. and Dale K. Van Kley (2011). *From Deficit to Deluge: The Origins of the French Revolution.* Stanford, Calif.: Stanford University Press.
Kaplow, Jeffry (1965). *New Perspectives on the French Revolution: Readings in Historical Sociology.* New York: Wiley.
Kettering, Sharon (1986). *Patrons, Brokers and Clients in Seventeenth-Century France.* Oxford: Oxford University Press.

Lefebvre, Georges (1939). *Quatre-vingt-neuf.* Paris: Maison du Livre Française.
Legay, Marie-Laure (2001). *Les États provinciaux dans la construction de l'État moderne aux XVIIe et XVIIIe siècles.* Geneva: Droz.
Legay, Marie-Laure (2011). *La Banqueroute de l'État royal: La Gestion des finances publiques de Colbert à la Révolution française.* Paris: ÉHÉSS.
Legay, Marie-Laure and Roger Baury (eds.) (2009). *L'Invention de la décentralisation: Noblesse et pouvoirs intermédiaires en France et en Europe.* Lille: Presses Universitaires du Septentrion.
Lilti, Antoine (2012). *The Society of Salons: Sociability and Worldliness*, trans. Lydia Cochrane. New York: Oxford University Press.
Linton, Marisa (2001). *The Politics of Virtue in Enlightenment France.* Houndmills: Palgrave.
Linton, Marisa (2006). "The Intellectual Origins of the French Revolution." In Peter R. Campbell (ed.). *The Origins of the French Revolution.* Basingstoke and New York: Palgrave. 139–159.
Lucas, Colin (1973). "Nobles, Bourgeois and the Origins of the French Revolution." *P&P*, 60: 84–126.
Markoff, John (1996). *The Abolition of Feudalism: Peasants, Lords and Legislators in the French Revolution.* University Park: Pennsylvania State University Press.
Mathiez, Albert (1922). *Histoire de la Révolution française.* Paris: Armand Colin.
Maza, Sarah (1993). *Private Lives and Public Affairs: The Causes Célèbres of Prerevolutionary France.* Berkeley: University of California Press.
McMahon, Darrin M. (2001). *Enemies of Enlightenment: The French Counter-Enlightenment and the Making of Modernity.* Oxford: Oxford University Press.
Mettam, Roger (1988). *Power and Faction in Louis XIV's France.* Oxford: Blackwell.
Michelet, Jules (1847–53). *Histoire de la Révolution française*, 5 vols. Paris: Chamerot.
Mornet, Daniel (1933). *Les Origines intellectuelles de la Révolution française.* Paris: Armand Colin.
Nicolas, Jean (2002). *La Rébellion française: Mouvements populaires et conscience sociale 1661–1789.* Paris: Seuil.
Palmer, Robert (1959–64). *The Age of Democratic Revolutions*, 2 vols. Princeton, N.J.: Princeton University Press.
Potter, Mark and Jean-Laurent Rosenthal (1997). "Politics and Public Finance in France: The Estates of Burgundy, 1660–1790." *Journal of Interdisciplinary History*, 27: 577–612.
Poussou, Jean-Pierre (1983). *Bordeaux et le sud-ouest au XVIIIe siècle: Croissance économique et attraction urbaine.* Paris: ÉHÉSS.
Price, Munro (1995). *Preserving the Monarchy: The Comte de Vergennes, 1774–1787.* Cambridge: Cambridge University Press.
Riley, James C. (1986). *The Seven Years War and the Old Regime in France: The Economic and Financial Toll.* Princeton, N.J.: Princeton University Press.
Roche, Daniel (1998). *France in the Enlightenment.* Cambridge, Mass.: Harvard University Press.
Saint-Jacob, Pierre de (1960). *Les Paysans de la Bourgogne du nord au dernier siècle de l'Ancien Régime.* Paris: Les Belles Lettres.
Skocpol, Theda (1979). *States and Social Revolutions.* Cambridge: Cambridge University Press.
Skornicki, Arnault (2011). *L'Économiste, la cour et la patrie: L'Economie politique dans la France des Lumières.* Paris: CNRS.
Smith, Jay M. (2005a). *Nobility Reimagined. The Patriotic Nation in Eighteenth-Century France*, Ithaca, N.Y.: Cornell University Press.

Smith, Jeremy (2005b). "Europe's Atlantic Empires: Early Modern State Formation Reconsidered." *Political Power and Social Theory*, 17: 103–153.

Sonenscher, Michael (1989). *Work and Wages: Natural Law, Politics, and the Eighteenth-Century French Trades.* Cambridge: Cambridge University Press.

Stone, Bailey (1986). *The French Parlements and the Crisis of the Old Regime.* Chapel Hill: University of North Carolina Press.

Swann, Julian (1995). *Politics and the Parlement of Paris under Louis XV, 1754–1774.* Cambridge: Cambridge University Press.

Swann, Julian (2009). "Power and the Provinces: The Estates of Burgundy in the Reign of Louis XVI." In Marie-Laure Legay and Roger Baury (eds.). *L'Invention de la décentralisation: Noblesse et pouvoirs intermédiaires en France et en Europe.* Lille: Presses Universitaires du Septentrion. 156–173.

Tackett, Timothy (1996). *Becoming a Revolutionary: The Deputies of the French National Assembly and the Emergence of a Revolutionary Culture (1789–1790).* Princeton, N.J.: Princeton University Press.

Taylor, George V. (1962). "Types of Capitalism in Eighteenth-Century France." *EHR*, 79: 478–497.

Taylor, George V. (1967). "Non-Capitalist Wealth and the Origins of the French Revolution." *AHR*, 72: 469–496.

Tocqueville, Alexis de (1856). *L'Ancien Régime et la Révolution.* Paris: Levy Frères.

Van Kley, Dale K. (1996). *The Religious Origins of the French Revolution.* New Haven, Conn.: Yale University Press.

Vovelle Michel (1990). *Ideologies and Mentalities.* Chicago: University of Chicago Press.

Wick, Daniel (1980). "The Court Nobility and the French Revolution." *Eighteenth Century Studies*, 13: 263–284.

Chapter Two

The Social and Economic Crisis in France at the End of the *Ancien Régime*

Jean-Pierre Jessenne

"Crisis": certainly one of the words most frequently used and heard at the start of the twenty-first century. Dictionaries stress its many meanings, from "sudden and violent manifestation" to "a serious phase in the evolution of things, events … depression, collapse, malaise" (Robert, *Dictionnaire de la langue française*). In any case, the drift toward the use of stereotypes has led to strongly contrasting uses, some indeterminate, notably in discussion of current affairs to justify policies said to be necessary, others on the contrary very specific – the "Crisis of 1929" being the most obvious, but also that of 1789. The latter has even been the subject of a major historiographical debate following the argument by Labrousse (1990 [1944]) and others that the French Revolution occurred at the end of an acute social crisis resulting from the impossibility of transforming what would from 1789 be called the *ancien régime*. In contrast with the views of Marxist economists and historians, since the 1980s another critique (notably Furet 1988) has, among other things, provoked a kind of inversion of interpretations, relegating the social crisis to an outmoded status, to place political culture and crisis at the very heart of the revolutionary process.

Since this turn towards the "tout politique" (Vovelle 1997), interpretations have for the most part gone beyond this simplistic seesawing to try to enable a historical understanding that combines all evolutionary elements that may have contributed to revolution. Therefore, to admit that the Revolution was first of all a political event that overturned the array of powers does not exempt us from asking why it arose within a context of deep economic and social crisis, which on the one hand made the situation intolerable for a large part of the population and on the other could find no resolution within the framework of social relations, of the monarchy and traditional structures generally. This perspective, which claims to approach the initial crisis with an essential but not exclusive explanation, requires,

A Companion to the French Revolution, First Edition. Edited by Peter McPhee.

in my view, several conditions. The first is to resist the teleological temptation to see all France before the Revolution in the light of the Revolution itself, as if everything led to it: for this reason we will avoid the use of the words "cause" and even "origins" so frequently found in the historiography of this question (e.g. Bertaud 1992; Campbell 2006; Doyle 1988 [1980]). In contrast, we will take into account the multiplicity of situations – change and archaism, wealth and poverty, solidarity and conflict, and so on. At the same time the inevitable question remains: why did these contradictions explode and crystallize into an acute crisis at a particular moment in time?

This endeavor requires a process that begins by recalling the essential, but occasionally forgotten, facts about a society of distinct inequalities that had, however, become more complex. This leads us to the consideration of the part played by prosperity in the eighteenth century and the rise in tensions, especially after 1760, including those relating to developments across the century. From then on the mixture of the economic and the political, notably because of financial and conjunctural problems, and the combination of crises creates a major part of the revolutionary dynamic.

Back to Basics: An Unequal and Fragmented Society

Despite the profound changes of the eighteenth century, French society remained basically a society organized into orders which assumed hierarchy on the one hand and on the other the location of individual or collective identities within recognized corporations or communities.

Orders, Hierarchy, and Privileges

Two fundamental principles governed the organization of society. First, Catholicism was still the state religion. This resulted in a rule of exclusion, at least until the Edict of Toleration of 1787: not to be Catholic meant to be on the margins of civil society. Moreover, the religious imaginary set up an essential hierarchy: on the one hand, the king was at the peak of the social pyramid by virtue of his sacred position as the representative of God on earth; on the other, the clergy made up the first order of the kingdom. In this it outranked those who fulfilled the other function judged to be superior according to the values passed down from the Middle Ages, namely combat in the service of the king, which was regarded, with other claimed distinctions, as legitimizing the superiority of the nobility, the second order of the kingdom.

According to this logic two orders benefited from privileges, of which it is interesting to recall the definition in the *Encyclopédie méthodique* of 1786: "All useful or honorable distinction enjoyed by certain members of society and which others do not enjoy." The legitimacy of these distinctions was therefore presented as intangible. In the long list of privileges, that of fiscal indemnity, notably from royal taxes and especially the *taille*, ranked first, but there were also honorific and political distinctions such as one's place in ceremonies or traditional representation in the Estates-General (with the intangible rule that an order was equivalent to a voice, the questioning of which lay at the heart of pre-revolutionary debates). These were differences in rights to which we should add a number of specific advantages. For instance, even if they were not the only seigneurs, most of those enjoying privileges were nonetheless the principal seigneurs. Moreover, they had control over a considerable share of the wealth of property – about 10 percent belonged to the clergy and 20 percent to the nobles – although there were significant regional variations, even between villages, which could totally change the social profile of that locality. We should add that the clergy was the most important proprietor of buildings in cities.

As a result, at the beginning of 1789, Sieyès expressed a fundamental social fact, not just a political slogan, when he observed that since about 97 percent of the French did not belong to the first two "estates" they formed the Third Estate (*Qu'est-ce que le Tiers-État?*). This third order was thus defined above all in negative terms: its members, unworthy of benefiting from privileges, were thus subject to taxation and relegated to the bottom of a cascade of contempt. But they did not thereby constitute a simple aggregation of individuals; belonging to a body or a community mattered to them. Amongst the variation in circumstances, we must remember that towns were more highly structured than the countryside, insofar as most towns had been granted statutes that endowed them with a certain number of rights (recognition of those inhabitants registered as bourgeois, specific administration and courts, fiscal exemptions); at its heart, most of the workers were organized into trade communities governed by regulations; these distinguished between masters, journeymen, and apprentices, they conferred various rights, and they imposed duties on various people. Toulouse, for example, numbered 81 trades, Paris six major bodies of merchants and 144 other "corporations." In 1776 Turgot, the Comptroller-General of Finance, tried to suppress them: they were re-established after his dismissal but the uncertainties this engendered formed part of the social uncertainties of a greater instability in recruitment and hierarchies (Kaplan 2001). In the countryside, the formal organizational cells were the *seigneurie* and the parish, but even if they had no legal status, the communities of inhabitants formed the crucial cells of collective life.

Thus, on every level, people were to be found each in his proper station, each in his own group. Hierarchy was continually highlighted: the allocation of pews in church or of graves in the cemetery, the order of precedence in religious or royal processions, even one's place at table, scrupulously signaled the differences in status between groups and within them. These elementary divisions were also subjected to many adjustments, however, as recent research has demonstrated.

The Thousand Splinter Groups of the Orders and Social Categories

For a long time the real heterogeneity of the orders, demonstrating the fiction of their unity, led us to make simple distinctions, notably between the high and low clergy and between the high and petty nobility. The symptoms of these differentiations remain valid. The high clergy of prelates, canons, and abbots was characterized by the accumulation of revenues from diverse sources (benefactions, pensions, seigneurial revenues) and by often being recruited from the high nobility. This, made up as it was of princes and the great men of the kingdom, displayed in any case the same characteristics of the accumulation of wealth. Presence at court and participation in its displays forged a common melting-pot, in spite of often sharp rivalries, for what the revolutionary generation would designate by the negative term "aristocracy," at the end of a long disparagement of this minority that continued to believe in its essential superiority even while the voices of utilitarian critics such as Mably gathered strength (Doyle 2009).

In any case, the contrast with others who enjoyed privileges is striking. It is true that the income of between 300 and 1,500 *livres* (which may or may not have been supplemented by casual payments) of the lower clergy, especially the parish priests and curates who were strongly linked to the people, was, although limited, above real poverty. The situation of the ordinary regular clergy was also very variable. A real crisis in recruitment meant that monastic orders and great abbeys, with considerable incomes, had only a derisory number of members. In contrast, the hospital, charitable, and teaching orders retained an undeniable social presence in most towns. The same heterogeneity can be seen among the nobility (Chaussinand-Nogaret 1984). One can in particular distinguish a provincial *bonne noblesse*, consisting of about 10,000 families, with incomes of between 4,000 and 50,000 *livres*, who often owned a country château and town house, with a considerable domestic staff and imposing lifestyle, involving hunting, maintaining a salon, theater-going, and travel. The *noblesse de robe*, particularly members of a *parlement*, constituted a small world notable for keeping to itself and maintaining a culture and lifestyle that were often more austere. The nobility, which was more numerous and consisted of about 50,000 families, disposed of mediocre incomes, sometimes amounting to less than 1,000 *livres*, more often of a few thousand *livres*; its members were country squires who had only a more or less rustic country house to live in and maintained a modest lifestyle. They are described as frequently being very attached to their titles and prerogatives.

Obviously the Third Estate was no more homogeneous, starting with those who lived in the country. We must remember that at the end of the eighteenth century about 80 percent of the French population was rural and that a stereotypical view, as evident in the elites of the period as it is among many historians, tends to lump everyone together as the peasantry, while the works of many scholars on French rural society underline the great heterogeneity that we have tried to summarize in Table 2.1.

We can thus identify at least five non-privileged rural categories, with a dominant rural group at its summit, notably made up of tenant farmers or sharecroppers who leased large farms, but which also included some members of the liberal professions and merchants, a group which in many ways could meld into a rural bourgeoisie; with at the bottom a truly vast category of dependents living by various means: farmers of plots, day laborers, wage-earners, and domestics with few qualifications: a category which at its fringes was hardly to be distinguished from those devoid of means. Between the two extremes were middling categories consisting of people who were more or less independent according to the amount of their land or the quality of their workshop. Altogether, in addition to this basic heterogeneity, we should stress that the majority of country-dwellers did not attain

Table 2.1 The heterogeneity of the rural Third Estate

SOCIAL CATEGORY	*% of country-dwellers*	*AGRICULTURAL ACTIVITIES*			*Non-agricultural professions (15–30 % of country dwellers)*
		Types of cultivator	*Designation*	*Types of cultivation*	
Dominant rural group	5–10	Large-scale cultivators	*fermiers*, *censiers*, and *gros laboureurs*	From tens to more than 100 hectares (ha.), mostly tenant-farmed, more rarely under sharecropping or freehold	– Liberal professions (notaries etc.) – Wholesale merchants (grains, textiles) – Millers
Independent	15–20	Medium-scale cultivators	– *laboureurs* (Parisian Basin, the East) – *ménagers* (Midi) – *metayers* (cente-west) Winegrowers [cusp of independence]	– *c.*10–20 ha. – A plowing team – Some freehold; some tenant-farmed or *métayage*	– Local shopkeepers (innkeepers) – Qualified tradesmen (farriers, carpenters, coopers)
Semi-independent	20–25	Small-scale cultivators	– *Ménagers*, *tabaquiers*, *haricotiers* (the north or Picardy) – *Closiers*, *bordiers* (west, southwest)	– 3–10 ha – No plowhorses – Variable status	– Tradespeople not highly specialized (building) – Textile workers
Dependent	35–50	– Cultivators of allotments – Non-cultivators	– *manouvriers*, *journaliers*, *brassiers* – *domestiques agricoles* (shepherds etc.)	Micro-exploitation plus salaried agricultural work and non-agricultural work (textiles)	– Workers – Servants
Needy	10–20	Aid-dependent and beggars			

Source: Jessenne 2006.

a state of economic independence that enabled them to support a family from their farm or workshop. Moreover, this general table hides considerable differences in the distribution of the various categories depending on different regions and agricultural systems.

The same need to differentiate applies to the analysis of urban society. Without forgetting that in most towns the nobility made up the richest category, we must remember the classic distribution into three or five "levels of commoner" proposed in *Histoire de la France urbaine* (Le Roy Ladurie 1976). At the top, a high bourgeoisie consisting of traders, bankers, high-level non-noble officials, and very well-off people of independent means made up 2–5 percent of the urban population. The intermediate class of the middling bourgeoisie consisted of merchants, legal men, liberal professions, qualified employees, officials with independent means, and shopkeepers with a house of their own, adding up to 10–20 percent depending on the town, and highly indicative of their main urban functions – with, for example, the legal professions being extremely important in towns that accommodated a bailiwick or sovereign court. It constituted the pivotal class in urban society. What is left is a majority of around three-quarters of the inhabitants which we can amalgamate into the composite category of townspeople, but more clearly break down into three groups: the petite bourgeoisie of independent people, grouping shopkeepers and tradesmen (the stallholders), innkeepers, drivers, and so on. Those who lived mainly from wages or the monies accumulated from various small revenue sources made up what is most commonly known as the *menu peuple* and offers the archetypal image of the urban populace, such as it is rehabilitated in the *Cris de Paris* and its companions, with its small street traders, numerous domestic servants, and so on (Milliot 1995).The remainder were the more or less indigent and the delinquents whom historians sometimes respectfully call the "third estate of the people" (*tiers peuple*) and those less concerned with their dignity designate as "the dregs of the people" or that part of the population frequently described as "vile."

Blurred Social Identities

Order or class? The debate during the 1960s about the knowledge we have of the principle governing French society during the *ancien régime* (Goubert 1969) seems to have been overwhelmed by the complexity of the social reality, which leads us to a detailed deconstruction of different categories according to multiple criteria in which wealth and income are linked to economic independence, prestige, and the mode and place of residence. In addition, the historiography of recent years has demonstrated the fluidity of social identities that defy simple attempts at classification. We can illustrate these approaches through three examples – of the bourgeoisie, of the people, and of colonial society.

As far as the first is concerned, what is at stake is obviously the matter of size, since it is a matter of nothing less than starting the debate on the bourgeois revolution from scratch. Some research stresses that the self-representations of certain groups embody the ideas embraced by Alfred Cobban (1984 [1964]), according to which a bourgeoisie that does not call itself by that name or recognize itself as such could not constitute a class capable of playing a major part in the social and political dynamic and is rather the result of a myth forged *a posteriori* (Maza 2000). The approach of others (Garrioch 1996; Jessenne et al. 2003; Jones 1991) stresses that it is precisely the characteristics of being heterogeneous, intermediate, hesitant, and unexpressed that gave this middle class its decisive influence on the changes taking place. The diverse components of the bourgeoisie shared a faith in individual merit and in money and were free to break through the "glass ceiling" of the high functions reserved by the state for those who made the most of titles and at the same time to establish an order that guaranteed equality before the law and freedom of the individual, property, and enterprise. Before 1789, these aspirations were manifested through diffuse outlooks and contradictory social practices that linked the growth in business and consumption with purchase of land and bourgeois domestic or family life, and with a taste for display. These various ways of behaving certainly did not arise from a coherent social project set out in advance, all the more because these bourgeois elites had still, like Beaumarchais, not decided whether they wanted to enter the world of privilege or change the rules of the game (Petitfrère 1989). Moreover, this diversity of aspirations was accentuated by the fact that some socio-professional groups were happy to cultivate their singularity, such as lawyers, who had not yet organized themselves into a national order, but made common rules for themselves on questions of training and recruitment and happily promoted specific values which were in any case equivocal since they mixed honor and social utility, thus providing a good example of divided identity (Leuwers 2006).

The same complexity of a people – at a moment which is seen as almost mythical following Jules Michelet in the mid-nineteenth century – becoming a homogeneous force capable of overturning all social barriers once they began to crumble is stressed in recent research. Both the way in which society is thought of within the multiple strands of economic and philosophical thought of the second half of the eighteenth century (physiocracy, egalitarian liberalism, and so on) and the sociocultural practices of tradespeople demonstrate a weakening of corporate conduct (less respect for rules of corporations, lessened prestige of the masters, a less hidebound choice of traditional first and family names, and so on) and a growing individualism in both matrimonial and professional behavior (Cohen 2010; Lethuillier 1993). Cohen ends her study with this diagnosis: "More than a popular identity, it is truly an open combination of possible behaviors [that one observes]. Political discourse constructs groups that start from a state of heterogeneity, of individuals who are not necessarily the same in terms of their relation to the means of production, but who have in the circumstances the same political outlook" (2010: 416). But one essential fact remains: the stigma imposed on the "dominated" by the elites could, in certain circumstances, such as the "Revolt of the Masked" in the Vivarais of 1783, turn into a slogan adopted by "the people" themselves to forge its union against a hegemony considered unbearable. We shall come back to this.

Even the society of the French colonies in the Antilles, which were for a long time examined only in relation to the opposition between white colonizers and black slaves, provides us with the opportunity for analyses that reveal a more complex social distribution, with the importance of the category of free people of color (the descendants of freed slaves who were themselves slave-owners and played a major role in the social dynamic of the Caribbean Islands) in Guadeloupe, for example (Régent 2004).

We have thus a paradox crucial to an understanding of French society in the eighteenth century: the rules of the social orders remained in place and were closely linked to the monarchical state, but social identities and practices were seen as more and more fractured. We must note that, contrary to a long-held view of the *ancien régime*, France had changed during the century and had known a prosperity that may seem paradoxical, at first blush, within an eighteenth century that finished in crisis.

Growth and Prosperity in the Eighteenth Century: Evidence and Ambiguity

A Snapshot of Some Growth Indicators

Within today's frontiers France had about 22.5 million inhabitants in 1715 and 28.5 million in 1789. This means there was a growth of about 25 percent over the period. The France of the 1780s was a young country: people under 20 made up more than 40 percent of the population. This growth, however, was not the result of any radical change in demographic behavior. The rates of birth and death were still above 35 per thousand; life expectancy did not rise above 27.5 years for men and 28.1 for women. As Jacques Dupâquier emphasizes, this fact conceals a situation of great contrasts: "During the *ancien régime* one did not die 'young', one died very young or old" (1988: 154). Medical conditions and the prevention of disease had not progressed much and vulnerability, especially of children, remained omnipresent. The growth of the French population resulted above all from the disappearance of great epidemics after the 1720 plague in Marseille and from a lessening in the spikes in mortality resulting from food shortages. Growth in production, while unequal, occurred in many sectors, starting with agriculture.

Agriculture had not undergone any technical revolution; it progressed by small steps: more extensive cultivation of corn, and, gradually, of potatoes, more frequent plantation of crops for fodder or wholesale, regional specialization in stock feed, clearances, and so on. Although it is hard to estimate the global evolution in agricultural production and the figures remain open to debate, it appears to have grown at a similar rate to that of the population, estimated, according to scholars, at between 20 percent and 60 percent (Béaur 2000; Duby and Wallon 1976). One of the striking characteristics of the state of agriculture was undeniably the regional differences in the figures. Craft and industrial production showed the same level of disparity (Béaur and Minard 1997; Braudel and Labrousse 1970; Lemarchand 2008). The textile industry, the most significant activity, underwent very different evolutions with a remarkable growth (of the order of 4 percent a year) in cotton, printed, and chintz fabrics, notably in Alsace and Normandy. Coal and metal mining also took a great step forward, although total production remained low. We must add to this the vitality of the building industry, which played an important part in inspiring expansion because of the size of its workforce. Other sectors evolved more slowly. Traditional textiles, such as woolens manufacture, experienced modest growth (of about 1 percent a year), which conceals a regression in certain regions like Brittany.

But certainly, the sector that made the greatest gains during the eighteenth century was trade. Foreign trade, above all with the colonies – especially the Antilles – showed the most spectacular growth, thanks to the efforts of ship-fitters and private traders. The value of the exchanges multiplied by five for foreign trade overall and by ten in the case of colonial trade alone. Two further indicators of colonial activity: from 1720 to 1780 sugar production in Saint-Domingue grew from 700 to 80,000 tonnes and the number of slaves in the French Antilles grew from 40,000 to 500,000. The Atlantic ports, notably Bordeaux and Nantes, were the great beneficiaries of this growth. There was a real growth in domestic trade but it was weaker by comparison (Braudel and Labrousse 1970). In any case, the long-held view that France lagged overall behind England is from this time on in question, especially where trade is concerned.

The climate of general prosperity was then translated into price rises, linked to three factors: growth in population and therefore in demand, increase in the arrival of gold and silver from the Americas, and the wider use of bills of exchange which enabled an expansion in the amount of money in circulation. Labrousse (1933) examined these simultaneous developments and showed, for instance, that average agricultural prices between 1771 and 1789 were 60 percent higher than those of the period from 1726 to 1741, that the fastest increase occurred after 1763 and would last until 1775–80 (the increase ranges from 66 percent for wheat to 91 percent for wood). Economic growth benefited to the extent that "money attracts activity, activity attracts money." But land rent also profited greatly from this: between 1730 and 1739 and 1780 and 1789 it rose between 20 and 50 percent (discounting price rises). At this point we can see the problem of distribution of the fruits of this growth and the first weak point in this development.

Inequalities in Development and the Social Consequences

France was still a country of contrasts. These were first of all geographic and sectoral: strongly growing little islands of capitalist modernity (port cities, a few textile and mining areas, Paris, and so on) were caught within a dense economic fabric fed by a powerful agricultural sector, but within which traditional production and sales methods endured. The absence of a unified national grain market and the differences in prices between regions were highly revealing signs of this economic heterogeneity (Margairaz 1997: 32–33). These disparities are explained as much by the difficulties of transportation, despite the improvements in the royal roads and the work of the Ponts et Chaussées, as by the many shackles on exchange (seigneurial tolls, food laws, and so on).

French development was also based on a financial system that lent itself to uncertainty. Following the failure of the Law system in 1720, there was no question of a national bank along the lines of those in Holland or England and a dual arrangement continued, with financiers dealing with royal finance and bankers devoted to trade and private loans. The separation between these two activities was never absolute, but links multiplied during the last decades of the *ancien régime*. They ended in the creation, in 1776, of the Caisse d'Escompte which brought together foreign and Parisian bankers and the great financiers, of whom the best known is the tax-farmer Lavoisier. Through its capital it contributed to economic stimulus and public expenditure, but did this by favoring the business of a small group and by maintaining the confusion of private and royal interests.

We can extend this observation to the whole of society by examining the chances different people had of benefiting from this growth. Property owners who did not farm their own land profited from the rise in rents, but the privileged had additional opportunities of increasing their wealth: lands, forests that gained considerably in value from the rise in the price of wood, seigneurial taxes offset by the price rises. In the wider context all sellers of products benefited: renters and owners of large farms who could sell their grain, vignerons, craftsmen, traders, shopkeepers, and, of course, wholesalers. Transatlantic traders came off best in this game. However, at the top of the pyramid we find those who accumulated all this revenue, especially aristocrats dealing in commercial, industrial, and financial matters – like Orléans, Luynes, Montmorency, Broglie, and a few businessmen.

The contrast between those who benefited from prosperity and those left behind became far starker. Between 1726 and 1741 and 1771 and 1789, wage-earners felt a reduction in their real earnings of around 25 percent, and although payment in kind, availability of work, and extension of working life may have attenuated the effects of this decline for several decades, the low level of purchasing power remained no less obvious. In Sedan in 1774 almost three-quarters of the textile workers earned less than 20 *sous* a day (Gayot 1998). More generally, most day workers and unskilled wage-earners found themselves below this level by as much as 10 *sous*. In these conditions, most wage-earners spent most of their earnings on food, particularly bread, and their vulnerability to the price of goods increased, which in itself affected growth.

Inequalities and Distortions in Growth

Distribution of the benefits of prosperity depends on the nature of demand: it remained strong for luxury goods bought by the well-off class, but leveled out when it came to products in current demand, such as coarse fabrics, despite a certain spread of "everyday things" (Roche 1993). And this last fact alone was able to inspire an increased development with the same trend as the growth in population.

Moreover, productive investments were offset by royal taxes, status spending, or "social" investments: real estate for commoners seeking the status of landed gentry and incomes that would allow them to live on the interest of their investments alone. This milking of copious funds partly explains the comparatively weak effect, with the exception to some extent of Bordeaux, that the activity in the Atlantic had on the hinterland, and more generally the scattered nature of development in France. Thus Livesey shows a real battle for influence in Languedoc, concerning the Provincial Estates and fiscal organization, where the issue was to determine whether revenue from taxation and public borrowing was to be used in the region for economic investment (roads, drains) or was to be consumed by external taxes, notably from the King (Livesey 2010).

In an evolution in France where two troubling factors were constant – the state of the royal finances and privileges – economic growth could paradoxically definitely lead to a simultaneous exacerbation of structural antagonisms.

Overt Social Frictions

Much research, notably that by Jean Nicolas on rebellions (2002), reveals an increasingly confrontational French society in the second half of the eighteenth century (see Tables 2.2 and 2.3).

From this increasing number of conflicts seven principal fronts emerge: taxpayers or tax evaders opposing taxes and taxation authorities; subjects opposing judicial or police authority; rural and particularly urban people against all those they held responsible for penury and the price of foodstuffs; masters and journeymen craftsmen against those who benefited from freedom of work or trade (both the free production of textiles in the countryside after 1762 and competition from products from overseas); villagers with problems with the seigneur; and the lower clergy and parishioners against the high and the regular clergy, especially if they took tithes without performing religious duties. We can demonstrate this through two scenarios.

The first, which became more and more common, pitted villagers against the seigneur. The seigneurial system, that is to say the sum of the taxes and prerogatives weighing on those who lived on a domain, affected most of the countryside (as free land was hardly known outside the Midi). Even though serfdom, which constituted the heaviest and most archaic aspect of feudalism, had become rare – although almost a million peasants, concentrated mainly in the east of France were affected – taxes were generally imposed, whether in

Table 2.2 Multiplication and exacerbation of antagonisms: the five main kinds of rebellion in France 1661–1789 (total number of actions noted: 8,528)

Nature	*Number of rebellions*	*% of total*
Against state taxes	3,336	39
Against police or justice administration	1,212	14
Food	1,497	18
Against landowners	439	5
Work conflicts	441	5
Other (six kinds)	1,603	19

Source: Adapted from Nicolas 2002: 34.

Table 2.3 The five-yearly rhythm of rebellions during the second half of the eighteenth century

1750–54	*1755–59*	*1760–64*	*1765–69*	*1770–74*	*1775–79*	*1780–84*	*1785–89*
412	350	307	513	670	679	619	869

Source: Adapted from Nicolas 2002: 36.

money or in kind. It was rare for the taxes of all the *seigneurie* to be cumulated, but the total was never negligible and could amount to 25 percent of the agricultural production of Auvergne or Burgundy. Moreover, the seigneur enjoyed various exclusive rights and privileges over his lands: hunting rights, pigeon-coops, mills, and so on; he or his officials dispensed justice, called assemblies of the inhabitants, and published local regulations (such as banns). And the number of reasons why rural groups rose against seigneurial dominion grew as the century progressed. For instance, edicts inspired by physiocrats that encouraged the partition of common lands envisaged that one-third should revert to the landowners; this right of "triage" was regarded by many communities as plunder. Some seigneurs, inspired by the success of agronomy and wishing to increase revenues from their domains, enclosed even more of their land and forbade its collective use. Was this a matter of a "seigneurial reaction" (Goubert 1969; Soboul 1966) or a sign of the modernization of the privileges of great property-owning, "the womb of capitalism" (Le Roy Ladurie 1976)? Motives are so intermixed and linked as far as the protagonists are concerned that this seems in fact to be a false debate but, on the social level, what is most important is that these initiatives exacerbated the tensions between seigneurs and villagers and embedded this cleavage at the heart of rural communities. Thus Nicolas demonstrates that in the total rise in seditious acts, actions against seigneurs alone add up to some 250 events from 1760 to 1789, nearly three times the number in the preceding century. Nonetheless, depending on the state of village communities, the virulence of the antagonisms, the capacity of dominant groups of villagers to direct them, the demonstrations and the length of conflicts varied greatly. There is nothing to indicate, at the beginning of the 1780s, that they will converge to endanger a whole system; the implosion will be based on other convergences.

In any case, until the 1780s there was no lasting convergence with another ever-hidden object of contention: food scarcity. While this may have originated in the countryside, it spread well beyond it and the most spectacular demonstrations concerning it occurred in the cities. The Flour War in the Île de France of 1775, after the liberalization decreed by Turgot, was one which most struck people: from 20 April to 5 May the movement spread from the Oise Valley as far as Fontainebleau, passing through Paris and Versailles; demonstrators everywhere prevented grain convoys from leaving by road or river, obliging them to sell in the market at prices they considered fair, and confronted suspected hoarders (Gauthier et al. 1988). What is striking about this was the strong political dimension: opposition to the Comptroller-General or the Chief of Police of Paris affected the whole monarchy and from then on the fear of disturbances haunted economists and officials. It explains the shilly-shallying in policy relating to the grain trade: despite liberal proclamations, local administrations continued to intervene extensively in the policing of *bleds* and both *intendants* and *parlements* constantly wavered between regulation, assistance, and repression, especially in big cities like Rouen (Miller 1999). How could this tenuous equilibrium be maintained? There is no doubt that it depended in part on the elites sticking together behind the king.

The Illusion of the Coalescence of the Elites

We know the analysis of the *intendant* Sénac de Meilhan, who in 1790 asserted that, beyond the orders, successful newcomers had in his time become able to penetrate French high society. This analysis was followed by historians (Chaussinand-Nogaret 1984). It is true that the quick promotion of descendants of famous newly rich people gave hope to those who dreamed of emulating the daughters and granddaughters of Crozat, the farmer-general who had married into the high nobility. But does this not over-emphasize a few shining examples and retrospective illusions about the "beautiful years" of the *ancien régime*?

In fact, we can just a easily find signs of the closing of ranks, starting with the desire of reserving the upper ranks of the army to the old nobility demonstrated by Ségur's edict, which was adopted in 1781 and made it obligatory for potential officers to prove that they possessed four quarters of nobility. It was not because the high nobility supported Beaumarchais in the matter of Figaro's marriage that the valet's famous comment to his master – "Nobility, wealth, rank, positions! What did you do for so much? You took the trouble to be born, and no more" (*Le Mariage de Figaro*, Act V) – failed to resonate as a manifesto against inherited privileges and did not express irreducible opposition between two concepts of social superiority, which found notable expression in innumerable displays of the contempt of the nobility for commoners. We must note that financial problems came back ever more frequently to this differentiation.

The Crisis in Public Finances was also an Economic and Social Crisis

The monarchical state was far from ineffective in the eighteenth century, but the stubborn financial problem became neuralgic after the American War of Independence, the cost of which has been estimated at 2 billion *livres* and caused a chronic deficit. There are three reasons why peace did not in fact allow the situation to be restored. The failure of fiscal reforms, maintenance of exemptions for the privileged, and various provincial statutes prevented the general imposition of direct taxes, whereas the system of indirect taxation (resistance by farmers-general to rises in their rents, for instance) limited the amount raised by those taxes. The result: the state profited so little from the prosperity of the times that the net revenue of 1783 was slightly lower than that of 1740. Finally, administration remained peppered with archaisms and showed very little foresight (Legay 2011). Thus, by borrowing more and more, by the time Calonne became Comptroller-General in 1783, almost half of the 600 million *livres* received annually was devoted to servicing the debt. Bankruptcy threatened. But counting on a resumption of activity and wanting to avoid essentially destabilizing reforms, Calonne extended the policy of borrowing, facilitated by recourse to the Caisse d'Escompte.

In fact the Comptroller-General could not measure the impact of a phenomenon established later by Labrousse (1990 [1944]): the economy had, since 1775, entered a cycle in which the slightest rise in prices was accompanied by an economic slowdown. Consequently, it was harder to accumulate tax revenues, whereas the interest rates on royal borrowing rose in tandem with the decline in confidence.

In the wider world, from shipbuilders who were hoping for an increase in business with the declaration of peace to sellers of agricultural produce, all who profited from the rise found their profits less certain. Winemakers were especially affected by weaker prices. Furthermore, in 1785 a dearth of fodder and an epidemic among cattle afflicted all graziers.

Making matters worse for the monarchical state, its liberal initiatives seeking to modernize led to new tensions: on 6 February 1786 France signed a trade treaty with England (known as the Eden–Rayneval Treaty after its negotiators) which involved lower duty on wine and spirits crossing the Channel in exchange for a reduction in taxes on English textiles and metals. These arrangements brutally increased the textile crisis already set in motion by the stagnation or lowering of the income of many of the French.

Population growth itself was not constant, with mortality rising slightly, promoting social tension, and employment became more competitive, access to land became all the more difficult because the great properties, notably the privileged, were not subject to division. More generally, the rise to employment age of the numerous people born in the 1760s caused problems for the youngest seeking to join different trades and bodies. A consequence of this concatenation of circumstances was that more or less marked underlying social contrasts emerged spectacularly.

Accentuated Social Contrasts

The effects of rising wages, increasing fragmentation of small and large landholdings, and job scarcity combined to multiply the number of dependents for whom survival was a daily struggle. In the Pays de Caux the noticeable growth in the numbers of the most vulnerable was an obvious indication of the increased numbers of rural people who were dependent, even destitute (Lemarchand 1989). Begging, vagrancy, applications for aid, and rural exodus increased notably and reinforced each other. In the villages that make up the Haute-Marne of today, 15 percent of the population was in need of assistance (Clère 1988); in Paris, Necker stated that 33 centers received between 7,000 and 8,000 beggars between July 1784 and June 1785 (Kaplow 1971). Increased vagrancy was accompanied by delinquency, banditry, and theft.

Nonetheless, Enlightenment society seemed to sparkle more brightly than ever and flourished in a new art of living and consumption (chocolate, crockery, colored fabrics, clothing accessories). Patrons of cafés and theaters participated in this *joie de vivre*. At the same time, social cleavages became more visible: in urban planning for example, differentiation between floors in buildings was replaced by a stronger sociological demarcation of districts, with the densely populated sectors of the old neighborhoods and working-class suburbs given over to the poor and migrants, and the rich and the aristocracy taking areas renovated or constructed according to the Enlightenment rules for geometric, well-aerated urban construction, of which the west of Paris is a good example.

In fact Paris, with some 600,000 inhabitants (of whom, in 1793, only 27 percent of the male adults were born in the city) offered an especially striking view of these contrasts. Thus the capital city was both hypersensitive to all "events" and liable to produce ambivalent responses, notably from writers split between the attractions of

Paris, the intensity of life there, and revulsion against a "place of perdition" counter to the celebrated natural health of other places. Everything united to make the city a sounding board for a crisis beginning to become more general.

Crystallization of Crises between 1785 and 1789

In the space of a few months, especially from 1785 onwards, the conjunction of problems and their cumulative effects resulted in what we may call the pre-revolutionary crisis. It is then that lively but scattered social antagonisms transformed themselves into simplified and explosive socio-political actualities. Without specifically constituting a social crisis, the financial crisis of the monarchy constituted one of the decisive elements of this fluid process.

The Impossible Financial Solution

The 1788 budget, considered to be one of the most reliable in the history of the monarchy, also revealed the seriousness of the impasse in which the state found itself. Expenses amounted to 620,000 *livres* and receipts came to a little more than 500,000. Over half the receipts were already devoted to debt and interest repayments. Even if the expenses of the court and its pensions amounted to some 6 percent of the total, they seemed a manifest abuse, especially since the 1785 scandal of the queen's necklace had exacerbated public sensitivity to the sumptuous spending of a minority with which the monarchy was associated.

From the moment when the most audacious attempt to develop a new financial solution, the *Plan d'amélioration des finances* presented by Calonne to the Assembly of Notables in 1787, was doomed to failure by the double opposition to the ministers and to the fiscal measures that would reduce privileges, we may speak of an inexorable start to the financial crisis, which Arthur Young perfectly diagnosed in October 1787: "The finances are in too great a state of disarray [for the king] to have any means of restoring them without appealing to the Estates-General of the kingdom and such a meeting cannot occur without occasioning a revolution in the government" (2009 [1790]). In fact lenders made themselves scarce despite very alluring rates; the royal borrowings were not covered and did not allow for ordinary expenses to be met. Finally, Loménie de Brienne, the prime minister, persuaded Louis XVI to call the Estates-General on 8 August 1788. The financial tensions were not eased, however, and the state was forced to take out a compulsory loan on 16 August. The political and social repercussions are obvious: from the 28th to the 30th demonstrations celebrating the dismissal of Loménie de Brienne and symbolically saluting Good King Henry IV on the Pont Neuf gave rise to violent confrontations. The financial impasse began to crystallize all the crises.

The Focus of Antagonisms on Conflicting and Mobilizing Figures

Everyone knows the famous 1789 engraving showing a peasant bent and supported by his hoe, carrying on his back a priest and a nobleman that recalled the burdens weighing on the Third Estate, and the depiction of animals devouring the harvests. It constitutes an extraordinarily concentrated vindication, of the same standard as the wonderful formulation by Sieyès in "What is the Third Estate?" The caption to the image and its variants expresses the new course being taken by these antagonisms: "We must hope the game will soon be up."

In any case, in spring the *cahiers de doléances* offered the same repeated echoes formulated in various ways, but fiscal inequality and seigneurial charges always headed the list of complaints (Shapiro and Markoff 1998). However, before they appeared as one of the essential elements of the revolutionary dynamic of the Great Fear (Lefebvre 1989 [1932]), another crisis exploded.

The Harvest Crisis and Riots of 1789

In July 1788 violent storms destroyed part of the harvest. The winter of 1788–89 was particularly severe, preventing the circulation of goods and necessitating the use of stocks to replace winter grain. Food prices rose continuously. In the south of France, the price of corn doubled in a matter of months; it tripled in the north. For the first time in many years these price rises affected every region to a greater or lesser extent and their effect was extraordinarily increased on the social and political levels. While the crisis did not result in massive excess mortality as it had done in the seventeenth century, with the economy already depressed the rise in food prices provoked a decline in sales of mass-consumption manufactured goods and textiles of around half between 1787 and 1789. Unemployment, mendicancy, and vagrancy exploded.

In addition, in a climate of hypersensitivity in debates over the grain trade, the crisis engendered social and political demands beyond anything previously heard. Hoarders were denounced everywhere, free trade and exports were called into question, although Necker had swiftly suspended them. There were demands for the state and local authorities to fix price ceilings and provision markets. When intervention was seen as slow or insufficient, riots erupted. A wave of riots, which had begun in Brittany as early in January, spread from the north to the south of France in March. Authority reacted tardily. However, in April the repression for which the *parlements* were responsible duly struck: two hangings in Aix, condemnation to the galleys in Nancy. But these disturbances remained endemic. Paris was affected in turn on 27 and 28 April, with the spectacular Réveillon riot which saw demonstrators from the Faubourg Saint-Antoine protesting against the wallpaper manufacturer Réveillon who was thought to be about to lower wages; several houses and businesses were pillaged and the Garde Française, having intervened tardily, fired into the crowd, leaving 300 dead on the streets of the *faubourg*. What followed during the Revolution made people forget that this was one of the most deadly insurrections of the entire period.

Our conclusion will be brief: yes, the Revolution was certainly a social and political crisis, but it can by no means be reduced to being due to a single cause: bourgeoisie or people, peasants or overlords, the acute grain shortage of spring 1789 or the century's long boom. What matters in this revolutionary context, as in many others since, including the most recent, is the conjunction of all these contradictions at a particular moment, so as to make ordinary political solutions ineffective and to delegitimize the authorities in power. Nonetheless, the course of Revolution was not written in advance in spring 1789 any more than in the middle of the century, but the exceptional nature of the situation was felt by many observers and protagonists.

References

Béaur, Gérard (2000). *Histoire agraire de la France au XVIIIe siècle.* Paris: Sedes.

Béaur, Gérard and Philippe Minard (eds.) (1997). *Atlas de la Révolution française*, vol. 10: *Économie.* Paris: ÉHÉSS.

Bertaud, Jean-Paul (1992). *Les Causes de la Révolution française.* Paris: Armand Colin.

Braudel, Fernand and Ernest Labrousse (eds.) (1970). *Histoire économique et sociale de la France*, vol. 2. Paris: PUF.

Campbell, Peter (ed.) (2006). *The Origins of the French Revolution.* Basingstoke and New York: Palgrave Macmillan.

Chaussinand-Nogaret, Guy (1984). *La Noblesse au XVIII*e *siècle.* Brussels: Éditions Complexe.

Clère, Jean-Jacques (1988). *Les Paysans de la Haute-Marne et la Révolution française: Recherches sur les structures foncières de la communauté villageoise (1780–1825).* Paris: CTHS.

Cobban, Alfred (1984 [1964]). *Le Sens de la Révolution française.* Paris: Julliard.

Cohen, Déborah (2010). *La Nature du peuple: Les Formes de l'imaginaire social (XVIII*e*–XXI*e *siècles).* Seyssel: Champvallon.

Doyle, William (1988 [1980]). *Les Origines de la Révolution française.* Paris: Calmann-Lévy.

Doyle, William (2009). *Aristocracy and its Enemies in the Age of Revolution.* Oxford and New York: Oxford University Press.

Duby, Georges and Armand Wallon (eds.) (1976). *Histoire de la France rurale*, vol. 2. Paris: Seuil.

Dupâquier, Jacques (1988). *Histoire de la population française*, vol. 2. Paris: PUF.

Furet, François (1988). *La Révolution française, 1770–1880.* Paris: Hachette.

Garrioch, David (1996). *The Formation of the Parisian Bourgeoisie, 1690–1830.* Cambridge, Mass.: Harvard University Press.

Gauthier, Florence, et al. (1988). *La Guerre du blé au XVIII*e *siècle.* Paris: Éditions de la Passion.

Gayot, Gérard (1998). *Les Draps de Sedan.* Paris: ÉHÉSS.

Goubert, Pierre (1969). *L'Ancien Régime.* Paris: Armand Colin.

Jessenne, Jean-Pierre (2006). *Les Campagnes françaises entre mythe et histoire.* Paris: Armand Colin.

Jessenne, Jean-Pierre, Gérard Gayot, Hervé Leuwers, and Philippe Minard (eds.) (2003). *Vers un ordre bourgeois? Révolution française et changement social.* Rennes: Presses Universitaires de Rennes.

Jessenne, Jean-Pierre, and Hervé Leuwers (eds.) (2010). *Changements sociaux et dynamiques politiques.* Special issue of *AHRF*, 359.

Jones, Colin (1991). "Bourgeois Revolution Revivified: 1789 and Social Change." In Colin Lucas (ed.). *Rewriting the French Revolution.* Oxford: Clarendon Press. 69–119.

Kaplan, Steven (2001). *La Fin des corporations.* Paris: Fayard.

Kaplow, Jeffry (1971). *Les Noms des rois: Les Pauvres à Paris à la veille de la Révolution.* Paris: Maspero.

Labrousse, Ernest (1933). *Esquisse du mouvement des prix et des revenus en France au XVIII*e *siècle.* Paris: Dalloz.

Labrousse, Ernest (1990 [1944]). *La Crise de l'économie française à la fin de l'Ancien Régime et au début de la Révolution.* Paris: PUF.

Le Roy Ladurie, Emmanuel (1976). "Une croissance agricole." In Georges Duby and Armand Wallon (eds.). *Histoire de la France rurale*, vol. 2. Paris: Seuil. 428–441.

Le Roy Ladurie, Emmanuel (1981). *Histoire de la France urbaine*, vol. 3: *La Ville classique.* Paris: Seuil.

Lefebvre, Georges (1989 [1932]). *La Grande Peur de 1789.* Paris: PUF.

Legay, Marie-Laure (2011). *La Banqueroute de l'État royal.* Paris: ÉHÉSS.

Lemarchand, Guy (1989). *La Fin du féodalisme dans le Pays de Caux: Conjoncture économique et démographique et structure sociale dans une région de grande culture de la crise du XVIIe siècle à la stabilisation sous la Révolution (1640–1795).* Paris: CTHS.

Lemarchand, Guy (2008). *L'Économie en France de 1770 à 1830.* Paris: Armand Colin.

Lethuillier, Jean-Pierre (1993). "Idéologies et mentalités: L'Essor de l'individualisme en Basse-Normandie." Doctoral thesis. University of Rouen.

Leuwers, Hervé (2006). *L'Invention du barreau français, 1660–1830*, Paris, ÉHÉSS.

Livesey, James (2010). "Les Réseaux de crédit en Languedoc au XVIII siècle et les origines sociales de la Révolution." *AHRF*, 359: 29–52.

Margairaz, Dominique (1997). "Les Échanges." In Gérard Béaur and Philippe Minard (eds.). *Atlas de la Révolution française*, vol. 10: *Économie.* Paris: ÉHÉSS. 32–33.

Maza, Sarah (2003). *The Myth of the French Bourgeoisie: An Essay on the Social Imaginary, 1750–1850.* Cambridge, Mass.: Harvard University Press.

Miller, Judith (1999). *Mastering the Market: The State and the Grain Trade in the North of France.* Cambridge: Cambridge University Press.

Milliot, Vincent (1995). *Les Cris de Paris ou le peuple travesti: Les Représentations des petits métiers parisiens (XVIe–XVIIIe siècle).* Paris: Publications de la Sorbonne.

Nicolas, Jean (2002). *La Rébellion française.* Paris: Seuil.

Petitfrère, Claude (1989). *Le Scandale du "Mariage de Figaro".* Brussels: Éditions Complexe.

Régent, Frédéric (2004). *Esclavage, métissage, liberté: La Révolution française en Guadeloupe, 1789–1802.* Paris: Grasset.

Roche, Daniel (1993). *La France des Lumières.* Paris: Fayard.

Shapiro, Gilbert and John Markoff (1998). *Revolutionary Demands: A Content Analysis of the Cahiers de Doléances of 1789.* Stanford, Calif.: Stanford University Press.

Soboul, Albert (1966). *La France à la veille de la Révolution.* Paris: Sedes.

Vovelle, Michel (1997). "Du tout social au tout politique." *AHRF*, 310: 545–554.

Young, Arthur (2009 [1790]). *Voyages en France en 1787, 1788, 1789.* Paris: Tallandier.

CHAPTER THREE

The Cultural Origins of the French Revolution

SARAH MAZA

Thirty or forty years ago, this chapter would have been entitled "The Intellectual Origins of the French Revolution." For historians before the 1970s, the term "culture" meant either society's aesthetic realm (art, literature, music), or the non-material aspects of people's lives such as education and religion. None of these were assumed to have much, if any, bearing on political change, which was triggered by social, economic, political, and ideological forces. Ideas could change the world; "culture," which was slow-moving and had no direct bearing on politics, could not. Much has changed in the last thirty years. Nowadays, historians of the French Revolution talk about the "cultural" rather than "intellectual" origins of the upheaval that began in France in 1789. What does it mean for an event to have "cultural origins"? The answer to that question is not simple, but in recent years a number of works on the cultural environments of different groups in late eighteenth-century France have proposed a wealth of possible answers.

Ascribing "intellectual origins" to the Revolution is an altogether simpler matter. The classic account of the French Revolution posited that a constellation of brilliant thinkers collectively known as the *philosophes* began in the 1720s and 1730s to write subversive works critical of the church, the French monarchy, and of a social order which favored bloodlines over talent. Thanks to books, newspapers, and pamphlets, such ideas "spread" like a contagious disease, undermining the status quo. The connection between ideas and action was as simple and linear as the apocryphal remark attributed to Louis XVI after he read Beaumarchais' *Marriage of Figaro*: if that play were performed, the monarch supposedly said, the Bastille would fall.

Even outdated interpretations can be partly true, and it would be foolish to deny that Voltaire's bitterly funny attacks on the church, Montesquieu's warnings about the evils of "despotism," and the publication of a multi-volume heresy-studded

A Companion to the French Revolution, First Edition. Edited by Peter McPhee.

Encyclopédie right under the noses of the royal censors played a significant role in eroding respect for established authorities among the reading public. But the idea that something called "the Enlightenment" was a direct cause of the French Revolution was rejected by scholars several decades ago (Doyle 1999). On the one hand the major figures of the French Enlightenment, most of whom were long dead by 1789, never called for political or social revolution, never dreamt of democracy, much less regicide and terror. They confined their radicalism to attacks on the clerical establishment, calls for political reform and open access to knowledge, and humanitarian crusades. For all of their satirical bite, they were reformers, not revolutionaries. On the other hand, many among the socio-political elites of the late eighteenth century were open to the new ideas: royal administrators and wealthy nobles took a lively interest in *les lumières*, several of Louis XVI's ministers, such as Anne-Robert Turgot and Jacques Necker, belonged to "philosophical" circles, and Marie-Antoinette herself was an enthusiastic reader of Rousseau and Beaumarchais. How revolutionary could the Enlightenment really have been?

Could "revolutionary ideas" be found anywhere in eighteenth-century France beyond the Enlightenment as traditionally defined? One scholar, Robert Darnton, has proposed such an argument in a series of influential books on what he has called the "literary underground" of *ancien régime* France. Darnton's exhaustive studies of the inventories of eighteenth-century French booksellers and peddlers has revealed a "low enlightenment" of scurrilous reading matter which featured copious amounts of pornography, libel, and political gossip, all of which sold far more briskly than the canonical works of the Enlightenment. To the cumbersome and expensive *Encyclopédie*, or the learned *Spirit of the Laws*, readers preferred such titles as *Venus in the Cloister* or *The Private Life of Madame Du Barry*. Darnton has argued in different ways, over the years, that these sensational works – intimate details about alleged debauchery at court, graphic anticlerical pornography, atheistic treatises from the radical fringe of the Enlightenment – paved the way for revolution by directing ridicule and anger at governing elites and institutions (Darnton 1985, 1996). This account of the Revolution's intellectual origins emerged, in the 1960s and 1970s, out of the new field of the history of the book. Instead of assuming the importance of Great Works, Darnton and others argued, we should look to the archives of booksellers and publishers to find out what the reading public was actually consuming. What eighteenth-century French readers wanted may not have stood the test of time but it was, in its own way, he argues, "revolutionary."

As a result of Darnton's work, our understanding of the literary culture of eighteenth-century France is a lot richer and less conventional than it used to be. But even as what is known as Darnton's "Grub Street thesis" continues to generate controversy and debate, the link between the underground literature he studies and the origins of the Revolution remains problematic. Libels and political pornography may have been radically destructive, but they offered no script for revolution, no positive prescriptions for change. Usually written by court insiders to discredit hated rivals, censored *libelles* offered no real alternative to the status quo. While we now know that there was much more to "the Enlightenment" than the writers featured in classic anthologies, it is difficult to demonstrate that the reading of "dangerous" material provoked people to behave in politically subversive ways.

More broadly, the very concept of the Revolution's "intellectual origins" became problematic after the 1970s because of the general evolution of the field away from the proposition that the events of 1789 and after had determinate, linear causes. An older tidy scenario had it that the Revolution was the result of the advent of early forms of capitalism and of the bourgeoisie, and that Voltaire, Montesquieu, Rousseau, and others provided the latter with the ideological weapons to wield against the old order: merit over birth, tolerance over clerical dogmatism, free inquiry over censorship and repression. In the 1960s and 1970s most historians in the field rejected the classic view of bourgeois advent and began to argue that the Revolution was not the outcome of deep-seated social conflict but of a series of major political-fiscal crises which the monarchy proved unable to control. While the causes of the 1789 crisis were not trivial – staggering debt, dysfunctional institutions, discredited leaders – neither was its outbreak inevitable. At many different stages before July 1789 the king and his ministers could have worked with progressive leaders to implement the necessary reforms and instill confidence in the government. "Revisionism," now the standard interpretation of the Revolution's origins, does not diminish the importance of the event; rather, it proposes that an upheaval which had world-historical consequences and implications could have contingent causes (Doyle 1999).

The reorienting of the field away from deep-seated determinism and towards contingency had significant implications for the understanding of the Revolution's intellectual, ideological, or cultural origins. This evolution coincided with a turn in many fields of the humanities and social sciences towards methods inspired by linguistics and cultural anthropology aimed at deciphering "meaning" rather than explaining change. The upshot for the field of French revolutionary studies was that instead of looking for ideas which "inspired" or "caused" the upheaval, historians sought to uncover patterns of meaning, concepts, which may not have triggered events but would provide the means of understanding or shaping the Revolution once it broke out. "In this sense," writes Roger Chartier, "attributing 'cultural origins' to the French Revolution does not by any means establish the Revolution's causes; rather, it pinpoints certain of the conditions that made it possible because it was conceivable" (Chartier 1991: 2).

In the 1990s especially, historians worked at defining and describing the discursive patterns in eighteenth-century texts, especially texts relating to political matters. There may not have existed a full-blown "revolutionary ideology" before 1789, but its different components could be found in the writings of jurists, royal administrators, and others, available for the accidental convergence of events which brought them together in the spring and summer of 1789. The salient work in this vein has been done by Keith Baker, who writes in a recent synthesis of his work that "the language of the Enlightenment, in its various forms, provided a fundamental repertory of meanings and understandings upon which revolutionary actors drew as they sought to redefine the principles of French social and political existence in 1789" (Baker 2011: 178). Baker finds "the language of the Enlightenment" in a wide range of writings, by government ministers, lawyers and judges, political analysts and pamphleteers whose names are no longer familiar, as well as the canonical writers of the Enlightenment.

One of Baker's central arguments is that the ideological synthesis upon which French absolutism rested was undermined by the political tensions of the eighteenth century, as the ineffectual monarchs Louis XV and Louis XVI proved incapable of arbitrating between a reactionary church and rebellious courts of justice (*parlements*), or between reforming ministers and their enemies at court. The ideology that undergirded the French monarchy, Baker argues, was made up of the combination of three languages: that of justice, derived from the monarch's most ancient function as a judicial arbitrator; that of will, the king's authority to unite by his command the disparate elements of a polity based on a host of private legal systems (*privilège*); and that of "reason," the reliance on fundamental laws, religion, and counsel which kept wise and benevolent monarchy from devolving into despotic whim. With governing institutions under pressure in the later eighteenth century, these braided strands were pulled apart as competing voices appropriated them to mount ideological challenges to the political status quo.

The most vociferous of these claims emanated from the courts of high justice, the *parlements*, especially the Parlement of Paris. Over the course of a series of clashes with the monarchy from the 1730s to the 1770s, the magistrates of these courts asserted with increasing force that the *parlements* were the guardians of French law, an "essential branch of government," and had authority to represent the interests of "the Nation." They claimed for themselves the royal prerogative of "justice." At the same time, writers like Jean-Jacques Rousseau, Gabriel Bonnot de Mably, and Guillaume-Joseph Saige drew upon the language of classical republicanism to argue that government owed its existence to the "will" of the nation – Rousseau's and Saige's notion of a "general will" mirrored royal authority even as it undermined it. Physiocrats and other political economists, meanwhile, posited that the reason and rights of individuals derived from the laws of nature as much as did those of kings. In sum, while educated and critical writers in the eighteenth century did not produce an explicit script for the Revolution, the discursive elements of a new political order, built upon the ideological collapse of the absolutist synthesis, were available to be drawn upon when the time came and combined into documents like the Declaration of the Rights of Man and of the Citizen (Baker 1990).

The revolutionaries, then, drew upon discursive formations whose original intent was critical rather than outright revolutionary. Such was the case, for instance, regarding the principles of the social order. Under the *ancien régime*, while the nobility had come in for plenty of criticism, nobody imagined abolishing France's hereditary ruling class. A noisy debate on the subject in 1756–57 pitted the Abbé Coyer against the Chevalier d'Arc: Coyer denounced nobles as idle parasites who should be allowed and indeed urged to engage in commerce, while d'Arc heatedly responded that if nobles abandoned martial glory for the pursuit of profit the nation's moral and political order would be fatally undermined. None of the many participants in the debate came close to envisioning an end to the nobility, yet the controversy provided fodder for the Abbé Sieyès' campaign against "privilege" thirty years later (Smith 2000).

Religion is another case in point. In the traditional view, eighteenth-century progressive ideologies were anti-religious; few of the *philosophes* were outright atheists but most of them were harshly critical of the church as an institution and eager to relegate religion to the margins of human affairs. The Revolution, in this older view, was the outcome of secularizing forces. More recent work has shown, however, that religion was a central component of oppositional activity and ideas in the pre-revolutionary decades. In the early eighteenth century, the groups most conspicuously persecuted by the French monarchy were Protestants (whose right to worship was outlawed by the Revocation of the Edict of Nantes in 1685), and followers of Jansenism, a Catholic heresy with Augustinian roots which became popular among some segments of the French noble and commoner elites and eventually among broad segments of the urban population in the first half of the eighteenth century. While exile and brutal repression mostly silenced the Huguenot community, recent research has shown that Jansenists and their supporters played a pivotal role in undermining the ideological alliance of church and throne, and indeed the very justification for traditional monarchy.

As Dale Van Kley has argued in a series of classic studies, the church, the First Estate of the realm, had less to fear from Voltaire and company's rather traditional caricatures of lascivious monks, debauched nuns, and power-hungry popes than from a high-minded Catholic movement with powerful supporters which proposed a coherent alternative view of the nature of both religious and secular power (Van Kley 1996). Jansenism, a movement resembling Protestantism but which professed loyalty to the Catholic Church, took shape in the mid-seventeenth century, and by the reign of Louis XIV the heresy had a committed following among the magistrates of the Parlement of Paris and the capital's parish clergy. The Sun King obtained from the pope a bull, *Unigenitus*, which in 1713 condemned not only theological beliefs attributed to Jansenists but also the radical Gallican ecclesiological principles (the church assembled in council was superior to the pope) favored by the movement. The Parlement of Paris, home to a number of prominent Jansenist magistrates and smarting from Louis XIV's attack on its traditional "right of remonstrance," took it upon itself to defend Jansenist priests from persecution, thereby setting the stage for some fifty years of conflict between itself and the monarchy over religious affairs.

The Jansenist controversy put the French monarchy in a conceptual and political bind. The French kings, eager to control their own clergy and keep Rome out of their affairs, had traditionally espoused Gallican views, insisting, for instance on appointing their own bishops. In order to control dissenting "Gallican" Jansenists and their supporters in the Paris Parlement, the monarchy had to play down its long-sought role as absolute head of the French church, ultimately undermining its own claims to sacredness. According to Van Kley, "the effect of the conflict over *Unigenitus* was to align fragments of the Gallican heritage against each other, to drive a wedge between the king's person and the state, and ultimately to desacralise the monarchy forever" (Van Kley 2011: 127). In the mid-1750s, when the French church hierarchy triggered a crisis by refusing extreme unction to dying Jansenists, Louis XV proved incapable of taking sides in the "refusal of sacraments" controversy, tacking back and forth between support for the ultramontane archbishop of Paris and the stridently nationalistic Parlement. The resulting dismay among the king's subjects who followed such matters is symbolized by the dramatic act of one

Robert-François Damiens, a mentally unstable domestic servant who on 5 January 1757 plunged a dagger into Louis XV's side, wounding but not killing the monarch. Damiens explained that he had been driven to touch the king in order to assuage his own anxiety over the religious conflicts of the day; upon investigation it turned out that the would-be regicide had served in the houses of several members of the Parlement who espoused pro-Jansenist views (Van Kley 1984).

Beyond undermining the king's spiritual claims to authority, the Jansenist controversy also generated, via the analogy between church and polity, some of the most radical political scripts of the time. Starting in the 1720s, Jansenist clergy and laypersons sought the protection of the Parlement, rallying behind the latter's claim that it had a "constitutional" right to resist "despotism" from on high. Some Jansenist theologians and magistrates went even further than "constitutionalism" to espouse a radical "conciliarist" position: just as the authority of the church assembled in a general council outweighed that of the pope, so the nation convened in the form of the Estates-General was superior to the monarchy. In sum, it now seems that religion was a far more powerful force than Voltairean skepticism in undermining the ideological-political status quo. It was, for instance, not the *philosophes* but a phalanx of determined Jansenist magistrates in the Paris Parlement who engineered the expulsion of the Jesuit order from France in 1764.

Most of the central political concepts of the Revolution were first articulated, then, not in the writings of canonical *philosophes* but in the fractious zone, primarily centered on the Parlement of Paris, where religion met politics. (Rousseau's overly radical and abstract *Social Contract* was virtually ignored before the 1790s.) The most serious political crisis of the pre-revolutionary decades unfolded from 1771 to 1774 when Louis XV's minister Chancellor René de Maupeou forcibly "reformed" the Parlement of Paris, radically curtailing its jurisdiction, severely restricting its right to opine on national affairs, and summarily dismissing those many magistrates who refused to go along with his project. The so-called "Maupeou crisis" touched off an avalanche of political commentary, with hundreds of pamphlets hammering out concepts and slogans that would become ubiquitous again in the late 1780s. On one side the Parlement and its many supporters howled their indignation at this act of ministerial "despotism," invoking the violated "constitution" and the trampled rights of the "nation" or *patrie*. Supporters of governmental reform, including Voltaire himself, responded by excoriating the Parlement's supporters as selfish "aristocrats," whose "gothic" principles led them to champion anti-national "corporate" and "particularistic" interests. In 1789 the Third Estate would prevail ideologically through spokesmen like the Abbé Sieyes by fusing these two formerly opposite strands, articulating the all-important national interest by pitting it against the selfishness of parasitical "aristocrats" (Echeverria 1985).

Equally innovative and important, before the Revolution, was the concept of "public opinion," which was regularly invoked long before anyone thought of assembling the Estates-General. In the later eighteenth century, political actors of all stripes began to justify their positions rhetorically by claiming that they spoke for, or had the sanction of, "the public," "public opinion," or "the public spirit." Such items in the political lexicon of the eighteenth century were obviously abstractions, since there existed no means of gauging "public opinion," nor even would such measurement have mattered. Rather, repeated invocations of "the public" and its judgment were symptomatic of a desire to shift political legitimacy rhetorically away from absolutist power and towards the sanction of an audience for politics coterminous with "the Nation." The public's "opinion" or "spirit," deduced from what the writer considered the moral and rational position, were invoked as a touchstone external to the established mechanisms of power. The idea of "public opinion" prefigured representative politics in France: by the later 1780s the monarchy could only attempt to salvage its financial credibility by putting its fiscal proposals before "representative" bodies such as the 1787 Assembly of Notables or the 1789 Estates-General (Baker 1990).

A related phrase which appeared often in print from the 1750s on was "tribunal of the public" or "tribunal of the nation." Exploiting a loophole in the censorship laws, barristers were allowed to print and disseminate their briefs, and in a series of *causes célèbres* of the later eighteenth century these frequently served as vehicles for political criticism and commentary. In some cases the political import of famous trials was explicit, as when Queen Marie-Antoinette became unwittingly embroiled in the sordid swindle later known as the Diamond Necklace Affair, which fatally damaged her reputation. More frequently, particular cases involving private individuals were used by idealistic or ambitious lawyers as metaphors for larger social concerns. When the seigneur of a hamlet in Normandy tried in 1773 to bully his villagers over the details of a local festival, lawyers writing in defense of the peasant community portrayed the lord as a brutal tyrant and identified the cause of the village of Salency as that of "the Nation"; when a servant girl from Caen was falsely convicted of poisoning and narrowly escaped execution, the heart-stopping tale of her ordeal and of her rescue by an enlightened and compassionate lawyer served as a vehicle to make the case for judicial reform; bitter separation cases among well-to-do defendants gave the authors of trial briefs occasion to make the point that both the marriage contract and the social contract should be revocable. Throughout their briefs, which sometimes attained a circulation of tens of thousands, lawyers appealed to "the judgment of the public" or "the tribunal of the nation." They rhetorically expanded the reading public for whom they wrote into a broader judging entity whose purview extended beyond the tribulations of plaintiffs and defendants to the very nature of the legal and political systems (Maza 1993).

The trial briefs connected to salient pre-revolutionary court cases offer one example of the ways in which the ideologies of the Revolution were first articulated in the pre-revolutionary decades around private matters, and especially issues of gender and of family life. The very essence of traditional monarchy was the overlap between what we now call the public and private realms, since the king was father to his people, the court a household writ large, and courtiers who ceremonially handed the king his shirt in the morning functioned as the equivalent of domestic servants. The household model of the polity, unproblematic for centuries, was described by the eighteenth century as a source and symbol of corruption. If impartial reason and the public good were the proper basis and goal of government, private intrigue and the conspicuous role of women, traditional features of a court-centered government, now seemed like signs of decadence.

Jean-Jacques Rousseau argued as much in 1758 in his *Letter to d'Alembert on the Theater*. In that text, Rousseau offered a stark contrast between the customs of the ancient world, Sparta especially, where women were barred from public life, and the prominent role of women in French public life on stage, at court, and in high society. Rousseau began with a critique of the theater, an institution central to the lives of the French elite but which, in the view of the Swiss Calvinist *philosophe*, served as a school for hypocrisy and lasciviousness. While actresses were paid to be "public women" in both senses of the term (most of them became mistresses to the high and mighty), there was only a difference of degree between their behavior and that of the society women who ruled over salons, offering their opinions freely and courting the admiration of men. The social power of women entailed, for Rousseau, the emasculation of men: "Every woman at Paris gathers in her apartment a harem of men more womanish than she." Rousseau's fulminations move seamlessly from the realm of culture (the theater) to that of society (salons) to that of politics. French society's admiration for "public women" bespoke the corruption an entire system associated with the monarchy and the court, which functioned along feminine principles of vanity, deceit, and personal interest. If, in Rousseau's view, monarchy, which unmans all subjects, promotes gender-blurring, republics are necessarily built on the masculine principle: "Whether a monarch governs men or women ought to be rather indifferent to him provided he is obeyed; but in a republic, men are needed" (Maza 1993: 165–171).

Rousseau's essay on the evils of public womanhood was a precocious and lucid statement of a theme which was to run through French high culture in the pre-revolutionary decades. This leitmotiv found expression in the 1770s in best-selling books and pamphlets which retrospectively excoriated the influence of Louis XV's mistresses Madame de Pompadour and especially Madame du Barry. These women, pamphleteers tirelessly repeated, were social upstarts (the first a merchant's daughter, the second a former courtesan) who used sex to subjugate the king and draw him away from manly pursuits into "the private, slothful, and voluptuous life for which he had been yearning" (Maza 1993: 181).

Once the theme of the sexual decadence of the state had been sounded, there seemed no way that a French monarch could win. Louis XV, who kept a private brothel alongside his stream of official mistresses, was despised for his addiction to sex; Louis XVI, a paragon of domestic virtue, was ridiculed for his initial inability to consummate his marriage and for allegedly being dominated and cuckolded by his Austrian wife. In the 1780s, pamphlet diatribes against Marie-Antoinette picked up where the scurrilous literature about the former king's mistresses had left off: the "Austrian bitch" (*l'Autrichienne*), deceitful, manipulative, and power-hungry, was said to be sexually involved with half of the court, male and female, including both of the king's brothers, one of whom had sired her children. As Jeffrey Merrick has observed, political dysfunction under Louis XV and Louis XVI was always configured as both foreign and female: "Excess, tyranny in the Turkish style, and license on the part of the ruler, on the one hand, and weakness, anarchy in the English style, and licence on the part of the subjects, on the other hand, were identified with womanish passions" (Merrick 2011: 208).

The corrosive effects of "public womanhood" were conceptually linked to a set of broader themes developed in many texts, but especially in the era's large corpus of writings on political economy, bemoaning the catastrophic effects of something called "luxury." Drawing on a tradition stretching back to antiquity, eighteenth-century French anti-luxury polemicists painted an appalling picture of the effects of *le luxe*. Peasants were lured off the land by the material pleasures of city life, town-dwellers indulged in the pleasures of non-procreative sex, and depopulation ensued. The availability and society-wide pursuit of consumer items – clothing, ornaments, knick-knacks – erased social boundaries, as poorer folk aped their betters to the extent that one allegedly could no longer tell who was who. Luxury (etymologically close to the Latin term *luxuria*, debauchery) made for gender confusion as men powdered their hair and doused themselves with perfume, and paradoxically for both sexual excess and a loss of sexual vigor as all of society succumbed to *mollesse*, flaccidity. Underlying all these symptoms was a fundamental malady, the evil, corrosive effects of money. Luxury, in these texts, was usually contrasted with ancient ideals of stern and healthy morality (*les moeurs*) and with the Roman masculine ethos of virtue (Maza 1997).

The economic source of the anxiety around "luxury" was the century's surge in commercial activity and the new availability of consumer goods; ideologically, such themes were given new life by writings such as Jean-Jacques Rousseau's *Discourse on the Sciences and the Arts* (1750) and *Discourse on the Origins of Inequality* (1755) which waxed apocalyptic about the evil effects of modern civilization on public morality and justice. As John Shovlin has pointed out, the anti-luxury literature of the mid- and later eighteenth century reflected more specifically widespread anger at the growing wealth and influence of financiers, the richest group in society, whose members moved with ease into and within court society. Both non-nobles and lesser nobles were disgusted by the increasingly cosy relationship between high finance and the elites at court. The advent of Madame de Pompadour, who was born into a milieu of high finance and became Louis XV's mistress in 1745, was widely regarded as a symbol of the fact that "financiers were, literally, in bed with the court aristocracy by the middle of the eighteenth century" (Shovlin 2006: 31). The revolutionary clamors against "aristocracy" and calls for "virtue" can be traced back to the abundant anti-luxury literature with its denunciations of a corrupt plutocracy and of the corrosive effects of money.

Cultural historians have, in sum, tracked in the writings of the decades before 1789 significant prefigurations of revolutionary ideologies and cultures in a range of materials which include, but go far beyond, the writings of the canonical *philosophes*. Over the course of the eighteenth century, political economists, Jansenist magistrates, ambitious lawyers, obscure polemicists, and muck-raking pamphleteers hammered out the terms and ideas that would dominate public discourse after 1789: despotism, the nation, public opinion, patriotism, virtue, the general will, the menace of "luxury," the selfish designs of "aristocrats," and the corrupting influence of "public women." From such materials the leading actors of the Revolution fashioned a new political universe, huge assemblies of men speaking for their compatriots, oaths of loyalty to the fledgling nation, all-out war against omnipresent but ill-defined "aristocrats," festivals honoring virtue, armies marching to battle singing hymns to the *patrie*.

The elements of revolutionary culture did not emerge solely from the printed page of treatises or pamphlets, however. Equally important were certain practices:

ideas and slogans do not travel far without means of conveyance, and people learn from gestures, habits, and encounters with others as much as they do from the written or spoken word.

About twenty years ago, scholars in the field began to approach "the Enlightenment" broadly defined – all of the intellectual innovations of the eighteenth century – not just as an array of *ideas* but as a set of *practices.* Ideas never exist in a vacuum of course, and the institutional frameworks of *les lumières* had long been known. The *philosophes* and their followers developed their ideas by exchanging reams of letters, joining local literary and scientific academies, and conversing in regular drawing-room meetings, especially the famous Parisian salons run by prominent women. The intellectual leaders came together to publish collective works like the *Encyclopédie*, their admirers perused legal books in *cabinets de lecture* and bought illegal pamphlets from peddlers or from the back rooms of booksellers. Where the traditional view had been, however, that networks of people (*philosophes*, Encyclopedists, the "Party of Humanity" to use Peter Gay's phrase) create ideas, newer approaches stress that the process works both ways, that the desire to exchange ideas creates new forms of social connection (Gay 1954). The means and form of intellectual exchange, in other words, matter as much as its content.

The inspiration for this approach was a book-length essay by the German philosopher Jürgen Habermas, first published in 1962 but rediscovered and used by historians in this field mostly starting in the later 1980s (Habermas 1989). In *The Structural Transformation of the Public Sphere*, Habermas explained that the cultural dynamic which laid the groundwork for democratic revolution came from the growing tension between, on the one hand, the acknowledged public sphere of the state in which the monarch was the only officially "public" person, and on the other a nascent "literary public sphere" made up of individuals who came together to make critical use of their reason. This implicitly oppositional, unofficial public sphere took shape in salons, coffee-houses, literary academies, and even through networks of epistolary exchange. The objects of criticism in this "bourgeois public sphere" gradually shifted from only matters of taste – art, literature, and the like – to political issues. These networks of individuals making use of their critical faculties provided, in the eighteenth century, an alternative to the public sphere of the monarchy. The "Republic of Letters," according to Habermas, was no mere figure of speech but a blueprint for a democratic polity.

Critics of Habermas have been quick to point out that this emergent, oppositional public sphere was certainly not democratic in any modern sense since it included only the tiny minority of the eighteenth-century population with enough literacy to understand the new ideas, and sufficient resources of time and money to invest in intellectual exchange, and that because reason was considered a male prerogative the "bourgeois public sphere" was essentially male (Calhoun 1992). Other scholars, most notably Dena Goodman, have countered that the "critical public sphere" of the Enlightenment was in some measure open to women as well as men. The emblematic institutions of the French Enlightenment, according to Goodman, were the literary salons of Paris, places of mixed-gender sociability over which formidably learned and skilled women like Madame d'Épinay, Madame du Deffand,

Julie de Lespinasse, or Suzanne Necker presided (Goodman 1994). Goodman's thesis of a proto-feminist Enlightenment has been challenged (Lilti 2005), but scholars agree more generally that practices of sociability such as joining Masonic lodges or literary academies were important in laying the ground for French revolutionary culture. Here again, as with political discourse and Jansenist controversy, the argument is not that the new public sphere of readers "caused" the French Revolution, but that the practice of literary sociability and debate shaped the ways in which the French elites would respond – forming political clubs like the Jacobins, for instance – once the Revolution broke out.

The exchange of information and critical commentary about public matters was not limited to the elites or to conventional printed forms, at least in the large urban centers that would be the sites of the Revolution. Robert Darnton has recently described eighteenth-century Paris as an "information society" in which news and gossip circulated back and forth between oral and printed media (Darnton 2000). Parisians would assemble in specific places such as the "Tree of Cracow" in the Palais Royal gardens, certain benches in the Tuileries or Luxembourg gardens, or speakers' corners near the Seine; the wealthy sent their servants from house to house and then pooled their intelligence in meeting places like the salon of Madame Doublet. Courtiers composed salacious verses about the royals and had them disseminated in the marketplaces where they would be picked up by artisans who retailed them to lackeys; eventually the gossip made its way back to the halls of Versailles where their duplicitous authors would nudge their acquaintances: "Have you read them? Here they are. This is what is circulating among the common people of Paris" (Darnton 2000: 9–10). In early July of 1789 liberal leaders of the Third Estate disseminated incendiary information about royal and aristocratic "conspiracies" in the gardens of the Palais Royal, touching off an uprising whose political benefits they would eventually reap back in Versailles; although the elites by then were different, the looping pattern was the same. The police archives of pre-revolutionary Paris contain abundant records by government agents and spies of the dense circulation of stories and songs among Parisians of all social classes. The division between rumor, gossip, and legitimate "news" was porous, and the circulation of oral information reached far beyond Habermas' "public" of readers and salon-goers. The "mixed media" of the *ancien régime*, Darnton concludes, "transmitted an amalgam of overlapping messages, spoken, written, printed, pictured and sung" (Darnton 2000: 34).

The cultural origins of the French Revolution have been located, then, in ideas and texts, on the one hand, and in institutions and modes of communication on the other. Equally important, however, has been the argument advanced recently by historians of material culture about the ways in which the availability, marketing, and consumption of new objects acted as a solvent on older forms of social relations and prepared French subjects for their future identity as citizens. New research on the world of goods in eighteenth-century France represents a return to, and renewal of, a social interpretation of the origins of the French Revolution. Eighteenth-century France was an increasingly wealthy and commercial society: between the 1720s and the 1780s, the estimated rate of growth for the industrial sector was just short of 2 percent per year, and foreign trade quintupled in those years (Félix 2001). The traditional interpretation of the Revolution's origins held that this modernizing economic growth allowed for an increasingly assertive bourgeoisie to snatch power from a declining landed aristocracy. While this scenario has long been disputed, historians have recently argued that commerce and consumption did make for deep social change, albeit not in ways strictly consonant with the traditional Marxian scenario.

Research on after-death inventories has revealed that starting around the 1730s, town-dwellers in a range of social stations, from the rich to better-off artisans, experienced a sea-change in their domestic environments and their access to consumer goods (Pardailhé-Galabrun 1992; Roche 2000). The latter included new kinds of furniture such as chests of drawers, secretaries, and comfortable seating; decorative items such as wallpaper, prints, decorative objects, and mirrors; household goods such as dishes and tableware; and all manner of accessories including canes, wigs, snuff-boxes, fans, watches, and playing cards. Most visibly, clothing was transformed in those decades as the value of wardrobes in Paris increased threefold on average, and even more so for the working poor. People owned more sets of clothing, and – within limits, of course – fashions were less strictly class-specific: the one-piece dress, for instance, once worn only by wealthy ladies, now became an item in the wardrobes of many working women. As Jennifer Jones has argued, the logic of fashion was traditionally linked to rank, and was not gender-specific: men displayed their finery at court and on public occasions in order to reinforce their family's standing (Jones 2004). While such customs certainly endured – noble deputies to the Estates-General in 1789 arrived bedecked in silk, plumed hats, and swords – the eighteenth century saw the birth of a competing system of meaning in which gender, nationality, and above all taste governed changing styles of clothing: *la mode* was becoming the preserve of the "naturally" elegant and discriminating Frenchwoman.

It would be far too simplistic to conclude from this evidence that access to consumer goods was erasing or attenuating class distinctions. Jeremiads against *le luxe*, of which there were literally hundreds in those years, routinely warned that the flood of luxury goods washing over the nation's towns made it impossible to distinguish between nobles and socially ambitious artisans, between ladies and their chambermaids. Such pronouncements should not be taken literally – social distinctions were still visible at a glance – but as expressions of a more generalized anxiety about the effects of consumerism on society. Writers ranging from traditional Christian moralists to Rousseauvian critics of the new plutocracy allegedly ruling the land assumed that new patterns of consumption were dangerously disjunctive, and were tearing society apart. Particularly troubling to many contemporaries was the link between the booming colonial trade and new habits of consumption: "privileged" monopolies like the French Indies Company were flooding the nation with expensive delicacies such as chocolate and coffee while spurring France into costly military rivalries (Shovlin 2006).

One influential view holds that, to the contrary, the new market for consumer goods may have been a conjunctive force, creating new forms and patterns of connection within the eighteenth-century reading and buying public (C. Jones 1996). Starting in the middle of the eighteenth century, a flourishing provincial press developed in France in the form of local newspapers known as *affiches* or *annonces* whose primary, but not only, function was to carry advertisements: by 1789 there were forty-four such papers, with a total readership which may have been as high as 200,000. They published notices for property sales and leases, and for a remarkable array of goods and services. These included items both predictable, such as books, jewelry, horses, and clothing, and unpredictable, such as tame monkeys, bidets, and indoor fireworks. Medical goods and services featured prominently in the *affiches*; readers were offered medical books (one-quarter of the total books advertised), face creams, false teeth, endless varieties of health-restoring drugs and drinks, artificial limbs, as well as medical and scientific courses.

The evidence from these provincial newspapers lends itself to many layers of interpretation. The *affiches* demonstrate the penetration of a new world of goods, of a form of the "pursuit of happiness" well into the purported backwaters of the realm. The "luxury" they offered was not the reviled *luxe d'ostentation* associated with the court and the very rich, but the morally defensible *luxe de commodité*, the ordinary person's right to comfort and convenience. The prominent space accorded in their pages to bodily health and comfort can be read, Colin Jones suggests, metaphorically, "the body social and the bourgeois body both requiring improved 'circulation' and energy." Jones's principal argument about these papers is that they both reflected and created a new form of social connection, the "Great Chain of Buying." Such publications represented an important contribution to the increasing commercialization of eighteenth-century French society and their purpose was socially transformative in that they cut across geographical, social, and gender barriers: "The Great Chain of Buying was grounded in the social and cultural capillarity of the small ad, which conjoined the private and the public, the economic and the cultural, the macro economy with the micro level of individual wants and needs" (C. Jones 1996: 26). Consumer culture, in other words, sliced through the hierarchical, corporate, particularistic social structures of the *ancien régime*: in becoming consumers as well as subjects, French people were primed for the leap into citizenship.

Recent work by Michael Kwass also shows that the new consumer items – in this case the male wig – penetrated deep into the provinces and the countryside and were purchased by a broad swath of society (Kwass 2006). In eighteenth-century France the wearing of wigs was by no means confined to the aristocratic elites; they were worn by most men who had attained or aspired to a modicum of status, such as priests, doctors, lawyers, merchants, and successful artisans. The rationale invoked by taste leaders for the wearing of wigs had nothing to do with emulation of the nobility. Instead, the reasons invoked for wearing a fake head of hair, whether the short-haired *perruque ronde* or the more formal style curled on the sides and tied in back, had to do with convenience, nature, and the enhancement of one's "physiognomy." Wigs were marketed as a wholly sensible *luxe de commodité* which, when properly constructed, allowed for freedom of movement, comfort, and protection from bad weather. A well-made wig also compensated for one's physical shortcomings by skillfully creating a "natural" look. At the same time, such objects were specifically designed to work with the wearer's particular facial features so as to bring out his true "physiognomy." The wig, in sum, was marketed and touted as the emblem of a new consumer aesthetic which, far from following a top-down logic of emulation, promised to bring out the individuality of the wearer's face while providing the pleasures of convenience and of "natural" good looks. While far from egalitarian in practice, "utility, authenticity, and individuality" may well have paved the way for "liberty, equality, and fraternity."

The expression "cultural origins" ought probably to be jettisoned, since, at least in regard to current practice among historians, it looks very much like an oxymoron: "culture" refers to patterns of meaning which are usually studied at a synchronic point in time, whereas the term "origin" implies a causal, diachronic approach to a historical question. To speak of the French Revolution's "cultural origins" is therefore problematic but probably still necessary since otherwise we would have to resort to a long and unwieldy expression such as "the cultural patterns and materials that historical actors drew upon to make sense of their world once the Revolution had broken out." These cultural elements included the new political concepts ('the nation," "patriotism," "aristocracy," "despotism") forged in the religious and political struggles of the century; ideas about men and women, private and public life, disseminated by novelists, playwrights, and lawyers; communication networks both formal and informal including salons, learned societies, critical pamphlets, gossip, and songs, which would later serve as the structures for ever more radical commentary and action; and a new world of consumer goods which both reflected and created new forms of social connection and individual expression, a more fluid world which would soon be profoundly reconfigured. We have come a long way, in a few decades, from the view that small groups of *philosophes* wrote the script for the French Revolution, and if the link between "before" and "after" now appears more problematic, our view of eighteenth-century French society and ideas is the richer for it.

References

Baker, Keith Michael (1990). *Inventing the French Revolution: Essays on French Political Culture in the Eighteenth Century.* Cambridge: Cambridge University Press.

Baker, Keith Michael (2011). "Enlightenment Idioms, Old Regime Discourses, and Revolutionary Improvisation." In Thomas E. Kaiser and Dale K. Van Kley (eds.). *From Deficit to Deluge: The Origins of the French Revolution.* Stanford, Calif.: Stanford University Press. 165–197.

Calhoun, Craig (1992). *Habermas and the Public Sphere.* Cambridge, Mass.: MIT Press.

Chartier, Roger (1991). *The Cultural Origins of the French Revolution*, trans. Lydia G. Cochrane. Durham, N.C.: Duke University Press.

Darnton, Robert (1985). *The Literary Underground of the Old Regime.* Cambridge, Mass.: Harvard University Press.

Darnton, Robert (1996). *The Forbidden Best-Sellers of Pre-Revolutionary France.* New York: W.W. Norton.

Darnton, Robert (2000). "An Early Information Society: News and the Media in Eighteenth-Century Paris." *AHR*, 105: 1–35.

Doyle, William (1999). *The Origins of the French Revolution*, 3rd edn. Oxford: Oxford University Press.

Echeverria, Durand (1985). *The Maupeou Revolution: A Study in the History of Libertarianism, France 1770–1774.* Baton Rouge: Louisiana State University Press.

Félix, Joël (2001). "The Economy." In William Doyle (ed.). *Old Régime France*. Oxford: Oxford University Press. 7–41.

Gay, Peter (1954). *The Party of Humanity: Essays in the French Enlightenment*. New York: W.W. Norton.

Goodman, Dena (1994). *The Republic of Letters: A Cultural History of the French Enlightenment*. Ithaca, N.Y.: Cornell University Press.

Habermas, Jürgen (1989). *The Structural Transformation of the Public Sphere: An Inquiry into a Category of Bourgeois Society*, trans. Thomas Burger and Frederick Lawrence. Cambridge, Mass.: MIT Press.

Jones, Colin (1996). "The Great Chain of Buying: Medical Advertisement, the Bourgeois Public Sphere, and the Origins of the French Revolution." *AHR*, 101: 13–40.

Jones, Jennifer (2004). *Sexing La Mode: Gender, Fashion and Commercial Culture in Old Régime France*. Oxford: Oxford University Press.

Kwass, Michael (2006). "Big Hair: A Wig History of Consumption in Eighteenth-Century France." *AHR*, 111: 631–659.

Lilti, Antoine (2005). *Le Monde des salons: Sociabilité et mondanité à Paris au XVIIIe siècle*. Paris: Fayard.

Maza, Sarah (1993). *Private Lives and Public Affairs: The Causes Célèbres of Prerevolutionary France*. Berkeley: University of California Press.

Maza, Sarah (1997). "Luxury, Morality and Social Change: Why There Was No Middle-Class Consciousness in Prerevolutionary France." *JMH*, 69: 199–229.

Merrick, Jeffrey (2011). "Gender in Pre-Revolutionary Culture." In Thomas E. Kaiser and Dale K. Van Kley (eds.). *From Deficit to Deluge: The Origins of the French Revolution*. Stanford, Calif.: Stanford University Press. 198–219.

Pardailhé-Galabrun, Annick (1992). *The Birth of Intimacy: Privacy and Domestic Life in Early Modern Paris*, trans. Jocelyn Phelps. Philadelphia: University of Pennsylvania Press.

Roche, Daniel (2000). *A History of Everyday Things: The Birth of Consumption in France*, trans. Brian Pearce. Cambridge: Cambridge University Press.

Shovlin, John (2006). *The Political Economy of Virtue: Luxury, Patriotism and the Origins of the French Revolution*. Ithaca, N.Y.: Cornell University Press.

Smith, Jay (2000). "Social Categories, the Language of Patriotism and the Origins of the French Revolution: The Debate over *Noblesse Commerçante*." *JMH*, 72: 339–374.

Van Kley, Dale (1984). *The Damiens Affair and the Unraveling of the Ancien Régime: Church, State, and Society in France, 1750–1770*. Princeton, N.J.: Princeton University Press.

Van Kley, Dale (1996). *The Religious Origins of the French Revolution: From Calvin to the Civil Constitution, 1560–1791*. New Haven, Conn.: Yale University Press.

Van Kley, Dale (2011). "The Religious Origins of the French Revolution." In Kaiser and Van Kley (eds.). *From Deficit to Deluge: The Origins of the French Revolution*. Stanford, Calif.: Stanford University Press. 104–138.

Chapter Four

France and the Atlantic World

Miranda Spieler

Anglophone people in the seventeenth century referred to the Atlantic when describing coasts, water, and communities. French sources hint at a different sense of the world. The first volume of Diderot and d'Alembert's *Encyclopédie* (1751) was far more concerned with learned controversy over the coordinates and fate of the Île Atlantique (Atlantis) than with the Atlantic Ocean; for d'Alembert, who wrote the entry, the Atlantique straddled myth and fact to the point that the word seemed wrong to apply to an actual body of water. "Atlantique: it is thus one used to call, and sometimes still calls, that portion of the ocean which is between Africa and America and which is more commonly known by the name North Sea. See Ocean."

D'Alembert's article in the *Encyclopédie* was written too early to reflect the French people's new sense of nearness to faraway places during the second half of the eighteenth century. The Seven Years War, an inter-imperial struggle fought (for nine years) on a global scale (1754–55 undeclared; 1756–63), heightened French concern for the world beyond the metropolis not least because of the magnitude of the debacle. In 1762, the year that "France lost all her colonies," d'Alembert lost his sense of humor. "How can one have the courage to laugh when one sees so many men massacred for the folly of priests and kings?" (Voltaire 1881: 81–82, 100). When war resumed between France and England in 1778, Parisians gave themselves over to oceanic enthusiasm, or so it seemed to the city's chronicler, Louis-Sébastien Mercier: "Freedom of the seas is in the mouths of all our women; our elegant men chat about ships as though they had built them, while mistaking the masts for the cords, and Europe is suddenly transported to America, the globe covered from one pole to the other with nascent republics" (1783: 280).

In a jointly authored 1955 essay, Robert Palmer and Jacques Godechot promoted the study of "Atlantic Civilization," thus investing geography – a frame for human activity – with anthropomorphic and moral characteristics. Land and sea

A Companion to the French Revolution, First Edition. Edited by Peter McPhee.

merged with travelers and inhabitants to become a spatial consciousness, an animating spirit behind a particular story of political change that began in 1760 and ended with the break-up of Spain's American empire in the early nineteenth century. Palmer's investigation of this topic, *The Age of Democratic Revolution* (1959–64), recounted a struggle between aristocracy and democracy that reverberated throughout the hemisphere and spoke in many voices while concerning a single phenomenon, even a single protagonist: Atlantic Civilization was unmistakably a freedom-seeking *Weltgeist.* The Hegelian character of Palmer's Atlantic world helps to explain why Africans, Indians, and their descendants – Hegel's people without history – did not appear in his story of the struggle for equality.

Atlantic history in its original form Americanized the French Revolution by linking the European struggle for equality and justice to the founding of the American nation. "The first and greatest effect of the American Revolution in Europe was to make Europeans believe, or rather feel, in a highly emotional way, that they lived in a rare era of momentous change" (Palmer 1959: 239). It is unsurprising that scholars in France proved resistant to the idea of the French Revolution as an Atlantic inheritance. For Soboul (1969) the specificity of the French Revolution lay in its ability to think beyond itself, dream the future, and forecast the eventual violent destruction of the bourgeoisie at the moment of that class's social and political triumph; it was a new beginning, not one form of a general contagion. For Michel Vovelle (2004–5), it was violence, including its tactical use for political ends, that defined the *exception française* and set the French Revolution apart from other Atlantic phenomena. Post-Palmerian approaches to the Atlantic world have met with quite a different reception in France. Jean-Clément Martin (2011) has lately mused that the incorporation of slaves and indigenous peoples into the story of the revolutionary era reveals that "France is no longer the land of the violent exception."

This essay revisits the relationship between the American and French revolutions while eschewing Palmer's emphasis on liberty and equality. Instead I have sought to expand on Jean-Clément Martin's suggestion that the Atlantic world can supply a broader context for interpreting revolutionary violence – the Terror especially. More generally this essay takes instruction from Paul Gilroy (1993) by acknowledging that violence and coercion, due to their ubiquity and magnitude in the Atlantic space, must be the foundation of any investigation of this region's distinctiveness. Toward that end I emphasize the importance of two practices – war and slavery – in giving coherence to the eighteenth-century Atlantic world.

I

John Adams, writing to Jefferson in 1815, reflected back on the meaning of revolution in the American context. "As to the history of the Revolution, my ideas may be peculiar, perhaps singular. What do We Mean by the Revolution? The War? That was no part of the Revolution … The Revolution was in the Minds of the People, and this was effected … before a drop of blood was drawn" (Wilstach 1925: 116). Years earlier, the case of France had led Adams to argue that war, which magnified the despotic character of governments, could not be an agent of democracy or liberty. "Those who dread monarchy and aristocracy and at the same time advocate war are the most inconsistent of all men," he wrote in May of 1794. For Adams, the entanglement of war with revolution that became so manifest during the Terror made it necessary to cleave the American Revolution, however improbably, from the war that delivered the thirteen colonies from the sovereignty of Great Britain. There is no reason, however, to allow this mystification of the American Revolution to subsist into the present day. For eighteenth-century people, the American Revolution was inseparable from war and even synonymous with it.

The American war helped to redefine French understandings of the law of nations (*jus gentium*) in a manner that would prove of great significance to the Revolution. During the eighteenth century the law of nations had two quite different meanings, in referring to a body of usually written practices amongst European nations and to a set of universal principles that stood against and outside precedent. In the course of the eighteenth century, *jus gentium* became ever more associated with natural law principles, a shift that the American war helped to bring about.

David Armitage (2008) has shown that the Declaration of Independence was written to resolve a diplomatic problem for Americans, whose status as unlawful combatants made it impossible for them to enjoy the recognition of other sovereigns, to engage in diplomacy, and to contract with powers hostile to Britain for wartime supplies. Jefferson's text summarized English violations of the law of nations and defended the colonists' right to break off from the metropolis in the name of that law. The Declaration of Independence set forth a legal argument that reversed the identity of the parties in this conflict: it reconfigured the thirteen colonies as a single sovereign entity with the right to engage in treaties with other powers; and it achieved that end by recasting George III and his subjects as brigands. The justice of the American cause hinged on the need to withdraw from a criminal entity and enforce the law that bound mankind.

The American colonists' conception of the law of nations shaped representations of the Franco-American alliance on both sides of the Atlantic (Slauter 2012). In George Washington's 1782 address to Luzerne at the birth of the French dauphin, he praised Louis XVI as the "protector of the liberty of other nations" whose soldiers died "for the maintenance of rights engaging the sentiments of humanity and the privileges of free men" (*Gazette de France*, 10 September 1782: 360). Two years later, in 1784, the Académie des Jeux Floraux in Toulouse offered an essay contest on "la grandeur et l'importance de la Révolution qui vient de s'opérer dans l'Amérique." The winning entry, by the jurist and future revolutionary legislator Jean-Baptiste Mailhe, gave this answer: They "avenged humanity from the outrages of unjust domination; they stood up for the original and imprescriptible rights of peoples" (Mailhe 1784: 26). For practical reasons resulting from France's intervention on the side of American colonists, a language of universal human rights entered wide circulation in France and in French colonies: the monarchy could not go to war on behalf of a band of brigands. The American legal argument in defense of the war, as set forth in the Declaration, conferred legitimacy on French intervention in the conflict. It was a war that needed to be justified in the name of humanity.

In *The Cult of the Nation in France* (2001), David A. Bell suggests that the barbarous Englishman became central to French wartime rhetoric from 1754 to 1763 and then vanished until resurfacing during the Revolution. The fact that George Washington figured as a villainous savage in French writing from the Seven Years War, due to his 1754 confrontation with Jumonville at Fort Necessity, leads Bell to conclude that French propagandists were obliged to retire this form of Anglophobia in 1778, when the monarchy became allied with English rebels under the command of France's former nemesis. Bell's account nonetheless overlooks an important dimension of French patriotic rhetoric during and after the American war. American colonists and their French allies employed the language of natural law to define the English as brutes twice over: they were barbarians on land and pirates at sea.

On 3 February 1778, as Louis XVI and Franklin prepared to seal their pact to destroy the English, the *Affiches américaines*, Saint-Domingue's semi-weekly gazette, reported incidents of land devastation, prisoner abuse, the killing of people who surrendered, and brutality by England's Indian proxies in the American war. The theme of English savagery is central to Hilliard d'Auberteuil's *Miss McCrea* (1784), a novella set during the American Revolution about a real woman who became legendary after Mohawk Indians killed and scalped her. In the novel, English officers justify the Indians' conduct by noting that "a rebellion is not an ordinary war and there is nothing one ought to forbid to make the rebels submit" (1958 [1784]: 131). Similarly, Mailhe's 1784 discourse on the American Revolution, written in the voice of an American colonist, recalls that England had "ceased to abide by the laws of war" and associated "their furors with savage hordes: It is not against men, but against monsters that we have had to defend ourselves" (1784: 9–10).

Depictions of Englishmen as pirates during the American and French revolutions need to be read in light of the long history of the "free seas" as an international legal concept. The Treaty of Tordesillas (1494) dividing the globe between Spain and Portugal led rival imperial powers – first England, later the United Provinces – to contest the treaty's legality by insisting that water belonged to all mankind. Hugo Grotius' *Commentary on the Law of Prize and Booty* (1605) and its companion volume, *The Free Seas* (1609), led the protection of water – the alleged patrimony of all mankind – from seafaring predators to become a motif of Dutch patriot rhetoric (Porras 2005).

Grotian rhetoric is conspicuous in the Declaration of Independence, which denounced George III for having "plundered our seas, ravaged our coasts, burnt our towns, and destroyed the lives of our people." The defense of international waters against maritime outlawry became France's *casus belli*, as Mercier's 1783 *Tableau de Paris* reminds us: the *liberté des mers* became France's wartime slogan and figured in all visual and textual representations of the Franco-American alliance. Jean-Baptiste Coeuilhe's *La Liberté des mers*, a poem laureled in 1781 by the Marseille Academy, praised Louis XVI for "breaking the chains that stretched from one world to the other" in battling English "tyrants of the sea" (Coeuilhe 1781: 11). In *Fragment de Xenophon nouvellement trouvé* (1786), a pseudo-Hellenistic fable about the American war, the Abbé Brizard recounts the deliverance of an oppressed island people by Philip of Macedonia, "the liberator of the seas," who is repaid for "breaking the chains of slaves" with a monument in his name. An engraving published the same year as Brizard's text, *L'Indépendance des États Unis*

(1786), also features a republican monument to a savior prince, which is inscribed "Amérique et les mers, O Louis, vous reconnaît pour son libérateur."

In *La Liberté des mers*, Coeuilhe defined the freedom of the seas as the inapplicability of any legal norm or jurisdiction to the water ("no one has law to obey nor a law to prescribe"). That anomic maritime fantasy little resembled the official French view of the question (Belissa 2001). At the peace, France emerged as the patron of neutral commerce and seemed poised to impose an international privateering ban (*Gazette de Leyde*, 25 April 1783). No such thing occurred, and Benjamin Franklin continued heckling the English as a nation of seafaring highwaymen; "*Piraterie* as the French call it or privateering is the universal bent of the English nation, at home and abroad, wherever settled" (Sparks 1836: 483). The conflation of privateering with piracy, vital to the American case against Britain in 1776, later inspired Guy-Armand, comte de Kersaint, captain during the American campaign, to demand a general ban on privateering one day after France declared war on Austria. On 21 April 1792, Kersaint forecast a devastating campaign by counter-revolutionary rovers; he wanted "those brigands whom you called *émigrés* … enemies of the human race" taken from the crews of captured privateers and put to death (*AP*, 42: 225).

The story of the free seas during the Age of Revolution did not end when deputies beat back Kersaint's ill-timed scheme for maritime legal reform. Instead, French wartime rhetoric after 1793 looked back to French Anglophobia during the American war quite explicitly. Sophie Wahnich (1997) and Dan Edelstein (2010) offer different accounts of the decree of 7 Prairial II (26 May 1794) instructing French soldiers to refuse quarter to captured Englishmen, which meant treating the English as brigands, or what Grotius called "enemies of the human race." Wahnich interprets this story in light of changing attitudes toward the foreigner, whereas Edelstein emphasizes the violent potentialities of eighteenth-century natural law theory. Neither scholar mentions the American Revolution in relation to this decree, despite the claim of Bertrand Barère, when presenting this text to the Convention, that England's recent outrages were a "repetition of the outrages of George during the American Revolution" (*AP*, 91: 36).

Barère lifted much of his narrative about the enormities of the English people from the American *Acte d'indépendance* (as it was known then), which he splices, quotes from, and paraphrases without attribution. Here is the relevant section of the Declaration of Independence in its 1778 French translation together with a passage from Barère's speech:

> Il a exercé le brigandage sur nos mers, ravagé nos côtes, brûlé nos villes et fait couler le sang des Peuples Américains. Actuellement il fait passer en Amérique des armées considérables des mercenaires étrangers pour consommer ses oeuvres de morts, de désolation et de tyrannie, qu'il avoit commencées avec des recherches de cruauté et de perfidie, dont les siècles de barbarie fournissent à peine l'exemple et trop indignes du Chef d'une nation civilisée. Il a forcé nos compatriotes, pris à la mer, à porter les armes contre leur pays, et à devenir les bourreaux de leurs frères, ou à périr eux-mêmes de leurs mains. Il a excité parmi nous des soulevemens domestiques, & a essayé de faire tomber sur nous les Habitans de nos frontières, d'impitoyables sauvages, qui ne savent faire la guerre que par le carnage, sans distinction de sexe d'age ou de conditions. (La Rochefoucauld d'Anville 1778: 10)

> Dans l'Amerique septentrionale, l'Anglais a fait ravager les côtes, détruit les ports, brûlé les villes et massacré les habitants des campagnes. Il a forcé les Américains, fait prisonniers en pleine mer, à porter les armes contre leur patrie, à devenir les boureaux de leurs amis et de leurs frères, ou à périr eux-mêmes par des mains si chères. Il a couvert les américains de trahisons, corrompu leurs chefs, salarié les criminels condamnés, acheté des seigneurs et des princes d'Allemagne, des soldats, comme des troupeaux, et corrompît l'humanité des sauvages au point de les faire sortir de leur tactique ordinaire et de leur donner une récompense pour chaque crâne d'homme libre qu'ils apporteraient au commandant anglais. (Bertrand Barère, *AP*, 91: 40)

Barère's text varies the order of phrases in the Declaration and contains additions and elisions. Two differences are most important for our purposes. The first concerns the identity of the grammatical subject – the agent who performs the crimes; *he* in the American Declaration of Independence always refers to the English sovereign, never to the English people. Barère by contrast uses the pronoun *il* to refer to the *Anglais*, the Englishman. In consequence of this substitution, it becomes possible for Barère to argue that the war waged by Britain against France was of a private and hence criminal sort.

A second difference from the 1776 Declaration lies in the omission of the phrase "he has plundered our seas," whose absence becomes palpable because of Barère's several allusions to English maritime enormities in this speech. This elision may result from the extent of France's privateering campaign against English commerce, which included a coordinated attempt to destroy the English slave trade to avenge recent French losses in the Caribbean, which then included Martinique, Guadeloupe (which France soon recovered), and portions of Saint-Domingue.

Notwithstanding Barère's refusal to denounce privateering, his case for the status of the English people as a criminal group owed something to the *guerre de course*. As Kersaint observed in 1792, "considering that war is the supreme act of sovereignty, it can only be waged by nations and not by individual for their own profit" (*AP*, 42: 225). Privateering violated the norms of lawful war according to writers in the natural law tradition whether one looks to Grotius, Emerich de Vattel, or Jean-Jacques Rousseau. Through the figure of the corsair, "England" as a sovereign entity became indistinct from the English people as individuals.

II

"There is a sacred veil to be drawn over the beginning of all governments." Edmund Burke's remark at the 1788 trial of Warren Hastings might just as well have described America. In the United States the problem lay in curtaining war from peace. European newspaper articles from the 1780s about the American republic described a place beset by anarchy, ripe for a military coup, and overrun by an insurrectionary plebe of former soldiers who refused to pay debts or taxes. In 1784, when English papers denounced Washington as a rising dictator (*Gazette de Leyde*, supplement to 7 December 1784), the comte de Mirabeau (1785), writing from exile in London, exposed the subversion of *Amérique régénérée* by the new cosmopolitan officer club, the Society of Cincinnati. While defending Washington against English smears, the *Gazette de Leyde* acknowledged the chaos. "The mental ferment that endures after a civil war is made worse in the case of America by the lack of specie and resources," noted the paper after the 1783 Newburgh conspiracy, when officers of the Continental Army rose up to demand payment, prompting Congress to flee to Princeton, New Jersey (*Gazette de Leyde*, supplement to 24 June 1783; Kohn 1970). The America that reached French people in the 1780s was "a continuous scene of anarchy and troubles" (*Gazette de Leyde*, supplement to 7 December 1784).

Tumult in the United States under the Articles of Confederation led pessimistic French-language texts about the United States to acquire a significance for American politicians unrelated to the truth of the criticisms those texts contained. Two texts assumed particular importance: first was a 1778 letter by the economist Anne-Robert Turgot to the minister Richard Price, which circulated in various forms during the 1780s; second was *Observations sur le gouvernement et les loix des États Unis* (1784), by Gabriel de Mably. Both texts called into question Americans' aptitude for liberty and raised doubts about whether so anarchic a country would be able to levy taxes, control the monetary supply, enforce treaties, and repay the war debt.

Concern about the reception of these works abroad, especially by creditors and speculators, inspired John Adams to write *Defence of the Constitutions of the United States* (1787) as a series of letters from London, where he served as plenipotentiary (Potofsky 2011). Elsewhere in London, as Marie-Jeanne Rossignol (1994) observes, the state of Vermont maintained its own diplomatic corps, which is a measure of the weakness of the union at the time Adams wrote his *Defense*. In January 1787 the clergyman Price received news from Benjamin Rush that the United States would soon split "into three independent confederacies." Price answered that Congress had become "an object of derision rather than of respect" (Peach 1994).

At the time of the drafting of the Declaration of the Rights of Man and of the Citizen, it was the idea of a declaratory act like George Mason's widely circulated bill of rights for Virginia (called a *déclaration des droits* in French), not the rights themselves that legislators took from the United States. French deputies had no knowledge of the American federal constitution due to a news blackout on the federalist and anti-federalist debate in French-language papers (Toinet and Toinet 1972).

French revolutionaries across the political spectrum, from monarchists to republicans, looked to England for inspiration (Hammersley 2010). England's contribution to the French Revolution is not limited, however, to the political theory of seventeenth-century republicans. It is also likely that England transmitted a legal mechanism to France by way of the New World for defending the state against internal rebels.

Until 1789 martial law was an English practice, though one considered taboo on English home soil since the seventeenth century (which did not prevent its use in Ireland in 1798). After Charles I claimed the "exercise of Martial Law for the purposes of putting down rebellion and maintaining order in the army," Parliament submitted the1628 petition of right depicting the suspension of the jurisdiction of ordinary courts in times of peace as an outrage against the liberty of British subjects (Hussain 2003; Phillimore 1900). Martial law in the eighteenth century described two related practices of special importance to the British West Indies and eventually to North America. First, martial law referred to what one now would call military law – the code and system of justice binding on soldiers in peace and in war. Second, martial law referred to the imposition of military rule by a Crown agent to raise the militia and suspend the jurisdiction of normal courts when confronted with an invasion or rebellion (Benton 2009). In the New World context, rebellions usually took the form of slave revolts. The frequency with which martial law was declared in the British West Indies during and after the Seven Years War helped this practice to become a conventional, region-wide tool for managing invasion and revolt.[1]

The struggle that began in 1763 between colonists and Parliament helped to transform martial law from a device for containing slaves into a means of subjugating citizens. Amid colonial resistance to the Stamp Act, the *New York Gazette* reported that a declaration of martial law was expected "in two colonies" (*New York Gazette*, 2 January 1766: 2). Soon, newspapers throughout British North America began reprinting Parliament's 1628 petition of right. The American War of Independence began with declarations of martial law by General Carleton in Quebec (9 June) and General Gage in Massachusetts (12 June). In a famous decree of November 1775, Virginia's governor John Murray, fourth Earl of Dunmore, offered liberty to slaves and indentured servants who fought for the king (Brown and Morgan 2006; Schama 2005). The legal character and chief purpose of that decree have been largely forgotten, however. Dunmore's proclamation was a decree declaring martial law in Virginia that transformed a device for repressing slave revolts into a weapon against slave masters and a means of slave liberation.

The widespread use of martial law in the West Indies during the second half of the eighteenth century supplies a necessary context for understanding the adoption of this practice by French legislators. In October 1789, after tens of thousands of demonstrators marched on Versailles and fetched the king and queen to Paris, legislators with links to the West Indies and North America began clamoring for new police measures. On 10 October two Saint-Domingue deputies, Cocherel and Gouy d'Arsy, explained that the mob had threatened their lives at which Pierre-Victor Malouet, a Saint-Domingue proprietor and former colonial administrator, invoked the Declaration of the Rights of Man and of the Citizen to demand a crackdown on seditious publications and gatherings. The Maréchal Adam-Philippe de Custine, who fought in the battle of Yorktown, answered by demanding "a martial law" to assure the "security of citizens" (*AP*, 9: 397–399). The resulting law, voted on 21 October and signed three days later by the king, spelled out municipal procedures for declaring martial law that climaxed with the use of lethal force against the crowd by national guardsmen (*AP*, 9: 472–475). One week after the passage of the law, on 28 October 1789, the king's ministers drafted an open letter to Louis XVI recommending that special measures, unknown on domestic soil, be applied to the overseas empire to maintain "the security of slaves and citizens." After the public reading of that letter, which did not simply concern the colonies, the Saint-Domingue planter Moreau de Saint Méry pledged the support of "good citizens" in his Paris district to support "the martial law with their last drop of blood" (*AP*, 9: 592–593). Finally, it was General Lafayette on 17 July 1791 who led the National Guard on the *champs de la Fédération* (the Champ de Mars) against stone-throwing republicans under the red banner of martial law (*AP*, 28: 396–402).

III

In view of the many effects of the American Revolution on French legal and political culture, it is worth taking measure of precisely what that war did not change. In the British case, the American Revolution transformed the cause of anti-slavery from a moral crusade into a mass movement (Brown 2006). In the French case, outspoken enthusiasts of the American cause were chief among the 104 members of the Société des Amis des Noirs, founded by Jacques-Pierre Brissot in 1788 as an offshoot of the tiny Société Gallo-Americain, Brissot's creation of the previous year (Darnton 2003; Gainot and Dorigny 1998; Vaugelade 2005). Both societies were vanguard revolutionary groups in the mind of their founder; sanguine about the role of men of letters in the world, Brissot credited the American Revolution to *gazettes*. He believed that mass movements originated with the printed word: write and the people will come. Forty years ago, the historian Daniel Resnick (1972) attributed the club's smallness and ineffectuality to elitism, a feature of other Enlightenment-era *sociétés de pensée*. More recently, the society has been credited with inventing a revolutionary style of outreach politics (Popkin 2010). In view of this flattering reappraisal, it becomes all the more curious how little the group managed to accomplish.

The society agitated for the abolitionist cause during the drafting of *cahiers de doléances* that defined the mandate of deputies to the Estates-General. In my count a mere thirty-nine of these requested either the abolition of slavery, the abolition of the trade, or the improvement of conditions for slaves in the colonies. Nearly all the *cahiers de doléances* mentioned slaves, but the shackled bodies were most often metaphors, because the slavery that most concerned French people in 1789, which they theorized in natural law terms, was their own. The seigneurial right over ovens and mills was "slavery against the law of nations" (*AP*, 3: 784). Rent contracts that could not be annulled by sale were "slavery as complete as that which existed among the ancients and to which negroes are now subject in the colonies" (*AP*, 4: 197). The *cahier* for the Third Estate in Nemours, while depicting local people as negro slaves in the colonies, did not request the abolition of colonial slavery or otherwise address colonial problems (*AP*, vol. 3).

The remarkable scope of abolitionist support in eighteenth-century England in comparison to France should not be read naively, as though it expressed a difference in moral character. Conditions that made it possible for anti-slavery to become a mass movement in England were lacking in France. According to Christopher Brown (2009), the American Revolution induced a crisis in the imperial constitution in England, which led customary practices to undergo new moral scrutiny and drew attention to slavery's injustice. The need to defend the noble purpose of the British Empire in the face of criticism led slavery to seem contrary to the national interest. With a view to the national interest, abolitionists translated what began as a moral crusade into a project of social utility by developing an alternative economic vision for Britain's imperial future.

French territorial losses to Britain in the course of the eighteenth century, especially the loss of Canada and India during the Seven Years War, meant that the French Empire during the final years of the *ancien régime* centered on the slave plantation. This essential fact about France's eighteenth-century empire helps to explain why French political economists failed to rally around an overtly abolitionist program, in contrast to their British counterparts. Instead they translated discomfort with the violence and corruption that subtended global trade into an inward-looking program that aimed to ignore the empire and maximize the wealth generated by domestic soil (Shovlin 2006). For some the slave empire seemed not only a necessary evil but also a condition of possibility for radical political change in France. As Paul Cheney (2010: 224) notes, Antoine Barnave – lawyer, legislator, and enthusiast of "democratic revolution" – embraced the cause of slave-owners because he believed that colonial wealth produced by slavery would enable the destruction of antiquated forms of social and political power in the metropolis.

The French Revolution coincided with the peak of France's plantation system and slave trade. The colony of Saint-Domingue, with more than 400,000 slaves and a surface area resembling that of New Hampshire, produced 40 percent of the world's sugar at the end of the *ancien régime.* In 1790, 48,771 slaves boarded French ships for the New World, of whom 47,855 were bound for Saint-Domingue (www.slavevoyages.org). Commodities produced by slaves and shipped to France from the colonies accounted for two-fifths of all French trade in 1787 (Doerflinger 1976). At the time that French revolutionaries approved the Declaration of the Rights of Man and of the Citizen, the monarchy depended on slavery more than it ever had.

Slavery's importance to the French economy might lead one to expect that legislators would simply exclude the colonies from the revolutionary project altogether, and many people tried to. Perhaps the most striking feature of French colonial policy during the first years of the new regime, apart from the fact that slavery still existed, lies in precisely how difficult it proved to avoid talking about the colonies. To exclude the empire from the revolutionary project legislators needed to be able to locate the colonies in a separate political reality. Instead, however, the early years of the French Revolution witnessed a collapse between metropolis and empire from a legal point of view. Confronted with this strange and unexpected occurrence, white planters, merchants involved in the slave trade, their advocates in the legislature, and even deputies who supported equal rights for free colored people sought legal tools to resurrect the metropolis–colony distinction. Ultimately the problem of how to sustain slavery in the era of the Declaration subtended all colonial legislation from the early revolutionary period and explains the highly evasive rhetoric found in that body of law.

The collapse in 1789 of the distinction between metropolis and colony raises the question of how to understand that development in light of pre-revolutionary history. In the course of the eighteenth century, the French juridical maxim "there are no slaves in France" assumed several new significances (Peabody 1996). The maxim described the specialness of metropolitan earth: slaves sued successfully for their freedom by showing that they had set foot in France. Every freedom suit heard by an eighteenth-century French court of the admiralty was decided to the slave's advantage. Yet the same maxim, "there are no slaves in France," also furnished pro-slavery administrators with rhetorical and legal grounds for prohibiting the unrestricted entry of slaves into France; those efforts culminated in a 1777 decree banning "blacks" from the realm. The lawyers who sought the slaves' deliverance in France and administrators who sought the slaves' exclusion from France had more in common than it first appears: both envisaged the metropole and the colonies as opposing legal realities.

In the years before 1789, the world of chattel slavery began to overtake the metropolis and merge with it. Slaves under the jurisdiction of the Parlement of Brittany were judged in eighteenth-century France according to colonial law in civil matters (Pruitt 2007). Even Paris did not count as free soil: it was a town where the police hunted impudent slaves for a fee and locked them up in *prisons d'état*. The Paris Parlement's refusal to register edicts relevant to slaves did not keep the city's police from enforcing those legal texts. On 10 March 1752, "Monsieur Coustard, honorary councilor to the Great Chamber, asked for a royal order to enable the arrest of a slave belonging to Monsieur Coustard, inhabitant of Saint-Domingue; and as he showed that this inhabitant had met the formalities for the passage of this slave in France, the order was expedited." From this source we learn that kinship linked Saint-Domingue planters to the Parlement; that Parisian police enforced provisions of unregistered edicts concerning declarations by slave masters; and that the Parisians who solicited *lettres de cachet* for slaves included jurists in the Parlement.[2]

The 8 September 1778 issue of Saint-Domingue's *Affiches américaines* included a short list of names and descriptions of slave fugitives, including two Congos, an Igbo, a Creole from the colony, a teenage hairdresser from the Carolinas, and an "English Negro." The same issue included an open letter from the king justifying war with England to avenge attacks on "the maritime commerce of my kingdom and American colonies." The people on the fugitive list were the face of that commerce; the war that Frenchmen celebrated in the name of freedom began as a defense of the French slave empire.

While Atlantic slavery led the monarchy into war, war also shaped the character of French slave society at the end of the *ancien régime*. Escalating demand for slaves coincided with a period of endemic civil war in what remained of the Kingdom of the Kongo. David Eltis (1990) and John Thornton (1998) dispute the contention by Paul Lovejoy (1989) that Atlantic slavery significantly affected the internal politics and economies of early modern African states. This quarrel is not germane to the character of late eighteenth-century French colonial society, however. The fact that civil war in west-central Africa and brigandage relating to it coincided with the height of European demand for young able-bodied African males turned Saint-Domingue circa 1789 into a place crammed with tens of thousands of deported warriors who came from the same places and spoke the same languages (Geggus 2001; Thornton 1998). The situation in Saint-Domingue at the end of the *ancien régime* was highly propitious to a massive revolt. The consumption of sundries and stimulants in Europe depended on field labor by rebel soldiers from the Kongo; the more sugar and coffee that Europe consumed, the greater the demand for experienced African fighters in the Americas. There is no more extreme case of a capitalist regime destroyed by internal contradiction than eighteenth-century Saint-Domingue.

White demands in 1789 owed a great deal to the wars of the eighteenth century. Trevor Burnard (2009), writing of the British Empire, underlines the importance of early modern war as a phase of rupture between center and periphery that encouraged the growth of autonomous political institutions and a sense of particularity on the part of colonial settlers. War shaped the revolutionary-era demands of Saint-Domingue planters. War scrambled normal communication networks, weakened communications with the metropolis, and loosened the bonds of empire in a legal, administrative, and commercial sense, which made the return of those imperial constraints all the more palpable. The frequency of war in the eighteenth century (1701–14, 1740–48, 1756–63, 1778–83) meant that this cycle occurred with annoying frequency: colonial settlers enjoyed the advantage of open ports and metropolitan distractedness for extended periods, followed by robust reassertions of metropolitan power. This pattern encouraged the rise of a "spirit of autonomy" among Saint-Domingue planters (Debien 1953). According to John Garrigus (2006), race laws introduced to Saint-Domingue after the Seven Years War were a bone thrown to whites by the monarchy to sweeten the return of crown control. After the American war, the Crown reasserted control over the internal affairs of the colony by seeking to extend its control over the slave body to an unprecedented degree. The building of a slave hospital in Le Cap (*Étrennes américaines*, 1788: 168–169) and attempts to prosecute masters for barbarism toward slaves (Ghachem 2011) bear witness to this tendency. At the time of the convocation of the Estates-General, the whites of Saint-Domingue embraced a reform program that involved strengthening local autonomy through new representative institutions, a new local code of laws, and an end to mercantile restrictions, in the form of the *exclusif*.

In 1789 colonial slave-owners witnessed the collapse of the metropolitan–colony distinction just as France became a blank land of liberty awaiting new law. The absorption of Saint-Domingue by the metropolis resulted from imprudent lobbying efforts by courtiers with fortunes in Saint-Domingue – the marquis de Gouy d'Arsy chief among them – who sought colonial representation in the Estates-General. Gouy d'Arsy centered those lobbying efforts on a demand for the legal assimilation of all colonies to provinces of the realm. It seemed necessary to argue that colonies be treated as provinces from a legal standpoint so he might justify Saint-Domingue's right to representation. The National Assembly embraced this argument on 4 July 1789 to justify admitting colonial deputies. One month later, however, the Saint-Domingue deputation confronted the magnitude of its folly. On 4 August 1789, when abolishing noble and clerical entitlements, the National Assembly annulled the privileges of French provinces, "whose sacrifice is necessary to the intimate union of all parts of the empire" (*Patriote françois*,

7 August 1789: 2). A mere two weeks later came the real disaster. Saint-Domingue deputies later confessed to being struck with "a type of terror, when we saw the Declaration of the Rights of Man posed as the basis of the new constitution, absolute equality, identity of rights, and liberty of all individuals" (*Correspondance secrète* 1790: 29). On 20 August 1789, when the Assembly finalized the text of the Declaration (formally adopted on the 26th), the French Colonial Corresponding Society, later known as the Club Massiac, convened for its first meeting. Its members aimed to disavow the colonial deputies; to keep colonial matters out of the Assembly; and to ensure that the colonies might exist as a separate legal order beyond reach of the Assembly's decrees.

Neither the rhetoric of metropolitan legislators nor of slave-owners in 1789 can be understood without reference to Atlantic slavery. In autumn 1789, the assumption by everyone including Saint-Domingue deputies that the empire and metropolis belonged to the same legal reality makes it possible to connect debates on the colonial question to a problem that I noted earlier in this essay, namely the introduction of martial law in October 1789. It was Gouy d'Arsy, deputy for Saint-Domingue, who first demanded a law of repression after the march on Versailles with support from Malouet and eventually from Moreau de Saint Méry. Their desire to empower the army to suppress *attroupements* (seditious gatherings) needs to be read in light of the apparent indistinctness of metropolitan from colonial territory at the time. Since the colonies and metropole were presumed to consist of one land under one law, the *loi martiale* would also apply overseas. This circumstance gives new interest to Moreau de Saint Méry's pledge on 28 October 1789 to "defend the martial law to the last drop of blood." What the new law promised slave-owners was the possibility of military rule overseas – an escape hatch from the new rights culture – to enable slavery to remain intact. It is likely that Moreau's pledge in October 1789 did not concern the defense of martial law – which was a means, not an end – but slavery.

For slave-owners, the proclamation of universal rights summoned a desire for that law's suspension and brought to mind an American device for accomplishing this. Here and in other respects the Atlantic world in the Age of Revolution helped to create what Michel Vovelle called the *exception française*. In the end, the entangled practices of eighteenth-century war and slavery were at least as significant as philosophical myth (Edelstein 2010) in producing legal concepts and instruments that became active during the Terror. From the beginning of the French Revolution, the New World helped to define the Old World's machinery of political violence.

Notes

1 On uses of martial law during the Seven Years War and after, see *New York Gazette Weekly* of 10 Jan. 1757, 3 (Jamaica); *New York Mercury*, 7 Mar. 1757, 2 (Jamaica); *Pennsylvania Gazette*, 14 July 1757, 3 (Jamaica); *New York Gazette*, 1 Dec. 1760, 3. (Jamaica); *Boston Evening Post*, 5 Apr. 1762, 3 (Jamaica); *Boston Evening Post*, 13 Apr. 1761, 2 (Jamaica); *Boston Evening Post*, 15 Mar. 1762, 2 (Bermuda); *New York Mercury*, 24 May 1762, 3 (Jamaica); *New York Gazette*, 27 May 1765, 1 (Curaçao and Saint Eustatia); *Newport*

Mercury, 30 June 1766, 2 (Virginia); *Providence Gazette*, 26 Mar. 1768, 2 (Antigua); *Pennsylvania Chronicle*, 24 Apr. 1769, 111 (Isle of Nevis); *New York Gazette*, 26 Feb. 1770, 2 (Jamaica); *Boston Newsletter*, 22 Mar. 1770, 2 (Jamaica): *Pennsylvania Gazette*, 24 May 1770, 3 (Jamaica); *New London Gazette*, 28 Dec. 1770, 1 (Cuba).

2 See MSS 11,793, 12,252, and 11,807, Archives de la Bastille, Bibliothèque de l'Arsénal, Paris.

References

Adams, John (1787). *A Defence of the Constitutions of Government of the United States of America*. London: C. Dilly.

AP: *Archives parlementaires de 1787 à 1860. Recueil complet des débats législatifs et politiques des chambres françaises, imprimé par ordre du corps législatif sous la direction de mm. J. Mavidal et E. Laurent. Première série, 1787–1799* (1867–1913), 82 vols. Paris: P. Dupont.

Armitage, David (2008). *The Declaration of Independence: A Global History*. Cambridge, Mass.: Harvard University Press.

Belissa, Marc (2001). "Les Lumières contre les corsaires (1763–1795)." *Dix-huitième siècle*, 33: 119–132.

Bell, David A. (2001). *The Cult of the Nation in France: Inventing Nationalism 1680–1820*. Cambridge, Mass.: Harvard University Press.

Benton, Lauren (2009). *A Search for Sovereignty: Law and Geography in European Empires*. New York and London: Cambridge University Press.

Brown, Christopher Leslie (2006). *Moral Capital: The Foundations of British Abolitionism*. Chapel Hill: University of North Carolina Press.

Brown, Christopher Leslie and Philip D. Morgan (eds.) (2006). *Arming Slaves: From Classical Times to the Modern Age*. New Haven, Conn.: Yale University Press.

Burnard, Trevor (2009). "The British Atlantic." In Jack P. Greene and Philip D. Morgan (eds.). *Atlantic History: A Critical Appraisal*. New York: Oxford University Press. 111–136.

Cheney, Paul (2010). *Revolutionary Commerce: Globalization and the French Monarchy*. Princeton, N.J.: Harvard University Press.

Coeuilhe, Jean-Baptiste (1782). *La Liberté des mers; poème qui a remporté le prix de l'Académie de Marseille en 1781*. Paris: Gueffier.

Correspondance secrète des députés de Saint Domingue avec les comités de cette île (12 août 1789 – 9 avril 1790). Paris.

Darnton, Robert (2003). *George Washington's False Teeth: An Unconventional Guide to the Eighteenth Century*. New York: Norton.

Debien, Gabriel (1953). *Les Colons de Saint-Domingue et la Révolution: Essai sur le Club Massiac, août 1789–aôut 1792*. Paris: Armand Colin.

Doerflinger, Thomas M. (1976). "The Antilles Trade of the Old Regime: A Statistical Overview." *Journal of Interdisciplinary History*, 6: 397–415.

Edelstein, Dan (2010). *The Terror of Natural Right: Republicanism, the Cult of Nature, and the French Revolution*. Chicago: University of Chicago Press.

Eltis, David (1990). "The Volume, Age/Sex Ratios, and African Impact of the Slave Trade: Some Refinements of Paul Lovejoy's Review of the Literature." *Journal of African History*, 3: 485–492.

Étrennes américaines chronologiques et historiques pour l'Année bissextile 1788. Port au Prince: Chez Bourdon.

Gainot, Bernard and Marcel Dorigny (1998). *La Société des Amis des Noirs, 1788–1799: Contribution à l'histoire de l'abolition de l'esclavage*. Paris: Éditions UNESCO.

Garrigus, John (2006). *Before Haiti: Race and Citizenship in French Saint-Domingue.* New York: Palgrave Macmillan.

Geggus, David Patrick (2001). "The French Slave Trade: An Overview." *William and Mary Quarterly*, 3rd series, 58: 119–138.

Ghachem, Malick (2011). "Prosecuting Torture: The Strategic Ethics of Slavery in Pre-Revolutionary Saint-Domingue (Haiti)." *Law and History Review*, 29: 985–1030.

Gilroy, Paul (1993). *The Black Atlantic: Modernity and Double Consciousness.* New York and London: Verso.

Godechot, Jacques and R.R. Palmer (1955). "Le Problème de l'Atlantique du XVIIIième au XXième siècle." *Relazioni*, 5 (Storia contemporanea; Florence): 175–239.

Hammersley, Rachel (2010). *The English Republican Tradition and Eighteenth Century France: Between the Ancients and the Moderns.* Manchester: Manchester University Press.

Hilliard d'Auberteuil, René (1958). *Miss McCrea: A Novel of the American Revolution.* Gainesville: University of Florida Press.

Hussain, Nasser (2003). *The Jurisprudence of Emergency: Colonialism and the Rule of Law.* Ann Arbor: University of Michigan Press.

Kohn, Richard H. (1970). "The Inside History of the Newburgh Conspiracy: America and the Coup d'Etat." *William and Mary Quarterly*, 3rd series, 27: 187–220.

La Rochefoucauld d'Anville, Louis-Alexandre (1778). *Recueil des loix constitutives des colonies angloises confédérées sous la dénomination d'États-Unis de l'Amérique septentrionale, auquel on a joint les actes d'indépendance, de confédération & autres actes du Congrès général Philadelphie, et se vend à Paris, chez Cellot & Jombert.*

Lovejoy, Paul (1989). "The Impact of the Atlantic Slave Trade on Africa: A Review of the Literature." *Journal of African History*, 30: 365–394.

Mably, Gabriel de (1784). *Observations sur le gouvernement et les lois des États Unis d'Amérique par l'Abbé Mably.* Paris and Amsterdam: Hardouin.

Mailhe, Jean-Baptiste (1784). *Discours qui a remporté le prix à l'académie des jeux floraux en 1784, sur la grandeur et l'importance de la révolution qui vient de s'opérer dans l'Amérique septentrionale.* Toulouse: Desclassan.

Martin, Jean-Clement (2011). "Le Bon Usage des malentendus." *AHRF*, 363: 151–160.

Mercier, Louis-Sebastien (1783). *Tableau de Paris*, new edn., vol. 4. Amsterdam.

Mirabeau, Honoré Gabriel Riqueti, comte de (1785). *Considérations sur l'ordre de Cincinnatus … accompagné de réflexions et de notes du traducteur.* London: Johnson.

Palmer, Robert Roswell (1959). *The Age of the Democratic Revolution: A Political History of Europe and America, 1760–1800.* Princeton, N.J.: Harvard University Press.

Palmer, Robert Roswell, and Jacques Godechot (1955). "Le Problème de l'Atlantique du XVIIIe au XXe siècle." In *Relazioni del Xo Congresso internazionale di Scienze storiche.* Florence, Sansoni. 5: 175–239.

Peabody, Sue (1996). *"There are No Slaves in France": The Political Culture of Race and Slavery in Old Regime France.* New York and Oxford: Oxford University Press.

Peach, William Bernard (ed.) (1994). *The Correspondence of Richard Price*, vol. 3: *February 1786–February 1791.* Durham, N.C.: Duke University Press; Cardiff, University of Wales Press.

Phillimore, George Grenville (1900). "Martial Law in Rebellion." *Journal of the Society of Comparative Legislation*, new series, 2: 45–72.

Popkin, Jeremy (2010). "Saint-Domingue, Slavery, and the Origins of the French Revolution." In Thomas Kaiser and Dale Van Kley (eds.). *From Deficit to Deluge: The Origins of the French Revolution.* Stanford, Calif.: Stanford University Press. 220–248.

Porras, Ileana (2005). "Grotius's de Iure Praedae – the Law of Prize and Booty, or on How to Distinguish Merchants from Pirates." *Brooklyn Journal of International Law*, 31: 741–804.

Potofsky, Allan (2011). "Le Corps consulaire français et le débat autour de la "perte" des Amériques: Les Intérêts mercantiles franco-américains et le commerce atlantique, 1763–1795." *AHRF*, 363: 33–57.

Pruitt, Dwain (2007). "'The Opposition of the Law to the Law': Race, Slavery, and the Law in Nantes, 1715–1778." *FHS*, 30: 147–174.

Resnick, Daniel (1972). "The Société des Amis des Noirs and the Abolition of Slavery." *FHS*, 7: 562–563.

Rossignol, Marie-Jeanne (1994). *Le Ferment nationaliste: Aux origines de la politique extérieure des États Unis 1789–1812*. Paris: Belin.

Schama, Simon (2005). *Rough Crossings: Britain, the Slaves and the American Revolution*. London: BBC Books.

Shovlin, John (2006). *The Political Economy of Virtue: Luxury, Patriotism and the Origins of the French Revolution*. Ithaca, N.Y.: Cornell University Press.

Slauter, Will (2012). "Le Paragraphe mobile: Circulation et transformations des informations dans le monde atlantique du 18e siècle." *Annales*, 2: 363–389.

Soboul, Albert (1969). "La Révolution française dans le monde contemporain: Étude comparative." *Information historique*, 3: 107–123.

Sparks, Jared (ed.) (1836). *The Works of Benjamin Franklin*, vol. 2. Boston: Tappan & Whittemore.

Thornton, John (1998). *Africa and Africans in the Making of the Atlantic World 1400–1800*, 2nd edn. New York and London: Cambridge University Press.

Toinet, Marie-France and Paul Toinet (1972). "La Presse française et la Constitution américaine en 1787." In Elise Marienstras (ed.). *L'Amérique et la France: Deux révolutions*. Paris: Publications de la Sorbonne. 31–41.

Vaugelade, Daniel (2005). *La Question américaine au 18ème siècle: Au travers de la correspondance du duc Louis Alexandre de La Rochefoucauld (1743–1792)*. Paris: Éditions Publibook.

Voltaire (1881). *Œuvres complètes*, vol. 42. Paris: Garnier.

Vovelle, Michel (2004–5). "1789: L'Exception française." *Les Révolutions du monde moderne*, Studien des Frankreich-Zentrums der Alert-Ludwigs Universität Freiburg, 15: 31–48.

Wahnich, Sophie (1997). *L'Impossible citoyen: L'Étranger dans le discours de la Révolution française*. Paris: Albin Michel.

Wilstach, Paul (ed.) (1925). *Correspondence of John Adams and Thomas Jefferson*. Indianapolis: Bobbs-Merrill.

Part II

Reshaping France, 1789–91

Chapter Five

The Principles of 1789

Michael P. Fitzsimmons

Today the best-known precepts of the French Revolution – *liberté, égalité, fraternité* – comprise the national motto of the French state and are generally familiar to educated people around the world. Their prominence has served to confer upon those ideals an air of destiny and virtual inevitability. In fact, the formulation and achievement of the principles of 1789 were much more a product of chance and contingency than of fixed goals or intent, and developed in stages. The fortuitous manner in which the principles of 1789 emerged in no way detracts from their grandeur, magnificence, or legacy – one must simply recognize that they did not begin as fully formed objectives and, before August 1789, would have had little claim to universality or capacity to inspire.

***

The catalyst for the sequence of events that led to the French Revolution was a worsening of the fiscal situation during 1786. The weakened fiscal position of the Crown, due in large measure to the American War of Independence, led the Controller-General Charles-Alexandre de Calonne to present a memorandum to Louis XVI delineating his ideas for ameliorating the situation. After characterizing France as an imperfect kingdom in which "privileges tear asunder all equilibrium," Calonne encouraged Louis to undertake an extensive reform of the state, and particularly urged him to attack fiscal privilege. The memorandum outlined several administrative, economic, and fiscal proposals, but its most pivotal and controversial component was a "territorial subvention," a proportional land tax to be paid in kind by all landowners, without exception.

Calonne knew that *parlements* and provincial estates would oppose his program, so he devised a stratagem designed to outmaneuver them. He advocated the

A Companion to the French Revolution, First Edition. Edited by Peter McPhee.

convening of an Assembly of Notables, which had not occurred since 1626, to which he would present his proposals. Confidently expecting approval by the Assembly, Calonne believed that its endorsement would pre-empt opposition by the Parlement of Paris, which would have to register the measures before they could be implemented. Calonne presented his project during August 1786, but Louis delayed giving his approval to the plan until December, which meant that the Assembly did not open until 22 February 1787.

Beginning with the opening session, the Crown made clear that the decisive issue in the resolution of the fiscal crisis was privilege. Whereas Louis took an understated tone – concluding his brief opening address to the Notables by expressing the hope that they would not favor private interests over the public good – Calonne was more pointed in his remarks. After presenting an analysis of the fiscal situation, he told the Notables that it was no longer possible to rely on expedients of the past and contended that only two courses of action were available, but one of them, admission of bankruptcy, was out of the question. The only feasible solution was to eliminate social, political, and fiscal abuses, and it was clear that by "abuses" Calonne was alluding to the privileges enjoyed by many Notables. After summarizing his proposals, Calonne emphasized that their goal was the public good and implied that the monarch had endorsed his program, suggesting that there was little provision for discussion and that it was simply a matter of the Notables approving the plan.

Angered by their apparent relegation to a compliant role and by Calonne's attack on privilege, the Notables opposed his program from the outset and avoided the pitfalls in which he had hoped to ensnare them. In an effort to create a favorable impression, the Notables endorsed the principle of fiscal equality and renounced their proposed exemption from a minor direct tax, the *capitation*. During the next several weeks, however, the Notables did not act upon Calonne's program, particularly the land tax, and Calonne's frustration grew. He commissioned a pamphlet critical of their inaction, seeking to influence perceptions of the Assembly, which was closed to the public.

The pamphlet declared that the re-establishment of financial equilibrium was in the interest of all and, to reassure the populace that there would not be an increase in taxation, asserted that the burden of the proposed measures would not fall on the Third Estate. The pamphlet contended that privileges would be sacrificed and asked whether the Notables preferred to overburden the non-privileged – the people. The tract ostensibly defended the Notables by observing that they had already agreed to sacrifice their fiscal privileges and had committed themselves to the principle that all should be subject to the land tax. It concluded by noting that it would be wrong to believe that reasonable doubts on the part of the Notables represented malevolent opposition because such an assumption would be harmful to the nation, but the clear intent of the pamphlet was to dissuade the Notables from further opposition (Calonne 1790: 436–440).

Calonne also took the exceptional action of having the pamphlet disseminated without charge, not only in Paris but also in provincial towns. Its publication and extraordinary diffusion embittered relations between Calonne and the Notables, one of whom said that the purpose of the pamphlet had been to reduce "everything to a combat between privilege and the interests of the people" (Hardman 2010: 203). With the reform program stalled and relations between Calonne and the Notables having all but broken down, Louis dismissed Calonne on 8 April.

Although Louis dismissed Calonne, he nevertheless wished to enact the reform program Calonne had formulated, but he recognized that the proposals needed to be modified. Consequently, on 23 April Louis addressed the Notables and, after offering concessions that met nearly all of their objections, urged them to pass the land tax. Moreover, on 1 May Louis appointed Loménie de Brienne, a member of the Notables and an opponent of Calonne's program, as minister without portfolio, and Brienne soon took control of finances for the Crown. He proposed a variant of Calonne's land tax, modified in accordance with recommendations suggested by the Notables. The Notables, however, delayed consideration of Brienne's proposal until 19 May, when a majority stated that they could not approve the land tax. With the linchpin of the reform agenda rejected, Brienne dissolved the body on 25 May.

The Assembly of Notables has drawn renewed interest from scholars and has been variously interpreted. In his seminal article, Albert Goodwin portrayed the Notables as selfish defenders of privilege, especially fiscal privilege, against royal efforts at reform (Goodwin 1946). Jean Égret did not contest that view, but shifted the focus to measures that followed afterward, including the establishment of provincial assemblies, greater civil status for Protestants and others – an aggregation of substantial reforms so directed toward renovation and reconstruction that he argued they represented a "pre-Revolution" (Égret 1962). Peter Jones also emphasized the accomplishments subsequently enacted and used the reforms of 1787 to suggest that the distinction postulated by Égret of "pre-Revolution" and Revolution needed reconsideration (Jones 1995). Vivian Gruder argued that the Notables were willing to yield some of their fiscal privileges in return for a broadened share of political power and also asserted that the meetings of the Notables should not be seen as part of the "pre-Revolution," but as an integral part of the Revolution itself (Gruder 2007). John Hardman has recently countered Jones and Gruder by emphasizing that the initial goal of the Notables was to remove the threat to their interests that Calonne represented and that the years 1787–88 are distinct from the Revolution. Hardman attributed the failure of the Assembly to the unwillingness of the Crown to sacrifice its absolute power and the disinclination of the Notables to yield their privileges for a share of that power (Hardman 2010).

To whichever view one subscribes two aspects of the Assembly of Notables stood out to contemporaries. The first was the publication of Calonne's commissioned pamphlet, which William Doyle characterized as the most ambitious attempt to cultivate public opinion since Necker's *Compte rendu* of 1781 (Doyle 1999: 96) – it had provided the first glimpse into the proceedings and made the workings of the Assembly a matter of larger interest (Fontana et al. 1997: 90). Furthermore, the pamphlet's framing of the Assembly as pitting privilege against the greater national interest became a defining theme during subsequent years.

The second was the lack of success of the Assembly – after three months it had disbanded without resolving the issue that had been the primary reason for its convocation. Its failure created a perception that the Notables were unwilling to give up their fiscal privileges to restore the solvency of the state, leading many contemporaries to infer that privilege had prevailed over the welfare of the nation. The pamphlet sanctioned by Calonne had legitimized the questioning of privilege, and the collapse of the Assembly became the catalyst for a reconsideration of the nature of the French state – was it primarily an agglomeration of privileged individuals and corporations or was it a grander entity defined by deeper bonds and common ideals (Fitzsimmons 1987: 276–277)?

***

The dissolution of the Assembly of Notables left the Crown in a difficult position because its edicts still needed to be registered in the Parlement of Paris. The effort by the Crown to achieve their registration led to the exiling of the Parlement of Paris to Troyes, an action that generated accusations of despotism and, for its part, the Parlement sought to align itself with the cause of the nation by advocating the convening of the Estates-General. The stance of the Parlement was largely a delaying tactic, but its advocacy of the Estates-General, along with the perception that it was involved in a struggle against despotism, enabled the Parlement to become increasingly identified with the nation and to begin to emerge as its chief symbol, although its opposition to the Crown was nearly as self-interested as that of the Notables had been (Égret 1962: 147–203; Stone 1986: 83–84).

Several provincial *parlements*, however, continued to defend fiscal privileges during 1787, which maintained the issue as a center of attention. Indeed, the resolute defense of privilege by provincial *parlements* made privilege a greater issue in the provinces than in Paris, which remained focused on despotism. Furthermore, events during 1788 allowed provincial concerns to dominate political developments – in May 1788 the Keeper of the Seals, Chrétien-François Lamoignon, reorganized the judiciary, creating a supreme plenary court that stripped the Parlement of Paris of its political role and substantially redefined its judicial functions. Lamoignon suspended the *parlements* and placed their members on indefinite adjournment, but only the Parlement of Paris complied.

The submissiveness of the Parlement of Paris shifted focus from Paris to the provinces, enabling provincial concerns to gain greater strength – unrest broke out in several provincial cities as inhabitants rallied in defense of their Parlement (Fontana et al. 1997: 190–194). On 5 July 1788, the Crown yielded and announced, without providing a date, that the Estates-General would be called, a decision the Venetian ambassador characterized as having important consequences, although they were currently incalculable (Fontana et al. 1997: 210). The decree also solicited ideas about the manner in which the Estates-General should be constituted, suggesting that all possibilities were open. On 8 August the Crown set May 1789 for the meeting of the Estates-General, and on 16 August suspended interest payments on the debt, an announcement of bankruptcy. On 23 September the Lamoignon edicts were withdrawn and the Crown recalled the *parlements*.

The bankruptcy and retreat of the Crown clarified what had been concurrent issues – despotism and privilege. With a date set for the meeting of the

Estates-General, bankruptcy, and the return of the *parlements*, despotism was no longer an issue – as the Venetian ambassador noted, the authority of the monarch had been compromised (Fontana et al. 1997: 222). Privilege therefore became the principal concern because bankruptcy effaced any uncertainty about the extent of the fiscal crisis – indeed, Sieyès began to form his ideas on privilege during August 1788, for his pamphlet *Essai sur les privilèges*, published during November 1788 (Archives Nationales (Paris) 284 AP 3, dossier 2, part 2; on the impact of the pamphlet, see Doyle 2009: 173–174).

The contrast between the obvious fiscal needs of the state and the pecuniary privileges of the clergy and nobility established an antithesis between them, making privilege and the nation mutually exclusive categories. Against this backdrop, the composition and procedure of the Estates-General took on elemental importance – because reform was imperative, and because the privileges of the clergy and nobility were the defining question, vote by order, which effectively gave the first two orders veto power, was unacceptable. As the debate proceeded, the issue of the composition and procedure of the Estates-General coalesced with that of fiscal privilege to create the dichotomy between privilege and the nation.

After the withdrawal of the Lamoignon edicts, the Parlement of Paris returned to the city but quickly forfeited all of the popularity it had accrued when it issued a ruling that the Estates-General should utilize the forms and procedures of 1614. Although Bailey Stone argued that the Parlement was seeking to provide a sense of orderliness to the debate by offering established principles, and Peter Jones contended that it sought to fill a political void in the absence of leadership from the government, contemporaries viewed it as a self-interested attempt to take control of the Estates-General (Fontana et al. 1997: 236; Jones 1995: 158; Stone 1981: 167).

The ruling embarrassed Necker, who had succeeded Brienne on 27 August, and led him unexpectedly to reconvene the Assembly of Notables to solicit its opinion (Fontana et al. 1997: 236–237). The Assembly opened on 6 November, and although Necker inaugurated it with a speech that allegedly moved many of the Notables to tears (Fontana et al. 1997: 241), the deliberations were difficult. The meeting concluded with the Notables also supporting the forms of 1614, provoking deep resentment – the Venetian ambassador wrote that if Louis XVI followed their opinion it could incite a general uprising (Fontana et al. 1997: 249).

As the controversy over the composition of the Estates-General continued, the Crown did not take a clear position, allowing each side to assume that the Crown might side with it. Each camp had valid grounds for such a belief – on the one hand, with the impression that the Crown had challenged privilege at the Assembly of Notables and been defeated, it could be considered a victim of privilege (Browning 1909–10: vol. 1, 227). On the other hand, as the source and guarantor of privilege, the Crown could equally be perceived as complicit in the system of privilege. The ambiguous position of the Crown and the emerging polarity between privilege and the nation were apparent in a pamphlet that appeared after the second Assembly of Notables. The anonymous author noted that the king had twice called the Notables to consult them on the interests of the throne and the nation. In 1787, he wrote, the Notables had defended their privileges against the throne, and in 1788 they had defended their privileges against the nation (Cérutti n.d.: xi).

Of all of the issues of composition and procedure for the Estates-General, the most critical was the doubling of the representation of the Third Estate (Fontana et al. 1997: 244–245, 251). Seeking to stem growing discontent, on 27 December 1788 the Crown authorized the doubling of the representation of the Third Estate to make it equal to that of the clergy and nobility. Although the action placated the Third Estate and angered elements of the clergy and nobility, it also left matters unsettled because the decree did not specify the rules to be followed at the Estates-General (Fontana et al. 1997: 256, 261).

During early February 1789 the Crown sent out letters convoking the Estates-General and authorizing the election of deputies – one indication of the magnitude of the event is that, according to the Venetian ambassador, it involved the dispatch of at least 156,000 letters (Fontana et al. 1997: 268; Browning 1909–10: vol. 2, 155 has the British ambassador putting the number at 126,000). The elections, however, were conducted with diametrically opposed ideas of the method by which the Estates-General would operate. Many within the clergy and nobility viewed the doubling of the Third Estate as a discrete act that did not necessarily modify the traditional format of vote by order, whereas the Third Estate believed that vote by head was implicit in the doubling of its representation. The nobility, and to a lesser extent the clergy, were prepared to accept the abrogation of their fiscal privileges, but many among them believed in the distinction of orders as a fundamental political, social, and constitutional principle. For its part, the Third Estate was willing to accept social differentiations by order, and to acknowledge honorific privileges of the clergy and nobility, but it would not acquiesce in the idea of orders as a political institution, particularly as the means of voting at the Estates-General (Fitzsimmons 1994: 143–144; Fontana et al. 1997: 269).

As Kenneth Margerison argued, among the Third Estate there was hope for a union of orders at the Estates-General, and this was embraced by the liberal nobility associated with the Society of Thirty. The idea of a union of orders envisioned distinction of orders but a doubled Third Estate and vote by head. Sieyès' most famous pamphlet, *Qu'est-ce que le Tiers-État?* signaled his disagreement with this approach, but his argument failed to gain traction – the union of orders was the prevailing sentiment within the Third Estate (Doyle 2009: 178–181; Margerison 1998). Despite the arresting answer given to the question posed by his pamphlet, Sieyès' stance was rejected (Margerison 1998: 98–103) – indeed, far from being influential, he was the last member chosen for the Third Estate delegation in the original elections to the Estates-General during the spring of 1789. Consequently, there were no stirring phrases on the eve of the opening of the Estates-General, but the goals of the Third Estate indicate that any slogan would have included the concepts of parity and mutual respect. Although important to participants, principles built on such ideals would not have made the events of 1789 of enduring significance.

***

The Estates-General opened on 4 May 1789 with an impressive ceremony but no guidance from the Crown. Louis XVI gave a brief speech that made no mention of the procedure to be followed by the Estates-General, and Necker, who was enthusiastically applauded by the Third Estate when he entered the hall, did not reach the rhetorical heights that he had achieved at the opening of the second Assembly of Notables – rather, he delivered a lengthy and tedious analysis of the financial situation that disappointed even his most ardent supporters (Fontana et al. 1997: 287). It was at this juncture that the Crown lost control of events because deputies were seeking direction from the Crown and, as a contemporary subsequently observed, no group would have begun the Estates-General with direct disobedience of the king. If Louis had mandated meeting in common and vote by head, he would have won over the Third Estate, and had he stipulated meeting in separate chambers and vote by order, he would have had the support of the clergy and nobility (Bénétruy 1951: 47).

The lack of Crown leadership allowed events to escape its control and to acquire a direction of their own, and the next day the nobility and the Third Estate sought to take control through the question of verification of credentials. The nobility met in a separate chamber, authenticated the credentials of its members, and declared itself constituted as an order, whereas the Third Estate met in the common meeting room and affirmed that credentials must be verified by the three orders meeting together. Although the clergy met separately, it stopped short of constituting itself as an order, but the mutually exclusive positions of the nobility and Third Estate threw the Estates-General into a deadlock.

It soon became clear that neither the clergy nor the nobility would appear in the common room, but the Third Estate was better prepared to withstand the stalemate that followed. Although some deputies wished to proceed unilaterally from the outset, the Third Estate pursued its goal of a union of orders in a unified fashion, with little division on what to do, only when to do it (Ligou 1961: 21–22). The clergy, and to a lesser extent the nobility, were more divided, with elements in each prepared to accommodate the demands of the Third Estate. Even as it met with boorish behavior by the nobility, the Third Estate nevertheless participated in two unsuccessful conciliatory conferences that continued into early June.

It was only because of mounting anger at the stalemate and recognition of the fact that it would not be possible to achieve an accord with the nobility that the Third Estate, which, to undercut vote by order, had renamed itself the commons, decided to act unilaterally. Sieyès offered a motion to invite the clergy and nobility to come to the common meeting room for the accreditation of credentials jointly; if they did not accept, verification would proceed without them.

On 13 June three *curés* entered the common room to have their credentials verified, which gave momentum and legitimacy to the initiative of the commons, and others entered during the following days. On 17 June the commons adopted Sieyès' motion and, rejecting appellations that could potentially have excluded upper clergy and nobility, approved the denomination of National Assembly for itself (Blackman 2007). Although the separation of orders had been breached, the National Assembly maintained distinction of orders – the *curés* who entered were seated in an area designated for the clergy (Creuzé-Latouche 1946: 103).

The assumption of the title of National Assembly at last led the Crown to take action. Louis decided to convene a royal session at which he would enjoin separate chambers and vote by order, but on 20 June, when members of the Assembly went to their meeting room they found it closed and secured by soldiers, allegedly to prepare it for the royal session set for the 23rd. Worried that the presence of soldiers presaged the possible dissolution of the Assembly, deputies repaired to a nearby tennis court and pledged not to separate until they had given France a constitution.

At the royal session on 23 June Louis submitted an agenda that would almost certainly have been accepted had it been offered at the opening of the Estates-General. After the resentment and resolve generated by the stalemate, however, and after the actions of 17 June and 20 June, which Louis specifically nullified, his intercession was dilatory and inapt. Despite Louis' instruction that discussion and votes be conducted by order, the commons remained in the chamber and defied orders to retire. The maladroitness of the monarch's intervention quickly became apparent – the next day the clergy met separately as an order, but when the meeting ended a majority of its members joined the National Assembly. The following day, 25 June, the resistance of the nobility began to crumble when forty-seven noble representatives joined the Assembly.

In a tacit acknowledgment of the failure of the royal session, Louis, on 27 June, without employing the term "National Assembly," wrote to the recalcitrant deputies of the clergy and nobility to ask them to join "the other two orders," and during the late afternoon most of the obdurate deputies entered the Assembly. The ostensible attainment of the union of orders buoyed deputies and sparked celebrations in Versailles and Paris – emotions ran so high that the Assembly adjourned for two days to honor the event.

The achievement, however, was more apparent than real. Not only was the Crown planning to dissolve it, but the National Assembly, as an improvised *sui generis* body, had no sense of identity or purpose – indeed, many clerical and noble deputies mocked the Assembly and used the recess to plan methods to undermine it with procedural questions (Bibliothèque Historique de la Ville de Paris MS N.A. 22, folios 1–5). Consequently, although the union of the three orders on 27 June was widely acclaimed, it did little to settle the impasse. On the contrary, in an undisguised show of contempt, when the Assembly reconvened on 30 June most of the formerly recalcitrant clerical and noble deputies arrived hours late and then asserted that they could not participate without receiving new instructions from their constituents.

The Assembly defeated their ploy on 8 July, when it abolished imperative mandates and then returned to its proclaimed goal of drafting a constitution. Finding the prospect of a different project from each of the thirty subcommittees into which it had divided itself cumbersome, the Assembly decided to elect a Committee on the Constitution to take the lead in drawing up the document. The structure of the committee conformed to the union of orders, with two clerical deputies, two noble deputies, and four deputies of the commons. The popular rising in Paris obscured the election of the committee on 14 July, but the effect of the insurrection was to establish the ascendancy of the Assembly over the Crown. When Louis went to Paris to recognize the new municipal government, he went as a defeated man and at times could barely speak (Browning 1909–10: vol. 2, 245; Vassal 1976: 440).

Although the uprising enabled it to draw up a constitution unimpeded, the Assembly remained a deeply fractured body. After the turmoil in Paris, a number of noble deputies who had continued to assemble separately in the evening after 27 June ceased their meetings, but absented themselves from evening sessions of the Assembly. Deputies had a clearly defined goal – to draft a constitution – but no agreed-upon criteria to inform it. The Assembly had begun a discussion of a declaration of rights, but its members were anxious to complete the constitution and return home, and the impatience emerged on 24 July when the Assembly ordered the Committee on the Constitution, formed only ten days earlier, to present a report on its work immediately.

The committee gave its report on 27 July and it provides insight into the outlook of the Assembly at this early stage of its existence. With little cohesion in the Assembly, the proposals offered by the committee were modest and vague – the project was much less bold and comprehensive than the program advanced by Louis during the royal session on 23 June (Vassal 1976: 411–412). It is little wonder that a contemporary observer in Dijon lamented the timidity of the report, which was so indeterminate that a British diplomat had trouble summarizing it (Bibliothèque Municipale Dijon MS 2522, no. 3, letter of 30 July 1789; Browning 1909–10: vol. 2, 257–258).

It is clear that had the drafting of the constitution proceeded along the path outlined in the report it would have been, even with a prospective declaration of rights, which was still inchoate, a conventional and largely uninspiring document. The National Assembly would almost certainly have disbanded after a few more weeks and the events of 1789 would in all probability have been remembered as a transition from absolute to constitutional monarchy, with little societal change or larger import – similar to the revolution of 1688 in England but without even the change of dynasty. Just over a week later, however, the meeting of the night of 4 August 1789 changed the trajectory of the French Revolution and enabled it to become an event of world-historical significance.

***

During late July, as unnerving reports of violence in the countryside poured into Versailles, deputies devised a plan to stem it whereby one of the largest landowners in France, Armand-Désiré Vignerot-Duplessis-Richelieu, duc d'Aiguillon, would give up seigneurial rights, perceived as a major source of peasant grievances, in exchange for a long-term pecuniary redemption (Fitzsimmons 2003 offers a fuller treatment of the meeting of 4 August and its ramifications). The arrangement, however, did not proceed as expected – before the duc d'Aiguillon could present his recommendation, Louis-Marie, vicomte de Noailles, a minor landless noble who would not have been affected by any disposition involving seigneurial rights, offered a proposal similar to that which the duc d'Aiguillon had been slated to submit. Understandably disconcerted and uncertain, the duc d'Aiguillon nonetheless continued with the plan and supported the recommendation put forward by the vicomte de Noailles.

In a body fraught with unresolved anger from weeks of bitter struggle and demonstrations of bad faith, as well as apprehension stemming from rural unrest, the gesture by the two men seemed extraordinary and other deputies vigorously applauded it. The prolonged applause in turn generated a powerful wave of emotion that induced other members of the Assembly to surrender rights and privileges that might be viewed as a source of antagonism or discord. A striking series of relinquishments ensued, driven by emotion, competition, and even a sense of theater, and continued for hours until, by the end of the session, the framework of the French state had effectively been dismantled (Fitzsimmons 2003: 14–15). Although deep divisions lay ahead as the Assembly remade France during the following two years, the source of conflict was more the degree than the fact of change.

The driving force behind the meeting of 4 August had been the proscription of privilege – one deputy wrote that the Assembly wanted to remove the word "privilege" from the French vocabulary (Bibliothèque Municipale, Nantes, Collection Dugast-Matifeux, vol. 12, folio 78). Privilege, which David Bien argued was the "functional equivalent" of a constitution, had been the defining quality of the French state (Bien 1978: 159). Consequently, the eradication of privilege made possible a new model for the polity, grounded in freedom, equality, and fellowship under the salutary authority of the nation – the principles of 1789.

The foundation of those principles was the nation as the focal point of one's identity and loyalty, supplanting all former corporate allegiances or delineations. Jean-Pierre Boullé, a deputy from Brittany, a province with a strong regional identity, wrote that during the meeting "one hastened to be French, to be completely French, and one no longer wanted any other title" (Archives Départementales, Morbihan, 1 Mi 140, no. 20, letter of 4 August 1789). The primacy of the nation as the new and exclusive focus for loyalty is equally evident in a letter written days after the meeting of 4 August by Charles-Élie, marquis de Ferrières, one of the recalcitrant noble deputies who had not entered the Assembly until 27 June. On 7 August, however, he wrote to a constituent that the meeting had produced something that twelve centuries of the same religion, the same language, and habits of common manners had not been able to accomplish – the reconciliation of interests and the unity of France toward a single objective, the common good of all (Charles-Élie 1932: 115). The next day another deputy, Jean-François Fournier de la Charmie, captured the new outlook more succinctly when he wrote to the municipal officials of Périgueux that "one wants to be French and nothing else" (Archives Départementales, Dordogne, OE DEP 5004, letter of Fournier de la Charmie to municipal officers of Périgueux, 8 August 1789).

This sentiment would grow during the following years, particularly after 1792, when France declared war on Austria. The sense of mission that inspired France in 1789 sustained it during early defeats and subsequently propelled it to victory over its adversaries. As the principles of the Revolution were carried across Europe by French conquests, an analogous attitude giving primacy to the concept of the nation took hold, generating similar pride. Ultimately, French armies were, in part, defeated by a principle to which the Revolution had given birth, and nationalism, as a mobilizing agent during the next two centuries, would be one of its most powerful legacies. It culminated with World War II, after which a chastened Europe, with France as one of the leaders, sought to forge a broader continental identity without disavowing a national one.

The repudiation of privilege required a new organizing principle to oversee the new purpose of the nation, the common good of all, as Ferrières had written, and the new ethos was the antithesis of privilege – laws common to all. The Assembly was so convinced of the validity of its new ideal that it universalized it before the end of the month in the Declaration of the Rights of Man and of the Citizen, which one contemporary proudly stated was "a benefit conveyed to all humankind" that had been created for "the happiness of all humanity" (Gautier 1791: 141, 173). Inspired by his experience in America, Marie-Joseph du Motier, marquis de Lafayette, initially proposed a broad declaration of rights on 11 July, and the American influence is underscored by Thomas Jefferson's involvement in Lafayette's endeavor. After formulating the renunciations of 4 August into a decree on 11 August, the Assembly resumed work on the Declaration of Rights, which would form a preface to the constitution. If there is a single document that captures the principles of 1789, it is the Declaration of Rights, and, particularly in the Assembly's desire to surpass the American example and make its declaration universal, the influence of the meeting of 4 August upon it is unmistakable.

Two weeks later, after ratifying seventeen articles, the Assembly hastily concluded the Declaration in order to turn to the drafting of the constitution. The Assembly decided to return to the Declaration after it completed the constitution, but in 1791 it declined to revisit the Declaration, which meant that what was originally regarded as a draft became the final version. Despite its unpolished and unfinished origins, the Declaration of the Rights of Man and of the Citizen continues to be commemorated – indeed, subsequent revisions of the Declaration in the Constitution of 1793 and the Constitution of the Year III are all but forgotten.

Article two of the Declaration of Rights proclaimed that the purpose of all political association was the preservation of the natural and imprescriptible rights of man, which were specified as liberty, property, security, and resistance to oppression. All of these were remarkable claims, but none more than the last. During an age in which concepts of divine-right monarchy lingered, and on a continent on which absolute monarchy was accepted, the stipulation of a right of resistance to oppression was an extraordinary shift. The Assembly was aware of the boldness of the assertion – it voted down a proposal to remove resistance to oppression from the declaration (*Bulletin de l'Assemblée Nationale*, 18 and 20 August 1789). Indeed, enthusiasm for a war on tyrants would be a factor in the drive for war in 1792.

The centrality of law to achieve and guarantee the preservation of rights is evident in its mention in a majority of articles – indeed, in more articles than any other single concept, including rights. Law was impersonal, universal, and not dependent on the will of the monarch, formerly the source of privilege. The place of law established in the Declaration of Rights also generated the most commonly known words associated with the principles of 1789. The declaration defined "liberté" as the ability to do anything that did not harm another, with the limits to be determined by law, and "égalité" signified equality in rights under the law. "Fraternité" ensued not only from the harmony that resulted from liberty and equality, but also from the shared sense of pride in being French – a dictionary published in 1791 defined "Français" as a citizen of a free country as well as a member of a sovereign nation and asserted that "the name of French is now the most exalted title that a man can carry around the world" (Gautier 1791: 213).

However naive it may seem in hindsight, in the immediate aftermath of the meeting of 4 August, deputies believed, as Ferrières' letter shows, that all differences and inequalities had been swept away. His sentiments were echoed in a letter of Grégoire de Roulhac to his constituents that stated that "all animosities, all vengeance ought to cease. The most cordial fraternity ought to reign among all citizens of all orders, henceforth bonded by the same interests, leaving no other goal than the happiness of all" (Archives Municipales, Limoges, AA 4, letter of 5 August 1789). On 11 July Lafayette's proposal for a declaration of rights had received polite applause but little support. As late as 1 August, Pierre-Victor Malouet, a conservative representative of the commons, had expressed reservations about drafting a declaration of rights, viewing it as impractical in a country with a long history of inequality. Although the spirit of goodwill was transitory, the new outlook enabled members of the Assembly to expand their thinking and to produce a document of enduring value. Indeed, it is a testament to the lasting importance of the Declaration of Rights that when the United Nations promulgated a Universal Declaration of Human Rights in 1948 – reportedly the most translated document in the world – it did so in Paris, with the U.N. document closely following the 1789 blueprint.

Another abiding principle of 1789 reflected in the Declaration of Rights was a product of the confidence created by the meeting of 4 August – the proclamation in Article 3 that sovereignty resided in the nation. The assumption of the title of National Assembly on 17 June had transformed a traditionally consultative body into a deliberative, policy-making one, but the Assembly had not appropriated sovereignty. The Tennis Court Oath of 20 June had opened the possibility of such an appropriation, but on 27 July the Committee on the Constitution had left it to the Assembly to decide whether to submit laws to sovereign courts for registration. Just a month later, however, it proclaimed sovereignty as belonging to the nation and disallowed the exercise of sovereign authority by any individual or body without authority from the nation.

An additional noteworthy idea enshrined in the Declaration of Rights was that enumerated in Article 16, which stated that any society in which the guarantee of rights is not ensured or the separation of powers not systematized had no constitution – a euphemism for lack of legitimacy. The right of resistance to oppression stipulated in Article 2 was essentially reactive, a response to acts of despotism. Article 16 expanded the right of resistance because it did not require the provocation of an unjustifiable action to be invoked. Sovereign power itself could be held accountable if its structure was fundamentally flawed or if it failed to preserve the natural and imprescriptible rights of man. In answer to a question posed by Robert Darnton in 1989, the accountability of sovereign power was a major element of what was revolutionary about the French Revolution (Darnton 1990).

In their influential dictionary of the French Revolution, François Furet and Mona Ozouf asserted that the contrast between the inequality and absolute monarchy of the *ancien régime* and the rights of man and sovereignty of the people that came into existence in 1789 represented the "most profound expression of the nature of the French Revolution," but characterized the rupture as an "enigma" (Furet and Ozouf 1989: xiii). This essay has argued that the fault line in 1789 is the meeting of the night of 4 August – a breach all the more apparent when set against the report of the Committee on the Constitution presented just days earlier. Indeed, the meeting of 4 August would also be the source for Robert Darnton's characterization of the spirit of 1789 as "energy – a will to build a new world from the ruins of the regime that fell apart in the summer of 1789" (Darnton 1990: 5).

The National Assembly formulated the principles of 1789 on 4 August, universalized them in the Declaration of Rights, and codified them in the Constitution of 1791 – a dictionary dedicated to the Constitution of 1791 defined the word "constitution" as "a body of fundamental laws that constitute the government of a people" (Gautier 1791: 100). It was the principles articulated during August 1789 that endowed the French Revolution with its world-historical quality, and it was the meeting of 4 August that enabled these principles to emerge. Rather than overlooking or dismissing it, one should recognize the meeting, despite the calculated fashion in which it was planned and the clumsy manner in which it evolved, as the breakthrough event that it was. The Assembly of Notables and the first twelve weeks of the Estates-General/National Assembly had demonstrated the failings of incremental change – any attack on privilege had to be comprehensive to achieve significant reform. However clumsily and inadvertently, this occurred on 4 August, increasing the range of possibilities exponentially, and deputies seized the opportunity. The National Assembly remade French society so extensively that it proscribed virtually all that had existed immediately before to what it pejoratively characterized as the *ancien régime*.

Although the dictionary of the Académie Française had allowed, in its third definition of the term, that "revolution" could metaphorically represent change in public affairs or the ways of the world, the French Revolution altered the meaning of the word to make it non-metaphorical and primarily a political event – the dictionary dedicated to the Constitution of 1791 defined revolution as "a sudden and strong change in the government of a people" (Gautier 1791: 533). The principles of 1789 proclaimed the right of a people to break with its past and to create a constitution, laws, and institutions that it believed best met its needs, an assertion that permanently transformed the nature of revolution by henceforth making it a process of change and improvement.

The spirit of goodwill established by the meeting of 4 August dissipated within weeks as disagreements about the scope of change soon emerged in the National Assembly. The Constitution of 1791, fatally undercut by Louis' flight from Paris during June 1791, passed into oblivion in less than a year. As for the Declaration of Rights, the Assembly's refusal to recommence work on it meant that it was never fully realized. Whether by neglect, by design, or through exhaustion, it had flaws – women were omitted and slavery in the colonies tolerated. Yet, despite its faults, during August 1789 the men of the Assembly crafted a document that, however incomplete or imperfect, was of enduring significance. It was the principles of 1789 conceived by the Assembly and enshrined in the Declaration of Rights that endowed the French Revolution with world-historical stature.

For all of its remarkable accomplishments, the National Assembly has also been an object of criticism. A modern critique has been that the Assembly, with its concept of sovereignty consolidated in the legislature, gave rise to the notion that dissent was subversive, thereby legitimizing the suppression of opponents. The argument posited that the roots of the Terror were to be found in the period 1789–91, particularly in the total reconstruction of society (Gueniffey 2000 is a recent iteration).

This criticism is misguided. Although it faced direct defiance on several occasions during the autumn of 1789, the National Assembly never resorted to coercion (Fitzsimmons 1994: 90–92, 165–167). Moreover, of all of the legislatures during the revolutionary decade 1789–99, only the Assembly did not pass punitive legislation against *émigrés* or refractory priests. In addition, and again uniquely, in September 1791 the Assembly granted a comprehensive, unconditional amnesty for all individuals arrested for political crimes (Fitzsimmons 2003: 43–44). Although the growing mistrust generated by Louis' flight would subsequently lead it to evolve into something more harsh and coercive, the political culture to which the principles of 1789 gave birth was generous, broad-minded, and moderate.

Two hundred years later, a final underlying ideal to which the events of 1789 gave rise was optimism – a belief in the possibility of forging a better nation and ultimately, by example, to bring into being a better world, which was the reason the National Assembly universalized the precepts it had conceived. Indeed, with survivors from Tiananmen Square receiving a silent and somber tribute at the head of the procession immediately prior to the start of otherwise exuberant festivities, attendees at the parade commemorating the bicentennial of the French Revolution in Paris were tragically and unexpectedly reminded of the continuing capacity of the principles of 1789 to inspire people around the world to strive to create a better society.

References

Primary Sources

Archives Départementales, Dordogne
Archives Départementales, Morbihan
Archives Municipales, Limoges
Archives Nationales (Paris)
Bénétruy, J. (ed.) (1951). Étienne Dumont. *Souvenirs sur Mirabeau et sur les deux premières assemblées législatives.* Paris: PUF.
Bibliothèque Historique de la Ville de Paris
Bibliothèque Municipale, Dijon
Bibliothèque Municipale, Nantes
Browning, Oscar (ed.) (1909–10). *Despatches from Paris 1784–1790.* London: Offices of the Society.
Bulletin de l'Assemblée Nationale, 1789–91
Calonne, Charles-Alexandre (1790). *De l'état de la France, présent et à venir*, 5th edn. London: Laurent.

[Cérutti, Joseph-Antoine-Joachim]. n.d. *À la mémoire auguste de feu de Monseigneur le Dauphin, père du roi.* n.p.

Charles-Élie, marquis de Ferrières (1932). *Correspondance inédite (1789, 1790, 1791).* Henri Carré (ed.) Paris: Armand Colin.

Creuzé-Latouche, Jacques-Antoine (1946). *Journal des États-Généraux et du début de l'Assemblée Nationale, 18 mai–29 juillet 1789.* Jean Marchand (ed.). Paris: Didier.

Fontana, Alessandro, Francesco Furlon, and George Saro (eds.) (1997). *Venise et la Révolution française: Les Dépêches des ambassadeurs de Venise au Doge, 1786–1795.* Paris: Robert Laffont.

Gautier, P.N. (1791). *Dictionnaire de la Constitution et du gouvernement français.* Paris: Guillaume.

Ligou, Daniel (ed.) (1961). *La Première Année de la Révolution vue par un témoin (1789–1790): Les "Bulletins" de Poncet-Delpech, député du Quercy aux États-Généraux de 1789.* Paris: PUF.

Vassal, Anne (ed.) (1976). Nicolas Ruault. *Gazette d'un Parisien sous la Révolution: Lettres à son frère 1783–1796.* Paris: Librairie Académique Perrin.

Secondary Sources

Bien, David (1978). "The Secrétaires du Roi: Absolutism, Corps and Privilege under the Ancien Régime." In Ernst Hinrichs, Eberhard Schmitt, and Rudolph Vierhaus (eds.). *Vom Ancien Régime zur Französischen Revolution.* Göttingen: Vandenhoeck & Ruprecht. 153–168.

Blackman, Robert H. (2007). "What's in a Name? Possible Names for a Legislative Body and the Birth of National Sovereignty during the French Revolution." *FH*, 21: 22–43.

Darnton, Robert (1990). *What was Revolutionary about the French Revolution?* Waco, Tex.: Baylor University Press.

Doyle, William (1999). *Origins of the French Revolution*, 3rd edn. Oxford: Oxford University Press.

Doyle, William (2009). *Aristocracy and its Enemies in the Age of Revolution.* Oxford: Oxford University Press.

Égret, Jean (1962). *La Pré-révolution française, 1787–1789.* Paris: PUF.

Fitzsimmons, Michael P. (1987). "Privilege and the Polity in France, 1786–1791." *AHR*, 92: 269–295.

Fitzsimmons, Michael P. (1994). *The Remaking of France: The National Assembly and the Constitution of 1791.* Cambridge: Cambridge University Press.

Fitzsimmons, Michael P. (2003). *The Night the Old Regime Ended: August 4, 1789, and the French Revolution.* University Park: Pennsylvania State University Press.

Furet, François and Mona Ozouf (1989). *A Critical Dictionary of the French Revolution.* Cambridge, Mass.: Harvard University Press.

Goodwin, Albert (1946). "Calonne, the Assembly of French Notables of 1787 and the Origins of the Révolte nobilaire." *EHR*, 61: 202–234, 329–377.

Gruder, Vivian R. (2007). *The Notables and the Nation: The Political Schooling of the French, 1787–1788.* Cambridge, Mass.: Harvard University Press.

Gueniffey, Patrice (2000). *La Politique de la Terreur: Essai sur la violence révolutionnaire, 1789–1794.* Paris: Fayard.

Hardman, John (2010). *Overture to Revolution: the 1787 Assembly of Notables and the Crisis of France's Old Regime.* Oxford: Oxford University Press.

Jones, P.M. (1995). *Reform and Revolution in France: The Politics of Transition, 1774–1791.* Cambridge: Cambridge University Press.

Margerison, Kenneth (1998). *Pamphlets and Public Opinion: The Campaign for a Union of Orders in the Early French Revolution.* West Lafayette, Ind.: Purdue University Press.

Stone, Bailey (1981). *The Parlement of Paris, 1774–1789.* Chapel Hill: University of North Carolina Press.

Stone, Bailey (1986). *The French Parlements and the Crisis of the Old Regime.* Chapel Hill: University of North Carolina Press.

Chapter Six

Reimagining Space and Power

Alan Forrest

The remaking of France during the revolutionary years was based on a shared belief in the common identity of the French people whatever their social or geographic origin, a belief that all were equal before the law, that all shared the rights and duties associated with citizenship. All were defined as French, and in revolutionary thinking it was France – the nation, the people, the revolution, the republic, or whatever designation they gave it according to the fashion of the moment – that should be the focus of their loyalty and that defined their identity. Revolutionary language emphasized the unity of the nation over its constituent parts. This was a fundamental change in the relationship between the center and the periphery, between the state, its provinces, and the citizenry. In every aspect of public life – whether in administration, the judiciary, the armed forces, or the church – the traditions of corporate rights, appointment, and hierarchy which had defined France under the Bourbons gave way to civic equality, accountability, and elections within national structures. The extent of this transformation should not be underestimated: it changed the most basic principles on which eighteenth-century France had been built. For if the social structure of what the revolutionaries chose to describe (and by implication vilify) as the *ancien régime* was constructed on notions of privilege and precedence, its institutional structure was characterized by an extraordinary provincial diversity controlled by a network of royal appointees. This structure was now reversed and new administrative principles introduced. The interests of the state were paramount, while at every level of public administration officials were elected and made answerable to local people. But the template of administration left little room for maneuver: the institutions in which they worked were everywhere the same.

A Companion to the French Revolution, First Edition. Edited by Peter McPhee.

Administrative Space

Though France was among Europe's earliest nation-states, the kingdom had been built up progressively and in a rather haphazard manner, the result of dynastic marriages and territorial acquisitions as its borders were extended through a series of European wars. The more peripheral provinces of Artois, Flanders, Franche-Comté, Roussillon, and Alsace had been French only since the seventeenth century, with Lorraine the last major province to be absorbed, in 1766, and the Mediterranean island of Corsica amalgamated two years later into what was still referred to as the "Kingdom of France and Navarre," a status of which the Pyrenean territory remained jealously proud. Diversity did not stop at provincial boundaries. *Ancien régime* France had no single law code, nor had it any shared tradition of law: the northern half of the country was ruled according to various common-law codes, whereas the south was subject to written codes and Roman law traditions. In fiscal terms the country was also divided, between *pays d'états* and *pays d'élection*. A few of the *pays d'états* did still have their own estates, though in the majority they had long since atrophied; where they existed, as in Brittany, Burgundy, and Provence, they could bargain over tax levels with the Crown and apportion taxes between the different regions they controlled. In the *pays d'élection*, on the other hand, royal government was more direct, and the king gathered in tax revenues through a network of officials and tax-farmers (Jones 1995: 12–24). No one model fitted all the regions of France, and though the provinces were little used for the purposes of royal administration, Calonne was, as late as 1787, proposing to revive them by creating provincial assemblies across the whole country, hoping by this means to bring conformity to local government and impose a greater degree of royal authority. But the scheme had to be dropped in the face of fierce opposition from those who felt that their own role risked being diminished, most notably the royal *intendants* and some of the more powerful provincial *parlements* (Égret 1977: 125–126).

Administrative, military, ecclesiastical, and judicial units varied hugely in size and importance and often overlapped wildly. Some of the old provinces, like Champagne or Languedoc, covered vast areas; others were relatively tiny, like the twin provinces of Aunis and Saintonge in the hinterland of La Rochelle. Bishoprics had been established without any apparent regard for the numbers of people they had to administer, and in extreme cases we find two sees only a few kilometers apart. It was much the same with the *parlements*, France's principal civil courts and courts of appeal, for if the authority of the Parlement of Paris extended over almost half the land area of the country, some provincial *parlements* had responsibility for small and relatively under-populated regions. The area of the Parlement of Pau, for instance, deep in the Pyrenees, was defined by the historic lands of Navarre, while in the north Picardy and Flanders had two sovereign courts, in Arras and Douai. Under these circumstances it was difficult to argue that the benefits of administration and justice were equally available to all, and for people from isolated communities, going to law often involved long and costly journeys to courts in faraway cities. Indeed, from *intendances* and *généralités* to *sénéchaussées* and *bailliages*, local institutions followed the lines of historical precedent, and paid little regard to the needs of local people.

But in reality, of course, these territorial divisions were in no sense random. Administrative bodies, whether royal or provincial, lay or ecclesiastical, represented power and especially the power of local families, a power that made a clear statement about status and privilege. The great landed *seigneurs* and the legal aristocracy of the provincial magistracy – which by the end of the eighteenth century had often become hereditary – were power-brokers in local towns and cities, where public and private interests were often conflated and public buildings were adorned with coats of arms or armorial bearings. Noble chateaux glowered down on the community, their mills and dovecotes underscoring their privileged status. The regiments of the royal army bore the names of provinces and noble families; they, too, reflected power structures in a France where central government still struggled to impose itself on tradition and privilege. The church, too, reflected the power of the great landed families who provided it with high functionaries, its bishops and abbots; and it remained a major landowner in its own right, imposing rents and seigneurial dues on its tenants while also levying tithes and other clerical exactions. Meanwhile, those in the king's service proudly displayed the insignia of royal favor, while in Paris the fact that many nobles used their town houses as ministries served to confuse further the distinction between private property and that of the state, between private and public interest. Noble houses were grand and imposing, and the administration used such buildings to impress the populace and to impose its authority on the physical fabric of the city. Power and monumentality went naturally hand in hand (Coquery 2000: 152).

At the apex of the pyramid was the king himself. The Crown owned well over 90 percent of the land in some areas of France – most particularly, of course, in the highly atypical city of Versailles – and buildings housing royal administrations sported the royal arms or were engraved with the Bourbon emblem of the *fleur-de-lys*. In this sphere, too, space, and especially urban space, reflected power and its representation to the people, and the monarchy had never been reluctant to emphasize to ordinary people the dignity of the king's office or to display before them the majesty of his person. Since the reign of Louis XIV the king's advisers had taken good care to present the monarch in the most glorious terms, as a military conqueror, as a statesman of genius, or, where appropriate, as the defender of the Catholic faith. Coins and medals, poems and plays, allegorical paintings and sculptures brought home to a widely diverse audience the power and glory of the monarchy; while equestrian statues, dominating squares and public thoroughfares, were often a preferred medium for royal propaganda, just as triumphal arches made the perfect entry point for a king on a tour of his provincial subjects (Burke 1992: 77–83). It was considered important that a monarch should be seen and publicly displayed: hence the sporadic tours organized by French kings of the principal provincial cities. These visits, like royal statues and sculpted images, served to remind the people of the power of the Bourbons and of their reputation in Europe and overseas. They were symbols every bit as potent as the Te Deum sung to celebrate the birth of a royal prince or the gibbet that stood on the place of execution. The use of space almost always told a political story.

The New Division of the Territory

If the *ancien régime* had been built around privilege, the revolutionaries set out to construct a polity based on the ideal of citizenship. In a nation where the people were sovereign, it followed that they must be equal in rights and must enjoy equal access to the state. In practice, as it was understood in 1790, that meant two things: an insistence that public bodies should be answerable to the people they served, and an assurance that all should enjoy equal access to local government and to justice. In political terms this was quickly translated into an almost obsessive belief that offices should be elected rather than lie in the gift of others, with the consequence that the early Revolution saw the introduction of elections at every level of local government, elections for posts in the judiciary, elections for the majority of promotions in the army. People who had never before been asked for their opinion on matters of governance were now repeatedly called on to express their views through the ballot-box and to exercise their rights as part of the sovereign people (Crook 1996: 8–29). And the radical decentralization of power was reflected in the multiplication of local offices that had to be filled: Peter McPhee has estimated that over half a million men were elected to positions in local government, the judiciary, and other administrations, and it was these men who played a key role in taking the Revolution to the people, bridging the gap in custom and understanding that separated the legislators at the center and the exigencies of the local situation (McPhee 2006: 57). Of course, this concern for electoral answerability could not last: with the passage of the months polls were greeted by increasing levels of public apathy and disillusionment, while the centralist philosophy of the Jacobins ensured that by 1793 control passed rapidly out of the hands of local people. But in the administrative and judicial spheres it was the early reforms of 1790 that were of more lasting consequence, with the National Assembly doing much to transform the administrative map of the country, devolving powers that had formerly belonged to the *parlements* or the royal *intendances* to local people. Their localism, however, was not boundless. The goal of equality which they had set themselves demanded elements of both centralism and devolution: centralism in that one law must be applicable to all, regardless of wealth or status, devolution in order to fulfill their stated purpose of bringing government closer to people's lives and making justice accessible to all.

The changes required nothing less than a redrawing of the administrative map of France, starting from principles of equity and an almost mathematical obsession derived from the Enlightenment. Privilege and antique tradition should not be allowed to stand in the way of people's rights. The Committee of the Constitution made it a priority to carry out a reform of local government, creating a special subcommittee to deal with the issue of how best this could be done. Its chairman was scathing about the system he had inherited and about the waste and inefficiency caused by overlapping jurisdictions. The need to create divisions roughly equal in size was considered paramount, administrative units of equal area and equal population that would truly represent a given fraction of France and its people. But so were issues of access: the new administrative units should be user-friendly, accessible to peasants and artisans, and sited at points that would concord with the normal commercial practices of local people. And finally, the committee took the decision that it would, wherever possible, work within existing provincial boundaries so as to reduce the risk of running counter to traditional bonds and customs. If the people of Brittany or Provence were in the habit of organizing their affairs at provincial level, it had no desire to disrupt these practices or to sow uncertainty: they should be allowed to trade, sue, and petition as far as was possible where they had traditionally done, through local bodies situated in the towns to which they were in the habit of traveling. Geography played an incisive part here. The committee was also keenly aware that there were serious constraints on travel, especially in winter, imposed by raging torrents and snow-capped mountains: in parts of the Massif Central roads and mountain tracks would be impassable for months on end. Habits were formed by the location of fairs and markets, which did most to determine where people went about their ordinary business. The revolutionaries therefore vowed to consult with local people and inform themselves about local conditions before making rash decisions about where the various jurisdictions should be sited and about which towns should be rewarded with administrative and judicial functions. Idealism had to be tempered with practical necessity. France could only be regenerated with one eye to local opinion, or at least to the opinion of the local elites (Ozouf-Marignier 1989: 39–42).

There is no questioning, however, that the redrawing of the administrative map of the country was done boldly and incisively. The territory of France was divided into new administrative units of roughly equal size and far smaller than the majority of the former provinces: the *départements*, eighty-three of them in 1790, rising to eighty-six during the Revolution itself, which still form the backbone of the country's administrative structure to this day. The committee had not been dogmatic about the number, insisting only that they should be small enough to offer easy access, and decreeing that there should be "between 75 and 85" in all, the precise number to be dependent upon the outcome of local consultation. In practice, of course, such consultation often ended in tussles between rival cities to obtain a prized administration or a tribunal that would bring litigants and lawyers – who would not only seek justice in its courtrooms but would bring welcome custom to its shops and hotels, with the influx of outsiders offering an artificial stimulus to the local economy. It was perhaps to be expected that allocations were not always made on the most scientific grounds or that local power-brokers and political leaders came to exert an often decisive influence on the outcome. For a lot was at stake. It was not just the division of France into departments that was carried out in 1790, but their further division into districts and cantons, and the allocation of tribunals, justices of the peace, schools, and colleges, all of which were prized assets and could spell the difference between prosperity and relative neglect. Towns felt that they could not afford to lose out, and many lobbied hard to be awarded a place in the new administrative structure (Margadant 1992: 205–219).

Departments were to be divided into districts, which were themselves distributed according to need and population: no department could have fewer than three, none more than nine. The provision of this secondary layer of administration was intended to fulfill the revolutionary goal of bringing administration closer to the people, allowing ordinary townsmen and villagers to access responsible officers of the state, while at the same time providing Paris with a valuable conduit through which to disseminate its laws as widely as possible. And below the districts were the 44,000 communes into which the territory of France was subdivided, each with its mayor and municipal officers, each elected by local people, yet with duties and obligations that were prescribed by the state. Administration now flowed down to the most isolated hamlet; the texts of decrees were to be posted in every commune across France, texts that were supposed to produce tribute in the form of taxes for the state coffers and soldiers for its armies, as well as to spread the values of citizenship to the farthest-flung corners of the kingdom. In that respect local government can be seen as a key part of the revolutionaries' project for the modernization of the country, a modernization that derived from an enlightened desire to create rational frameworks in which administration could function efficiently so that there would be no further need for middlemen, tax-farmers, or military recruiters serving the state from a position of privilege and self-interest.

It might seem that it worked well, surprisingly well, if we judge from the fact that the departmental system still applies today, the districts renamed as *arrondissements*, the mayors, still largely elected and still answerable for their office to the minister of the interior in Paris. It is true that under the Napoleonic Empire the concern for public accountability was diluted, and the electoral principle abandoned in favor of the interest of the state. But the system itself, as a blueprint for effective local government, remained largely intact. It was extended to French colonies in the Caribbean, as it would be in the nineteenth and twentieth centuries to the coastal plains of the Maghreb. And at the height of the Empire it was exported to many of France's continental neighbors as they were progressively annexed to the motherland, until, in 1812, Napoleon ruled over a France of 130 departments that stretched into northern Italy and, further north, to the banks of the Rhine, the historic foreign policy objective of Louis XIV and all the Bourbon monarchy. The Grand Empire boasted departments that extended from northern Germany to Rome, from Holland to Dalmatia. All, like their French counterparts, were baptized with the names of their most salient geographical features, such as rivers and mountain ranges. And all had the same administrative hierarchy: the only difference was that under the Empire they no longer answered to the local elites, but reported through their prefect directly to the government in Paris.

Winners and Losers

The division of the territory was carried out amidst a groundswell of petitioning and protest, and not everything would be left to reason or to the cold logic of the cadastre. Local interests often expressed themselves noisily, pleading, petitioning, and protesting until they had achieved the result they wanted, and it soon became clear how much, in the provinces at least, desire and ambition drove the decentralizing agenda. The petitions that landed on the table of the Committee of Division in Paris pulled few punches, testifying to the depths of animus that local communities harbored against their neighbors (Margadant 1992: 257–286).

The case of Bertrand Barère, the future Jacobin leader and president of the National Convention, is instructive in this regard. Barère was a powerful figure in the upland valleys of the Pyrenees, and he lobbied strongly for a department for his home town of Tarbes. This was not the most obvious choice for a departmental *chef-lieu*, located as it was in a region with a sparse population and remote from the major through-routes to Spain. But he took advantage of the fact that the southwest proved one of the most difficult regions to subdivide: regional traditions remained strong in Navarre and the Béarn, and the Convention had itself been uncertain whether the region merited five or six departments. It proved fertile ground for intrigue and manipulation. Barère got his way, and Tarbes got its department (the future Hautes-Pyrénées). But in the resultant scrum, if Pau and Tarbes both achieved their ambitions, it meant that the city of Bayonne had to be overlooked, and that a department had to be created to the north, in the Landes, based on the relative backwater of Mont-de-Marsan (Forrest 1996: 78–81). The scramble for trophies inevitably produced losers as well as winners. The winners were often towns that were established centers for the local agricultural community, market towns which acted as magnets for the people of their hinterland and where peasants were frequently seen mingling with the townsfolk, towns that were appreciated for their market days and their seasonal fairs, towns deemed to be useful by neighboring communities.

As for the losers, those cities for whom the new division of the territory proved damaging and at times humiliating, prominent among them were the great merchant cities that looked outwards to the ocean and relied on foreign countries and France's colonial possessions for their wealth and *raison d'être*. Bayonne was not alone in being left bereft and poorly esteemed. If Bordeaux and Nantes did get the departments that they assumed to be theirs by right, other trading ports were less fortunate. In Normandy Le Havre was unable to wrest even a district from its rivals; it lost out to the claims of the market town of Montivilliers, "which," Paris was assured, "would redistribute the fruits of its position amongst the local population" (Forrest 2004: 91). Time and again historic connections or agricultural self-interest marginalized the merchant community. Even Marseille, the third city of France and a town proud of its mercantile prosperity, proved a poor runner-up to the old legal capital of Aix-en-Provence. And it lost precisely because of the power of its merchant interests, its extravagant wealth, its assumed superiority, and its imperial ambition. The deputies of Provence favored Aix: in their words, "the richer Marseille becomes the less it needs help; the more it grows and becomes more important than other towns, the less it should be given the means by which to stifle them" (Joutard 1990: 10). The great merchants were too outward-looking, too divorced from agriculture and the land, to win much support from the rural areas of their hinterland, for whom they were, quite simply, not useful enough to fulfill the role of a local capital.

Dispensing Justice

The judicial system, too, was reformed, the new jurisdictions copying faithfully the territorial divisions that had been established for local government. Law, like the administration, had to be easily accessed by the population at large, many of whom had seen distance as one of the major obstructions to getting justice under the monarchy. From 1790, therefore, justice was devolved. Each department was assigned a *Tribunal criminel* for the more serious criminal cases that came to trial; each district was given a lesser court, a *Tribunal correctionnel.* Both had elected judges and citizen juries. And, with considerable imagination, the Revolution adopted the institution of the justice of the peace to take minor areas of litigation out of the law courts altogether. Disagreements within families over inheritance rights, between neighbors over the ownership of a strip of land, between villagers over grazing rights: these were the very stuff of civil disputes in the eighteenth century. The revolutionaries' response was to free the courts of such relatively minor matters and hand them instead to the communities themselves. Rural communes were grouped together into cantons, each of which would appoint a local man of substance, someone whose role in the community commanded respect, to serve as a *juge de paix.* Usually the person who was selected was not a notary or a trained lawyer; rather, it was on the basis of common sense and his knowledge of how the local community functioned that he formed opinions about the rights and wrongs of such disputes and made his ruling, a judgment which the law made binding on all parties. The bigger villages, the more important communes, thus acquired standing in rural society through their role in settling neighborhood disputes and their status as the seat of a justice of the peace (Crubaugh 2001: 133–142).

Even the site of a canton might be bitterly fought over between rival towns and communities, and the animus with which towns attacked their rivals in their petitions to Paris betrays an abiding fear of losing face and with it whatever fragile claim they might have to a degree of prosperity. Towns and cities feared loss of status not only because they saw is as degrading and dishonorable – their attitude to questions of honor and primacy betrayed a sentiment that still smacked of *ancien régime* privilege – but for more basic material reasons, too. The loss of a court or of some administrative distinction meant not only that people from the outside would stay away, but also that they would lose their wealthiest residents, people whose role as consumers they so greatly valued. "The desertion of magistrates, notaries, solicitors, and wealthy bourgeois is going to reduce this unhappy town to the state of a simple village," claimed the special deputy sent from Meulun to plead his town's case. He was not alone. Across France the threatened loss of courthouses, and of the legal luminaries and urban elites they attracted, was seen as an economic disaster, and we hear the same stereotyped wails from the four corners of the country. Tarascon declared that without a tribunal it would be an "object of mockery" for its neighbors; Richelieu announced that it would be nothing more than "a collection of hovels." But their fear was social as well as economic. Communities that had enjoyed something of a bourgeois or noble presence had seen the growth of refined manners and polite society. Now all that was put at risk and the outlook for the next generation seemed suddenly grim. As two judges from the *sénéchaussée* of Concarneau admitted, "we will lose the hope of transmitting these offices to our children as a sacred property, the most inviolable of laws" (Margadant 1992: 112–115). As so often in *ancien régime* France, privilege, wealth, and office were tightly entangled in a complex web of interest.

Religion and Public Space

If civic, administrative, and judicial administration were best served by the new divisions into departments and districts, there seemed little reason why they not be used also for other purposes as the revolutionaries turned their attention to other forms of *ancien régime* administration. The church seemed to many an obvious target for their zeal, an institution where bishoprics were of grossly unequal size and importance, where wealth was concentrated in the hands of the few, and where clerical stipends were inequitable and in some cases failed to provide a living wage. And though it was argued by some that the state had no right to interfere in matters that were the prerogative of the clergy and ultimately of the pope himself, rationalism prevailed. To sons of the Enlightenment, this was not a question of faith but of administrative expediency: a bishop or archbishop was a clerical administrator, appointed and paid to manage the affairs of his diocese rather as secular administrators ran their departments or ministries. There was no reason, therefore, why anomalies should not be righted in the interests of logic and efficiency, why the size of sees and parishes should not be standardized, why clerical affairs, like secular ones, should not be organized with the convenience of the people the main priority.

The Civil Constitution of the Clergy may be most famous for the oath which it imposed on the clergy, forcing them to swear allegiance to the revolutionary state, and in the process driving a wedge between jurors and non-jurors, and in some cases between priests and the communities they served. But that was only part of its purpose. At heart it was an administrative document, bringing the church into line with the newly established norms of local government. In future there would be only one bishop for each department and historic sees were swept away in favor of more bureaucratic offices like those of the bishop of the Meuse or of the Saône-et-Loire; in the process some of the 135 existing bishops would be culled and the episcopacy reduced to eighty-three. It did not matter that some fifty bishops would lose their jobs, or that the powers conferred on them by the pope were arbitrarily annulled. The reforms operated at parish level as well. In towns with fewer than 6,000 inhabitants it was decreed that there should in future be only one parish and that other parishes should be suppressed and merged with the principal church. The bishops, like other officials, were to be elected by the people they served, a principle that was dear to the Revolution, but which in this case ignored issues of faith, so that Protestants, Jews, and atheists were all entitled to take part in the vote. Clergy were to be allocated decent living conditions, and they were to be paid by the state according to a common scale: bishops would be paid between 12,000 and 50,000 *livres* (the salary offered to the archbishop of Paris), while *curés* would get between 6,000 *livres* (again, in Paris) and 1,200 in the more thinly populated rural parishes. The huge inequalities that had marked the salary structures of the eighteenth-century church were abolished at a stroke. But, significantly, the clerical authorities were not consulted, and these changes were imposed on the church by the French state. Religious space was now treated in the same way as any other, and the Civil Constitution was another step in reforming France's administrative landscape.

Revolutionary Vandalism and Symbolic Space

From the earliest months the revolutionaries were determined to obliterate all signs of privilege and to replace them with a new symbolic order, a narrative emphasizing the rights of citizenship and equality before the law. The obliteration came principally in the form of what has been termed "revolutionary vandalism," or the deliberate and forced destruction of symbols, statues, and inscriptions that recalled the authority of the rich and privileged. This had its roots in the anti-feudal demands of the *cahiers de doléances* of 1789 and in the more or less spontaneous outbursts of violence directed at chateaux and their owners in the early years of the Revolution. Between 1789 and the fall of the monarchy the outward symbols of feudal privilege were progressively stripped away. Dovecotes were ether abandoned by their owners or attacked by angry villagers. The private pews reserved for the *seigneurs* and their families in village churches were the subject of complaints, denunciations, and physical attacks; some were publicly burned in front of the church as a signal that noble privilege had finally been ended. Archives and decrees establishing rights and privileges were another favored object of attack, while in many towns stonemasons were hired to strip away all reminders of the old order: pulling down armorial bearings from walls, chipping away family crests from the gates of chateaux, and removing royal arms from above the doors of public buildings (Bernard-Griffiths et al. 1992: 158–159). A clear message was being sent to local people: space was liberated from all vestige of privilege.

If one major target for the vandals was any lingering sign of feudalism, another, especially during the months of the Jacobin Terror, was the rich and varied symbolism of the church itself. The church was, of course, as much a temporal power as a spiritual one, and Rome was a supranational power, too, at a time when the Revolution was becoming more and more narrowly nationalistic. And at local level the physical presence of the church was often imposing: the rich materials that had gone into its construction, its place at the very center of the community, its symbolic power as a place of prayer and thanksgiving, the natural destination for every ceremony or procession in French towns and villages. It was seen by many as making a statement about power and privilege, a statement that was increasingly at odds with the ideology of revolutionary France.

Unsurprisingly, the revolutionaries became increasingly intolerant of external symbols of faith and Christian piety, of those day-to-day reminders of religious practice that were so ubiquitous in the towns and villages of the eighteenth century (Desan 1990: 31–75). Catholic saints were taken from the niches where they had stared down on generations of passers-by. Streets that had borne the names of Christian saints and martyrs were renamed, first after more prosaic landmarks like the town hall or the courthouse, but later they were given more ideologically charged names that would inspire political loyalty and spark republican fervor. Villages, too, were de-baptized as traditional saints' names were discarded along with those of powerful noble families in what was seen as an orgy of democratization; in all the names of around 3,000 communes – over 7 percent of the total – were transformed in this way, usually on the initiative of local people (McPhee 2006: 149). At times the raw energy that was expended on acts of physical desecration suggested something approaching an ideological frenzy, as with the attacks on church fabric mounted by units of the Paris *armées révolutionnaires.* Altars were overturned and Christ's disciples guillotined in stone. A good instance occurred in late 1793, when a detachment from Paris arrived in Auxerre on the feast of Saint Martin, and it soon became clear that any form of clerical symbolism was open to attack. Richard Cobb takes up the story. "This detachment had committed along the way all kinds of frenzied excesses against religious objects, battering down church doors, smashing altars, flinging down statues and images of saints." Their enthusiasm was quickly imitated by others, including young people from Auxerre itself, "who fanned out through the neighboring parishes, demolishing crosses, images and statues; nothing escaped their rage, they had no respect for the antiquity of the monuments, the most touching images only irritated them, in less than a week every external mark of Christianity had disappeared from the Auxerre area and from the neighboring parishes" (Cobb 1987: 460). Such acts of destruction shocked opinion and left a deep scar on many in the local community. But for the perpetrators, there was an element of carnival in their orgy of destruction. The symbols of privilege and fanaticism were seen as fair game.

By the time of the Jacobin republic the symbolic significance of such acts of vandalism was clear: to make a clean break with the past, and particularly with belief systems that were equated with fanaticism and superstition. No one was too mighty to resist humiliation and debasement. Kings were toppled from their bronze horses on a myriad public squares across France, men vying with one another for the honor of pulling on the ropes that would send them tumbling. And as the guillotine gained in sanctity to become a symbol of revolutionary virtue in its own right, the statues of saints and effigies of the Virgin Mary that decorated the churches of the Île-de-France risked the ultimate humiliation of decapitation in stone. At the same time graveyards were often relocated away from parish churches to the outskirts of towns or to near the village edge – a measure of public health as much as of ideology – and they were forbidden by law to retain their traditional religious imagery. Gone were the crucifixes, gone, too, the statues of Christ and the tears of the Virgin; burial was now marked by a secular ceremony, the only statue permitted in the graveyard was a representation of death, while the inscription above the gate confidently proclaimed it to be "an eternal sleep." Instead of a priest, civic officials and members of the National Guard now accompanied the deceased on his final journey. These acts of "revolutionary vandalism" took place, in this or like forms, across the country. They were not dismissed by contemporaries as purely destructive acts of popular vengeance; rather, they were seen as a deliberate form of political education, a cleansing of public space so that it could be restored to the public as its rightful owners. Frenchmen could scarcely remain unaware of it. A symbolic transfer of power was taking place before their eyes, one that brought the full meaning of the Revolution into their town halls, their churches, their local communities (Bernard-Griffiths 1992: 423–434).

Something of the same symbolic importance was attached to the army, one of the most recognizable outward signs of royal authority under the *ancien régime.* Though many of the Revolution's military reforms had more prosaic purposes – the mass desertion of soldiers and the emigration of up to one-third of their officers meant that the army they inherited simply had to be reformed – the measures they took also reflected the ideology of the revolutionary years. The provincial names of regiments were abandoned in favor of simple numbers; and the regiments, with their aristocratic associations and traditions of regional recruitment, were replaced by smaller, more maneuverable *demi-brigades* composed largely of young volunteers. The old military honors were dispensed with, too, as was the white uniform of the Bourbon army. The blue tunics that replaced it were a symbol of the regime as much as of the army, underlining its commitment to the nation, to the revolutionary cause, and to the French people. Both on the battlefield and on the parade ground the troops symbolized dedication to the national cause, while its structures and politicization emphasized its new role as a democratic space within the republic (Bertaud 1979: 91).

Building the Revolution

This does not mean that the revolutionaries wished to abolish the traditional pomp that was attached to public space and civic architecture. They belonged to an era when the rich had sought to secure status by adopting a noble lifestyle, and when provincial bourgeois – men like themselves, lawyers and royal office-holders and Atlantic traders – had built luxurious townhouses and invested in country estates that would reflect their fine taste and inscribe their achievements in stone. They were well aware of the value of such buildings in establishing authority and in impressing others; they had no desire to end the habits of a lifetime, and lavished money on the public sphere, on civic buildings that would, by their size and majesty, instill in the citizenry a sense of awe for the new political order. Their attack on privilege led to the destruction of the majority of the administrative and judicial institutions of the old order, with the consequence that by the early 1790s there were hundreds of disused public buildings, many of them former palaces and noble *hôtels*, lying vacant across France. The attack on the Catholic Church and the expulsion of the regular orders produced in turn a clutch of clerical buildings, among them abbeys and monasteries, nunneries and presbyteries, almost crying out to be put to a new use. The revolutionaries did not hesitate to do so, seizing them as national lands and putting them to a rich variety of uses, from grain stores and armories to the meeting rooms of popular societies like the Jacobins and the Cordeliers. They destroyed surprisingly little of the rich heritage they had assumed, preferring to replace signature buildings of the *ancien régime* with new ones of their own. In Paris, most memorably, the former church of Sainte-Geneviève was resurrected as the Pantheon to France's heroes (Bouwers 2011: 91), while the royal palace of the Tuileries was regenerated as an art gallery for the people of France. The symbolic significance of what was being undertaken was made clear by the minister of the interior, Jean-Marie Roland, on commissioning the project. The museum, he declared, "will embrace knowledge in all its manifold beauty and will be the admiration of the universe. By embodying these grand ideas, worthy of a free people," it would "become among the most powerful illustrations of the French Republic" (McClennan 1994: 91–92).

It was not so much the physical geography of towns and cities that was transformed as the uses of public space, uses that sent a powerful message to the inhabitants about the structures of power and the priorities of the revolutionary state. As they wandered around their towns they could see, wherever they looked, evidence of the new administrative order and of the obligations which it imposed on them. Isser Woloch expresses it well: "The spires of a cathedral or the largest parish churches would still command the horizon. But as one moved about the town one could readily identify its civic institutions: the departmental administration (later the prefecture); the town hall or *mairie*; the local schools; several new courts or tribunals; the institutions of poor relief such as an *hôpital* or workhouse"; and finally, and not the least important reminder of the outreach of state power, the often hated "*dépôt* for mustering conscripts" (Woloch 1994: 15). The townscape reflected with deliberate precision the different ways in which the Revolution intervened in the lives of its people.

At certain moments towns and cities were transformed into stages on which civic or moral messages could be explored and expounded to the population through military parades and civic festivals. Festivals were among the Revolution's preferred methods of spreading civic virtue and educating public opinion. At first this was done cautiously, the symbolism and the structure of the festival mimicking the festivities of the *ancien régime*, with processions winding through narrow streets on their way to High Mass in the parish church. But if these processions had the benefit of familiarity – their route was the traditional one that had been followed for generations – they did not offer a clean break with the past. By the time of the first Festival of the Federation, in Paris in 1790, the Revolution was already thinking along quite different lines: gone was the procession with its natural sense of hierarchy and precedence, to be replaced by vast human tableaux on public greens and in large open spaces like the Champ de Mars in Paris, the Quinconces in Bordeaux, or the Boulingrin in Rouen and Toulouse. These displays were in no sense spontaneous: groups of citizens were assigned particular roles in the celebration – mayors and town-hall dignitaries, soldiers and national guardsmen, young girls and nursing mothers, all had a designated part as the actors played out their theme in a carefully choreographed show that was presented to be seen and admired. They were intended to impress, and to be impressive, and to this end the organizers made full use of the topography of the city in a symbolic mapping out of public space (Ozouf 1988: 132–136). Public buildings provided the backcloth to the drama being played out before them, a drama that appropriated to the realm of politics many of the roles that had formerly been fulfilled by the church and which conveyed to those present an abiding sense that the nature of authority had changed (Biver 1979: 87).

If the revolutionaries made full use of open spaces and the city skyline, they did not build many landmark buildings of their own. In part this was a question of time: the Revolution did not last for more than a few short years, money was in short supply, and the political leadership had other things on their minds. But, like Napoleon in the years that followed, they did not lack ideas for transforming the urban spaces they controlled, filling Paris and the major provincial cities of France with huge squares, elegant classical facades, and the neoclassical temples that the taste of the age demanded. Most of these projects were no more than dreams on some architect's plan or entries for one of the many architectural competitions so favored by the regime. It is the drawings that remain: drawings of public squares and gardens with didactic statues representing the core values of the Republic, of cold, classical memorials to such revolutionary martyrs as Simoneau and Marat, and of proud, imposing buildings to house the great institutions of the state. There are plans for courthouses, for temples of reason, for triumphal arches and victory columns that would have transformed the face of Paris, while some of the new squares and triumphal arteries would have necessitated massive demolition before they could be realized. Happily, few were. Provincial cities, too, were subjected to a glut of plans for new buildings and monuments, some of which went beyond mere classicism to produce an ideological landscape and educate the citizenry. Among the buildings proposed in Bordeaux, for instance, were new club rooms for the Jacobins on the site of a former cloister, while architects vied with one another to design elaborate symbolic buildings that would represent the sacred Mountain to the populace. The architect Brongniart also devoted himself to the creation of suitably dignified public space in the city: he planned a majestic Place de la Révolution on land in front of the old Château-Trompette, the city's nearest equivalent to the hated Bastille; and round the cathedral he proposed a vast square surround by identical classically styled buildings, each with three courtyards. The scheme – again never implemented – would have involved sweeping away a medieval bell tower, but that did not worry the architect. As James Leith remarks, "Brongniart's plan not only anticipated some of the changes made in the area in the nineteenth century, but also some of the ruthlessness of Haussmann in effacing historic buildings" (Leith 1991: 225).

Conclusion: Reordering Space and Time

The message conveyed by the reorganization of administrative space was both pointed and ubiquitous – a reminder every time the citizen walked the streets and went about his daily business that the political order had changed and that privilege had given way to a new civic equality. The revolutionaries sought to popularize the Revolution, and the reordering of public space was one of the most potent weapons at their disposal. They did not, of course, stop at administrative reorganization. They sought to rationalize in other ways too: through metrification and the invention of new systems of weights and measures; through the reform of the currency and the attempt to impose *assignats* on an unwilling population; and above all, perhaps, through the abolition of the Gregorian calendar and the introduction of revolutionary time. The experiment did not markedly affect the way ordinary people lived and calculated their daily rounds; but it had a clear ideological aim as well as roots in a tenacious rationalism. The new day was decimal, the twenty-four hours divided into ten units to replace the more familiar system; and while the year followed the dictates of astronomy, months were refined to units of thirty days divided into three ten-day periods (*décades*), which offered a spurious air of rationality to the exercise. Alarmingly for Catholics, Sundays and saints' days were abolished, while the first year of the new era was deemed to have begun, not with the supposed date of Christ's birth, but with the most significant moment of modern times, the beginning of the First French Republic. Like the new divisions of the territory, called after rivers and other natural features of the landscape, the new days and months were given functional names like *nivôse* and *fructidor* that reflected the climate at the various seasons of the year and broke with the habits of the past. Seen in this way, the revolutionary calendar offered a new and radical approach to what was for the revolutionaries a constant challenge: how to bring an awareness of the Revolution into people's everyday lives and to make it relevant to their daily existence. As Matthew Shaw has noted, there was far more to it than the evocation of an "empty modernity", and it was consistent with the Revolution's ideals in that it marked a step towards a greater toleration of difference. It was, he believes, devised with revolutionary ideology at its core, "a conscious move to a secular, religiously neutral calendar" which "privileged neither Catholic nor Protestant" (Shaw 2011: 152).

References

Bernard-Griffiths, Simone, Marie-Claude Chemin, and Jean Ehrard (eds.) (1992). *Révolution française et "vandalisme révolutionnaire"*. Paris: Universitas.

Bertaud, Jean-Paul (1979). *La Révolution armée: Les Soldats-citoyens et la Révolution française*. Paris: Robert Laffont.

Biver, Marie-Louise (1979). *Fêtes révolutionnaires à Paris*. Paris: PUF.

Bouwers, Eveline G. (2011). *Public Pantheons in Revolutionary Europe: Comparing Cultures of Remembrance, c.1790–1840*. Basingstoke: Palgrave Macmillan.

Burke, Peter (1992). *The Fabrication of Louis XIV*. London and New Haven, Conn.: Yale University Press.

Cobb, Richard (1987). *The People's Armies*, trans. Marianne Elliott. London and New Haven, Conn.: Yale University Press.

Coquery, Natacha (2000). *L'Espace et le pouvoir: De la demeure privée à l'édifice public. Paris, 1700–1790*. Paris: S. Arslan.

Crook, Malcolm (1996). *Elections in the French Revolution: An Apprenticeship in Democracy, 1789–1799*. Cambridge: Cambridge University Press.

Crubaugh, Anthony (2001). *Balancing the Scales of Justice: Local Courts and Rural Society in Southwest France, 1750–1800*. University Park: Pennsylvania State University Press.

Desan, Suzanne (1990). *Reclaiming the Sacred: Lay Religion and Popular Politics in Revolutionary France*. Ithaca, N.Y.: Cornell University Press.

Égret, Jean (1977). *The French Pre-Revolution, 1787–1788*. Chicago: University of Chicago Press.

Forrest, Alan (1996). *The Revolution in Provincial France: Aquitaine, 1787–1799*. Oxford: Oxford University Press.

Forrest, Alan (2004). *Paris, the Provinces and the French Revolution*. London: Arnold.

Jones, P.M. (1995). *Reform and Revolution in France: The Politics of Transition, 1774–1791*. Cambridge: Cambridge University Press.

Joutard, Philippe (ed.) (1990). *L'Espace et le temps reconstruits: La Révolution française, une révolution des mentalités et des cultures?* Aix-en-Provence: Publications de l'Université de Provence.

Leith, James A. (1991). *Space and Revolution: Projects for Monuments, Squares and Public Buildings in France, 1789–1799*. Montreal: McGill-Queen's University Press.

McClennan, Andrew (1994). *Inventing the Louvre: Art, Politics and the Origins of the Modern Museum in Eighteenth-Century Paris*. Cambridge: Cambridge University Press.

McPhee, Peter (2006). *Living the French Revolution, 1789–1799*. Basingstoke: Palgrave Macmillan.

Margadant, Ted W. (1992). *Urban Rivalries in the French Revolution*. Princeton, N.J.: Princeton University Press.

Ozouf, Mona (1988). *Festivals and the French Revolution*. Cambridge, Mass.: Harvard University Press.

Ozouf-Marignier, Marie-Vic (1989). *La Formation des départements: La Représentation du territoire français à la fin du 18e siècle*. Paris : ÉHÉSS.

Shaw, Matthew (2011). *Time and the French Revolution: The Republican Calendar, 1789–Year XIV*. London: Royal Historical Society and Boydell Press.

Woloch, Isser (1994). *The New Regime: Transformations of the French Civic Order, 1789–1820s*. New York: Norton.

Chapter Seven

"The Case against the King," 1789–93

Barry M. Shapiro

As the remains of the decapitated Louis XVI were being carted away from the Place de la Révolution on the morning of 21 January 1793, some in the crowd of spectators were reported as commenting: "Let them take him wherever they like. What do we care? We always wanted him; he never wanted us" (Beaucourt 1892: vol. 1, 341). While the political and juridical dimensions of the accusations of treason lodged against the former king have been of primary interest to historians over the years, what is especially striking about this comment is the intensely personal reaction that it seems to register, the sense of personal betrayal and bitter disillusionment that it conveys. Indeed, at the risk of evoking the language of a trashy romance novel, it might almost be said that the comment transports us seamlessly into a quite particular region of personal emotion, the region of unrequited love. Yet whatever feelings of personal betrayal may have existed among the crowd that morning or, for that matter, among the deputies of the Convention or the French people in general, a consideration of the relevance of the notion of unrequited love to the building of the "case against the king" requires a return to the primal crisis of the Revolution, the spring–summer 1789 confrontation between the monarch and the deputies of the Third Estate.

Despite recent historiographical emphasis in French revolutionary studies on the degree to which what Roger Chartier (1991: 122) calls an "affective rupture" between the king and his people had gravely eroded the ideological viability of the monarchy well before the actual arrival of the deputies in Versailles in spring 1789, my own recently published study on the Constituent Assembly (Shapiro 2009) supports Timothy Tackett's assertion (1996: 120, 149) that, during the early days of the Estates-General, the vast majority of Third Estate representatives were firmly convinced that Louis XVI was "on their side" and that "all reforms must be accomplished under the auspices of the monarchy, in close cooperation with a king

A Companion to the French Revolution, First Edition. Edited by Peter McPhee.

for whom they continued to show strong filial devotion." Moreover, while the term "filial devotion" here may well have been intended to be taken in a largely metaphorical sense, my own affinity for psychoanalytic theory inclines me to a more literal reading of the frequent familial references to the relationship between the French people and the king with which all historians of the early Revolution are so familiar. Hence, rather than seeing the routine depictions of the king "surrounded by his subjects like a father amid his children" (Chartier 1991: 111) or gazing "tenderly" upon the deputies "as his cherished children" (Ménard de la Groye 1989: 21–22) as little more than hyperbole or empty convention, I would argue that such expressions reflect the deeply significant quasi-parental role played by the monarch as an "internal object" in the inner psychological world of his subjects (Garland 1998: 9–10). For the French people and, in particular, for the deputies of the Third Estate, Louis XVI was a figure in whom a large amount of emotional capital had been invested, a figure with whom, regardless of growing intellectual skepticism regarding issues of political authority, their relationship still carried a strong emotional charge.

Now the use of parental and familial language in the effort to forge a political bond between the king and his subjects had been part of the ideological arsenal of royal propagandists since the medieval period, when, as Thomas Kaiser (1998: 133) observes, the idea that the king and the people "were tied together by a special divine love" first emerged. But in the face of a deep-seated process of secularization associated with the dawn of modernity, eighteenth-century propagandists, recognizing the dwindling impact of attempts to associate their royal client with the paternal aura of the Heavenly Father, sought instead to create emotional ties with a more down-to-earth monarch. Thus, David A. Bell (2001: 67) indicates the emergence in the pre-revolutionary decades of a heightened emphasis on a "language of love" which consistently highlighted the theme of "the mutual love of king and subjects" as a new basis of royal authority. As Kaiser (1998: 135–137) suggests, noting the contrast between forbidding images of Louis XIV as a "godlike figure well beyond the status of ordinary mortals" and efforts to teach Louis XV that "love, not fear, should bind him to his people," pre-revolutionary stress on the king's loving concern for the happiness of his people was "notable for its narrowing of the social and political distance between subject and sovereign."

Assuming the reality of such a "narrowing" in distance, what might its psychological and political consequences have been? Echoing current historiographical emphasis on the ideological nullity that the monarchy had supposedly acquired by 1789, one might well contend, as does Kaiser, that it served to dispel the king's mystique, thereby leaving him more vulnerable to the challenges soon to be posed by the revolutionaries. But it might just as easily be argued, and perhaps with more psychological verisimilitude, that the representation of the king as a more genuinely human figure enabled royal propagandists to connect monarchical paternalism more directly to subjects' internalized and often idealized images of their own parents, thereby setting up new possibilities for the creation of strong emotional and ideological ties between king and people. Such an analysis, moreover, resonates with more general eighteenth-century cultural trends which saw the rise of what Lynn Hunt (1992: 17–52) calls the ideal of the "good father." With tyrannical and patriarchal fathers who ruled more through fear than love being increasingly replaced as cultural ideals by sensitive, caring, and affectionate fathers who may sometimes have even been prepared to share their authority, we can reformulate the strategies of late eighteenth-century royal propagandists as efforts, in effect, to construct powerful images of the king as a "good father" in the inner psychic worlds of his subjects. Indeed, in terms of the depth and intensity of emotional involvement, the kinds of psychological bonds fashioned with a "good father" might well tend to be deeper and stronger than those forged with a traditional patriarch. Or, putting it another way, a "democratic" father, with whom one struggles to work out the terms and conditions of one's independence, could easily assume more weight and importance within one's "inner world" than a cold and remote patriarch.

While François Furet (1989: 238–240) is no doubt essentially correct in declaring the absolute monarchy "already dead" before Louis XVI's ascension to the throne, it does not inevitably follow, as Furet further states, that a viable constitutional monarchy "could never have been implemented." For if, as I will be suggesting, there is good reason to believe that royal propagandists had had some success in the pre-revolutionary decades in promoting strong ties with a more down-to-earth and "democratic" monarch as a new basis of loyalty and devotion to the Crown, the emotional and ideological foundations for a workable constitutional monarchy can be said to have been present. While the monarchy may well have been "desacralized" (see especially Merrick 1990; Van Kley 1984), in the sense that associations of the king to the realm of the sacred were increasingly giving way to more down-to-earth associations, this by no means signifies that, on the eve of the Revolution, Louis XVI did not occupy a position of enormous importance in the "inner worlds" and personal lives of his subjects and, in particular, of the deputies of the Third Estate. Rather, to return to the matter of the "case against the king," the position that he occupied in the "inner worlds" of the deputies was, to say the least, weighty enough that his abject failure to act as a "good father" in the weeks leading up to the fall of the Bastille was sufficient to generate a profound sense of personal betrayal on the part of many of these deputies. Though Louis was not formally arraigned on charges of treason until December 1792, the idea that he had betrayed the trust of the representatives of the Nation first began to take on psychological reality in the summer of 1789.

With the controversy concerning the way in which the Estates-General would be organized largely consuming the attention of the deputies during the early weeks of the meetings of the Estates, the assumption, mentioned above, of most of the deputies of the Third Estate that the king was "on their side" slowly and grudgingly changed into a realization that Louis was aligning himself with the privileged orders. Though historians remain divided on the question of whether or not the royal government planned to use the military forces it had summoned in the midst of this controversy to dissolve the newly proclaimed National Assembly, it was, for purposes of understanding the emotions of the deputies, "the perception [that] mattered" (Hardman 1993: 145). And as Hardman states, "having virtually called the Third Estate into existence as a political force, the King was perceived to have betrayed their trust and thrown in his lot with the nobility."[1] Moreover, the dominant perception among the deputies of the Third Estate was not only that

Louis was prepared to use his military assets to carry out what amounted to a counter-revolutionary coup against the National Assembly, but also, as the study of their correspondence and diaries makes clear (Shapiro 2009: 91–98), that he was prepared to use these forces to kill, or at least to arrest, many or even all of them. In short, the betrayal in question was not only political, it was intensely and viscerally personal. The beloved and supposedly benevolent and kindly Louis XVI, who had almost seemed to have been sent by an eighteenth-century version of Central Casting to play the role of the king as good father, had suddenly turned into their would-be murderer.

Although the "trepidations," as Michelet (1967: 183) put it, of the deputies that each moment "would be their last" are well known and have long been part of the standard narrative of the events of summer 1789, these fears and terrors have generally been treated as mere fleeting emotions and their possible impact on subsequent events generally ignored. In my view, however, the intense fear and stress experienced by the representatives in the weeks preceding Louis XVI's 15 July agreement to withdraw his troops and the psychic trauma induced by this fear and stress should be regarded as the emotional impetus for the first traces of what would become a judicial case against the king. While there were, as we will see, many good reasons why Mme Roland's late July 1789 call for the National Assembly to "put two famous heads [presumably those of Louis and Marie-Antoinette] on trial" (Lefebvre 2005: 117) was not immediately heeded and instead placed on hold for more than three years, what Hardman (1993: 233), highlighting for us again the language of personal betrayal and unrequited love, calls "the great hurt of 1789" would never be forgiven and would figure prominently in the Convention's formal accusation of Louis Capet.

Among thirty-four paragraphs enumerating a "multitude of crimes" and making up the official indictment (*acte énonciatif*) of 11 December 1792 (Mavidal and Laurent 1867–1913: vol. 55, 3–5), the very first three paragraphs relate specifically to the king's actions of June and July 1789. First, referring to the closing on 20 June 1789 of the newly proclaimed National Assembly's meeting hall, which led directly on that day to the taking of the celebrated Tennis Court Oath, the king was notified that he had "attacked the sovereignty of the people in suspending [the assembly] of its representatives and in driving them from their meeting place." Second, referring to the royal session of 23 June, at which Louis repudiated the proclamation of the National Assembly and declared all of its actions null and void, he was told that he had "surrounded [the nation's] representatives with troops" and had "tried to dictate laws to the nation." Third, moving from the monarchy's confrontation with the deputies to its confrontation with the representatives' most crucial source of support, the Parisian popular movement, he was told that he had "ordered an army to march against the citizens of Paris," that "your satellites had made their blood flow [at the Bastille and other Parisian locations]," and that "you only sent them away when the taking of the Bastille and the general insurrection showed you that the people were victorious." Moreover, pointing to the extent to which perceptions of what had happened in summer 1789 became consolidated in the collective memory and set the tone for later readings of the king's actions, Louis was informed that, with respect to the violence perpetrated by royal soldiers in July 1789, "*the massacres at the Tuileries depose against you*" (my emphasis); that, in other words, the blood that he had "made flow," as the very last paragraph in the indictment charges, at the Tuileries Palace on 10 August 1792 constituted valid and admissible evidence of his criminal responsibility for causing blood to flow in July 1789. Putting it another way, in terms of legal responsibility and criminal intention, the "recidivistic" violence of August 1792 is construed in this document as a continuation of a pattern that was first established in summer 1789.

Now, looked at from the perspective of the early twenty-first century, especially considering the history of countless subsequent political trials carried out against deposed heads of state (Laughland 2008), the case that could potentially have been mounted against the king in the aftermath of the events of summer 1789 might be thought of as a fairly routine one. After all, Louis had (or, what is more important in these kinds of political trials, was at least believed to have) summoned and deployed military force in an effort to retain his authority. He had had "command responsibility" for the civilian deaths and injuries incurred in the course of this perceived attempt to retain his authority, and, as is being highlighted in this essay, he had also had "command responsibility" for the perceived threats to the lives and/or personal liberty of his key political challengers generated by the presence and movements of his forces. In addition, he had rejected and had indeed shown contempt for the newly emerging legitimating myth of the new regime, the idea of popular sovereignty, and had interfered with the activities of the political challengers who claimed to embody this idea. Moreover, though he had obviously not been removed from the throne in summer 1789, his attempts to retain his authority had failed completely and he had suffered an ignominious and severe political defeat from which he would never recover. All of this, if it had occurred in the more recent "post-Nuremberg" past or in our own contemporary world, would surely have been enough to ensure that the individual in question would have had to face some form of "transitional justice," some kind of legal reckoning, whether a trial or, if a premium were to be placed on the need for some accommodation with the *ancien régime*, perhaps some kind of "truth commission."

But we are not of course talking here about the recent past or the contemporary world: we are talking about the French Revolution. In basic outline, the events of summer 1789 may well appear quite similar to those of countless other failed attempts by defeated regimes all over the world to quash a popular uprising and prevent a transfer of authority and sovereignty, failed attempts which in countless other cases have led relatively quickly to the institution of procedures designed to effectuate some kind of "settlement with the past" (Walzer 1992: 6). Why, then, was Mme Roland's call for an immediate trial of the royal family such an isolated voice in the wilderness? Why was it that even the most radical Parisian newspapers uniformly praised the king throughout 1789 and indeed through much of 1790 (Censer 1976: 111–115)? Why was it not until the abortive flight to Varennes of June 1791 that the idea of such a trial entered the mainstream of revolutionary discourse (Tackett 2003)?[2]

The most standard answer provided by historians over the years to these kinds of questions is that, despite growing intellectual doubts about the ideological foundations of the monarchy (currently updated as monarchical "desacralization"), the level of confidence among the early revolutionaries that a republic could possibly be an effective form of government in any polity larger than a classical city-state was so low that the notion of doing without a king or even doing without the incumbent monarch was largely unthinkable. Moreover, if doing without a king was unthinkable, it would seem that the idea that a king could commit, or be held accountable for committing, a crime was just as difficult if not more difficult to imagine. Additionally, though the monarchy had been dealt a grievous blow in July 1789, the royal government still retained some control over the levers of power, especially with respect to loyal elements of the military, and it still possessed a significant degree of active political support among the population at large. Hence, it might be said that some combination of residual loyalty, inertia, and prudence led the Constituent Assembly to attempt to steer Louis down the path of constitutional monarchy rather than to summon him before it to face a judicial procedure. It would, of course, be three years before conditions had "ripened" to the point that a different set of representatives of the Nation were prepared to go in a different direction.

The "ripening" process being posited here can be examined more substantially in connection with the very first crime cited in the *acte énonciatif* of December 1792, the charge that the king had "attacked the sovereignty of the people" on 20 June 1789 in deploying military force to prevent the newly proclaimed National Assembly from meeting. Now, popular sovereignty was formally declared as a central operating tenet of the new regime in August 1789 as part of the Declaration of the Rights of Man and of the Citizen, and we can probably assume that, though it certainly meant very different things to different people, it was an idea that had enjoyed wide support (or at least possessed a certain fashionable cachet) within the National Assembly during the unfolding of the June–July confrontation with the royal government. But it is one thing to support an ideological precept; it is something quite different to assert that an "attack" upon that precept is a crime. In the French Revolution, it took time for the former to "ripen" into the latter.

For the members of the Convention who composed the *acte énonciatif*, Louis XVI's deployment of troops in June 1789 to interfere with the deliberations of the representatives of the Nation clearly constituted an attempt to interfere with the implementation and operation of popular sovereignty itself. But it seems highly unlikely that any more than a tiny number of deputies were thinking in these terms in the summer of 1789, and even of those that may have been, not one, so far as I can determine, actually said so publicly. Yes, the vast majority undoubtedly "supported," "subscribed to," or "believed in" the idea of popular sovereignty. But they had never, to that point, actually experienced it as a day-to-day reality, had never, that is, lived in a world in which the sovereignty of the people and the exercise of that sovereignty by the people's representatives were understood to be the normal operating principles of politics, a world in which interfering with or otherwise infringing upon the activities of the people's representatives could easily (and one might almost say "naturally") be conceptualized as criminal behavior. As the French became more and more accustomed, as the Revolution unfolded, to the exercise of sovereignty and authority by the Representatives of the Nation, the idea that the violation of the prerogatives of the new authorities could be a crime became more and more imaginable.

In examining the immediate reaction of the National Assembly to the monarchy's failed counter-revolutionary efforts of summer 1789, what is perhaps most striking is how hard the deputies seemed to work to avoid accusing Louis of anything. Despite the intense fears of imminent death that many had just experienced, the man who was ultimately responsible for triggering these fears was greeted, in his 15 July appearance before the Assembly, with a torrent of acclaim and affection. At the "moving sight" of the king's arrival without any accompanying military guard, "the Assembly," as one deputy put it, "lost its fears and anxieties and saw only a father coming to console his too unfortunate children" (Delandine 1789: 3, 141). "Clothed in majesty like a father in the midst of his children," as another stated in language that was entirely typical, "he filled our eyes with tears by his goodness, his frankness and by the loyal stamp of his discourse" (MacDonogh 1992: 60). Putting a familiar trope into overdrive, many of the representatives displaced blame for recent events onto the king's "evil advisers." Thus, for example, the deputy Lofficial (1897: 90) wrote to his wife on 17 July that Louis had been "seized with indignation" upon learning of plans to attack the Assembly. "Knowing then," continued this deputy, "that he had been deceived, since they angrily proposed to him to have the throats slit of the elite of his people, he resolved to come all by himself to be with us without delay." In separating the king, moreover, from the evil that had been perpetrated in his name and in seeing him now as "finally free from deception" (Pellerin, entry of 15 July), the deputies were able to construe Louis' appearance before them as a manifestation of the true nature of this "most cherished and best of kings" (Chaumiel 1940: 58). As the deputy Visme (entry of 15 July) put it, he had finally "returned to himself." But if the king had somehow magically "returned to himself" on the morning after the fall of the Bastille, what of the deputies themselves? What kind of a "return" might they have been seeking?

As indicated in the clinical literature on psychic trauma, most individuals who have been subjected to intense fear of imminent death experience some degree of traumatic reaction, especially if they (1) have hitherto been, as was true of the vast majority of Third Estate deputies, totally unaccustomed to and unprepared for anything like the perceived dangers with which they are suddenly confronted; (2) are subjected to fears and terrors that escalate over an extended period of time (in this case a span of three to four weeks); and (3) face perceived threats from a human source in whom strong feelings of trust and affection have previously been invested. In brief, it is my contention that, without any significant number of representatives necessarily developing the kind of severe long-term reaction that would today be identified as Post-Traumatic Stress Disorder (PTSD), a large number of Third Estate deputies appear to have experienced the kind of traumatic reaction that clinicians describe as a relatively short-term "normal response" to an "abnormal situation" (Horowitz 1986: 242–243). As such, the deputies in question would have tended to manifest a pattern of behavior that clinicians call the "dialectic of trauma" (Herman 1992: 37–50), a pattern of behavior in which periods of denial or "forgetting" oscillate with periods of hypervigilant repetition or "remembering." Though the general public, which often hears about traumatic "flashbacks" in the popular media, is more familiar with the notion of traumatic repetition, it is the phase of traumatic denial that is most relevant to our present enquiry.

As trauma researcher Daniel Weiss (1993: 16) explains, traumatic denial is driven by a powerful need "to avoid accepting the reality of vulnerability [and] lack of safety." When individuals, like the deputies of the Third Estate, are exposed to situations in which their existential feelings of "being safe in the world" have suddenly and unexpectedly been ripped away from them by a terrifying threat to their lives, they typically try to find ways to ward off or otherwise avoid the painful recollection of what has happened to them. As Weiss tells it, denial and other forms of the inability to fully absorb the shattering of one's accustomed sense of safety and security are rooted in the desperate desire to believe that "the stressor [could not] really have happened." In envisioning Louis XVI as "returning to himself" on 15 July in what they further sought to construe as an essentially voluntary decision "to throw himself into our arms," "to join together with his subjects and children," or "to abandon himself to the National Assembly" (Desgraves 1967: 31; Gallot 1961: 117; Bouillé 1887–89: vol. 14, 117; Roulhac 1991: 154), the deputies, it can be suggested, were trying to convince themselves that their emotional connection to the king which his evil advisers had put at risk had now been restored. For in finding a monarch who had "returned to himself," the deputies could, in an important sense, "return to themselves" as the respectable and law-abiding pillars of society who had come to Versailles to cooperate with the "good father" who was "on their side," rather than to rebel against him. In straining to re-create the sweet and comforting feelings of love and affection for the "most cherished and best of kings" that they had brought with them to Versailles, the deputies could almost believe, if only until traumatic denial had run its course, that the terrifying events of recent weeks had not really occurred and that the feeling of "being safe in the world" that they had until then taken for granted was not now gone for good.

Discussing the need of abused and traumatized children to retain some semblance of a positive image of their parents, psychiatrist Judith Herman (1992: 101) writes that these children, though they know deep in their hearts what their parents have done, "will go to any lengths to construct an explanation for [their] fate that absolves [their] parents of all blame and responsibility." Now there are obviously huge differences between how children relate to their actual parents and how adults relate to a figure, like the king, who functions in some manner as a kind of parental surrogate. Moreover, there is clearly an enormous gulf between abused and powerless children, who generally remain totally dependent on their parents, and the deputies of the Third Estate, who had access to a variety of resources (most importantly the support of "the People") that gave them the ability to exercise a great deal of control over (and ultimately to emerge victorious from) the situation with which they were confronted. Nonetheless, the sense of desperation conveyed here by Herman strongly reverberates with the intense and persistent efforts of the deputies to retain some semblance of faith and trust in the king by pushing away awareness or otherwise "forgetting" his recent course of conduct. We have just seen how these efforts manifested themselves in the immediate aftermath of the de facto transfer of power from the monarchy to the National Assembly. Moreover, as I seek to demonstrate in some detail in *Traumatic Politics: The Deputies and the King in the Early French Revolution*, such periods of denial would continue to manifest themselves intermittently over the next several months (in conjunction with alternating resurfacings of disturbing memories of recent betrayal), and these periods of denial would intermittently incline the Assembly to pursue policies of cooperation and accommodation with regard to the monarchy. But the most fundamental policy of cooperation and accommodation pursued by the Assembly was the unstated one of immunity for the king from all thought of prosecution.[3] As we can now see, the deputies' traumatic need to deny that their good father had betrayed them was instrumental in protecting Louis from early prosecution, while the gradual tapering off of that need was part of the "ripening" process that would eventually bring him before the bar of justice.

As this essay has sought to suggest, the importance of the events of summer 1789 to the building of the "case against the king" cannot be overestimated. Though Louis' attack on popular sovereignty on 20 June had, of course, no standing in positive law in 1789, it was the first deployment of physical force against the Third Estate deputies, in effect the first public declaration of political war against the revolutionaries, and it would eventually be construed as a cardinal violation of revolutionary "higher law" or "natural law."[4] Indeed, as the first open act of betrayal of a group of men who desperately wanted to believe that the king was "on their side," it can be viewed as the "primal crime" from which all his later crimes flowed. Yet, at the same time that this essay has emphasized how easily Louis' course of behavior on 20 June and during the succeeding weeks leading up to 14 July *could* have been regarded as criminal by the deputies of the Constituent Assembly (and *would* be regarded as such by the deputies of the Convention), it has also stressed the factors which prevented the deputies of 1789 from consciously seeing their "good father" as a criminal conspirator. In particular, it has stressed the strength of the deputies' devotion to the king on the eve of the Revolution, and the lengths to which they subsequently went to maintain and, in some sense, even reinforce their feelings of connection to him in the face of the potentially murderous course of action that he had pursued against them. Given the strength of this need of the deputies to preserve the representations of the king as good father that had been built up within their "inner worlds" by a lifetime of exposure to the new style of royal propaganda discussed earlier, one is led to wonder what it could imply about the possibilities that might have existed in the summer of 1789 for the establishment of a viable constitutional monarchy.

If we take the residual degree of loyalty to the monarchy that seems to have prevailed among the deputies on the eve of the Revolution as good grounds for believing that a workable constitutional compromise was indeed possible, then we are left with the proposition that the revolutionary conflagration that emerged that summer resulted from what can be regarded as a failure of elite political management. Despite weeks of conferences and negotiating sessions in May and June and beyond, the various segments of the "political class," the elected deputies of the three estates and the leaders of the royal government, were unable were to reach a viable agreement among themselves, thereby creating space for a rush of popular energy onto the center of the political stage where it quickly became the driving force of events. While the question of what enabled the revolutionary genie to find its way out of the proverbial bottle is one which can hardly be answered in this essay, the king, of course, would eventually be forced to assume criminal responsibility and blame for the escalation of what began as a contentious but essentially peaceful political dispute into a life-and-death struggle. "We always wanted him; he never wanted us," murmured elements in the crowd as Louis' remains were being carted away on 21 January 1793. But let us, in this regard, go back to the days just before and just after the Third Estate declared itself to be the National Assembly on 17 June 1789, the key revolutionary moment in which the deputies first publicly asserted their claims to embody national sovereignty. Conveying a point of view expressed in the correspondence of many Third Estate deputies, one representative wrote to a friend on 9 June that "we will address ourselves to the king so that he can *permit* [my emphasis] us to constitute ourselves as the nation and join with us in working together on the great project for which he has convoked his people," while another wrote to his wife on 18 June that the Third Estate's declaration was an expression of "how much his [the king's] people will be devoted to him" (Bouchette 1909: 227; Lepoutre 1998: 52). Thus, even as (or perhaps especially as) they defiantly carried out what William Doyle (2001: 40) calls "the founding act of the French Revolution," many of the deputies anxiously continued to insist on their loyalty and devotion to Louis and to deny that any serious conflict between him and them could possibly exist, thereby reminding us again of the longing of the representatives to cling to the images of their relationship with the monarch that they had brought with them to Versailles.

Yet if the king's decision to summon and deploy his military assets against the defiant representatives led, as we have seen, to an even more intense effort on the part of the deputies to cling to the idea of Louis as good father, the post-14 July denial featured in this essay constituted only one phase of the "dialectic of trauma." For the desperate attempts of those who have been traumatized to deny or forget what has happened to them cannot possibly be entirely successful in the face of the relentless and inexorable intrusion of their nightmarish memories into conscious awareness. In the case of Louis XVI, the culmination of the ultimate failure of traumatic denial to banish unwanted memories can be found in the opening paragraphs of the *acte énonciatif* of December 1792. But what is especially interesting about the relationship of the trauma of summer 1789 to the playing out of the "case against the king" is the bifurcated vision of the monarch which traumatization seemed to foster. For the traumatized deputies of 1789, depending upon whether denial or repetition was ascendant, Louis was either a saintly good father deceived by his evil advisers or a traitorous enemy who, in their heart of hearts, they believed was willing to have them killed to protect his own interests. Conversely, struggling in either case to avoid seeing their own role in activating the dynamics of confrontation, the deputies construed themselves as loyal and devoted subjects of their good father or as the innocent potential victims of their betrayer. In keeping with the difficulty that those who have been traumatized tend to have in cognitively processing and "fully knowing" the events to which they have been exposed (Caruth 1996: 4; Leys 2000: 9), what is missing from this bifurcated landscape is a more nuanced and more balanced evaluation of the political situation in which the deputies and the king had become entangled. In particular, what is missing is a recognition on the part of the deputies that the repressive and violent policies pursued by the royal government were, to some degree, a reaction to their own defiant and rebellious course of action, a recognition, that is, that just as their own fears and anxieties were being triggered by aggressive governmental policies, so too might the challenges which they were posing to royal authority induce fears and anxieties on the part of Louis and his agents, fears and anxieties that, at least in part, could be seen as driving these aggressive royal policies.

Reinforcing moralistic tendencies in pre-revolutionary French political culture (Linton 2001; Maza 1993), the traumatization of many of the deputies in summer 1789 made it extremely difficult for these deputies to see themselves, with some degree of emotional detachment and political realism, as engaged in a political version of a chess game in which opponents react and counter-react to each other in making their moves and counter-moves. After all, it is hard enough for political adversaries to act on the basis of this sort of detached perspective under the least frantic of political circumstances, and, as I argue in *Traumatic Politics*, the traumatization of summer 1789 ultimately severely undermined and perhaps largely foreclosed the possibility of establishing a viable constitutional monarchy in which the representatives and the monarch could have worked out ways of relating to each other as opponents rather than as enemies. With respect to the process which eventually brought Louis to the scaffold, the tendency of the traumatized deputies to see him in sharply moralized and exaggerated terms as either saint or villain helped to preclude the possibility of negotiating with or accommodating the "real Louis" who, being subject to the same kinds of emotional vulnerabilities to which they were subject, was trying, however stubbornly, to navigate and indeed to bumble his way through the minefields of a frighteningly novel political situation. As the confrontational dynamic of summer 1789 became a way of life in the months and years that followed, and as pre-revolutionary images of the saintly good father accordingly became harder and harder to square with any semblance of reality, it was the image of Louis as the betrayer of the Third Estate that, while largely pushed away from conscious awareness in the early months of the Revolution, had the greater staying power and that, as we saw in the *acte énonciatif* of December 1792, eventually mainlined itself into the revolutionary bloodstream. In their inability to see Louis more prosaically as "neither saint nor villain," the deputies of the Constituent Assembly were the first to elevate him, however intermittently, to the exalted status of political enemy and therefore the first to launch him on what would become the path to the guillotine.

Notes

1 Though Hardman (2007: 65–67; 1993: 155–157) argues that, in reality, plans for the troops largely centered around defending Versailles from a potential attack by Paris revolutionaries and on other defensive operations, my own inclination is to believe that long-held assumptions by generations of historians that the intent was to dissolve the Assembly were indeed correct (Shapiro 1993: 36–37; 2009: 83).

2 In regard to Timothy Tackett's approach in *When the King Took Flight*, it might be noted that, in contrast to much recent French revolutionary historiography, he and I are in broad agreement that the possibility for the emergence of a viable constitutional monarchy had not necessarily been foreclosed before the outbreak of the Revolution. However, whereas Tackett gives pride of place to the flight to Varennes as the key event

that grievously undermined and perhaps doomed the system being set up by the Constituent Assembly, my aim in this essay and in *Traumatic Politics: The Deputies and the King in the Early French Revolution* is to call attention to the serious damage to the possibility for a stable constitutional monarchy that I believe occurred as a consequence of the summer 1789 crisis. I would argue that one important reason why historians have so markedly underestimated the extent of this damage is that much of the hostility and distrust towards the king that resulted from the summer 1789 crisis was, as will be seen, pushed away from the conscious awareness of the deputies, thereby depriving future historians of the kind of hard evidence which any researcher normally seeks. While much of what follows in this essay will perhaps be easily dismissed by those who find it hard to acknowledge the role of the unconscious in shaping human behavior, I ask only that the reader maintain an open mind as to the possible validity or at least plausibility of the argument I am making.

3 As I discuss elsewhere (Shapiro 1993), judicial proceedings were launched against some of the king's "evil advisers" in the aftermath of the Paris Revolution of 12–14 July. Though these proceedings were, for various reasons, not very vigorously or successfully pursued, the relevant point here is that immunity for the king did not extend to his agents, who were from the beginning thought quite capable of committing crimes against the nation.

4 For the role of higher or natural law in the trial of the king, see Edelstein 2009: 147–158.

References

Primary Sources

Beaucourt, marquis de (ed.) (1892). *Captivité et derniers moments de Louis XVI: Récits originaux et documents officiels*, 2 vols. Paris: A. Picard.

Bouchette, François-Joseph (1909). *Lettres de François-Joseph Bouchette.* Camille Looten (ed.). Lille: H. Champion.

Bouillé, Jean Pierre (1887–89). "Ouverture des États-Généraux de 1789." In Albert Macé (ed.). *Revue de la Révolution: Documents inédits*, 10: 161–171; 11: 11–20, 45–53, 113–120; 12: 7–14, 35–42, 49–58, 109–112; 13: 11–17, 65–79; 14: 26–32, 42–51, 82–92, 114–123; 15: 13–28, 99–120; 16: 15–29, 45–84.

Chaumiel, Louis (1940). *Les Journées de 89, d'après Delavilleleroulx, député de Lorient aux États-Généraux.* Lorient: Nouvelliste du Morbihan.

Delandine, Antoine-François (1789). *Mémorial historique des États-Généraux*, 5 vols. n.p.

Desgraves, Louis (ed.) (1967). "Correspondances des députés de la sénéchaussée d'Agen aux États-Généraux et à l'Assemblée nationale (1789–1790)." *Recueil des Travaux de la Société Académique d'Agen: Sciences, Lettres, et Arts*, 3rd series, 1–191.

Gallot, Jean-Gabriel (1961). *La Vie et les oeuvres du Dr. Jean-Gabriel Gallot (1744–1794).* Louis Merle (ed.). Poitiers: Société des Antiquaires de l'Ouest.

Lepoutre, Pierre-François (1998). *Député-paysan et fermière de Flandre en 1789: Les Correspondances des Lepoutre.* Jean-Pierre Jessenne and Edna Hindie Lemay (eds.). Villeneuve d'Ascq: Centre d'Histoire de l'Europe du Nord-Ouest.

Lofficial, Louis-Prosper (1897). "Lettres de Lofficial." In C. Leroux-Cesbron (ed.). *La Nouvelle Revue Rétrospective*, 7: 73–120, 169–192.

Mavidal, Jérôme and Émile Laurent (eds.) (1867–1913). *Archives parlementaires de 1787 à 1860: Recueil complet des débats législatifs et politiques des chambres françaises, première série (1787–1799)*, 82 vols. Paris: P. Dupont.

Ménard de la Groye, François-René-Pierre (1989). *Correspondance (1789–1791)*. Florence Mirouse (ed.). Le Mans: Conseil Général de la Sarthe.
Pellerin, Joseph-Michel. "Journal." Bibliothèque Municipale de Versailles.
Roulhac, Guillaume-Grégoire de (1991). "Lettres de Grégoire de Roulhac, député aux États-Généraux (mai–août 1789)." In Paul d'Hollander (ed.). *Bulletin de la Société Archéologique et Historique du Limousin*, 119: 144–167.
Visme, Laurent de. "Journal des États-Généraux." Bibliothèque Nationale de France, Paris.

Secondary Sources

Bell, David A. (2001). *The Cult of the Nation in France: Inventing Nationalism, 1680–1800*. Cambridge, Mass.: Harvard University Press.
Caruth, Cathy (1996). *Unclaimed Experience: Trauma, Narrative, and History*. Baltimore, Md.: Johns Hopkins University Press.
Censer, Jack Richard (1976). *Prelude to Power: The Parisian Radical Press, 1789–1791*. Baltimore, Md.: Johns Hopkins University Press.
Chartier, Roger (1991). *The Cultural Origins of the French Revolution*, trans. Lydia Cochrane. Durham, N.C.: Duke University Press.
Doyle, William (2001). *The French Revolution: A Very Short Introduction*. Oxford: Oxford University Press.
Edelstein, Dan (2009). *The Terror of Natural Right: Republicanism, the Cult of Nature, and the French Revolution*. Chicago: University of Chicago Press.
Furet, François (1989). "Louis XVI." In François Furet and Mona Ozouf (eds.). *A Critical Dictionary of the French Revolution*, trans. Arthur Goldhammer. Cambridge, Mass.: Harvard University Press.
Garland, Caroline (ed.) (1998). *Understanding Trauma: A Psychoanalytical Approach*. New York: Routledge.
Hardman, John (1993). *Louis XVI*. New Haven, Conn.: Yale University Press.
Hardman, John (2007). "The Real and Imagined Conspiracies of Louis XVI." In Peter R. Campbell, Thomas E. Kaiser, and Marisa Linton (eds.). *Conspiracy in the French Revolution*. Manchester and New York: Manchester University Press. 63–84.
Herman, Judith Lewis (1992). *Trauma and Recovery*. New York: Basic Books.
Horowitz, Mardi Jon (1986). "Stress-Response Syndromes: A Review of Posttraumatic and Adjustment Disorders." *Hospital and Community Psychiatry*, 37: 241–249.
Hunt, Lynn (1992). *The Family Romance of the French Revolution*. Berkeley and Los Angeles: University of California Press.
Kaiser, Thomas E. (1998). "*Louis le bien-aimé* and the Rhetoric of the Royal Body." In Sara Melzer and Kathryn Norberg (eds.). *From the Royal to the Republican Body: Incorporating the Political in Seventeenth- and Eighteenth-Century France*. Berkeley and Los Angeles: University of California Press. 131–161.
Laughland, John (2008). *A History of Political Trials: From Charles I to Saddam Hussein*. Oxford: Peter Lang.
Lefebvre, Georges (2005). *The Coming of the French Revolution*, trans. R.R. Palmer. Princeton, N.J.: Princeton University Press.
Leys, Ruth (2000). *Trauma: A Genealogy*. Chicago: University of Chicago Press.
Linton, Marisa (2001). *The Politics of Virtue in Enlightenment France*. New York: Palgrave.
MacDonogh, Giles (1992). *Brillat-Savardin: The Judge and his Stomach*. London: Ivan R. Dee.
Maza, Sarah (1993). *Private Lives and Public Affairs: The Causes Célèbres of Prerevolutionary France*. Berkeley and Los Angeles: University of California Press.

Merrick, Jeffrey (1990). *The Desacralisation of the French Monarchy in the Eighteenth Century*. Baton Rouge: Louisiana State University Press.
Michelet, Jules (1967). *History of the French Revolution*, trans. Charles Cocks. Chicago: University of Chicago Press.
Shapiro, Barry M. (1993). *Revolutionary Justice in Paris, 1789–1790*. Cambridge: Cambridge University Press.
Shapiro, Barry M. (2009). *Traumatic Politics: The Deputies and the King in the Early French Revolution*. University Park: Pennsylvania State University Press.
Tackett, Timothy (1996). *Becoming a Revolutionary: The Deputies of the French National Assembly and the Emergence of a Revolutionary Culture, 1789–1790*. Princeton, N.J.: Princeton University Press.
Tackett, Timothy (2003). *When the King Took Flight*. Cambridge, Mass.: Harvard University Press.
Van Kley, Dale (1984). *The Damiens Affair and the Unraveling of the Ancien Régime*. Princeton, N.J.: Princeton University Press.
Walzer, Michael (1992). "Regicide and Revolution." In Michael Walzer (ed.). *Regicide and Revolution: Speeches at the Trial of Louis XVI*, trans. Marion Rothstein. New York: Columbia University Press. 1–90.
Weiss, Daniel S. (1993). "Psychological Processes in Traumatic Stress." *Journal of Social Behavior and Personality*, 8(5): 3–28.

Part III

Church, State, and War

CHAPTER EIGHT

The *Ancien Régime*, Catholic Europe, and the Revolution's Religious Schism

DALE VAN KLEY

In a phrase that has since entered into the historiographical lexicon, the late Denis Richet and François Furet argued in 1965 that at some point the French Revolution "skidded" off course, diverting it from its liberal beginnings in 1789 toward the Terror of 1793–94 (Furet and Richet 1970: 122–146). If a single decisive moment of "skidding" can be identified, the National Assembly's attempt to give the French Catholic or Gallican Church a new "civil" constitution in 1790 is as good a candidate as any. The Civil Constitution of the Clergy split the Gallican Church even before it incurred papal condemnation. By creating a religious schism, the National Assembly's ecclesiastical legislation lent religious coherence to hitherto dispersed aristocratic and "feudal" grievances, channeling their energy into a veritable counter-revolution in the service of a holy cause. The sanctioning of this legislation also put a pious king on the "schismatic" side of Catholicism, troubling the royal conscience and leading quite directly to Louis XVI's attempted flight from Paris in 1791. That flight in turn already implicated the Austrian Habsburgs and pointed toward the war of 1792. Besides creating enemies with weapons without, the war made opponents of the Revolution into traitors within. It was counter-revolution that would justify the Terror.

But to focus on the circumstances of the Civil Constitution and the schism is only to displace the questions that have long bedeviled the historiography of the Terror. To what extent was the schism avoidable or necessary? Or to what degree was it a product of contingent circumstances or of non-negotiable ideology? Most obviously on the side of "circumstances" lie the fact of France's national debt and deficit and the vagaries of France's diplomacy with Rome. On the side of ideology lie the nature of Revolution's principles and the theological outlook of the papacy. But to pit circumstances against ideology is to ask a badly posed question. As Keith Baker has aptly put it, events contain ideas; ideas, when acted upon, create events

A Companion to the French Revolution, First Edition. Edited by Peter McPhee.

(Baker 2011: 166–167). History appears "inevitable" only in retrospect. Better therefore to mix the two up; nothing illustrates the mixture better than the origins of the religious schism of 1791.

Given the close connection between the Gallican Church and the realm in *ancien régime* France, it is hard to imagine a revolution in the state that would not have affected the church. Given the nature of the French Revolution, it is hard to imagine it without an attempt to reform that church. Given the nature and outlook of the papacy of Pius VI, finally, it is equally hard to imagine him not condemning that reform, especially if enacted only by the state. So much, then, for the unlikelihood of a schism. But it is less difficult to imagine a schism that would have taken a form less destructive for the French Revolution, perhaps even for Catholicism – a differently imagined sundered community, as it were. The area of the greatest "give" turns out to be French revolutionary ideology, or rather ideologies, and the mix between them that in the circumstances of 1790 went into the making of the Civil Constitution of the Clergy.

A Brief Overview[1]

A brief account of what has to be explained is in order. The Gallican Church first became a target during the run-up to the French Revolution when, having convoked an Assembly of Notables to consider his plans to deal with the royal deficit and debt, the Controller-General Alexandre de Calonne proposed to subject clerical as well as noble property to his proposed land tax as well as to oblige the church to sell some of its property to liquidate its corporate debt. The proposal to liquidate that debt also threatened the *raison d'être* of the church's periodical general assemblies, which, although they met in order to finance that debt, also gave the clergy a corporate political power unique in all of Europe. Bishops such as Loménie de Brienne of Toulouse were also among the most vociferous critics of Calonne's proposals, a situation that did not change even after Brienne replaced the disgraced Calonne and revised his proposals in an attempt to make them more palatable for the Assembly. Associating itself in an unprecedented way with the "patriotic" opposition to ministerial and monarchical "despotism," the General Assembly of the Gallican clergy refused to give Brienne much more than a pittance in response to his request for a loan when it met for the very last time in June 1788.

By then the *parlements* led by the Parlement of Paris had taken the place of the dismissed Assembly of Notables at the head of the "patriotic" resistance to new taxes, with the episcopacy still on the patriotic side. But that brief moment of episcopal "patriotic" popularity came to an end when, having obtained from an all but bankrupt monarchy the convocation of the long defunct Estates-General, the Parlement ruled that they should meet in the form last observed, in 1614. For if, as many thought, that ruling meant that France's three traditional orders would meet and vote separately and thereby reduce the Third Estate to a single vote, one result would be to put the clergy as the realm's first order on the wrong side of a redefined patriotic cause. That result became a reality after episcopal members indeed construed the meaning of the "forms of 1614" in this way when consulted on the matter in a second meeting of the Assembly of Notables called by Jacques

Necker in November 1788. For his part, Necker, who had replaced the fallen Brienne as de facto first minster, continued Calonne's and Brienne's tactic of subsidizing rhetoric critical of the clergy's fiscal and other privileges and its alliance with the forces of "aristocracy."[2] This tactic got the ministry nowhere against the first Assembly of Notables and the *parlements* until the autumn of 1788, but gained purchase after the issue of the forms of 1614 put "aristocracy" next to "despotism" as patriotism's twin *bêtes noires.*

It was also Necker who helped divide the clergy by favoring the largely commoner parish clergy at the expense of the bishops and monastic and cathedral clergy in regulations for the elections to the Estates-General, now due to meet in May 1789. The result was not only a vast pamphlet literature touting the virtues of parish priests versus the vices of their "aristocratic" superiors and other tithe-owners, but also a veritable "revolt" by *curés* during the electoral process that gave them a majority of about two-thirds within the delegation of the First Estate (McManners 1998: 705–744). In the meeting of the Estates-General itself, the revolt of commoner *curés* also produced a defection by priests from their order and in favor of the Third Estate. That defection began with individual decisions on 13 June 1789, but culminated in a vote within the first order of 149 to 134 in favor of accepting the Third Estate's invitation to join it, apparently for the purpose of a common verification of credentials. The heroes of the hour, these *curés* gave crucial – perhaps indispensable – help in enabling the Third Estate to make good its claim to be the "National Assembly," only to realize days later that in voting to join the Third Estate they had also voted to end the clergy's existence as a separate order (Hutt 1955; Necheles 1974).

That consequence became clear on 2 July when a tearful archbishop of Aix, Jean de Cucé de Boisgelin, proved unable to exempt concerns unique to the clergy from common deliberation.[3] It became far clearer during the holocaust of privileges of 4–11 August 1789, when the clergy sacrificed the income from the tithe only to learn that, unlike those who had given up feudal dues or venal offices, the clergy was to receive no compensation for its sacrifice at all. It was also during these debates that the deputy François-Nicolas Buzot ominously observed that the clergy only enjoyed the usufruct of landed property that ultimately belonged to the "nation."[4] The implication was clear that the nation might well reclaim that property if it needed to use it to finance the royal debt for which National Assembly had assumed responsibility in one of its first acts of sovereignty. It was basically on these grounds that, after a long debate in late October, the National Assembly acted on a motion by the bishop Charles-Maurice de Talleyrand of Autun and declared church property to be "at the disposition of the nation" on 2 November 1789.[5] While this motion did not yet declare that property to be the nation's, the debate made that implication clear enough. In principle if not yet in practice, it left the entire Gallican Church without fiscal resources, dependent either on the national budget or the generosity of the French "faithful."

Whether and to what extent this "regenerated" nation would remain Catholic had meanwhile also become a cause for clerical concern. While allowing for religious toleration, the debates that went into the writing of the Declaration of the Rights of Man and of the Citizen also turned back the first of three attempts by

Catholic clergymen to persuade the National Assembly to proclaim Catholicism to be the official religion of France, in part on the grounds that it threatened the religious toleration recently granted to Protestants. The following two occurred in February and April 1790, as the National Assembly decided, first, to dissolve all religious orders except for those indispensable to the work of charity or education; and, second, to begin the sale of clerical property as backing for its bonds or *assignats*. What helped to turn the tide against Bishop La Fare's motion of 14 February was Dupont de Nemours' reminder of the Assembly's resolve to include the expenses of the Catholic "cult" in its budget. For shortly before that date, on 5–7 February, the National Assembly decided to renew the membership of its Ecclesiastical Committee, the task of which was to reform the Gallican Church in view of its incorporation into the new constitution.

No surprise therefore greeted the proposal to defray the expenses of Catholic worship by means of public revenues when, with the deputy Louis-Simon Martineau reporting, this ecclesiastical committee submitted its plan to reform the Gallican Church to the National Assembly on 28 May 1790.[6] Nor could monks such as the Carthusian Antoine-Christophe Gerle be surprised by the suppression of all contemplative and mendicant orders, a measure already decided several months earlier. More shocking for the clerical deputies were the committee's plans to suppress all cathedral and collegial clergy and reduce the number of dioceses – hence also bishops – from 135 to 83. Besides reducing costs, the proposal's intent was to redraw the boundaries of these dioceses as well as parishes in view of bringing them into conformity with the new constitution that had replaced the old provinces and the *ancien régime*'s other jurisdictions with departments and cantons. A similar aim to integrate the church's "civil" or external form into the new constitution underlay the equally novel proposal to subject bishops and priests alike to election by the same "active" and mainly lay electors who were to designate their representatives at the departmental and cantonal levels.

Complementing these surgical proposals were others designed to replace the confirmation of newly designated bishops by the papacy with that of by "metropolitan" bishops, who were to replace the old archbishops. Lest the implication of this measure was unclear, another annulled the jurisdiction of all "foreign" ecclesiastical authorities, including the papacy itself, while yet a third provision enhanced the power of bishops in relation to this "foreign" authority by allowing them to grant hitherto papal dispensations from canon law. A fourth provision subjected the power of bishops in turn in relation to their parish clergy by subjecting episcopal decisions to the approval of diocesan councils composed of *curés* who, though named by bishops, were destined to replace the repressed cathedral chapters. Still other provisions sharply curtailed the income of bishops and raised that of *curés*.

Together these measures unilaterally abrogated the Concordat or Treaty of Bologna of 1516 between François I and Pope Leo X that had given the king the right to nominate candidates to major benefices and the pope the right to confirm them. The total effect was further to nationalize the Gallican Church in relation to the Catholic Church while also so subjecting it to the state as to make it a salaried department of state.

With few revisions, the Ecclesiastical Committee's proposals prevailed and became law in short order. The most important debates and decisions took place between 31 May and 2 June; those that occupied the National Assembly until 12 July concerned only details. Perhaps the most important of these adopted the *abbé* Henri Grégoire's motion to add to the provision disallowing the jurisdiction of bishops under a "foreign power" the clause, "without prejudice to the hierarchy of the Sovereign Pontiff."[7] As it happened, it came to depend on the Sovereign Pontiff to bless or refuse to bless these reforms – and thereby either to avoid or provoke a schism – because the National Assembly refused to accede to Archbishop Boisgelin's plea to allow the Gallican Church to convene a national council and provincial councils in order to lend its "spiritual" authority to the new legislation.

As of 2 June 1790, therefore, the question of whether the National Assembly possessed the competence as a purely lay body to undertake such an extensive ecclesiastical reform without treading on the church's "spiritual" jurisdiction became the main if largely undebated issue, the closest the debate got to the domain of doctrine. It was on the grounds that a lay assembly had no such power that, on Bishop François de Bonal of Clermont's motion of 2 June, most of the episcopal delegates – some fifty-two in all – refused to debate much less vote on the measures that went into the making of the Civil Constitution of the Clergy. As these bishops persuaded numbers of lesser clerics of their point of view, their boycott took crucial votes away from efforts to amend particular provisions so as to make them more "canonical." To the "right" of the likes of Boisgelin, moreover, sat other clerical delegates such as Bonal or the ultramontanist *abbé* Jean-Claude Goulard, who would never have settled for anything less than papal approval.

In the absence of a national council, or even an invitation from the National Assembly to negotiate with the papacy, the king's foreign minister, Armand Marc, comte de Montmorin, sought to engage the papacy with the advice of the king's ecclesiastical advisors, archbishops Jérôme Champion de Cicé of Bordeaux and Lefranc de Pompignan of Vienne, as well as with the help of the François Joachim, *abbé* de Bernis, France's resident minister in Rome since 1774. What they hoped to obtain from Pius VI was at least the papacy's provisional canonical acceptance of the Civil Constitution's chief features, which they summarized under five headings. From the Revolution's point of view, neither its diplomatic agent nor its partner was ideal, since its legislation had embittered Bernis by curtailing his income from the bishopric of Albi, while Pius VI was already all but at war with the Revolution as temporal sovereign of the papal enclaves of Avignon and the Comtat Venaissin. In fact, Pius VI condemned the principles of the French Revolution as early as in a secret meeting of the Roman Consistory on 29 March 1790.

It was moreover only under pressure that Louis XVI give his royal sanction to the National Assembly's ecclesiastical legislation, at first provisionally on 24 July, and then – even after the bishops of Bordeaux and Vienne had informed him of papal disapproval – more formally a month later. An agonizing wait followed, with Boisgelin and others still hoping that that Pius VI would approve the major headings while Pius VI for his part professed to be waiting to hear from the French episcopacy. Hear from thirty of them he did on 30 October via an *Exposition des principes*, which he chose to interpret as condemnation of the Civil Constitution.

When, in the days that followed, as the National Assembly became aware that the existing metropolitan and even other bishops might refuse to consecrate new bishops elected in accordance with the Civil Constitution's procedure, the Assembly further radicalized the Civil Constitution by stipulating on 15 November that district tribunals might designate any bishop in France to consecrate a newly elected nominee if this candidate met with a refusal by all the bishops in his diocese. It was by means of this decree that Talleyrand consecrated the first two "constitutional" bishops in Paris on 24 February, thus creating bishops who could consecrate other bishops in turn and maintain the principle of episcopal succession.

One of the new bishops that Talleyrand consecrated replaced an existing *ancien régime* bishop because this bishop had refused to take the oath to the new constitution that an impatient National Assembly had imposed on all would-be benefice holders on 27 November. Sanctioned under pressure by the king a month later, this decree first affected the clerical delegates in the Assembly itself, among whom only eighty-one, led by Grégoire, out of 263 took the oath. This number included only two bishops: Talleyrand and Jean-Baptiste Gobel, auxiliary bishop of Basel. So partial was the oath-taking as a whole that the Assembly found itself obliged on 27 January to ask non-jurors to continue to serve their churches until replacements could be recruited. In France as a whole, a mere seven bishops including Loménie de Brienne took the oath as compared to 55 percent of the parish clergy. The same "constitutional" consecrations by Gobel and Talleyrand in late February also forced Pius VI to break his silence with two papal briefs dated on 10 March and 13 April 1790, the first addressed to Boisgelin and Cardinal Dominique de la Rochefoucauld and the other bishops and archbishops in the National Assembly, the second to all the cardinals and the entire clergy of France.

Although neither fulminated any excommunications, these condemnations completed the creation of rival "constitutional" and pro-papal or "refractory" French Catholic clergies and already provoked enough defections from the ranks of the first to the second to take the percentage of oath-swearing clergy members to below 50 percent. Since the rise of the papacy and its curia in the high Middle Ages, no surer way to provoke an intra-Catholic schism had developed than to consecrate bishops without papal confirmation. The consecrations of 24 and 27 February did not fail to do so again.

The Making of the Civil Constitution

The social and geographical map and distribution of the resultant schism has best been tracked by Timothy Tackett in his study of the subject (1986). To a large degree, local histories and particular conditions "on the ground" explain the reception of the Civil Constitution by the clergies and their parishioners in different parts of France. But the variegated nature of that reception is inseparable from the content of the Civil Constitution – what was in it that clergies and people were being asked to accept. This briefest of résumés reveals that the geography of the Civil Constitution's ideological origins is almost as complex as that of its reception.

The simplest explanation for the content of the Civil Constitution would be to insist on the "hard" circumstance of the royal debt and the National Assembly's decision to nationalize it, and therefore the need to nationalize the only body of readily available wealth large enough to pay the nation's creditors. As soon as it found itself obliged to defray the costs of the Catholic cult – or so might go the argument – it was only "natural" for the National Assembly to enlarge its constitution to include the civil or external aspects of the Gallican Church as well. It would also seem to follow that the citizens who now directly paid for the Catholic cult and its clergy should be given a decisive "say" in the choice of what and whom they paid for.

But while the royal debt and deficit may be a necessary condition for the Civil Constitution, it is no more a sufficient cause of its content than it is for the coming or course of the Revolution itself. Toward the end of the debate on the status of church property, the clergy, in the person of Archbishop Boisgelin, offered the National Assembly "whatever it could give" in addition to bearing its fair share of taxes, help that Boisgelin later specified as 400,000 *livre* loan secured against a graduated sale of ecclesiastical property.[8] Had it been accepted, the offer might have prevented the National Assembly from using paper notes simply to meet current expenses instead of liquidating the debt or fashioning a more viable system of taxation (Velde and Weir 1992). But the "patriotic" majority's answer was Isaac-Guy Le Chapelier's peremptory warning to beware bishops bearing gifts. Like Le Chapelier, Adrien Duport and the comte de Mirabeau made it clear that they argued for the nationalization of church property as a matter of principle, and not to pay the state's debts.[9] With no taxes coming in, the deteriorating fiscal situation did not really begin to exert an influence on the National Assembly's decisions until mid-April, when indeed the Assembly turned over the administration of church property to the departments and communes in preparation for sale. But by that time decisions taken in the name of high principle barred any retreat.

Anything beyond the nationalization of the royal debt takes the explanation into territory decidedly ideological, and the ideological influence often invoked is that of Jansensim.[10] Much recommends this hypothesis, if by "Jansenism" is understood the radicalization of Gallicanism in Jansenist hands in alliance with the Parlement of Paris that had justified the independence of the Gallican Church in relation to Rome, the rights of the parish priesthood against their bishops, and the intervention of the state for these and other reasons in the "spiritual" affairs of the church. Thus characterized, Jansenism made a certain contact with the French Enlightenment, especially by way of a residually Cartesian tendency to define the "spiritual" in terms so opposed to the external as to make the church's institutions fair game for reform by a lay assembly in the name of "reason" alone. This thesis of Jansenist influence found contemporary advocates on either side of the revolutionary spectrum. The future ultra counter-revolutionary *abbé* Jacques-Julien Bonnaud announced his "discovery" that the Civil Constitution embodied the Jansenist ideal of the "little church" as early as on the morrow of its passage while, as the schism drew nigh in November 1790, the revolutionary periodical, the *Moniteur*, printed a letter that blamed "the little Jansenist constitution foisted onto the National Assembly in a moment of distraction" for all that was already going awry at that early point.[11]

What can be said at the outset for this hypothesis is that deputies with connections to Jansenism or to Gallican canon law dominated the debate over the provisions of what became the Civil Constitution. These include the barristers Jean-Denis

Lanjuinais, Louis-Simon Martineau, Durand de Maillane, and Jean-Baptiste Treilhard, all of them members of the Ecclesiastical Committee; as well as the barrister Armand-Gaston Camus, the *abbés* Henri Grégoire, Jacques Jallet, and Claude Jacquemard, and still others.

Further, the Civil Constitution undoubtedly contained many features that implemented long-standing Jansenist ideas of ecclesiastical reform. Throughout the eighteenth century, Jansenists had inveighed against the "despotic" behavior of bishops; the Civil Constitution made their decisions subject to the advice and consent of a council composed of *curés.* Jansenists had similarly stood for the right of *curés* to appoint their own curates; the Civil Constitution accorded them that right. For more than a century, mandatory oaths to formularies and bulls condemning Jansenism had disbarred many from the clergy; the Civil Constitution disbarred all such oaths. Toward the end of the century, Jansenism gave theological cover for a movement by *curés* to raise their material condition; the Civil Constitution raised that condition while lowering that of bishops. Increasingly too, Jansenists had championed the cause of the secular clergy in general against the regular clergy and all benefices without cure of souls; the Civil Constitution all but eliminated the non-pastoral clergy. Some Jansenists even came to stand for the "restoration" of the role that the early church had given the "people" in the election of their clergy. The Civil Constitution "restored" that right, although not in the form that Jansenists would have preferred.

While the Civil Constitution failed to restore provincial and national councils or to allow the clergy to participate as a clergy in its own election – both Jansenist desiderata – it did indeed call for regular synods or mini-councils at the diocesan level and factored the "people" into the designation of the clergy. And by abrogating the Concordat of Bologna of 1516, the Civil Constitution bypassed papal consecration entirely in favor of consecration by metropolitans. That the most recent model of such a consecration was that of an archbishop of Utrecht by a dissident – and Jansenist – clergy in the Dutch Republic in 1723 did not escape the attention of the pro-papal deputies in the National Assembly, such as the *abbé* Goulard.[12] Where the suppression of abuses and the restoration of pristine discipline were concerned, most Jansenists could console themselves, as did Grégoire, with the thought that the Civil Constitution had "done more in a moment than a host of councils."[13]

Jansenists also took the lead in defending the Civil Constitution as well as the required oath to the constitution for members of the clergy as soon as both had become objects of intense controversy in 1791. At issue was a purely lay or secular assembly's right to reform the Gallican Church without the formal concurrence of either that church or the papacy – of the "spiritual" power in some form – as well as the nature of the reforms themselves, in particular the ruthless suppression of more than fifty dioceses and the election of bishops and parish priests by "active" citizens alone.

In defense of the National Assembly's competence, the most audacious line of Gallican argument, best articulated by Noël de Larrière, was that because the church was by definition the "assembly of all the faithful," and because with few exceptions in France the "faithful" were also the newly empowered French "citizens" represented by both clerics and laypeople in the National Assembly itself, the Assembly was fully competent to legislate in matters spiritual as well as material.[14] A second argument was that even such reforms as having active citizens act as the clergy's electors and the redrawing the dioceses to conform to France's new administrative divisions did nothing more than restore ancient ecclesiastical discipline that, endowed with every kind of "spiritual" authority, had once allowed the lay "faithful" to elect their clergy and had enshrined the principle that ecclesiastical divisions should follow or conform to imperial ones. In this argument, the needed "spiritual" concurrence or authority was always already at hand in the form of ancient ecclesiastical practice and conciliar decrees, among them the Council of Chalcedon of 451's canon that ecclesiastical divisions should "follow" the imperial ones.[15]

In the end, nothing was more influential in "selling" the Civil Constitution to the part of the clergy that accepted it than the conviction that the combination of poverty and the restoration of putatively original canonical forms would bring about the return of apostolic virtues. Defending the Ecclesiastical Committee's proposals on 30 May, Treilhard spoke for many when he assured the Assembly that, "[f]ar from doing any damage to religion, your decrees will bring back its pristine purity; you will then find yourselves reborn as Christians of the evangelical era, Christians like the apostles and their first disciples."[16]

But if, as even the Civil Constitution's defenders admitted, an electoral form of providing for benefices that excluded the clergy's own participation was without precedent in church history, then a third argument came to the rescue. This argument was that, in reforming the church as it did, even a purely lay assembly acted within its rights because its reforms affected only the external aspects of the church and did not violate the "holy of holies" of a purely spiritual jurisdiction. Against the counter-argument that to alter diocesan boundaries or to orphan fifty bishops was to break the "spiritual" bond or marriage between the bishops and their flocks, the defenders of the Civil Constitution invoked the principle – a genuinely Jansenist one – that only the church's power to preach and administer the sacraments conferred by the sacrament of ordination was spiritual, while its assignment of that power to this or that particular territory was merely material or "ecclesiastical." It was in order to invalidate these arguments as best articulated by Camus and Treilhard in the National Assembly that Bishop François de Bonal of Clermont announced on 2 June that he and his fellow bishops did "not wish to take part in the debates," much less to vote on the Civil Constitution.[17]

Binding and undergirding all of these arguments was the radically Gallican principle that Christ had given the spiritual power or "keys" to the kingdom of heaven, not just to all the apostles and their successors, much less to Peter alone, but to the whole church, and that the clergy merely administered them. Since this same principle defined the "church" as the "assembly of all the faithful," the arguments in defense of the Civil Constitution followed in due course, as so many corollaries from this axiom. While this principle's pedigree went back to late medieval Gallicanism, it was above all French Jansenists in alliance with the *parlements* against the episcopacy and the Jesuits who revived it and drew out its most radical implications. Hammered into shape and honed in the course of a century's

Jansenist-related disputes, all of the arguments saw duty on behalf of the Revolution's ecclesiastical legislation, whether wielded by Jansenists or Gallican canonists versed in this thought. Although the National Assembly abolished the *parlements*, it did so only by stepping into its shoes.

Left to their own devices, however, neither Jansenist nor Gallican Catholics nor any combination of the two would ever have come up with so surgical an implementation of these principles. Never would any or all of them have nationalized all church property, suppressed all cathedral chapters and contemplative orders, eliminated the clergy qua clergy from its own elections, cut and tailored dioceses in order to make them correspond to the new departments, or all but forgo any reference to the papacy. Symptomatic of this diagnosis is that Jansenist opposition to the Civil Constitution emerged outside the National Assembly's confines, as venerable veterans led by the canonist Gabriel-Nicolas Maultrot also criticized the Civil Constitution's most controversial features, challenged the National Assembly's competence, and also squared off in public against such equally Jansenist defenders of the Civil Constitution as Camus and Noël de Larrière, author of the influential *Préservatif contre le schisme* (Fauchois 1990).[18]

The divisive effect of the Civil Constitution on even the relatively small late eighteenth-century Jansenist group holds *a fortiori* for the much larger Gallican community including the bishops both within and outside the National Assembly. Although heretofore nominated by the monarchy, as bishops in the Gallican Church they had an interest in that aspect of the Gallican tradition that gave their church a modicum of independence from the state as well as from the papacy. And although France's "absolute" monarchy had never permitted the Gallican Church to hold national councils since the late Middle Ages – its periodical general assembly had met for fiscal purposes only – its members were bound as good Gallicans to try to compensate for the loss of their property and status as the state's first order by enhancing their "spiritual" authority in the form of national and provincial councils.

The hoary Gallican tradition stood for two distinct sets of liberties. The first and most obvious was the church's liberties in liturgical usages and canon law and right to "concur" with the papacy's doctrinal judgments – liberties vis-à-vis the papacy – while the second consisted in the monarchy's independence from any temporal effects of the papacy's judgments – its answerability to God alone. Although the royal state had traditionally stood by and protected the Gallican Church's liberties from the papacy, its defense of its own temporal jurisdiction from the church's judgments had often translated into an erosion of the Gallican Church's independence in relation to the state. On the rise since the sixteenth-century wars of religion, this trend reached its apogee during the eighteenth-century Jansenist conflict when the Parlement of Paris all but usurped the role of articulating the Gallican tradition by taking the Jansenist side against the monarchy and most bishops. The conflict had placed a part of Gallican episcopacy in the ironic position of defending papal or "ultramontanist" authority against Gallicanism as interpreted by Jansenists and the *parlements*.

But that was back then. The cooling of the Jansenist controversy after 1765 plus an entente between the *parlements* and the bishops in defense of "property" had allowed the bishops to recover a Gallicanism free from contamination by Jansensim, in least in the sense of their independence from Rome. Never perhaps in the eighteenth century were the Gallican bishops more Gallican than on the eve of the French Revolution. It was hence their singular misfortune in 1790 to find themselves confronted by a constitution that, besides giving them more independence from the papacy than they had ever wanted, also made them more dependent on the state in revolutionary form than had the Parlement at its most Jansenist. By disallowing the convening of a national or series of provincial councils, the National Assembly also put the Gallican clergy at the mercy of the papacy for the canonical "baptism" they thought it needed. If ever there was a formula for re-creating a Gallican episcopacy as papal if not more so than the pope, the Civil Constitution of the Clergy was it.

It was perhaps also a misfortune for the episcopal delegates in the National Assembly to be represented in its first Ecclesiastical Committee by two of their least Gallican or flexible bishops: Marie-Charles-Isidore de Mercy, bishop of Luçon, and François de Bonal, bishop of Clermont. It was they, according to Pierre-Toussaint Durand de Maillane, who pursued a policy of passive resistance to the work of the committee, beginning with the implementation of the decree nationalizing church property, even though numbers of other bishops had accepted that decree with good grace. The chief casualty of their resistance was a more "moderate" project that would have included the clergy and even the king as well as the "people" in the nomination of bishops and selection of *curés*. Aware that the committee was deadlocked, and with the issue of monastic orders coming up, an impatient National Assembly doubled the number of deputies on the committee on 5–7 February 1790, whereupon Bonal and Mercy as well as others resigned from it. The result was a committee more radically inclined than the first, reinforced by "philosophic" deputies such as Dupont de Nemours and Dionis du Séjour.[19]

Is it here, in the "influence" of such "philosophes," that the roots of the radicalism of the Civil Constitution are to be found? The French Enlightenment, it is true, stands out among national variants of enlightenment for its virulent anti-clericalism and anti-Catholicism – even its hostility to all revealed religion. That hostility in turn had to do with two structural factors that are similarly salient in France in contrast to the rest of Catholic as well as Protestant Europe. In the form of the Jansenist controversy, first of all, France produced the most virulent and durable religious conflict of the entire century of lights. Not only did this conflict produce fissures between Gallican and ultramontanist Catholicism that, barely healed after 1765, began to reassert themselves in the early Revolution, but also a variety of anti-clerical *philosophes* to whom the National Assembly gave an unprecedented platform. One reason why this controversy had so festered, second, was that both sides found strongholds within institutions that the monarchy could not do without and had no counterparts elsewhere in Europe: Jansenism in the Parlement of Paris and episcopal opposition to it in the General Assembly of the Gallican Clergy. While the "absolute" monarchy could in principle override the opposition of either institution, its very policy of circumventing national consent to taxes in order to maintain its absolute authority had ironically made it fiscally dependent on both: on the office-owning magistrates of the

Parlement for registration of new taxes and loans, and on the general assembly to finance its loans from the clergy. This unique power of the Gallican clergy further fueled French anti-clericalism.

Present in the diffuse form of a general concern for moral and social "utility" in Jansenist and "philosophical" parlance alike, the "influence" of the French Enlightenment in the making of the Civil Constitution remains elusive in detail. In the vast pamphlet literature accompanying the crisis of the *ancien régime*, expressions of vulgar Voltairianism or hell-bent Holbachianism surface only as trace elements, even when the subject is the clergy.[20] In the debates of the National Assembly leading up to and including the Civil Constitution, only Mirabeau and Jérome Pétion de Villeneuve allowed themselves a few anti-clerical barbs such as those against pious "ignorance" and "superstition" in the accumulation of ecclesiastical property, in Mirabeau's case reminders of the clergy's intolerance as displayed in the St. Bartholomew's Day Massacre and the revocation of the Edict of Nantes.[21] Although at street level cries of "down with the [clerical] cap" made themselves heard as popular attention turned toward ecclesiastical property in the autumn of 1789, nothing more specifically "enlightened" characterized these catcalls than those from the galleries that hissed down speeches by the militantly clerical *abbé* Jean-Siffien Maury.

In one precise respect, however, the contribution of the Enlightenment – or a certain aspect of the French Enlightenment – proved decisive in the shaping of the Civil Constitution, accounting for its curiously incompatible aims of restoring the primitive church while reducing it to a department of state.

The aspect of enlightenment in question is the Rousseauvian hostility to the "particular interest" of partial associations paradoxically combined with a physiocratic hostility to the interest of artificial corporate bodies, most especially in the domain of landed property. Although never cited in these debates, Rousseau spoke through Pétion and Maximilien Robespierre. The only eighteenth-century *philosophe* whose name was explicitly invoked was the sometime Controller-General Anne-Robert Turgot on the subject of foundations. Opining that "to cite Turgot was to attest to the truth itself," Isaac-René-Guy Le Chapelier, for example, appealed to his authority to support the contention that "foundations exist only by virtue of the law," the law being the will of the nation.[22] Best articulated by Mirabeau and Jacques-Guillaume Thouret, this principle was that individuals alone were the bearers of "natural" rights, including the right to own property, and that corps only existed and at most acted as the "dispenser" of donated property by virtue of laws enacted by the collective will of individuals after they formally bonded as nations.[23] Against this principle it was in vain that critics including Grégoire and Joseph-Michel Pellerin among others argued to the effect that corps probably preceded the formation of nations, that the "nation" was a corps as well, or that the real owners of corporate property were the particular institutions that donors' bequests had founded.[24]

The foundational acts to which all proponents of this argument appealed were the ones whereby the Estates-General decided to become a "National Assembly" – 16, 20, 23, and 27 June 1789 – and even more so the legislation of 4–11 August 1789, which in principle abolished all privileges attached to particular corps, cities, and provinces. Nothing intrinsically anti-clerical characterized the anti-corporate corollary drawn from these premises, as it was made to apply to guilds and workers' associations by Le Chapelier in 1791. But the extension of these foundational decisions to strip the church of every semblance of corporate presence probably went well beyond the intentions of most of the willing parties to these acts.

Lest this "philosophic" anti-corporatist contribution to the mix itself remain unmixed, it should be added that these deputies only clearly articulated a deeply embedded and widely shared absolutist political apriority that, as classically defined by Jean Bodin, could not think of sovereignty in other than indivisible terms. All parties to the *ancien régime*'s political conflicts including the clergy and the *parlements* shared in it to one degree or another, holding against each other the very corporate power and "independence" from the monarchy that venality and the monarchy's fiscal needs had given them.

In any event, it was the anti-corporate argument that lay behind the National Assembly's refusal to leave any landed property in the hands of the clergy. It was with this rebuttal, for example, that Le Chapelier cut down pleas by such "patriotic" priests as the *abbés* Grégoire and Jean-Louis Gouttes to endow the parish clergy with land: to leave any property in the hands of clergymen, he held, was to give them an excuse to administer it and "to rise from [their] ashes and to reconstitute [themselves] as an order."[25] When again, on 9 June, the *abbé* Jacquemard came close to persuading the National Assembly to allow the clergy to take a hand in the election of its own members, his canonically correct argument fell victim to the guillotine of Robespierre's refutation that to give the clergy "a particular political influence," even in filling its own ranks, was tantamount to "reconstituting a solitary corps."[26] The defeat of Jacquemard's attempt to make some of the provisions of the Civil Constitution more canonical was all the more devastating in that it was due in part to the refusal of many of the clerical deputies to debate or vote at all. Why? Because to do so would be to recognize the National Assembly's right to reform the Gallican Church on its own "secular" authority alone. Why did the Assembly maintain this right? Because to allow the Gallican clergy to meet in order to give its canonical blessing to the reform would be to recognize its existence as a separate corps.

It goes without saying that revolutionary ideology's exclusion of separate corps also excluded the possibility of separating the church from state on the recent American model, or as even Alexandre de Lauzières-Thémines, the bishop of Blois, seriously suggested in 1791.[27] To separate the Gallican Church from the regenerated state would leave it free as a separate corps. Out of the Jansenist, Gallican, and "enlightened" conceptual elements in the ideological magma, what emerged was the implausible project of restoring the primitive church as a department of state.

The Making of the Papal Condemnation

Unable to "baptize" the Civil Constitution itself, the Gallican clergy therefore ironically found itself at the mercy of the papacy for the canonical "baptism" that so many of its members thought it needed. So it was with the National Assembly's tacit if not explicit permission that Montmorin, seconded by Champion de Cicé, an ailing Lefranc de Pompignan, and even Boisgelin tried to persuade the papacy to provide the same kind of canonical enabling that it had done for the suppression of annates earlier on. In one of the best books he ever published, the great French socialist historian Albert Mathiez stretched an argument for contingency to the breaking point, reasoning that if only Montmorin had been served at Rome by an ambassador less duplicitous than Cardinal Bernis, or if only the National Assembly had held out the prospect of a possible restoration of papal authority in Avignon and the Comtat Venaissin a little longer, or if only the same assembly had imposed its oath and ultimatum to the episcopacy a little earlier – if only the chief actors in this tragedy had played their roles a little differently – the drama might have ended with the needed papal blessing and the tragedy of a schism avoided (Mathiez 1911).

What is true is that both the ministry and much of the episcopacy sincerely hoped that a canonical enabling act by the papacy was possible, that the papacy waited until after the first episcopal consecrations to publicize its disapproval, and that the seven long months the papacy allowed to elapse – from 24 July 1790 to 10 March 1791 – fostered illusions that an accord might be within reach even while they gave time for an indigenous clerical opposition to the Civil Constitution to gain traction. That opposition enabled Pope Pius VI to speak for at least part of the Gallican clergy when speak he finally did.

The cardinal Giovanni Angelo Braschi, who became Pius VI in 1775, donned the tiara determined not to endure the kind of humiliation just suffered by his predecessor at the hands of the Bourbon monarchies, which had forced the papacy to dissolve the Society of Jesus. No degree of counter-factual imagination makes it easy to imagine him signing on to something like the Civil Constitution. That said, it was still during his watch that Emperor Joseph II of Austria also suppressed monasteries, redrew dioceses, limited the contact between Austrian bishops and Rome, took over the determination of degrees of consanguinity for marriage, inaugurated a policy of civil toleration of Jews and Protestants, and even altered forms of Catholic piety – all this while avoiding papal condemnation. Meanwhile his younger brother Peter Leopold not only promulgated similar ecclesiastical legislation in nearby Habsburg Tuscany but also sponsored an anti-papal synod in Pistoia that professed a very Jansenist credo while also enshrining the Gallican liberties as revealed truths. True it is too that Pius VI "baptized" the creation of the entirely new diocese of Mohilew in the part of Poland newly annexed by Catherine the Great of Russia, who, though not even a Catholic, had named her own protégé to this see and unilaterally raised it to the level of an archdiocese (Plongeron et al. 1997: 123–124). If the king's ministers hoped to persuade the papacy to "swallow" the Civil Constitution, it was not without these proximate precedents in mind.

But it is equally true that, in thumbing their noses at papal authority, neither the Habsburg powers, much less Catherine the Great, had asked for papal approval. In the French case, however, it was not only the king of France but the notoriously independent Gallican bishops themselves who, on 30 October 1790, published an "exposition" of their principles that, though still asking for the National Assembly's permission to hold provincial councils, concluded with a supreme appeal for an approving reply "from the successor of Saint Peter."[28]

Then too, neither the Habsburgs nor Catherine the Great had produced any censurable pronouncement accompanying their acts such as the Civil Constitution, while Pius VI not only had that document before him but also the Declaration of the Rights of Man and of the Citizen. As it was, the papacy condemned nearly every publication that justified the actions of the Habsburgs, including Johann Nikolaus Von Hontheim's (alias Febronius's) *De statu ecclesiae* in 1764 and Josef Eybel's *Was ist der Papst?* When, inspired by Febronius' German adaptation of Gallican episcopalism, the four imperial archbishops of Mainz, Trier, Cologne, and Salzburg issued a statement of the rights of bishops against the papal project of establishing a new nuncio in Bavaria in the *Punctatio* at Ems in 1788, Pius responded with a point-by-point refutation in 1789.[29] On the very day that Pius VI convoked the first meeting of a congregation of cardinals to examine the Civil Constitution – 24 September 1790 – the first of three successive congregations that judged and condemned the acts of the synod of Pistoia finished its work (Pelletier 2004: 78). The same cardinals who judged the synod of Pistoia took their places on the new congregation; and if, as it happened, their judgment of the unmistakably Gallican and Jansenist acts of Pistoia was to end in the resounding condemnation of the bull *Auctorem Fidei* in 1794, little chance remained that their judgment of the far more radical Civil Constitution would be any more charitable.

Last but not least, none of these other acts or documents emanated from "below" or came accompanied by the watchwords of "liberty, equality, and fraternity" as did the Civil Constitution. Reacting to the National Assembly's suppression of religious orders and refusal to declare Catholicism to be the religion of the regenerated France, Pius VI had in fact already condemned these acts along with the principles of religious and civil toleration – even "the vain phantom" of political liberty – in a closed meeting of the papal consistory on 29 March 1790 (Pelletier 2000: 797–798).

What Mathiez did not take into account was the direct influence of a militantly Roman and unapologetically "ultramontanist" school of theology and ecclesiology that, supported by Pius VI himself and, grouped around the periodical *Giornalo ecclesiastico di Roma*, had gathered momentum in reaction to the exportation of Gallicanism in the form of Josephism and Febronianism and the radical program of national and anti-curial ecclesiastical reform to which these labels refer (Pignatelli 1974). Prominent among the cardinals who judged the Civil Constitution was a significant contributor to this school, namely Hyacinthe Sigismund Gerdil, author of a widely read refutation of Rousseau's *Émile* as well as two defenses of the Pius VI's brief *Super Soliditate* against Eybel's *Was ist der Papst?*

Published on the eve of the Revolution, that brief enunciated many of this school's chief theses in adamantly unadorned form. The bishop of Rome was Peter's only successor and sole vicar of Christ, the Roman see the only truly apostolic one. Far from being the merely honorific first among episcopal equals as in Eybel's ecclesiology, the pope was the only universal bishop, as Christ's vicar the only unique bishop, and the sole pastor of the entire church including all the other pastors, who received their jurisdictions only by ecclesiastical law as applied by him. And far from deriving his authority from church councils, his authority preceded the tenure of any councils, the decrees of which were binding after papal approval alone. Given such principles, it followed that the Roman see alone possessed the authority to confirm – or infirm – episcopal consecrations, without which they were schismatic. Last but not least, all of these tenets belonged to the domain of dogma rather than that of ecclesiastical law alone. Thus did the brief condemn all of the premises and provisions of the Civil Constitution in advance.[30]

Nor did it advance the chances of the Civil Constitution in Rome that the same principles underwrote the challenge to Pius VI's authority as temporal sovereign of Avignon and the Comtat Venaissin, where pro-French revolutionary "patriots" had come close to cutting their ties with Rome. At same time, however, revolts and revolutions from "below" elsewhere in Catholic Europe tended to take a pro-papal turn. In Habsburg Brabant and Flanders, violent popular and priestly reaction to Joseph's Gallican-like ecclesiastical legislation widened in 1789 when the emperor suspended the "joyous constitution" for fiscal reasons, culminating with the defeat and expulsion of Austrian troops in 1790. Closer to home in Habsburg Tuscany, revolts against Grand Duke Peter Leopold's Jansenist-style ecclesiastical reforms including the synod of Pistoia in 1787 broke out anew in the spring of 1790 and caused Leopold's successor and son Ferdinand III to rescind all of his father's "enlightened" legislation. Feeling the tide turning and the wind behind him, well might the pope have hoped for a similar turn of events in France. He was eventually to get a religious revolt, but not before the Vendée and parts of the south erupted in revolt against the Convention in 1793.

Louis XVI assured the National Assembly of his intent to approve the Civil Constitution on 22 July – a day before his ministers received the pope's warning that to do so would be to take the road toward schism. That letter did not deter the king from giving the law his approval the next day, nor from having Montmorin send proposals for papal action on 1 August. What the foreign secretary asked for was the pope's provisional canonical blessing on key propositions, including the new diocesan map of France, the popular election of bishops and *curés*, the replacement of cathedral chapters with episcopal councils, and the power of bishops to grant dispensations from canon law (Mathiez 1911: 268–272; Pelletier 2004: 84). Assuring the papacy of the National Assembly's intention not to touch doctrine, as well as of the possibility of revising the substance of the legislation later, the foreign minister stressed the need for speed in order to avoid a schism.

The person Montmorin depended on to persuade Pius VI to bless these propositions was Cardinal Bernis, who still represented France in Rome despite his distaste for the Revolution at home. In figuratively as well as literally translating his instructions for papal consumption, Bernis subtly altered their tenor by holding that the king's approval had been forced, by inviting an examination of the Civil Constitution itself, and by even suggesting that the papacy's canonical blessing might begin with a condemnation of the "erroneous" principles of the French Revolution.[31] Far from the quick action pleaded for by Montmorin, Pius VI appointed a congregation of twenty cardinals that did not meet until 24 September, then took another month to digest the cardinals' different opinions. The effect of Bernis' diplomacy was also to direct papal attention away from the king and toward the Gallican bishops, a direction reinforced on 21 September when the news reached Rome that meanwhile Louis XVI had officially promulgated the Civil Constitution without waiting for the pope's judgment. From that point forward, Pius VI justified his repeated delays by alleging the need to hear from the French bishops.

A recent analysis of the opinions of the cardinals consulted reveals a surprising flexibility at the level of detail by some of them, even among the so-called *zelanti* or pro-curial hardliners. But none deemed the provisional propositions, much less the actual provisions, of the Civil Constitution acceptable as they were, nor did any think them free of doctrinal implications. Beneath the details of the legislation, the cardinals most hostile to the propositions perceived a "schismatic system tending toward the total extermination of religion," indeed, nothing less than the aim of "undermining all power both human and divine," behind which threats not a few of them descried Jansenism at work (Pelletier 2004: 125–161, esp. 137). Nor of course did any of the cardinals accept the authority of the National Assembly to legislate at all on ecclesiastical matters.

But neither for the most part did the Gallican bishops, including those still in the National Assembly, which, failing a national council, is why they had looked to the royal ministry that included two bishops for help in getting papal approval in the first place. Yet Pius VI's undoubted awareness of this situation did not prevent him from invoking his desire to hear from the Gallican bishops. Reported by Bernis on 17 August, the first reason given by Pius VI for not approving the propositions was the fear of angering some of the French bishops, although only two of them had publicly rejected the Civil Constitution at that point (Mathiez 1911: 294–296). But another reason the pope alleged for his public silence, that he was fearful of further "irritating" already fired-up French emotions, may be taken at face value, since that anger would have been directed against Rome.[32]

Yet the pope's dominant reason that he needed to hear more precisely from the French episcopate persisted even after the publication of the thirty bishops' *Exposition des principes* of 30 October. While repeating the reservations about the canonicity of the Civil Constitution previously stated by Boisgelin, that exposé was all in favor of accommodation and compromise and finished with a plea for Rome's canonical aid and succor. In lieu of any such help, Pius chose to read the *Exposition* as an outright condemnation of the Civil Constitution and, still asking for the bishops' opinions, on 14 December convened another meeting of the cardinals whose advice was to reject Boisgelin's eleventh-hour reformulation of the enabling propositions. Whether intended or not, the effect of the papal insistence on postponing public papal judgment until the Gallican bishops had been heard from was to hoist the Gallican bishops on their own petard, or to allow enough time to elapse for French episcopal sentiment to become sufficiently "irritated" against the Civil Constitution, so that the Gallican bishops would be seen as exercising their cherished concurrence in a papal condemnation of a constitution embodying a one-sided version of – Gallicanism.

Pius VI took nearly three more months before sending his long-awaited brief entitled *Quod Aliquantum*, dated 10 March 1791. When it came, it addressed the bishops in the National Assembly rather than the king, whose lack of liberty the brief noted. The brief rejected the National Assembly's distinction between doctrine as spiritual and the ecclesiastical as temporal, instead condemning the distinction itself as heretical. As Bernis had advised the pope, the brief condemned the revolutionary concept of "rights in society" including "absolute liberty," a principle the brief attributed to the National Assembly's usurpation of both spiritual and temporal power and intention of "destroying the Catholic religion" along with "the obedience due to kings." While the main target was "modern *philosophes*," the brief traced the ancestry of the National Assembly's principles to the history of heresies running from the Waldensians to Gallicans and Jansenists by way of Luther and Calvin.[33] Instead of following Bernis' advice in granting provisional canonical status to the ministry's propositions, the brief condemned them all in line with the harshest of the most hard-line cardinals' opinions.

Yet that condemnation did not prevent Pius from persisting in challenging the Gallican bishops to "find ... some [canonical] expedient that does no injury to Catholic dogma and the universal discipline of the church" in order to avert a schism, as though they had anything left to say or do about it.[34]

For that reason, perhaps, *Quod Aliquantum* withheld its formal fire, although it took Talleyrand to task for taking the oath to the constitution imposed on would-be benefice holders by the National Assembly on 27 November 1790. In France, meanwhile, push had come to shove between departmental officials and "*ancien régime*" bishops who refused either to take the oath or to vacate their sees. Papal patience ran out after the news reached Rome on 24 February 1791 that Talleyrand had taken the place of the oath-refusing metropolitan of Rennes by consecrating Louis-Alexandre Expilly as bishop of Quimper along with another newly elected nominee in place of the oath-refusing bishop of Soissons – a performance repeated three days later by another of the seven oath-taking bishops, Jean-Joseph Gobel, the future constitutional bishop of Paris. Promulgated on 13 April, the papal brief *Charitas* was therefore less charitable. It declared all these bishops to be schismatic, their consecrations sacrilegious, suspended all these churchmen and others from their functions, and gave all those who had sworn the oath of 27 November 1790 forty days to retract it on pain of the same penalties.[35] Thus did the careers of the rival "constitutional" and "refractory" churches begin, as did the schism that separated them.

Conclusion

Like a circle of dominoes in serried falls, the ecclesiastical schism that began in 1791 set off other schisms, each less ecclesiastical and more political in its turn before they all together impinged on the religion and its relation to the revolutionary state. But as these dominoes were arranged in a circle, with none of them perfectly aligned with its nearest neighbors and some of them farther apart than others, the various schisms came in various degrees of unavoidability before coming, as did the Revolution, full circle.

Most unavoidable was the strictly ecclesiastical schism that split the oath-taking clergy on the one side from the papacy and "refractory" clergy that sided with the papacy on the other. But this schism was already multiple. For while the papacy never formally excommunicated the constitutional clergy, portions of the refractory clergy eventually did so in effect, since they refused to recognize the validity of the sacraments of baptism and marriage performed by members of the constitutional clergy and, like Donatists of old, insisted on rebaptism and remarriage for laypeople who changed sides. At "ground level" the schism was hence religious as well as ecclesiastical, much to the torment, even graveyard, of lay consciences.

Although after the Concordat of 1801 the papacy eventually reintegrated members of the constitutional clergy into the hierarchy, numbers of the formerly refractory clergy similarly refused to do so in fact.

Given the National Assembly's decision to integrate the Gallican Church more tightly within the state rather than to separate the two – a big given – a political schism was just about as unavoidable as the ecclesiastical one. This political schism divided the papacy and the refractory clergy on the one side from the Revolution and those who sided with it on the other. Reading the bishops' *Exposition* of 30 October exactly as did the papacy – as a flat rejection of the Civil Constitution – the National Assembly interpreted attempts to get adhesions to it as the first signs of a "counter-revolution" as early as November 1790.[36] In the event, this assumption was to prove self-fulfilling. Attempts to apply the Revolution's principle of religious toleration to the "refractory" church fell prey to popular hostility on the revolutionary side. The result was not only the transformation of the refractory clergy into opponents of the Revolution as well as of opposition to the Revolution into a veritable Counter-Revolution, but the recruitment of the monarchy to that cause. This much already entailed terror.

Most contingent and elusive but just as momentous was a third hybrid political and ecclesiastical schism that split the Gallican tradition. An incoherent product of the ideologically heterogeneous mix that went into its making, the Civil Constitution entirely sacrificed the conciliar and associative to the royal or statist side of the Gallican tradition. The result was a refractory clergy that was as Gallican in one sense as was the constitutional clergy in another, and also – with the exception of the episcopacy – just about as plebian as well. The Revolution therefore found itself unable to interpret this clergy's opposition as either uniquely ultramontanist or aristocratic, leaving it with only with Catholic religious "fanaticism" and "superstition" against which to channel its ire. Revolutionary hostility therefore eventually fell on constitutional and refractory clergies alike, depriving the Revolution of all traditionally religious support and making the Terror more terrible still. If schism there had to be, the Revolution might have finessed a more usable schism.

The long-term consequences could not have been more momentous, not only for France but for the rest of Catholic Europe: the transformation of late eighteenth-century conflict between forms of Gallicanism and ultramontanism into one between militant republican unbelief and an intransigent conservative Catholicism, the replacement of the conflict between the temporal and spiritual powers by a tension between the public sphere and a privatized religion, and the eventual disappearance of Gallicanism from Gaul itself.

Notes

1 In order to minimize the references, I have regarded much of the following information as common knowledge, for which we are indebted to classic works on this subject by historians from Pierre de la Gorce to Bernard Plongeron. In addition to the editor, Peter McPhee, I wish to thank my friend Carolina Armenteros, my colleague James Bartholomew, my fellow *dix-huitièmiste* Thomas Kaiser, and my graduate student Mircea Platon for their helpful suggestions for improving this chapter.

2 Besides being textually evident, the existence of ministerial patronage of pamphleteering is alluded to in Hardy 1764–89: MS 6686, 17 Aug. 1787, 180; or MS 6687, 18 July 1788, 21.
3 *Archives parlementaires* (1867–1913), henceforth *AP*, 2 July 1789, 8: 182–183.
4 *AP*, 6 Aug. 1789, 8: 354; 8 Aug. 1789, 8: 369–370; 10 Aug. 1789, 8: 380–382.
5 *AP*, 10 Oct. 1789, 9: 402; 12 Oct. 1789, 9: 408–409; 2 Nov. 1789, 9: 649.
6 Martineau 1790.
7 *AP*, 2 June 1790, 16: 44.
8 On Boisgelin's offers, *AP*, 31 Oct. 1789, 9: 622, but in general 615–625; and 12 Apr. 1790, 12: 691–698.
9 *AP*, for Le Chapelier, 2 Nov. 1789, 9: 639; Duport, 23 Oct. 1789, 9: 484–485; Mirabeau, 30 Oct. 1789, 9: 607–609.
10 This subject has provoked an imposing scholarly literature, at the center of which lies Edmond Préclin, *Les Jansénistes du XVIIIe siècle* (1929). Estimates of degrees of Jansenist "influence" in the making and defense of the Civil Constitution rate it as strong or weak depending on the width or narrowness of the operative characterizations of "Jansenism." My own "take" on the subject is spelled out in some detail in Van Kley (1996: 352–360), and assesses the Jansenist contribution more generously than does Préclin. What has become clear in recent work on the Roman side of the schism is that the papacy perceived the Civil Constitution though the lens of its recent jousts with forms of Italian Jansenism. What is essential in this analysis is that the "Enlightenment" and "Jansenism" not be reified as mutually exclusive categories, but rather recognized as mutually porous and influential phenomena.
11 Bonnaud n.d.: 9–10; and *Le Moniteur* (1853–68): no. 314, 10 Nov. 1790, "mélanges," 1298.
12 *AP*, 31 May 1790, 16: 13–14.
13 Grégoire 1791: 30.
14 Larrière 1791b: 10.
15 Charrier de la Roche 1791: 63–65.
16 *AP*, 30 May 1790, 15: 571.
17 *AP*, for Camus, 31 May 1790, 16: 3–10; 1 June 1790, 16: 33–35; 2 June 1790, 16: 45. For Treihard, 30 May 1790, 15: 744–751.
18 Larrière 1791a.
19 Durand de Maillane 1791: 6–7, 26–28, 33–34, 38–41, 71.
20 For example, *Les Sept péchés capitaux* (1787): 3–4.
21 *AP*, 31 Oct. 1789, 9: 625; 13 Apr. 1790, 12: 717–718.
22 *AP*, 2 Nov. 1789, 9: 639.
23 *AP*, for Thouret, 23, 30 Oct. 1789, 9: 485–487, 611; for Mirabeau, 30 Oct. and 2 Nov. 1789, 9: 607–609, 639–645.
24 *AP*, 23–24 Oct. 1789, 9: 492, 518.
25 *AP*, 2 Nov. 1789, 9: 639.
26 *AP*, 9 June 1790, 16: 154–156; Royou and Montjoie 1791: 10 June 1790, 39.
27 Lauzières-Thémines [1791]: 12.
28 Boisgelin et al. 1790: 24–26.
29 Pius VI 1790.
30 Pius VI, *Super Soliditate*, in Pelletier 2000: 3: 789–796.
31 This conclusion emerges from a close examination of Mathiez' case against Bernis in *Rome et le clergé français sous la Constituante* in Mathiez 1911: 283–289; and Pelletier's attempt to clear Bernis of his charges of betrayal of his diplomatic mission in Pelletier 2004: 125–130, 152, 164, 166–167.

32 Pius VI, "Recentia decreta," a letter to Jean-Georges Lefranc de Pompignan, 10 July 1790, in Pelletier 2000: 802 ; "Intimo ingemiscimus," letter to Louis XVI, 22 Sept. 1790, ibid., 809; and *Quod Aliquantum*, 10 Mar. 1791, ibid., 810.

33 Pius VI, *Quod Aliquantum*, in Pelletier 2000: 813–814, 816, 819–822, 827–828. That Pius VI's main target was "enlightened" philosophy is evident in his excoriation of the "furors of incredulity" in "Recentia decreta," ibid., 802; against the "profound incredulity and the stubbornness of this century" in "Intimo ingemiscimus," ibid., 805, and *Charitas*, ibid., 846.

34 *Quod Aliquantum*, in Pelletier 2000: 833.

35 Pius VI, *Charitas*, 13 Apr. 1791, in Pelletier 2000: 843–844.

36 The expression is Mirabeau's in *AP*, 26 Nov. 1790, 21: 10.

References

Primary Manuscript Sources

Hardy, Siméon-Prosper (1764–89). "Mes loisirs, ou Journal d'événements tels qu'ils parviennent à ma connaissance," 8 vols. Bibliothèque Nationale, Manuscrits Français 6680–6687.

Primary Printed Sources

AP: Archives parlementaires de 1787 à 1860. Recueil complet des débats législatifs et politiques des chambres françaises, imprimé par ordre du corps législatif sous la direction de mm. J. Mavidal et E. Laurent. Première série, 1787–1799 (1867–1913), 82 vols. Paris: P. Dupont.

Boisgelin, Jean de Cucé de, et al. (1790). *Exposition des principes sur la Constitution civile du clergé, par les évêques, députés à l'Assemblée nationale.* Paris: Herissant.

Bonnaud, Jacques-Julien (n.d. [1791]). *Découverte importante sur le vrai système de la Constitution du clergé, décrétée par l'Assemblée nationale.* Paris: Crapart.

Charrier de La Roche, Louis (1791). *Questions sur les affaires présentes de l'Église de France, avec des réponses propre à tranquiliser les consciences.* Paris: Le Clere.

Durand de Maillane, Pierre-Toussaint (1791). *Histoire apologétique du Comité ecclésiastique de l'Assemblée nationale.* Paris: F. Buisson.

Grégoire, Henri (1791). *Légitimité du serment civique exigé des fonctionnaires ecclésiastiques, par M. Grégoire, curé d'Embermenil, député du département de la Meurthe.* Paris: Imprimerie Nationale.

Larrière, Noël Jean-Baptiste Castera de (1791a). *Préservatif contre le schisme, ou Questions relatives au décret du 27 novembre 1790.* Paris: Le Clere.

Larrière, Noël Jean-Baptiste Castera de (1791b). *Suite du Préservatif contre le schisme, ou Nouveau développement des principes qui y sont établis.* Paris: Le Clere.

Lauzières-Thémines, Alexandre (n.d. [1791]). *Lettre de M. l'évêque de Blois à MM. les administrateurs du département du Loir-et-Cher.* n.p.

Le Moniteur universel, also known as the *Gazette national* (1853–68). 68 vols. Paris: H. Agasse.

Les sept péchés capitaux, ou Exemples tires de l'état ecclésiastique, occupant actuellement le clergé de France, par un ex-ci-devant soi-disant j... (1787). Paris: chez le prieur de l'abbaye de St-Germain des Près.

Martineau, Louis-Simon (1790). *Rapport fait à l'Assemblée nationale au nom du Comité ecclésiastiaque, par M. Martineau, député de la ville de Paris, sur la Constitution du clergé.* Paris: Imprimerie Nationale.

Pie VI (2000). "Recueil des principaux brefs du pape Pie VI." In Gérard Pelletier (ed.). "La Théologie et la politique du Saint-Siège devant la Révolution française (1789–99)." Ph.D. dissertation. Université de Paris, Sorbonne IV, and Institut Catholique de Paris, vol. 3.

Pius VI (1790). *Responsio ad Metropolitanos Moguntium, Trevirensem, Coloniensem, et Salisburgensem Super Nunciaturis postolicis.* Liège: Jacobi Tutot.

Royou, Abbé Thomas-Marie, Galard de Montjoie, et al. (eds.) (1791). *L'Ami du roi, des français, de l'ordre et sur-tout de la vérité, par les continuateurs de Fréron.* Paris: Crapart.

Secondary Sources

Baker, Keith Michael (2011). "Enlightenment Idioms, Old Regime Discourses, and Revolutionary Improvisations." In Thomas E. Kaiser and Dale K. Van Kley (eds.). *From Deficit to Deluge: The Origins of the French Revolution.* Stanford, Calif.: Stanford University Press. 165–197.

Fauchois, Yann (1990). "Les Jansénistes et la Constitution civile du clergé." In Catherine L. Maire (ed.). *Jansénisme et Révolution.* Paris: Bibliothèque Mazarine. 195–207.

Furet, François and Denis Richet (1970). *The Revolution*, trans. Stephen Hardman. New York: Macmillan. 122–146.

Hermon-Belot, Rita (2000). *L'Abbé Grégoire. La Politique et la vérité: L'Abbé Grégoire et la Révolution française.* Paris: Seuil.

Hutt, Maurice (1955). "The Role of the *Curés* in the Estates-General of 1789." *Journal of Ecclesiastical History*, 6: 190–220.

McManners, John (1998). *Church and Society in Eighteenth-Century France*, vol. 2: *The Religion of the People and the Politics of Religion.* Oxford: Clarendon Press.

Mathiez, Albert (1911). *Rome et le clergé française sous la Constituente: La Constitution civile du clergé, l'affaire d'Avignon.* Paris: Armand Colin.

Necheles, Ruth (1974). "The Curés and the Estates-General of 1789." *JMH*, 46: 124–144.

Pelletier, Gérard (ed.) (2000). "La Théologie et la politique du Saint-Siège devant la Révolution française (1789–99)." Ph.D. dissertation. Université de Paris, Sorbonne IV, and Institut Catholique de Paris, vol. 3.

Pelletier, Gérard (2004). *Rome et la Révolution française: La Théologie et la politique du Saint-Siège devant la Révolution française (1789–99).* Rome: École Française de Rome.

Pignatelli, Giuseppe (1974). *Aspetti della propaganda cattolica a Roma, da Pio VI a Leone XII.* Rome: Istituto per la Storia del Risorgimento Italiano.

Plongeron, Bernard, et al. (1997). *Les Défis de la modernité 1750–1840.* Paris: Desclée.

Préclin, Edmond (1929). *Les Jansénistes du XVIIIe siècle: Le Développement du richérisme, sa propagataion dans le bas clergé.* Paris: Gamber.

Tackett, Timothy (1986). *Religion, Revolution, and Regional Culture in Eighteenth-Century France: The Ecclesiastical Oath of 1791.* Princeton, N.J.: Princeton University Press.

Van Kley, Dale K. (1996). *The Religious Origins of the French Revolution: From Calvin to the Civil Constitution of the Clergy, 1560–1791.* New Haven, Conn.: Yale University Press.

Velde, François R. and David R. Weir (1992). "The Financial Market and Government Debt Policy in France, 1746–1793." *Journal of Economic History*, 52: 1–39.

Chapter Nine

The Origins and Outcomes of Religious Schism, 1790–99

Edward J. Woell

Introduction

> What did the National Assembly do? Did it change our faith? Did it take away our holy mysteries, the doctrine we believe? Did it establish principles contrary to those of the Gospel? No, certainly not. On every occasion it displayed its respect for the one Religion and its firm resolution to never take that away …
>
> Because the National Assembly re-established divine worship in all its primitive purity; … because it re-established the institutions of the first beautiful centuries of the Church, notably in allowing you to choose your Bishops and your Pastors rather than leaving these nominations to corrupt ministers; and lastly, because the National Assembly destroyed all the abuses that dishonor the one Religion and allow impiety to triumph, those who profit from these abuses want to persuade you that the one Religion is in danger, and that you must rise up against the law.[1]

Staunchly defending revolutionary policy regarding the Catholic Church in January of 1791, the Departmental Directory of the Côte-d'Or published these words just as priests in its jurisdiction were weighing submission to state religious reforms through the taking of an oath. The apology stands as a stark reminder that in a revolution noted for its secularizing rigor, there nevertheless was a critical moment when the state became deeply invested in religious politics. Yet given that this same administrative body presided over attempts to dismantle Catholicism in the Côte-d'Or less than three years later, the defense is also telling of the complicated relationship between religion and revolution in France throughout the 1790s.

The complexity is evident even when three basic questions about this relationship are raised, as they will be in this essay. First, was the 1790 Civil Constitution of the Clergy more the product of culture rooted in the *ancien régime*, on the one hand, or of an unpredictable political dynamic immediately preceding such legislation on

A Companion to the French Revolution, First Edition. Edited by Peter McPhee.

the other? Though not a novel question, it has been raised anew by recent scholarly focus on the Enlightenment's connections with the Revolution and on eighteenth-century struggles over Jansenism. Second, what accounts for the varied responses to the 1791 Ecclesiastical Oath requirement, particularly by the clergy, the laity, and the state? Much of this query is owed to Timothy Tackett, whose masterful study of the 1791 oath revealed the enigmatic pattern of reaction to the requirement as well as its greater significance (Tackett 1986). And third, how does the religious crisis of 1791–92 correlate with subsequent revolutionary developments regarding Catholicism, most notably dechristianization in Year II and recovery from it during the Directory period? An answer now seems more elusive because of recent reappraisals indicating that Catholic culture from 1794 to 1799 was more vibrant and resourceful than previously claimed.

Addressing these questions here nonetheless allows for the making of two broader points regarding the nexus of Catholicism and the French Revolution. One is that interaction between the state and Catholics was central to the fate of French democratic culture in the 1790s. Although the beliefs and actions of Catholicism and those of democracy are often seen as parting ways during the Revolution, a deeper analysis shows that these cultures continued to shape each other. The other is that religion helped facilitate the centralization of political power and therefore unprecedented state expansion. This was most evident in the national takeover of ecclesiastical property, state efforts to quell religious conflict and promote conformity in the wake of the 1791 oath, the official oversight of dechristianization, and republican surveillance of Catholic clergy and laity. As other essays in this book may show, democratic development and the growth of centralized power remain crucial to today's understanding of the French Revolution. The following suggests that Catholics were fundamental to both.

Precursors to Crisis: The Late *Ancien Régime* and Early Revolution, 1764–90

Although the structures and cultures of Catholicism during the late *ancien régime* were vital to revolutionary events, surprisingly little consensus about these exists among current scholars. True, Michel Vovelle's extensive study of eighteenth-century wills confirmed previous research regarding a decline in clerical vocations, bequests of masses for the dead, and reception of Easter Communion in urban areas (Vovelle 1973). But for some scholars this evidence is illustrative of not so much a *laïcité*,[2] but rather a new spirituality in which flamboyant expressions of piety were considered crass (Aston 2001: 54–60; Clarke 2007: 42–48). Furthermore, John McManners argued that, far from losing influence among the French at this time, the Catholic Church had never enjoyed such a prominent cultural standing. Both the clergy and laity were educated in the faith more than ever before, and attendance and Communion reception were at an all-time high in the countryside (McManners 1998: vol. 1, 3–4; Van Kley 2003: 1089–1095).

Such contradictory evidence suggests that the Catholic Church of the late *ancien régime* was marked by not only geo-demographic variations but also acute internal divisions. This was most evident in a clerical corps distinguished by socio-economic segregation between many underprovided parish priests and relatively few affluent prelates (Tackett 1977). But other rifts among the clergy and laity were pervasive as well. While the political chasm dividing Jansenism and the Society of Jesus generally ceased to be pivotal after the French suppression of the Jesuits in 1764, Dale Van Kley adeptly showed that the religious polarity between *parlementaires* and the Crown transformed itself into wider political factionalism in the 1770s and 1780s (Van Kley 1996: 249–302). Though often struggling over constitutional prerogatives and growing royal debt, these factions also quarreled over questions of Gallicanism: what was to be the correct balance of French ecclesiastical authority between officials in the kingdom and those in Rome; who specifically in France was to exercise the church's power; and what the church's relationship with the state should be (Aston 2000: 103–121; Van Kley 1996: 195–203).

Behind some of these divisions stood another Catholic fissure identified by new scholarship. For decades most studies concluded that the Enlightenment was the basis for a protracted struggle pitting secularism against religiosity – as reflected in Peter Gay's title for one part of his study on the Enlightenment: *The Rise of Modern Paganism* (Gay 1966). But more recently specialists have shown that, far from being opposites, religion and enlightenment frequently intersected. Catholics, Protestants, and Jews throughout Europe, according to David Sorkin, discovered ways of integrating enlightened thought with theological perspectives and spiritual traditions (Sorkin 2008). Darrin McMahon observed, on the other hand, that the Enlightenment was accompanied by a "Counter-Enlightenment" through which some Catholic clerics and laypeople shaped arguments later made by counter-revolutionaries in the 1790s (McMahon 2001). Yet just as significant is his inference, recently corroborated by Jeffrey Burson, that the Enlightenment divided French Catholics as well (Burson 2010).

This splintering within the Catholic Church proved pivotal at the meeting of the Estates-General in May and June of 1789, particularly when several priests from Poitou became the first representatives not of the Third Estate to join what became the National Assembly. Still, such divides cannot fully account for legislation affecting the church in the early days of the assembly. As a recent analysis by Michael Fitzsimmons showed, the spontaneity marking the abolition of privileges on the night of 4 August indicates how much of the first constitution was subject to contingency. Tracing the first few months of the National Assembly, Fitzsimmons also demonstrated that deputies quickly became polarized over ecclesiastical issues. A factional dynamic arose not only in the contentious fight over the tithe but also in protracted debates first over Article 10 of the Declaration of the Rights of Man and of the Citizen, which established a right to religious freedom, and then later over the nationalization of ecclesiastical property (Fitzsimmons 2003: 47–71). While there were scattered protests by the Catholic clergy and laity when the National Assembly formally abolished Catholic religious orders on 13 February 1790, specialists have identified two symbolic developments that widened existing divides within and beyond the Assembly: the election of a Protestant pastor, Jean-Paul Rabaut de Saint-Etienne, as its president; and Dom Gerle's failed motion to designate Catholicism as the state religion. When conservatives in the assembly reacted adversely to both, progressive deputies became more adamant about decoupling religion from citizenship and proceeding with the sale of *biens nationaux*. Meanwhile, Catholics in religiously troubled Nîmes violently mobilized against local authorities, most of whom were Protestants (Aston 2000: 133–139; Fitzsimmons 2003: 72–76; Tackett 1986: 16–22).

Amid these unsettling circumstances the National Assembly's Ecclesiastical Committee drew up the Revolution's most important religious decree, the Civil Constitution of the Clergy, which the Assembly then approved on 12 July 1790. In light of subsequent events, numerous scholars have concluded that the Assembly was remarkably reckless in both creating the law and approving it. Though some have argued that the decree reflected an ideological preference for a political solution to an intractable cultural divide, or was based on polarized politics in which compromise became increasingly difficult, an explanation still preferred by many specialists is that the Assembly simply neglected to foresee the intense reaction that the Civil Constitution would provoke. Thus to the extent that one might consider the decree a debacle, it derived from a failure of political and religious imagination. Refusing to negotiate with a general assembly of the French clergy because it would signify recognition of a corporative body of the *ancien régime*, most deputies underestimated how much resentment would arise over reforms such as standardizing clerical salaries, eliminating fifty-two dioceses and hundreds of parishes, and severely circumscribing episcopal authority and high-church offices. Nor did they fully appreciate the theological underpinning of opposition by many priests, most bishops, and (later) the papacy. But perhaps above all, they failed to fathom the extent to which the decree's requirement of indirect elections for bishops and *curés* would be perceived as radical (Aston 2000: 140–162; McManners 1970: 38–46; Tackett 1986: 14–16).

Even so, most current scholars are equally disposed to agreeing that the Civil Constitution's supporters were never as blind as partisan historiography has suggested. Perhaps aside from elected bishops and *curés*, many of the outcomes were moderate in the sense that they merely echoed what the Catholic Joseph II had attempted to do in the Austrian Empire. The legislation also enjoyed substantial support among clerical deputies in the assembly, with many believing – in keeping with progressive Richerist and Jansenist theologies – that the decree was a providential opportunity to recover the virtues and sanctity of primitive Christianity. Moreover, specialists today are apt to argue that the political intransigence appearing shortly after the decree's passage belonged as much to the papacy and many prelates in France as to the National Assembly (Aston 2000: 196–198; McManners 1970: 42–46).

On the basis of such perspectives, one may rightly conclude that the Civil Constitution and its immediate reception mirrored both divides in Catholic culture during the late *ancien régime* and political polarity in the National Assembly over the previous year. But does it follow that religious and political ideologies of the *ancien régime* and the early Revolution all but prescribed the schism that was to come? Much contemporary scholarship seems wary of making this leap if only because it has uncovered increasing complexity within and beyond France's Catholic Church. For many scholars, this intricacy implies that numerous outcomes regarding the church were feasible once a fluid revolution began. *Ancien régime* religious ideology and political culture clearly influenced the Civil Constitution of the Clergy and thus were implicit in the trouble that followed. Yet one would be hard pressed to explain the subsequent crisis apart from capricious events and unimaginative leadership in 1789 and 1790.

The Ecclesiastical Oath and Birth of a Schism, 1790–92

No longer able to ignore substantial opposition to the Civil Constitution, the National Assembly decreed on 27 November 1790 that all clerics take an oath of fidelity signifying their assent to the law, which was then approved by the king on 26 December. While most contemporary scholars have seen the Ecclesiastical Oath of 1791 as one of the most critical turns in the Revolution, they have offered diverse arguments for why. Views of the oath have ranged widely – from the impetus for a "cultural revolution" that defined modern France, to a foundation for factionalism that made the constitutional monarchy unworkable, to a basis for broader popular counter-revolution, to another episode in a broader church–state struggle that resembled the Jansenist controversies during the *ancien régime* (Fitzsimmons 2003: 91–92; Furet 1996: 91–92 Sutherland 1986: 97–99; Tackett 1986: 287–300). Despite such differences, there is broad consensus that since almost all of the episcopacy and a little less than half of the parish clergy initially refused to take it, the 1791 oath became the catalyst for an acute political and religious divide throughout France.

The rift's most striking characteristic, according to Timothy Tackett's analysis, is the regional variation in clerical reaction to the oath. Whereas the majority of priests took the oath in the Parisian basin, the Berry-Bourbon center, southern Poitou, the Guyenne-Gascon southwest, and the Alps, by and large the clergy refused the oath in Brittany, western Normandy, northern Poitou, the Midi, Alsace, Franche-Comté, and Flanders. Tackett attributed the clerical response to multiple social and cultural variables, not the least being the personal perspective of a priest. Yet he also argued that clerical density was the most reliable predictor of oath reaction. Thus priests who refused the oath were mostly from parishes where the clerical community was robust, while clerics who took the oath likely resided in parishes having a lone pastor or relatively few *vicaires* (Tackett 1986: 34–56). Tackett agreed with many previous studies, moreover, by perceiving clerical reaction to the oath as crucial not only of its own accord but also because of its influence on the laity. Skillfully providing a multi-layered description of reaction – often through quantifiable data, he considered the laity's complex relationship to the clergy in different contexts and in light of pre-existing regional religious cultures, revolutionary reforms coinciding with the oath, mitigating factors like gender and the siege mentality of Catholics residing among Protestants, and the critical role of the urban elite in revolutionary politics (Tackett 1986: 159–300).

As influential as Tackett's study has been on recent scholarship, however, it may actually minimize the full scope and quality of the troubles. To cite one instance of how: if oath-taking and refusal rates are taken as strict indicators of the crisis, the impression given is that some regions were more prone to conflict over the oath than others. But recent research on geographically varied small towns, which were often epicenters of religious reform, suggests that a regional approach tends to veil the many troubles that arose in 1791 and 1792, to say nothing of the numerous issues at play. A few examples make this clear. As one might expect, many of the district seats in the Ille-et-Vilaine, which had a paltry oath-taking rate of 17 percent, saw an explosion of conflicts over the oath between the politically active proponents of the Civil Constitution and the many supporters of priests who had refused the oath (Tackett 1986: 330). Accordingly, in December of 1791 the prosecuting attorney of the district of Saint-Malo explained to his superiors that "visceral divisions" regarding the oath were thriving in his district "among the most tightly united families, troubling the best marriages, raising a wall of separation said to be impenetrable between father, mother, children, and the espoused." Officials in the Ille-et-Vilaine's small towns of Montfort, Redon, Fougères, and Vitré also reported animated conflicts in 1791 and 1792 that foreshadowed the more violent acts of *chouannerie* several years later.[3]

Nonetheless, there seemed to be equally numerous incidents of civil unrest in the small towns of the Haute-Garonne, which recorded a modest oath-taking rate of 40 percent (Tackett 1986: 327). In the district seat of Grenade, the town became scandalized over a midwife who had convinced new parents that their infants would be damned if baptized by the constitutional pastor. Unrest was also rife in the nearby towns of Rieux, Castelsarrasin, and Muret.[4] Even in a department like the Isère, where the oath-taking rate reached 85 percent, civil and religious conflict abounded (Tackett 1986: 332). A case in point is the town of Saint-Marcellin – coincidentally portrayed in Tackett's study as a haven of constitutional support, most notably (and anomalously) among women (Tackett 1986: 172–173). On the night that the constitutional pastor was installed in 1791, a crowd sympathetic to the refractory clergy that had gathered outside the parish church became so large and unruly that sentinels saw the need to fire their guns to keep protestors at bay. A few days later, the municipal prosecutor reported that refractory priests had been gathering at a defunct convent chapel and that some women who attended their masses threw rocks at sentinels stationed at the parish church door. When Marie Brun, the wife of a *journalier* (day laborer) living just outside the town, was later prosecuted for fomenting civil unrest at Saint-Marcellin she was asked by authorities

> if at the time of the installation of the [constitutional] *curé* Barre, she did not cry publicly that his mass was worth nothing, that he was a schismatic, that he would later be dead if he went into the countryside, that they wrote him a letter in which they asked him to carry nothing more than two shirts: one for him and one for his burial ...[5]

Aside from showing that religious and civil unrest was regionally ubiquitous in 1791 and 1792, such examples reveal why the "oath crisis" is a somewhat misleading term. For once the oath is taken out of isolation and placed in context, we not only uncover issues that are harder to detect and therefore less easy to quantify from afar – the actions of a community midwife, for example – but also other revolutionary religious reforms such as parish circumscription, the suppression of religious orders, and the confiscation and selling of *biens nationaux*. To an extent the economic fallout of such reforms motivated some of the discontent, but thoroughly social and cultural repercussions cannot be dismissed as sources either. In any case, the immediate effect of reform was the creation of a milieu suitable for religious rebellion. As evident at Saint-Marcellin, resistance to the Constitutional Church became formidable thanks to an accommodating venue: the town's abandoned convent chapel. Yet this was available only because religious orders had been suppressed and their property nationalized before passage of the Civil Constitution.

While most scholars today are aware of such conflict, few have speculated on what the crisis of 1791–92 meant for the Revolution's broader goal of democratic governance in the countless villages and small towns throughout France. As some political scientists have recently argued, establishing a democratic government has usually involved not only free elections and the observance of a rule of law guaranteeing basic civil rights, but also the ability of a citizenry to deliberate openly and make collective decisions based on such considerations. One can see that this was what was missing throughout much of France in 1791 and 1792 due to religious conflict. Building democratic governance faltered during these years not so much because many were denied the vote or individual rights were ignored, but rather because the oath and other religious reforms divided many communities so profoundly that there was little chance of France becoming a "deliberative democracy" (Elster 1998).

In addition to circumscribing a democratic potential, the unrest personified by the prosecution of Marie Brun and the other women at Saint-Marcellin points to another critical dimension of the crisis: the response by the state. When France became sharply divided over the oath and other religious reforms, state officials intervened to mitigate the conflict as well as to enforce the law. The state's progressively heavy-handed reaction to oath resistance has prompted scholars to query whether this response was due to explosive circumstances or an ideological mandate. Somewhat overlooked by this inquiry, however, is that regardless of its motivation state intervention likely exacerbated local hostilities instead of subduing them. Events in a *bourg* of the Seine-Inférieure in 1791 and 1792 are a clear example of this. In Gournay-en-Bray a conflict between the parishes of Saint-Hildevert and Notre-Dame erupted due to the Civil Constitution's stipulation that the town have only one parish. Although there likely had been tension between the parishes for some time, their mutual antagonism became acute in 1791 once departmental officials decreed the closure of Notre-Dame. Rewarded by the decision, parishioners from Saint-Hildevert became more derisive toward those from Notre-Dame, who in response became even more rebellious. The conflict ultimately subsided, but only after departmental authorities threatened the entire town with military force and financial penalty in the spring of 1792.[6]

One other implication of the state's intervention at Gournay is that just as popular reaction to the oath cannot be viewed in isolation, neither can the response of the state – especially given its role regarding *biens nationaux*. The closure of parish churches and other spiritual edifices, together with the seizure and selling of this property, have rarely been recognized as integral to the crisis of 1791–92. Yet the considerable research done on *biens nationaux* can be used to argue as much. While disputes stemming from the oath were unfolding, preparations were well under way for the suppression of redundant parishes, the dispersion of religious communities, and the selling of former church property. Most districts began auctioning off plots of land that had belonged to orders or other Catholic institutions in January of 1791, just as the oath requirement went into effect. On 6 May 1791, just as conflict over the oath was reaching new heights, the National Assembly voted to sell off the churches, chapels, and *presbytères* formerly belonging to parishes and religious orders, thereby confirming numerous laws previously approved. By the end of the year, much of what had been church property had already been sold (Bodinier and Teyssier 2000: 25–32, 123–132, 333–362). McManners concluded that:

> the effects of this vast auction on the national life and on the course of the Revolution were incalculable. Inventories, sales, haggling, demolitions; officials, clubs, and committees installed in ecclesiastical premises – all added a faint, sacrilegious perversity to ordinary existence that reinforced the great groundswell of anti-clericalism that was sweeping into the revolutionary events as tempers became frayed over the Civil Constitution of the Clergy. (McManners 1970: 30)

Such anticlericalism, nonetheless, was also accompanied by a perception among some Catholics that their way of life was under siege, causing them to call the Revolution's legitimacy into question.

The nationalization of ecclesiastical property in turn necessitated state payments to all church personnel – a monumental leap in the state's centralization of power. As Isser Woloch observed, the revolutionary state "took on new responsibilities and showered departments across France with growing lists of mandated obligations" (Woloch 1994: 145, 38). Yet often sidestepped by specialists is how compensatory payments to all church personnel constituted one of the most important of these mandates. Readily apparent in many of France's departmental archives are not only countless tables documenting payments to church personnel from 1791 to 1793, but also directives for this process intended for departmental and district officials. In the Puy-de-Dôme, for example, departmental officials explained that:

> The functions of the district directories are of major importance in everything touching the process of payment to the secular and regular clergy. ... Foreseeing the immensity of detail to be taken up by the directories of the administrative corps, and hoping to facilitate a prompt process, [the National Assembly] relies on the ability of the department and district directories to work together in this endeavor ...[7]

This coordination may seem unconnected with the troubles of 1791 and 1792, but only if one ignores how much it enabled the state to regulate church personnel – including those spearheading opposition to religious reform.

Related to such regulation is another mode of revolutionary centralization identified by Woloch and other scholars: policing. As in the case of state payments, though, most specialists have neglected to see how official actions against refractory priests became a building block for what Howard Brown aptly described as the "security state" (Brown 2006; Woloch 1994: 155–163). True, as Tackett found, the initial regulation of refractory clerics was uneven at best. Some regions were more repressive toward these priests than others, and many local authorities were reluctant to move against such clerics for fear of upsetting their constituents (Tackett 1986: 271–283). Yet in the context of a troubling war in 1792, among the effects of better administrative coherence was not only comprehensive enforcement of the Civil Constitution, but also a more standardized subjugation of the refractory clergy (Aston 2000: 179–183). Ironically, one sign of the state succeeding at this was the rise in resentment at the local level, particularly in the west where the new religious policy was hated and the ousted clergy found overwhelming favor. Recent scholarship has shown that the state's increasing restrictions on refractory priests helped feed the discontent that fueled popular counter-revolution in this region (Tackett 1982; Woell 2006: 95–136). But probably the best indication of state success in centralization was the decree of 26 August 1792, whereby the lame-duck Legislative Assembly ordered all able-bodied refractory priests to leave France within two weeks. The mere expectation that the law was enforceable reflected how much the regulation of clergy – amid other repressive acts in the religious crisis – had already furthered centralization (Aston 2000: 182).

As important as state power was in the crisis, however, it constitutes only one variable in the religious tumult of 1791 and 1792. What else accounts for such turbulence? Surely some of it was due to conflicting conceptions of the church and the new regime. Many Catholics justified their opposition to the Civil Constitution and the oath on the basis that, in keeping with Tridentine ecclesiology, decisions about church governance had to be made within the chain of clerical command, not by the National Assembly. Clerical and lay support for the legislation and the oath, on the other hand, was tied to an expansive notion of the National Assembly's role and a different conception of the church whereby the "citizen-priest" led the laity as his equals (Tackett 1986: 59–74). Nevertheless, the practical effect of broader ecclesiastical reorganization – too often conflated with the oath – was also a basis for popular unrest. Many Catholics were incensed by not only the expulsion of respected clerics and their replacement by "intruders," but also the elimination of episcopal sees, religious communities, and confraternities from which they derived many social and economic benefits, the sale of properties that had been popular spiritual sites and sources of charitable assistance to the poor, and the suppression or inadvertent division of parish communities that remained central to a citizen's identity. Thus the Catholic disposition toward religious reform hinged on both ideological and pragmatic considerations, thereby reflecting socio-economic context as well as differing politico-religious beliefs.

Church Destruction and Resilience, 1793–99

While the 1791–92 crisis generated much upheaval, the subsequent actions taken by officials and their supporters arguably led to even greater distress. Although the term itself has been called into question, "dechristianization" is usually invoked to describe the closing of churches, the destruction or profanation of religious articles and spaces, the redefinition or renaming of times, spaces, and places tangentially tied to Christianity, the prohibition on public worship, and the persecution of religious personnel occurring in Year II (22 September 1793 – 21 September 1794). Most recently two issues have recharged a debate about these phenomena. The first is whether dechristianization was propelled more by centralized authorities or by discontent toward the church within French communities. McManners, for example, emphasized the role played by the representatives-on-mission, many of whom had anticlerical axes to grind on arriving in the provinces (McManners 1970: 87–89). And he seemed to agree with Richard Cobb, who had argued that since the majority in rural France opposed dechristianization, line troops, ad hoc militias, and the notorious *armées révolutionnaires* had to effect its implementation (McManners 1970: 95–96). Nonetheless, some evidence suggests that dechristianization was self-perpetuating in many communities. Michel Vovelle's study of Year II – in line with his previous work on eighteenth-century wills – indicated that these phenomena were reflective not only of long-term cultural and ideological trends in place before the Revolution, but also of sharply contrasting attitudes toward the church that first came to light in the crisis of 1791–92 (Vovelle 1991: 121–166). The second contested issue is the clerical response to dechristianization. Vovelle's work compellingly suggested that over one-half of the constitutional clergy may have abdicated from the priesthood in Year II. But his study was much less clear on why these priests had made the choice. While acknowledging that many abdicated under the duress of local authorities or popular societies, Vovelle argued that other priests did so of their own free will, either in solidarity with their flock's perspective or because of their own revolutionary principles. That some went on to marry, moreover, suggested to Vovelle and subsequent scholars that many abdicating priests sought an irrevocable break with the church (Byrnes 2005: 13–46; Fenster 1999; Vovelle 1991: 62–97).

But many scholars have questioned Vovelle's conclusions. Some have surmised, for instance, that countless clerics considered the surrendering of their letters of ordination a state-mandated formality rather than a repudiation of their sacerdotal role. As for priestly marriages, the case has been made that dechristianizers remained unconvinced of priestly abdication without an ensuing marriage, and thus external pressure dictated this clerical decision as well. Though conceding some local support for dechristianization, critics of Vovelle's work see behind such backing a convergence of circumstances, most notably rebellion by intransigent Catholics in the west. This enabled the authorities to use a traditional antipathy toward the clergy to win over an unsophisticated constituency – the implication being that, similar to the trouble over the 1791 oath, this episode was also born of revolutionary contingency (Aston 2000: 260–261; McManners 1970: 106–117). Bernard Plongeron, for instance, argued that, when the French Church's experience during the Revolution is compared to that of other churches and their states in Europe at the same time, dechristianization appears highly exceptional. He took this rarity to mean that this episode was only one of several paths that the state and religion could have taken. In this sense, the crisis of 1791–92 was one of the contingencies through which dechristianization became a viable option (Plongeron 1997; Van Kley 2003: 1096–1101).

The debate over circumstance, however, can miss a larger point. According to Nigel Aston, what mattered most about dechristianization was the vast majority of priests overtly abstaining from ministry. If one estimate is correct, of the 40,000 parishes that had existed prior to 1789 only 150 were openly holding masses by the spring of 1794 (Aston 2000: 215–217). Coinciding with this was the appearance of state-mandated alternatives to Christianity, including the festivals of Reason and the cult of the Supreme Being. While these quasi-religious creations gained many adherents in revolutionary strongholds, recent scholarship has been more inclined to view them as political contrivances whose influence on Catholics in much of France was negligible (Aston 2000: 267–276; Byrnes 2005: 47–68; Clarke 2007: 193; Ozouf 1988). If anything, such alternatives may have further delegitimized the state among many Catholics.

Even so, dechristianization proved instrumental to centralization and the proliferation of democratic culture. Regarding the former, many official dechristianizing policies ensured that the central government's power would expand further at the local level, especially since for many representatives-on-mission the enforcement of secular standardization rose to the level of obsession (McManners 1970: 104–105). Furthermore, among many local officials the abdication of a parish *curé* meant that a potential threat to their authority and influence over citizens was eliminated; in theory if not in reality, there was one less potential competitor to whom citizens could defer. Dechristianization's relationship to democratic culture, on the other hand, was more complex. On one level the closing of churches eliminated a familiar medium whereby citizens could become immersed in democratic culture and, just as important, integrate it with a broader cosmology. Considered "patriots" as well as "civil servants," constitutional clerics were well poised for this endeavor (Aston 2000: 208–209; Chapman-Adisho 2006). On another level, though, dechristianization may have given many Catholics wanting to maintain their culture a tutorial about the Revolution's democratic limitations, particularly at a moment when populist demagoguery prevailed. It can be argued, moreover, that a dechristianizing repression led many Catholics toward embracing the value that democratic culture placed on challenging authorities who defied the popular will and violated individual rights.

While some consider the National Convention's decree of religious freedom on 18 Frimaire II (8 December 1793) a turning point in reining in dechristianization, arguably a more effectual law was that of 3 Ventôse III (21 February 1795), which declared the freedom of all religious practice undertaken in private. Implicitly striking down previous laws that thwarted Catholicism, the latter legislation freed the refractory clergy not subject to deportation in 1792, allowed parishioners to worship in those parish churches that remained unsold, and permitted what had been the constitutional clergy to minister in public provided they take a new oath signifying submission to the republic (Aston 2000: 279–280). Meanwhile, in 1794 numerous clerics who had taken the 1791 oath met secretly in Paris to revive what had been the Constitutional Church. Led by prelates like the *abbé* Henri Grégoire and Jean-Baptiste Royer, the "United Bishops at Paris" started work on a plan for church reorganization that they completed by the end of 1795. When they convened a National Church Council in 1797, thirty bishops who held sees, as well as representatives from many dioceses without one, attended. By the end of 1800 an additional twenty-eight bishops were ministering their dioceses, meaning that just twenty-nine sees in France remained vacant (McManners 1970: 123–125). Although many specialists have reduced the United Bishops to a revolutionary footnote, recent scholarship – most notably by Rodney Dean – has challenged this, arguing instead that this institution realized one goal of the Civil Constitution of the Clergy: a reformed Gallican Catholic Church compatible with a democratic state (Dean 2008).

Yet facing these bishops were two major problems. First, despite the reconciling overtures of the United Bishops, the refractory church – to say nothing of the papacy – continued to view takers of the 1791 oath as apostates. Given that the refractory church's presence in France remained in the shadows, many scholars have downplayed its significance as well. Recent research has nonetheless uncovered this group's striking resourcefulness. For example, in her study of the royalist journal *Gazette de Paris*, Laurence Coudart found that refractory clerics and their defenders were remarkably adept at attacking the Constitutional Church in 1791 and 1792, in part because they used the journal to network and coordinate their struggle (Coudart 1995: 235–251). While deportation, the Terror, and dechristianization disrupted the refractory clergy's efforts, its loyal laity tried to fill the void from 1794 to 1801. Many women, most notably former nuns, became proxies for refractory bishops and priests trying to administer their jurisdictions from afar, in addition to hiding refractory clerics who had defied deportation (Aston 2000: 239–241). The counter-revolutionary role of these believers, as Olwen Hufton long argued, should not be overlooked (Hufton 1992).

A second problem for the United Bishops was the state, which for much of the Directory period reverted to a default position of anticlericalism. Less than nine months after religious freedom was declared in 1795, legislators reimposed the 1792–93 laws against refractory priests and gave them fifteen days to either leave France or face execution. Although these decrees were lifted once more in late 1796, the left-wing coup of 18 Fructidor V (4 September 1797) represented another anticlerical turn. Requiring the new clerical oath of "Hatred of Royalty," the coup's allies purposely sought to make former constitutional clerics enemies of the state. Local officials returned to enforcing revolutionary commemorations, including that for the execution of the Louis XVI on 2 Pluviôse V (21 January 1798), and cultic practice on the *décadi*, the tenth day of the revolutionary calendar. In still another shift, though, the anti-Jacobin coup of 22 Floréal VI (11 May 1798) resulted in officials backing away again from stringent anticlericalism (Aston 2000: 280–315). Yet by maintaining that Christianity and citizenship were virtually incompatible, republicans of the Directory ensured not only widespread Catholic unrest, but also their own regime's democratic artifice.

Paradoxically, the frequent vacillation of religious policy during the Directory led to further growth in centralized power. Because the state's position on Catholic clerics was in constant flux, local authorities were forced to keep the clergy under constant surveillance. Shortly after Napoleon Bonaparte came to power, municipal, cantonal, and departmental authorities were keeping track of how many of the five required clerical oaths (those of 1791, 1792, 1795, 1797, and 1799) each and every priest in their jurisdiction had taken (Plongeron 1969: 74–100). This required no small amount of bureaucratic coherence, but it also meant that local authorities had to monitor religious practitioners and report about them to superiors. As departmental administrators of the Meurthe explained in their monthly report of Frimaire VI (21 November – 20 December 1797),

> The policing of religion is becoming noticeably more exact. Religious ministers know that the central administration has them under surveillance, and their inclination above all is to ask themselves who would be held responsible for infractions if they were committed; and this realization contains them.[8]

The Catholic laity encountered similar harassment under the Directory, yet despite this, recent scholarship has revealed an unexpected religious revival from 1794 to 1799. This development was particularly critical for democratic culture in France. As Suzanne Desan's invaluable study of the Yonne illustrates, many Catholics demanded the right to practice their religion during this time, in part through democratically petitioning local officials (Desan 1990: 122–135). While republican-friendly citizens resorting to this practice may be unexceptional, rather remarkable here is that some Catholic petitioners were unambiguous supporters of the refractory clergy. In an entreaty against the reimposition of laws against refractory priests, for example, citizens from the small town of Billom in the Puy-de-Dôme expressed their "terrible sorrow at never being able to continue their [religious] practice with confidence." Viewing the right to practice their religion as constitutionally guaranteed, they reminded departmental officials that "the Constitution [of Year III] became the handiwork of all the French through their solemn acceptance of it, it belongs to them, and nothing is able to take that away." Moreover, as "sincere souls of the Republic, scrupulous observers of the law," yet also the objects of attack by "Robespierre's shadow," they argued that "the law must be equal for all, whether it punishes or protects, it must strike down only the guilty and never their victims."[9] Thus even Catholics whom officials passed off as "royalists" were making democratic arguments by 1795, implying that notions of popular sovereignty deeply penetrated *la France profonde* – on account of religion, no less, which must have both vexed and perplexed the republican authorities.

Still, much of this democratic culture proved inconsequential to Napoleon Bonaparte, who after the Brumaire coup in 1799 quickly focused on the republic's problem of religious and civil unrest. Believing that a solution was to reconcile not only republican citizenship and religion but also the two de facto Catholic churches, Bonaparte pursued negotiations with Pius VII to this effect. While considering the 1801 Concordat is beyond the scope of this essay, it bears mentioning here that a Catholic renewal between 1794 and 1799 places the crisis of 1791–92, dechristianization, and even the Napoleonic accord in a somewhat new interpretive light. The comeback of Catholicism in the Revolution's second half suggests that neither the 1791–92 crisis nor dechristianization secured the supremacy of republican *laïcité* any more than they assured the demise of Catholic culture. Moreover, such resurgence implies that the Revolution's Catholic schism may be less responsible than is often thought for the pervasive chasm between the French Church and democratic culture in the nineteenth and twentieth centuries. Rather, since the Concordat of 1801 eliminated a democratically compatible, conciliar, and Gallican Church, turned its back on faithful Catholics who had embraced popular sovereignty, and paved the way for an authoritarian and ultramontane Catholicism, liability for this great separation seems more ascribable to Napoleon Bonaparte (Dean 2004: 705–716; Desan 1990: 217–230).

Conclusion

Among this essay's obvious conclusions is that current scholarship on Catholicism in the French Revolution has no shortage of interpretive and argumentative discrepancies. But at the risk of oversimplifying a vast array of recent historical literature, a case can be made that much scholarly debate pivots on two fundamental disagreements. The first involves how politically vital and culturally influential Catholicism was in France, both before the Revolution and while it unfolded. The other dispute – and one shared more generally by French revolutionary historiography – concerns whether the events discussed here were more ascribable to agency and contingency, or to an authoritative role played by either ideology or culture. The positions taken on these two sets of differences will inevitably determine one's views about where the Catholic schism originated, what it was all about, and how it influenced what followed.

In accentuating how Catholicism effected centralization and affected democracy in the Revolution, this essay mostly concurs with scholars who give an indispensable role to religion in eighteenth-century French society and thus in the Revolution as well. Nevertheless, such agreement is not synonymous with disregarding the Revolution's non-religious phenomena, much less dismissing the perceptible drift toward *laïcité* in the eighteenth century. Similarly, insofar as centralization and democratization are deemed as such, this essay shows a preference for the greater schemes of ideology and culture. But the specific examples from the archives included here are meant to show that state power and democratic culture were constantly subject to the capriciousness of those who took them up. For this reason, the two developments never assumed a linear path and their interplay with religion was enormously complex. If – as argued here – Catholicism helped develop centralization and democracy during the French Revolution, it did so erratically, even accidentally, and in the midst of numerous other elements doing the same.

Notes

1 *Adresse du Directoire du Département de la Côte-d'Or, aux municipalités de son arrondissement* (Dijon, 1791), 1–2; Archives Départementales de la Côte-d'Or, L 1138.

2 *Laïcité* defies simple definition in English. It generally refers to a secular vision of society in which religious authorities have no meaningful political power and religious practice is consigned to the private sphere.

3 Saint-Malo District Prosecuting Attorney to departmental officials, December 1791, Archives Départementales d'Ille-et-Vilaine, L 441. See L 996, L 436, L 1402, 1 Q 821, and 1 Q 839 for other examples of religious conflict in the small towns of the Ille-et-Vilaine.

4 The official response to the actions of Grenade's midwife can be found in the 1 May 1792 entry of the communal *registre*, Archives Départementales de la Haute-Garonne, 2 E 412. Documents in 1 L 1069, 1 L 368, 1 L 1057, and 1 L 1073 reveal more about religious conflict in the small towns of the Haute-Garonne.

5 Interrogation of Marie Brun, 29 June 1791, Archives Départementales de l'Isère, L 1765.

6 Most documents regarding the conflict at Gournay are found in Archives Départementales de la Seine-Maritime, L 1191. However, additional evidence is found in L 1193, L 1196, L 1777, and L 337.

7 *Conférence des décrets sur le traitement du clergé séculier et régulier, publiée en forme d'instruction par le Directoire du Département du Pui-de-Dôme* (Clermont-Ferrand, 1790), 16–17; Archives Départementales du Puy-de-Dôme, L 5360.

8 Monthly Report on the Material and Moral Situation of the Department of the Meurthe, 21 Frimaire VI (11 Dec. 1797), Archives Départementales de la Meurthe-et-Moselle, L 173.

9 Petition from Billom, 13 Brumaire IV (4 Nov. 1795), Archives Départementales du Puy-de-Dôme, L 2446.

References

Aston, Nigel (2000). *Religion and Revolution in France 1780–1804.* Washington, D.C.: Catholic University Press.

Bodinier, Bernard and Teyssier, Éric (2000). "*L'Événement le plus important de la Révolution": La Vente des biens nationaux (1789–1867) en France et dans le territoires annexés.* Paris: SÉR and CTHS.

Brown, Howard G. (2006). *Ending the French Revolution: Violence, Justice, and Repression from the Terror to Napoleon.* Charlottesville, Va. and London: University of Virginia Press.

Burson, Jeffrey (2010). *The Rise and Fall of Theological Enlightenment: Jean-Martin de Prades and Ideological Polarisation in Eighteenth-Century France.* Notre Dame, Ind.: University of Notre Dame Press.

Byrnes, Joseph F. (2005). *Catholic and French Forever: Religious and National Identity in Modern France.* University Park: Pennsylvania State University Press.

Chapman-Adisho, Annette (2006). "Patriotic Priests: Constitutional Clergy in the Department of the Côte-d'Or during the French Revolution". Ph.D. dissertation. University of Illinois at Chicago.

Clarke, Joseph (2007). *Commemorating the Dead in Revolutionary France: Revolution and Remembrance, 1789–1799.* Cambridge and New York: Cambridge University Press.

Coudart, Laurence (1995). *La Gazette de Paris: Un journal royaliste pendant la Révolution française (1789–1792).* Paris: Harmattan.

Dean, Rodney (2004). *L'Église constitutionnelle, Napoléon, et le Concordat de 1801.* Paris: Picard.

Dean, Rodney (2008). *L'Abbé Grégoire et l'église constitutionnelle après la Terreur 1794–1797.* Paris: Picard.

Desan, Suzanne (1990). *Reclaiming the Sacred: Lay Religion and Popular Politics in Revolutionary France.* Ithaca, N.Y. and London: Cornell University Press.

Elster, Jon (ed.) (1998). *Deliberative Democracy.* Cambridge and New York: Cambridge University Press.

Fenster, Kenneth R. (1999). "The Abdicating Clergy of the Gironde." *Catholic Historical Review*, 85: 541–565.

Fitzsimmons, Michael P. (2003). *The Night the Old Regime Ended: August 4, 1789, and the French Revolution.* University Park: Pennsylvania State University Press.

Furet, François (1996). *The French Revolution 1770–1814*, trans. Antonia Nevill. Oxford and Cambridge, Mass: Blackwell.

Gay, Peter (1966). *The Enlightenment: An Interpretation*, vol. 1: *The Rise of Modern Paganism*. New York: Knopf.

Hufton, Olwen (1992). *Women and the Limits of Citizenship in the French Revolution.* Toronto and Buffalo: University of Toronto Press.

McMahon, Darrin (2001). *Enemies of the Enlightenment: The French Counter-Enlightenment and the Making of Modernity.* Oxford and New York: Oxford University Press.

McManners, John (1970). *The French Revolution and the Church.* New York: Harper & Row.

McManners, John (1998). *Church and Society in Eighteenth-Century France*, 2 vols. Oxford and New York: Oxford University Press.

Ozouf, Mona (1988). *Festivals and the French Revolution*, trans. Alan Sheridan. Cambridge, Mass.: Harvard University Press.

Plongeron, Bernard (1969). *Conscience religieuse en Révolution: Regards sur l'historiographie religieuse de la Révolution française.* Paris: A. and J. Picard.

Plongeron, Bernard (1997). *Histoire du christianisme des origines à nos jours*, vol. 10: Jean-Marie Meyer, Bernard Plongeron, and Astérios Argyriou (eds.). *Les Défis de la modernité, 1750–1840.* Paris: Desclée.

Sorkin, David (2008). *The Religious Enlightenment: Protestants, Catholics, and Jews from London to Vienna.* Princeton, N.J.: Princeton University Press.

Sutherland, D.M.G. (1986). *France 1789–1815: Revolution and Counterrevolution.* Oxford and New York: Oxford University Press.

Tackett, Timothy (1977). *Priest and Parish in Eighteenth-Century France: A Social and Political Study of the Curés in a Diocese of Dauphiné, 1750–1791.* Princeton, N.J.: Princeton University Press.

Tackett, Timothy (1982). "The West in France in 1789: The Religious Factor in the Origins of the Counter-Revolution." *JMH*, 54: 715–745.

Tackett, Timothy (1986). *Religion, Revolution, and Regional Culture in Eighteenth-Century France: The Ecclesiastical Oath of 1791.* Princeton, N.J.: Princeton University Press.

Van Kley, Dale (1996). *The Religious Origins of the French Revolution: From Calvin to the Civil Constitution, 1560–1791.* New Haven, Conn. and London: Yale University Press.

Van Kley, Dale (2003). "Christianity as Casualty and Chrysalis of Modernity: The Problem of Dechristianization in the French Revolution." *AHR*, 108: 1081–1104.

Vovelle, Michel (1973). *Piété baroque et déchristianisation en Provence au XVIIIe siècle: Les Attitudes devant la mort d'après les clauses des testaments.* Paris: Plon.

Vovelle, Michel (1991). *The Revolution against the Church: From Reason to the Supreme Being*, trans. José, Alan. Columbus: Ohio State University Press.

Woell, Edward J. (2006). *Small-Town Martyrs and Murderers: Religious Revolution and Counterrevolution in Western France, 1774–1914.* Milwaukee, Wis.: Marquette University Press.

Woloch, Isser (1994). *The New Regime: Transformations of the French Civic Order, 1789–1820s.* New York and London: W.W. Norton.

Further Reading

Bonin, Serge, Timothy Tackett, Michel Vovelle, and Claude Langlois (eds.) (1996). *Atlas de la Révolution française*, vol. 9 : *Religion.* Paris: ÉHÉSS.

Brye, Bernard de (2004). *Consciences épiscopales en exil (1794–1814): A travers la correspondance de Monseigneur de la Fare, évêque de Nancy.* Paris: Cerf.

Cousin, Bernard, Monique Cubells, and René Moulinas (1989). *La Pique et la croix: Histoire religieuse de la Révolution française.* Paris: Centurion.

Chapter Ten

A Tale of Two Narratives: The French Revolution in International Context, 1787–93

Thomas E. Kaiser

When on 28 May 1789 Louis XVI reminded the Estates-General that he had convened it three weeks earlier "to collaborate with me on the regeneration of the kingdom," he no doubt had the "regeneration" of the state's failing finances principally in mind.[1] But he was also surely thinking of one of the most ominous consequences of the government's fiscal crisis, namely the decline in France's capacity to project power abroad. Indeed, if there was one thing that Louis' contemporaries could agree upon, it was that the days of French hegemony were long since over and that France might no longer play a major role in European affairs. The most conspicuous proof of French impotence came in the late summer and early fall of 1787. Forced to seek peace at almost any price because of its financial troubles, France not only ignominiously declined to support its ally, the Netherlands, which thereafter suffered invasion by Prussia, but also shamefully abandoned its "old friend" Turkey, which faced imminent dismemberment by Russia and its soon-to-be accomplice Austria (Murphy 1998).

These and other unmistakable demonstrations of French impotence abroad sent signals in two directions. To the other European states, it was now clear that for the foreseeable future they could safely act with minimal regard for French power and interests. In the eyes of the Germans, the baron de Groschlag reported from across the Rhine in July 1790, France appeared "enervated, divided, and ruined at home and isolated abroad. This impression of weakness piques the imagination of [foreign] princes … [who think] that once Europe is pacified, they will [be able to] to dictate to France at will."[2] To the French, their government's abject failure to defend national interests abroad and those of their allies signaled how much more was at stake in the fiscal crisis than "mere" government solvency. As the failures of French foreign policy became more conspicuous in the late 1780s, a nightmare scenario began to emerge in which a coalition of unfriendly states ganged up on a

A Companion to the French Revolution, First Edition. Edited by Peter McPhee.

prostrate France. "We are beginning to perceive," noted an anonymous observer in August 1787, "that a concert [of powers] fatal to our interests could be forming among the foreign powers, [and] could even have existed for a long time under the appearance of sham divisions, to execute great designs that our dilatory politics has made all the easier."[3] As historians have insufficiently appreciated, an atmosphere of intense insecurity surrounded all the great events of the early Revolution, during which France grimly faced the prospect of Europe's next "general war."

On paper, France's security position seemed far from hopeless at the end of the *ancien régime*. In 1756, France and Austria had formally buried their ancient rivalry and formed an alliance to stabilize the frontier between them so that both could focus their energies on fighting other adversaries – in the case of France, England, and in the case of Austria, Prussia. Then in 1761 France had capitalized on the installation of Bourbon rule in Spain at the beginning of the century by forging with its cousin kingdom a third *pacte de famille*, an alliance that proved more durable than two previous attempts at intra-Bourbon solidarity (Blart 1915). Although the *pacte de famille* was formally closed to non-Bourbon powers, France's two major alliances were conjoined by a flurry of inter-dynastic marital unions with the Habsburgs in the 1760s that culminated in the marriage of the archduchess Marie-Antoinette to the future Louis XVI in 1770. Thus did Austria acquire, as one contemporary put it, "a kind of admission ... to the *pacte de famille*."[4] In 1789, it looked as if this system of loosely interlocking dynastic alliances among France, Spain, and Austria might be enlarged and strengthened, when Russia, seeking French guarantees of its borders from Prussian attack while militarily engaged in Turkey, expressed interest in acceding to the Bourbon–Habsburg coalition as a member of a much-anticipated, but never concluded, Quadruple Alliance (Kaiser 2011).

In reality, however, all the links in the French security chain were weaker than they appeared on paper. The Franco-Austrian alliance of 1756 had suffered many stresses and strains over the years, particularly after the Empress-Queen Maria Theresa had died in 1780, and her son Joseph II had embarked on a belligerent foreign policy that France refused to support (Beales 1987, 2009). Marie-Antoinette's plunging reputation did nothing to improve French perceptions of their Austrian ties, and in the run-up to 1789 rumors abounded that France faced bankruptcy because she was exporting "all the gold in France" to finance her brother Joseph II's wars of conquest (Kaiser 2000). The *pacte de famille* was somewhat less battle-scarred and unpopular in France than the Austrian alliance, but it, too, had failed to live up to expectations. Never did it provide France with a solid phalanx of Bourbon powers as originally intended because of disputes between its Spanish and Italian branches; defense of the Spanish Empire against English attacks had created new vulnerabilities for France to cope with; and many of the expected commercial benefits of the *pacte de famille* had failed to materialize. Although Spain had voiced welcome support for France in the Dutch crisis of 1787, less than six months later the French foreign minister, the comte de Montmorin – in a stunning assessment of the nation's security posture – noted that France "has no friend, no ally on whom it can count, and if it faced a war on the continent, it would probably be left to its own devices."[5] Thus was dynasticism proving to be a broken reed in French foreign policy. In hopes that the Quadruple Alliance would remedy this situation, Montmorin and most of the royal council supported French accession to it. But ultimately Louis XVI failed to do likewise, not because he opposed it in principle, but because he was persuaded that it would impose on France a currently unbearable financial burden. Once again, financial crisis at home prevented France from exerting its "natural" weight abroad, and France entered into the Revolution of 1789 with a much weaker diplomatic hand to play than it might otherwise have enjoyed (Kaiser 2011).

The Two Nightmare Narratives

This sense of weakness and vulnerability provided a perfect ground for the elaboration of two principal nightmare narratives regarding the international scene on the eve of the French Revolution. I shall call one the "ministerial" narrative and the other the "Jacobin" narrative.

The "ministerial" narrative, which featured England as France's main adversary, was woven out of long-standing Anglophobic strands drawn from the "second Hundred Years War" France had fought with England over the previous century (Dziembowksi 1998). It acquired a fresh relevance with the formation of a Triple Alliance among England, Prussia, and the Netherlands in the wake of the 1787 Dutch crisis. Although historians today have no trouble spotting the conflicting, ultimately destabilizing objectives among these powers, the Triple Alliance looked all too solid to the French ministry and its adherents, who feared that it was but the first step to English hegemony over all Europe. "Drunk on its success in the Netherlands," warned Montmorin in July 1788, England was covertly trying to organize an expanded coalition that, in addition to Prussia and the Netherlands, would include Sweden, Denmark, and the Protestant German principalities. If that plan were realized, Montmorin predicted, "the English government will be able to lay down the law to the house of Bourbon; it will shackle [the house] of Austria; contain Russia in the East; dominate Germany; in a word, it will make England the predominant power in Europe ... The house of Bourbon will be deprived of the role it has played until now; its trade and possessions will be at the mercy of its natural enemy."[6]

In counterpoint to this "ministerial" narrative emerged another one, dear to most Jacobins, based on what I have called the "Austrian Plot" (Kaiser 2000; Savage 1998). The "Austrian Plot" arose out of long-standing French fears that Austria had been conspiring for centuries to weaken and destroy its only true continental rival by draining French resources through ruse and betrayal. It was reconfigured during the last decades of the *ancien régime* by the "devout party" at court, which had sought to discredit Louis XV's mistress Mme de Pompadour, a strong promoter of the 1756 Austrian alliance, and the foreign minister, the duc de Choiseul, who had done his best to maintain it. Claiming that the Austrian alliance was a deception whereby Austria had seduced France into bankrolling its efforts to retake Silesia from Prussia, the "devout party" had frequently crossed swords with Marie-Antoinette and her creatures under Louis XVI. On the eve of the Revolution, the anti-Austrian message of the "devout party" was recycled in more popular form by publicists like Charles Peysonnel and Jean-Louis Carra, whose indictment of

Austrian subversion of French foreign policy resonated all the more loudly when France deserted Turkey, apparently at Vienna's instigation.

Unlike the "ministerial" faction, most Jacobins did not dwell on the Dutch debacle as a prime example of English perfidy; rather, they feared that it would push France more deeply into the arms of Austria and its evil ally Russia. Far from viewing the pending Quadruple Alliance as a means to salvage France's sinking fortunes abroad, the many Jacobins who subscribed to the "Austrian Plot" considered it but another Austrian ruse to milk France dry of resources and render the nation defenseless. Because of Marie-Antoinette's real and imagined association with France's tilt in the Austrian direction, it was inevitable that the "Austrian Plot" became associated with the counter-revolution – another example of the conjoining of domestic and foreign politics in public discourse. The reportedly harsh Austrian campaign to repress a rebellion in neighboring Belgium was repeatedly represented in the Jacobin press during the spring of 1790 as a dress-rehearsal for an even bloodier Austrian invasion of France to come, while rumors of a secret "Austrian Committee" devoted to the internal subversion of France began to spread (Kaiser 2009).

The Nootka Sound Crisis

Until the spring of 1790, the great French implosion of 1789 had allowed other powers to focus on the resolution of the Turkish war and the fate of Poland. Thus was France able to focus on its own reconstruction at the cost of abdicating its role as a major player in European affairs. But matters changed in the spring of 1790 – long before France's domestic "regeneration" was complete and its army, racked by internal dissension, was again a credible military force (Scott 1978). On 14 May, Montmorin informed the National Assembly that Spain and England were about to fight a war over the Spanish seizure of English ships in Nootka Sound off Vancouver Island, the result of their long-standing conflicting colonial claims in the Pacific. The king, Montmorin assured the deputies, was seeking a peaceful settlement of this dispute. But Montmorin also asked the Assembly for funds to equip fourteen ships that the king had already mobilized as a preventive measure against an English assault on France.

Limited as this request was, its passage would clearly increase the likelihood of French involvement in a war the nation did not seek, was unlikely to benefit from, and was ill prepared to wage – all in the now dubious cause of fulfilling its commitments to the Bourbon dynasty under the *pacte de famille*. Therein lay the galvanizing power of the crisis. Not only did it ignite the Revolution's first major debate on foreign policy in the Assembly, but it also attracted great attention in the press and mobilized crowds of tens of thousands to the site of the Assembly's debates. The debates generated a spectrum of different opinions on many different aspects of the crisis, including the extent of the king's war powers under the new constitution and the status of French treaties with other powers under the new regime (Belissa 1998: 179–204; Whiteman 2003: ch. 4). But the two most clearly staked out positions on the Nootka Sound crisis itself corresponded closely to the two "ministerial" and "Jacobin" narratives already in play. Both were apocalyptic in tone and at the same time "realistic" according to their first premises.

To Montmorin and other subscribers to the "ministerial" narrative, England's behavior provided further confirmation of its long-suspected perfidious intention to dominate Europe. The English response to the Spanish seizure of its ships, Montmorin claimed, was wholly disproportional to the provocation and indicated that the English ministry would use it as a pretext to disrupt the *pacte de famille.*

> London believes the moment has come to shatter our union with Spain. The British ministry would like to think that this power, obligated to ask for our help, will meet with a refusal on our part; that finding itself incapable of fighting Great Britain, will seek an accommodation [with her] and that France, unfaithful to its commitments, will lose all consideration ... [and] find itself isolated and at the mercy of the court of London.[7]

Not only was England intimidating Spain by brandishing its arms, claimed Montmorin, but it was also subverting the king's efforts to salvage the *pacte de famille* by lobbying members of the National Assembly to vote against subsidies to Spain – a charge that we now know was perfectly true.

This language was echoed in the Assembly by supporters of the ministry, who acceded to the left's position that all future foreign policy had to be premised on the interests of the nation, not the dynasty, and built their case upon that new foundation. Arguing that the *pacte de famille* was in reality a "national treaty" although dynastic in form, these supporters recalled Spain's support for French efforts to contain English power since the end of the Seven Years War. Without sufficient support from France, warned Bengy de Puyvallé, Spain risked losing its colonial empire and the wealth it shared with France, and it ultimately might have "to make its peace [with England] at your expense."[8] It was precisely because France was presently so vulnerable, argued the comte de Custine, that the Assembly must give the king a free hand in settling the current crisis.

To subscribers to the Jacobin narrative, history and prudence dictated a notably different course of action. The proper year from which to view the current crisis, they contended, was not 1763, but 1756, date of the first Franco-Austrian alliance. "You well know," intoned Pétion de Villeneuve, "the fatal consequences of the famous treaty of 1756 ... [when] France – victim of the house of Austria's cunning policy, without any real and solid interest, without proportion or reciprocity in its obligations – became entangled in the ambitious projects of this power, exposed to perpetual wars with its numerous enemies ... [and thereby] lost its consideration in Europe."[9] Such entanglements, argued the Jacobins, were typical of dynastically based treaties like the *pacte de famille*, which the marquis de Condorcet branded as "veritable conspiracies against the people." "France," he declared, "must be free, as if the reigning princes in Madrid, Naples, and Parma, were not [members] of the Bourbon or Capet family."[10] Although some Jacobins favored a truly "national" alliance with Spain, rushing to its aid now, they insisted, would entail supporting a regime that in banning the importation of French publications the previous December had displayed its true colors as the pre-eminent champion of the counter-revolution. Indeed, argued Charles de Lameth, it would mean fostering a counter-revolutionary coalition composed of "a power that fears the

Revolution [abroad], a power that would like to destroy the Constitution [at home], and a family possibly motivated by its [own particular] interests."[11] Referring to the Quadruple Alliance, Carra charged that Spain, in connection with its dynastic Italian allies, had become party to a secret treaty that linked it not only to Russia, but also to Vienna. Hence, adoption of the ministry's policy of support for Spain entailed falling for another Austrian ruse to profit at French expense. Indeed, insisted Carra, the ministry had now become a tool of the "Austrian Committee."[12] From this perspective, "realism" dictated a policy of judicious restraint and, if anything else, an open hand extended to England, the one foreign nation that, according to Jacques-Pierre Brissot, understood the meaning of liberty.[13]

In the face of mounting Jacobin opposition that he feared would carry the Assembly and tie his hands, Montmorin instructed the chevalier de La Luzerne, French ambassador to England, to use everything in his power to settle the crisis with the English prime minister William Pitt, while Montmorin stalled at home. He not only delayed sending the formal Spanish request for French support to the National Assembly for six weeks, but also dismissed the French ambassador to Spain, the duc de La Vauguyon, after Charles de Lameth charged La Vauguyon with complicity in a royalist plot to plunge France into war. Notwithstanding these efforts, Montmorin's request for ship money produced not an authorization from the Assembly but a wide-ranging debate on the nature and conduct of foreign policy under the new constitution. The best Montmorin could achieve for the moment was passage on 22 May of a compromise resolution on the king's war powers crafted and pushed through the Assembly by the new secret advisor to the court, the comte de Mirabeau. In its forthright assertion that the "nation" – not the dynasty – would henceforth be the foundation of foreign policy and in its proscription of wars of conquest (as opposed to "defensive wars"), the resolution constituted an ideological victory for the left. But in its operative clauses – which reserved to the king the power to conduct ordinary foreign and military affairs and required his consent, as well as the Assembly's, to declare war – the resolution played into the hands of the ministry.[14]

Not surprisingly, Mirabeau's resolution, for all its historic importance as a statement of revolutionary principles, hardly reassured the left that the "plot" against the nation they detected behind the ministry's policies had been effectively quashed. But neither did the resolution provide Montmorin with the means to resolve the present crisis, since it left unclear how much support for Spain the Assembly would ultimately authorize. This uncertainty, La Luzerne reported from London, was stoking English expectations that popular pressure would eventually force France to abandon its ally altogether. Such was exactly what the Spanish feared might happen, and they immediately called upon their reluctant ally for pledges of tangible support. "If we do not see these measures taken soon," observed the Spanish foreign minister, the conde de Floridablanca, on 21 May, "we will have to look [for help] elsewhere, beyond friends and even allies. We will try to maintain the respect due to friendship and kinship ... but [only] insofar as that does not expose us to ruin" (cited in Mousset 1923: 202–203). Thus, just when France was abandoning its Bourbon dynastic ties because of their excessive risk, Spain was discounting them for yielding too little, and seemingly too late.

While France was seeking a peaceful, cost-free resolution of the crisis, England continued to arm and Spanish patience wore increasingly thin. Never, charged Floridablanca in July, would England have dared act so resolutely had it not been sure that Spain would receive no assistance from an ally "whose critical situation prevented it from taking part in the events of Europe," an accusation that must have been especially wounding to Montmorin because it underscored his own worst fears of French impotence.[15] Yet so fearful was Montmorin of the Assembly's response that he only dared submit Spain's formal request for assistance in early August. What finally moved him to act was less Spanish pressure than the new political entente he was establishing with Mirabeau. As the author of the 22 May resolution and the dominating figure on the subcommittee of the Assembly charged with re-examining all France's foreign treaties, Mirabeau was ideally positioned to act as the ministry's point-man, and on 25 August he submitted the subcommittee's report on the *pacte de famille* to the full Assembly (Masson 1977: 82–83).

In a masterpiece of discursive *bricolage*, Mirabeau managed to thread together pieces of the seemingly irreconcilable ministerial and Jacobin narratives by once again granting to the left its principles and to the right its operative demands. Although he avoided all reference to the "Austrian Plot," he conceded to the left that England was not France's inveterate enemy, but rather a fellow-traveler in liberty that made it France's natural ally. Yet sharing France's "political religion," Mirabeau conceded to the right, did not ensure England's commitment to peace. If England did not seek a military conflict and was arming merely to secure a better peace agreement, French fulfillment of the defensive clauses of the *pacte de famille*, which is what Mirabeau proposed, would not be viewed as a provocation and thus not lead to war. But if England did seek a war, France's support for Spain was critical for defending its ally from an English attack, which could only be succeeded by a second one, motivated by the "same ambition and an even more animated vengeance," upon a still vulnerable France.[16] Nodding once again to the left, Mirabeau insisted that France would stand by only the defensive clauses of the *pacte de famille*. But if France abandoned the *pacte de famille* altogether, Mirabeau warned, Madrid might wind up making concessions to England that were highly damaging to French credit and commerce. On that argument he proposed arming thirty war ships, which the Assembly raised to forty-five in the course of enthusiastically ratifying Mirabeau's proposal on 26 August.[17]

It has recently been argued, against standard views, that in reaffirming the French commitment to the defensive clauses of the *pacte de famille* backed by the commissioning of forty-five ships, Mirabeau's amended motion signaled not a repudiation of the alliance, but its reaffirmation (Belissa 1998: 203). To be sure, because the English expected the French to forsake the alliance altogether, the vigor of the resolution did catch Pitt off-guard, and he did, much to Montmorin's relief, come to terms with Spain on 28 October. Yet to view that settlement as a reaffirmation of the *pacte de famille*, let alone a victory for French diplomacy, would entail misconstruing the process by which England and Spain retreated from war as well as the consequences. To begin with, the Assembly's authorization of forty-five warships hardly forced the English to the bargaining table, as

La Luzerne and Montmorin preferred to think. For widespread reports of mutinies in the Brest shipyards and Montmorin's own indiscreet hints that France was in no rush to expand its navy – undoubtedly made to dissuade Pitt from waging war – weakened the impact of the 26 August resolution on English decision-making (Black 1994: 248). Indeed, it is probable that Montmorin cynically intended to use the Assembly's resolution more to placate Madrid with specious assurances of support than to intimidate London with real warships. But the Spanish were not deceived by Montmorin's duplicity. Resentful of France's repeated failures to support them over the previous three decades, Spain could only regard France's temporizing in the current crisis as another instance of French bad faith. Thus, in July 1791 Floridablanca, recalling the "treaties that we [the French] had broken so often they could no longer be relied upon," bitterly dismissed France's self-serving claims that it had acted as Spain's loyal ally during the crisis. The Assembly's authorization of arms for only defensive purposes, he insisted, meant "that the provisions of the *pacte de famille* had not been fulfilled."[18]

The French had no more reason to celebrate the settlement of the crisis than the Spanish. To be sure, France had escaped involvement in a possibly ruinous war. But England – France's pre-eminent enemy in the ministerial narrative – had won a clear victory without firing a shot. As Louis XVI told the Spanish ambassador Fernan Nuñez, "your convention [with England] is nothing but a bundle of thorns" (cited in Mousset 1923: 225). Although the unexpectedly strong resolution of 26 August had temporarily boosted French credibility abroad, that credibility – particularly among the dreaded English – declined again once Europe learned of the settlement. As a dismayed La Luzerne reported, a London theater, which during the crisis had staged a play commemorating English victories over Spain, replaced it, when the crisis was over, with a farce that "covered the National Assembly with ridicule."[19] Worse still was the alienation of France's closest ally. Indeed, having lost faith in its dynastic cousin, Spain began slipping into England's diplomatic orbit, and the impact was felt as far away as Russia. During the crisis, the French *chargé d'affaires* in the Russian capital, Edmond Charles Genêt, had labored hard with the Spanish ambassador Galvez to construct a defensive league among their two nations, Russia, Denmark, and Sweden in opposition to the Triple Alliance. But upon resolution of the crisis, Galvez abruptly stopped communicating with Genêt, and in early 1791 Genêt realized that Spain had given up on the defensive league that he and Galvez had tried to assemble. Instead, Genêt reported, Galvez was now working on Pitt's behalf to reconstruct ties between London and St. Petersburg![20]

It was, of course, true that the *pacte de famille* had been a mixed blessing for both parties, and Spain, not being a first-rank power, alone posed no major threat to French security. But deep and wide as Montmorin's suspicions of English ambitions had run since the Dutch crisis of 1787, he had not anticipated the unraveling of the *pacte de famille* before the Nootka Sound crisis erupted; and he surely could take no comfort in a report of July 1791 indicating that "some plan among foreign powers" was brewing in Madrid and that Floridablanca had spookily warned revolutionary France it would "surely be punished" because it stood "guilty" in the eyes of Providence.[21]

Like Montmorin, the Jacobins could find some relief in the fact that France had not been drawn into a war on behalf of its dynastic ally. Nevertheless, the new signs of Anglo-Spanish collusion bred suspicions that the Jacobins' faith in English good intentions had been misplaced, and these suspicions were compounded by fears of a growing coalition of counter-revolutionary forces at home and abroad. For if it was true that Spain – dynastically linked to the French royal family and to the Habsburgs – had been acting in harmony with the evil "Austrian Committee," it seemed entirely possible that in its settlement with England, about which Floridablanca had kept Montmorin in the dark, Spain had secretly offered Pitt the use of its fleet to support England in a joint crusade against France. Indeed, warned the radical journal *Orateur du peuple*, an Anglo-Spanish attack on French colonies and ports now seemed imminent, and many people, according to one anonymous source, were convinced that "Spain and England must be uniting to destroy the French Revolution."[22] Camille Desmoulins went even further. "All courts are conspiring against the French constitution," he declared: "Vienna, Turin, Madrid, Naples, and the cabinets of St. James and St. Cloud."[23]

The Unimaginable Alliance and the Resurgence of Austria

Serious enough in isolation, the effective rupture of the *pacte de famille* was all the more grave because it occurred at the same time that France's other major alliance, with Austria, was also collapsing. Under strain for many years, the Austrian alliance came under renewed pressure in 1789 when Vienna tried to resolve a crisis generated by an armed revolt in Belgium, insurgency in Hungary, a costly and still unresolved war with Turkey, and most intimidating of all, the likelihood of a Prussian attack. Given its own weakness, there seemed little France could or would do to assist their embattled ally. Thus even before the Austrian emperor Joseph II died in February 1790 and Leopold II succeeded him, Austria sent out diplomatic feelers to England in hopes of restoring their long-lapsed partnership and thereby apply English leverage to contain Prussian aggression. Negotiations failed to yield a settlement largely because England and Austria were still too closely tied to their respective allies (Hochedlinger 2003: 391–392). Nevertheless, the mere possibility that Vienna might desert Paris for London – at the very moment that the *pacte de famille* was dissolving – sent chills up Montmorin's spine. "We can influence nothing," he wrote in despair to the French ambassador to Austria, the comte de Noailles, in August 1790. "Instead of directing events, we face the painful necessity of following them ...We have more than one reason to be distrustful of [Austria]: everything depends on the extent of the ties established between [Vienna] and London."[24]

Although Vienna did not sacrifice Paris for London at this juncture, France encountered another aspect of the Austrian crisis that was far more unexpected and bristled with no less serious implications – the emerging reconciliation of Austria and Prussia (Hochedlinger 2003: 392–396; Lord 1915: ch. 7). For a half-century, France had been able to project power in eastern Europe by playing off these two apparently "natural enemies" against each other. But in July 1790 Prussia – frustrated in its territorial ambitions – and Austria – seeking to reverse its sinking fortunes – began settling some of the outstanding issues between them in the Convention of Reichenbach. Austria agreed to exit the Turkish war with the possibility of making only minor territorial gains, while Prussia agreed to broker the Austrian reoccupation of Belgium with the other members of the Triple Alliance. Not surprisingly, the deep suspicions between the two German rivals did not melt away overnight and the possibility of war between them lingered. But Austria did escape invasion, and a major corner in its relationship with Prussia had been turned, leading to the signing of a preliminary alliance between the two powers in July 1791 and a formal alliance in February 1792. That slowly emerging reunion plus the stamping out of revolt in Belgium and of opposition in Hungary put Austria by the summer of 1791 in the strongest international position that it had enjoyed for years, while France lost almost all its leverage in eastern Europe.

To believers in the ministerial narrative, who were inclined to take a benign view of Leopold II's intentions, Austria's recovery and its rapprochement with Prussia did not appear immediately threatening to French interests. Despite increasing talk of a German "national" war over the French government's refusal to compensate German princes for the loss of their seigneurial rights in Frances's eastern provinces via negotiations with the Imperial Diet, Montmorin at the end of 1790 discounted rumors that Austria and/or Prussia would exploit the dispute to provoke an armed conflict (Belissa 1998: 219; Muret: 1899–1900). Likewise, the pro-ministerial *Gazette universelle* dismissed the notion that the German states were plotting the violent re-annexation of Alsace and Lorraine. "There will be no war between the Empire and France, other than that of the pen," editorialized the journal on 14 July 1791. "We will be attacked by written matter and brochures, and nothing else."[25]

But to the Austrophobic Jacobins, who had been inclined to believe and were encouraged (and bribed) by the Prussian agent Ephraim to advertise that Frederick William II was a friend of the Revolution, the unthinkable, but undeniably emergent Berlin–Vienna axis presented a terrible prospect, indeed the latest turn in the "Austrian Plot." Having previously urged his countrymen to look to Prussia as one of France's strongest allies against Austrian aggression, Carra, by the end of 1790, was deploring Prussia's acquiescence in the Austrian recapture of Belgium as sealed at Reichenbach. "Thus," he wrote in despair, "did the house of Austria, which the tyrannical follies of Joseph II had brought within two steps of its ruin, revive with more power and audacity than ever; thus did the [supposedly] benign Leopold expand his empire, despite its imminent dissolution; thus did the weak [Frederick] William, seized by a panic fear of revolution in his own states, play the dupe of his wily and mortal enemy the Austrian Caesar in the treaty of Reichenbach."[26] Already in March 1790 Peysonnel had laid out what an Austro-Prussian rapprochement might mean. "Who could guarantee that the forces of Prussia and Austria, joined within our borders, would not attack French Flanders, Hainault, Cambrésis, our first and second line [of defense], and would not perhaps try to attack Alsace and Lorraine?"[27] In March 1791, with the Vienna–Berlin axis harder than ever, Brissot could be more definite and specific. The convention of Reichenbach, he charged, contained a secret plan to "descend on France." Austria and Prussia would commission the prince de Cobourg to lead their combined armies. If their offensive were successful, Austria would annex Alsace and Lorraine, while Prussia would expand outward from Silesia and in the Netherlands. Troops were currently being deployed along the Rhine, and the primary attack would come through Flanders. "The plan is to reach Paris, concluded Brissot, "and to strangle the Revolution."[28]

The Road to War[29]

In reality, neither Leopold II nor Frederick William II had any intention of invading France, alone or in combination. Indeed, both princes had been initially sympathetic to the French Revolution, and neither wished to see a return of the *ancien régime*, which might well have resurrected France as a major military power. But the revolutionaries' increasingly hostile treatment of the French royal family, which set a bad example to their own subjects, in combination with the danger that revolutionary principles might be exported, led these two princes to change perspective by the end of 1790. As brother to the endangered French queen Marie-Antoinette, Leopold II was especially sensitive to her plight. When the royal family began planning to flee Paris and she naturally turned to him for support in late December 1790, the Austrian emperor responded by pledging to deliver financial aid and military assistance once and so long as the royal family eluded their revolutionary captors (Price 2002: ch. 7). Because after fleeing Paris incognito on 21 June 1791 they were intercepted at Varennes and forced to return to Paris, Leopold II was freed from making good on his commitment. But he had not lost interest in the fate of the royal family, which henceforth became increasingly entangled in the larger struggles among Europe's great powers (Blanning 1986: ch. 3).

This point needs emphasis because most historians have portrayed Leopold II's response to Varennes as timid, if not accommodationist. Although the Padua Circular, issued by Leopold II in July, and the Pillnitz Declaration, issued jointly with Frederick William II in August, threatened military action against France, Leopold II's commitment, these historians point out, was binding only in the unlikely event that the other European powers participated in this intervention. This stipulation and the mustering out of 25,000 troops from the Austrian army during the summer of 1791 do indeed indicate that for the time being the Austrians believed war was neither desirable nor likely.

Nevertheless, the Padua Circular and the Pillnitz Declaration were neither politically meaningless nor innocent, and the French, now more isolated than ever, were not delusional for viewing them as threats to be taken seriously. The Padua Circular and the Pillnitz Declaration may have freed Leopold II from any obligation to send his troops across the Rhine unilaterally; but by the same token they were mechanisms to sound out potential future allies that could *threaten* France with war in the short term and possibly *wage* war later if these threats proved unavailing. For this reason, as Hamish Scott has rightly argued, the summer of 1791 was a decisive moment in crystallizing the coalition that would eventually fight France (Scott 2006: 254). Moreover, although Leopold II surely intended to stop short of war, in the summer of 1791 he proposed taking measures that were not far from it, such as an economic and diplomatic boycott of France. Such measures shocked even the relatively bellicose Frederick William II. Although he favored the drafting of a "fixed plan" of coordinated attack with which to intimidate France and thereby repress "the contagion ... of license and insubordination," the Prussian king doubted that an economic boycott would work; and he rejected outright the Austrian proposal to recall all foreign ambassadors as the "equivalent of a declaration of war that the very dignity of the allied courts would not permit until the moment of actual rupture" (Vivenot 1873–93: vol. 1, 218–219).

In the end, what made Austrian-inspired threats so dangerous was not so much the fears they naturally aroused among French Austrophobes as the false conclusion drawn by the Austrians that their threats had been effective. For having been arrested and suspended of his functions after the Varennes episode, Louis XVI was reinstated in the fall of 1791 under a new constitution that he formally swore to uphold, and at first he got along reasonably well with the new Assembly and moderate Feuillant ministry. This unexpected return to calm promoted the Austrian belief that allied intimidation had moderated French politics once, and, if necessary, could do so again (Blanning 1986: 89).

It would not take long before another round of bullying seemed in order, for Louis XVI's honeymoon with the Assembly had ended by November. In addition, the Brissotin coalition in the Assembly, hoping to ride to power by stalking the issue, began whipping up war fever against Austria in October, which Vienna took as a sign that further action was needed to prevent the "factions" from coming to power and again endangering the royal family. There can be no question that the Brissotins bore a heavy responsibility for igniting the first war of the French Revolution, which erupted six months later. They actively lobbied for war in the press and in the Assembly, contending, on the one hand, that counter-revolutionary armies, abetted by the "Austrian Committee," were about to put the *patrie* to the sword, and on the other that these armies were easily vanquished paper tigers.

But as historians have insufficiently recognized, Austria – by resuming its policy of brinksmanship – made it infinitely easier for the Brissotins to win their case for war before the French public. On 21 December 1791 the Austrian chancellor Wenzel Anton Kaunitz warned that any provocative French action would be countered by a league of "sovereigns together united to maintain public tranquility and the security and honor of their crowns."[30] These words were subsequently recalled and deplored, not only by the Jacobins, but also by the ministerial faction, which, hoping to preserve the 1756 alliance in the interests of peace and the royal family, had hitherto taken a relatively benign view of Austrian policy. Now the ministerial faction confronted what they had every reason to regard as evidence of Austrian bad faith. The new foreign minister Delessart – a Feuillant later purged for insufficient vigilance against Austria – saw in Kaunitz's words "the sign of a league formed without the knowledge of France and possibly directed against it." "We are shocked," he declared, "that the Emperor, brother-in-law and ally of the king, did not inform him of this concert formed among the sovereigns of Europe, at the head of which His Imperial Majesty appears to be placed."[31]

Despite repeated warnings sent to Vienna by Delessart, Noailles, and even Mercy-Argenteau that French sensibilities were at their rawest and the slightest threat could unleash a war, the Austrians, having once, they thought, bullied the French into submission, returned to their policy of intimidation. Far from moderating his threats in response, Kaunitz, under growing pressure from Prussia and Austrian advocates of a hard line, warned again and again that Austria and its confederates, notwithstanding their standing as foreign powers, had the right and duty to punish Jacobin violations of the new French constitution. On 17 February 1792 he proclaimed that while Leopold II had done all he could to restrain the *émigrés*, the Austrian-led coalition intended to "force the king and nation to accept the laws they had made" – that is, ensure the inviolability of the king and the monarchy.[32] Of course, Austria continued to count on getting what it wanted on the cheap rather than by putting its troops in the field; but this made no difference in the end in French calculations. As Jean-Joachim Pellenc reported on 15 January 1792, the French were increasingly persuaded "that there is a coalition hatching among the powers; that the emperor is the leader of it; that he will ultimately attack us, if he is not checked; that delays will thus end in our destruction by giving our enemies the time to prepare" (Glagau 1896: 288).

Fearing, in other words, that if it delayed any longer France would lose the advantage in any likely military encounter, the National Assembly on 20 April 1792 declared war nearly unanimously on the new Austrian ruler Francis II after the new foreign minister Charles Dumouriez delivered a speech that firmly situated recent Austrian provocations within the context of the historic "Austrian Plot."[33]

This war and those that followed soon sucked in most other major European powers, partly because of the coalition-building that had preceded it. Having ridden to power on the war issue as they had planned, the Brissotins tried to limit the scope of the war through some instant diplomacy with England and Prussia that would at least keep them neutral. But just as the ministerial faction had to abandon some of its illusions about Austria, so did the Brissotins have to swallow some hard truths about these "natural allies." Faithful to his alliance with Austria, Frederick William II declared war on France on 21 May 1792, and although it was France that declared war on England the following February, this was in anticipation of an imminent English declaration of war on France, which thereafter pre-emptively declared war on Spain and the Netherlands.

Final Assessment

Whether the virtual encirclement of France by a hostile counter-revolutionary coalition in 1793 was the "inevitable" result of the French Revolution of 1789 is impossible to determine definitively, for the chains of cause and effect between them extended in both directions and were in many respects indirect. It is true that the Revolution, as it became more radical and anti-dynastic, became proportionally more noxious in the eyes of the foreign powers, thereby generating common interests – or at least a common language – among them. Yet Blanning and others are certainly correct to deny that for ideological reasons the other European powers could never have learned to live peaceably alongside revolutionary France. Had Prussia and Austria not diplomatically reconciled; had Leopold II and Francis II not believed they enjoyed at least the moral support of counter-revolutionary regimes like Spain and Russia; and above all, had the Austrians not assumed they could easily defeat a power so bankrupt and so racked by revolution as France, it is hard to imagine that Austria, in collaboration with Prussia, would have pursued the high-risk strategy it adopted after Varennes, thereby inciting the French declaration of war. In other words, ideological conflict may been a *necessary* precondition of war, but it was not a *sufficient* one.

If French weakness invited Austria and its allies to regard the Revolution as not only a rude disruption to be quashed but also a golden opportunity to be exploited, it was also critical in framing French perceptions and generating French responses – more so than dreams of conquest. As recent research has shown, such dreams did not have much purchase on the French political imagination until late 1791 and derived less from a new forward revolutionary global strategy than from the search for like-minded "friends of liberty" in the face of increasing diplomatic isolation (Belissa 1998: 287). Similarly, far from precipitously discarding established public and international law in a fit of ideological fervor as counter-revolutionaries then and many historians since have alleged, the revolutionaries were very much at pains between 1789 and 1791 to invoke that law when justifying their incorporation of French "national" rights in Corsica, Avignon, and Alsace (Kolla 2010). Thin as these justifications might have appeared, they were hardly thinner than those proffered by the very members of the counter-revolutionary coalition, which, while indignant at the "license" exhibited by revolutionary France, had themselves within recent memory seized Silesia, raped Saxony, carved up Poland, and nonchalantly rearranged the map of Italy to suit their own interests. Of course, the revolutionaries always professed that once France was "regenerated," its plentiful resources, exceptional enlightenment, and stainless virtue would empower the nation to recapture its "natural" pre-eminence, restore its lost national honor, and make the new France a light to the world. Nor can it be denied that once the war began, the French appetite for conquest intensified. *L'appétit vient en mangeant.* But before that vision and that feast could be realized, revolutionaries acted at least as much out of fear as out of hope, at least as much in defense as offense. Differently as the ministerial and Jacobin "narratives" mapped the political geography of Europe, both were "realistic" enough to acknowledge that for the indefinite present the nation was at risk and vulnerable to the designs of its enemies. This is one reason why they were so apocalyptic in tone. It is also why, when an Austrian-led coalition of powers seemed prepared to embark on a counter-revolutionary crusade in the spring of 1792, the two narratives worked awkwardly in tandem to convince the National Assembly and the nation that the only reasonable response was war.

Notes

The author would like to express his gratitude to Hamish Scott for his close reading and helpful suggestions for revision of an early draft of this chapter.

1 *Archives parlementaires* (1867–1913) (henceforth *AP*), 8: 55. The translation is mine, as are all those that follow.

2 Archives du Ministère des Affaires Étrangères (henceforth AAE), Correspondance Politique (henceforth CP), Allemagne 661, folio 197.

3 Lescure 1866, vol. 2, 176.
4 Favier 1866: vol. 2, 109.
5 AAE Mémoires et Documents Russie 16, folio 313.
6 AAE CP Espagne 625, folios 33–4.
7 AAE CP Angleterre 573, folio 117.
8 *AP*, 15: 616.
9 *AP*, 15: 538.
10 Jean-Antoine-Nicolas de Caritat, marquis de Condorcet, *Extrait du pacte de famille*, in Condorcet O'Connor et al. 1847–9: vol. 10, 44–5.
11 *AP*, 15: 530.
12 *Annales patriotiques et littéraires*, no. 279 (8 July 1790 – supplement), 115, and 226 (16 May 1790), 3.
13 *Patriote français*, no. 320 (24 June 1790), 4.
14 *AP*, 15: 661–662.
15 AAE CP Espagne 629, folio 112.
16 *AP*, 18: 265.
17 *AP*, 18: 293.
18 AAE CP Espagne 630, folios 404–405.
19 AAE CP Angleterre 575, folios 384–385.
20 AAE CP Russie 133 and 134, *passim*.
21 AAE CP Espagne 630, folio 286.
22 *Orateur du peuple*, no. 22 (1790), 171; Lescure 1866: vol. 2, 482.
23 *Révolutions de France et de Brabant*, no. 50 (8 Nov. 1790), 495.
24 AAE CP Autriche 360, folio 110.
25 *Gazette universelle*, 2 no. 195 (14 July 1791), 778.
26 *Annales patriotiques*, no. 454 (30 Dec. 1790), 854.
27 Peysonnel 1790: 20.
28 *Patriote français*, no. 579 (10 Mar. 1791), 258.
29 The following section is a condensed version of the argument elaborated in Kaiser 2008.
30 AAE CP Autriche 362, folio 287.
31 AAE CP Autriche 363, folio 55.
32 As published in the *Moniteur universel*, 11 (3 Mar. 1792), 525. Brissot roundly criticized this statement in a speech to the Assembly published in the *Moniteur universel*, 11 (12 Mar. 1792), 602–603.
33 *AP*, 42: 195–199.

References

Primary Sources

Archives du Ministère des Affaires Étrangères

AP: *Archives parlementaires de 1787 à 1860. Recueil complet des débats législatifs et politiques des chambres françaises, imprimé par ordre du corps législatif sous la direction de mm. J. Mavidal et E. Laurent. Première série, 1787–1799* (1867–1913), 82 vols. Paris: P. Dupont.

Condorcet O'Connor, A. and M.F. Arago (eds.). (1847–49). *Oeuvres de Condorcet*, 12 vols. Paris: Firmin Didot.

Favier, Jean-Louis (1866). *Conjectures raisonnées sur la situation actuelle de la France*. In M. E. Boutaric (ed.). *Correspondance secrète inédite de Louis XV sur la politique étrangère avec le comte de Broglie, Tercier, etc.*, 2 vols. Paris: Plon.

Lescure, Adolphe Mathurin de (ed.) (1866). *Correspondance secrète inédite sur Louis XVI, Marie-Antoinette, la cour et la ville de 1777 à 1792*, 2 vols. Paris: H. Plon.

Peysonnel, Charles (1790). *Discours prononcé à l'Assemblée de la Société des Amis de la Constitution … le mercredi 10 mars 1790*. Paris: Chez Gattey.

Other Sources

Beales, Derek (1987, 2009). *Joseph II*, 2 vols. Cambridge: Cambridge University Press.

Belissa, Marc (1998). *Fraternité universelle et intérêt national (1713–1795): Les Cosmopolitiques du droit des gens*. Paris: Éditions Kimé.

Black, Jeremy (1994). *British Foreign Policy in an Age of Revolutions, 1783–1793*. Cambridge: Cambridge University Press.

Blanning, T.C.W. (1996). *The Origins of the French Revolutionary Wars*. London: Longman.

Blart, Louis (1915). *Les Rapports de la France et de l'Espagne après le pacte de famille jusqu'à la fin du ministère du duc de Choiseul*. Paris: Félix Alcan.

Dziembowksi, Edmond (1998). *Un nouveau patriotisme français, 1750–1770: La France face à la puissance anglaise à l'époque de la guerre de Sept Ans*. In *Studies on Voltaire and the Eighteenth Century*, vol. 365. Oxford: Voltaire Foundation.

Glagau, Hans (ed.) (1896). *Die Französische Legislative und der Ursprung der Revolutionskriege, 1791–1792*. Berlin: E. Ebering.

Hochedlinger, Michael (2003). *Austria's Wars of Emergence, 1683–1797*. London: Longman.

Kaiser, Thomas E. (2000). "Who's Afraid of Marie-Antoinette? Diplomacy, Austrophobia and the Queen." *FH*, 14: 241–271.

Kaiser, Thomas E. (2008). "La Fin du renversement des alliances: La France, l'Autriche et la déclaration de guerre du 20 avril 1792." *AHRF*, 351: 77–98.

Kaiser, Thomas E. (2009). "Entre les mots et les choses: Le Fantôme du 'comité autrichien'." In Annie Duprat (ed.). *Révolutions et mythes identitaires: Mots, violences, mémoire*. Paris: Nouveau Monde. 31–47.

Kaiser, Thomas E. (2011). "From Fiscal Crisis to Revolution: The Court and French Foreign Policy." In Thomas E. Kaiser and Dale K. Van Kley (eds.). *From Deficit to Deluge: The Origins of the French Revolution*. Stanford, Calif.: Stanford University Press. Ch. 4.

Kolla, Edward James (2010). "*Legality, Legitimacy, and the Will of the People: The French Revolution and the Transformation of International Law, 1789–1792*." Ph.D. dissertation, Johns Hopkins University.

Lord, Robert Howard (1915). *The Second Partition of Poland: A Study in Diplomatic History*. Cambridge, Mass.: Harvard University Press.

Masson, Frédéric (1977). *Le Département des Affaires Étrangères pendant la Révolution 1787–1804*. Geneva: Slatkin-Megariotis. Reprint of 1877 edn.

Mousset, Albert (1923). *Un témoin ignoré de la Révolution: Le Comte de Fernan Nuñez, ambassadeur d'Espagne à Paris (1787–1791)*. Paris: Édouard Champion.

Muret, Pierre (1899–1900). "L'Affaire des princes possessionnés d'Alsace et les origines du conflit entre la Révolution et l'Empire." *RHMC*, 1: 433–456, 566–592.

Murphy, Orville Theodore (1998). *The Diplomatic Retreat of France and Public Opinion on the Eve of the French Revolution, 1783–1789*. Washington, D.C.: Catholic University Press of America.

Price, Munro (2002). *The Road from Versailles: Louis XVI, Marie-Antoinette, and the Fall of the French Monarchy*. New York: St. Martin's Press.

Savage, Gary (1998). "Favier's Heirs: The French Revolution and the *Secret du Roi*." *HJ*, 4: 225–258.

Scott, Hamish (2006). *The Birth of a Great Power System 1740–1815*. Harlow: Pearson.
Scott, Samuel F. (1978). *The Response of the Royal Army to the French Revolution: The Role and Development of the Line Army, 1787–93*. Oxford: Clarendon Press.
Vivenot, Alfred Ritter von (ed.) (1873–93). *Quellen zur Geschichte der Deutschen Kaiserpolitik Oesterreichs während der Französischen Revolutionskriege, 1790–1801*, 5 vols. Vienna: Wilhelm Braumüller.
Whiteman, Jeremy J. (2003). *Reform, Revolution and French Global Policy, 1787–1791*. Aldershot: Ashgate.

Part IV

Contesting the Limits of Revolution

Chapter Eleven

Whose Revolution?

Serge Aberdam

The title of this chapter has two interpretations in French, and these alternatives are meaningful in terms of the groups involved. If we ask "To whom did the Revolution belong?" we risk essentializing the Revolution by assuming that one or more actors were in charge. The other wording, "Whom did the Revolution concern?", is less mechanical, since the Revolution did not "concern" only those involved in it but society as a whole, those for whom it was a thousand miles from their preoccupations as well as those who took risks for it. From this logic, however, not everybody was equally concerned with the Declarations, those of 1789, 1793, and 1795, which did not necessarily contain the essential meaning of the Revolution.

Rights and Exclusions

If we begin with four categories excluded from rights at one time or another – slaves, mulattoes (in the French juridical sense "free persons of color"), women, and one group of Jews – a demonstration of the slowness of emancipation may be sketched. This was more accurately a delay for mulattoes and Jews; a refusal of political rights for women; advances and then spectacular reversals for the civic status of women and slaves. Any deeper study reveals nuances in each case, in the sense that civic and political rights did not march in step. From that comes an overall impression of limited results that at the time was immediately apparent to interested parties.

It should be noted above all that the universal conception of rights, which is too often examined *a posteriori*, was not necessarily understood in the same way by contemporaries. Thus the consequences which might have flowed from certain articles must be carefully stipulated. Even the Declaration of 1793, the most liberal and wide-ranging (Aberdam 2006–7), left considerable room for interpretation to

A Companion to the French Revolution, First Edition. Edited by Peter McPhee.

both readers and jurists. Hence it stipulated in Article 3, in a direct link to the first article of the Declaration of 1789, that "All men are equal through nature and before the law," but it equally made clear in Article 18 (repeated in Article 15 in that of 1795) that "Any man may commit his services or his time; but he may neither sell himself, nor be sold. His person is not alienable property." For us, the meaning of these phrases and their applicability to slavery seems obvious. It does not appear, however, that such was the case at the time: the operability of the text was not obvious. In reality, it was the slave revolts and the need to mobilize them to resist the counter-revolution which led to the official abolition in Saint-Domingue, later taken up and expanded by the Convention – and we know that the abolition was temporary.

Are there not other cases where measures at first taken pragmatically, under pressure from interested parties, were afterwards more or less accurately inscribed in law, then rethought in the context of the applicability of rights? Much depended on the manner in which different classes of people reacted to their situation and were able to impose change. There were many intermediary cases between admission to "equal" rights and exclusion from them, between the abrupt abolition of orders and honorific privileges, linked to the night of 4 August and the first declaration of rights, and demands which would not be accepted as stemming from a claim of rights for a long time. Those of women, for example, precisely because their formulation called into question the organization of the whole of society and the family, quickly became the object of a pure and simple rejection, and were dismissed as farcical.

The exclusion of women, however, was not unequivocal. In politics, it took several years to reverse the tendency of local communities to count widows or female property-owners among taxpayers and therefore among those whose vote must be sought. In civic rights, inequality of inheritance was the rule under the *ancien régime*, whether between brothers or between brothers and sisters. The situation of younger siblings and daughters was doubly unequal, since the laws on inheritance depended on the place of residence and the diverse legislations of the *parlements*. This juridical heterogeneity of the kingdom then became part of campaigns in favor of the uniformity of laws, taxes, administration, weights and measures, languages, and so on. Equality of inheritance was only adopted after almost four years, in March 1793, and it would be definitive, albeit difficult to apply. That was not the case for divorce, made possible in September 1792 but the object of an abrupt turnaround under the Consulate.

In the late eighteenth century other exclusions from common law equally concerned more marginal groups, such as freethinkers, *libertins*, and atheists, but also homosexuals, labeled as *sodomites* or even just *onanistes*, who could at any moment become the object of legal persecution or public stigmatization, from which were exempt neither actors nor children of people who had committed suicide. In similar fashion, descendants of lepers (*cagots*) were excluded from normal social life. These archaic forms of discrimination disappeared very slowly, even when their legal basis had been removed. Actors, treated as pariahs in the system of civic rights, recovered common law rights despite the jibes directed towards Collot d'Herbois and other actors and actresses active in public life. The articles of the Penal Code adopted in September–October 1791 abolished capital punishment for the crime of sodomy, but the mass of "offenses against decency" continued, and for a long time. At the same time unbelievers, if not atheists, were accepted or at least tolerated by virtue of the endless nuances between public *conduct* and personal *opinion*. Nevertheless, neither the liberty proclaimed in 1789 nor the relative independence enjoyed for a time by civil society with regard to the moral norms of the official church prevented a continuity of repression.

Well beyond the declaration of 1789, the separation – in fact then in law – between religion and the state was a novel experience for which, exceptionally, the context was provided by the declarations of 1793 and 1795. The former only declared separation by affirming religious freedom without any place whatsoever for an official religion, but the second stipulated it explicitly. This separation unleashed powerful forces, such as the vigorous anticlericalism and dechristianization of the autumn of 1793, the Gallican Presbyterianism of the Église Nationale of 1795–99, or the mysticism of Catholic reaction around the return to the *catacombes*. Put back on track by Bonaparte with the 1801 Concordat, the Roman Catholic Church – which had remained dominant – hurried to smother its rivals, whether the republicans of the Église Nationale or the traditionalists (*enfarinés*) of the Petite Église. Catholicism would impose its public worship and control of education and daily life until the separation of 1905.

In the space of three or four years, limits were removed on rights to worship for Protestants, members of different Jewish rites, and other minority religions. But we need to be mindful about the survival of local discrimination which could, for example, keep Jews on the margins of political rights. The strength of anti-semitism drew surprising support from leaders of the most integrated communities: for the so-called "Portuguese" Jews of Bordeaux, Bayonne, and around Avignon, the fear of losing their few privileges was a powerful motive in the toleration of discrimination against the Ashkenazi Jews of Alsace and Lorraine, who themselves had something to lose compared with Jews in the Holy Roman Empire. A universalist logic was not spontaneously embraced by the oppressed. Even Zalkind Hourwitz hesitated between various approaches. A Parisian Jew from Poland (Malino 2000), whose essay was awarded a prize by the Société des Arts et Sciences of Metz in 1789, he replied to the question "Are there ways to make Jews more useful and fortunate in France?" On the one hand, he pleaded for universal rights, not hesitating to mock the "paternalist" assumptions of the Académie in contemporary sardonic style (Bourguinat 1998). But Hourwitz also admitted that means had to be found to "liberate" Alsatian Jews from their practice of usury, and the persistence of anti-semitism led him to note sadly: "the lamb of the fable is indeed stupid if, instead of fleeing, he wastes time in protesting his innocence to the wolf who knows it as well as he does." As a consequence, with Napoleonic legislation on the organization of minority religions, the *ancien régime* situation where people were considered members of "communities" because they practiced particular religions was only slowly left behind. However, during the Empire as well as the Restoration, while political rights became more constrained, access to civil rights continued to expand in practice.

Rare were those who concerned themselves with the lot of prisoners or mentally ill detainees. Their situation was not only invisible to the majority of activists: it was far from being formulated in terms of rights. The third declaration (1795, Article 14) made very clear that "any treatment which worsens the punishment determined by law is a crime," but the practical outcome was very limited. A woman whom we would describe as a militant feminist, Théroigne de Méricourt, was interned in 1793 for the rest of her days, chained to the wall of her cell (Godineau 1988; Roudinesco 1989). There was no recourse against this incarceration, which reduced feminist politicization to madness. The fiction of Peter Weiss (*Marat-Sade*, 1963) is perhaps closest to the mood of the time than our endless debate about the role of the liberal "aliéniste" Philippe Pinel in 1793–98 (Foucault 1964, 2003; Sémelaigne 2001; Swain 1997; Weiner 1999). What must be kept in mind, however, is the Bonaparte brothers' regime of politico-psychiatric internment, which met hardly any resistance. In sum, when considering the applicability of rights, not only must the active existence of a particular group be borne in mind, but it must equally be remembered that the conception of rights was far more restricted than that to which we habitually refer.

It is true, however, that eighteenth-century French men and women were aware of, experienced, or on the contrary criticized an endless number of more or less flagrant inequalities. Knowledge of all these rules of subordination was part of their culture, absorbed from childhood and indispensable for living in their society. Many situations which, in hindsight, we would define as exclusions from rights were elemental ground rules which contemporaries knew made up the social terrain. They were the same rules as those that historians of the *ancien régime* and the Revolution seek to keep in mind as they undertake research. If they forget them they create misunderstandings and anachronisms, which their colleagues highlight. But contemporaries who ignored them risked being placed in the pillory, imprisoned, whipped with canes, or thrown in the river, unless they were regarded as insane, which was much worse. Between privileges and properties, rights and duties due to others from each person and considered as being natural, feudal, or contractual in origin, every individual would have had difficulty in forming a clear image of his or her position with regard to rights, but the resolution of several major issues helped clarify them.

Rustics, Peasants, and Commoners

Numerous rules of subordination governed every layer of *ancien régime* society, described significantly as a "cascade of contempt," in which everyone was supposed to scorn those who were weaker. What we would now call exclusions from rights then took a perfectly legal form, with important economic consequences. So statutes applying to persons or land or both and proclaimed as having a "feudal" origin had been renegotiated periodically across the centuries while also being held to be immutable. In 1789, the servitude of *serfs* had practically disappeared and those subject to *mainmorte* (seigneurial control over land at the owner's death) were few in number, even if some remained; but it was quite the opposite concerning tenant farmers and others who were liable for dues (*redevables* or *censitaires*), all of them subject to the tithe, peasants who were freeholders but equally perpetually liable to an extraordinarily diverse mass of dues, rents, services, and obligations. These constraints had been reinforced by the "seigneurial reaction" of the eighteenth century, provoking in response a juridical thicket of lawsuits between rural people and "owners" of rights. In the final decades of the absolute monarchy, it mattered little to those who were liable that their obligations were tied to their personal status or to that of the land that they "held": they had no choice other than to cling to the land and to win time through guile against the owners of titles, charters, lists, and registers, whether authentic or falsified.

It was to be expected then that questions were raised once again in the *cahiers de doléances* of 1789, where "anti-feudal" grievances were often the object of additional articles suddenly imposed on the elite during the local assemblies of the Third Estate (Robin 1970). After the night of 4 August and the Declaration of Rights, some of the constraints weighing on the "rustics" were abolished but most were subsumed by the lawgivers into contractual obligations and made redeemable. It was mainly a question of "seigneurial" rather than "feudal" rights, but the latter, more pejorative term was used freely as a series of *jacqueries* – a vast guerrilla war reactivated each summer – erupted from 1790 to 1793. This deep anger has been detailed by Anatoliï Ado (1996), correcting a hate-filled stereotype established earlier by Hippolyte Taine; but both showed that refusal was the motivation which pushed the Revolution forward, when those liable to pay dues freed themselves by sheer force. They won legal decisions for abolition, culminating in the great law of 17 July 1793, and this rough, iron will interacted with other conflicts over clerical property, the king, the communes, and other bodies, and then the *émigrés*. The equality of personal status of rural people progressed but, along the way, a new juridical context was created for agricultural production in the Civil Code (1804), then the Forest Code (1827).

Fundamental inequality in personal status, the constant cause of scandals addressed in the Declaration of Rights, also stemmed from membership of each person in an order and especially by the exclusions linked to commoner status (*roture*). Most often this membership was marked by the commoner obligation to pay the tithe, which was immediately abolished, and royal taxes. Even more common in the *cahiers de doléances* than seigneurial rights, ancient anti-fiscal claims were transformed, within a few months changing from local or regional equality to a national perspective, a change of such exceptional breadth that it deserves to be more widely known. But if the end of fiscal inequality freed the great mass of peasants, artisans, and tradespeople from the burden of being the only taxpayers, it did not eliminate of itself all the ancient consequences of being a commoner, for both rich and poor. Those capable of defending their property and income were less able to escape their origins, because, under the *ancien régime*, to remain a boor (*manant*) meant to drag behind oneself the "baseness" of an "ignominious" birth and be hampered in one's path in life.

From the desire to camouflage this stigma stemmed the success of sales of seigneuries or, even better, of noble titles, above all when, towards the end of the *ancien régime*, requirements for the "purity" of noble origins were strengthened for those wanting access to high ranks of the army or clergy. From this stemmed too, and on a larger scale, the use of "social whitewashing" (*savonnettes à vilains*), which the monarchy had created at the start of the seventeenth century, selling public offices and making money from the wealthiest subjects. This system introduced new "dignities": purchasable pathways to a nobility known as "of the robe." These pathways were a lasting success and for two centuries governed the appointment of judges at all levels of the magistracy. However, once the Revolution had begun, it was plain that the sale of offices was so despised that its immediate suppression was advocated. There was a unanimous cry for the state to reimburse the purchasers, to finish with the system, and for new judges to be elected immediately. With the subsequent upheavals in military and civil office-holding from the wars and territorial conquests, equality of the right of access to public office, formulated in the declarations, became a fundamental belief in French society. Appointment by nomination, elections and competitive recruitment and advancement remained variable, as elsewhere, but right up to our own times any deviation from these rules would create real tensions. This shows the point to which, from the outset, the application of the Declarations of Rights necessitated complicated collective procedures, never definitively established.

At the other extreme of the Third Estate, that of the poorest, specific exclusions from rights concerned huge groups of servants, laborers, wage-earners, and apprentices of all types, classed as "dependants," and vagrants and beggars whether incarcerated or assisted, either by the church, the town, or the state. Those whom publicists in 1789 described as the "Fourth Estate" were not all deprived of rights in the same way. A journeyman (*compagnon*) could enjoy real independence, but notions of dependence, of "belonging to the master's house" and of personal service, were often bound together by wage-earning. Slipping from one category to another was all the easier in that such people could not become involved in legal acts such as a contract or bearing witness. From this stemmed much local and legislative hesitation about their political rights. After successive decrees in the summer of 1792, the Declaration of 1793 pronounced a formal abolition: "The law recognizes no domestic service whatsoever; only an agreement of care and recognition between the working man and the employer may exist" (Article 18, already cited concerning slavery). This was reflected in the extent of the right to vote for several years, but not longer. Concerning wage-earners in general, the Le Chapelier et d'Allarde laws, adopted in 1791, sought to prohibit, on the one hand, strikes or collective action and on the other associations formed between citizens in the same trade and, something that is less commonly noted, even the possibility of intervening collectively in public meetings. From our twenty-first-century perspective, these rules constitute a major restriction of rights. At the time, the contradiction was hardly apparent: strikes were common during the Revolution and it would only be under later regimes that their outlawing would be effective, when workers were constrained by the regime of the passbook (*livret*). This legal situation would last more than a century, until wage-earners finally obtained clear political rights and the right of association.

One could examine at length how, sector by sector, exclusions were passed over, crushed, or eliminated by revolutionaries. This historiographical method, both productive and fertile, has allowed us in particular to understand better the enormous rural population which certain French traditions of research unfortunately treat as homogeneous (Bodinier 2010). But by detailing the categories of which this chapter can give only a simplified picture, when we try to find out to what extent and when this or that group benefited from the Revolution, we end by having difficulty in knowing just what the Revolution was or whether indeed there was one. By losing sight of the overall picture, we can underestimate the dynamic of new, basic institutions governing society which, without necessarily placing everyone on the same footing, simultaneously created a new universalism and new forms of discrimination.

Assemblies of Citizens

The processes through which society reconstituted itself therefore need to be considered. Between lawmakers, more or less inspired, and activists, more or less aggressive and determined, a lively dialectic bound Assembly, neighborhood, and village. We now know that this interaction happened first in particular public places where groups of people exercised their essential rights: political participation and the bearing of arms which were embedded respectively in assemblies of citizens and the National Guard. Property-owners had immediate access to these rights, but debate quickly began over whether the poor, dependants, servants, and wage-earners, as well as soldiers and sailors, had the right to *exercise* the rights of citizens. The question was raised periodically and accelerated the proliferation of texts, laws, decrees, proclamations, and circulars. We have undertaken a collection of "electoral" documents (Aberdam et al. 2006), and counted no fewer than 178 of these from December 1789 to December 1799, without including either the elections to the Estates-General or votes from the Consulate and Empire. Even if many of these texts in fact sought to define transitional processes between successive systems, behind all these models we found implicit and quite consistent rules according to which it would be gatherings of citizens who ultimately decided the forms of their meetings and decisions. Whether they gathered at the level of the municipality (*assemblées communales*) or canton (*assemblées primaires*) or decided which of them should meet as "electors" at the district or department level (*assemblées électorales*), all their assemblies were as much deliberative as elective and resembled a type of local congress. In 1790–93, in a land of some 28 million people, with 44,000 communes, between 4.5 and 6.5 million citizens were qualified to elect perhaps 1 million public and military office-holders. The reader can judge from this the universality of the issues and passions raised.

The powers of citizens' assemblies were at issue throughout the period: their deliberations were virtually forbidden in 1790–91, were at a maximum in 1792–93, and often lasted into 1795–99. Above all, in all these assemblies, the rule of equality of social rank was in stark contradiction to respect for the timeless order of prerogatives. The complex hierarchy of ranks had experienced its final flourishing during the multiple meetings for the formation of the Estates-General. Following well-known rules, and after minor if ferocious clashes, the ecclesiastical, civil, and military authorities sized each other up, but were also confronted by the "vulgar" people. Once the first article of the Declaration of 1789 had been adopted – "Men are born and remain free and equal in rights. Social distinctions may only be based on common usefulness" – it had then to be applied, in the most opulent towns as well as in the smallest villages. The progressive introduction of alphabetical order of names or first names for the roll-call of those present or voting, an apparently minor detail, represented in fact a visible step towards the equality of citizens. This advance was made only once in each place, but it encountered hesitations and reaffirmations with regard to the election of new civil servants. There would later be long-term reversals, with arbitrary nomination at times taking precedence over elections and, with the passion for etiquette, pompous titles would be restored to many dignitaries, but never again without irony.

The Sharing of Weaponry

The profound desire for social equality was the basis of another fundamental creation, the National Guard. At first it was a response to popular fears, both those identified explicitly ("brigands") and those that were implicit, of the nobility and foreign princes (Bianchi and Dupuy 2006; Dupuy 1972, 2010). On the initial formation of the National Guard, command might be given to a retired officer. The desire for social equality then became clear in the preference for authority to be invested in commoners rather than men from the *noblesse d'épée* whose birth supposedly endowed them with superior military ability. Soon, as an inversion of privilege, national guards would systematically conduct searches of chateaux looking for the aristocracy's weaponry. They were at the same time democratically organized units, because officers and under-officers were elected. In this way, the Guard resembled a citizens' assembly which began to reverse noble privilege, with the right to bear arms extended to all, and which then inverted the principle of hierarchy: election by subordinates became legal and functional. It was difficult not to experience an extension of rights thereby. The juridical right to possess weapons, after centuries of severe restrictions, was not only practiced within the Guard. The exercise of the right to hunt flowed naturally from it, a clandestine practice until then and more or less violently repressed depending on location. The popular tradition of possessing weapons in order to feed oneself as much as to kill dangerous animals, made possible more important activities, such as self-defense and also smuggling. France today still counts, despite significant attempts at outlawing them, some millions of hunting rifles, with or without permits.

The democratic transformation of the National Guard facilitated a radical revolution at the heart of military society which, under the absolute monarchy, had been governed by markedly inegalitarian rules, imposing severe discrimination and physical punishment on tens of thousands of soldiers and sailors. The totality of seamen, sailors in the royal navy, in trade or fishing, had been covered by a royal statute of naval conscription (*inscrits maritimes*). The Revolution afforded those over 12 years of age the right to elect delegates (*syndics*) for their area (*quartier maritime*) (Cabantous 2000). That did not facilitate the exercise of their civic rights. More directly concerned, the sailors of the royal navy, like those enlisted in the king's regiments, nevertheless had to insist on being treated as free men. On ships, in garrisons, and in arsenals, a ferocious repression was unleashed in 1790–91 against what were considered full-scale "mutinies." In fact it was more often a question of economic claims about payment and demands for dignified treatment.

The most famous of these uprisings was that of the garrison at Nancy, crushed by the troops of General Bouillé. The soldiers who escaped the broadsides were sent to the galleys. Their freedom, finally obtained by "patriots" in April 1792 at the end of a long public campaign, would become the symbol of change. At the time of the demonstration which met their arrival in Paris, they affirmed their citizenship by hoisting their prisoners' red caps, which thus came to be associated with the liberty cap.

When, in February 1792, it was decided to amalgamate the professional battalions with those of the national volunteers to form the regiments (*demi-brigades*) of the new national army, the processes of election of officers by their subordinates, forged in the National Guard, was extended to the entire army. These elections were integrated into a new system of promotion which took account of the earlier debate on careers in the public service and the respective roles to be played by seniority and by merit (Blaufarb 1997, 2002). So the army began, without too much difficulty, to elect most of its officer corps. This system, both democratic and bureaucratic, would be a key characteristic of the revolutionary armies inherited by the Empire.

Minorities and Universalism

The assemblies of citizens and the National Guard, new institutions, opened unexpected political possibilities. They were thenceforth the context within which new rights were formulated, the right of existence for example, and where, from claims for better supplies, the general question of subsistence and the role of hoarding was posed. The political radicalism of the Revolution was based on popular foundations of all types and it would be necessary to outlaw them to deprive the sans-culottes of a voice, through closing clubs, societies, and most newspapers. As living proof of the scale of the movement, citizens' assemblies remained vigorous until 1799 and were resurgent in 1815. People could express themselves divergently in these different democratic theaters, and could also participate in decision-making or carve out a career. These spaces, open to talent, attracted many young men and women, although they also practiced exclusion. With citizens' assemblies, with the extension of the right to vote, with the National Guard, and with battalions of *fédérés*, of *volontaires*, or of *défenseurs de la patrie*, they became real communities of citizens, all able to vote, all egalitarian. They were republics of brothers and friends whose closure to women was in its own way a means of self-expression. From that perhaps came, alongside demands about subsistence, the two political demands made by different minorities of women: on the one hand the right to bear arms, on the other the right to vote, both of which appeared during 1792–93 (Godineau 1988, 1995, 1996).

In April 1793 Gilbert Romme failed to have the political rights of women accepted in his proposed declaration of rights. During the fierce summer that followed, in the primary assemblies where the Declaration of Rights and the first republican constitution were accepted, women's right to vote seemed more an issue than that of bearing arms. At the same time, other primary assemblies adopted stridently misogynist motions against the access of women to divorce or against the division of common land (10 June 1793), for which women had received the right to vote (Aberdam 2005). The exceptionally strong democratic surge between the summer of 1792 and that of 1793 went as far as a proposal to abolish husbands' power over their wives (in the Civil Code of Cambacérès, 9 August). It is revealing that it was after this moment of open and even anarchic expression that the brutal measures of autumn 1793 followed against the political and associational rights of women, the consequences of which, as we know, would last for 150 years regarding the vote. We are here at the heart of the matter since this defeat, which concerned the majority, was only felt strongly by a tiny minority. If, in the light of an obviously complex situation, it is simply affirmed that the exclusion of women from the suffrage "was complete from 1789" (Verjus 2009), then obviously nothing has been understood about what happened in 1793. Certainly, attempts which were "before their time" and partial must not be confused with a more general evolution; but taking account of contradictions and conflicts is the very basis of our work. It is all the more necessary that, navigating between Taine and Tocqueville, one should underline the continuities between the *ancien régime* and that of Napoleon, to show how the regimen formerly imposed by the Parlement of Paris was taken up again in the Civil Code, and to highlight the slowness of change, rather than misinterpret through an anachronistic reading of events.

When we study a revolution, when we research who was involved, and if we suspect that it involved everybody, then we are interested in whatever might have increased its impact. The effect on lived experience is attested by hundreds of witnesses from the time: "as if our life had lasted several centuries," Portalis would write in 1804. Daily reality was the individualization of older juridical relationships and the acceleration of the circulation of goods and people. The appearance of new types of relations between humans for the production of goods to satisfy their material needs was all the more surprising because it was the result of measures apparently thought through in a perfectly reasonable manner but which unleashed changes which were totally foreign to the intentions of their initiators, with implications for the entire population. In evoking these new relations of production, I am not moving any mountains or attacking any windmills, but taking up points that have been treated at length by others and linked to recent research.

The Universalizing of Circulation and Revolutionary Currency

Without dealing here with quantifiable economic history, it can be emphasized that the immediate beneficiaries of the Revolution – large farmers and large landowners, traders, lawyers, bankers, state financiers, and military suppliers – were relatively few in number and that, unsurprisingly, they were exactly those who would have done well under other circumstances. Our perspective must be broadened if we are to understand what else changed. Poor returns from taxation, paralyzed by privilege, such as the lack of credit and liquidity which systems like that of Law had sought to remedy, were the norm in France before the *cahiers.* It has been said that the sale of national property was "the most important event of the French Revolution" (Bodinier and Teyssier 2000). It was even more so when these sales were combined with the abolition of tithes and the creation of the *assignat.* Without rehearsing here the sales of national property (see Chapters 13 and 27 below), these occurred only well after the massive refusal to pay tithes, seigneurial dues, tolls, and former taxes, and then the long paralysis of the new system of taxes, had had very contradictory economic consequences (Postel-Vinay 1989).

With the breakdown of all the traditional mechanisms of extracting rent, monetary circulation became still more constrained, starving the luxury goods trade in the large towns and the outlets for colonial produce, while peasant incomes increased accordingly. An improved diet for peasants (through *autoconsommation*) and the settling of usurious debts at first held back financial reorganization, but from 1790–91 the internal market slowly expanded, less by means of barter than by exchange with those in close proximity, ensuring a certain prosperity from products of lower quality, not valuable but saleable (Cornette 1986). During these early years, the *assignats* did not circulate like ordinary currency because of the high face value of the notes issued. Quite a different paper money appeared "spontaneously," familiar to collectors (Kolsky 2004), but less so to historians. The spontaneous production of these notes (*billets de confiance*) in a wide variety of denominations was the work of a multitude of entrepreneurs from some 1,660 municipalities. In practice, these notes were issued with only a modest global value, of the order of 100 million *livres*, but they included a great quantity in small denominations to supply wages and daily needs. Despite the pious affirmations of the authorities, it seems that these private issues of promissory notes were more than tolerated, and were considered as normal and to be encouraged. They ensured a large part of the daily monetary circulation in 1790–93, sometimes later, until the issuing of small-denomination *assignats* met people's needs. This remarkable recourse to a private currency in the early years of the French Revolution resembled nineteenth-century America and its abundant issues of currency (Wood 2011), but it is also a revealing indicator: the spontaneous issuers were entrepreneurs who were "concerned," and their currency "concerned" the entire population.

The free production of paper money was based in the final analysis on those who could not refuse it, because they lived from day to day on their wages, but it affected everything. Before any link with metallic currency disappeared in 1795, the use of the *assignat* spread from the purchase of national property and the payment of taxes to the economy as a whole, enabling the payment of debts and all forms of speculation, in particular to buy consumer goods, especially the cereal grains so important to urban neighborhoods. On the side of the right to existence as much as on that of the right to profit, everyone was affected by the commercialization of social relations. The liberal remaking of society was a reality which occurred through monetary practices, inflationary explosion, and finally the hyper-inflation under the Directory, by no means accidental policies.

Legislative Constraints

Whatever the temporary concessions the Committee of Public Safety had to make to the urban masses, the freedom of contracts and market mechanisms was finally applied, but within limits defined by legislators. From a longer-term perspective, one can see the emergence of durable public policies. That was the case for the management of the countryside. When successive versions of revolutionary laws were being elaborated, a cautious movement for "codification" was already at work. That was not so much when the great law on rural policing of March 1791 was incorrectly designated as a Rural Code but rather when Cambacérès himself came officiously to the Convention on 9 August 1793 to present his proposal for a Civil Code as a prelude to the announcement of the results of the referendum on the republican constitution. Between this modernizing proposal, long considered as a model, and the Napoleonic Code of 1804, which was much more conservative, much water would flow under the bridge, but nevertheless a distinctive milieu of jurists from the revolutionary assemblies would be constituted. Even if its members fervently denied forming a group and still more so representing vested interests, the way they presented themselves in fashioning the new world of which they dreamed must be taken seriously, as well as the manner in which the context thus established became a juridical norm to be carefully preserved.

I have already emphasized the hierarchy of accumulated personal and landed status, the stack of obligations and exactions which the *jacqueries* of 1789–92 would overthrow, obtaining abolition in 1793. But the relationship between obligations presented as "immemorial property" and others issuing from "customary" contracts already constituted an imbroglio under the *ancien régime*. Given the rush of "polite society" towards ways of "living nobly," the tendency had been, at least since the sixteenth century, to change the clauses in contracts of agricultural production towards furnishing payments enveloped in the decorum and social prestige due to seigneurs. Various traditional forms of production had thus been "invested" with the task of ensuring landed proprietors the income and lifestyle compatible with the seigneurial model. But by the end of the *ancien régime*, direct leasing, farming, tenant farming, and other ways of temporarily "holding" the land had become widespread. They had moreover given birth to a gradual movement undermining landed property, or rather of agricultural concentration, on the one hand in the large lease-held farms in the Paris Basin and the north and on the other in the "general leases" over small-scale lease-holding of the center and southwest. In this multiplicity of ways of accessing land, the exact limits between that which could be abolished, as of "feudal" origin, and that which could continue were neither obvious nor fixed in advance nor formulated in the Declaration of Rights.

The laws of abolition were discussed at length, under direct pressure from peasants, by jurists such as Merlin de Douai who had to arbitrate in such matters into the Restoration period. In a way which is not surprising, the liquidation of seigneurial obligations, combined with the sales of national property, resulted in a simplification and reinforcement of large landed property. There is no paradox in this outcome, which resulted from the failure of the poorest peasants to impose subdivision (Ado 1996). A range of sources demonstrates the crushing weight of these great properties at the dawn of the nineteenth century. Before Balzac, and more bluntly than him, Benjamin Constant wrote in 1819 that "it is obvious that, if the nobles, in their role as large landholders, seize majority control of France's destinies, then in a few years, perhaps in just one, France would lose the fruits of forty years of struggle." But the jurists were on the look-out!

When the Civil Code was adopted in 1804, preceding other codes (criminal, commercial, legal process, forests, and so on) by a few years, one of the draft proposals was set aside and would remain so for 150 years. It was the proposal for a Rural Code (Aberdam 1982–84, 1988, 1990), which was to have regulated the system of traditional methods of agriculture in regions of smallholding, sharecropping, of leasing (*domaine congéable*) in Brittany, the *gouvernorat* of the Perche region, the contracts of lessees (*baïlets* and *maîtres-valets*) in the southwest, and so on. It was also a question of agricultural wage-earners, the regulations for water, paths, hedges, and fences, and the resolution of rural conflicts. The Napoleonic Conseil d'État refused to ratify this proposed code from fear that it would be the shield for the return of the total power of the great landowners. Neither it nor its successors would accept particular rural regulations, specifically rural contracts, rural courts, or the militarization of rural police: in sum, nothing which resembled Andalusia, Ireland, or Latin America.

Sharecropping and other forms of cultivation would be tolerated but leasing alone would be regulated according to the Civil Code, just as the hiring of labor would be the only work contract admitted in actuality. However, every regime, and at times every government, throughout the nineteenth century would encounter the machinery of proposals for rural codes, inquiries, votes from departmental councils (*conseils généraux*), and attempts to create a detailed code on the basis of local customs. Nothing was done, and this refusal lasted until the Third Republic, and even then the articles adopted in 1889 were completely secondary in nature. The real decisions about a rural code were only taken in 1944–46, with the "statute governing farm-leasing and sharecropping" and the round-table tribunals for rural leases, and even then it was in order to liquidate the remains of sharecropping to the benefit of a very controlled form of leasing. Thus was completed the dismantling of a compromise of great significance, at first designed to block peasant attacks on large property but which had also sought to maintain contracts as the sole basis of social relationships in metropolitan France, to prevent the return of "customary" and "imprescriptible" rules, and thus to conserve a tenuous but real link with the declarations of rights.

Conclusion

The classic definition of a revolution is that the great mass of individuals tries to take its destiny into its own hands. The political memories of participants would bear detailed testimony: in the army and still more the navy, antagonism between the ranks and their officers would be still clearly discernible fifty years later, in the votes of 1848–49 (Salmon 2001), just as particular share-cropper conflicts in the twentieth century referred directly to 1789. The limits of emancipation in these cases are well known; but what must be borne in mind is that at the start of this adventure many of the issues we regard as crucial were only raised by tiny minorities, while we have difficulty in understanding the real intensity of contemporary feelings. If the *cahiers de doléances* were not just liberal catechisms, it was because sharp barbs from the people sometimes found their target. The deputy Beugnot recalled: "the editor had accumulated a mass of more or less exaggerated wishes, and he ended with these insolent words: 'let us authorize our deputies to solicit from his royal majesty his consent to the demands above; to thank him for that if he agrees; and, should he refuse, to see his downfall', the last word being underlined."

Fear did not change sides when political equality appeared on the street corner but rather when crowds climbed the walls. The declarations were adopted in very uncertain circumstances. The real question is above all that of which group became revolutionary or not, did or did not gain satisfaction, and in which circumstances. The hope of freeing oneself was not enough in itself, and circumstances saw it rejected, delayed, or finally achieving a mixed outcome. This was not so much the case for the unification of weights and measures, for the new decimal system, or for the rational new subdivision of national territory, but it was so for human groups torn apart by vested interests and the difficulty of setting goals when oppressed or exploited.

Inversely, the example of the disjuncture between the Civil Code and the Rural Code highlights an actor, the Conseil d'État, a veritable fount of power, the repository of the collective juridical memory of successive regimes of the French bourgeoisie, and which has unceremoniously ensured its own survival until our own times. So we need to return to the choice outlined at the beginning of this chapter, that the French Revolution was above all a revolution of those who managed its conclusion and created from it a particularly durable order. Except that the care that they have taken to remain in charge makes us think too that this ownership was not an foregone conclusion!

References

Aberdam, Serge (1982–84). *Sur les origines du code rural, un siècle de conflit, 1789–1900.* Nantes and Paris: INRA.

Aberdam, Serge (1988). "Profil d'un codificateur, l'expérience révolutionnaire de Verneilh-Puyraseau, rédacteur du projet de code rural de 1814." In M. Pertué (ed.). *La Révolution et l'ordre juridique privé*, 1st vol. Paris: PUF. 205–217.

Aberdam, Serge (1990). "Histoire des usages locaux: Ambiguïtés, discontinuités, Guide d'exploitation." In Louis Assier-Andrieu (ed.). *Une France coutumière.* Paris: CNRS. 43–68.

Aberdam, Serge (2005). "Deux occasions de participation féminine en 1793: Le Vote sur la Constitution et le partage des biens communaux." *AHRF*, 339: 17–34.

Aberdam, Serge (2006–7). "La Convention en campagne: à propos des éditions du projet de Constitution de 1793." *Le Temps des média, Revue d'histoire*, 7: 20–34.

Aberdam, Serge, S. Bianchi, R. Demeude, É. Ducoudray, B. Gainot, M. Genty, and C. Wolikow (2006). *Voter, élire pendant la révolution française, 1789–1799: Guide pour la recherche.* Paris: CTHS.

Ado, Anatoli (1996). *Paysans en Révolution: Terre, pouvoir et jacquerie 1789–1794*, trans. from the Russian. Paris: SÉR.

Beugnot, Jacques-Claude (1959). *Mémoires publiées par son fils.* Paris: Lacour-Gayet, Hachette.

Bianchi, Serge and Roger Dupuy (eds.) (2006). *La Garde nationale entre nation et peuple en armes: Mythes et réalités, 1789–1871*, Rennes: Presses Universitaires de Rennes.

Biard, Michel (1995). *Collot d'Herbois: Légendes noires et Révolution.* Lyon: Presses Universitaires de Lyon.

Blaufarb, Rafe (1997). "Démocratie et professionnalisme: L'Avancement par l'élection dans l'armée française, 1760–1815." *AHRF*, 310: 601–625.

Blaufarb, Rafe (2002). *The French Army, 1750–1820: Careers, Talent, Merit*. Manchester: Manchester University Press.

Bodinier, Bernard (2010). "La Révolution française et la question agraire." *Histoire et sociétés rurales*, 33: 7–47.

Bodinier, Bernard and Éric Teyssier (2000). "*L'Événement le plus important de la Révolution*": *La Vente des biens nationaux en France et dans les territoires annexés, 1789–1867*. Paris: SÉR.

Bourguinat, Élisabeth (1998). *Le Siècle du persiflage: 1734–1789*. Paris: PUF.

Cabantous, Alain (2000). "Communautés maritimes et Révolution (1790–1791): Un apprentissage démocratique?" In G. Le Bouëdec (ed.). *Pouvoirs et littoraux du XVe au XXe siècle*. Rennes: Presses Universitaires de Rennes. 119–128.

Constant, Benjamin (1837). *De la division des propriétés foncières*. In *Cours de politique constitutionnelle*. Brussels: Société Belge de Librairie.

Cornette, Joël (1986). *Un révolutionnaire ordinaire: Benoît Lacombe, négociant 1759–1819*. Paris: Champ-Vallon and PUF.

Dupuy, Roger (1972). *La Garde nationale et les débuts de la Révolution en Ille-et-Vilaine, 1789–mars 1793*. Paris: Klincksieck.

Dupuy, Roger (2010). *La Garde nationale, 1789–1872*. Paris: Gallimard.

Foucault, Michel (1964). *Folie et déraison: Histoire de la folie à l'âge classique*, 2 vols. Paris: UGE.

Foucault, Michel (2003). *Le Pouvoir psychiatrique: Cours au Collège de France, 1973–74*. Paris: Gallimard–Seuil.

Godineau, Dominique (1988). *Citoyennes tricoteuses: Les Femmes du peuple à Paris pendant la Révolution française*. Aix-en-Provence: Alinéa. Réédition (2004) Paris: Perrin.

Godineau, Dominique (1995). "Femmes en citoyenneté: Pratiques et politique." *AHRF*, 300: 197–207.

Godineau, Dominique (1996). "Privées par notre sexe du droit honorable de donner notre suffrage … Le vote des femmes pendant la Révolution française." In E. Viennot (ed.). *La Démocratie "à la française" ou les femmes indésirables*. Paris: Presses Universitaires de Paris 7. 199–211.

Hourwitz, Zalkind (2001). *Apologie des Juifs (1789)*. Paris: Syllepse.

Kolsky, Maurice (2004). *Les Billets de confiance de la Révolution française, 1790–1792*. Collection Histoire du Papier Monnaie Français, vol. 13. n.p.

Malino, Frances (2000). *Un juif rebelle dans la Révolution et sous l'Empire: La Vie de Zalkind Hourwitz: 1751–1812*. Paris: Berg International.

Postel-Vinay, Gilles (1989). "À la recherche de la révolution économique dans les campagnes (1789–1815)." *RÉ*, 40: 1015–1046.

Robin, Régine (1970). *La Société française en 1789: Semur-en-Auxois*. Paris: Plon.

Roudinesco, Élisabeth (1989). *Théroigne de Méricourt, une femme mélancolique sous la Révolution*. Paris: Seuil.

Salmon, Frédéric (2001). *Atlas électoral de la France, 1848–2001*. Paris: Seuil.

Semelaigne, René (2001). *Philippe Pinel et son œuvre, au point de vue de la santé mentale*. Paris: Harmattan.

Swain, Gladys (1997). *Le Sujet de la folie: Naissance de la psychiatrie*. Paris: Calmann-Lévy.

Verjus, Anne (2009) intervention dans "Femmes, genres, Révolution. Regards croisés de Dominique Godineau, Lynn Hunt, Jean-Clément Martin, Anne Verjus et Martine Lapied." *AHRF* 358: 143–166.

Weiner, Dora B. (1999). *Comprendre et soigner: Philippe Pinel (1745–1826), la médecine de l'esprit*. Paris: Fayard.

Wood, Gordon S. (2011). "American Dream Money" *The New York Review of Books*, 10 Nov.

Chapter Twelve

Gender, Sexuality, and Political Culture

Anne Verjus

Today gender and sexuality are commonly linked. If gender is the system by which the world of men and women is divided, in other words which invents sex as the natural criterion of division of the social world so as to order it hierarchically (Delphy 2001), then it is linked to sexuality. Sexuality, however, does not necessarily need gender: militant feminist homosexuality has in the main constructed itself on the postulate of the disappearance of gender as a system of dominance. Gender, on the contrary, requires sexuality, or rather one of its particular social forms: heterosexuality. According to female historians it is, together with marriage and paternity, one of the conditions for the functioning of patriarchal societies (Miller 1998; Pateman 1988). For, if sexuality is a practice, a playful demonstration of human inventiveness that is a matter of free choice of the private individual from 1791, heterosexuality is a social norm (Darmon 1979; Merrick and Ragan 1996). Until the twentieth century, and therefore until the Revolution, it was the only norm, most often tacit, governing marriage, that most obvious of social contracts, the foundation of the basic element of society, the family. It is through this that gender and (hetero)sexuality and cultural politics meet.

Cultural politics may be very loosely defined as the totality of the laws and manifestations that govern the holding of legitimate power in society, whether this power is exercised at the high state level, through intermediate institutions like national or local assemblies, through professional associations like guilds, or indeed in the public space (*cité*) and family in a democracy. Far from being concerned only with the public domain, we know that from then on it penetrates all social relations, including private ones.

We know this, although it is not a matter of course. For a long time historians and political scientists adhered to the division of social space born out of the Revolution: on the one hand the public realm governed by the law, on the other

A Companion to the French Revolution, First Edition. Edited by Peter McPhee.

the personal realm shielded from politics. According to the 1804 Civil Code, the law was not supposed to intrude on personal matters. It is in fact for this reason that this space is defined as *private*. Deprived of all state intrusion, shielded from public scrutiny, the law placed it behind a "wall" intended to preserve the fundamental freedom of the individual, notably sexual freedom. Of course, this wall lost no time in demonstrating how porous, even fragile, it was, to the point of being, in the eyes of certain lawyers, no more than an illusion (Iacub 2008). The idea of a line of separation endured, however, particularly among some social scientists. A logical consequence of this imaginary division of space is that the private was most commonly associated with the feminine domain: the public one for men, the domestic one for women. It thus seems difficult, or in any case seemed so for a long time, to imagine the political character of this space that was in theory protected from state interference. Along the same lines, during the Revolution, people were equally used to thinking that action regarding the law and morals was defined according to both space and gender: the former was the province of men and in the political sphere, while women within the closed realm of the family were responsible for the conservation and transmission of the latter. It was thus that for years political history, heir to this body of ideas, was constructed on the study of the public domain of laws and institutions alone, ignoring anything to do with family relations and norms of gender and sexuality. We had to wait for the feminist scholarship of the 1970s and all the theoretical research on "the politics of the personal" for this separatist conception of political culture to be interrogated and qualified.

A chapter in a book on the Revolution that links, as this one does, gender, sexuality, and political culture is thus the result of a lengthy process. This process is still not regarded as entirely convincing by some writers, because in France it is still possible to formulate a serious and convincing account of equality without interrogating the gender norms that have governed its acceptance through time (Rosanvallon 2011). Nonetheless, looking at the revolutionary period through the lens of gender and sexuality has not only deepened our understanding of the construction of democracy, but also changed how we define its most basic figure: the individual.

This process was neither linear nor homogeneous. On the one hand our questions have evolved; and the disciplines involved, whether history, philosophy or legal or political sciences, have each seen the problem from a particular angle. Nevertheless, beyond the diversity of viewpoints, paradigms stand out. They are mostly related to women's history, since it is through this that gender studies developed and consolidated. But these two paradigms are equally valid for the history of masculinity. Bringing light to bear on them allows us to understand not only why the Revolution had such an asymmetrical effect on the rights of men and of women, but also how historiography has dealt with this inequality. The first paradigm regards women as a social group that has been subjected to particular political treatment; it leads us to observe and explain the modalities through which a society constructs and mobilizes the category of sexual cohort. The assumption is that women form a homogeneous political grouping, both in the eyes of the law, which excludes them all, without distinction of rank or estate, and in the light of their interests. We shall call this the sexualist paradigm. The second paradigm places women in a different cohort than a sexual one: this time they are regarded as members of a family. This has the effect of dissociating them from each other, while at the same time bringing them closer to other social categories: thus a woman of the aristocracy will be considered as politically closer to her husband than to a peasant woman. This leads to a totally different view of the political situation of women, linked to other excluded people who had been forgotten until then; going so far as to call back into question the dogma of the separation of the public and the private, the familial and the political. This paradigm, which we shall call patriarchalism, first appeared in Anglo-Saxon historiography of modern Europe and the American Revolution; it impacted upon the history of the French Revolution only in the last years of the 1990s and still has difficulty gaining acceptance.

The Sexualist Paradigm

Women were present from the dawn of the Revolution, they acted individually with men, for example in the assault on the Bastille; or else in groups, for instance when they brought the king back to Paris on 5 October 1789. They participated in drafting the *cahiers de doléances*, petitioned (Fauré 2006), established political clubs (Desan 1992), and claimed the title of citizeness (Godineau 1996), the rights to education, work, an equitable wage, divorce, and abolition of the dowry (Devance 1977) and even the right to bear arms and join the war effort. They were present in the assemblies either to applaud in support of the motions of the deputies – these were the notorious *tricoteuses* (Godineau 1988) – or in order to overthrow the government, as on 1 Prairial III (20 May 1795). We know about the canteen-keepers and camp followers, but there were also those who, assuming men's clothing, fought on the front line (Cardoza 2010; Hopkin 2009). They took advantage of all forms of writing, from the most modest petition to the henceforth famous Declaration of the Rights of Women by Olympe de Gouges, and including novels and treatises, which made the revolutionary period a significant milestone in a process of individualization that was already well under way (Hesse 2001). They wrote, but they also made a lot of ink flow. Innumerable texts, such as those of Pierre-Louis Roederer (Verjus 2008) expressed anxiety about their influence; damned them, like Chaumette (Badinter 1989) when they stepped beyond the bounds of domesticity; praised them to the skies when, like Charlotte Corday, they made themselves into instruments of judgment (Mazeau 2009); demanded, like Sylvain Maréchal, that teaching them to read be prohibited; or, on the contrary demanded, following Condorcet, that they be taught. Finally their faces and their bodies were used to represent Reason, the Republic, and the Motherland (Heuer and Verjus 2006).

If women were present throughout the Revolution, were they citizens with the same status as men? This question has elicited two kinds of response: those of women historians of the law, for whom women were citizens like any others; and those of women cultural historians for whom the Declaration of the Rights by its nature excluded all women.

The Political Exclusion of Women

We know that at the time of the Revolution citizenship could be understood in electoral or civil terms. It could therefore be limited to electors or be extended to include those subject to the law – this was the famous distinction drawn by Sieyès between active and passive citizens, all claiming the protection of the law. It did not, however, extend to all who held French nationality, as the Revolution created the category of "non-subjects in law" which included the *émigrés* (civilly dead) and unworthy public officials (Simonin 2008). According to this distinction, women clearly were never citizens in the electoral sense of the word since they were not entitled to vote throughout the Revolution (and well after that). But women were citizens according to the civic meaning of the word: in theory they enjoyed the same legal protection as men, children, and servants. Proof of this lies in the fact that when they defined marriage as a civil contract in 1791, the legislators assumed that the parties to the contract enjoyed a priori equality before the law: they thus made women completely subject to the law. This is the thesis of legal historians when they rely, as in the present case, on a strictly juridical interpretation of the law. If citizenship refers to being part of the public space and that space is the legal system that confers the right of protection under the law, then women are certainly citizens.

If women existed as civic entities, if between 1791 and 1792 the family had become an "association governed, like the body politic, by liberty and equality" (Sagnac 1899), it is difficult to understand the "political disinheritance" of women, that is to say their exclusion from all participation in civic matters (Azimi 1991). How could the legislators confer civic individuality on women with one hand while taking away their political individuality with the other? The answer is chronological: whether it began in 1793 with the ban on women's clubs or in Year III, a reactionary tendency caused the Revolution to swing from progressive individualism towards a return to order, rejecting the whole idea of equality, whether civil or political between men and women (Devance 1977; Martin 2006). On 4 Prairial II (23 May 1794), the Convention banned women from the section assemblies and in Prairial III (May–June 1795) from political assemblies; soon afterwards it ordered the arrest of assemblies (*attroupements*) of more than five women. Finally, in response to popular demand for the judicial security of hereditary property, the Directory revoked most of the reforms relating to family law (Desan 2004). For some women historians this reaction served to "create space and legitimacy for male democratic politics" (Desan 1992); the exclusion of women was thus not only one means among others of reinstating social discipline; it also served to create a community of citizens on the basis of a sexual identity that could transcend class differences. From being a means, it became a necessity.

Not everyone agrees with this interpretation, for two reasons.

First, it is not clear that the first revolutionary period, from 1789 to 1793 was a golden age for women; though they benefited from the laws of 1791 and 1792, they did so only indirectly. Marriage was certainly envisaged as between equal parties. The laws did not, however, overturn the status of married women: though they entered the state of marriage as an equal party, within it she became a minor.

Equal administration of property was never voted in and while divorce appeared to give them a new freedom, it did not grant them equality with men (Bigot 2010). Other legal historians have shown that the Revolution did not provoke any "break" in the position of women under the law, since legislators had taken "no measure to directly and exclusively favor women with the intent of ensuring their equality with men" (Portemer 1962). Indeed, their conditions were improved almost "accidentally" by the new laws (Ourliac 1966); improved, for instance, as equal heirs among siblings, but not within marriage. In fact the married estate is the sole and unique instance in which the law touched on the status of women. This is an absolutely fundamental matter. Since women did not, unlike Jews, make up a "constituent group" within the nation, they were not considered separately but were treated as part of other categories, such as in marriage, where they were always given the status of minors (Marc 2002).

Second, women never cut themselves off from politics, for the very good reason that they had never been included. Participating in the revolutionary events was never enough to establish citizenship with regard to an electoral right they had never enjoyed. Certainly one can understand that the strong involvement of some women might imply (or arouse) an awareness of citizenship. One can also assume that from the point of view of legislators, such as Amar and Chaumette, it was this involvement regarded as threatening that justified women being banished back to domesticity. From this point of view, 1793 and the ban on women's clubs certainly represented a break in political life and the law. We must be careful, however, not to confuse the disenfranchisement of militant women in 1793 with a general exclusion of women from legal citizenship (Geoffroy 1989). We can certainly not deny that from the outset, in other words from 1789, the idea of having women participate in the electoral process occurred to almost nobody, women or men. Those who, like Condorcet and Guyomar, ventured to consider it, were careful not to express themselves within the precincts of the Assembly, being well aware that feminism was an idea of the elites (Devance 1977). If a consciousness of citizenship existed, it was thus most often confined to specific roles and duties: it was as women workers, mothers, wives, possible soldiers that women wrote in the *cahiers de doléances*, petitioned, joined demonstrations, or claimed the right to express themselves. It was as moral guardians rather than guardians of the law, the primary educators of future citizens, peerless organizers of festivals and ceremonies that inspired and rewarded masculine heroism that they were recognized as having power and influence (Desan 1992; Verjus 2008). Some women experienced a major set-back in 1793 but most considered themselves excluded from electoral citizenship from 1789.

A Sexist Democracy

Though the word "citizeness" was used, it resulted from a kind of "involuntary" linguistic adoption of the word "citizen" (Sewell 1988). Moreover, Roederer, well acquainted with the law of the time, suggested putting an end to the use of this appellation, since "citizen" was not a title like "president" that conferred on a wife the right to use the feminized version of the title. The "title" of citizen was like that of a doctor that of "a profession which one must earn personally" and not a usage obtained by favor: women, who were merely "family members" and had "no political rights within the state," should therefore stop calling themselves citizenesses and revert to the more appropriate term of "madame" (Roederer 1796).

Some feminist philosophers and political scientists have considered that women had never been citizens: liberal democratic political theory never granted them a share of political authority. They were not individuals in the political sense of the word either, that is to say they did not establish public space and did not, from a theoretical viewpoint, take part in the social contract. Their outsider status, however, was not irrelevant: on the contrary, it was a constituent part of the construction of democracy. "Only men are endowed with the attributes and capacities necessary to enter into contracts. The most important of these is ownership of property in the person: on this basis, only men are individuals" (Pateman 1988). Consequently, the Declaration of Rights applies only to men. Beyond the question of the French Revolution, the entire theory of the social contract needs to be revised in order to integrate the marriage contract or "sexual contract," otherwise we can explain the externality of women only as an expression of "resistance to the emergence of an individualist society" (Rosanvallon 1992). However, according to patriarchal theory, the political right that forms the basis of the social contract rests on the conjugal right (or "sexual right') of Adam over Eve. In other words, before political society existed, there existed a state of nature composed, not of socially undifferentiated individuals, but, on the contrary, made up of men and women of already unequal status of which the origins are believed to be based on the Bible. Civil society is therefore not the result of that Hegelian division between the society of citizens under the state and the economic society of private persons, but truly the fraternal community of equal males.

We find this interpretation applied to the French Revolution in Landes, Fraisse, and Scott. According to these female historians and philosophers, masculinity is a fundamental principle of the public sphere. Olympe de Gouges, who drafted a Declaration of the Rights of Women and the Citizeness, intended to make her contemporaries aware of the gendered, particularistic nature of the Declaration of the Rights of Man and of the Citizen, moreover, had certainly grasped it (Scott 1998). The man of 1789, the political individual subject to the law, was man with a small "m": the person possessed of exclusive rights which he recognizes as his only insofar as he represents his gender group. The Declaration of Rights was from the outset, in other words as soon as it was promulgated and not when it was interpreted and applied for the purposes of the different revolutionary constitutions, a declaration of the rights of man of the masculine gender.

This analysis from a chronological and thus historical point of view is more convincing: the rupture of 1793, which gave meaning to the laws that revised some of the radicalism of the propositions of 1791–92, tells only part of the story. For it was from as early as 1789 that women were left by the roadside electorally. We should, therefore, speak of non-inclusion rather than exclusion.

It is this non-inclusion that female historians of political culture are interrogating, even though they continue to prefer the term exclusion. Democracy needed to work out an external boundary: in order to imagine equality based on a natural homogeneity (all men are born free and equal under the law), it was necessary to destroy internal boundaries. Some women historians have shown that in the eighteenth century "fraternalism" could favor the appropriation of the idea of equality among all men (Clawson 1989) and that gender difference, regarded as a new and more just category for analysis than the hierarchy of orders (Steinberg 2001), had reached the point of permitting the notion of fraternity.

What this approach brought with it is fundamental: from being a text beyond the grasp of men and badly understood, or contested by more or less reactionary political actors, it came to be a text that conformed to the representations and dominant political culture embodied in and represented by the legislators. The Declaration was no longer out of step with its times, it is of its time.

What brings these two approaches together despite their differences is clear: one rests on the internal logic of legal texts, from the Declaration to marriage laws; the other demonstrates on the contrary that legal texts conform to representations that give men the lion's share. What brings these two approaches together is a presupposition: the fundamental antagonism between the category of woman and the category of man. On the one hand, some legislators had reacted to a threatening female force by removing its means of imposing itself politically; on the other, men had seized the symbols of power in order to construct the democratic space from the beginning, with gender difference serving as an auxiliary to equality. Antagonism is assumed between the interests of women, without representation in the nation, and the interests of men. Women are unrepresented in the nation, men represent only themselves: they are therefore excluded.

It is to be expected that interrogation of the political situation of women should have come out of women's history: it alone apprehended the silence concerning their non-citizenship insofar as it alone shone a light on the gap between the worth and the rights of women. Until then, in political history, this gap was at best taken for granted. When history is only that of the problems debated in the Assembly, assumptions remained unchanged from one century to another.

Nevertheless, this was not the way the revolutionaries spoke about women. If their non-citizenship was recognized and assumed, this was because it was regarded as legitimate. It was even regarded by some as the obvious state of affairs as far as morality (Sieyès) and institutions (Roederer) were concerned. For the former, women would be citizens when they were better educated. For the second, the question was more subtle. If women were part of the body politic, they could have only two options at the ballot box. They could vote for themselves, as a group whose interests could not be represented by men, and then, the professor inquired with a feigned naivety, who would decide between the feminine half and the masculine half in parliament? Or they would vote for their husbands, and then who would re-establish the inequality this set up between husbands and bachelors (Roederer 1859 [1793])? The option of an individualist vote, of women who voted according to their own views, was not thought of. Thus, this distance between the foundations of the attribution of rights (legal individualism) and assumptions of electoral behavior did not affect women only: it fostered many of the representations steeped in traditionalism on voting in general (Gueniffey 1993) and voting by the men of the family.

When we look further, and despite appearances, we can see that it is not the category of men that enjoyed the right to vote, but only some men. It is the patriarchal paradigm that allows us to distinguish politically between men.

The Patriarchal Paradigm

Universalist and republican philosophy excludes special categories; historians who have worked on corporations have stressed how difficult it was to think of interest groups in the dawning Republic (Kaplan and Minard 2004). How could it conceive of a distinct political group? Men could no more than women form a category with particular interests within the political nation "presumed one and indivisible." Beginning with these interrogations, other schemas were put forward in order to understand the political situation of women and the role of gender in political culture: the familial paradigm on the one hand and the patriarchal one on the other. What both have in common is that they make the family, and not only gender, the operating principle in the distribution of rights and attribution of political authority.

Familialism or Women in the Political System

The masculine character of the citizen was the result of a deduction rather than an observation. Since all women were denied the right to vote, a sexist policy was operating. From that sexist policy came the deduction that a citizen was a masculine individual. Which is incontestable, but not a priori incontestable. Certainly, all citizens were men, but not all men were citizens. Masculinity was not the sole criterion for the attribution of political authority. Gender studies, seeking to discover hitherto unknown traces of women's participation, neglected a close scrutiny of the figure of the citizen. And it is only by identifying the constructed nature of political masculinity that we have been able to restore the coherence of the non-inclusion of women and the implicit criteria of electoral citizenship. To do this, we had to traverse the political connection between men and women.

In the Republic, the theory of representation rested on the link uniting the person doing the representing and those represented, rather than on antagonism and conflict of interests. This theory assumes a continuity of interests between citizens and inhabitants, between the deputy and the nation, between the state, departments, and communes. It is thus that the representative, the incarnation of the general interest, could and was obliged to speak in the name of the Nation and not in order to defend a special interest. The citizen, even if male, was invested with the capacity of speaking in the name of what transcended him as an individual and member of a gender group. Deputies made laws not for those who elected them, but for the entire nation. Sovereignty was one and indivisible: no one was excluded from it, except for the stigmatized categories such as the nobles whom Sieyès explicitly placed outside the nation. Even foreigners, if they had lived in France for five years, formed part of the citizenry if they took the civic oath, were married to a Frenchwoman, or owned real estate. *A fortiori* the same went for women, children, and servants, that is to say all those "categories" hitherto considered as so many distinct cases (Hincker 1991; Le Cour Grandmaison 1992). However, these three categories made only a single one in the eyes of the electoral law, and from that came three points of view: all these people remained without the right to vote from 1789 to the eve of 1848; their political situation was never debated within the Assembly; and finally, their position was ascribed to a natural particularity, that of gender, age, or servitude. The family is the social category that produced these three conjoined effects.

The family was used as the basis for calculating the electoral census throughout the revolutionary period and up until 1848. It allowed a citizen to avail himself of the taxes paid by his spouse, parents, and parents-in-law as well as by his children (Verjus 2002). Thus four generations in a family may be involved in the construction of the right of what was referred to as a citizen's "individual" vote. The only thing that changed during this time was the passage from the patriarchal family to the conjugal family when, in August 1792, the power of paternal authority over adult children was abolished (Verjus 2010a).

The family makes up a unit of interests and opinions politically embodied by the person who holds power within it: the paterfamilias. The paterfamilias as the Romans understood the term is the person who is or can be the head of a family. In electoral terms this left out all who occupied a subordinate position in the "natural" family as the reference point for the allocation of citizenship rights, regardless of any rights they might have over their property or persons. Giving voting rights to one of these subordinates, be they men or women, children or adults, married or unmarried, would be to double the vote of the head of the family since it is assumed that everyone would vote as he did. It was thus in the spirit of equality of all citizens, in order not to give weight to the family other than through the medium of the "single and indivisible" patrimony, that the legislators did not accord voting rights to family members.

Jennifer Heuer's work on the *émigré* families who were required by the Revolution to choose between loyalty to the family and loyalty to the nation has revealed two fundamental elements. First the demand by the legislators that wives of *émigrés* demonstrate their loyalty to the fatherland through divorce certainly assumed that a spouse shared her husband's interests and political choices. Second, in the face of claims by their defenders that "outside society" they would be unable to betray their country, the legislators remained unmoved: women belonged to the nation and their loyalty must be shown in homage to the nation, otherwise they would in their turn be subject to the law against *émigrés* (Heuer 2005).

This changes our representation of the political position of women: although they were not granted voting rights as citizens, this was not so much the result of legal differences in status based on gender as of the inclusion of the family in the definition of political categories. One can see how women could be deprived of all voting rights and be regarded, nonetheless, as stakeholders in the sovereignty of the nation. Electors were not representatives of the interests of the family within the nation, but as heads of families they were regarded as able to speak for family members. From a political point of view, women were thought of as an extension of the citizen and not as a group apart. The difference that we perceive from a distance between women and men does not separate them, but unites them.

The difference between the sexes determined position within the "natural" family. Gender was not absent from the organization of the natural family, but it must be considered with age, generation, and servile status if we are to understand why some men and all women remained outside the community of electors until 1848. This connection between position within the family and enjoyment of authority has often been noted in other areas, both historical and national, through studies of gender. It was noted by Anglophone historians who very early employed the concept of patriarchy, which is far better applicable to the description of American and European societies of the eighteenth century than the study of gender groups, quite distinct from it.

The Patriarchy and the Question of Spheres

Those who consider the family in terms of gender groupings see it as a private space of relegation (Sewell 1988) or indeed of emancipation when individualized by the great reforms of 1791–92 (Desan 2004). In this case the family is of political concern but is not political: it is not approached as an area for the allocation or distribution of rights.

In the contrary case, research on the patriarchy during the *ancien régime* since 1980 has shown that the family, in Europe and the United States, was a political space and organizational unit. Bennett, who draws a distinction between patriarchy and Filmer's "patriarchialism" (Lessay 1998; Schochet 1975), defines it as a political, ideological, and familial system dominated by men who decide what role women are to play (Bennett 2006). This hierarchical organization bases its legitimacy on a previous (super)natural state from which the family emerges ready-made. Patriarchy is a system within which differences between men are not hidden.

Though the patriarchy has still been insufficiently studied from a historical standpoint, even in Bennett's opinion, and though it has never been employed by historians of the French Revolution – something we have yet to understand – its usefulness has been shown by scholars of British political society. The points of similarity between English voters of 1832 and French voters during the Revolution are enlightening in this case. According to Amanda Vickery's research, the English voter of the reforms of 1832 was linked to the figure of "male householder," meaning paterfamilias (Vickery 2001). English citizenship rested principally on independence, which heads of families alone possess: in Georgian England politics and the family are inseparable (McCormack 2005). All men are not men in political terms: they must display a quality, an independence of character that can be achieved only through a particular position within the family. Thus, in political terms, male minors and male servants are not truly masculine. We can see here a gendered perspective that goes so far as to conceive as feminine everything pertaining to the family, regardless of a person's identity or sexual attributes. This in no way lessened the heavy weight of the attribution of rights within the family on individual members of English society.

For the United States, Jan Lewis has demonstrated that, at the end of the eighteenth century, persons and not property formed the basis for representation and that these persons could be of any age, sex, or station (Lewis 1995). Deprivation of the right to vote did not involve exclusion from the realm. A political link bound those with the right to vote and other members of the nation. The similarities (and no doubt the circulation of ideas) go further, since we find James Wilson asserting that government was created only for the protection of the family unit that pre-dated it. Roederer had used the same formulation in his 1793 lectures on social organization. Finally, in nineteenth-century Portugal and Germany we find this same attribution of political rights only to heads of families in the Roman sense (Cassidy 1897; Romanelli 1998).

These convictions did not necessarily imply belief in the inferiority of women. In a hierarchical system subordination did not assume inferiority (Dumont 1970). Thus a son, although without political rights because of his subordinate position within the family until 1792, was not regarded as an imbecile. It was the patriarch's authority that induced dependence. This was to change with the coming of the democratic republic: it became difficult to justify power, even within the family, other than by invoking the necessity of protecting the weaker members. From that time on the medical argument about the innate inferiority of women became decisive in justifying their exclusion from civil, family, and political rights (Verjus 2010b; Knibielher 1976; Laqueur 1990).

Some historians have observed this influence of the private and familial on political organization operating in different ways: they note the extent to which the matrimonial relationship, through marriage law, had been endowed with a political power of which the sexual relationship had been deprived (Desan 2004; Hunt 1995). The Revolution tried to regenerate marriage through divorce (Ronsin 1990); it also tried to encourage priests to marry for at least two reasons: first, because it assumed that intimacy, the yeast of sensibility, would allow them to transcend their individual interests in favor of the general will (Desan 2004); second, because it regarded marriage and fatherhood as matters of patriotic service and civic obligation (Cage 2011). We can see that this approach has progressed from being the study of the impact of the familial on political relationships and of rights between men and women to the study of the influence of the private on the political. From the sexual grouping to the family as "the basic unit of political society" (Guiraudet 1797), the perspectives of historians of the men and women of the revolutionary period have evolved and now place greater emphasis on interactions between the personal and public spheres.

At the same time as she researched the male householder, Amanda Vickery was able to demonstrate how much power was conferred by property, rank, and heritage on privileged Englishwomen. She suggests extending the definition of the public sphere to include the supposedly "private" life of family connections and friendship networks, "*fora* within which political ideas were discussed and new social practices imagined" (Vickery 2001). When we read what certain political scientists and historians have called "informal politics" we can see the extent to which family, social, and political relations were combined at the end of the eighteenth century. Women from the political class were far from being excluded from the careers of their husbands, even of their fathers; they took part in the long and fastidious work on relationships that were a condition of every political transaction.

The historical separation that has been taken up again between the domestic and the political was very strict: it touches not only on the collaboration of the masculine and the feminine within couples, but equally of the interior and the exterior, the dining room and the minister's office, the public and private face of the actors on the political stage. So, starting from women's participation in political events in order to demonstrate their status as citizens in deed if not in law, as a kind of retrospective reparation, we have rediscovered this participation of women. No longer as unrecognized, crushed, or "broken" citizens but as "endowed with the authority" of their husband, in a situation that, without being irreversible, established many bridges between a public man and his wife or mother.

The notable silence about researches on sexuality in this chapter is because they generally lack political interrogation, in the sense that they still avoid the question of attribution of legitimate political power. It is possible that this problem is the result of the essentialist nature of a position that links penis and power, as we see in the revolutionary rhetoric about the sexuality of the king and of men in general (André 1993; Baecque 1991; Hunt 1991). If the patriarchalist paradigm is the one that best accounts for the organization of public space, however, we should study its effect on the discourse on sexuality. In other words, can we not envisage a distinction between different sexual practices (and the discourse surrounding them) of a group of men we know is not homogeneous in political terms? A paterfamilias and a servant share as men, in sexual terms, the common condition of manhood; but the relationship is social. As a result, the sexuality of the head of a family is probably not that of a servant. In making these distinctions, might we not find data that would enrich our understanding of the links between gender, sexuality, and political culture?

Historians of masculinity have stressed how far we have, in our concentration on the abstract individual and universal man, "subordinated the gender identity" of the public man (Kann 1998; Roper and Tosh 1991) and almost forgotten that he was also a man of flesh and blood. Even a Citizen. The paterfamilias is much more than an empirical father. He is the incarnation of the political man and woman. Thus the revolutionary paterfamilias and his wife are not a male and a female. This is where the change in perspective occurs. Beyond personal history confined to domestic and familial history and the political history of biographies, political culture is nourished by studies of gender and sexuality: when history, rather than bringing to light the specific acts of citizens governed by their emotions and individual interactions, illuminates the way they are represented and the perspectives through which a society thinks, organizes public space, and apportions the rights of its members.

Acknowledgments

I should like to express my deep gratitude to Jennifer Heuer and Grégoire Bigot for their careful reading and their advice, as perceptive as it was welcome.

References

André, Jacques (1993). *La Révolution fratricide: Essai de psychanalyse du lien social.* Paris: PUF.

Azimi, Vida (1991). "L''Exhérédation politique' de la femme par la Révolution." *Revue historique de droit français et étranger*, 69: 177–216.

Badinter, Élisabeth (1989). *Paroles d'hommes, 1790–1793.* Paris: POL.

Baecque, Antoine de (1991). "The 'Livres remplis d'horreur': Pornographic Literature and Politics at the Beginning of the French Revolution." In Peter Wagner (ed.). *Erotica and the Enlightenment.* Frankfurt: Peter Lang. 123–165.

Bennett, Judith M. (2006). *History Matters: Patriarchy and the Challenge of Feminism.* Philadelphia: University of Pennsylvania Press.

Bigot, Grégoire (2010). "Impératifs politiques du droit privé: Le Divorce 'sur simple allégation d'incompatibilité d'humeur ou de caractère' (1792–1804)." In *Clio@Themis, Revue électronique d'histoire du droit*: 3.

Cage, Claire E. (2011). "Unnatural Frenchmen: Priestly Celibacy in Enlightenment and Revolutionary France." Ph.D. dissertation. Johns Hopkins University.

Cardoza, Thomas (2010). "'Habits Appropriate to Her Sex': The Female Military Experience in France during the Age of Revolution." In Karen Hagemann, Jane Rendall, and Gisela Mettele (eds.). *Gender, War and Politics: Transatlantic Perspectives 1775–1830*, Basingstoke: Palgrave Macmillan. 188–205.

Cassidy, Jessie (1897). *The Legal Status of Women.* New York: National American Women's Suffrage Association.

Clawson, Mary Ann (1989). *Constructing Brotherhood: Class, Gender, and Fraternalism.* Princeton, N.J.: Princeton University Press.

Darmon, Pierre (1979). *Le Tribunal de l'impuissance: Virilité et défaillances conjugales dans l'ancienne France.* Paris: Éditions du Seuil.

Delphy, Christine (2001). *L'Ennemi principal*, vol. 2; *Penser le genre.* Paris: Éditions Syllepse.

Desan, Suzanne (1992). "'Constitutional Amazons': Jacobin Women's Clubs in the French Revolution." In Bryant T. Ragan and Elizabeth A. Williams (eds.). *Re-creating Authority in Revolutionary France.* New Brunswick, N.J.: Rutgers University Press. 11–35.

Desan, Suzanne (2004). *The Family on Trial in Revolutionary France.* Berkeley: University of California Press.

Devance, Louis (1977). "Le Féminisme pendant la Révolution française." *AHRF*, 229: 341–376.

Dumont, Louis (1970). *Homo hierarchicus: Essai sur le systeme des castes.* Paris: Gallimard.

Eaubonne, Françoise d' (1990). "Prairial an III: L'Interdiction des clubs de femmes." In Michèle Dayras (ed.). *Liberté, égalité – et les femmes?* Paris: Éditions du Libre Arbitre. 141–144.

Fauré, Christine (2006). "Doléances, déclarations et pétitions, trois formes de la parole publique des femmes sous la Révolution." *AHRF*, 2006: 5–25.

Geoffroy, Annie (1989). "Citoyen/citoyenne (1753–1829)." In *Dictionnaire des usages sociopolitiques (1770–1815)*, 4: 2.

Godineau, Dominique (1988). *Citoyennes tricoteuses: Les Femmes du peuple à Paris pendant la Révolution française.* Aix-en-Provence: Alinéa.

Godineau, Dominique (1996). "'Privées par notre sexe du droit honorable de donner notre suffrage...': Le Vote des femmes pendant la Révolution française." In Eliane Viennot (ed.). *La Démocratie "à la française" ou les femmes indésirables.* Paris: Publications de l'Université Paris 7 – Denis Diderot. 199–211.

Gueniffey, Patrice (1993). *Le Nombre et la raison: La Révolution française et les élections.* Paris: ÉHÉSS.

Guiraudet, Charles-Philippe-Toussaint (1797). *De la Famille considérée comme l'élément des sociétés.* Paris: Desenne.

Hesse, Carla A. (2001). *The Other Enlightenment: How French Women became Modern.* Princeton, N.J.: Princeton University Press.

Heuer, Jennifer Ngaire (2005). *The Family and the Nation: Gender and Citizenship in Revolutionary France, 1789–1830.* Ithaca, N.Y.: Cornell University Press.

Heuer, Jennifer and Anne Verjus (2006). "Les Mères de la patrie révolutionnaire: Entre représentation et incarnation du politique, 1792–1801." In *Les Mères de la patrie. Représentations et constructions d'une figure nationale.* Caen: Maison de la Recherche en Sciences Humaines. 45: 259–270.

Hincker François (1991). "La Citoyenneté révolutionnaire saisie à travers ses exclus." In Nathalie Robatel (ed.). *Le Citoyen fou.* Paris: PUF, Nouvelle Encyclopédie Diderot. 7–28.

Hopkin, David (2009). "The World Turned Upside Down: Female Soldiers in the French Armies of the Revolutionary and Napoleonic Wars." In Karen Hagemann, Alan Forrest, and Jane Rendall (eds.). *Soldiers, Citizens and Civilians: Experiences and Perceptions of the French Wars, 1790–1820.* Basingstoke: Palgrave Macmillan. 77–98.

Hunt, Lynn (1991). *Eroticism and the Body Politic.* Baltimore, Md.: Johns Hopkins University Press.

Hunt, Lynn (1995). *Le Roman familial de la Révolution française.* Paris: Albin Michel.

Iacub, Marcela (2008). *Par le trou de la serrure: Une histoire de la pudeur publique, XIXe–XXIe siècle.* Paris: Fayard.

Kann, Mark E. (1998). *A Republic of Men: The American Founders, Gendered Language, and Patriarchal Politics.* New York: New York University Press.

Kaplan, Steven L. and Philippe Minard (2004). *La France, malade du corporatisme: XVIII–XXe siècles.* Paris: Belin.

Knibiehler, Yvonne (1976). "Les Médecins et la 'nature féminine' au temps du Code civil." *Annales,* 4: 824–843.

Laqueur, Thomas Walter (1990). *Making Sex: Body and Gender from the Greeks to Freud.* Cambridge, Mass.: Harvard University Press.

Le Cour Grandmaison, Olivier (1992). *Les Citoyennetés en révolution, 1789–1794.* Paris: PUF.

Lessay, Franck (1998). *Le Débat Locke-Filmer: Avec la traduction du Patriarcha et du premier traité du Gouvernement civil.* Paris: PUF.

Lewis, Jan (1995). "'Of Every Age Sex and Condition': The Representation of Women in the Constitution." *Journal of the Early Republic,* 15: 359–387.

McCormack, Matthew (2005). *The Independent Man: Citizenship and Gender Politics in Georgian England.* Manchester: Manchester University Press.

Marc, Yann-Arzel (2002). "Des femmes-citoyennes: Aperçu sur les caractères de l'activité politique des femmes au début de la Révolution (1789–1790)." In Christiane Plessix-Buisset (ed.). *Ordre et désordre dans les familles: Études d'histoire du droit.* Rennes: Presses Universitaires de Rennes. 151–201.

Martin, Jean-Clément (2006). *La Révolte brisée: Femmes dans la Révolution française.* Paris: Armand Colin.

Mazeau, Guillaume (2009). *Le Bain de l'histoire: Charlotte Corday et l'attentat contre Marat, 1793–2009.* Seyssel: Champ Vallon.

Merrick, Jeffrey, and Bryant T. Ragan (1996). *Homosexuality in Modern France.* New York: Oxford University Press.

Miller, Pavla (1998). *Transformations of Patriarchy in the West: 1500–1900.* Bloomington: Indiana University Press.

Ourliac, Paul (1966). "L'Évolution de la condition de la femme en droit français." *Annales de la Faculté de droit de Toulouse,* 14/2. Toulouse. 43–71.

Pateman, Carole (1988). *The Sexual Contract.* Stanford, Calif: Stanford University Press.

Portemer, Jean (1962). "Le Statut de la femme en France depuis la reformation des coutumes jusqu'à la rédaction du Code civil." In *La Femme. Recueils de la société Jean Bodin pour l'histoire comparative des institutions*, vol. 10. Brussels: Éditions de la Librairie Encyclopédique. 243–254.

Roederer, Pierre-Louis (1859 [1793]). *Cours d'organisation sociale (1793): Oeuvres du comte P.-L. Roederer, publiées par son fils, A. M. Roederer*, vol. 8. Paris: Firmin Didot.

Roederer, Pierre-Louis and Corancez (1796). "Aux auteurs du Journal de Paris." *Journal de Paris*, 19.

Romanelli, Raffaele (1998). *How Did They Become Voters? The History of Franchise in Modern European Representation*. The Hague: Kluwer Law International.

Ronsin, Francis (1990). *Le Contrat sentimental: Débats sur le mariage, l'amour, le divorce, de l'Ancien Régime à la Restauration*. Paris: Aubier.

Roper, Michael and John Tosh (1991). *Manful Assertions: Masculinities in Britain since 1800*. London: Routledge.

Rosanvallon, Pierre (1992). *Le Sacre du citoyen*. Paris: Gallimard.

Rosanvallon, Pierre (2011). *La Société des égaux*. Paris: Seuil.

Sagnac, Philippe (1899). *La Législation civile de la Révolution française, la propriété et la famille (1789–1804)*. Paris: A. Fontemoing.

Schochet, Gordon J. (1975). *Patriarchalism in Political Thought: The Authoritarian Family and Political Speculation and Attitudes Especially in Seventeenth-Century England*. Oxford: Blackwell.

Scott, Joan Wallach (1998). *La Citoyenne paradoxale: Les Féministes françaises et les droits de l'homme*. Paris: Albin Michel.

Sewell, William H. Jr. (1988). "Le Citoyen/La Citoyenne: Activity, Passivity, and the Revolutionary Concept of Citizenship." In Colin Lucas (ed.). *The French Revolution and the Creation of Modern Political Culture*, vol. 2. Oxford: Pergamon Press. 105–123.

Simonin, Anne (2008). *Le Déshonneur dans la République: Une histoire de l'indignité, 1791–1958*. Paris: Grasset & Fasquelle.

Steinberg, Sylvie (2001). *La Confusion des sexes: Le Travestissement de la Renaissance à la Révolution*. Paris: Fayard.

Verjus, Anne (2002). *Le Cens de la famille: Les Femmes et le vote, 1789–1848*. Paris: Belin.

Verjus, Anne (2008). "'Rétablir les moeurs par la police domestique': 'Influence des femmes' et 'organisation sociale' dans la pensée de P.-L. Roederer à l'issue de la Révolution française." In Irène Théry and Pascale Bonnemère (eds.). *Ce que le genre fait aux personnes*. Paris: ÉHÉSS.

Verjus, Anne (2010a). *Le Bon mari: Une histoire politique des hommes et des femmes à l'époque révolutionnaire*. Paris: Fayard.

Verjus, Anne (2010b). "L'Homme de la Révolution, un Pater Familias? Le Porteur de droits civils dans le concours de l'Institut sur l'autorité des pères en République (1798– 1801)." In *Clio@Themis, Revue électronique d'histoire du droit*, 3.

Vickery, Amanda (2001). *Women, Privilege, and Power: British Politics, 1750 to the Present*. Stanford, Calif.: Stanford University Press.

Further Reading

Dudink, Stefan, Anna Clark, and Karen Hagemann (2007). *Representing Masculinity: Male Citizenship in Modern Western Culture*. New York: Palgrave Macmillan.

Elshtain, Jean Bethke (1981). *Public Man, Private Woman: Women in Social and Political Thought*. Princeton, N.J.: Princeton University Press.

Fliegelman, Jay (1982). *Prodigals and Pilgrims: The American Revolution against Patriarchal Authority, 1750–1800*. Cambridge: Cambridge University Press.

Fraisse, Geneviève (1989a). "La Double Raison et l'unique nature." In Irène Théry and Christian Biet (eds.). *La Famille, la loi, l'État: De la Révolution au Code civil.* Paris: Imprimerie Nationale. 45–52.

Fraisse, Geneviève (1989b). *Muse de la raison: La Démocratie exclusive et la différence des sexes.* Aix-en-Provence: Alinéa.

Guibert-Sledziewski, Élisabeth (1984). "Naissance de la femme civile, la Révolution, la femme, le droit." *La Pensée, Recherches marxistes, Sciences, Société, Philosophie*, 238.

Hardwick, Julie (1998). *The Practice of Patriarchy: Gender and the Politics of Household Authority in Early Modern France.* University Park: Pennsylvania State University Press.

Heuer, Jennifer, and Anne Verjus (2002). "L'Invention de la sphère domestique au sortir de la Révolution." *AHRF*, 327: 1–28.

Hunt, Lynn (1991). *Eroticism and the Body Politic.* Baltimore, Md.: Johns Hopkins University Press.

Klein, Lawrence E. (1995). "Gender and the Public/Private Distinction in the Eighteenth Century: Some Questions about Evidence and Analytic Procedure." *Eighteenth Century Studies*, 29: 97–109.

Landes, Joan B. (1988). *Women and the Public Sphere in the Age of the French Revolution.* Ithaca, N.Y.: Cornell University Press.

McPhee, Peter (2002). *The French Revolution, 1789–1799.* Oxford: Oxford University Press.

Smith, Hilda L. (2002). *All Men and Both Sexes: Gender, Politics, and the False Universal in England, 1640–1832.* University Park: Pennsylvania State University Press.

Théry, Irène (2007). *La Distinction de sexe: Une nouvelle approche de l'égalité.* Paris: Odile Jacob.

Théry, Irène and Christian Biet (eds.) (1989). *La Famille, la loi, l'État de la Révolution au Code civil.* Paris: Imprimerie Nationale.

Yazawa, Melvin (1985). *From Colonies to Commonwealth: Familial Ideology and the Beginnings of the American Republic.* Baltimore, Md.: Johns Hopkins University Press.

Chapter Thirteen

The Peasantry, Feudalism, and the Environment, 1789–93

Noelle Plack

Introduction

It is often said that the peasantry played a fundamental role in the French Revolution. But it is difficult to describe *the* role the peasants played as they were not a unified, undifferentiated mass. Indeed, historians have argued about the peasantry's role in the origins, course, and outcomes of the French Revolution ever since it began over 200 years ago. Were they active agents, pushing the Revolution forward; docile witnesses, serving as a brake on the Revolution; or hostile adversaries, openly engaging in counter-revolutionary acts? Georges Lefebvre (1947) argued that the peasantry experienced their own revolution in 1789 through their struggle against seigneurial lords and that this was one of the most distinctive features of the French Revolution. His assessment, however, ends in a dichotomy: while the peasantry destroyed feudalism, they also consolidated the traditional agrarian structure of France, based on smallholding subsistence farmers, which thwarted capitalist development in the countryside (Lefebvre 1954). More recent work has argued that these smallholders may not have been as "backward" as previously thought and that at least some of them turned towards more commercialized forms of agriculture (Ado 1996; McPhee 1999). While there is debate regarding the second part of Lefebvre's contention, his first assertion about the peasantry's independent revolution against their lords has stood the test of time – there was some sort of peasant revolution in 1789 and it was independent of, but interactive with, the "bourgeois" revolution.

This chapter will focus on some of the key issues in that independent and interactive peasant revolution. It will begin with a brief description of the peasantry and their grievances in 1789. This will lay the foundation for the chapter's main themes, which coalesce around three areas: lords, land, and the environment. The first

A Companion to the French Revolution, First Edition. Edited by Peter McPhee.

theme to be explored is peasant insurrection and the abolition of feudalism. This is one of the fundamental components of the peasant revolution and one that is central to the entire revolutionary decade. Landholding was another issue that galvanized most peasants during the Revolution and demonstrates well the interactive nature of the revolutionary experience as both people in the countryside and legislators in Paris engaged with the question of access to land and resources. This is the second theme. The final theme seeks to discover the impact of the French Revolution on the environment. What effect did land clearance, tree felling, or marsh draining have on the environment, and did the revolutionary decade change how people interacted with their physical surroundings? These questions represent some of the latest thinking on the subject as historians of the French Revolution begin to engage with the field of environmental history. The chapter will end with a brief conclusion that will highlight key arguments and point the way towards future research.

The Peasantry and their Grievances in 1789

The French word *paysan*, meaning people of the land (*pays*), is usually employed to refer to the rural population, but this term cannot begin to describe the complexities of French rural society in the eighteenth century. One noted historian of rural France has identified and described "twenty contrasting peasantries" (Goubert 1974). It is estimated that the French population totaled about 28 million in 1780. At least 22 million of these people lived in the countryside and some 18 million of these were engaged in agriculture (Moulin 1991: 5). Therefore, three out of four people were peasants on the eve of the Revolution. In the broadest sense these people farmed the land and, because of their close links to the soil, shared a common lifestyle and outlook. However, there were a number of ranks within the internal hierarchy of the peasantry. By far the most numerous group, perhaps 55 percent, were the owners of small plots who had to supplement their income by renting, sharecropping (*métayage*), or wage labor. Above them were the well-to-do tenant farmers (*fermiers* or *tenanciers*) or large landowners (*laboureurs*) who needed to employ farmhands to work their vast tracts of land. These *fermiers* and *laboureurs* would have been the most powerful peasants in their respective communities (*coqs du villages*) and are sometimes referred to as the "rural bourgeoisie." At the bottom of the peasant hierarchy were the landless poor, who made up approximately 30 percent of the rural population; they were hired as day laborers or domestic servants on large farms. Their numbers ranged tremendously, however, across France; from only 5 percent in the Auvergne to some 55 percent around Versailles (McPhee 2004). All of these people lived in a diverse kingdom with different linguistic and cultural practices as well as contrasting economic structures and topographic features.

In January 1789, in preparation for the upcoming Estates-General, the monarchy called on all adult male taxpayers to assemble in their village communities at a special meeting to draw up a list of grievances and appoint delegates to represent their parishes. These parish grievance lists or *cahiers de doléances* represent a unique source for historians, not only because of their sheer number (some

40,000), but also because through them we can hear some of the voices of rural France. Although these documents must be approached with caution as they were often influenced by model *cahiers* from larger cities and towns, and because they were most likely drawn up by the more affluent members of a community (sometimes with pressure from a local seigneur or priest), they are still invaluable as they contain the hopes and anxieties of the peasantry. Gilbert Shapiro and John Markoff (1998) have investigated a sample of 748 of these rural parish *cahiers* and their findings provide a statistical analysis of the peasantry's grievances on the eve of the Revolution. First and foremost, the most common complaint in the parish *cahiers* was the theme of surplus extraction either from the state (in the form of taxation), seigneurs (in the form of dues, produce, or labor), or the church (in the form of the *tithe* and the *dîme*). Indeed, the claims of others on peasant income make up almost one-half of all peasant grievances (Markoff 2006). It must be remembered that if we add up all the various claims on peasant income, between one-quarter and one-half of their revenue was lost through extraction from the state, lords, or the church. But what this work has also revealed is that the inhabitants of rural France were able to make distinctions between these various forms of extraction. In contrast to arguments of historians, such as George V. Taylor (1972) and William Doyle (1980: 198), who claim that peasants lacked any radical revolutionary consciousness or even the intellectual capacity to grasp "feudalism as a whole," Markoff (1996) has been able to demonstrate that peasants had quite a sophisticated understanding of the complex web of institutions that impinged upon them. Indeed, these findings have helped to change our perceptions of the eighteenth-century French peasantry in that they reveal an autonomous and discerning group with considerable awareness of their world.

However, state taxation and seigneurialism were not the only themes to appear in the parish *cahiers de doléances* as both land and environmental issues were also on the minds of country dwellers on the eve of the Revolution. At the heart of the rural world stood the edifice of communal rights. These usage rights, such as gleaning, stock grazing, and woodcutting, applied to both private property and common land and ensured the survival of many poor peasants as well as the proper functioning of the rural economy (Jones 1988). According to Markoff (1996), some 70 percent of Third Estate *cahiers* discuss communal rights, with woods, common land, and enclosures being the most widely mentioned issues. The question of who "owned" these lands was of the greatest significance as there was much tension surrounding, and pressure on, these spaces in the run-up to the Revolution. Another theme that can be gleaned from the parish *cahiers* is a concern for the ecological degradation of collective resources. It is clear that many communities recognized the link between land clearance and soil erosion. In several regions across France, but particularly in the south, complaints surfaced about the extent of land clearances. Across the Midi, hillsides had been cleared in previous years and some of the best land was subject to being washed away when rainwater rushed down the ravines, taking trees, crops, and vineyards with it. A related environmental thread in the *cahiers* was hostility to wood-fueled industries, such as glass or brick works, which devoured precious resources and forced some peasants in the *bailliage* of Mirecourt to burn their fruit-trees for firewood (McPhee 2001). Thus, the *cahiers* reveal the variety and depth of peasant disenchantment and apprehension at the end of the *ancien régime*; all of these issues were played out in the revolutionary dynamic of 1789–93.

Insurrection and the Abolition of Feudalism

Although the Tennis Court Oath of 20 June and the storming of the Bastille on 14 July 1789 are often seen as the opening acts of the French Revolution, the peasantry in France had been in open revolt since at least the spring of 1789. These revolts took various forms, from tax rebellions and food riots to land conflicts and attacks on seigneurial chateaux, and varied in intensity during the period 1789–93. In other words, there were peaks and troughs of peasant insurrectionary action during the French Revolution. The Russian historian Anatoliï Ado (1996) has identified seven different waves of peasant insurrection, while John Markoff (1996) has argued that key periods of unrest were followed by legislation, which dismantled the seigneurial regime. By analyzing over 4,700 incidents of rural unrest, Markoff (1996) has been able to track peasant insurrection during the French Revolution through time and space and has demonstrated that the abolition of feudalism was a complex dialectical process between legislators in Paris and the rural inhabitants of France. Even though it was the successive Assemblies that passed over one hundred pieces of legislation to abolish seigneurialism in its entirety, they were not acting on their own. Indeed, Peter Jones (2001: 80) has described the dismantling of the feudal regime as "an object lesson in how the nominally weak and supposedly illiterate get their own way in the end." This section will focus on four main periods of insurrection and the corresponding legislative acts, which by growing more radical in scope and content ultimately brought down the seigneurial regime.

During the spring and summer of 1789, peasants rose up across France. They were both angry and hungry, but because the calling of the Estates-General and the drafting of the *cahiers* served as a massive *prise de conscience*, they were also hopeful. Virtually every region of France was touched to some degree by insubordinate action or collective violence. However, there were eight main epicenters of revolt: Franche-Comté, Dauphiné, Provence, Hainaut and Cambrésis, Lower Normandy, Mâconnais, Alsace, and the southwest (Jones 1988). Many of the insurrectionary actions, which occurred in April and May, displayed elements of both traditional subsistence revolts and newer anti-feudal antagonisms. In May bands of hundreds of peasants armed with knives, scythes, and pitchforks attacked grain stores throughout northern France, confiscated the stocks, and then sold them at a "just price" in local markets. This practice, known as *taxation populaire*, often involved entire communities, including women and children. However, throughout the spring of 1789 these subsistence events were transformed more and more into mass movements against seigneurial lords. In his magisterial study of the Nord department, Lefebvre (1959) argued that the struggle against feudalism mobilized the peasantry *en masse*, and more recent research has certainly confirmed this contention (Jones 1988). From Paris and Versailles to Provence and the Dauphiné, peasants, during the spring of 1789, began to invade and ransack chateaux and to take back usurped land by destroying enclosures and letting their livestock loose to pasture (Ado 1996).

These actions only intensified once the news of the events of 11–14 July in Paris reached the countryside. Beginning on 20 July in six or seven flashpoints throughout France waves of fear, panic, and revolt took hold. Angry rumors and imagined sightings of "brigands," or agents of vengeful seigneurs, sparked off the events of late July and early August which are known as "the Great Fear" (Lefebvre 1973). Peasants armed themselves for defense against malfeasant outsiders, but very quickly used their weapons to attack seigneurial chateaux instead, burning manorial tax rolls and destroying weathercocks and lords' private pews in churches. Although there was relatively little physical violence against the lords themselves (most of the violence was directed at destroying the symbols of their power), some peasants were put to death in this first summer of revolution. In Burgundy, there were improvised trials and summary justice that condemned thirty-three peasants to death in late July 1789 for attacks on seigneurial chateaux and abbeys (Clère 2005). While there has been much debate about violence in the French Revolution, with some historians, like Simon Schama (1990), claiming that "violence *was* the Revolution itself," John Markoff (1996: 442n) reminds us that to focus only on victims of crowd violence and the Terror overlooks and disregards the "peasants (who were) shot, hung, and broken at the wheel … for hunting, invading fields, and taking food from the lord's stocks" during the summer of 1789. Regardless of whether these insurrectionary actions were punished or not, the events of the summer of 1789 had direct consequences in the National Assembly.

On the night of 4 August 1789 liberal noble deputies, led by the viscount de Noailles and the duc d'Aiguillon, presented a program that sought to suppress all seigneurial rights in return for reimbursement. These initial declarations produced an emotional response in the hall with many deputies from all three orders lining up at the podium to renounce various privileges until the small hours of the morning. The meeting on the 4 August made it possible for the National Assembly to achieve what Michael Fitzsimmons (2001: 16–17) has called "a functional consensus." While this did not necessarily mean that all deputies agreed on every issue, it did ensure that they were able to move forward on a program that addressed feudalism. From this night on, the National Assembly never considered reverting to a system of privilege. A number of decrees were passed in the days that followed this historic night and culminated in the law of 4–11 August 1789. The first article of the new law boldly declared: "The National Assembly destroys, in its entirety, the feudal regime." This proclamation, however, was soon to disappoint as the rest of the decree made the distinction between "personal servitude" which was abolished outright and "property rights" which were to be redeemed by a payment.

The decree of 4–11 August 1789 abolished many features of seigneurialism including exclusive hunting rights, seigneurial courts, the tithe, tax exemptions, civil distinctions, venal offices, perpetual rights, and harvest dues. However, many of these reforms were to require further legislation before they could be put into effect. Thus, harvest dues, seigneurial courts, and the tithe were all to remain in force until additional legislative work was done. This created what Clère (2005: 139) has described as "an insurmountable contradiction" in that the decree of

4–11 August 1789 promised to destroy the feudal regime while at the same time it guaranteed a certain number of seigneurial rights for at least a period into the foreseeable future. In the countryside, the peasantry focused on the first sentence of the decree and looked no further. Only slowly did they realize that they would still be subject to harvest dues and other payments and consequently regarded this law as "a monstrous fraud" (Jones 1988: 81). After the autumn harvest, collectors of seigneurial rights and the tithe tried their best to extract these payments from a reluctant peasantry, who either refused outright or willfully claimed misunderstanding. The winter of 1789–90 witnessed a second wave of insurrection across France in which the peasantry was growing more and more politicized in their reaction to the continued collection of seigneurial dues. In the epicenters of this rebellion, notably parts of Brittany and the southwest, peasants continued their destruction of seigneurial chateaux and symbols of the lords' power, but also used in their protests the new rhetoric of the Revolution. In the Dordogne, after crowds ransacked local chateaux in January 1790, numerous liberty trees were planted in village squares to symbolize the inhabitants' liberation from feudalism (Ado 1996; Sutherland 1985).

This second wave of peasant insurrection forced the National Assembly to clarify the terms of the original August decree on feudalism in the spring of 1790. The law of 15–28 March 1790 was a much more conservative document than its predecessor. Merlin de Douai, head of the Feudal Committee, attempted to turn "lords" into "proprietors" by using the language of contractual rights, so the new law continued the distinction between "personal obligations" and "real rights." It spelled out which "coerced" rights would be abolished outright (*corvées*, *triage*, and *banalités*), but also which ones would only be relinquished through indemnity because they were derived from a concession of land once freely made. The latter were viewed as "real rights" and could only be extinguished, according to the Declaration of the Rights of Man "on condition of a previous just indemnity." They included lucrative monetary and harvest dues (*cens*, *champart*, and *tasque*) as well as the right of *mainmorte*, which had been abolished under the August 1789 decree. This backsliding caused much resentment, but even more disturbing for the peasantry, perhaps, was the fact that the burden of proof for the remaining rights lay not with the former seigneurs, but with the village communities themselves.

The property-owning elites who dominated the National Assembly charged the Feudal Committee to work out the rates for buying out the remaining "real rights." The law reached the statue books on 3–9 May 1790 and set the rate of redemption at twenty times the amount of annual cash dues and twenty-five times the annual amount of dues payable in kind. Although there has been some debate whether these rates were fair given the circumstances, there is no doubt that the peasantry *en bloc* rejected the idea of indemnification of seigneurial dues as the evidence for the number of actual redemptions remains very thin. Clère (2005) has estimated that with the set rates, this could have easily represented 50,000 or 60,000 *livres* for the inhabitants of a single village; this sum would have been equivalent to the amount of direct taxes paid by a village over twenty years or more. Nevertheless, the laws of March and May 1790 represented what Peter Jones (1988: 90) has called "an exercise in the art of the possible" as they opened a window through which the peasantry could glimpse the end of their burdens. They were by no means satisfied with the contradictory and ambiguous terms of the legislation and continued their resistance through willful non-payment during the rest of 1790 and 1791, until the spring of 1792 when the peasantry rose in a third great wave of insurrection.

From February until June 1792 there was widespread rebellion in rural France on a scale not seen since the summer of 1789. The escalation of tensions over the war added to the anxiety, as many rural dwellers feared a return to the *ancien régime* if France was defeated. In the southeast during the spring of 1792 there was a wave of violent attacks, known as the *guerre aux châteaux*, which was predominantly anti-feudal in character but which also contained religious and patriotic elements (Vovelle 1980). This charged atmosphere served as the prelude for the second revolution of 10 August 1792 when members of the National Guard, working people from Paris, and army volunteers (*fédérés*) stormed the Tuileries palace, effectively ending the reign of Louis XVI. The crisis of the spring and summer of 1792 served as a major turning-point: the revolutionaries were committed from then on to passing legislation that satisfied the common people of France, both urban and rural. Indeed, after the *Dix Août* there was a veritable cascade of legislation, which addressed the desires of the peasantry. In terms of seigneurialism, the law of 25 August 1792 declared that all feudal dues were to be abolished without indemnity, except in cases where the *ci-devant* seigneur could produce the original title. This decree, which reversed the burden of proof from communities back to former lords, ended anti-seigneurial protest in the countryside for the most part, as it was now almost impossible for *ci-devants* to collect what dues, in principle, remained (Markoff 1996).

However, there were further protests in late autumn 1792 and spring 1793, which although they had different targets (subsistence and counter-revolution), constituted the fourth wave of insurrection that spurred further anti-seigneurial legislation. Indeed, it seems that the Jacobins realized that by ignoring peasant demands they risked engendering massive defection from the Revolution's cause; so they committed themselves to satisfying popular rural desires. Although peasants were not revolting against their lords in the summer of 1793, as they had done in previous years, the deputies in the Convention felt it was necessary to pass one final piece of legislation, which ended the feudal regime in its totality. The law of 17 July 1793 abolished all feudal dues and rights, even if the former lords could produce a title. This legislation was the crowning act that finally made good on the promise of the decrees of 4–11 August 1789. In fact, part of this law ordered all feudal title deeds to be turned over to municipal officials and solemnly burned during the *fête nationale* on 10 August 1793. It seems that most of the *auto-da-fés* took place during the autumn of 1793 in front of decorated liberty trees and accompanied by large crowds singing *La Marseillaise*. Anatolï Ado (1996) has argued that historians have not given enough attention to this aspect of the law. The open, public, and legally sanctioned burning of feudal titles was very important to many peasant communities because this act had always been previously described as *jacquerie* (peasant revolt). While historians have found it difficult to trace how many feudal titles were actually destroyed after 17 July 1793, recent work has estimated that around 4,000 titles were burned, almost one in five, from 1789 to 1793 (Bianchi 2002; Soboul 1976). Regardless of whether the titles were actually set alight, for four years the peasantry rose in waves of protest and insurrection, which ultimately forced legislators in Paris to abolish once and for all the feudal regime. We should not underestimate the impact of these actions, for without this determined and often violent battle, peasants in France would have most likely been responsible for seigneurial obligations until at least the middle of the nineteenth century (Markoff 1996).

Access to Land: Actions and Results

Because of the fundamentally agrarian nature of the French economy, ownership of and access to land were important issues in the French Revolution. However, the complex nature of landownership that existed at the end of the eighteenth century meant that reform was far from straightforward. The Rural Code (28 September 1791) attempted to codify the agricultural practices of the new nation. Its opening article proclaimed "the territory of France is free, like the people who inhabit it," yet the actual text of the law is often seen as a compromise between the bourgeoisie and the peasantry – one that did not really satisfy either group. The problem was that large landowners wanted their freehold property rights vindicated; they believed that with the abolition of feudal dues, the long-standing collective and communal rights of the countryside must also be rescinded. In contrast, the peasantry, or at least the majority of small proprietors and the landless, desired two things that were probably incompatible. They wanted private property that was free from servitude or feudal dues, but at the same time they desired to retain their communal rights, such as collective pasturing on private lands (*vaine pâture*), on the lands of their better-off neighbors (Jones 1988). Because of the impossibility of abolishing these collective rights in the face of mass agrarian revolt, the Assembly passed a law which tried to satisfy competing claims. Many of the collective rights, such as *vaine pâture*, survived, as well a concession for the landless poor to keep up to six sheep and a cow with calf in the *troupeau commun*. However, the right of enclosure and the right to remove land from the jurisdiction of *vaine pâture* were vindicated as well as the freedom to cultivate any produce desired. Compulsory crop rotation was also abolished. Even though the Rural Code of 1791 was essentially a compromise, it seems to have struck the right balance between the maintenance of large sections of rural society and guaranteeing individual property rights – many of its main tenets remained in revisions of the Rural Code throughout the nineteenth and twentieth centuries (Clère 1982; Plack 2008).

While the Rural Code dealt with collective rights and private property, there was another aspect of the Revolution's land policy. Essentially two types of land were made available in reaction to a widespread and sustained movement by the peasantry for access to resources. The first were the *biens nationaux*, the lands of the church and *émigré* nobles, which had been nationalized and sold at auction from 1791. Ordered by the decree of 14–17 May 1790, the lands of church were seized and put on the market in large blocs; these church lands became known as the lands of first origin. After the popular uprising on 10 August 1792, deputies decided to confiscate and sell off the property of *émigré* nobles as well; these lands were seized under the law 14 August 1792 and became known as the lands of second origin. A further decree passed by the Jacobins on 3 June 1793 ordered the subdivision of the *émigré* lands into small plots aimed at helping the poor gain access. The second type of land that helped to transform ownership in the countryside was the privatization of village common lands, known as the *biens communaux*. On 14 August 1792 a law ordered the partition of all common land in France, and on 28 August another allowed for communities to reintegrate any common land that had been unjustly taken from them by their former seigneurs. But these laws were inoperable because the *mode de partage*, or how the commons were to be divided, was not decided. After the popular uprising of 31 May – 2 June 1793, the law of 10 June 1793 was declared and allowed for the egalitarian partition of non-wooded common land between all members of a village community, regardless of age or sex, provided one-third of all residents over 21, including women, voted for such an action. Peter McPhee (2006: 137) has called the law of 10 June 1793 "one of the most ambitious attempts of the revolutionary government to meet the needs of the poor." But what were the results of these laws that sought to provide access to land for so many in the countryside?

Historians have been trying to assess the impact of the sale of the *biens nationaux* for almost two centuries, but most of these studies have focused on individual regions and departments. Recently, Bernard Bodinier and Éric Teyssier (2000) performed the monumental task of gathering and analyzing all of the regional studies to present a national portrait of the sales of *biens nationaux*; they have entitled their volume *The Most Important Event of the Revolution*. Two of the most fundamental questions relating to the *biens nationaux* are: how much land was sold, and who acquired it? According to Bodinier and Teyssier (2000), around 8.5 percent of the entire surface area of France, or around 4.75 million hectares, was sold as *biens nationaux*, with most transactions occurring in 1791 for church lands and between 1793 and 1797 for *émigré* lands. Around 600,000 people benefited from the sales of nationalized lands, or around one in ten households. It is often said that the bourgeoisie purchased most of this land, but detailed analysis of the sales revealed that the peasantry also gained significant amounts of land from this exercise. For the sales of church lands, peasants acquired 30 percent of the lands, while that number rose to perhaps 40 percent for the *émigré* lands. Bodinier and Teyssier (2000) are certain that the peasantry benefited from the Jacobin policy of subdivision of *émigré* lands as they secured a higher percentage of land sold. In total then, the peasantry added around 1.5 million hectares of land or 3 percent of the total surface area to its ownership. However, these global results varied tremendously according to region. There were hardly any peasant acquisitions in the zones of *grande culture* in the Paris Basin where the land was of good quality. In the Ardèche, Aveyron, and the Hérault, however, the peasantry acquired between 50 percent and 70 percent of all *biens nationaux* (Bodinier 2010). So without doubt, the peasantry gained land from the sale of nationalized church and *émigré* lands and benefited from the Jacobin policy to subdivide plots; this substantial transfer of land to the peasantry should not be underestimated and may indeed represent, if not the most important, at least a very significant event of the Revolution.

The global results for the partition of common land under the law of 10 June 1793 are more difficult to quantify. Support for the division or preservation of the commons depended in large measure on the local economy. In some areas the poor insisted on preserving communal land and collective access to it, while in others, the poor were keen to divide these spaces. Historians have been studying the impact of this law for over a century and it is now clear that there were specific areas where it was widely applied and zones where it was virtually ignored (Vivier 1998). While the west, southwest, center, and Alps tended to be areas where the division of common land was not a widespread practice, the departments north of Paris, the northeast, and south were zones where the law of 10 June 1793 was implemented with greater success. Even in these regions there was still much tension surrounding this issue as many smallholding peasants desired a plot, while their better-off neighbors, who tended to monopolize the commons for pasture, were not as supportive of egalitarian division. Still, a significant amount of communally held land was privatized during the revolutionary and Napoleonic decades. In the Oise some 30,000 peasants, almost 10 percent of the population, received a plot of land, while in Burgundy and Champagne perhaps as much as one-quarter of all commons were divided (Ikni 1996; Vivier 1998). In the Midi there was a widespread desire on the part of many *petits* peasants for a parcel of land on which to grow grapevines. Although these actions were usually usurpations rather than legal divisions, much land was turned over to viticulture in the years following the Jacobin partition decree (McPhee 1999; Plack 2009). Thus, although the results were perhaps not as great as legislators hoped, there were still many in France who benefited from the opportunity to divide up common land, and the ranks of the smallholding peasantry were bolstered as a result.

The Impact on the Environment

Historians of France have been concerned with the environment since the early twentieth century as many have exhibited a deep and abiding interest in agricultural landscapes and have been concerned with the symbolic meanings with which the natural world has been invested. Historians working in the Annales tradition have carried out much of this work out, but there are also cultural-literary approaches as well as institutional ones to French environmental history (Ford and Whited 2009). However, it is also true that "environmental history" in its purest form has only recently taken off in France compared to its initial launch in North America during the 1970s (Ford 2001; McNeill 2003). For too many historians in France environmental history has become synonymous with forests, but there were other types of spaces that experienced ecological change. One interpretation has dominated the historiography in terms of the impact of the French Revolution on the environment: the *légende noire*. This black legend contends that the Revolution of 1789 unleashed a reckless and unmitigated environmental disaster in the countryside. The blame is placed squarely on the shoulders of the French peasantry who took advantage of the breakdown in rural authority to invade and pillage forests and to clear wasteland. Despite warnings and complaints from local officials and countless decrees by successive assemblies, illegal tree cutting and occupation of wasteland continued unchecked until, according to the legend, the re-establishment of order under the Empire and Restoration. It was contemporaries who first began to describe the 1790s as the period when a massive wave of environmental destruction commenced. Several deputies and former legislators penned memoires at the end of the decade cataloguing the ecological degradation since 1789. Coupé de l'Oise claimed that parts of Midi suffered so greatly from deforestation that the climate was affected, while Rougier de la Bergerie argued that the peasantry's "newly found freedom" led many to usurp or clear a piece of wood or wasteland or to pasture their beasts in forested areas that were previously off-limits (McPhee 2001; Plack 2010). Historians have also perpetuated this *légende noire* of the French Revolution. Jules Michelet, in his *Histoire de France* written in the 1830s, claimed that the poor began their work of destruction during the Revolution when every barrier had fallen. Modern-day historians have targeted 1789 as the date when state supervision of forests, which had been regulated with varying degrees of success since Colbert, collapsed. Simon Schama (1995) contends that with the proclamation of "liberty, equality and fraternity," forests were henceforth open to everyone and, as such, the rural poor helped themselves to as much wood as they wanted. Much of the writing within the paradigm of the *légende noire* has focused on the destructive mentality of the peasantry and the "anarchy" of the peasant revolution. It is assumed that because the peasantry called for the abolition of the seigneurial regime and attacked chateaux that there was a destructive *mentalité* common to all rural people. During the French Revolution, this pernicious attitude was not only aimed at aristocrats, but towards the rural environment as well, much to the dismay of both contemporaries and (some) modern historians.

What is certain about this phenomenon is that forests and the forested regions of France have been at the center of the debate. These spaces, which today cover almost one-quarter of France's territory and hold important economic resources and cultural meanings, have been the focus of much study, carried out primarily by the Groupe d'Histoire des Forêts Françaises led by Andrée Corvol. They argue that the French Revolution unleashed a "politics of nature" and had both short- and long-term impacts on the environment (Corvol and Richefort 1995). On the one hand the Revolution's material inscription on the landscape must be examined, and on the other the imprint that it left on *mentalités* in terms of private property must also be considered. The revolutionaries paid much legislative attention to forests, passing over forty-five laws and fifty decrees. Very early on, in reaction to reports of widespread pillage, legislators passed a law on 11 December 1789 which stated that forests were now under the control of the nation and all infractions would be punished, while on the day following the proclamation of the Rural Code, the revolutionaries passed their Forest Code (29 September 1791) with the goal of preserving the 3 million *arpents* of wooded land within France's borders. Under this law all forests not privately owned came under the same jurisdiction as those belonging to the nation, while those in private hands were not subject to this central administration and each proprietor was free to dispose of their resources as they wished. This liberty was diminished by the Napoleonic Code of 9 Floréal XI (29 April 1803), which required all individuals who wanted to clear a piece of woodland to make a declaration to the forest administration six months prior. However, these laws seemed to have little effect as the battle over the use and control of rural resources continued for much of the 1790s (McPhee 1999). By 1793 half of all *bailliages* in France reported conflicts over forests and the rights of use and ownership of forested spaces (Markoff 1996).

Yet despite all of this evidence, the *légende noire* of the French Revolution is misconceived in several ways. First, contemporary documents, upon which many historians have based their interpretations, must be seen as alarmist rather than objective evaluations of the situation (Woronoff 1989). These *mémoires* and *observations* may have been written to get the attention of legislators and/or to punish rural dwellers' actions; in no way do they quantify the amount of forested land cleared or destroyed. Second, the focus on 1789 is misplaced. Although the Revolution may have accelerated the clearing of woodland, these trends began under the Bourbon monarchy during the final decades of the *ancien régime*. The land clearance edicts of the 1760s and 1770s started the fervor for land clearance while at the same time the physiocratic ideals which underpinned them tended to valorize cultivated lands to the detriment of woods (McPhee 2001; Plack 2005; Woronoff 1989). And finally, the peasantry were but one of the consumers of wood in the eighteenth century. Timber was used in all forms of construction, including ships and buildings, as well as serving as the primary fuel in many industries from ironworks, to tanning and glass-making, to distilling. Wood, of course, was also used for making barrels and many other objects including tools, furniture, and clogs. Andrée Corvol (1984) has argued that the conservation and administration of forests became more difficult as the eighteenth century progressed because of population growth and the more commercial attitudes of owners and users of these spaces. The navy, industry, and the urban population all consumed wood on a much larger scale than most rural inhabitants. And not all rural dwellers had a pernicious, destructive attitude towards their environment. Some of them expressed a complex understanding of who the main consumers of wood were in the late *ancien régime* – seigneurs, industrialists, and rich city dwellers who "by their multitude of fires, consume a terrifying amount of wood" and also how best to practice agriculture in a fragile ecosystem (McPhee 2001: 257). Yet there were periods, to be sure, when the peasantry invaded forests to procure wood and these peaks of activity were related to the larger context. There seem to have three periods of peasant over-consumption of wood during the 1790s: at the beginning of the Revolution in 1789–90, during the terrible winter of 1795, and again at the end of the Directory (Woronoff 1989). However, the *légende noire*, which characterizes the peasantry's widespread destruction of the environment during the French Revolution, is far from reality as forests in France had decreased by one-quarter in 1820 (McPhee 2006). This is certainly a significant reduction in woodland, but in no way is it "total devastation" and it varied tremendously from region to region. Furthermore, forests were not the only spaces affected by ecological change as *garrigues* also experienced clearance and cultivation during these decades. Without doubt the environment was put under increased strain at the end of the eighteenth century because of rising population, industrial activities, and warfare, but it is an error to condemn the peasantry alone for these pressures. Some of them exhibited quite a complex awareness of environmental issues in the *cahiers de doléances* analyzed by McPhee (2001). The ecological change that occurred during the French Revolution needs to be viewed in terms of the *longue durée* of environmental history, as human transformation of the natural world did not suddenly begin in 1789, nor did it end with Napoleon or the restored Bourbon monarchy.

Conclusion

As this chapter has discussed key themes in the peasantry's experience of and involvement in the French Revolution, some general concluding observations are necessary. Firstly, it is now clear that the French Revolution is best understood as an interaction between a government and its citizens. Peter McPhee (2006) has argued that the French Revolution was a rare period when "ordinary" people, such as peasants, laborers, craftsmen, tradespeople, and even the indigent expressed themselves directly to the authorities through petitions, letters, and legal actions as well as through riots and revolts. These interactions formed the core of the revolutionary process, which was characterized by negotiation and confrontation between locals and government officials. Markoff's work has demonstrated how the legislative dismantling of the seigneurial regime was in large part due to peasant insurrection in the countryside. Yet it must be remembered that not everyone in the countryside viewed the changes wrought by the Revolution as positive. Donald Sutherland (1985) has argued that the entire French Revolution can be understood as a struggle against a "massive, extensive, durable and popular" counter-revolution and that reforms of the National Constituent Assembly benefited certain groups more than others. The church and nobility are certainly groups who lost out, but the some of the rank and file also found revolutionary reforms hard to swallow. The grievances of sharecroppers and tenant farmers, in particular, had not been addressed and they had no reason to support a regime of landowners. However, for a large section of peasantry, the transformative nature of the revolutionary process must be stressed. The peasant revolution became more and more emancipatory and egalitarian as it pushed legislators beyond their initial positions; the violence committed by the peasantry exhibited choices of targets and tactics guided by reason (Markoff 1995). But it was not just the issue of seigneurialism that changed peasants as they were radicalized in their quest for land as well. This process clearly took place in Meurthe where only 7 percent of parish *cahiers* mention common land, but by 1793 one-quarter of all communes demanded partition legislation (Jones 1991). Anatolï Ado (1996) reminds us that every petition sent to legislators echoes the many conversations which took place in markets, taverns, and village squares; the petitions were only the paper manifestations of rural politicization.

A larger awareness of the natural world and environmental degradation can also be seen in a number of peasant *cahiers* (McPhee 2001). So the interactive and transformative nature of the revolutionary process and experience is certainly an avenue of future research for historians. Another area for contemplation is the challenging years of the Terror. Although 1793–94 brought unprecedented suffering, fear, and conflict, these years cannot be remembered for those things alone. David Andress (2006: 197) has recently characterized the measures of the summer of 1793, which were directed towards improving the lives of the poorest members of rural society, as "little more than propaganda." This is certainly wide of the mark as the complete and total abolition of feudalism and widespread acquisition of land had a profound, direct, and material impact on rural society. For all their flaws, the Jacobins were the only ones to devise practical policies to improve the conditions of the lowest tier of the peasantry and these measures were pursued with conviction throughout the Year II (Gross 1997; Jones 1991). There were fundamental social and economic issues at stake in the Revolution, which cannot be solely understood in terms of political discourse. While it is difficult to capture *the* role of the peasantry in the French Revolution and *the* impact that the cataclysm had on this diverse group, the people who lived in France's rural communities were forever changed after 1789 and many of them helped to make the world around them anew.

References

Ado, Anatoli (1996). *Paysans en Révolution: Terre, pouvoir et jacquerie, 1789–1794.* Paris: SÉR.

Andress, David (2006). *The Terror: Civil War in the French Revolution.* London: Abacus.

Bianchi, Serge (2002). "Terriers, plans-terriers et révolution." In Ghislain Brunel, Olivier Guyotjeannin, and Jean-Marc Moriceau (eds.). *Terriers et plans-terriers du XIIIe au XVIIIe siècle.* Paris: Association d'Histoire des Sociétés Rurales. 309–324.

Bodinier, Bernard (2010). "La Révolution française et la question agraire: Le Bilan national en 2010." *Histoire et Sociétés Rurales*, 33: 7–47.

Bodinier, Bernard and Éric Teyssier (2000). "*L'Événement le plus important de la Révolution*": *La Vente des biens nationaux.* Paris: SÉR.

Clère, Jean-Jacques (1982). "La Vaine pâture au XIXe siècle: Un anachronisme?." *AHRF*, 54: 113–128.

Clère, Jean-Jacques (2005). "L'Abolition des droits féodaux en France." *Cahiers d'histoire. Revue d'histoire critique*, 94–95: 135–157.

Corvol, Andrée (1984). *L'Homme et l'arbre sous l'Ancien Régime.* Paris: Économica.

Corvol, Andrée and Isabelle Richefort (eds.) (1995). *Nature, environnement et paysage: L'Héritage du XVIIIe siècle, guide de recherche archivistique et bibliographique.* Paris: L'Harmattan.

Doyle, William (1980). *Origins of the French Revolution.* Oxford: Oxford University Press.

Fitzsimmons, Michael (2001). *The Night the Old Regime Ended: August 4, 1789 and the French Revolution.* University Park: Pennsylvania State University Press.

Ford, Caroline (2001). "Landscape and Environment in French Historical and Geographical Thought: New Directions." *FHS*, 24: 125–134.

Ford, Caroline and Tamara Whited (2009). "Introduction: New Directions in French Environmental History." *FHS*, 32: 343–352.

Goubert, Pierre (1974). "Sociétés rurales françaises de XVIIIe siècle: Vingt paysanneries contrastées, quelques problèmes." In Fernand Braudel (ed.). *Conjoncture économique, structures sociales: Hommage à Ernest Labrousse.* Paris: Mouton. 375–387.

Gross, Jean-Pierre (1997). *Fair Shares For All: Jacobin Egalitarianism in Practice.* Cambridge: Cambridge University Press.

Ikni, Guy-Robert (1993). *Crise agraire et révolution paysanne: Le Mouvement populaire dans les campagnes de L'Oise de la décennie physiocratique à l'an II.* Paris: Université de Paris I.

Jones, P.M. (1988). *The Peasantry in the French Revolution.* Cambridge: Cambridge University Press.

Jones, P.M. (1991). "The "Agrarian Law': Schemes for Land Redistribution during the French Revolution." *P&P*, 133: 96–133.

Jones, P.M. (2001). "Agrarian Issues during the French Revolution, 1787–1799." In James C. Scott and Nina Bhatt (eds.). *Agrarian Studies: Synthetic Work at the Cutting Edge.* New Haven, Conn.: Yale University Press. 69–85.

Lefebvre, Georges (1954). "La Révolution française et les paysans." In *Études sur la Révolution française.* Paris: PUF. 246–268.

Lefebvre, Georges (1959). *Les Paysans du Nord pendant la Révolution française.* Bari: Laterza.

Lefebvre, Georges (1973). *The Great Fear: Rural Panic in Revolutionary France* trans. Joan White. Princeton, N.J.: Princeton University Press.

Lefebvre, Georges (1989 [1947]). *The Coming of the French Revolution*, trans. R.R. Palmer. Princeton, N.J.: Princeton University Press.

McPhee, Peter (1999). *Revolution and Environment in Southern France, 1780–1830: Peasants, Lords and Murder in the Corbières.* Oxford: Oxford University Press.

McPhee, Peter (2001). "'The Misguided Greed of Peasants'? Popular Attitudes to the Environment in the Revolution of 1789." *FHS*, 24: 247–270.

McPhee, Peter (2004). *A Social History of France, 1789–1914.* New York: Palgrave Macmillan.

McPhee, Peter (2006). *Living the French Revolution, 1789–99.* New York: Palgrave Macmillan.

McNeill, John R. (2003). "Observations on the Nature and Culture of Environmental History." *History and Theory*, 42: 5–43.

Markoff, John (1995). "Violence, Emancipation, and Democracy: The Countryside and the French Revolution." *AHR*, 100: 360–386.

Markoff, John (1996). *The Abolition of Feudalism: Peasants, Lords and Legislators in the French Revolution.* University Park: Pennsylvania State University Press.

Markoff, John (2006). "Peasants and their Grievances." In Peter Campbell (ed.). *The Origins of the French Revolution.* New York: Palgrave Macmillan. 239–267.

Moulin, Annie (1991). *Peasantry and Society in France since 1789*, trans. M.C. and M.F. Cleary. Cambridge: Cambridge University Press.

Plack, Noelle (2005). "Agrarian Reform and Ecological Change during the *Ancien Régime*: Land Clearance, Peasants and Viticulture in the Province of Languedoc." *FH*, 19: 189–210.

Plack, Noelle (2008). "Collective Agricultural Practice and the French State: Aspects of the Rural Code from the 18th to the 20th Century." In Nadine Vivier (ed.). *The State and Rural Societies: Policy and Education in Europe 1750–2000.* Turnhout: Brepols. 95–110.

Plack, Noelle (2009). *Common Land, Wine and the French Revolution: Rural Society and Economy in Southern France, c.1789–1820.* Burlington, Vt.: Ashgate.

Plack, Noelle (2010). "Environmental Issues during the French Revolution: Peasants, Politics and Village Common Land." *Australian Journal of French Studies*, 47: 290–303.

Schama, Simon (1990). *Citizens: A Chronicle of the French Revolution.* New York: Vintage Books.

Schama, Simon (1995). *Landscape and Memory.* London: HarperCollins.

Shapiro, Gilbert and John Markoff (1998). *Revolutionary Demands: A Content Analysis of the Cahiers de Doléances of 1789.* Stanford, Calif.: Stanford University Press.

Soboul, Albert (1976). "Le Brûlement des titres féodaux (1789–1793)." In *Problèmes paysans de la Révolution 1789–1848.* Paris: François Maspero. 135–146.

Sutherland, Donald (1985). *France 1789–1815: Revolution and Counterrevolution.* London: HarperCollins.

Taylor, George V. (1972). "Revolutionary and Nonrevolutionary Content in the *Cahiers de Doléances* of 1789: An Interim Report." *FHS*, 7: 479–502.

Vivier, Nadine (1998). *Propriété collective et identité communale: Les Biens communaux en France 1750–1914.* Paris: Publications de la Sorbonne.

Vovelle, Michael (1980). "Les Troubles sociaux en Provence de 1750 à 1792." In *De la cave au grenier: Un itinéraire en Provence au XVIIIe siècle. De l'histoire sociale à l'histoire des mentalités.* Quebec: S. Fleury. 221–262.

Woronoff, Denis (1989). "La "Dévastation révolutionnaire" des fôrets." In *Révolution et espaces forestiers.* Paris: L'Harmattan. 44–52.

Part V

Revolutionary and Counter-Revolutionary Violence

CHAPTER FOURTEEN

Urban Crowds, Riot, Utopia, and Massacres, 1789–92

DONALD SUTHERLAND

Urban crowds in the French Revolution have generated a huge literature. For over half a century, George Rudé's *The Crowd in the French Revolution* has dominated. Rudé's crowd is exclusively Parisian, one that intervenes in the revolutionary *journée* to save the bourgeois revolution or resolve a crisis within the political class. The *journée* itself is based on anxieties about food supply and prices. Ordinary people only acquire a higher political consciousness thanks to the activities of middle-class agitators, without whom "such movements would have remained strangely purposeless and barren of result" (1959: 208–209).

Once one expands the conceptual horizon to include the provinces, however, the subject becomes larger and more complex. Subsistence issues, for instance, never appear in a pure form, at least in the larger cities. Classic bread riots in which people fixed the price of bread were extremely rare in the big cities in the spring and summer of 1789. Instead, subsistence issues were always linked to suspected official malfeasance over supply or adulteration; or linked to indirect taxes, like the *octroi*. Popular politics also included deep feelings of injured pride and worthiness, and, most important, of justice. Finally, any consideration of the transition to radical politics that was so evident in 1792 has to include the inheritance of the *ancien régime*. The utopianism that emerged among ordinary people even before the Estates-General met and that continued after, followed state breakdown. This had occurred before. In earlier centuries when the state teetered on collapse, ordinary people saw a chance to eliminate millennial oppressions (Bercé 1987: 114–119). Although the language of popular politics clearly changed between 1789 and 1792, the aspirations for a better life remained the same. Moreover, the acquisition of the language of sovereignty did not eliminate another inheritance from the past: cruelty toward bodies of presumed malefactors.

A Companion to the French Revolution, First Edition. Edited by Peter McPhee.

Even in 1789 and even in Paris, the rising anxiety over the fate of the Estates-General was not at all a function of the rising cost of bread. In Paris, officials fixed the price of the 4-pound loaf at an unwavering 14 *sols* 6 *deniers* from February 1789 until just after the fall of the Bastille on 18 July when the city reduced the legal price (Chassin 1888: vol. 3, 414; Monin 1889: 319). If there had been mounting anxiety, it would have to have been over shortages. Yet on 13 July, the day before the Bastille fell, the *lieutenant général de police* reported that there was enough food on hand to feed the capital for two weeks (*Moniteur*, 1: 218, column 2).

There was, to be sure, a food emergency that followed the terrible weather of 1788: alternating dry spells and heavy rains and thunderstorms in the spring, followed by a freak hailstorm on 13 July that began near Poitiers and ended in Holland. Some hailstones weighed up to half a pound and killed several people and grazing cattle. The following winter was the coldest in generations. Below freezing temperatures lasted for fifty days after 25 November.

A whole series of expedients staved off the worst. From the summer of 1788 onwards, the government intervened to set prices, restrict grain and flour sales to official markets, forbid exports, subsidize imports, and subsidize bakers. By the spring, officials ordered a census of grain stocks in barns and mills and forced farmers to sell on designated markets (Bord 1887: 50). The government also took over imports. It managed to import substantial amounts, nearly 1.5 million *quintaux* costing 25 million *livres*, according to the Director General of Finances, Jacques Necker (*AP*, 8: 191–3, session of 4 July 1789). Bailly, the mayor of Paris from July 1789 onwards, credited Necker with saving Paris from famine (Bailly et al. 1821: vol. 1, 288–289).

At least for Paris, government struggled successfully. Still, the subsistence question mattered, not because of a failure of the market, but because Parisians were extremely sensitive to the politics of the food question. They feared that evil officials and agents of the spendthrift court were conspiring to withhold supplies to achieve their nefarious political ends (Kaplan 1982: 6). The Estates-General gave Parisians the hope that they had the means to foil the conspiracy.

The public focused this hope on Necker and on the Estates-General. He was extraordinarily popular because several significant groups projected their hopes onto him. They believed he was many things: financial genius, the man who had tried to rein in court expenditures and had suffered for it, a man with vast international connections. Many claimed he sympathized with the Third Estate, and that he spoke for the nation in an otherwise hostile ministry.

The heavy official intervention in securing supply meant that any official could find himself accused. Indeed, the crowd killed officials because they suspected they profited from the subsistence crisis to benefit themselves, their business associates, or their political masters. Thus the *intendant* of Paris, Berthier de Sauvigny, and his father-in-law, Foulon de Doué, were beheaded and dismembered on 22 July. The crowd alleged they withheld grain from Paris markets to promote the court's conspiracy against the Estates-General. This is an instructive example because it shows that even at a very early stage the crowd was aware of wider issues and that what mattered was the politics of subsistence rather than the price of bread alone.

Georges Lefebvre contributed a great insight when he argued that the calling of the Estates-General stimulated expectations among ordinary people for a dramatic change in their condition. Because it had not met since 1614 and memories of its role in monarchial government were hazy, they could project all sorts of hopes on to the Estates and a benevolent king. The Estates-General provoked revolutionary expectations. Thus in Provence, "The insurrection of the people against the clergy and the nobility is as vigorous as it is general ... The people believe they will be relieved of all taxes ..." (AN H 1274, *pièce* 82). One official was baffled that, "The greatest benefit of the sovereign [is] interpreted in the most bizarre manner by an ignorant populace ... The lowest classes of the people have persuaded themselves that the time of the Estates-General ... must be that of a total and absolute change, not only in present institutions [*formes*] but in Conditions and fortunes" (AN H 1274, *pièce* 173).

Such extraordinary expectations were quite compatible with older, even archaic ways of conceiving the ideal polity. Thus, for example in Troyes, witnesses claimed one rioter in September 1789 had cried out, "They thought we were sheep, I showed them we weren't, vengeance of the Nation ... The owners of these houses [we have pillaged] have been eating white bread for a long time, [now] they have to eat black [bread]" (*Jugement prévôtal*, 18). Injured pride, resentment, and primitive egalitarianism exploded in numerous rebellions in the *ancien régime* as well. Some slogans about the king and taxes would have been as familiar in the 1640s as they were in 1789. In Provence, for example, when rioters pillaged the home of the farmer of the leather tax at Brignoles in 1789, they cried out "Vive le Roi!" (AN H 1274, *pièce* 84). As soon as the population heard of the meetings to elect deputies to the Estates-General and draft *cahiers*, the people of Marseille began to complain about taxes. On 23–24 March, rioters attacked and pillaged the house of the town's tax-farmer and threatened the warehouses storing cod and bread. The mayor and his assessors had to flee over rooftops. All the while people shouted, "Vive le Roi!" and later when they lowered the price of bread and meat, "Vivent les Consuls [the municipal officials]!" (AN H 1274, *pièce* 84). The slogans and goals of the riots in 1789 reassembled those of the previous century in their cobbling together of hostility to taxes and loyalty to the Crown.

Unlike the 1640s when there was no Estates to capture people's hopes, the calling of the Estates-General in 1789 raised hopes for permanent relief exponentially. Such hopes also tie the great variety of the urban and small-town insurrections of 1789 together. Thus in places, like Lyon, food prices were nowhere as important as local taxes in generating disturbances. From Lyon to the Mediterranean, cities and small towns financed local expenditures and paid royal taxes not only through the *octroi*, but through various taxes on flour, meat, wine, and oil. This in turn raised the issue of political power since local grandees used their position to lighten their burden and impose it on humble consumers. People understood this. The furniture-makers of Arles in Provence explained that taxes would have weighed less on working people "if the artisan ... could have voted on the distribution of burdens like the other landowners [*terriers*], members of the [municipal] council" (cited in Cubells 1991: 32).

Parisians had similar views of politics. For them, politics was as much about justice as it was about factional or ideological competition. The Réveillon riots of

27–28 April showed supply and price of bread were not particularly strong grievances for the rioters; these were not classic bread riots. Instead, the crowd wanted vengeance for a remark Réveillon, a wealthy wallpaper manufacturer in eastern Paris, had allegedly made that workers' wages ought to be lowered. Réveillon denied this but he soon became a hate figure for the crowds anyway. Moreover, the riots resembled those in the Midi because of the elections to the Estates-General. They occurred as the electors of the city of Paris were meeting to elect their deputies to the Estates-General and the crowds tried to influence them. Apparently, up to 3,000 people carried an effigy of Réveillon to the electoral assembly where they intended to seize him and put him to death (Anon. 1789). Such threats were not isolated. The bookseller Hardy encountered a crowd of 300 on the Montagne Sainte-Geneviève. One marcher carried a card that proclaimed "Decree of the Third Estate which judges and condemns the named Réveillon and Henriot to be hanged and burned on the public square" (cited in Chassin 1888: vol. 3, 50). Expressions of popular sovereignty in 1792 would retain these judicial undertones. The continuing rioting and repression the next day, 28 April, resulted in 200 rioters killed and about 300 wounded. It was the largest Parisian insurrection since the Fronde nearly 150 years before and one of the bloodiest acts of repression in the entire Revolution.

As debate in the Estates-General deadlocked over the issue of verification of powers in common, opinion grew alarmed at the delay. Opinion in Paris interpreted the delay as a prelude to dissolution. Moreover, the court party, not the aristocracy as a whole, was behind these machinations. At Orléans, on the day the Estates first met, a pamphlet appeared claiming, "The princes, tied through interest with the nobility, the clergy and all the *parlements*, have hoarded all the wheat in the kingdom. ... Their abominable intentions are to prevent the holding of the Estates-General, in sowing famine throughout France and thus have a part of the people die of hunger, and have the other part rebel against the king" (cited in Lefebvre 1963: vol. 2, 17).

The decisive event that panicked opinion was the *séance royale* of 23 June 1789 in which the king attempted to resolve the deadlock over verification of powers. The decision shocked the patriot party because the king allowed the clergy and nobility to preserve or surrender their privileges as it suited them. Although they had already surrendered their tax exemptions, the privileged orders would still have jurisdiction over feudal prerogatives and preferential access to high civilian or military positions.

Opinion blamed the cabal around the king's younger brother, the comte d'Artois, for seducing noble deputies at Versailles with sumptuous dinners and endless flattery. The ambassador from Saxony, the very well connected comte de Salmour, claimed reactionaries had advised Artois to break up the Estates-General, turn over the leaders and Necker to the Parlement of Paris, which would then have them hanged as traitors (Flammermont 1896: 232–233). Hardy reported that the ministry intended to imprison one deputy per bailiwick in the Bastille, the proof being that many beds and mattresses had been moved there recently (Caron 1906–7: 21).

People feared retaliation that would surely follow the defiance of the king's decisions. Thus began the final crisis of the *ancien régime*. In Paris, the Electors for the Estates-General quickly displaced the formal legal municipality with themselves and former councilors. The Electors of the Hôtel de Ville, as they were called, became revolutionaries, worthy of being hanged, when they endorsed the National Assembly's rejection of the king's proposals. They were not violent men but every step they took cracked the legal shell in which they would have preferred to shelter. They petitioned for a *garde bourgeoise* to keep order, but when the king ignored the request they established it anyway on 13 July. Once the Electors began to arm this embryonic National Guard from the Hôtel de Ville's own stocks, and then from royal armories in the Arsenal, the Invalides, and the Bastille, they became fully fledged revolutionaries, even though they distrusted the poor and the down-and-out.

The most significant feature of the outcry following the king's speech was the defection of the French Guards. These were an elite unit responsible for policing Paris and the immediate environs. They had refused to fire on 5,000 or 6,000 protestors who broke into the grounds of the Château de Versailles on the 23rd. After this, radicals from the Palais Royal feted both them and soldiers arriving from frontier garrisons. Although the French Guards' defections had more to do with their intense dislike of their commander's modernizing reforms than it did with politics, commentators saw only the crumbling of military discipline. Other regiments also suffered desertions.

Possibly as a response to the defiance of the king's speech, possibly too in response to the mutiny of the French Guards, the government began to move troops up to the Paris region in early July. No one believed the government's explanation that the troop build-up would protect grain shipments into the capital. Opinion interpreted the troop movements as part of the machinations of the court party. Whatever the government's intentions, rumors had been flying of a coup against the Estates-General for weeks. Thus when Parisians heard the news around noon on the 12th that Necker had been dismissed, they took it as the opening strike in the coup.

The cry went up immediately at the Palais Royal for the people to arm themselves. One of the most prominent agitators was Camille Desmoulins, a young lawyer who is often credited with being the first to raise the call to arms. But the cry to arm the population occurred in several places at once, notably at the Hôtel de Ville where the Electors distributed arms. At the same time, a long procession closed theaters as a sign of a public calamity, pillaged a waxworks, and paraded wax heads of Necker and the duc d'Orléans (demonstrators believed the cabal would exile him too). They ended up at the Palais Royal. There, some enthusiasts decided to march to Versailles to continue the protest. As they entered the Place Louis XV (the present day Place de la Concorde), troops tried to stop them. After a skirmish, the Prince de Lambesc's Royal Allemand cavalry charged into a crowd in the nearby Tuileries Gardens, injuring some and terrifying others. This certainly stopped the march on Versailles, but in the inevitable exaggerations the charge became a massacre, an assault on peaceful strollers and old people. Parisians' demands for weapons to defend themselves became ubiquitous and irresistible (Alpaugh 2009: 336–359; Spagnoli 1991: 466–498).

These events not only stimulated Parisians to arm themselves; for the Electors they also signaled a broader social collapse. With no police or military forces in sight, crowds began to attack and burn the customs posts that ringed the capital. Between the night of the 12th and sometime during the day of the 14th, forty of the fifty-four customs posts had been torched – a reflection of the deep hatred of taxes on basic articles of consumption (Buchez and Roux-Lavergne 1834: vol. 2, 73–74, 82; Rudé 1959: 49).

Throughout the night of the 12th, the Hôtel de Ville received reports that crowds of "vagabonds and homeless, armed and threatening, [are] roaming neighborhoods" (Bailly and Duveyrier 1790: vol. 1, 177). The pillaging of the monastery of Saint-Lazare added to the fear of disorder. The fires from the burning customs posts and Saint-Lazare, the random gunshots, the marching of improvised militias through the streets, the constant ringing of the church bells or tocsins (a sign of emergency) threw the city into a terror. The Hôtel de Ville ordered the city's districts into action. Huge crowds milled about the Palais Royal and the Hôtel de Ville. Women forced half-hearted men to salute the *Tiers-État*.

In the early morning of the 13th, the Electors took matters into their own hands. They formed the *garde bourgeoise* to defend against the military attack everyone feared. The Electors also formed a Permanent Committee of twenty-two men drawn partly from the old municipal council, but mostly from the Electors themselves. It would coordinate with the districts, take charge of subsistence issues, and supervise the newly named "Parisian Militia" (Bailly and Duveyrier 1790: vol. 1, 182–191).

The new militia needed arms. The Electors first wanted to negotiate with royal officials for them. But events overwhelmed them. A heterogeneous crowd of delegates from the Hôtel de Ville, the French Guards, a priest and his parishioners, and several thousand others took arms stored in the Invalides in several waves on the 14th. The Bastille was also a target for some of the same reasons the Invalides was, a source of weapons. Yet the aftermath was very different.

The Bastille represented many things to Parisians (Lüsebrink and Reichardt 1997). As a state prison it was a symbol of the cruelest despotism, and several *cahiers* that spring had demanded its demolition. The liberation of the prisoners, few as they were, was therefore a great triumph. More immediately, the Bastille stored a fabulous amount of arms and munitions that had been moved there from the nearby Arsenal a few days before. Moreover, as fears spread that the army was preparing to assault Paris, control of the Bastille had an obvious strategic advantage. Whether there was such a plan of attack or not, the government certainly did order the military to hold it.

The ancient fortress capitulated after a six-hour siege that ended at 5 p.m. on 14 July. The violence that followed was a consequence of the indecision of the Bastille's governor, the marquis de Launay, the crowd's bitterness at de Launay's apparent violation of the truces, his troops firing into the besiegers, and the crowd's distrust of their own leaders. Despite orders to hold out, de Launay surrendered when French Guards brought up cannon and trained them on the main gate. The crowd rejected the surrender, however, and if they had had their way they would have slaughtered every one of the defenders. Instead, the crowd's leaders, Hulin and Élie, both junior officers, accepted de Launay's surrender and escorted him down the rue Saint-Antoine to the Hôtel de Ville, possibly for a trial before the

Electors. The escort soon lost control, however, and the crowd beat de Launay to death. An unemployed cook then cut off his head and paraded it about. Five other soldiers were hanged or beaten to death. Finally, the crowd demanded de Flesselles, the *prévôt de marchands*, or mayor, for his equivocal role in the crisis. There was an agreement to imprison him in the Abbaye but no sooner had he left the Hôtel de Ville than someone shot him. He too was decapitated. The crowd then hoisted the two heads on the end of long poles, and took them by torchlight to the Palais Royal. Although a few were shocked, onlookers applauded the triumph. The same crowd that cheered the prisoners liberated from the Bastille cheered the executions.

The capitulation of the Bastille was significant for several reasons. The first and most long-lasting was the symbolic triumph over despotism. At the time, the meaning was also military and political. The city was now entirely in the hands of the insurgents. If this had been the only problem, the government might have been able to reconquer the city as future governments would do in the nineteenth century. Yet commanders of some regiments reported serious morale and desertion problems among the troops. Some regiments, but not all, were considered unreliable. More serious still, over the next several days, there were many reports that the huge, newly armed Paris militia was going to attack Versailles. Even the queen's life was in danger. Consequently, the king agreed to withdraw the troops from Paris, and on 17 July visited the Hôtel de Ville where he donned the symbol of rebellion, the tricolor cockade.

The king's reception in Paris on the 17th also showed the profound loss of faith in the monarch. From the moment he entered the city at a western gate until his arrival at the Hôtel de Ville in the center of the capital, no one cheered him. The crowds, more than 100,000 strong, four deep on either side of the route, were eerily silent. Although the Electors and the deputies in Versailles tried to maintain that the king had been duped – as they would claim in 1791 – Parisians' loss of trust in Louis XVI would be permanent.

The collapse of authority would last for over a decade. Artois and at least fifty courtier families fled Versailles for the frontiers in fear of their lives from the vengeful Parisians. The agitators at the Palais Royal drafted lists of participants in the courtier conspiracy and dispatched runners to hunt them down. Although the insurrections had begun in the provinces in the early spring of 1789, the events in Paris and Versailles accelerated them and they spread to new areas. The withdrawal of the troops removed protection from enemies and so raised the level of violence. The inability to protect markets provoked more riots as ordinary folk in the countryside and small towns feared supplies would disappear. So they anticipated further shortages by halting grain convoys or shipments out of markets. This, of course, only aggravated the supply situation, even, this time, of Paris itself.

All rioting in 1789 had a political component but it differed from place to place. It rarely involved national issues that had enraged Parisians. Instead, rioters contested fiscal and subsistence issues in different ways. The weighting of these two varied according to local circumstances. Besides demanding a lowering of the bread price, rioters frequently displayed their hatred for indirect taxes, especially those on food like the *piquet* in Provence that taxed flour, or the *ésquivalent* in Languedoc that taxed meat, fish, and wine. Targets varied enormously too. Frequently these included town councilors, tax-farmers and clerks in their offices, lords, grain dealers of whom there were many different types: millers and merchants, of course, but also innkeepers, petty dealers called *blâtiers*, itinerant charcoal burners, and many others. In dozens of cases, and significantly in the big provincial cities, the *maréchaussée*, the royal mounted police, and the army were faithful defenders of law and order – an interesting comment on the supposed unreliability of the army in 1789. Unlike Paris and its region, the military occupied Lyon for a few months after the riots. Marseille was under virtual martial law until early 1790.

***

The transition from crowd action ostensibly concerned primarily with subsistence issues to the revolutionary crowd of 1791 and after presents a problem. Rudé argued that radicals transformed the primitive consciousness of the bread riot into revolutionary consciousness. Some very fine work highlights the role of the Cordeliers Club in Paris and other groups and newspapers in instilling working people with the ideology of direct democracy. They proclaimed the right of insurrection, petition, recall, and referendum. The success of these efforts became apparent in the petition campaign following the king's fatal attempt to flee Paris in June 1791. Ordinary people demanded, if not a republic outright, then at least a "change in the executive power" (Rudé 1959: 87).

This is a Paris-centered explanation. It assumes the moral economy of subsistence existed in a vacuum. Two other factors need to be added to the mix: the conflict over order and the persistence of fiscal grievances. Deep-seated suspicions against officials and the rich preceded 1789 but the events of the summer aggravated them. Urban elites were determined to protect the fiscal *ancien régime* partly because consumption taxes favored them as property owners and partly because, without them, municipal services like wash houses, hospital subsidies, lighting, water fountains, and so on would be impossible.

However ordinary folk attained Rudé's higher consciousness – propaganda from the clubs, lingering resentments, frustration at a revolution that had yet to live up to its dazzling promises – few could have anticipated how wildly spontaneous, creative, and cruel popular mobilization would be. By the spring of 1792, large areas of the country, including Paris, had entered a liminal or lawless period where "the people" – the clubs, the national guards – dictated its wishes with no intermediaries. This was the climax of the urban crowd. It spilled over urban boundaries to defend the country and mete out justice directly. It climaxed with the massacres in Paris and elsewhere that followed the overthrow of the monarchy.

One sign was the poetry of the language of popular sovereignty during the protest against Louis XVI's sacking the patriot ministers in early June 1792. For militants, a constitution that permitted the king to corrupt officials through an inflated civil list was intolerable. Thus formal law no longer applied and the people resumed its direct sovereignty. A petition and demonstration from the Faubourg Saint-Antoine in Paris expressed this popular outrage dramatically. After complaining about the slowness of the National High Court to judge traitors, the petition reclaimed the right for the people to take "this sword and avenge with a single blow, the law outraged, to punish the guilty and the pusillanimous custodians of this same law" (*AP*, 45: 417). Statements like this justified the *journée* of 20 June 1792. An estimated 8,000 demonstrators from the *faubourgs* Saint-Antoine and Saint-Marcel paraded before the Legislative Assembly. Afterwards, they invaded the Tuileries where they forced the king to don the red cap of liberty.

The bigger cities did not need a signal from Paris. The Central Club at Lyon denounced "the head of the executive power, as cowardly as he is inconsequential … this false and perjured king" (cited in Wahl 1894: 535–536). The inspiring address of several "citizens of Marseille" sent the left of the Legislative Assembly into delirious applause: "French liberty is imperiled. The free men of the Midi have all arisen to defend it. *Le jour de la colère du peuple est arrivé*" (*Adresse d'un grand nombre de citoyens actifs*, repr. in *AP*, 45: 397).

Marseille quickly organized its battalion of 500 *fédérés*. This grand adventure to the capital, like the others in the region earlier, had a multiple purpose. Defeating the enemy was an obvious goal but they had political purposes, too. When the *fédérés* left Marseille on 2 July, a Jacobin official defined one of these goals as vetoing the king's vetoes. "Go, turn the cheeks of the tyrant pale! He occupies a throne he no longer merits … Go tell him that the sovereign people are there to ratify the decrees that he has struck down with his monstrous *veto*!' (cited in Pollio and Marcel 1881: 141). The *fédérés* were also apostles of liberty, their purpose to support oppressed comrades and to spread the sweet light of reason. "We have every reason to believe," the mayor of Marseille wrote, "that this ray of liberty emanating from the Midi, will ignite the inflammable air of the regions it will traverse, and we will see what material anyone can use to extinguish the sacred flame of liberty whose light offends the eyes of the cowardly partisans of despotism" (Pétion et al. 1866: 463).

This was an army of experienced militants, singing, of course, the *Marseillaise*. According to Michelet, the "little band of Marseillais, passing through towns and villages, exalted, terrified France by their frenetic ardor to sing the new song. In their mouths, it took a tone quite different from the original inspiration, a ferocious, murderous accent; this generous and heroic song became a song of anger …" (Michelet 1899: vol. 3, 503; Mason 1996: 97–100). Other cities mobilized their *fédérés* too: Brest, Rennes, Caen, Montpellier, Bordeaux, and others.

Unlike the *journées* of July and October 1789, the overthrow of the monarchy on 10 August 1792 was a planned assault, even though the execution was incredibly chaotic. This time, there was no question of a motive based on subsistence. There were three loose and occasionally interlocking organizations that cooperated in the planning: the *fédérés*; the Cordeliers Club and the Paris sections; and finally a combination of the first two, a "secret committee." No prominent politician had a direct role in the planning, although plenty of them claimed greater credit than they deserved after the event. None of the organizations ever had full control over their followers or over the ordinary men and women who participated in the overthrow of the monarchy. This weakness may explain the massacres that followed.

The first meeting of the secret committee on 26 July, at the *Soleil d'or* near the Place de la Bastille decided to launch the call to arms immediately. One member of the "secret directory," the journalist Carra, invented a red banner that captured the moment when ordinary law was suspended: it read, "Martial Law of the Sovereign People Against the Rebellion of the Executive Power" (Jaurès 1900: vol. 2,

1287–1288). Besides that, nothing was prepared. The plan had been to kidnap the king from the Tuileries and imprison him in the fortress of Vincennes, but poor coordination with the patriot national guards throughout the city doomed the plot (Buchez and Roux-Lavergne 1834: vol. 16, 270–271).

Even before the Marseillais and the equally militant Brestois arrived, the *fédérés* emerged as the most active force. Two addresses, presented on 12 and 23 July, demanded a suspension or removal of the king (Aulard 1897: vol. 4, 94–95; Lemny 2000: 248). They denounced the court, Lafayette (now an enemy because he had denounced the Jacobins), and the bloated civil list that allowed the king to corrupt politicians. They also demanded the king be judged, and claimed that pending the calling of the primary assemblies to elect a national Convention, they represented the sovereignty of the French people. Most interesting, however, was the declaration of conditional loyalty to the Assembly. "We will march alone, if we must," they insisted, "and all the friends of the *patrie*, and the entire people will throw themselves with us on our enemies" (*AP*, 46: 560–561; 47: 69–70; Aulard 1897: vol. 4, 110).

After this, at least a dozen major addresses from the *fédérés*, the Paris sections, or from masses of ordinary citizens repeated these themes. A few demanded the calling of a national Convention to replace the Legislative Assembly and a few claimed the right to act if the Legislative Assembly did not. Until the very eve of the insurrection against the monarchy, none demanded a violent solution. All of them looked in one way or another to the Legislative Assembly for action. Only when the politicians overtly refused to remove the king and Lafayette did the *fédérés*, the sections, and Parisians respond violently.

This occurred on 8 August when the Assembly decided it would not indict Lafayette. The Assembly had rejected two major planks of the radicals' agenda: deposition of the king and arrest of Lafayette. As in 1789, rumors flew through the city of a heinous plot that only a vigorous attack from the patriots could forestall: some said patriots would be lured to the Tuileries, executed before the king, and their heads displayed on the grille work in plain view of the queen's apartments. Patriots in the provinces would be slaughtered. Even families would be punished. Women would have to drag the corpses of their husbands, children would be spattered with their fathers' blood and have to wear clothes soaked in dried blood until the age of 15 (Chaumette et al. 1893: 50; Hébert 1792: 1–2; Anon. 1792: 110).

The defenders heard rumors too. Ever since they arrived, the royalist press had depicted the Marseillais as the worst jetsam of the Mediterranean. Now on the eve of battle, some heard that the Marseillais "would show no mercy to anyone and that any armed National Guard captured would be torn to pieces" (Viard n.d.).

The secret directory and the central committee of the sections coordinated the neighborhood sections, national guards, and *fédérés*. Just before midnight on 9 August, the tocsin sounded in the various sections. By dawn, national guards and *fédérés* were marching to the Tuileries (Assemblée Nationale: n.d.; Buchez and Roux-Lavergne 1834: vol. 16, 271–272; L'Héritier et al. 1890: 74). By 7 a.m., commissioners from the sections had moved into the Hôtel de Ville, where they promptly replaced the legal municipality. They sacked the legal National Guard commander. A crowd then promptly murdered him (Peltier et al. 1792: vol. 1, 112). Nor was this the only killing before the much better-known slaughter of the

Swiss Guards. A patrol of constitutionalist national guards on patrol on the Champs-Élysées was set upon and executed. Eight of them were decapitated and their heads paraded about on the tips of pikes. The corpses still lay on the Place Vendôme the next day (Hébert 1792: 3; *Révolutions de Paris* 1792: vol. 13, 230–231).

By mid-morning, the defenses of the Tuileries had begun to crumble. Loyal national guards became squeamish about firing on fellow Parisians, while the gendarmes' morale sank. Both groups began to slip away. Some, most significantly the artillery, changed sides. At first, the king was going to fight; then, typically, he changed his mind. He acceded to his advisors and led the royal family to refuge in the nearby Legislative Assembly. They stayed in an anteroom behind the speaker's chair. This made the fight for the Tuileries moot. Still the Legislative Assembly delayed deposing the king. This inaction cost hundreds of lives.

Although the insurgent leadership had a hard time getting organized, popular enthusiasm was high. Passive citizens in the eastern neighborhoods broke into arms shops and stole weapons. They too marched to the Tuileries, leaderless. "The insurrection was becoming universal," said Prudhomme (Monnier and Santerre 1989: 37–39; *Révolutions de Paris* 1792: vol. 13, 234). The tocsins ringing, heads being paraded about, it was more of an unruly crowd than a military formation that gathered in the Place du Carrousel.

Somehow, the crowd broke through a door that led to the *cour des princes* in the Tuileries. With the Marseillais in the lead, they ran into the Swiss defenders who appeared to lay down their arms. Nevertheless, as with the poor communications on 14 July 1789, other Swiss fired on the insurgents from the upper windows or from the staircases.[1] Crying betrayal, the insurgents stormed through the chateau killing as many defenders as they could, refusing all gestures of surrender, chasing some even into the gardens, apartments, staircases, and latrines. They threw some defenders from the windows onto the paving stones below where, impervious to their cries for mercy, other insurgents ran them through with pikes. Others escaped to the streets where they were stabbed with cutlasses and pikes. "Their bodies were stripped, naked, and mutilated, for the most part in their secret parts, were piled up on the pavement in layers mixed with straw and left exposed to public view until the next day. More than a hundred of Louis's servants suffered the same fate." The day after the battle, crowds searched the chateau, found some Swiss hiding in the cellars, and killed them too. Others hid in the chateau's chimneys and fireplaces for three days until they escaped (Anon. 1882: 103; Sagnac 1909b: 280).

This was the bloodiest *journée* so far: 376 insurgents killed or wounded, including 83 *fédérés*, a figure that includes 42 Marseillais; on the other side, 900 defenders, including 600 Swiss. A few women also died fighting on the patriot side (Sagnac 1909b: 300).

Nor was all the killing the result of a crazed search for revenge. Like the parades of 1789, reminiscent of the *amendes honorables* of the *ancien régime*, Swiss prisoners were marched a couple of miles east to the Hôtel de Ville where sixty of them were shot in the head, "par le droit de la guerre." There was a trial of sorts, on the street, where they were sentenced to death without appeal. Forty-seven of them were decapitated (Hébert 1792: 6; Reinhard 1969: 584). For the insurgents, the new Convention's purpose was not to draft a new constitution but to represent the entire French people's demand for a trial of the king. The Convention would be a court, an executor of the people's justice, not a legislative body.

On 13 August at 6p.m., the royal family was transferred to the Temple Prison in the heart of the Marais. Like the procession of 17 July 1789, national guardsmen and immense crowds lined the route on either side. To show their scorn, people wore their hats or, if they had none, covered their heads with handkerchiefs (Anon. 1882: 107).

***

The horrible killings in Paris had horrible counterparts in the provinces. Although crowds had executed enemies as early as the spring of 1789, the Legislative Assembly's declaration of the *patrie en danger* (11 July) heightened the idea that public safety overrode formal law. In Paris, militants used the declaration to browbeat officials and politicians into taking bolder action. In the provinces, it stimulated municipal officials and clubs to search for arms, go into permanent session, encourage volunteers to join the army, and to undertake pre-emptive arrests. In a few places, the declaration set off a chain of events that led to murder.

The declaration of *patrie en danger* made everyone more vigilant and therefore suspicious. At Marseille, the excitement led to the murder of six individuals, including two monks. Women stripped the monks naked, and dragged the corpses through the streets. The crowd then hanged the bodies from various lampposts, and finally dragged and dumped them near the homes of the rich (AN: F^7 3659^3).

These murders were part of a series of outbreaks that had begun in the late winter of 1791. Some followed the declaration of the *patrie en danger*. Others followed the news of 10 August in Paris. All of them followed local rhythms too, as had other disturbances. The most atrocious killings were the September Massacres in Paris. Between the 2nd and the 7th, groups of killers broke into the city's prisons and sometimes in the courtyards, sometimes on the streets, killed between 1,200 and 1,400 men, women, and children. Pierre Caron, whose book on the subject appeared nearly seventy-five years ago, is still very persuasive. Caron argued that the massacres varied with the fear of the internal enemy that haunted many other aspects of the revolutionary imagination. Thus as the Prussians crossed the frontier and took the fortresses of Longwy and Verdun, the fear of the internal enemy intensified. The massacres were pre-emptive strikes intended to prevent the junction of the internal and external enemies.

This is quite reasonable, but not all massacres of the summer of 1792 can be fitted into Caron's framework. The narrative of the massacres at Versailles on 9 September, for instance, never mentioned the military situation (AM, Versailles, carton 227, dossier prisonniers d'Orléans; AN, F^7 3689^7; Buchez and Roux-Lavergne 1834: vol. 17, 434–435). Elsewhere, the utopianism of the Revolution played an enormous role. Thus, the Electoral Assembly of the Seine-et-Marne, meeting at Meaux, heard two commissioners from Paris harangue them in extremely incendiary language. "They announced that there were no longer any laws, that we were masters to do what we wanted, that we were sovereign. They electrified our assembly. They harangued the people and that very evening, 14 heads were cut off. These people, so-called friends of liberty are therefore only arsonists, thieves and assassins" (*AP*, 52: 136). At Reims, which witnessed grisly killings of priests and a noble, authorities denounced "fermentation ... against priests, nobles and well-off citizens that opinion affects to designate as aristocrats." At the same time, a radical municipal councilor asserted that "the people have been vexed for too long, that we have to get rid of aristocrats and that the day of vengeance has arrived" (AD, Marne, 10 L 37).

***

Georges Lefebvre explained the violence of the Revolution as a defense against violent aristocratic counter-revolution. This is a powerful insight. Certainly one reason the Revolution was violent was resistance, not only from aristocrats, but from ordinary people too. Another reason is that the stakes were so high. From the earliest days of 1789, ordinary folk in many parts of the country knew the breakdown of the state was an opportunity to rid themselves of oppression – fiscal, seigneurial, and much else. As in earlier times of trouble, people attempted to impose a utopia of true justice, meaning a society that permitted simple communities to live without the burdens of unfair and opaque taxation, without useless tithes and archaic dues, and without the contempt of the high-born. The Revolution also taught ordinary folk to express their aspirations in democratic language. That changed them but not completely. It was not a big step from the egalitarianism of 1789 to the violent democracy of 1792. It would be another couple of generations before the rule of law would be entrenched in France and people, including the elites, would learn to respect the results of elections. This was the ordinary, normal politics of the future. Clearly 1792, the year of the second, the democratic, revolution, was very different.

Acknowledgments

I should like to thank Tim Le Goff for his comments on this chapter.

Note

1 The betrayal story is one version. Another makes no mention of a fake surrender, has the Swiss firing on the poorly armed insurgents until running out of ammunition, killing 400 patriots. Then the killing of the Swiss began (Sagnac 1909a: 274–282). There is nothing about deception in the Swiss account, which says the gestures of fraternity originated with the assailants who then fired on the Swiss (Altishofen and Villevieille 1824: 12; *Révolutions de Paris* 1792: vol. 13, 234; Sergent-Marceau 1835: 332; Viard n.d.: 8).

References

Primary Sources

(a) Archives

AD: Archives Départementales
Marne 10 L 37: procès des septembriseurs, An III.
AM: Archives Municipales
Versailles, carton 227, dossier prisonniers d'Orléans
AN: Archives Nationales
F7 3659³, 3689⁷: Police générale
H 1274: émeutes en Provence

(b) Printed sources (pamphlets, newspapers, letters, memoirs)

Altishofen, P. and L. Villevieille (1824). *Récit de la conduite du régiment des gardes suisses à la journée du 10 août 1792.* Geneva: Chez Abraham Cherbuliez.

Anon. (*c.*1789). *Acte patriotique de trois électeurs du tiers état, ou la sédition dissipée (27 avril.).* BNF Lb[39] 1620.

Anon. (1792). *Adresse d'un grand nombre de citoyens actifs de la commune de Marseille, lue à l'assemblée nationale, dans la séance du 19 juin 1792; imprimée par ordre de l'assemblée nationale, et l'envoi aux quatre-vingt-trois départemens.* Paris: Imprimerie Nationale. BNF Le[34] 92, repr. in *AP*, 55: 397.

Anon. (1882). "Lettres inédites du conventionnel Pinet sur le 10 août." *RF*, 3, no. 1: 97–113.

AP: Archives parlementaires de 1787 à 1860. Recueil complet des débats législatifs et politiques des chambres françaises, imprimé par ordre du corps législatif sous la direction de mm. J. Mavidal et E. Laurent. Première série, 1787–1799 (1867–1913), 82 vols. Paris: P. Dupont.

Assemblée Nationale (n.d.) *Procès-verbal de l'assemblée nationale: Séance permanente du vendredi 10 août 1792, l'an quatrième de la liberté*, Paris: Imprimerie Nationale.

Aulard, F.A. (ed.) (1897). *La Société des Jacobins: Recueil de documents pour l'histoire du club des Jacobins de Paris.* Paris: Librairie Jouaust.

Bailly, Jean Sylvain, Saint-Albin Berville, Jean-François Barrière, and Frères Baudoin (1821). *Mémoires de Bailly.* Paris: Baudouin Frères.

Bailly, Jean Sylvain and Honoré Nicolas Marie Duveyrier (eds.) (1790). *Procès-verbal des séances et délibérations de l'assemblée générale des électeurs de Paris, réunis à l'hôtel-de-ville le 14 juillet 1789.* Paris: Baudouin.

Buchez, Philippe Joseph Benjamin and Pierre-Célestin Roux-Lavergne (1834). *Histoire parlementaire de la Révolution française. Ou journal des assemblées nationales, depuis 1789 jusqu'en 1815.* Paris: Paulin.

Chassin, Charles and Conseil Général de la Seine (1888). *Les Élections et les cahiers de Paris en 1789; documents recueillis, mis en ordre et annotés.* Paris: Jouaust et Sigaux.

Chaumette, P.G., F.A. Aulard, and Société de l'Histoire de la Révolution Française (1893). *Mémoires de Chaumette sur la révolution du 10 août 1792.* Paris: Au Siège de la Société.

Flammermont, Jules (1896). *Les Correspondances des agents diplomatiques étrangers en France avant la Révolution, conservées dans les archives de Berlin, Dresde, Genève, Turin, Gênes, Florence, Naples, Simancas, Lisbonne, Londres, La Haye et Vienne.* Paris: Imprimerie Nationale.

Hébert, Jacques-René (1792). *Grande relation du siège et de la prise du château des tuileries: Détail de tous les événemens arrivés depuis le 10 août dernier…* Paris: De l'Imprimerie de la rue Sainte-Barbe. Lb[39] 10627.

Jugement prévôtal et en dernier ressort, Rendu publiquement, Audience tenante, Par M. Lucot d'Hauterive, … Sur le massacre du sieur Huez, Maire de la ville de Troyes … (1789) Troyes: De l'impr. de la Veuve Gobelet. Médiathèque de Troyes – Patrimoine RR 48–4218.

L'Héritier, C.F., F.-A. Aulard, and Société de l'Histoire de la Révolution Française (1890). *Mémoires secrets de Fournier l'Américain: Publiés pour la première fois d'après le manuscrit des archives nationales.* Paris: Au Siège de la Société.

Peltier, J.G., F.J. Saint-Méard, and H.S.J. Bolingbroke (1792). *Dernier tableau de Paris: Ou récit historique de la révolution du 10 août des causes qui l'ont produit, des evénemens qui l'ont précédés, et des crimes qui l'ont suivi.* London: the authors.

Pétion, J., F. Buzot, C.J.M. Barbaroux, and C.A. Dauban (1866). *Mémoires inédits de Pétion et mémoires de Buzot & de Barbaroux.* Paris: H. Plon.

Ray, A. (1847). *Réimpression de l'ancien moniteur.* Paris: H. Plon.

Révolutions de Paris: Dédiées à la nation et au district des Petits Augustins (1792).

Sagnac, Philippe (ed.) (1909a). "Une relation inédite de la journée du 10 août 1792 [by the bookseller Nicolas Ruault]." *RHMC*, 12: 274–282.

Sergent-Marceau, Antoine (1835). "Notice historique sur les événemens du 10 août 1792 et des 20 et 21 juin précédens." *Revue rétrospective, ou, bibliothèque historique*, 2nd series, iii: 328–346.

Viard, F. (n.d.). *Rapport fait à l'assemblée nationale, par le commandant de garde au poste des appartements du traître louis xvi* ... Paris: Imprimerie de P. Provost. Lb[39] 6098.

Secondary Sources

Alpaugh, Micah (2009). "The Politics of Escalation in French Revolutionary Protest: Political Demonstrations, Non-Violence and Violence in the *Grandes Journeés* of 1789." *FH*, 23: 336–359.

Bercé, Yves-Marie (1987). *Revolt and Revolution in Early Modern Europe: An Essay on the History of Political Violence.* Manchester: Manchester University Press.

Bord, Gustave (1887). *Histoire du blé en France: Le Pacte de famine; histoire–légende.* Paris: A. Sauton.

Caron, Pierre (1906–7). "La Tentative de contre-révolution de juin–juillet 1789." *RHMC*, 8: 5–34, 649–78.

Cubells, Monique (1991). "La Ville d'Arles au printemps de 1789." In Jean Sentou (ed.). *Révolution et contre-révolution dans la France du midi*: 1789–1799. Toulouse: Presses Universitaires du Mirail.

Jaurès, Jean (1900). *Histoire socialiste (1789–1900)*, vol. 1, pt. 12. Paris: J. Rouff.

Kaplan, Steven L. (1982). *The Famine Plot: Persuasion in Eighteenth-Century France.* Philadelphia: American Philosophical Society.

Lefebvre, Georges (1963). *Études orléannaises: Contribution à l'étude des structures sociales à la fin du xviiième siècle.* Commission d'Histoire Économique et Sociale de la Révolution. Mémoires et Documents 15. Paris: Bibliothèque Nationale.

Lemny, Stefan (2000). *Jean-Louis Carra (1742–1793): Parcours d'un révolutionnaire.* Paris: L'Harmattan.

Lüsebrink, Hans-Jürgen and Rolf Reichardt (1997). *The Bastille: A History of a Symbol of Despotism and Freedom.* Durham, N.C.: Duke University Press.

Mason, Laura (1996). *Singing the French Revolution: Popular Culture and Politics, 1787–1799.* Ithaca, N.Y.: Cornell University Press.

Michelet, Jules (1899). *Révolution française: La Constituante et la législative.* Paris: Calmann-Lévy.

Monin, H. (1889). *L'État de Paris en 1789: Études et documents sur l'ancien régime à Paris.* Paris: D. Jouaust [etc.].

Monnier, Raymonde and Antoine Santerre (1989). *Un bourgeois sans-culotte, le général Santerre. Suivi de l'art du brasseur par A. Santerre.* Paris: Publications de la Sorbonne.

Pollio, J. and A. Marcel (1881). *Le Bataillon du 10 août: Recherches pour servir à l'histoire de la Revolution française.* Paris: G. Charpentier.

Reinhard, Marcel R. (1969). *La Chute de la royauté, 10 août, 1792.* Paris: Gallimard.

Rudé, George (1959). *The Crowd in the French Revolution.* Oxford: Clarendon Press.

Sagnac, P. (1909b). *La Révolution du 10 août 1792: La Chute de la royauté.* Paris: Hachette.

Spagnoli, Paul G. (1991). "The Revolution Begins: Lambesc's Charge, 12 July 1789." *FHS*, 17(2): 466–498.

Wahl, M. (1894). *Les Premières Années de la Révolution à Lyon (1788–1792).* Paris: Armand Colin.

CHAPTER FIFTEEN

The Vendée, *Chouannerie*, and the State, 1791–99

JEAN-CLÉMENT MARTIN

Commonly referred to as "the wars in the West," the "Vendée rebellion" and *chouannerie* have logically been considered together, if not simply confused with each other. Victor Hugo's *Quatre-Vingt-Treize* provides a perfect example: he places the action "in the Vendée," not far from Fougères, a town in Brittany! Identified as counter-revolutionary, prosecuted in the name of throne and altar by peasants to a greater or lesser extent led by minor nobles and refractory priests, these events are differentiated in historical memory only by the clothing of the combatants. Thus Vendéans were the ones wearing large-brimmed felt hats, wide pants and jackets, whereas the *chouans* were the ones in Breton-type clothing.

If it were only a matter of costume, this confusion would raise a smile and be of no more than passing interest to historical scholars. In their relations with the state, however, the Vendée and *chouannerie(s)* have fewer characteristics in common than they have structural differences, placing them in two distinct categories of opposition to the Revolution. Conflating them involves, on the one hand, denying the specific ruptures that engendered the existence of these two instances and on the other, and more significantly, erasing the importance of the question of the state at the time of the Revolution. Moreover, the difference between the Vendée and *chouannerie* brings into question the very nature of the French Revolution. The aim of the following pages is not only to examine the differences essential to an understanding of these historical events but also to account for the Revolution itself. The Revolution and counter-revolution are less distinct than ever before; it is their various links that allow us to comprehend the complexity of the history of the period (Martin 1998).

A Companion to the French Revolution, First Edition. Edited by Peter McPhee.

Identical Beginnings

The terms "Vendée rebellion" and "chouannerie" began to be used only in 1793 and 1794, but, if we look at the uprisings in order to find their antecedents, they started simultaneously and in the same way at the end of 1790 and beginning of 1791. In this they are no different from other rural insurrections that arose against the application of the Civil Constitution of the Clergy. In February 1791, peasants from around the Breton town of Vannes invaded it in support of the bishop who was refusing to take the oath. At least four peasants were killed in the ensuing repression. In April, peasants from the Machecoul region, south of Nantes, took up arms against a detachment of the National Guard which had come to install a constitutional priest. It was to the cry of "Give me back my God!" that one of the insurgents, later recognized as the first to die in the Vendée rebellion, was killed.

Beyond mere imagery, we should note that in various parts of the Loire region, the protest movements that formed were identical. In a region in general massively opposed to the Civil Constitution of the Clergy (with whole cantons going so far as to number themselves among the refractory), the rural people found themselves in conflict with the new institutions represented by the presence of the districts and departments. Beyond the religious dispute, this became progressively a conflict that encompassed every political and social dimension. The religious differences were not, in fact, between groups by definition hostile to each other, as was the case between the Catholics and Protestants in the south of France. In the west, memories of Protestantism were genuine but weak to the south of the Loire and virtually non-existent to the north. What was in play was the attachment of the rural populations to forms of religious observance marked by spectacular display linked to rituals, notably concerning the Sacred Heart, and to processions, linked to the teaching of Grignion de Montfort and his followers, that distinguished them from the inhabitants of hamlets and towns, with their greater intellectual sensibility, impregnated with Jansenism. Even in the Machecoul area, the break between the peasants of the villages and the residents of the little town is clear (Perouas 1989; Woell 2006).

The discord gradually became glaring as priests who had refused the oath and who therefore enjoyed the marked support of their parishioners, who stood behind them virtually unanimously, were expelled and replaced by priests brought in by force. The National Guard, as well as elements of the army, was then sent in at the request of the departmental and district authorities to enforce the orders of the National Assembly. All over the west, peasants confronted this in various ways. In the Mauges, rural communes contacted each other to organize federations of Catholic national guards, in the name of the first principles of the Revolution. Everywhere alliances were made between refractory priests and their curates, who were often even more determined to fight. These men organized more or less clandestine church services and administered the sacraments to the detriment of "juring" clergy, abandoned by their flocks. The nobility of Brittany and Poitevin had refused the reforms suggested by Louis XVI and even participation in the Estates-General. They had confronted the "patriots" as early as 1788–89, since the first blood of the Revolution had been spilled in Rennes in January 1789. They had distanced themselves from political life since then, but after 1791 and the failure of the king's flight at Varennes, a few of them organized groups of rural counter-revolutionaries. This was notably the case in Brittany, around a veteran of the American War of Independence, La Rouërie, as well as of the La Lézardière family, not far from Machecoul (Sutherland 1989).

Thus an alliance – unexpected, considering how deep earlier cleavages had been – gradually formed between rural people, priests, and nobles opposed to the revolutionary state and its representatives on the one hand, and administrators, national guardsmen, landowners, and bourgeois notables on the other. Differences in the way of life between town and country, however this contrast is defined, provoked different confrontations depending on the area (demonstrated by Dupuy 1972, 1988). The antagonisms thus varied, but the mechanisms in play pitting rural people, peasants, and weavers against the *vignerons* of the Mauges, peasant-*vignerons* against villagers (*bourgadins*) in the Nantes region, peasant farmers against farm-owners in Ille-et-Vilaine, peasants against weavers in Sarthe, were identical (see the work of Bois 1960; Sutherland 1982; Tilly 1964, 1967, 1970). But fighting the state and its representatives was more important than fighting against "the town" or the market. We should note that the graziers of the Mauges sold their animals as far away as the markets of Paris and that the producers of muscadets and other wines in Loire-Inférieure partly supplied the port of Nantes. For different reasons, but following an almost identical process, it was clearly rural communities which, in the name of their own identity, rose up against the state control that had been increasing over decades and was accelerated by the Revolution. All over the country people renting land were henceforth subject to increases in taxation from which property owners were exempt. In a certain number of regions the uniformity imposed by the creation of departments suppressed the exemptions (*marches séparantes*) that separated Brittany from Maine and Poitou and which encouraged smuggling of contraband or which guaranteed privileges. This change drew into opposition to the Revolution groups of rural people used to living on the margins of the state and who no longer benefited from the differences in taxation that had until then existed between Brittany and its neighboring provinces.

Religious questions crystallized this conflict-ridden situation, bringing into play autonomous and unified groups of people. The juring clergy, defended by the mayors and National Guard of small communes, made a point of baptizing the new-born and above all of burying the dead, often provoking physical fights and sometimes murders. Communities and even families were divided between partisans of the "juring priest," who became "the intruder," and those who followed and protected the "refractory," the "good priest." From the end of 1791, the National Guard no longer contented itself with pursuing people processing through the woods or around miraculous fountains and oak trees where signs of God were believed to appear. They felled the trees, broke up the processions, and sometimes destroyed relics or ritual objects that had become suspect, before finding themselves confronted by groups of people armed with sticks and even pick-axes. At this moment and even more so in 1792 the emissaries of the Legislative Assembly noted that the whole region was close to civil war. Alongside more muted disturbances, those that attracted the most attention were two rebellions that shook the west in

August and September 1792. One, of adherents of a certain Jean Cottereau, alias Jean Chouan, a former smuggler who narrowly escaped hanging under the *ancien régime*, took place on the border between Brittany and Maine. This uprising was linked to La Rouërie. The other took place in the north of the department of Deux-Sèvres, where several thousand peasants rallied round Bressuire. In both cases the rioters were dispersed: in the Poitevin case not without considerable violence.

Comparison with other regions of France enables us to specify the distinctive nature of the west. After all, actual wars were also raging in the Rhône Valley and around the edges of the Massif Central with Catholics opposing Protestants since 1790, and successive waves of peasant uprisings were sweeping through the whole southwest and Massif Central, with the last of them, in 1792, being especially violent. However, in the southeast it was competing communities, grouped around strong local identities, which confronted each other, whereas in the southwest nobles and priests and even influential individuals did not take part in confrontations led by peasants unless they were themselves under attack (see Delpont 2002; Lapied 1996; but cf. Bercé 1980; Gérard and Heckmann 1994). In the western Loire and Brittany, even if it is hard to prove conclusively, we need to recognize that the use by Marcel Faucheux of the phrase "uprising of the whole population" (Faucheux 1964: 143, cited in Sutherland 1989) evokes what must have been an increasing cohesion among large groups of the rural population, supported by the local nobility and refractory priests, defining themselves in distinction to identified opponents.

The March 1793 Rupture

This solidarity logically extended into the first months of 1793 when the Convention decreed the conscription of 300,000 men, destined for frontier combat, provoking a general repudiation of the "ballot," that is to say the identification of young men by the communes and districts. The assemblies called for this purpose turned against the authorities and became the locus of refusal. Similar reactions occurred in many regions, with the same general political, economic, and religious motives. Supporters of the Revolution found themselves in a state of opposition which was unexpected in terms of its size and virulence, since many supporters, national guardsmen, administrators, and elected officials were abducted, assaulted, and even killed. Acts of violent resistance took place around Orléans, in the north of Puy-de-Dôme, and in Alsace, giving rise to the formation of rural bands violently demonstrating their opposition to the Revolution. The Mauges around Cholet rose from the beginning of March, but the rioters were swiftly repressed. This was not the case for those who rebelled from 10 March in Brittany, Maine, north of Nantes, from the Guérande peninsula to the Maine heathlands, along the right bank of the Loire, and to the south of the river, as far as the Vendée. The movement was significant, since within a few days small towns were seized, and representatives of the Nation were imprisoned, sometimes put to death, or forced to flee.

This is particularly true of La Roche-Bernard, midway between Rennes and Nantes, where the president of the district, Joseph Sauveur, died heroically beneath the blows of those who can from that time correctly be called counter-revolutionaries.

Their political orientation was exposed with notable clarity by Jacques Gaudin de la Bérillais, a noble officer who had retired to Saint-Étienne de Montluc, north of Nantes, and who drew up a precise list of the complaints and demands of the insurgents. It was not a question of returning to the *ancien régime*, but of demands for guarantees of the autonomy of rural communities against national power, notably in religious observance like that envisaged by King Louis XVI in the speech he had given on 23 June 1789 in his attempt to reach a compromise with the "patriots" in the Estates-General. The steps taken in 1793 by the insurgents still resembled the usual processes of rural revolt of earlier centuries: the explosion of rage occurred in expectation of the opening of negotiations rather than of the creation of a new society. The insurgents were not, in any case, following the directions of the exiled princes or *émigrés*, about whom they knew nothing (in support of this, see Martin 1987). Should they be described as "anti-revolutionaries" rather than "counter-revolutionaries"? Their gatherings, even though poorly organized, devoid of clear demands and in fact independent of the nobility, placed them nonetheless in opposition to the Revolution. They expected at least to recover their social and religious autonomy: they clearly blamed the birth of a state linked to the Revolution.

What is important is that the movement was identical all over the Loire region and sometimes better organized to the north, most notably for example in Léon. Nantes was immediately surrounded by armed rebels, who besieged it from 12 to 16 March (Bourgeon 1986; Bourgeon and Hamon 1993; Guin 1993). As far as we know, no link was established between the insurgents to the north and south of the river, while a semblance of organization occurred to the north between the rebels of the eastern part of the department of Loire-Inférieure and those of Anjou, foreshadowing the creation of a lasting zone of counter-revolutionary combat. After a few battles against detachments of patriots from the town, the siege was broken on 18 March and the rebels retreated, without disappearing, however, leaving the most important avenues of communication – to Rennes and Paris – open. To the south of the Loire, the situation in the *faubourgs* of Nantes was less urgent, but the uprisings around certain centers, especially Machecoul, Montaigu, and Legé, and in the Mauges, were significant and coherent. However, there was no ideological, social, or geographical continuity between the regions traversed by groups of rebels who hunted down patriots and began organizing themselves for combat against companies of the National Guard or small groups of soldiers of the line who found themselves in the area. Leaders were appointed either because they had distinguished themselves under fire or, especially, because they were already known for their part in the battles of the last two years. This was notably the case for Cathelineau in the Mauges, known since 1792 as a ringleader, who placed himself at the head of a troop which was immediately swelled by some thirty members of his family.

From then on, the destiny of the left and right banks of the Loire diverged. The news of the events surrounding 16 to 18 March that reached Paris alarmed the Convention. The disagreements between the Girondins, who then held power, and the Montagnards, not supported by the majority of the members of the Convention, were bitter and increased by the rivalry between the deputies and the actions of the sans-culottes, of whom Marat presented himself as the representative within the Assembly. In this three-cornered conflict, when the Girondin presses had just been forcibly closed and the decision to create an extraordinary revolutionary tribunal had been taken, members of the Convention were engaged in battles against counter-revolutionary enemies and in mortal inter-factional rivalries. On 18 March the Assembly decreed the death penalty against anyone demanding the agrarian law, in other words the division of property. This was aimed at the most radical of the sans-culottes. The next day, the majority acted when the threat emanating from Brittany was announced. In the ensuing battle, in which the Girondins were accused of moderantism, referring to their attitude during the trial of the king and their desire to "appeal to the People" to avoid the immediate execution of Louis XVI, some Montagnard deputies put to the vote a motion that any person found bearing arms or wearing a white cockade would be judged and executed within twenty-four hours. In some ways, this measure followed procedures put in place earlier, notably after 1788 in the summary courts invested with powers of this kind in order to break up riots. The new context changed their meaning.

The decree initially aimed at the Bretons and indirectly at the Girondins coincided with a conflict nobody expected which took place on the same day in the heart of the department of Vendée, not far from Saint-Fulgent, at a place called Pont-Charrault (Valin 1992, 1993, 1997). A troop made up of soldiers of the line, national guardsmen, and volunteers had left La Rochelle, where the general in charge of the region was stationed, and was defeated by rural groups of armed rebels which had taken them by surprise. The repercussions were threefold. First, the defeated fled, frightening the populace by announcing the imminent arrival of counter-revolutionaries bent on massacre. Second, the south of the Loire in general was suddenly given over to the rebels since no other revolutionary force was there to take them on. And finally, the representatives on duty on the spot made the news known in Paris in the following days, accusing local Girondins of complicity with the rebels. At the same time, the rebels to the north of the Loire, confronted by well-commanded armies which had been consistently victorious, were defeated several times, with heavy loss of life. The communes judged to be responsible for the insurrection were severely punished. During March and early April important pockets of Angevin and Breton rebellion were crushed, and the best-known leaders obliged to hide or flee south of the Loire.

In this area, in contrast, the military vacuum had allowed the existing armed rebel groups to consolidate and give each other mutual recognition, more or less readily depending on the difference in aims. Many, following the conflicts of earlier years, described themselves as "Catholic and Royal armies," while some had been set up simply to take revenge on neighbors who had held power until then. This was the case of the rebels round Machecoul, who herded together and massacred at least 160 local patriots, causing other supporters of the Revolution to flee to Nantes, and thus nourishing every phobia. In the Assembly from 23 March 1793 onwards, the deputies referred to the "war in the Vendée and surrounding departments," a formulation soon abbreviated to the "war in the Vendée," forgetting the neighboring departments in which the rebellion had nonetheless been strong, but which had no desire to be designated as counter-revolutionary or "moderate" in the same way as the Vendée. Thus within a few days, following a specific event, the interpretations constructing the national political space differentiated between rebellions that had nonetheless the same nature, appearance, and aims, providing public opinion with enemy number two, the Vendée – Coblenz and its *émigrés* constituting enemy number one. The counter-revolution thus had two faces – internal and external – against which the armed forces had to mobilize not just to win, but above all to enable the identification of the most effective revolutionaries, who would be destined to achieve political power as a result. Chronology was here more discriminating than the strength of the rebellion itself, since understanding of this incomprehensible victory of peasants over soldiers, who were revolutionaries into the bargain, occurred in the context of the internal divisions that consumed the French Revolution. It was these divisions that, from August to September 1792, literally transformed the course of the Revolution into a civil war, that is to say a situation in which the legitimate authority incarnated by the state was contested, divided, and uncertain, giving the opposition some sway over the state's monopoly of violence. The Vendée became exceptional because it permitted, in this undefined but emblematic context, those fighting for control of the revolutionary state to confront, in mortal combat, not only counter-revolutionaries but also each other. This kind of iconic war did not exist in any other region with the same degree of ferocity.

The Drift of the Civil War

It is not a question here of retelling the story of the war in the Vendée but rather of stressing within this particular context – namely the relationship between the rebellions in the west and the state – what was specific to it: the central role of the state and of internal conflicts in this "war," the only insurrection identified in this way in the entire Revolution. "The Vendée," as it was to become generally known after 1793, was at first linked to the most important decisions taken by the central state. The Committee of Public Safety owed its very existence to it, since it was set up to remedy the deficiencies of the existing committees, made up, it is true, of Girondins, and thus suspect following the trial of the king. It was to receive news of the war in the Vendée at midday every day, and its most strenuous efforts were directed against it. Troops to fight it were requisitioned from all over France. The disadvantages of this policy would prove to be considerable. Political, tactical, and regional rivalries between the troops would weaken command, particularly since they consisted of a mixture of soldiers of the line, volunteers, and sans-culottes. The last refused to accept military discipline unless they were allowed to elect officers who shared their sense of independence, and for some of the men their taste for pillage.

The result of this political direction of an ideological war would prove catastrophic through to October. The clashes between Montagnard generals, Girondins, Dantonists, and sans-culottes were such that the armies under sans-culotte control failed in September 1793 and allowed the Vendéans to block an offensive which could not be coordinated. A month later, once the sans-culottes had gained total control over the armies of the west, they could, by concentrating their forces, crush the Vendéans in a decisive battle. The deputies in Paris, who had been unable until then to provide a rational explanation of the surprising victories of the Vendée revolt, described this as "inexplicable," as a phoenix rising from the ashes. The reality, proclaimed by a few generals as early as the summer of 1793, was less enigmatic. Political disunity and underhand dealings were responsible for this military mess, aggravated by destruction, rape, and pillage committed by some soldiers even at the risk of their own safety. The retreats of the Vendée armies can only be blamed on the Vendéans themselves, who failed at Luçon and Nantes because they too were divided and incapable of coordinating their attack. The battle of Nantes on 29 June 1793 is particularly important from this point of view since the revolutionaries themselves united *in extremis* to resist, while the Girondins and Montagnards were engaged in open warfare in Paris and Lyon. Failures in the chain of command then explain the extraordinary success of the long meander of the Vendéan column from the Loire to the port of Granville in Normandy. Reinforcements from the Breton or Norman *chouans* would not have been enough to ensure a rapid advance. Their defeat at Granville was due to their poor preparations for a siege, rivalries at the heart of their general staff, and their lukewarm relations with the English. Their ill-prepared return was a disaster because the most competent republican generals, Marceau and Kléber, organized the counter-offensive by taking advantage of the loss of influence and departure of generals who were incompetent and linked to the sans-culottes, themselves victims of the purges decreed by the revolutionary government in Paris at the end of 1793.

Throughout this time, the Vendée, regarded as the counter-revolutionary threat, served as the yardstick by which other uprisings were judged. In April, for instance, the press and the Assembly referred to the Vendée in order to describe the disturbances stirring in the Massif Central. The Vendée was a scarecrow used to justify and impose any measures, however exceptional. This was especially evident on 1 August and 1 October 1793 when Barère, in his famous speeches, spoke of destroying the Vendée and "its brigands" allied with Pitt's England, Marie-Antoinette, and the *émigrés.* A terrorist rhetoric thus arose around the Vendée, to which all were linked who, for one reason or another, were at any given moment characterized as counter-revolutionary. The administrators of the department of the Vendée particularly were targeted, and with them anyone within the insurgent zone who had held office. The ephemeral but spectacular victories of the Vendéan troops thus created a military and administrative vacuum stretching broadly from Saumur to Sables d'Olonne, from Nantes to Chantonnay. The Vendéan "fiefdoms" remained few in number, although important areas continued to be disputed between enemies, thus constituting a kind of "no man's land" through which combatants from either side circulated, confronting local populations regarded as adversaries by the republicans.

In the summer and autumn of 1793, conflict at the highest echelons of the state placed the country in a state of civil war during which all the important political groups tried to take control of state violence. Even though the consequences were the same in other regions, notably in Lyon, and similar in the Basque country or Toulon, the results in the Vendée were particularly frightening, because the combat zone was vast, the number of soldiers considerable (there were over 70,000 permanently deployed), and the displacement of populations had been enormous, with at least 200,000 people voluntarily or involuntarily fleeing their homes. While no limit and no precise definitions were provided, "the Vendée," the mythical enemy, was left to the soldiery from autumn 1793 until March–April 1794, when the Convention and the Committee of Public Safety decided to intervene forcefully in the conduct of operations. In the meantime, Carrier, the "representative-on-mission" on the spot and close to the Hébertists, allowed repression to reach appalling levels, while some of the incendiary columns set up on the orders of the general-in-chief, Turreau, protected by Carnot, committed the worst acts of violence possible through poorly led men who had themselves been placed in danger and were inclined to kill anyone they encountered.

Even if it is not possible to establish precise figures, the war conducted in this way in the Vendée ended up costing the lives of at least 170,000 people, killed, massacred, executed, or simply "disappeared." It is impossible to assess the "republican" elements in these figures, particularly because 40,000 inhabitants of the region left it in chaotic circumstances, making calculation even more complicated (Hussenet 2007). It is equally impossible to exclude the soldiers, volunteers, or people conscripted into the revolutionary armies who died as a result of the war. Most of the deaths, as far as we can tell, were due to illness and the results of wounds rather than to combat, even though these became deadlier and deadlier. Perhaps we could estimate that 100,000 "republicans" might have died in these wars? The complexity of this war and its unimaginable violence have continued to fascinate memorialists and historians. Even though we must obviously regard Turreau and a certain number of his troops as war criminals, we cannot accuse the Revolution, as has been suggested, of deliberately initiating genocide, or even exterminating a population. It was precisely the absence of unity among the revolutionaries that facilitated this violent outburst as opposed to any systematic planning (cf. Secher 1986; equally the over-systematic approach of Gérard 1999; see also Martin 2007).

The elimination of the Hébertists and sans-culottes who had taken over the Ministry of War, followed by the resolution of the Committee of Public Safety, enabled the recall to Paris of those representatives-on-mission who had been guilty of excess – Barras, Fouché, or Carrier in Nantes, then Turreau, who was stripped of his command. The war in the Vendée then entered, after May–June 1794, a more military phase, with generals who paid attention to discipline, to the protection of civilians, and to non-ideological aims. First Canclaux, then Hoche thus succeeded in waging war against the Vendéan generals who were still dangerous because the local population had no choice, on pain of death, but to support them. The change of policy in the Convention therefore led to negotiations with the principal Vendéan leader, Charette, and a declaration of peace with him in February 1795. This was certainly a cessation of hostilities rather than a true peace, made all the more necessary by the exhaustion of both camps. Nonetheless, the end of the Vendée was near. Since neither the *émigrés* nor the English had supported it until then, and since its impetus came from the ideological repression by which it was assailed, it was Charette's support of the Quiberon expedition of June–July 1795 that set its final defeat in train. Effectively abandoned by the comte d'Artois and the English, Charette, followed by the other Vendéan leaders, Stofflet among them, was stripped of all popular support through the effective operations of Hoche, before being captured and shot. After March 1796, the war of the Vendée as such was only a memory, one which would have considerable importance in giving rise to a regional memory and as a universal symbol – but that is another story (Martin 2006).

The *Chouan* Guerrilla

The history of *chouannerie* is very different. The generals in Brittany prevented the rural armed groups from coalescing and taking control of the region. At the end of April 1793 republican control had been re-established, despite the fact that those opposing it remained in general totally hidden, sometimes concealed underground, most often in wooded areas or isolated villages, benefiting from the support of the peasants, whether voluntary or forced. A certain number of Bretons or insurgents from Maine and Anjou traveled to the south of the Loire, joining one of the Catholic armies being set up. After July 1793 complex confrontations between Girondins and Montagnards split the revolutionary camp even further: some of the defeated Girondins defected to the counter-revolution, the most famous of these being Puisaye, who entered into negotiations with various groups of resisters and succeeded in being named general-in-chief of the *chouans* at the end of the year (Hutt 1983). In the meantime, the name *chouans* was applied to all of them, giving general application to a nickname originally relating to bands of smugglers who imitated the call of the owl.

The arrival across the Loire of Vendéans heading for Granville after October 1793 changed the situation. The *chouans* rallied and joined in the battles before going back into hiding once the counter-revolutionaries had been repelled. But the arrival of the Vendéans upset the regional balance to the benefit of the *chouans*, who were freed from the pressure of the republican troops they had been fighting and which were redirected against the Vendéan column. Moreover, even though the Vendéans had been crushed, the republican armies emerged greatly weakened by a succession of battles. By the beginning of 1794 the republicans held the towns, main roads, and those parts of the countryside where the locals had stayed faithful to the Revolution. But several informal groups of *chouans* established themselves here and there along the coast of Brittany as far as the south of Caen, to the east of Le Mans and Angers. The leaders, mostly commoners identified by their peers and thereafter recognized for the leadership they had demonstrated in combat, had established fairly strong links. The factions that had developed within the revolutionaries and the exhaustion of their armies led to a certain stasis, confirmed by the peacemaking efforts of a few representatives on the spot, notably in Rennes. During the autumn of 1794, insurgents stopped being referred to as "bandits" and became once again "misguided brothers," who might be pardoned if they agreed to lay down their arms. The process, as in Charette's Vendée, ended with a peace treaty between the *chouan* general Cormatin and the Republic, signed at Mabilais, not far from Rennes, in April 1795. But, as in the Vendée, where the counter-revolutionaries had split over this point, some *chouans*, of whom the best known is Cadoudal, the powerful leader from the Morbihan, rejected any peace deal.

But peace did not last there either. It served only to allow preparations for fresh battles, with the *chouans* benefiting from direct aid from the English and from the gratitude of the *émigré* princes, thanks to Puisaye, who had gone to England. This support, which the Vendéans had lacked, benefited the *chouans*, but transformed the movement by placing it under the de facto control of the nobles wanting to conduct a war in France against the Revolution and who saw an opportunity to regain their power and prestige. The limitations of this new situation became obvious as early as July 1795, when the *émigrés* and soldiers who had landed from English ships in the bay of Quiberon were defeated, imprisoned, and shot by troops commanded by Hoche. Bad relations between the expedition leaders and the difficulty of commanding peasant armies unused to any form of military discipline led to a resounding defeat of the whole undertaking. While Brittany had mostly escaped the Republican ascendancy, the failure of the landing at Quiberon had catastrophic consequences. The radical counter-revolution seemed incapable of changing the balance between the armies. The comte d'Artois spent two months off the Île d'Yeu before landing in France. His abnegation was not merely tactical: the Paris uprising was crushed, the royalist networks dismantled or weakened, and the strategy of the constitutional monarchists was henceforth to take power through the electoral process.

Thus between 1796 and the summer of 1797 a period of indecision over the fate of the armies ensued. *Chouannerie*, however dangerous, was not accorded the same priority as the Vendée. It needed only to be contained; it did not endanger the republican state, which had more to fear from enemies on its borders and the possible alliances of royalists in the southwest of the country. In Brittany and Normandy armed groups were crossing the countryside engaging in surprise attacks or individual assaults and were frequently assisted, notably in Normandy, by poor people driven by destitution. Young noblemen joined these groups, helped by links with England which had become entrenched via the Channel Islands. Facing them, republicans watched, organized, and repressed, sometimes barely within the limits of the law, as "counter-*chouans*" undertook what were real commando operations. A state of general insecurity reigned. Assassinations and the settling of old scores occurred, as well as executions of political opponents. The inhabitants were subjected to the passage of opposing troops and were themselves committed to one camp or the other. However, the local administrative framework was often respected, even if it was difficult to find municipal officials to appoint or to know whether some were covert royalists. Taxes were poorly collected and the presence of armed forces was indispensable, but extending the conflict to the rest of the country was unthinkable, and the moderate royalists who were competing with the republicans were not inclined to support the *chouans* and their noble leaders who wanted to return France to a bygone era (see the case-study in Bourgeon 1986).

After 1797, and the failure of the attempt by constitutional monarchists and conservative republicans to take power, the position of the radical counter-revolutionaries was strengthened. The *chouans* became a sort of shadow army, with a general staff in which nobles played a greater part, even if the established leaders, such as

Cadoudal, remained in place. The *chouan* leaders, Bourmont, d'Andigné, Scépeaux, and Frotté, led henceforth an organized and hierarchical guerrilla war, with a more or less stable body of troops, depending on safe chateaux or forests, with arms and money from England. When needed, the nebulous *chouannerie* hidden within the peasantry could always be mobilized. The links with the *émigrés*, England, and the king thus give *chouannerie* its ideological importance, especially as networks of secret agents were criss-crossing France and preparing to retake the country by force of arms. The political aim of *chouannerie* is clear: the movement was participating in the counter-revolution in order to restore a monarchical, Catholic, and seigneurial state, in other words, essentially France as it was before 1787.

This militarization reached its peak in 1799, linked to the great offensive launched against the Republic by the coalition. On every front – Italian, Dutch, Swiss, German – armies were engaged in significant operations. In the west, war resumed after overt preparation by the *chouan* leaders, who rallied their troops and organized their offensive operations by placing whole regions under military control. The counter-revolutionary offensive was, however, brought up short; there was no similarity in outcome between different theaters of war and, while Italy had virtually rid itself of French republicans, the latter were fighting to the death in Switzerland, defeating the Anglo-Russians in the Netherlands and had scattered the thousands of men who had laid siege to Toulouse.

In October 1799, the *chouans* succeeded in seizing a few towns in the west (Le Mans, Saint-Brieuc, and Nantes) before falling back to their preferred territory. The armies that had been raised to the south of the Loire had not been victorious, confirming the military defeat of the Vendée. Bonaparte, as soon as he was made Consul, opened negotiations with the *chouan* leaders, granted freedom of worship, made contact with Stofflet's former secretary, the *abbé* Bernier, in order to prepare the Concordat, and tried to win over the *chouan* leaders, by force or persuasion. Cadoudal resisted but left France for the time being; Frotté was taken and shot as a general warning; and others fell into line sporadically. The glory days of *chouannerie* were at an end.

Between Glory and Disdain

In the years that followed, the distinction between the Vendée and *chouannerie* became ever clearer. Reconstructing the "Vendéan" departments was difficult, lengthy, and expensive; many areas ended up with a population made up mostly of insurgents and their families who were in charge of the local councils. Arriving at a frequently hard-earned compromise with consular and imperial authorities, these groups ensured an armed peace, while retaining the memory of the "martyrs" who began to be commemorated. From 1813–14 they supported groups opposing the emperor, culminating in a resumption of hostilities in 1814, and above all during the Hundred Days, when *chouans*, who had also been active from 1813, helped to form armies against the Empire. The insurrection failed, but required an army to be deployed, thus weakening the emperor on the field of Waterloo. The Vendée became henceforth, thanks to the pen of the marquise de La Rochejaquelein, the exemplar of a land of fidelity to the monarchy, the church, and France before the error of the Revolution. In 1832, the half-baked attempt by the duchesse de Berry to rouse the country, starting with the Vendée, on behalf of her son the duc de Bordeaux, did not dim this picture of an exceptional region crystallizing royalist nostalgia and republican rancor for the next two centuries.

To the north of the Loire, the disappearance of the noble leaders sent the *chouans* back to their original banditry. With the murder of tax-collectors and mayors, stage-coach hold-ups and setting up of guerrilla groups, *chouannerie* found itself unable to decide whether it consisted of honorable rebels or highway robbers. The nobility, who had joined Napoleon or returned overseas, viewed the *chouans* with suspicion and disdain. As Michel Denis (1977) notes, their alliance was a matter of pure chance and the very memory of *chouannerie* collapsed as soon as "Celtic Brittany" became fashionable. But unlike the case of the Corsicans, the *chouans* did not form an immediate focus of this dawning romanticism. One need only look at the low status they were accorded by Balzac (1845) in the novel that bears their name. Peasants hostile to the state are seen merely as backward country folk, who are dangerous and hunted down with the consent of all those who count. It is only after 1850 that the first histories of *chouannerie* would be written and romantics would paint masses at sea and *chouans* in animal skins fighting against the revolutionaries, confusing the Vendée with *chouannerie*. Finally, from 1880 to 1890, when noble and royalist priests opposed the Third Republic, the *chouan* achieved national, although ambiguous, recognition. By virtue of his uncouthness, he would incarnate Natural Man, hostile to modernity and politics, whereas the Vendéan retained a religious, if not downright bigoted, dimension. It was only in the twentieth century that a combination of the *chouan* and Vendéan would come to embody the peasant resistant to the centralized and egalitarian state.

The wars in the west have thus seen two kinds of trajectory, with different chronologies, human and regional consequences, and even different meanings, despite their undeniable similarities in so far as their relations to the state as adversaries or pawns were not unalike. To try to unite them within the counter-revolution is thus a serious historical error. Their specific characteristics make clear that, depending on the occasion, links between the Revolution and counter-revolution were not the same in both cases, since the passage of the *chouans* from simple rejection of the Revolution to the counter-revolutionary camp was a matter of contingency, whereas the Vendée has become emblematic of the counter-revolution by virtue of being at the heart of the struggles over the control of the state. So it is a question of two distinct historical moments in the constitution of the French state during the revolutionary period, corresponding to the separate pinnacles of the Vendée and of *chouannerie*.

References

Balzac, Honoré de (1845). *Les Chouans*. Paris: Furne.

Bercé, Yves-Marie (1980). *Révoltes et révolutions dans l'Europe moderne*. Paris: PUF.

Bois, Paul (1960). *Paysans de l'Ouest*. Le Mans: Vilaire.

Bourgeon, Jean (1986). *La Vie est dans le pré*. Nantes: ACL.

Bourgeon, Jean and Philippe Hamon (eds.) (1993). *L'Insurrection de mars 1793 en Loire-Inférieure*. Nantes: Nantes-Histoire.

Delpont, Hubert (2002). *La Victoire des croquants*. Nérac: Les Amis du Vieux Nérac.

Denis, Michel (1977). *Les Royalistes de la Mayenne et le monde moderne XIXe–XXe siècles*. Paris: Klincksieck.

Dupuy, Roger (1972). *La Garde nationale et les débuts de la Révolution en Ille-et-Vilaine, 1789–mars 1793*. Paris: Klincksieck.

Dupuy, Roger (1988). *De la Révolution à la Chouannerie*. Paris: Flammarion.

Faucheux, Marcel (1964). *L'Insurrection vendéenne de 1793: Aspects économiques et sociaux*. Paris: Commission d'Histoire Économique et Sociale de la Révolution.

Gérard, Alain (1999). *"Par principe d'humanité...": La Terreur et la Vendée*. Paris: Fayard.

Gérard, Alain and Thierry Heckmann (eds.) (1994). *La Vendée dans l'histoire*. Paris: Perrin.

Guin, Yannick (1993). *La Bataille de Nantes*. Laval: Siloë.

Hussenet, Jacques (ed.) (2007). *"Détruisez la Vendée!"*. La Roche-sur-Yon: Centre Vendéen de Recherches Historiques.

Hutt, Maurice (1983). *Chouannerie and Counter-Revolution*. Cambridge: Cambridge University Press.

Lapied, Martine (1996). *Le Comtat et la Révolution française*. Aix-en-Provence: Presses Universitaires.

Le Roy Ladurie, Emmanuel (1974). *Le Territoire de l'historien*. Paris: Gallimard.

Martin, Jean-Clément (1987). *La Vendée et la France*. Paris: Seuil.

Martin, Jean-Clément (1998). *Contre-révolution, Révolution et Nation: France 1789–1799*. Paris: Seuil.

Martin, Jean-Clément (2006). "The Vendée, Region of Memory." In Pierre Nora (ed.). *Rethinking France*, vol 2. London and Chicago: Chicago University Press. 383–408. Revised version, first published 1984.

Martin, Jean-Clément (2007). *La Vendée et la Révolution: Accepter la mémoire pour écrire l'histoire*. Paris: Perrin.

Perouas, Louis (1989). *Grignion de Montfort et la Vendée*. Paris: Éditions du Cerf.

Peschot, Bernard (1999). *La Chouannerie en Anjou, de la Révolution à l'Empire*. Montpellier: Université Paul Valéry.

Secher, Reynald (1986). *Le Génocide franco-français: La Vendée-Vengé*. Paris: PUF.

Sutherland, D.M.G. (1982). *The Chouans: The Social Origins of Popular Counter-Revolution in Upper Brittany, 1770–1796*. Oxford: Clarendon Press.

Sutherland, D.M.G. (1989). "L'Association bretonne: La Conspiration du marquis de La Rouerie." *Annales de Bretagne et des Pays de l'Ouest*, 96: 433–455.

Tilly, Charles (1964). *The Vendée: A Sociological Analysis of the Counter-Revolution of 1793*. Princeton, N.J.: Harvard University Press.

Tilly, Charles (1967), *The Vendée*. New York: Wiley. Paperback edn., with preface not translated in the French edn.

Tilly, Charles (1970). *La Vendée: Révolution et contre-révolution*. Paris: Fayard.

Valin, Claudy (1992). *Autopsie d'un massacre*. Saint-Jean d'Angély: Bordessoules.

Valin, Claudy (1993). "La Bataille inaugurale dite de Pont-Charrault: Réalité et résonance." In Jean-Clement Martin (ed.). *La Vendée et le monde*. Enquêtes et Documents 20. Nantes: Ouest-Éditions et Université de Nantes. 35–64.

Valin, Claudy (1997). *La Rochelle-La Vendée: 1793*. La Rochelle: Le Croît Vif.

Woell, Edward J. (2006). *Small-Town Martyrs and Murderers*. Milwaukee, Wis.: Marquette University Press.

Part VI

Political Choice and Practice

CHAPTER SIXTEEN

Friends, Enemies, and the Role of the Individual

MARISA LINTON

Introduction

Friendship and enmity played an important – though often underestimated – role in revolutionary politics. This chapter addresses the interaction between personal and political factors in the politics of the Jacobins between 1790 and 1794. It focuses on the tension between loyalty to one's friends and the demands of the revolutionary ideology of political virtue. It then goes on to focus on the examples of three men who, at different stages, were dominant figures in the Jacobin Club: Antoine Barnave, Jacques-Pierre Brissot, and Camille Desmoulins. It will investigate the ways in which their political choices and ultimate fates were intertwined with the shifting patterns of both friendship and enmity between them. Lastly we shall relate these examples of individual agency to a key question about the politics of Jacobinism – which is how it relates to the system of Terror sustained by the Jacobins from 1793 to 1794. There have been many ideological interpretations of the Terror, which we do not have the space to explore here. Nevertheless, the argument in this chapter relates to the Terror. The Terror cannot be fully explained in terms of ideas. By examining Jacobin politics through personal experience and the agency of individuals, it becomes evident that ideology alone does not explain the choices that individual Jacobins made, and that often much more personal factors also played a decisive part, including friendship, enmity, trust, distrust, loyalty, and betrayal.

The Terrain of Revolutionary Politics: Ideological, Tactical, Personal

As I argue in a forthcoming work (Linton, *Choosing Terror*), Jacobin politics can be understood not only through its ideology, but also in terms of a whole terrain of

A Companion to the French Revolution, First Edition. Edited by Peter McPhee.

politics. Jacobin politicians operated on three levels, which together formed this terrain. These levels were closely interconnected, and can be better understood if we grasp them in relation to one another. Such an approach brings us a little closer to the ways in which Jacobin politics were actually experienced by the people involved in them. The first level was that of ideology. This was the public face of Jacobinism. It is primarily traced through public writings and speeches. But politics is not just conducted on the level of official discourses. It is also a business, something that people do. The second level of Jacobin politics therefore was the tactical business of "doing politics." This level was characterized by polemics and in-fighting, deals and strategies, managing assemblies and clubs, networking and advancement. There was also a third level of politics: this was the personal dimension. The personal dimension of politics can be further subdivided into two related categories. The first category was that of individual circumstances. These included relationships with friends and family, which affected political choices and alignments. The second category was that of personal emotions and psychology. Emotions (whether acknowledged or not) were a driving factor in Jacobin politics. Visceral feelings – including patriotic fervor, friendship, and loyalty, as well as dislike, distrust, and fear – all contributed powerfully to revolutionary politics.

The psychological and emotional history of the Revolution is beginning to assume a new importance amongst historians and there is a growing literature on the personal dimension of revolutionary politics. This new literature is explored, and its implications reflected upon, in Hunt (2009) and Rosenfeld (2009). Individual studies which incorporate the study of emotions include Shapiro (2009), Martin (2006), Wahnich (2003), and Reddy (2001). The related topics of individual experience, the sense of self, and the role of imagination in the revolutionary psyche are also being explored. The work of Goldstein (2008), though she focuses mostly on the period after the Revolution, offers valuable insights into the changing idea of the self, and the importance of the imagination in this construction. Individual agency and consciousness in the period leading up to the Revolution are explored in Smith (2001). New work on the experience of Revolution, including the studies collected in *Experiencing the French Revolution* (Andress forthcoming), is exploring how individuals struggled to make sense of the Revolution as a lived experience, and how they sought to give the Revolution meaning, by drawing on revolutionary ideology and relating it to their own circumstances. When revolutionary politics are studied at this level it is apparent that individual revolutionaries were able – within certain constraints – to negotiate and manipulate revolutionary ideology and official pronouncements in accordance with their own needs and aims.

Virtue or Friendship?

In common with many others of their time, the Jacobins saw politics in moral terms – as founded on political virtue. They believed that their leaders should act as "men of virtue," which meant they were supposed to set aside self-interest, ambition, and personal loyalties and consider only the public good. As I have shown (Linton 2001), the revolutionaries' idea of political virtue originated from two main traditions: the first was the classical republican tradition, derived from antiquity and reinterpreted by eighteenth-century thinkers; the second was the tradition of natural virtue, which stemmed from innate feelings. The "political virtue" of a revolutionary politician was meant to be an authentic emotion, written on his heart. As Hunt (1984) demonstrates, revolutionary politics were meant to be "transparent" so that nothing about the conduct of politics was hidden. Revolutionary politicians were answerable to public opinion. The public had the right to scrutinize not only the words and actions of their political leaders, but also their inner motives and private lives. This was because the private life and motives of a politician were meant to match up with his public identity as a "man of virtue."

Friendship was central to revolutionary politics. Friendship has always played an important (if frequently under-acknowledged) part in political life. But friendships forged against the backdrop of the French Revolution were often more intense than those made under more normal circumstances. The changes wrought by the Revolution broke down the rigid social conventions of the *ancien régime*, and brought together people who would otherwise have moved in very different circles. For the Jacobins the early years of the Revolution were personally, as well as politically, liberating. Shared sympathies and a common purpose could lead to close friendships. Increasingly, however, the reverse was also true: revolutionaries made at least as many enemies as friends, and former friends could make the bitterest enemies of all – not least because they had been party to one another's personal lives, and their unguarded selves.

Jacobin ideas about friendship were ambiguous and conflicting. In the absence of an official party structure, and a bureaucratic system for securing appointments, friendship was central to the way in which much of the actual practice of revolutionary politics was conducted, but this was something that the Jacobins found difficult to admit – even to themselves – as it contradicted their ideas of what politics ought to be about (Linton 2008). On the one hand the Jacobins prized friendship as an ideal form of human association. Friendship also served as an important emotional outlet: a way of escaping from the constraints of old-regime society. On the other hand, friendship had many negative connotations in revolutionary politics. First, there was an ideological problem with political friendships. According to the Jacobins' ideology, the highest love was that for the *patrie* (Campbell 2010). Loyalty to a friend could be seen as a betrayal of the imperative to serve the people as a whole. Friendship between individuals was thus potentially in conflict with the demands of political virtue. These conflicting demands were illustrated in a familiar story from antiquity. This was the account of Lucius Junius Brutus who had brought about the downfall of the Roman kings. So great was his virtue that when his own sons conspired against the Republic he had them both executed. Many radical revolutionaries consciously adopted the model of Brutus as part of the self-fashioning of their identity as "men of virtue" (Linton 2010). In a further dangerous modification, there was an association between friendship and political conspiracy. Friendship networks, with their exclusivity and private meetings, could be seen a cloak for counter-revolutionary conspiracy. In all the major trials of political factions in the Year II, great play was made of the supposed link between networks of friends, illicit factions, and political conspiracy.

There was also a more practical reason for the Jacobins to be wary of friendships in politics. This was the association of political friendships with the old-regime style of politics. Much of the actual practice of the old-regime politics was conducted in private, behind closed doors, often over dinner. Friendships struck in these circumstances could serve as a means for mutual social advancement. This practice of conducting politics "behind closed doors" was seen as incompatible with the new revolutionary forms of "transparent" politics. From the outset, revolutionaries were aware of this potential conflict. In September 1789 Desmoulins was offered just such an "old-regime" form of friendship by the comte de Mirabeau. Desmoulins wrote to his father to describe the friendliness and generosity of Mirabeau, and what he, Desmoulins, was meant to give in return – the service of his pen. He described a world of *ancien régime* sociability which could be all too seductive for a young, nearly penniless lawyer:

> For the last eight days I have been staying with Mirabeau, at Versailles. We have become great friends; at least, he calls me his dear friend. At each moment he takes my hand, he punches me playfully on the back; then he goes to the assembly, resumes his dignity as he gets to the vestibule, and achieves marvels; after which, he returns to dine with excellent company, and sometimes his mistress, and we drink excellent wines. I fear that his table, too laden with delicacies, is corrupting me. His Bordeaux wines and his maraschino come at a price which I try in vain to hide from myself, and I have all the difficulty in the world in resuming afterwards my republican austerity and to detest the aristocrats, whose crime is to give such excellent dinners. (Desmoulins 1836: 40–41)

To accept proffered friendship and hospitality was a choice that brought favors and patronage, but also laid one under an obligation. It was thus contrary to the obligation of a "man of virtue" to remain independent. In practice, though, during the early years of the Revolution a lot of political business was conducted in this "behind closed doors" manner. To some extent this practice continued, even through the Terror, but it was an activity that became seen increasingly as "suspect." During the Terror many trials of politicians included as "evidence" dinners and friendships with people who had come under suspicion. As I have shown (Linton 2007), during the Terror these private contacts were all too easily seen as "conspiratorial."

Barnave, Brissot, Desmoulins, and the Jacobins of the Constituent Assembly

Barnave, Brissot, and Desmoulins had very different characters and social backgrounds, but they were brought together by their shared enthusiasm for the Revolution. All three became important figures in the Jacobin Club in its early period, during the Constituent Assembly. Barnave was a lawyer from an affluent family in Grenoble, not quite noble himself, but living in a noble milieu, and with noble family (his mother was noble, his father had personal nobility), yet his sympathies were very much with the Third Estate. He was astute, an excellent speaker, skilled at improvising and getting to the heart of a question; he was also the kind of man who made friends readily, and was good at keeping them. Barnave was one of the co-founders of the Jacobin Club along with a group of patriot nobles and leading members of the Third Estate. Three men from this group, Alexandre Lameth, Duport, and Barnave, became the effective leaders of the Jacobins. From late 1789 to the summer of 1791 they dominated Jacobin politics. They became known as the "triumvirate" – a name given them by their opponents as it recalled the triumvirate that had dismantled the Roman Republic and shared power for themselves. They were so closely united, politically and personally, that Barnave lived with Lameth and his brothers during the period of their involvement at the Jacobins.

In order to become a leader of the Jacobins a man needed to acquire skills at three things: oratory, networking, and the projection of a Jacobin identity. To master the oratory of the Jacobins he had to speak as a patriot and a "man of virtue," and convince his audience that he was not motivated by personal ambition. Duport and Alexandre Lameth were skilled public speakers, but it was Barnave who was the outstanding orator of the three, fluent and able to improvise on his feet. The emotional side of Jacobinism was never his forte, however, and Brissot's friend, Madame Roland, who preferred her rhetoric much more effusive, found his language chilly; she described Barnave ungraciously as "a lemon fried in snow" (Roland 1966: 128).

The Jacobins' ideology made it unacceptable to have formal leaders who sought to use the Jacobins to promote their own political ambitions. Leaders were redolent of English-style "party politics" – a launching pad for the machinations of a group to gain political power. Barnave and his friends could unleash the power of the popular radical movement in the Jacobins to achieve power for themselves and achieve their ambitions, but they could only do this by presenting themselves as patriots and men of virtue. Like Cincinnatus, in order to be worthy of power, they had to deny that they wanted it. There were many potential advantages for a would-be leader in having the support of the Jacobins behind him; by harnessing the power of the Club he could exert considerable sway over public opinion. There were also, however, considerable risks, for he would be offering himself to the judgment of people who came from a very different background to his own. This set up a profound tension between personal ambition and the demands of political virtue.

In contrast to Barnave and his friends, the great majority of the Jacobins were commoners, many of them men of limited means. These socially "humbler" Jacobins included several deputies, Robespierre, Pétion, and Buzot. A number of Jacobins came to prominence through their journalism. Desmoulins was one of these. Like Robespierre he had trained as a lawyer, but he had lived a hand-to-mouth existence until the coming of the Revolution brought him sudden fame for his skill as a journalist, and the dramatic role he had played before the storming of the Bastille. Brissot was another revolutionary journalist, editor of the *Patriote français*. Before the Revolution Brissot already had a long career as a writer and would-be "man of letters," though often this had been a precarious, somewhat hand-to-mouth existence (Burrows 2003; Ellery 1915). He was an enthusiast for natural virtue, and for liberty. He became a leader of the Société des Amis des Noirs, a group devoted to the abolition of slavery. During the 1780s he had engaged in political writing, partly for powerful patrons, including the duc d'Orléans. Brissot later recounted this experience in terms of himself as a "man of virtue" confronted by d'Orléans and his circle, who epitomized the excesses of a privileged lifestyle: "They should have prepared the Revolution by means of good morals, by vigorous writings, by which one could attach the people weary of despotism to the prince, and instead they confined themselves to thinking up projects over the most sumptuous dinners, in front of lackeys most of whom were spies. I counseled against this step, I extolled, but it was in vain. They called me *the virtuous man*, and continued to find fault, a glass of wine in hand, or on the sofa with the girls" (Brissot 1912: vol. 2, 64–65).

Brissot's Letter to Barnave

Robespierre, Desmoulins, Brissot, Pétion, and Buzot were all members of a network of radicals amongst the Jacobins. During the first year of the Revolution there were friendly relations between many of this group and the triumvirate. Desmoulins and Barnave were good friends at this time, as Desmoulins would later attest. Not all of them got on well, however; Brissot seems to have taken against Barnave personally from the early days of the Revolution, at a point well before political choices had come between them (Bradby 1915: 330).

The early camaraderie began to change, however, as over the winter of 1790–91 Barnave and the other members of the triumvirate grew closer to the court. The radical Jacobins suspected that their leaders were deserting them and seeking a separate role for themselves as king's men. Barnave's reputation was further damaged by his active involvement in the defense of French colonial interests, when he headed the Assembly's colonial committee and used his position to resist political rights for mulattoes. Charles Lameth owned extensive property in Saint-Domingue, and Barnave's involvement was seen as motivated by his personal friendship with the Lameths, though Barnave denied this. Brissot was outraged at what he saw as Barnave's betrayal of the principles underlying the rights of man. Charles Lameth had offered to sacrifice his colonial property early on, though according to Brissot this was a ruse to gain popularity amongst the Jacobins and Charles was not in earnest (Brissot 1912: vol. 2, 121–123). Brissot became Barnave's chief attacker in the Jacobins. In November 1790 Brissot published an open letter, his *Letter to Barnave*, in which he denounced Barnave for having acted out of personal motives, and in support of the vested interests of his friends – in short for his lack of political virtue. The letter ended with a description of the characteristics of a true patriot, which Brissot listed one by one. A patriot should "want liberty for all men"; he should "hate monarchy," he must "not allow a lie to sully his lips"; he does not "manoeuvre to arrive at positions of pre-eminence"; he "does not have a court of numerous clients in his antechamber." When he is in a position of power a true patriot will model his behavior on Cato, or Cincinnatus: "He will stay in mediocrity even in the midst of the most brilliant places; and often he will leave to his children only his memory and the recognition of his fellow citizens" (Brissot 1790). Brissot then went on to examine Barnave's own conduct and how it measured up to these standards. Brissot concluded that Barnave was only imitating the conduct of a patriot: his political identity was assumed, to further his own ambition.

The *Letter to Barnave*, as both Brissot and Barnave acknowledged, had a big impact on the public and was highly influential in undermining Barnave's reputation as a "man of virtue." After the publication of the letter, it was at a dinner at a restaurant at which several prominent Jacobins had planned to be present that the depth of the personal enmity became apparent. Lameth had brought Barnave, but when they heard that Brissot was also coming, they and all the other guests departed in order to avoid a confrontation if Brissot and Barnave met (Bradby 1915: vol. 1, 355). Subsequently the two men faced up to one another in the Jacobin Club. Brissot won the encounter and the oratory of the triumvirate never dominated the Jacobins again as it had once done. Brissot's letter illustrates Brissot using ideology (that of patriotism and virtue), in a tactical manoeuvre to denounce Barnave by means of a "letter" couched as though it were a personal disagreement between them, but published so as to damage Barnave's public reputation.

Brissot's attack was in part motivated by his strong opposition to slavery. Yet that was not the only reason he wrote the letter. We know from Brissot's own words that he nursed a profound enmity for Barnave, one that outlasted the period of their political power. When, nearly three years later, in 1793, both men were imprisoned under the Terror, Brissot's *Memoirs*, written partly as a personal justification of his actions, presented an unforgiving portrait of Barnave's shortcomings. Though both men were by this time under the shadow of death, Brissot was still intent on establishing his own authenticity and Barnave's perfidy, both in his own eyes and in those of posterity: "Barnave, as I reproached him, never had true patriotism, but only the vanity of the orator and the ambition of the tribune. It was not my love for the blacks, as people believed, it was not a blind indignation that animated me against him. I had seen into the depths of his soul …" Brissot felt no regret at having written the *Letter to Barnave*, which had done so much to demolish Barnave's reputation. He expressed his satisfaction at having written it, saying it was "one of the best and most useful works to have come from my pen" (Brissot 1912: vol. 2, 111–113).

Desmoulins' Brissot Unmasked

In 1790 Desmoulins and Brissot were on very good terms, so much so that Brissot, along with Robespierre, Pétion, and Mercier, was a witness at Desmoulins' wedding in December of that year. Desmoulins knew most of the inner circle of the Jacobins of this time and many of them were present at that wedding. Yet Desmoulins was a very different character to Brissot. Whilst Brissot took himself very seriously as a "man of virtue" and prided himself on his scrupulous austerity, Desmoulins was much more ambiguous and changeable. In his journalist writing he liked to play with his own public image, revealing intimations of a life not up to the high moral standards of the Jacobin Club and then backtracking, like a child that knows he has said something shocking in front of the grown-ups. It was this reckless, uncontrolled characteristic that made other revolutionaries talk about him, and that goes some way to explain why he was not trusted with high office. He was known to be indiscreet – he could not help himself. Thus Desmoulins' own enjoyment of intimate dinners *chez* the aristocratic party was too well known – largely through his own indiscretion – for him to deny it. He said in his defense: "I am taunted with having dined recently with some of the great props of the royalist aristocracy. The harm is not in dining with these gentlemen, but in holding their opinions" (Claretie 1876: 103–105).

Brissot had grown rapidly in stature to become one of the leading figures within the Legislative Assembly. He was also a key player in the Jacobin Club, where his role in discrediting Barnave's reputation had helped to cement his own. Yet over the winter of 1790 and spring of 1791 a second division began in the Jacobins. It started over a conflict between Brissot and his supporters, who were pursuing a pro-war policy, and Robespierre, who was opposed to declaring war. Brissot's group later became known as the Girondins. In 1791 the ties between this group were based more on personal choice and friendship groups than on a separate "Girondin" ideology. Insofar as Brissot's group had a collective identity at this time, it was primarily through their friendships (Linton 2008; Linton forthcoming). Brissot dominated partly by virtue of his great facility for bringing people together and forging connections. He himself admitted: "I have always loved to bring my friends together" (Brissot 1912: vol. 1, 176). Brissot was the kind of man who operated very much in terms of friendships and personal connections. But the favoring of friends had adverse resonances of old-regime culture and private loyalties over the public good. It was a path that needed to be trodden with care by an aspiring revolutionary politician. When Brissot was seen to have a hand in appointing his friends to key posts in the so-called Girondin or patriot ministry, other Jacobins outside Brissot's group began to suspect him of personal ambition.

One of the earliest, most comprehensive, and damagingly articulate of the attacks on Brissot was Camille Desmoulins' pamphlet *Brissot Unmasked* (*Brissot démasqué*). It was highly successful, and is said to have made more stir than any other revolutionary pamphlet. It set the tone and the style for the series of deadly attacks on political leaders that were made during the period of the Terror. This was achieved by unpicking the conduct of the person "unmasked"; mingling personal and political allegations; calling into question the person's claims to authentic virtue; and depicting him as a secret enemy of the Revolution. It appeared in February 1792, in the midst of the controversy over the war, and it included a defense of Robespierre, who may well have known about this pamphlet beforehand. It must be seen in the context of the growing divisions between Brissot's group and other Jacobins. But Desmoulins had an additional, personal motive to go all out to get Brissot. What galvanized him into writing was his outrage at an article in the *Patriote français* which had attacked him as an unworthy patriot for his defense of people's rights to engage in gambling. Brissot saw gambling as a sign of aristocratic culture, corruption, and decadence. The article had ended with a harsh judgment against Desmoulins' moral and political integrity: "This man calls himself a patriot only in order to calumniate patriotism" (Desmoulins 1874: vol. 1, 252). Brissot had long nurtured a low opinion of Desmoulins' ability to resist the various temptations in which Paris abounded. Brissot later recalled how Desmoulins had once admitted in his newspaper, *Les Révolutions de France et de Brabant*, to a weakness for "bacchic distractions." Brissot suggested contemptuously that drunken dissipation had closed

Desmoulins' eyes to the iniquities of Barnave, whose principles Desmoulins had defended in the same issue (Brissot 1912: vol. 2, 115).

Desmoulins used *Brissot Unmasked* to inflict a very personal revenge on the former friend who had slighted him. Desmoulins recast Brissot's role in the Revolution, turning him from patriotic hero to self-seeking and duplicitous villain. Despite abstract references to the Republic and the good of the people, the world Desmoulins wrote about here was relatively enclosed – a small group of people who knew one another, who liked or disliked one another, trusted or distrusted one another, and who chose sides accordingly. As part of this personalization of politics, Desmoulins addressed Brissot directly: "I warn you that you shall not succeed in your attempt to *brissoter* my reputation: it is I who will tear the mask from your face ..." The term "brissoter," first coined by Brissot's enemy Morande, and given the meaning "to steal," had earlier been taken up by the right-wing press and used against Brissot. Here Desmoulins was seizing on this word and using it to discredit Brissot's reputation as a true Jacobin (Desmoulins 1874: vol. 1, 259). Desmoulins proceeded to take his revenge by calling into question the meaning of Brissot's conduct since the beginning of the Revolution, and even before it. The fact that Brissot and Desmoulins had been friends gave Desmoulins insider information which he could use to inflict additional damage on Brissot's public reputation. Desmoulins proved well up to the task, as his words punched holes in the mask of Brissot's public face.

Desmoulins repeated the allegation that even before the Revolution Brissot's bad faith had been evident through his taking 150 *livres* a month to act as a spy for the police chief, Lenoir (Desmoulins 1874: vol. 1, 267). He poured scorn on Brissot's weaknesses of character: his rashness that had made more enemies for the Revolution than anyone else; his limitations as a writer, "as indefatigable as he is mediocre"; his ministerial ambitions, for himself and his friends (Desmoulins 1874: vol. 1, 277–280). Desmoulins went further: Brissot's devotion to the Revolution had always been highly questionable: "you have been in the worst of bad faith, a true Tartuffe of patriotism and a traitor to the *patrie* ..." (Desmoulins 1874: vol. 1, 268). The name Tartuffe invoked theatrical duplicity and sanctimonious hypocrisy. Desmoulins, with his talent for insinuation, mocked Brissot's public image. Like Tartuffe, Brissot's way of presenting himself, his austere clothes, his Puritan hairstyle, drew people's attention to his assumption of a virtue he did not possess. "Listening to you the other day at the tribune of the Jacobins proclaim yourself to be an Aristides ... I contented myself with laughing quietly with my neighbors at your stainless patriotism and the immaculate Brissot" (Desmoulins 1874: vol. 1, 266).

Even Brissot's republicanism was depicted as a sign of his bad faith. Desmoulins accused him of having affected a republicanism that could only further destabilize an already volatile situation in the days that led up to the Champ de Mars massacre, and of having been behind the petition that led to it (Desmoulins 1874: vol. 1, 281). According to Desmoulins, Brissot's republicanism showed him to be a reckless "ultra" revolutionary, when wiser heads than his – including Robespierre – thought that a republic was not appropriate for France at that time, and would only endanger the Revolution and precipitate conflict (Desmoulins 1874: vol. 1, 277–283).

Since Desmoulins himself had been one of the first to call for a republic back in 1789, for him to criticize Brissot for doing the same thing indicates that Desmoulins' attack on Brissot was personal and tactical rather than based on ideological differences. Desmoulins had made a choice to range himself with Robespierre and against what Desmoulins termed "Brissot's cabal." Desmoulins' praise of Robespierre's incorruptibility and virtue in this same pamphlet was designed to show that, unlike Brissot, Robespierre was the real thing (Desmoulins 1874: vol. 1, 268, 283–284).

In the closing sections of the pamphlet Desmoulins turned to his own "incorruptibility," detailing allegations that had been made against him by Roederer that had appeared in the pages of the *Chronique de Paris* accusing Desmoulins of being a "pseudo-patriot" who had with his journalism "sold himself to all the world, and been bought by no one." According to Desmoulins, Roederer was motivated by his hatred of Robespierre, and had attacked Desmoulins for his friendship and loyalty towards "his old college friend." In defending himself Desmoulins seemed a little uneasy about some aspects of his own past conduct, and whether these would meet the high standards required of a "man of virtue." He sought to excuse himself for his own past friendships with Mirabeau and with the Lameths, now seen by the Jacobins to be "intriguers" against the Revolution. Mirabeau, he said, had won him over by his esteem and friendship. The Lameths had "seduced him" by the only means possible – "that of swearing that they would never desert the Jacobins, that they would lose their heads on the scaffold in the cause of liberty." But he insisted that none of these men had "bought him." He had been won over by lies, flattery, and friendship – not money: "But regardless of whether I owe my incorruptibility to virtue or to the fear of infamy, it is none the less incontestable. People refer to the immense fortunes that the principal actors in the revolution have made, the lands, the mansions, the chateaux that they have bought. In the great upheavals of the revolution, I defy anyone to say that my field has increased by so much as a handful of earth ... the esteem of my fellow citizens, the only benefit that I have derived from the revolution ... I do not envy the heroes of the revolution their fortune, their advancement. ... It is my fortune not to have enriched myself in the revolution" (Desmoulins 1874: vol. 1, 284–290).

The pamphlet stopped short of declaring Brissot to be a counter-revolutionary, nor was it directed against anyone other than himself. But it made him look a fool, self-interested, and a false patriot, if not worse. Brissot made little attempt to respond to the damaging allegations (Ellery 1915: 242). Here, as elsewhere in revolutionary politics, personal friendship which had soured into enmity had political consequences. The allegations that Desmoulins made here (along with his subsequent *Fragment of the Secret History of the Revolution*), and the interpretation that he gave to Brissot's conduct, would subsequently form part of the basis of the case made against Brissot at his trial, and thus these words were used to kill him. Desmoulins himself understood this, too late. When Brissot and his friends were condemned to death, Vilate, a Jacobin who witnessed the trial, reported that Desmoulins collapsed in public, crying: "It is my *Brissot Unmasked* that is killing them!" (Wallon 1880–81: vol. 1, 418). Yet this repentance did not stop him two months later delivering in *Le Vieux Cordelier* a personal threat against Hébert, spokesman for the sans-culottes, that Desmoulins would serve him as he had Brissot: "I shall unmask you as I unmasked Brissot" (Desmoulins 1874: vol. 2, 212–213). Desmoulins' attack on Hébert, spokesman of the sans-culottes, should be seen in the context of the factional fighting in the Jacobins during the Year II (Linton forthcoming). It is notable, however, that here too there was a very personal and vindictive dimension to the way in which Desmoulins and Hébert each sought to present the other as having assumed a false identity as a patriot to hide his corruption and true identity as a conspirator.

Barnave's Trial

After the overthrow of the monarchy Barnave was arrested and held in prison for over a year before he was brought to trial in November 1793. There was scant evidence against Barnave of conspiracy with the court. The letters he sent to Marie-Antoinette which made it clear that his loyalty was to her cause did not come to light till long afterwards. In the absence of more concrete evidence Barnave was charged with vague crimes relating to his conduct which had not been that of a "man of virtue." Thus he was accused of personal ambition, of aspiring to be a minister, of corruption, of intrigue, of letting himself be bought by the court, and of letting himself be influenced by his friendships, particularly his friendship for the Lameths. In his own defense he said that all he had done was to defend constitutional monarchy at a time when this was the accepted thing – even Robespierre had accepted it. Barnave claimed that the damning image of him as a false patriot had been largely the invention of Brissot in his *Letter to Barnave* three years earlier. "It is Brissot," Barnave protested, "it is Brissot almost alone who devised this notion of an alteration in my principles ..." (Walter 1968: 416). Ironically Brissot himself had been executed the previous month as a "conspirator" against the Revolution, but the impact of his *Letter to Barnave* outlasted his own death and made itself felt in Barnave's own trial for "conspiracy."

In his defense Barnave gave a courageous vindication both of his friends, and of friendship. It was all the more courageous since the Lameths and Duport had emigrated and were out of harm's reach, whilst he himself was under the threat of execution. No one could have blamed him if, in such circumstances, he had repudiated his friends, but that was not what he chose to do. He said:

> The public accuser has spent a lot of time proving that the Lameths and Adrien Duport were intimately connected with me. A woman's letter, inviting me to dine at the home of the latter, was read, at the last session, as proof of this conviction.
>
> Well then! What need was there to reveal so many little details, citizen accuser? All that is well known.
>
> Never would I be so base as to disavow my friends. I loved, I still love the Lameths. Certainly, they had faults, and I was not the last to reproach them. They kept something of the manners of the Court ... But what profound and genuine qualities didn't I know in them? ...
>
> After two or three months' trial, my friendships were fixed and have never since changed. They united me with men full of defects, but of great honesty, fine character, and great courage. Those who followed the stream of prejudice have added these

> friendships to the number of my crimes. Perhaps the observant will judge that men, who were placed during three years at the center of the most important affairs, and saw a thousand coalitions form and dissolve, without knowing one single instant of misunderstanding among themselves, deserve at least to be heard before they are condemned. (Walter 1968: 418–419)

Desmoulins' Friends

By the summer of 1793 many things had changed. The Jacobins were now the ones in power. At this time Desmoulins had another compromising friend with whom he reportedly liked to enjoy excellent meals, and copious amounts of wine. This was the general Arthur Dillon, a former noble with military ambitions. Desmoulins had tried to promote Dillon's interests with the Committee of Public Safety. In July Dillon came under suspicion for royalism and was arrested. Desmoulins attempted to defend his friend, an effort which brought him too under suspicion of protecting former nobles in the army (Desmoulins 1874: vol. 2, 202–206). Desmoulins published an open *Letter to General Dillon* in which he not only defended Dillon, but used his inside knowledge to poke fun at several leading Jacobins, including Saint-Just and Billaud-Varenne. It was amusing – but it was a dangerous tactic, as Desmoulins himself acknowledged when he wrote to his father about the popularity of his "letter" with opponents of the Jacobins: "Its prodigious success in the past two days makes me fearful that I have avenged myself too much. I need to look into my heart and find there the same patriotism, to excuse myself in my eyes, when I see how much the aristocrats are laughing at it: and to appreciate why I am attacked with such indignity" (Desmoulins 1836: 176).

Towards the end of that year the Jacobins conducted a "purifying scrutiny" whereby members had to answer questions about their past conduct before having their membership renewed. It was a process that reflected the Jacobins' growing anxiety about the authenticity of their identity as "men of virtue." On 14 December it was the turn of Desmoulins. Partly because of Desmoulins' defense of Dillon, attention focused on his friendships. Desmoulins was asked to explain his connection with Dillon. He was also questioned about his show of sensibility at the Revolutionary Tribunal when the Girondins had been condemned, and his reported words that "they were true republicans" and that "they would die like Brutus." Before the eyes of the watching Jacobins Desmoulins stammered as he pleaded his extenuating circumstances. He admitted to having been "deceived" by Dillon, with whom he had not communicated in the last three months. He denied that he had spoken in support of Dillon; he had only asked that Dillon be brought to judgment. Regarding his show of grief at the condemnation of the twenty-two Girondins, he offered this explanation, "of the 60 people who signed my marriage contract, I only have two friends left, Robespierre and Danton. All the others have either emigrated or been guillotined. Seven of the 22 were amongst these friends. It is surely pardonable therefore that I showed my sensibility on this occasion." Under pressure from the Jacobins, he conceded that, though he "cherished the Republic," he had often made a poor choice of friends, including Mirabeau and the

Lameths. In his justification he said: "I was always the first to denounce my own friends; from the moment that I realized that they were conducting themselves badly, I resisted the most dazzling offers, and I stifled the voice of friendship that their great talents had inspired in me" (Aulard 1889–97: vol. 5, 559).

Why should Desmoulins make such a chilling statement? This was after all the man whose latest journal, *Le Vieux Cordelier*, was supporting a policy of clemency, and the winding down of the Terror. He said it partly out of fear. We should not underestimate the importance of fear in Jacobin politics during the Terror. As I argue elsewhere (Linton forthcoming), the words and actions of the Jacobin leaders themselves need to be understood in relation to the claustrophobic atmosphere of suspicion, stress, acute anxiety, and sheer panicky terror which characterized Jacobin politics in the Year II. The Jacobins had chosen to maintain the Republic through terror, but this was also a system that they inflicted upon themselves. This "politicians' terror" was one of the most ruthless forms of terror. Those who fell victim to it were subjected to what amounted to political show trials in which they were given a minimal chance to defend themselves.

In early January 1794, in issue 5 of *Le Vieux Cordelier* (1874: 201–202) Desmoulins came back voluntarily to the subject and defended his record for putting the Revolution before his attachment to individuals, and denouncing his own friends. His motives for this avowal seem to have been complex: it was partly self-defense; partly to give himself credibility as a "true" patriot; but he was also stating a simple truth – he had done this – and it is hard to avoid the thought that on some level he was taking pride in what he had done. He said, "Can anyone cite me a single conspirator whose mask I haven't raised well before it fell? I have always been six months, and even eighteen months ahead of public opinion." He then gave a list of former political leaders of the Revolution whom he had denounced long before they had been formally accused, including Lafayette, Mirabeau, the Lameths, Pétion, d'Orléans, Sillery, Brissot, and Dumouriez. He conceded that he had been friendly with the majority of these men, but claimed that this showed, not his own corruption, but the depth of his devotion to the *patrie*. Could there have been any "more difficult test than to renounce the friendship of Barnave and the Lameths, to tear myself away from Mirabeau whom I loved to idolatry, like a mistress." He claimed: "I have been more faithful to the *patrie* than to friendship." As final proof of this he stated that he had refused to take Barnave's hand until after Barnave been condemned. Desmoulins' close friend Fréron, in a letter to Desmoulins' wife, Lucile (Desmoulins 1836: 190), passed on his congratulations to her husband for his gesture repudiating Barnave: "Give him my compliments on his proud response to Barnave; it is worthy of Brutus, our eternal model ...".

Conclusion

These examples have served to illustrate the importance of personal relationships, friendship, enmity, and how these affected the choices made by individuals in the inner circle of Jacobins between 1790 and 1794. These personal factors can be integrated with ideology and tactics to help us to better understand the whole terrain of politics. This personal dimension of politics can throw new light on the Terror of the Year II, and the ways in which a few individuals, many who had whom were former friends, became bent on killing one another in a "politicians' terror." In this chapter I have attempted to reconstitute some of the personal elements of the complex and multi-faceted motivation that lay behind the individual choices of men like Barnave, Brissot, and Desmoulins. This is an important task – though admittedly a difficult one – but one that helps us to understand how far choosing terror was also a decision that individuals made, one that had consequences for individual lives.

Brissot's *Letter to Barnave* helped to destroy Barnave's reputation as a true patriot and "man of virtue," a process which facilitated his condemnation during the Terror. Desmoulins' *Brissot Unmasked* performed a similar act of destruction against Brissot's reputation as a "man of virtue"; this "unmasking" in turn helped structure the accusations made against Brissot at his trial. We have not discussed the trial and death of Desmoulins here (that story is well known), but we should note that he too was to suffer from a process whereby his reputation was destroyed as a prelude to killing him, and that some of the personal details for that attack were put together by two men with whom he had once been friends, Robespierre and Saint-Just. This chapter is not suggesting for a moment that these personal attacks were the only factor involved in the political divisions between the successive factions of Jacobins. What it does argue, however, is that to understand the Terror it is necessary to situate this personal dimension within the context of revolutionary politics, and to recognize that at key moments individuals were often inspired by motives that were much more personal and much more bitter than pure ideology.

References

Primary Sources

Aulard, François (1889–97). *Société des Jacobins: Recueil de documents pour l'histoire du club des Jacobins de Paris*, 6 vols. Paris: Léopold Cerf; Noblet; Quantin.

Brissot, Jacques-Pierre (1790). *Lettre de J.P. Brissot à M. Barnave.* Paris, 20 Nov.

Brissot, Jacques-Pierre (1912). *Mémoires (1754–1793), publiés avec étude critique et notes par Cl. Perroud*, 2 vols. Paris: Picard et Fils.

Desmoulins, Camille (1836). *Correspondance inédite de Camille Desmoulins, député à la Convention Nationale.* Paris: Ébrard.

Desmoulins, Camille (1874). *Œuvres de Camille Desmoulins.* J. Claretie (ed.). 2 vols, Paris: Charpentier.

Desmoulins, Camille (1987). *Le Vieux Cordelier.* Pierre Pachet (ed.). Alençon: Belin.

Roland, Marie-Jeanne (1966). *Mémoires de Madame Roland.* Paul de Roux (ed.). Paris: Mercure de France.

Wallon, Henri (1880–81). *Histoire du Tribunal révolutionnaire*, 6 vols. Paris: Plon.

Walter, Gérard (ed.) (1968). "La Défense de Barnave transcrite par son avocat." Reproduced in *Actes du Tribunal révolutionnaire, recueillis et commentés par Gérard Walter.* Paris: Mercure de France.

Secondary Sources

Andress David (ed.) (forthcoming). *Experiencing the French Revolution*. Aldershot: Ashgate.

Bradby, Eliza Dorothy (1915). *The Life of Barnave*, 2 vols. Oxford: Clarendon Press.

Burrows, Simon (2003). "The Innocence of Jacques-Pierre Brissot." *HJ*, 46: 843–871.

Campbell, Peter R. (2010). "The Politics of Patriotism in France (1770–1788)." *FH*, 24: 550–575.

Claretie, Jules (1876). *Camille Desmoulins and his Wife: Passages from the History of the Dantonists*, trans. Mrs Cashel Hoey. London: Smith, Elder.

Ellery, Eloise (1915). *Brissot de Warville: A Study in the History of the French Revolution*. Boston: Houghton Mifflin.

Goldstein, Jan (2008). *The Post-Revolutionary Self: Politics and Psyche in France, 1750–1850*. Cambridge, Mass.: Harvard University Press.

Hunt, Lynn (1984). *Politics, Culture, and Class in the French Revolution*. Berkeley: University of California Press.

Hunt, Lynn (2009). "The Experience of Revolution." *FHS*, 32: 671–678.

Linton, Marisa (2001). *The Politics of Virtue in Enlightenment France*. Houndmills: Palgrave.

Linton, Marisa (2007). "'Do You Think That We're Conspirators?" Conspiracies Real and Imagined in Jacobin Politics, 1793–94." In Peter R. Campbell, Thomas E. Kaiser, and Marisa Linton (eds.). *Conspiracy in the French Revolution*. Manchester: Manchester University Press.

Linton, Marisa (2008). "Fatal Friendships: The Politics of Jacobin Friendship." *FHS*, 31: 51–76.

Linton, Marisa (2010). "The Man of Virtue: The Role of Antiquity in the Political Trajectory of L. A. Saint-Just." *FH*, 24: 393–419.

Linton, Marisa (forthcoming). *Choosing Terror: Authentic Identity and Jacobin Politics in the French Revolution*. Oxford: Oxford University Press.

Martin, Jean-Clément (2006). *Violence et révolution: Essais sur la naissance d'un mythe national*. Paris: Seuil.

Reddy, William (2001). *The Navigation of Feeling: A Framework for the History of the Emotions*. Cambridge: Cambridge University Press.

Rosenfeld, Sophia (2009). "Thinking About Feeling, 1789–1799." *FHS*, 32: 697–706.

Shapiro, Barry M. (2009). *Traumatic Politics: The Deputies and the King in the Early French Revolution*. University Park: Pennsylvania State University Press.

Smith, Jay M. (2001). "Between *Discourse* and *Experience*: Agency and Ideas in the French Pre-Revolution." *History and Theory*, 40: 116–142.

Wahnich, Sophie (2003). *La Liberté ou la mort: Essai sur la Terreur et le terrorisme*. Paris: La Fabrique.

Chapter Seventeen

Choosing Revolution and Counter-Revolution

Peter M. Jones

Introduction

Do men and women choose to participate in a revolution, or are they simply swept along by the tide of events? When the *status quo* suddenly changes, is it not those refusing change who exercise the faculty of choice? These bald questions are not often raised by historians; they belong instead to the conspiratorial literature on the French Revolution where agency counts for everything. It is true that some historians have reached the conclusion that a conceptual break with the *ancien régime* occurred in men's minds before the meeting of the Estates-General – initiated perhaps by *abbé* Sieyès' famous pamphlet *What Is the Third Estate?* Finding evidence in support of this argument is difficult, though. Most researchers argue that the events set in motion in 1789 can best be understood as a transformative process in which the French became unintentional actors in their own drama. As Lazare Carnot, who was never very far from the center of the revolutionary stage put it, "one is not born a revolutionary but becomes one" (Garrone 1959: 14).

But if men and women did not become revolutionaries (or counter-revolutionaries) overnight, or even over a period of weeks or months, we are bound to ask how this process started and where it ended. What were the way-stations on the road to political consciousness? Could political choices be made by degrees? And were choices, once made, binding for ever after? We might question, too, the binary character inherent in a process of "choosing" between revolution and counter-revolution. To lump everybody into one camp or the other risks distorting the day-to-day reality of the events unfolding after 1789. Were all the individuals who offered passive resistance to the new regime's unrelenting drive for renewal counter-revolutionaries by definition? By 1793 revolutionary rhetoric had determined that they were, but we should not be so hasty in our judgments.

A Companion to the French Revolution, First Edition. Edited by Peter McPhee.

Historians have long sought to lay bare the process of becoming a revolutionary (Applewhite 1993; Mitchell 1984; Patrick 1972, 1990; Tackett 1996). Becoming a counter-revolutionary, by contrast, has attracted much less research. For reasons that are readily understandable, the historiographical focus tends to be placed on the leaders of the Revolution. Parliamentarians leave external traces of their allegiance, even if it is not always possible to probe effectively the question of motivation as individual choices evolved or shifted under the pressures of events. However, those individuals of the second rank who did not occupy the spotlight, save perhaps in small-town Jacobin clubs, are harder to pin down and label. As for the great mass of ordinary men and women whom historians commonly enlist either on one side or the other, their motivations lie beyond the reach of sustained analysis. We are reduced to plausible conjectures as to why one section of the fledgling French nation might have rallied to the new regime and another might have clung to the old. Parliamentary histories can only take us so far, then. Yet if the evidence of opinion formation at the parliamentary level is interpreted sensitively it does allow us to reach out in the direction of the faceless masses. For the deputies in the revolutionary legislatures dialogued with the nation-at-large. The choices they made, and remade, powerfully influenced the choices made by countless others.

Choosing Revolution

Although it has been suggested – a little mischievously – that the Revolution was a "magnificent irrelevance" for most French people (Cobb 1972: 125), it is unlikely that the majority and the poor in particular, were simply spectators of events, or carried along as passengers. This said we need to be cautious when attempting to construe the politicization of the masses. Researchers disagree about how alert ordinary town and country dwellers were to the possibility of change before 1789. Yet there are grounds for supposing that on the streets of eighteenth-century Paris absolute monarchy was an object of discussion even among the capital's poorest inhabitants (Farge 1994: 123–195, 196–199), and John Markoff (1996: 20) has concluded from his analysis of the *cahiers de doléances* that ordinary country dwellers were likewise capable of "a considerable intellectual grasp of their world."

What is certain is that the interactive face of proto-revolutionary politics soon became apparent. The encounter of Arthur Young with a poor woman on the road to Metz on 12 July 1789 ("*something was to be done by some great folks for such poor ones, but she did not know who nor how*") has often been cited (Young 1900 [1792]: 97), but the riposte of a band of insurgents to the Marquise de Longaunay is perhaps more eloquent. Having carried off her title-deeds and rent rolls, they gave the seigneur a receipt signed "The Nation" (Dwyer and McPhee 2002: 22–23). By the summer of 1789 ordinary people were starting to feel empowered and they were learning, very rapidly, how to express their sense of empowerment in the regenerative language of the Third Estate. Does this mean that they were "choosing" revolution? Not necessarily. If political acculturation was a two-way process, it was also highly malleable, even volatile. Many of the peasant insurrectionaries of 1789 no longer figured in the van of Revolution by 1793; in the west, indeed, a significant number of them were sullenly resisting the new order. Some had even changed sides.

The interactive character of early revolutionary politics is a relatively straightforward matter to document, unlike the shifts in alignment occurring subsequently, which are harder to capture. In the most thorough analysis to date of the "becoming" process, Timothy Tackett (1996) has examined many thousands of letters written by the men who came to Versailles in May 1789 – initially as representative members of the Estates-General and then as deputies to the National Assembly. It is safe to assume that a large proportion of these missives were written for their constituents to read. They therefore shed light both on the outlook of their authors and on the manner in which opinion was shaped in the country at large.

The speed of the transition in Versailles and in Paris during the summer of 1789 left many struggling to keep up after all. The commonplace wisdom that the whole country instantaneously embraced reform on receipt of the news of the fall of the Bastille belongs to the realm of myth. Some deputies, such as Jean-Baptiste Poncet-Delpech, wrote open letters to their constituents (Ligou 1961), whereas others penned missives to friends and family with the recommendation that they be circulated more widely. The marquis de Ferrières, who represented the Second Estate of the *sénéchaussée* of Saumur, urged a correspondent to inform local nobles that it was futile to oppose the changes agreed on the night of 4 August. The parts of his letter that were to be read out to the fief owners of the district were highlighted, as were those parts that were not to be made public (Carré 1932: 113–118). Similarly, Thibaudeau *père* dispatched to the administrators of the department of the Vienne a circumstanced account of the "abduction" of the king and royal family on 22 June 1791. In a follow-up letter he confided to a friend that he had hastened to put pen to paper so as to ensure that "there would be no uncertainty in Poitiers over the key facts" (Carré and Boissonnade 1898: 159). A month or so later he tutored the patriots of his home town on the subject of the split in the Paris Jacobin club, urging a circumspect stance until the outlook became clearer. His advice came too late: the Poitiers Jacobins had already submitted an address in support of the Feuillants.

During the critical transition period of 1789–91 it is clear that many deputies worked tirelessly to secure political compliance, then. Or at least they did their utmost to bridge the expectation gap between Paris and the provinces. As far as possible, dissonant opinion was toned down or filtered out, and the coteries of patriots that had sprung up in nearly every small town were schooled in the rhetoric of national belonging. This "choosing" process was played out for the most part during the eighteen months following the events of the summer of 1789. By the spring of 1791 it is probable that most men and women had managed to stabilize their views on the subject of the Revolution. Thereafter the dynamic grew more complicated as splits developed within the patriot camp, as initial supporters of change dropped from the ranks, and as a constituency came into being that not only objected to further change but sought to turn the clock back. The emergence to prominence from the spring of 1791 of numerous conditioning agencies (such as rural municipalities, National Guard militias, political clubs, and newspapers) was an oblique acknowledgment that the spectrum of political opinion now contained many more gradations than previously.

What of the deputies themselves; how did they choose? The fact that they had all presented themselves for election to the Estates-General implies a predilection for change of some description. No doubt a few visionaries with plans for national regeneration already mapped out in their heads were sent to Versailles, but historians now largely discount the argument that the men who faced down absolute monarchy and then dismantled the *ancien régime* were Rousseauvian intellectuals acting on principle (Baker 1990: 301–305; Furet 1981: 25–46; Hampson 1988: 5–7, 42). A significant minority had recent political experience which they owed for the most part to institutional reforms put in place by the Bourbon monarchy. Indeed, the letter correspondence of deputies indicates that many continued to assume that the kingdom would be rebuilt on the basis of provincial, district, and municipal assemblies even after the transfer of the National Assembly to Paris in the autumn of 1789. And of course they had to work alongside a large cohort of noble deputies; deputies whose ideas of reform, to the dismay of the metropolitan liberal nobility, scarcely extended beyond a fairer tax system.

Despite the seductive mystique of a nation reborn, many deputies in the first revolutionary legislature continued to think of themselves as provincials and as members of either the First, Second, or the Third Estate. Indeed, their initial political orientation often flowed from these sources. The anti-nobilism of Breton Third Estate deputies can be traced back to struggles over membership and tax immunities waged in the Provincial Estates. Several of the most outspoken members of the Third – the Rennes lawyer Le Chapelier is a case in point – came to prominence by this route. Quarrels of a similar type in the Dauphiné and in Provence also generated recruits to the first generation of revolutionary leaders.

On their arrival in Versailles the deputies often clung together in provincial caucuses, groupings which sometimes transcended allegiances by estate. But the challenge of law-making once the National Assembly had assumed the task of drawing up a constitution tended to undermine such pragmatic arrangements. Nevertheless, it can be questioned whether the shift which transformed provincial delegates with a narrow deliberative remit into full-blown "representatives of the nation" occurred as swiftly in men's minds as the historiography of the Revolution might lead us to suppose (Jones 1995: 183–191). Like many deputies, we suspect, Thibaudeau *père* took every opportunity to burnish his localist credentials – whether in smoothing away the rough edges of Parisian demagoguery or in badgering the committees so as to secure a share of the fruits of reform for his own locality. As late as the spring of 1791 he assured the administrators of the Vienne that he saw himself primarily as a delegate, not as a representative: "the first movement of my heartstrings is always for the department and the town which I represent" (Carré and Boissonnade 1898: 139).

With the possible exception of a hard core of deputies drawn from certain well-defined areas of the kingdom, there seems little reason to suppose that the erstwhile Third Estate in the National Assembly was anti-noble from the start. There existed an impatience with former members of the privileged orders whose behavior betrayed a reluctance to pull their weight, but that seems to have been all.

This impatience was not confined to the Third in any case. Sophisticated conservatives such as the marquis de Ferrières and the liberal aristocrats who had orchestrated the bonfire of "privilege" on the night of 4 August felt it as well. Of all the instincts marking out the commoner deputies the most pervasive was probably anticlericalism. Once a large contingent of the lower clergy began to repent their enthusiasm for root-and-branch reform – a process detectable as early as August 1789 when the ecclesiastical tithe nearly ended up on the bonfire – this instinct could be given free rein.

On the issue of monarchy no clear and consistent pattern emerged, whether at the popular or the elite level. Some historians discern a long-term decline in the mystique of monarchy, leading to an erosion of support for kingship (Shapiro 2009: 29–37). However, it is hard to square the contradictory attitudes towards Louis XVI on display during the early years of the Revolution with any such hypothesis. Nobles remained extraordinarily attached to the person of the monarch, whether in 1789 or in the midst of deposition crisis of 1792; this much is certain. But ordinary people blew hot and cold, and so did the deputies. The marquis de Sillery, who witnessed Louis XVI's entry to Paris three days after the taking of the Bastille, reported that the monarch was greeted by an armed populace shouting "Long Live the Nation; Long Live our Courageous Deputies" (Vaissière 1907: 63), but nothing more. Nearly two years later, when Louis and his queen returned to the capital under armed escort after the flight to Varennes, the Parisians neither greeted him nor took off their hats. Yet the king's formal acceptance of the constitution only three months later unleashed a huge emotional outpouring across the land. Madame Lepoutre, wife of an obscure commoner deputy from Flanders, told her husband that she had wept on hearing the news. Clearly, all parties badly wanted to believe in the good faith of the monarch. After the king appeared to give his blessing to the work of the National Assembly on 5 February 1790, Lepoutre wrote to his wife, "I regard yesterday as one of the finest of my life." He instructed her to read out the king's speech to the servants and serve them beer to drink his health (Jessenne and Lemay 1998: 189).

Noble deputies first expressed serious misgivings at the train of events in the aftermath of the 4 August session – even though members of their own order had been heavily involved in setting the agenda for the debate. But many Third Estate deputies concluded that the wholesale destruction of the *ancien régime* had been a step too far as well. They spent the next six months trying to unpick the legislation and neutralize the impact of the abolition of feudalized property rights. However, all sources appear to be in agreement that it was the passing on 19 June 1790 of an unanticipated measure to abolish hereditary nobility and all honorific titles that caused many members of the old Second Estates to wonder whether they had a role to play in the new regime. The marquis de Ferrières worried that nobles were being depicted as enemies of the Revolution, but he counseled against resistance on the ground that it might trigger a fresh wave of attacks on chateaux. Mirabeau correctly predicted that the passing of the law would lead to deeper divisions within the National Assembly (Bacourt 1851: vol. 2, 38–39). The abolition of noble status, together with the refusal of the deputies to acknowledge that the Catholic Church was anything more than the "religion of the majority of Frenchmen"

(Tackett 1996: 267–272) were probably the two legislative measures of 1790 that did most to catalyze educated opinion and to signpost a parting of the ways between the Third and the former privileged orders.

At less exalted levels more mundane concerns held sway. Sometime in February 1789 a nameless Parisian laborer came home from work and spent an hour writing out a petition to complain about the cost of living which he then carried off to the printers. The arcane debate about taxes and who should pay them was of little moment, he declared, "I want to deal with a subject which interests me and people like me much more, namely the diminution [in price] of bread" (*Réflexions* 1789: 3). He went on to describe how his family consumed 6 *livres* of bread each day which cost 22½ *sols* to purchase, leaving just 13½ *sols* from his daily wage for all other necessities. He was assuredly not alone in calibrating his adhesion to the Revolution in material terms. Provinces that had enjoyed significant exemptions (from state taxes), or privileges under the *ancien régime* faced a particular problem in this respect. By the end of the first year of revolution Pierre-François Lepoutre was deploring the lack of "patriotism" of his native Flanders as the local population weighed up the economic cost of regeneration in the name of the nation (Jessenne and Lemay 1998: 153–155). Bretons faced a similar dilemma. So sensitive was the issue of giving up their provincial rights and privileges that the deputies of the *sénéchaussée* of Nantes organized what amounted to a referendum in order to secure a mandate for the painful pecuniary sacrifices that lay ahead. The results provide a fascinating snapshot of the choosing process. Some parishes were clearly following debates in the National Assembly very closely and displayed considerable political acumen, but others were unprepared for the changes that were now being contemplated. In the minds of the parishioners of Sainte-Luce, the privileges of the province were not privileges at all but a species of property sanctified by the treaties that had united Brittany to France in the early sixteenth century (Archives Départementales, Loire-Atlantique 2Mi25).

All rhetoric aside, there is no doubt that cutting loose from the *ancien régime* could seriously damage one's wealth. But adhesion to the new regime carried cost–benefit implications as well. The livelihood of whole towns (Dijon and Toulouse are good examples) depended on the dispensing of administrative and legal services before 1789, and many of these localities would be cruelly exposed by the reforms of the National Assembly. In the vicinity of Paris at least fifteen towns competed for the status of department seats in a region that could scarcely accommodate more than four units of local government (Margadant 1992: 254). The rivalry between Soissons and Laon for the dignity of *chef-lieu* reached epic proportions; indeed there are grounds for supposing that urban rivalries to the northeast of Paris played an instrumental role during the elections to the Estates-General. Laon seems to have carried the day because parish delegates were deeply suspicious of the entrepôt function of Soissons in the capital's elaborate provisioning network. At a less exalted level the competition between the towns of Guise and Vervins almost descended into physical conflict in the spring of 1790. It is significant that Vervins, having emerged victorious in the contest for administrative power in the new department of the Aisne, displayed exemplary patriotism throughout the decade whereas Guise retreated into disdainful conservatism.

The federalist episode in the summer of 1793 exposed these faultlines afresh. Soissons tried to tar Laon with the brush of disloyalty to the Jacobin-dominated Convention, which thrust the Laonnais onto the defensive. Embarrassed by their political misjudgment in supporting Lafayette's call for the closure of the Paris Jacobin Club and legislative action against the sections a year or so earlier, the departmental administrators went out of their way to parade the patriotism of the town. In Laon the ballot on the Constitution of 1793 produced a near-unanimous turnout which included a contingent of 132 women voters (Brassart 2007: 21, 56–63, 137–152). In Marseille, by contrast, the Revolution was welcomed first and foremost as an opportunity to escape the political tutelage of nearby Aix-en-Provence. The merchant elite hailed the collapse of absolute monarchy as a vindication of utilitarian values which they had long espoused and they set out to stage-manage the elections to the Estates-General. When in February 1790 the first new-regime municipality was installed, over half the members turned out to be merchants.

Within a space of twenty-four hours, both Thibaudeau *père* and the marquis de Ferrières condemned the news that Poitiers would not after all become the seat of a major law court. No one anywhere, it transpired, was going to profit from the destruction of the *parlements.* This reminds us that in its first flush the Revolution left many disappointed parties and losers in its wake, whereas the future beneficiaries were far from immediately identifiable. Ferrières predicted that abolition of the plethora of minor legal jurisdictions would "plunge a multitude of ordinary families into a state of desolation" (Carré 1932: 287). He was right, for the new regime set its face firmly against corporate bodies of any description. The *procureurs* (attorneys) who had often bought their practices at some expense were among the first to go. They were followed, in 1791, by a host of minor customs officials whose services were no longer required following the abolition of excise duties on goods entering Paris and other major cities. "That puts 20,000 clerks out on the street," reported the marquis de Mesmon in a letter which also claimed that legislators had "ruined" many master-craftsmen by abolishing the guilds, thereby adding to the ranks of the discontented (Vaissière 1907: 267). All too often professional solidarities ensured that the numbers of those with grounds for dissatisfaction with the new regime rippled far and wide. In Toulouse the barristers sided with the magistrates of the local *parlement* and moved with them into the camp of opposition. It was the liberal nobles and prelates of Languedoc who had led the charge against absolute monarchy rather than the Third Estate.

The well-founded suspicion that many deputies regretted their enthusiasm for the abolition of seigneurialism on the night of 4 August kept large sections of the rural population on an active footing. Peasant insurrectionism, indeed, could produce some strange bedfellows. Bourgeois landowners were not always as scrupulous about mobilizing on the side of law and order as they would be later on in the Revolution, and it is even possible to find maverick nobles playing leadership roles. An inquest into peasant disturbances in the Lot department at the latter end of 1790 uncovered the fact that the invasion of the town of Gourdon had been spearheaded by a career soldier who had fought in America, the comte Joseph de Linars. Dissatisfied at the slow pace of promotion under the *ancien régime*, Linars flung himself into the movement for reform, becoming successively mayor of his village and commander of its National Guard. It was in this capacity that he put himself at the head of a formidable squadron of 4,500 peasant insurgents (*Rapport* 1790).

Yet by the summer of 1792 the winning and the losing constituencies in the countryside appeared more sharply etched. In Brittany, it has been suggested, poorer tenant farmers were coming to the conclusion that their material needs were not likely to be met and were moving into the camp of opposition (Hutt 1983: vol. 1, 9–11; Le Goff and Sutherland 1983: 65–87). However, in the southwest and the center sharecroppers kept faith with the Revolution by and large – in the belief no doubt that the deputies would eventually get round to land and tenure reform (Jones 1988: 77; Vovelle 1993: 293). The research of Claude Petitfrère (1979, 1988) on the west, where a mobilization possessing the characteristics of a civil war was in gestation, does reveal a polarizing countryside though. Those who had done well out of three years of revolutionary change and who were not unduly perturbed by the strident anticlericalism of legislators in Paris confronted a great mass of country dwellers who felt they had done rather badly in the division of the spoils. The rural bourgeoisie, whose stamina for change was sustained by the chance to buy church property at auction, decisively nailed their colors to the mast of revolution. So did the townspeople of Anjou and the Vendée, along with many craft outworkers whose occupations involved contact with urban markets and consumers.

Typical of the latter was Louis Simon (Fillon 1996), a muslin weaver with a bit of land who also carried on a modest trade in wine. As the only literate commoner inhabitant of the village of La Fontaine-Saint-Martin, it was perhaps inevitable that he should be elected syndic in the wake of the monarchy's short-lived reforms to widen the basis of consent to taxation. Thereafter the die was cast. Simon was prevailed upon to draw up the parish *cahier de doléances* and to carry it to Le Mans. The following year he became the first mayor. Whether by virtue of his several occupations and contacts or his administrative apprenticeship, he was now linked inextricably to the fortunes of the new regime. When the Vendéan army passed through his commune in December 1793, he went into the forest to hide. For understandable reasons, those who were preparing to resist further revolutionary intrusions counted few such men in their ranks. There were few bourgeois either. Antagonized by the Civil Constitution of the Clergy, the clerical oath and insensitive administrative schemes to amalgamate parishes, the peasantry of the west began to regret their earlier support for change. Whilst the majority seem to have refrained from any explicit declaration of allegiance for or against the Revolution, a significant minority were now in a mood to rebel.

In France's tropical colonies the issues were rather different, but just as thorny. The option of "choosing" revolution was available initially only to the free white population of the Caribbean islands. Neither the mulattoes (*gens de couleur*), nor the enslaved majority who were of African descent were considered to be participating members of the regenerated nation. When in September 1789 a vessel arrived in Guadeloupe bearing news of events in the metropole, the colonial authorities were thrown into confusion as the townspeople of Pointe-à-Pitre donned the red, white, and blue cockade. After some hesitation, it was decided that the mulattoes would not be prevented from wearing this emblem of liberty, but the governor warned of severe penalties if the slave population were to follow suit. The white plantation owners meanwhile procrastinated in the face of the invitation to cut adrift from the *ancien régime*. A campaign by mulattoes to widen the definition of citizenship was fought throughout 1790 and the year following, but it produced contradictory results in Paris. Not until 1792 were they welcomed into the nation's warm embrace. Too late, for by this time a massive slave rebellion had started in Saint-Domingue and the colonial revolution was degenerating into a civil war.

The chronic inability of the deputies to resolve the issue of citizenship in the colonies reminds us of the fluidity of political options during these early years. Not until the king had given his assent to the constitution was there a clear perception shared by all that a revolution had happened and was now irreversible. It follows that the men who came to power in the autumn of 1791, whether at the national or the local level, were individuals with a sense of commitment. They had chosen, to all intents and purposes. After all they were a self-selected group who had served an apprenticeship to the cause, either as department and district administrators, civil court judges, justices of the peace, or constitutional clergymen. The country had chosen, too, and in most regions it had endorsed the changes carried through since 1789. The evidence of popular reactions to the flight of the king is unmistakable in this regard. Mercy-Argenteau spoke true when he warned the fleeing royal couple that the Revolution had worked a shift in the mentality of ordinary people: "every village could be an insurmountable barrier to your passage" (Tackett 2003: 86). With the installation of the Legislative Assembly in October 1791, the terms of the debate changed, then. The world of orders and estates had now lost its purchase on men's minds. Deputies no longer ruminated on choices made, but rather on how far their capacity for change would take them in the years to come.

Choosing Counter-Revolution

The Flanders deputy Pierre-François Lepoutre mentioned counter-revolution in his letters home for the first time in April 1790 and the marquis de Ferrières did the same a month or two later. Yet it is worth emphasizing that there was no political project in existence from the beginning to purge the body of the nation of those who could not, or would not, keep in step. It is probable in other words that nobles and clergymen could have remained a part of the popular front which launched the Revolution had they wished to do so. Although William Doyle has suggested that the explosion of 1789 was "anti-noble almost from the start" (Carpenter and Mansell 1999: xv), it does not seem that overweaning hostility to the formerly privileged orders was an original characteristic of the French Revolution. It evolved. The National Assembly did not pass any legislation against *émigrés*. On the contrary, the deputies acknowledged the right of free movement – even when it was invoked by individuals closely linked to the royal family. Or at least they did so in theory, for after October 1789 neither the king nor the queen was able to leave Paris without permission. Ferrières and deputies like him, moreover, displayed an increasing reluctance to quit the capital for rest and recuperation lest their temporary absence be misconstrued.

So what went wrong? A case can be made that noble and clerical deputies led the way by choosing to opt out and, in so doing, allowing revolutionary politics to proceed in a direction that was detrimental to their interests. After all, on paper, conservative-minded deputies enjoyed a clear numerical advantage in the National Assembly. However they tended to absent themselves from debates in worryingly large numbers, with the result that their leaders found it difficult to command a majority when important motions came up for debate. The marquis de Ferrières, who never missed a session, came close to blaming his own "side" for the defeat on the issue of noble titles (19 June 1790). He noted that several members of the "right wing" actually withdrew in disdain rather than staying to vote (Carré 1932: 206, 214–215). Over the next fifteen months or so, nearly 20 percent of formerly noble deputies abandoned the parliamentary arena (Tackett 1996: 295). This phenomenon of withdrawal was confirmed by the comte de La Marck who observed in a letter to the Austrian ambassador that the ascendancy of the "patriots" was far from solidly rooted. On issues unrelated to the clergy their domination was precarious, so much so that "if the right wing did not have two hundred members missing roles might very well change" (Bacourt 1851: vol. 3, 70).

But were absenteeism and mounting disenchantment at the train of events the inevitable precursors to emigration and counter-revolution? Although he did not himself emigrate or even retire from Paris, Ferrières provides us with a running commentary on kinsmen and fellow members of the Poitou delegation who were planning to leave the country. The picture he paints scarcely conforms to the stereotypical image of a massive, homogeneous, and definitive exodus motivated by uncompromising ideological hostility to the Revolution. Research in this area is not well developed, though. It tends to focus on the arrival and sojourn of *émigrés* in foreign capitals – by which point the hesitations that were intrinsic to the project of political emigration had mostly been overcome. Nevertheless, it seems clear that expatriation was more of a dribble than a flood. Individuals left at irregular intervals and usually did so with the intention of returning after a few months. Having joined the first wave of departing court nobles, who mostly exited the kingdom within hours or days of the taking of the Bastille, the prince de Conti returned to Paris in April 1790. He presented himself to the king, took a civic oath, and donated 2000 *livres* to the poor, prompting a widespread expectation that all of the "fugitifs" would soon return (Lescure 1866: 438).

More chose to leave in 1791. With an employment crisis developing in Paris, a rumor went round that between 500 and 600 well-to-do families had left the capital after Holy Week – perhaps in reaction to the disturbances at the Tuileries which had deterred the king from going to the palace of Saint-Cloud. Most were said to have headed for the borders (Vaissière 1907: 399–400). Further departures occurred after the abortive flight and, perhaps more surprisingly, after the king's acceptance of the constitution and the dissolution of the National Assembly. Yet it is far from clear that in any of these cases a conscious decision to enlist in the ranks of the counter-revolution was involved. Former nobles and clergymen felt vulnerable, particularly during the summer when war seemed a real possibility, and they sought safety outside the kingdom and beyond the reach of reprisals. Many of the ex-nobles were military men, which occasioned a great deal of soul-searching since the officer corps had initially welcomed the Revolution (Blaufarb 2002: 88). Ferrières also reminds us that many departed under duress, or, at the very least, in a state of emotional turmoil – a prey to impulses of honor, pride, and perhaps shame. Despairing of the old Second Estate, he wrote to his wife, "emigration continues; noblemen arrive here and from here set out, often against their better judgment, but like idiots they have given undertakings, and there is no shortage of people here who are egging them on; they are given to believe that to retreat would be shameful" (Carré 1932: 431).

Outright counter-revolution waited on the moves towards European war and, in the west, on the mishandling of the campaign to replenish the armies with new recruits. Before 1793 it is hard to find evidence of counter-revolutionary actions as opposed to intentions. There were a few plots by isolated noblemen and, in the south of the country, mobilizations in defense of religion took place as the Legislative Assembly pushed ahead with the anticlerical agenda, that is to say the reforms enshrined in the Civil Constitution of the Clergy. Disaffected nobles and priests did their best to fish in these troubled waters. But the struggle to escape the grip of the feudal regime was not yet over. Most country dwellers were not prepared to push their dissatisfaction with the regime beyond a vaguely anti-revolutionary stance – despite anxieties over the closure of monasteries and dismay at the departure of familiar parish priests.

We may question, too, the motivations of the putative leaders of counter-revolution. For those who fled abroad and remained abroad, the issues were relatively straightforward, or they soon became so. Even if they had left the kingdom with mixed feelings the logic of their situation spawned political intransigence, particularly once boatloads of fleeing priests began to disembark on the coasts of England and the Channel Isles in the wake of the September 1792 prison massacres. But for the internal leaders of the opposition, "counter-revolutionary" scarcely seems an apt description. At best it telescopes a number of possible stances and denies the transformative character of the politics which the French Revolution was in the throes of creating. At worst it brackets all dissidents together using a label invented by their opponents.

The career of the noble Joseph de Puisaye, who emerged to head the Breton *chouannerie*, will illustrate this point (Hutt 1983: vol. 1, 23–97). He served a political apprenticeship in the district assembly of Mortagne, which would scarcely have distinguished him politically from the future "triumvir" leaders of the National Assembly. Indeed, he would go on to support moderate constitutional monarchy as a Second Estate delegate from the Perche to the Estates-General. Unable to continue his parliamentary career following the promulgation of the Constitution of 1791, Puisaye dropped out of sight, only to offer himself for election to the Convention a year or so later. Although he was not successful in his bid to re-enter national politics, he seems to have shared the distaste of many at the rise of Paris radicalism. It was this distaste that pushed him into the arms of the Norman federalists in the summer of 1793, although at this juncture he appears to have been more a Fayettiste in outlook than a royalist conspirator. At any event he fled into Brittany, where his visceral anti-Jacobinism was transmuted into militant royalism. When the Vendéan army succeeded in crossing the Loire in October Puisaye offered a military alliance, claiming that he commanded a substantial partisan force in the neighborhood of Rennes which he dubbed the "organisation provisoire de royalistes de la forêt du Pertre."

The Breton *chouannerie* posed an intermittent challenge to the power of the Republic in the West for a number of years. But was it a counter-revolutionary movement? British agents who were seeking to widen the maritime struggle against revolutionary France by instigating revolt in the interior persuaded themselves that it was. Yet this is to misunderstand the protean nature of the rural mobilizations we have touched upon in this chapter. Rather than opting for counter-revolution as such, it appears more likely that the Breton *chouans* were signaling their determination to refuse further installments of intrusive change. By this date those who wished, or who felt obliged, to "choose" had mostly done so in any case. Whether as a practical proposition or a rhetorical construct, the middle ground had dropped out of revolutionary politics.

The last two "choosing" moments followed in swift succession and they admitted of no ambiguity. In September 1792 the new legislature declared France a republic, and a couple of months later a vote was won to put the imprisoned ex-monarch on public trial. Louis Louchet, who had been dispatched to the Convention by the electors of the Aveyron, cheerfully reported that the towns through which he had passed on his way to Paris were all keenly anticipating the break with monarchy. Another well-placed source announced that the motion to establish the republic had passed on the floor of the Convention in fifteen minutes flat and without opposition. In reality many of the provincial deputies had yet to arrive in the capital (Ruault 1976: 314). Within a matter of days, however, Louchet was grumbling in a letter to the Jacobins of Rodez that the abolition of the monarchy had elicited nothing but silence from the authorities of his home department. "It is not enough simply to approve in the critical circumstances in which we find public affairs, it is necessary to manifest approval," he admonished (Combes de Patris 1912: 171). The times had changed, in other words: choices made must now be seen to have been made. A docile conformism was taking over from the interactive politics which had been the salvation of the early Revolution. That autumn local government elections enabled voters all over the country to take stock of what had happened in Paris. The outcome can scarcely have been to Louchet's satisfaction for the news of the execution of Louis Capet, ex-monarch, some three months later was again received in Rodez with deafening silence.

Conclusion

One final issue invites a comment. Were the choices made by a generation in possession of unprecedented freedom of expression steadfastly adhered to thereafter? It seems unlikely, if only for the reason that political awareness and commitment do not usually survive intact for an entire lifetime even in the most conducive settings. The building contractor Pierre-François Palloy, who fashioned a career as a patriot out of the demolition of the Bastille by his workmen, recorded in his journal that on the evening of the execution of "the last king of the French" (21 January 1793) he sat down with his family to a meal of stuffed pig's head (Romi 1956: 199). But times change and so did Palloy. In 1814 the man who had ordered a medallion to be struck to celebrate the fall of Robespierre received in his turn a decoration – from the Bourbons. The irony of the situation was not lost on him for he noted, "where now are the days of the stuffed pig's head? What stupidities youthfulness causes even the best of citizens to commit" (Romi 1956: 261). Yet allegiances forged during formative years of the French Revolution patently could persist. We know, for instance, that Jacobinism did not completely wither and die in the bleak years following the Terror. Its cadres remained active and fairly influential in both national and local politics throughout the Directory years (Gainot 2001). Indeed, in towns such as Toulouse (Fournier 1998), they survived as a political force until the time of the Bourbon Restoration.

Modern historians have often attributed the explosive energy of the French Revolution to an enduring struggle between the forces of revolution and those of counter-revolution (Sutherland 2003). This essay has taken a rather different tack and emphasized the fluid and contingent character of the politics which France gave birth to in 1789. But there can be no denying that the search for explanations of individual motivation also brings to light significant continuities. In some parts of the country the very phenomenon of revolution gestated its own traditions. By 1800 the political geography of the Vendée and the *chouan* districts of Brittany had settled into a pattern that would endure for decades to come. By contrast, the south of the country was neither consistently for nor consistently against revolution, yet here, too, evidence of extraordinarily tenacious political loyalties can be found. In southern upland regions revolution played the role of catalyst, converting territorial rivalries, kin loyalties, and sharply etched confessional differences into enduring political alignments. Southern Protestants are a good example. They chose revolution in the same breath as they repudiated an *ancien régime* which had dispossessed and persecuted them.

References

Applewhite, Harriet B. (1993). *Political Alignments in the French National Assembly, 1789–1791.* Baton Rouge: Louisiana State University Press.

Archives Départementales, Loire-Atlantique 2Mi25.

Bacourt, Adolphe de (ed.) (1851). *Correspondance entre le Comte de Mirabeau et le Comte de La Marck pendant les années 1789, 1790 et 1791*, 3 vols. Paris: Veuve Le Normant.

Baker, Keith M. (1990). *Inventing the French Revolution.* Cambridge: Cambridge University Press.

Blaufarb, Rafe (2002). *The French Army, 1750–1820: Careers, Talent, Merit.* Manchester: Manchester University Press.

Brassart, Laurent (2007). "La République à l'épreuve de l'ordinaire et de l'exception: État-Nation, pouvoirs locaux et comportements collectifs dans le département de l'Aisne, 1792–1795." Doctoral thesis. Université Charles de Gaulle-Lille 3.

Carpenter, Kirsty and Philip Mansell (eds.) (1999). *The French Émigrés in Europe and the Struggle against the Revolution, 1789–1814.* Basingstoke: Macmillan.

Carré, Henri (ed.) (1932). *Marquis de Ferrières, député de la noblesse aux États-Généraux: Correspondance inédite, 1789, 1790, 1791.* Paris: Armand Colin.

Carré, Henri and Pierre Boissonnade (eds.) (1898). *Correspondance inédite du Constituant Thibaudeau, 1789–1791.* Paris: H. Champion.

Cobb, Richard C. (1972). *Reactions to the French Revolution.* Oxford: Oxford University Press.

Combes de Patris, Bernard (ed.) (1912). *Procès-verbaux des séances de la Société populaire de Rodez.* Rodez: Carrère.

Dwyer, Philip G. and Peter McPhee (2002). *The French Revolution and Napoleon: A Sourcebook.* London and New York: Routledge.

Farge, Arlette (1994). *Subversive Words: Public Opinion in Eighteenth-Century France.* Oxford: Polity Press.

Fillon, Anne (1996). *Louis Simon villageois de l'ancienne France.* Rennes: Éditions Ouest-France.

Fournier, Georges (1998). "La Longue Survie du jacobinisme toulousain du Directoire à la Restauration." In Christine Le Bozec and Éric Wauters (eds.). *Pour la Révolution française: Hommage à Claude Mazauric.* Rouen: Publications de l'Université de Rouen. 365–370.

Furet, François (1981). *Interpreting the French Revolution.* Cambridge: Cambridge University Press.

Gainot, Bernard (2001). *1799, un nouveau Jacobinisme? La Démocratie représentative, une alternative à Brumaire.* Paris: CTHS.

Garrone, Galante (1959). *Gilbert Romme: Storia di un revoluzionario.* Turin: Einaudi.

Hampson, Norman (1988). *Prelude to Terror: The Constituent Assembly and the Failure of Consensus.* Oxford: Basil Blackwell.

Hutt, Maurice (1983). *Chouannerie and Counter-Revolution: Puisaye, the Princes and the British Government in the 1790s,* 2 vols. Cambridge: Cambridge University Press.

Jessenne, Jean-Pierre and Edna H. Lemay (eds.) (1998). *Député-paysan et fermière de Flandre en 1789: La Correspondance des Lepoutre.* Villeneuve d'Ascq: Université Charles de Gaulle-Lille 3.

Jones, Peter M. (1980). "Political Commitment and Rural Society in the Southern Massif-Central." *European Studies Review,* 10: 337–356.

Jones, Peter M. (1988). *The Peasantry in the French Revolution.* Cambridge: Cambridge University Press.

Jones, Peter M. (1995). *Reform and Revolution in France: The Politics of Transition, 1774–1791.* Cambridge: Cambridge University Press.

Le Goff, Timothy and Donald Sutherland (1983). "The Social Origins of Counter-Revolution in Western France." *P&P,* 99: 65–87.

Lescure, Mathurin de (1866). *Correspondance secrète, inédite sur Louis XVI, Marie-Antoinette, la Cour et la ville de 1777 à 1792.* Paris: Plon.

Ligou, Daniel (1961). *La Première Année de la Révolution vue par un témoin (1789–1790): Les "Bulletins" de Poncet-Delpech, député du Quercy aux États-généraux de 1789.* Paris: PUF.

Margadant, Ted W. (1992). *Urban Rivalries in the French Revolution.* Princeton, N.J.: Princeton University Press.

Markoff, John (1996). *The Abolition of Feudalism: Peasants, Lords and Legislators in the French Revolution.* University Park: Pennsylvania State University Press.

Mitchell, C.J. (1984). "Political Divisions within the Legislative Assembly of 1791." *FHS,* 13: 356–389.

Patrick, Alison (1972). *The Men of the First French Republic: Political Alignments in the National Convention of 1792.* Baltimore, Md.: Johns Hopkins University Press.

Patrick, Alison (1990). "The Second Estate in the Constituent Assembly, 1789–1791." *JMH,* 62: 223–252.

Petitfrère, Claude (1979). *Blancs et bleus d'Anjou, 1789–1793,* 2 vols. Paris: Atelier de Reproduction des Thèses, Université de Lille 3.

Petitfrère, Claude (1988). "The Origins of the Civil War in the Vendée." *FH,* 2: 187–207.

Rapport de messieurs J. Godard et L. Robin, commissaires civils envoyés par le Roi, dans le département du Lot, en exécution du Décret de l'Assemblée Nationale, le 13 Décembre 1790. Paris: Imprimerie Nationale.

Réflexions d'un ouvrier sur le rencherissement du pain. Le premier février 1789.

Romi [Robert Miquel] (1956). *Livre de raison du patriote Palloy.* Paris: Éditions de Paris.

Ruault, Nicolas (1976). *Gazette d'un Parisien sous la Révolution: Lettres à son frère 1783–1796.* Paris: Perrin.

Shapiro, Barry M. (2009). *Traumatic Politics: The Deputies and the King in the Early French Revolution.* University Park: Pennsylvania University Press.

Sutherland, Donald M.G. (2003). *The French Revolution and the Empire: The Quest for a Civic Order.* Malden, Mass.: Blackwell Publishing.

Tackett, Timothy (1996). *Becoming a Revolutionary: The Deputies of the French National Assembly and the Emergence of a Revolutionary Culture, 1789–1790.* Princeton, N.J.: Princeton University Press.

Tackett, Timothy (2003). *When the King Took Flight.* Cambridge, Mass.: Harvard University Press.

Vaissière, Pierre de (1907). *Lettres d'"aristocrates": La Révolution racontée par des correspondances privées, 1789–1794.* Paris: Perrin.

Vovelle, Michel (1993). *La Découverte de la politique: Géopolitique de la Révolution française.* Paris: La Découverte.

Young, Arthur (1900 [1792]). *Travels in France during the Years 1787, 1788, 1789.* Betham-Edwards edn. London: George Bell & Sons.

CHAPTER EIGHTEEN

The Course of the Terror, 1793–94

DAVID ANDRESS

In one very clear sense, the course of "the Terror" is starkly defined. A tightening spiral of repression, persecution, and the pursuit of ideological purity, ending with an accelerating procession of innocents to the guillotine, it is one of the archetypal modern examples of fanatical intolerance. At the time, it evoked comparison with the legendary excesses of the Roman emperors and the furies of the post-Reformation religious wars. In hindsight, it has often seemed to foreshadow – sometimes very directly – the merciless and wide-scale application of terror as a political weapon in the Soviet Union and elsewhere.

Such a clear picture, however, is misleading. Analogies and comparisons, especially those imposed in hindsight, or used to model later events, are more likely to obscure the reality of a historical period than to enlighten us. Unlike seventeenth-century Puritans or Russian Bolsheviks, the men who led France into Terror had no longstanding commitment to a fiercely partisan ideology. They had views which in the cold light of history were extreme – and acted on them in ways that we may find unpardonable – but such views and deeds emerged from a complex cultural heritage, and were refracted through the short, intense, and traumatic political tradition of the Revolution itself.

In the months of 1793 and 1794 that are at the heart of this period, many of those views and deeds intensified in ways which even the leaders of the Revolution had not foreseen. Understanding the complexity of the situation that brought this about should not diminish the awfulness of what did take place, but it should distinguish it from a pattern of mythology and demonization that began, extraordinarily, even before the Terror itself, and which particularly in its immediate aftermath was more concerned with scapegoating than justice.

A Companion to the French Revolution, First Edition. Edited by Peter McPhee.

When Does "the Terror" Begin?

For those hostile to the Revolution and all its works, there was no real dividing-line between political upheaval and all the excesses of "Terror." In 1790, the Anglo-Irish politician Edmund Burke described events that had already taken place in France in tones which suggested that massacre and mob rule were already the norm, and total anarchy shortly to arrive. Aristocratic enemies of the Revolution, present and active in politics, made little distinction between occasional violence with local and factional causes, and a general subversion of all order. The overthrow of the monarchy in August 1792 was heralded in apocalyptic tones that made the subsequent September Massacres a natural focus for legends of torture and depravity, completely overshadowing the horrible, but rather businesslike, quasi-judicial execution of over 1,000 people that did take place (Andress 2005: 5, 93–112).

Historians have not hesitated to roll Revolution and Terror together. Keith Michael Baker (1990: 305) declared that political choices made in 1789 meant that revolutionaries were "opting for the Terror," while Simon Schama (1989: xv) noted that "violence *was* the Revolution," and Terror its natural end-point. In the same year, J.F. Bosher declared in his own survey of the Revolution that "The Terror ... began on Friday, 10 August 1792." It was, according to him "based on the violence of the populace, led mainly by educated leaders who approved of popular violence on ideological grounds," and from that date all their enemies were facing "sudden death or the threat of it" (Bosher 1989: 178). Yet if "the populace," a phrase which echoes a dismissive eighteenth-century French term not far short of calling them "rabble," was so imbued with violence, why did this not erupt decisively until (as was the case on 10 August) enemy troops were well inside the national frontiers, and radical activists had decided to topple the monarchy to save the nation from its own treacherous leaders?

George Kelly (1980) offers a useful account of how multiple senses of the word "terror" wove through politics and culture before and during the Revolution. However, there is no "real" starting-point for "the Terror," because that label was only ever available in hindsight, and because the various identifiable elements of what we call "the Terror" were assembled gradually, partly from a repertoire of concerns and responses bred out of previous revolutionary experience, and partly out of a series of dramatic and potentially catastrophic new developments with consequences that required drastic new action. One of those concerns was with counter-revolution, and one response to that threat was, as it had been since the storming of the Bastille itself, relatively spontaneous and "popular" violence. Yet the tale of the Revolution was of violence from both sides – for the lynchings of 1789, there was the counterpoint of the massacre of military mutineers at Nancy in 1790, and of antiroyalist protestors in the heart of Paris in July 1791; in the south, there were episodes at Nîmes, Montauban, and Avignon that confronted "revolutionaries" with a potent mix of Catholicism and traditionalism, rolled up with a real presence of aristocratic agents of subversion, and exploding into mutual slaughter (Andress 2004: 113ff.).

Such confusion was not confined to the towns, either. In the years before the fall of the monarchy, there was no telling which region would be hit next by widespread rural protests – sometimes against aristocrats intent on continuing to claim their feudal dues, but sometimes against revolutionary authorities trying to enforce new tax policies, or (bitterest of all) install priests obedient to the new order (Andress 2004: 137–142). All of this was common knowledge, spread by a fulminating press, and by repeated efforts at official intervention to mediate or impose order. When a real external war against Austria and Prussia was layered atop this from the spring of 1792, the strains on the attempt to maintain social peace in a constitutional monarchy – especially a monarchy with a monarch regarded by many as a traitor – became simply unbearable.

"The Terror," taken analytically, must therefore be more than just the outbreak of violence, because violent confrontations were endemic to this period (though not in the one-sided fashion that Schama and others propose). The process of the emergence of "the Terror" is a process of the gradual acceptance by the political elite that extraordinary measures were needed for institutional survival, the steady implementation of more extreme versions of such measures, and the gathering implosion of revolutionary political culture under the weight of their consequences. In some ways, any brief summary of its course will be fatally incomplete, and a full narrative treatment – whether classic (Palmer 1941) or modern (Andress 2005) – will always give a more subtle picture.

The Vendée, Conscription, and Extraordinary Measures

Some of the first acts that pointed clearly towards a "terrorist" future came in the early spring of 1793, in the aftermath of the execution of Louis XVI, and as politicians, convinced of the international nature of the threat they faced, expanded the war to encompass Britain, Holland, Spain, and the Italian states. A key moment came at the end of February with the systematization of conscription to bring a further 300,000 men into the armies. News of this, striking regions of the west particularly aggrieved over changes to taxation, rents, and the church, fomented riots that became uprisings, and within weeks a major insurrectionary threat to the Revolution in the name of throne and altar.

Histories of this "Vendéan Revolt" have been dramatically partisan ever since, not least because the responses it occasioned were so extreme. Authors such as Jean-Clément Martin (2001, 2006) have struggled to bring balance to Francophone treatments of the topic, and many accounts (Gérard 1999) retain an air of grievance – often justified to all appearances by the atrocities they relate. Some (such as Secher 2003 [1986]) have gone so far as to call the conflict a genocide. Anglophone authors have largely steered clear of the core disputes here, though Gough (1987) offers a clear summary of their tortuous nature. What has become clearer in the last generation is the cultural origins of the conflict that erupted, demonstrating that it was deeply tied to the patterns of landholding and community structure, within which revolutionary demands were experienced as alien and harmful (Le Goff and Sutherland 1983; Petitfrère 1988).

With echoes of rebellion across other provinces, the National Convention created a raft of policies that took politics outside the bounds of normality. At the basic level, "surveillance committees" were created in every community, empowered to arrest suspicious individuals, and to grant (or withhold) "civic certificates" that soon became a necessity for work and travel. From the top down, members of the Convention were anointed as "representatives on mission," to be sent out across the country, initially particularly to rally recruitment, but eventually to interfere in all aspects of economic and political life, and to be granted literally unlimited powers (Biard 2002). Those like the Vendéans declared to be "rebels in arms" were condemned to summary execution, while at the center, a Revolutionary Tribunal was created in Paris to judge counter-revolutionary crimes.

In the debate on this, the orator Georges-Jacques Danton raised the image of Terror, proclaiming "Let us be terrible, so that the people does not have to be" (Wahnich 2003: 62). He was making direct reference to the September Massacres, and indicating unequivocally that, in such initiatives, there was a clear attempt to hold a line between actions that were legitimated by state authority and those that were dangerously uncontrollable. This in particular is the argument put forward by Wahnich, an intriguing challenge to older Marxist views that associated radical action with popular pressure, but also a more direct counter to the arguments that revolutionary politicians were simply sucked into a spiral of ideological commitment to violence (Furet 1981; Gueniffey 2000).

Girondins, Federalism, and the Template of Betrayal and Subversion

Danton's line was not easy to hold, however, and the next stage in the evolution towards "Terror" showed how crossing it was a temptation, and an opportunity, hard to avoid. During the same weeks and months that the first mechanisms of state "Terror" had been legislated, the National Convention was repeatedly racked by factional disputes, hovering on the brink of overt violence. Supporters of the "Girondin" grouping, that had tried to keep the king alive as a bargaining-chip, clashed with proudly regicide "Montagnards" in the Convention and their supporters in the Parisian local authorities, and the national network of Jacobin clubs (from which the Girondin leadership had been expelled the previous year).

In a political, and to some extent social, conflict that went back to late 1791, Girondins saw the more radical groups as "anarchists" who, for personal profit or possibly even counter-revolutionary ends, were spreading disorder and hindering the development of a stable republican system. Montagnards thought that the Girondins had secretly tried to maintain the monarchy, and were an elitist clique that would, if unchecked, sell the common people's liberty down the river in a deal with the aristocracy. Patrice Higonnet (1985) offers a good brief discussion of the emergence of these contrasting outlooks, complemented by the work of Lynn Hunt (1984) on the general revolutionary political culture, and Jon Cowans' work (2001) on the problem of defining just who spoke for the public in these disputes.

Legislative actions in the weeks of March, April, and May 1793 bore the scars of this conflict – while *émigré* aristocrats and advocates of royalty were more harshly penalized, so too were those in the press who advocated destruction of property or (political) murder, and anyone seeking the redistribution of land. While the Convention was creating a Committee of Public Safety to direct the government, the Paris Jacobin Club was petitioning its local affiliates to demand the expulsion of deputies who had voted against the king's execution. One of the first cases to come before the Revolutionary Tribunal – and face its only penalty, death – was that of the journalist and deputy Jean-Paul Marat, who had introduced that petition, and was impeached for it by the Convention under Girondin pressure. His dramatic acquittal only spurred new attacks, and in late May Girondins sought the arrest of several leading Parisian radicals for subversion. The Paris Jacobins, local authorities in the city, and other radical groups plotted insurrection to "save" the Convention from this "faction" that seemed to have seized it (Slavin 1986). Meanwhile in Lyon, France's second city, open violence broke out between radical Jacobins in the city's central administration and Girondin supporters in neighborhood committees, leading to the overthrow of the radicals. Further south in Marseille, events were heading in a parallel direction (Edmonds 1990; Scott 1973).

On 31 May, Parisian crowds, organized by the neighborhood "section" committees, demonstrated for a purge of the Convention. In a three-day crisis, with armed militias on 2 June literally threatening the lives of the deputies, almost thirty leading Girondin figures were removed from office. News of this compounded the unrest in Lyon and Marseille. Here, and also in Bordeaux, in Normandy, and briefly in several other centers, there was an overt rejection of this assault on the national representative body. Out of their factional disputes, the revolutionaries conjured a second civil war. By mid-July, pro-Girondin forces had been dispersed in Normandy, but consolidated in Lyon and Marseille, soon to be put under armed siege by government troops. In Paris itself, the hand of what was dubbed "federalism" reached out chillingly when on 13 July Charlotte Corday arrived from Normandy and stabbed Marat to death. Events were in the process of confirming every paranoid fear that radicals had ever had about the nefarious intentions of those Girondins who had once called themselves patriots. The work of Paul Hanson (2003) discusses in depth, and with some sensitivity, the emergence and escalation of what was ultimately a violent conflict from a sense of wounded political and social legitimacy.

To make matters worse, the Vendéan rebels were engaging ever larger numbers of republican troops, and despite some defeats, were showing no signs of giving up. On international battle fronts, from the north around Dunkirk, via Mainz in the Rhineland, to the Alps and the Pyrenees, a tide of enemies was poised to flood ever further onto republican soil. In the cities that remained loyal, prices rose and real shortages began to bite, despite earlier laws controlling the price of grains. The Convention was again pressed from the Parisian left to do more to support the common people, though some of the more politically isolated amongst the most radical – the *enragés* or "madmen" – were crushed by a tactical alliance between Montagnards and the Parisian municipal leadership, anxious to preserve their moral authority as directors of popular wrath (Rose 1965).

The Convention in this period did attempt to introduce measures that would carry forward a potentially pacific agenda – it decreed, for example, the final abolition of the hated feudal dues that the peasantry had, in any case, long stopped paying. But external pressures produced further harsh laws, creating a bureaucracy to track down food supplies and decreeing the death penalty for anyone judged to be "hoarding" or "speculating" with such stocks. A new, transparently democratic, constitution was written, and ratified by popular vote, in July and August, but the political leadership, now joined by Maximilien Robespierre on the Committee of Public Safety, shied away from allowing it to come into effect when so many citizens were revealing themselves to be traitors. What was decreed instead, on 26 August 1793, was a "mass levy" against all enemies. The population was effectively drafted into action, to be marshaled by the representatives-on-mission, for any functions necessary to raise, clothe, arm, and feed a mighty national army.

Terror Laws, Hunger, Revolutionary Armies, and "Anarchy"

The mass levy was decreed as the civil wars approached another critical phase. Federalists in Lyon, facing military defeat, were becoming more openly counter-revolutionary as they desperately sought outside aid. Meanwhile to the south, Marseille was retaken by the Republic's armies after its leading federalists had undergone a similar rapid evolution rightwards. Fleeing the city, these groups seized control of the naval port of Toulon, and at the beginning of September 1793 handed it, and the French Mediterranean Fleet, over to the control of the British Royal Navy and an expeditionary force of allied counter-revolutionaries. All this proved to Parisian opinion in particular that all their assumptions about the nature of treachery – and in particular the emptiness of Girondins' claims to be true republicans – were correct.

Meanwhile, there was continuing hunger on the streets of the capital. It was not at all surprising that a country in the midst of such deep turmoil should see rising prices and shortages, and that farmers should be more inclined to stockpile grain for their own future than sell it for a paper currency that continued to shrink in value, but revolutionaries saw all aspects of life through a political lens. When it came to the food supply this was a long-standing tradition. Belief in the abundance of agriculture, the wickedness of monopolists, and the duty of the state to intervene to provide fair access to supplies (of bread in particular) ran deep in the culture of the eighteenth century, as did a suspicion that "famine plots" could be cooked up at the highest levels to manipulate popular suffering. In this sense, some of the most apparently radical demands of the revolutionary era were in fact amongst the most time-honored. It was politicians of the educated classes, persistently extolling the benefits of free markets, that were in line with "advanced" thinking of the age, but anger on the streets trumped this, at least in appearance, in 1793 (Andress 2005: 178ff.).

In the first days of September, protests that began with groups of workers were seized on by all the various groups in the capital keen to press for a more radical agenda. Local section committees used them to pressurize the municipal government, or Commune, which in turn, allied with the Jacobin Club, directed popular anger at the Convention. In a tense showdown on 5 September, where memories of the Girondins' fate must have been vivid, demands for a more far-reaching program of popular mobilization, political repression, and economic control were conceded – again, at least in appearance. Petitioners openly demanded that "terror" be put "on the order of the day," but as Jean-Clément

Martin (2006: 188) carefully shows, the Convention avoided any such official pronouncement. One of the other measures passed on the day was a restriction on the meeting times of the local section assemblies. Justified, not unreasonably, by the assertion that honest workers needed to be working, not sitting in meetings, and that the sections' "permanence" was a license for idle agitators to take over, it was at the same time a clear signal from the national political class that street politics were not going to dominate the Convention (Burstin 2005: 92–113).

The Convention, however, was clearly intent on dominating counter-revolution. One of the first products of a post-5 September wave of legislation was the "Law of Suspects," which required the detention, or at least house-arrest, of anyone falling under a wide umbrella of politically unacceptable activities or identities. Within weeks, tens of thousands had been rounded up, rising to hundreds of thousands over the coming months. The relatives of *émigré* nobles were detained simply for who they were; many faced imprisonment for choosing the wrong side in any of the intricate political disputes of the previous years; some were simply the victims of vendetta, purged from power by the roving representatives-on-mission because their enemies caught the ears of power first, or put on a better show of popular virtue.

Those representatives, meanwhile, were paired with, on the one hand, the development of a huge national bureaucracy to administer a "general maximum" of price controls on all basic goods, and on the other, the formation of "revolutionary armies." These, sent not to fight on the front line, but to attack the supposed lurking counter-revolutionaries across the countryside, were manned by an extraordinary mix of zealots, draft-dodgers, sociopaths, and even occasional aristocrats in hiding. Together with the efforts of the representatives, pressured from Paris to do whatever it took to mobilize the people and strike fear into their enemies, the revolutionary armies – roaming, uncoordinated, self-righteous, often vindictive, sometimes criminal – did much to justify the label of "anarchic Terror" often applied to the closing months of 1793. Richard Cobb (1987) offers a monumental study of the complexity and confusion unleashed by the revolutionary armies, while Colin Lucas' study of the representative Javogues and his fight against "federalists" near Lyon (1973) remains an indispensable examination of the forces that swept ordinary people into extraordinary, and brutal, action. The work of Jean-Pierre Gross (1997), on the other hand, shows the remarkable success other representatives had in rallying some provincial communities to the war effort without overt violence.

War Effort, Show Trials, Revolutionary Government

If the "anarchic Terror" was not in fact anarchic – all its chaos came from men exercising the powers of the state in what they claimed as the public interest – it soon came to be seen in the National Convention as a threat to efficient government. Far from being a monolithic power, the national representative body was riven with factions and remained under considerable external pressure. Robespierre, for the Committee of Public Safety, had to defend its actions robustly as news of continued defeats arrived late in September. The movement towards more extraordinary structures of power – going beyond merely new specific laws – intensified on 10 October with a declaration that government would be "revolutionary until peace," suspending the implementation of the new constitution. In December this was followed up with new structures that began to consolidate a top-down version of power, in which the Convention's assumed legitimacy became justification for overruling elections elsewhere, imposing appointed local officials who reported directly to Paris, and more strictly monitoring the behavior of the many representatives and the "commissioners" and "revolutionary armies" they had spawned across the nation.

Meanwhile, the autumn of 1793 had seen high drama played out at the Revolutionary Tribunal, which had relentlessly worked through a series of prominent "enemies of the Revolution," beginning in mid-October with Marie-Antoinette. At her trial, the radical activist, journalist, and municipal prosecutor Jacques-René Hébert claimed that she was so depraved that she had sexually abused her own son, to weaken his mind and strengthen her influence over him. Real political evidence of traitorous correspondence and counter-revolutionary designs was pushed into the background by such charges, and a savage joy at defaming a woman whose physical reality had long faded behind a legend of monstrous proportions. After her execution, a long calendar of charges was worked up against the Girondin leadership, much of which relied on flimsy assertions and guilt by association. With a cohort of skilled orators and lawyers in the dock, the trial almost got out of hand, as charges were knocked down by robust arguments.

On 29 October, in yet another step on the road to outright Terror, the Convention directed the Tribunal that it could convict defendants after no more than three days' hearing, if the jury's "consciences had been sufficiently enlightened" by the preceding evidence. Thus, twenty Girondin leaders, defiantly singing the *Marseillaise*, went to the guillotine on the 31st. The next five weeks saw a parade of show trials as the ruling Jacobins settled scores with prominent figures from the revolutionary past. Prominence was also given to the trial and dispatch of Marie-Olympe de Gouges, on 4 November, and a month later Madame du Barry. The former was an outspoken feminist author, the latter the aging former mistress of Louis XV. They had little in common except a certain sympathy for royalty, and the disruptive quality of being female – something coming under increasing suspicion in these months.

At the end of October 1793, the Convention formally banned all female political associations, even (especially) those given to radical republican demands. This may have been in part a follow-up to the general restriction on Parisian popular activism signaled on 5 September, but it was also a signal that the new society the revolution was constructing would have some hard limits. The overt misogyny of the radical revolutionaries was overlooked by historians for too long, but has now been decisively scrutinized (Offen 1990). Joan Landes (1988) and Olwen Hufton (1992) demonstrate the structural and cultural underpinnings of such attitudes, while others (Hunt 1992; Outram 1989) explore the wider way in which masculinity itself helped shape revolutionary politics.

With dramatic appearances before the Revolutionary Tribunal playing such a part in the events of these months, it is worth noting some statistics about it.

In its first eight months of operation, prior to this series of show trials, it had sentenced 92 people to death – but it had acquitted 214. From autumn to midwinter, its pace of operations was much faster: some 196 death-sentences were handed down, as the net of revolutionary justice was flung wider. But there were also 298 acquittals. Despite measures such as those of 29 October, the Tribunal was still not a killing machine (Walter 1986: 29–31).

While Paris hosted a rising tempo of trials, the country was rallied for war. The federalists in Lyon were smashed in early October, and shortly afterwards armies in the north pushed back the Austrians, almost simultaneously with a turning-point victory against the Vendéan rebels in the west. To the southwest, Bordeaux and the Gironde were secured, and the Spanish invaders forced to withdraw to the Pyrenees. Later in the autumn, the Vendéans were hounded across Brittany after a failed attempt to find British support at the English Channel, and crushed in late December. Tens of thousands of both combatants and followers were harried to their deaths. With fighting stabilized in the east, and the British forced to evacuate Toulon, the huge internal and external crisis that had turned France towards Terror was at least partially resolved. Unfortunately, by now there had been further developments that would make ending Terror almost impossible.

Factions, Fear, and Fabrications

Part of the drive to centralize administrative power in December 1793 came from a perception that existing arrangements were being abused, and that such abuse was counter-revolutionary. Here we enter the heart of what made "the Terror" such an abrupt and disorienting spiral into paranoid repression. From an outside perspective, it is easy to see that all the revolutionary leaders were floundering. In part, this was because of a lack of practical guidance and constraint. They had no long-term structures to hold on to; their "Jacobinism" was not a party with a constitution and a heritage, but rather a hasty improvisation of ideas and associations. There was no hierarchy of leadership with long experience, and no respect for such experience as there was – notably, the leading revolutionaries became younger with every purge. Even amongst those not in the first flush of youth, there were many that political events had promoted well beyond their competence (Brown 1995; Campbell et al. 2007; Higonnet 1998).

Partly as a result of all this, there was also a moral floundering. Men like Hébert, whose words continually proclaimed them as united with the common people, held positions of power in which they were vulnerable to the blandishments of those with money who needed favors. Others within the Convention, including a whole series of important figures, went out of their way to engineer self-enriching schemes when given charge of difficult economic decisions. They may have had shining principles, but they lacked a heritage of disinterested public service: before 1789, it was normal to be richly rewarded for being important, and only a few could resist the urge to keep up this tradition.

Recent historiography has suggested just how complex the cultural trap was that Jacobins found themselves in. Their cultural heritage included a deep attachment to the melodramatic heroism passed down in narratives of classical antiquity

(Linton 2010), and also "sentimentalist" beliefs about human psychology emerging from recent scientific and literary developments (Andress 2011; Brown 2008; Reddy 2000). These placed an unbearable burden on the manifestation of emotional sincerity as a device to judge individual merit, and bred an increasingly corrosive fear about the fraudulent display of such attributes. As Charles Walton (2009) has recently suggested, a countervailing tendency towards reckless slander, a "culture of calumny" inherited from pre-revolutionary habits, amplified mistrust beyond the bounds of reason. When Jacobins also professed an allegiance to "Natural Law" (Edelstein 2009) that was supposedly clear and uniform, then the pressure to misunderstand differences as betrayals could only spiral out of control.

However clearly these developments can be understood from outside, their effects within the revolutionary leadership were extraordinarily destructive. Rather than accepting each other's faults, revolutionaries latched on to them as evidence of more dangerous flaws – partly out of malice and self-protection, but partly also out of real fear of the surrounding enemies. By November 1793, such suspicions were merging with other disputes to create a toxic cocktail of mutual recrimination. The populist radicals of the Paris Commune, and some of their sympathizers amongst the representatives-on-mission, had begun to attack the symbols and practices of religion. They had also engineered the replacement of various "aristocratic" army generals with more acceptably plebeian activists, especially in the war against the Vendée. Against them stood other representatives who denounced such new appointments as the fruit of cronyism and graft, with the resulting incompetence being effectively counter-revolutionary; and yet others who viewed the atheistic "dechristianization" as an immoral excess that would both alienate the rural masses and potentially lead to counter-revolutionary attitudes.

All this produced a series of angry disputes and counter-accusations that seemed to be going nowhere. Robespierre – always the pre-eminent voice of "virtue" – was handed a key to understanding what was happening when a colleague, fearful for his own safety, denounced some of the self-enriching plotters. To make his tale all the more convincing, he also tangled them up with a "foreign plot" that had been rumored for some time as the cause of the Republic's ills, which was lent support by the activities of several rather shady (and foreign) associates of Hébert mixed up in dechristianization's excesses (Hampson 1976). Events were highly complex, but what emerged by the late winter was a political scene in which the radicals around Hébert were pressing for intensified terror, a counter-faction (figure-headed by Georges-Jacques Danton) was demanding that excesses be reined in, and Robespierre had come to believe – with a certain amount of plausible evidence to hand – that both groups were motivated by material gain and counter-revolutionary intrigue.

Centralization, Victories, Purifications

In early February 1794, Robespierre made a landmark speech "On the Principles of Political Morality." It set out very starkly, and in tones which approached religious enthusiasm, his vision of the unprecedented social happiness that the revolutionary process could bring. Weaving its positive message around the notion of "democracy" or "popular government," the speech emphasized the need for "virtue" in the population to cement the good society. It also made clear that under revolutionary circumstances "both virtue and *terror*" were the "mainsprings" of the government: "virtue, without which terror is fatal; terror, without which virtue is impotent." What "terror" meant to Robespierre appears to have been something quite restrained: "nothing but prompt, severe, inflexible justice," which itself was an "emanation of virtue." However, the bulk of the speech was taken up with denunciation, both of the "indulgents" who called for "mercy for the scoundrels" threatened by terror, and of the "ultras," "false revolutionaries" whose radicalism was a dangerous facade for ideas "set by the committees of Prussia, England, Austria" (Baker 1987: 369–384).

Administrative centralization was being followed by ideological centralization. Hébert and his Parisian associates were seized on 13 March, the same day as new measures were hastily passed to tighten scrutiny of office-holders and loosen the definition of suspects for detention. The arrest was not merely about ideology – in their Cordeliers Club the radicals had been openly calling for an insurrection against the current political leadership – but it reflected a new willingness to resist pressure from the left of the kind that had inaugurated so much of the Terror's apparatus in the summer of 1793. The execution of the "Hébertists" ten days later, after a trial in which hearsay and fabrication bound them into the "foreign plot," was followed almost at once by the abolition of the Parisian revolutionary army, and then at the end of the month by the seizure of Danton and other leading "Indulgents" (Slavin 1994).

In its motivations, this act was perhaps even less ideological, and more purely power-political, than the preceding trial. Robespierre was only with some difficulty persuaded by more hard-headed members of the Committee of Public Safety that Danton had to die to safeguard the Republic. However, once persuaded, he helped to draft an indictment which turned all of Danton's disagreements with the virtuous Jacobin line into evidence of a treacherous heart and aristocratic goals. The farcical show trials of both groups, and others which followed shortly after, were accompanied by wider crackdowns on the possibility of dissent – the government ministries were broken up into smaller, more closely monitored "commissions," Parisian local politics was effectively closed down, replaced by obedient administrators, other independent bureaucracies and local tribunals were shut down or centralized, and a "Bureau of General Police" under the direct control of the Committee of Public Safety was established, encroaching even on the role of its "sister" Committee of General Security (Hardman 1999).

All this was happening as the material causes of the Terror – the internal and external conflicts – were developing in ways both successful and unsustainable. The massive mobilizing drive by representatives and agencies to produce new armies had paid off through the winter months, with literally hundreds of thousands of new recruits marshaled, drilled, and prepared for combat. As campaigns opened in the spring, the frontiers on the Pyrenees and Alps were secured, with the prospect of further advances. To the east, a winter campaign had already pushed towards the Rhine, and in the north a series of battles first secured against invasion, and then began a drive that would push Austrian and

British forces into effective evacuation of the Belgian territories by the summer (Forrest 1990; Gross 1997).

Meanwhile, triumph over the internal forces of counter-revolution and division had been followed with retribution on a massive scale. Not content with smashing and slaughtering the main Vendéan army, the Republic's leaders had directed a series of sweeping punitive expeditions through their home territories late in the winter. These "infernal columns" burned everything they found, and indiscriminately massacred men, women, and children that their leaders had successfully demonized as "brigands" from the cradle. In other centers of revolt, actions did not approach these levels of mass killing, but the drive for greater ideological purity from the center, assisted by complex local situations and score-settling, did produce a rising toll of condemned victims, even months after rebel cities had surrendered. Confused concerns about both potential local leniency and "ultra" destabilization caused the Convention to shut down tribunals in the regions in early May, ordering their prisoners to be transported to Paris for trial. This was one of the acts that set the stage for the final melodramatic months of the Terror.

Shining Future and Closing Circle

The month of May 1794 saw a determined effort by the leading figures in the Convention to consolidate the regime that in law remained "revolutionary" and provisional. Determined that mere laws could not remold a population to the virtue Robespierre had spoken of in February, they (and he in particular) promoted what was effectively a new religion as a core "institution" to provide this moral transformation. The "Cult of the Supreme Being" was an answer both to the corruption of traditional Christianity by the church and to the excesses of atheistic dechristianization. Tied to a ritual calendar around the new "revolutionary calendar" introduced the previous autumn, dispensing with Sundays and saints' days and naming new months after seasonal events, this cult reflected a vision of republican purity back onto the French (Ozouf 1988a).

Its god was formless and non-specific, but its practices were to be highly ritualized and focused on a wide range of social and familial virtues – in a sense, it was to be society worshiping itself (or at least its own better nature). This message was reinforced by demands for the arts to produce prose, poetry, paintings, sculpture, and architecture that would transmit and reinforce a narrative of republican heroism, self-sacrifice, and unity. Ambitious plans for a national education system to inculcate such values in the young already existed; now they were to be augmented by what amounted to a multi-media blitz on the perceptions of the whole population (though no more so, one might also argue, than that which church and monarchy had orchestrated for centuries). As Mona Ozouf (1988b) has noted, this was part of the psychological heritage of the age, that firmly believed in the malleability of the human mind – something which, ironically, reinforced the perception of how easy it was to be corrupted by bad influences.

The inaugural Festival of the Supreme Being was celebrated nationwide on 8 June. There is widespread evidence of real popular enthusiasm for what was taken to be a return to religion. However, just to be sure, in Paris almost literally the whole population was marshaled into taking some part, according to a detailed plan by the artist Jacques-Louis David. The parades and spectacles that wound through the capital were crowned by a speech from Robespierre. He held center-stage because he had been elected to chair the Convention – a brief and rotating honor – a few days before, but it was a performance which to some observers suggested his messianic tendencies were getting out of hand. Two days later, as provincial prisoners flooded into Paris because of the centralization of revolutionary justice, the forcing through of the "Law of 22 Prairial" raised new alarms in the Convention. Designed to accelerate the work of the Revolutionary Tribunal by stripping away the last few safeguards of procedure available to defendants, its wording also implied that members of the Convention might lose their defense against indictment without a vote of that body.

The rhetoric and practice of politics were slipping ever closer to something not far from paranoia. Significant political players who had led repression in the Vendée and the southeast now saw their actions called into question by Robespierre and his cohorts, and their bloodthirsty zeal itself depicted as potentially counter-revolutionary excess. Rather than suggest Dantonist "indulgence," the response of the "Robespierrists" was to hint ever more strongly at further purges of these new "ultras" and their questionable motives. By the middle of June, huge cracks were opening in the facade of unity even amongst the governing committees. The Committee of General Security launched a scathing attack on a group led by a religious mystic in Paris that was exalting Robespierre as a prophet – effectively accusing the latter of encouraging them. Only the plain fact that nobody really commanded the political initiative, as the management of the war that continued to rage on all fronts sucked up much of the Convention's time, prevented an even more rapid deterioration.

Robespierre, meanwhile, was frequently ill, incapacitated by his nerves. How far he as an individual was responsible for any or all of the excesses of Terror remains a vexed question. John Hardman (1999) presents him as a political "boss" in a fashion which is probably too clear-cut to be wholly accurate, while also noting the extent to which he became surrounded by self-serving cronies who persuaded him of their own virtue while promoting their friends. Peter McPhee's new biography (2012) goes to the limits of the available evidence in probing the enigmas of Robespierre's final months, but that evidence remains tantalizingly fragmentary. One wide-ranging collection of essays, playing off his nickname of the "Incorruptible," labeled Robespierre as potentially "incomprehensible" (Haydon and Doyle 1999: 3), and the mystery of what really drove him in these last months in particular may simply always continue.

While politics was paralyzed, the bureaucracy of the Terror ground on. The late spring months had seen some 863 death sentences from the Revolutionary Tribunal, most of which came even before the acceleration of the 22 Prairial law. In the next revolutionary month, Messidor, there were 796 death sentences. Acquittals continued, it should always be noted, but fell from around a quarter of cases in the spring to around a fifth in Messidor (Walter 1986, 32–33). Some of the grounds for conviction, based around transparently absurd "prison plots" denounced by paid informers, were so flimsy that it seems likely the acquittals came from cases where there was no evidence presented at all.

Endgames

The Terror ended in a welter of accusations and executions, yet one of the intriguing points about this process is how long it took to move from words to deeds. From early July, Robespierre used the platform of the Jacobin Club – now largely frequented by provincial visiting activists and "Robespierrist" office-holders – to name a series of prominent figures as traitors. These included Barras and Fréron, returned from missions in the southeast, Tallien likewise back from Bordeaux, and Dubois-Crancé, accused of crimes in Lyon, and recalled from Rennes by the Committee of Public Safety as a result on 14 July. On that same day, Robespierre had Joseph Fouché, an arch-dechristianizer, thrown out of the Jacobins, labeling him "a vile and miserable impostor," and "the chief of a conspiracy that had to be stopped" (Bienvenu 1968, 133–134).

Yet these men remained at liberty, increasingly actively working to save themselves, and by implication bring down Robespierre and his associates. Fouché by his own account lobbied other members of the Committee of Public Safety to persuade them that they, too, shared the danger from Robespierre's crusading zeal. When Dubois-Crancé reached Paris on the 24th, he openly demanded an investigation from the committee, and repeated the demand in the Convention the next day. On that 25 July, a prominent member of the Committee of General Security visited the seventy-three Girondin-leaning Convention members who had been in political detention since the previous autumn – thus establishing contact with the "right" of the political spectrum to gain further leverage. None of this activity would have been possible if the Terror had been the relentless and systematic death-machine it is sometimes presented as. Robespierre, meanwhile, did not have such men secretly seized, but like them sought open confrontation, appearing at the Convention on 26 July with a two-hour speech.

The text might have been designed to unite opposition. Not only did Robespierre attack the recalled deputies, he assailed several other Convention committees for their "counter-revolutionary" behavior, and even asserted that unnamed members of the Committee of Public Safety were part of the plot. The other main strand of the speech was a long account of his sacrifices for the Republic, and an appeal to the virtue of the listeners to support him in conducting a massive new purge. In the face of this, opposition in the Convention at last found its voice, and a confused, stormy, and inconclusive debate followed. In the evening, Robespierre repeated his charges at the Jacobin Club, where they were acclaimed – but no overnight *coup d'état* resulted. On the 27th, 9 Thermidor, the Convention gathered again to hear Robespierre's leading associate, Saint-Just, deliver a planned report on the political situation.

Now at last there was concerted action. Saint-Just was shouted down almost before he had begun, and there were melodramatic scenes as Robespierre tried to speak out and was howled down, then placed under arrest, along with a handful of devoted defenders. As darkness fell, confusion ensued. Robespierrist municipal officers initially rallied, and the arrested deputies ended up amongst friends at the City Hall. But with a vote of the Convention to formally outlaw them, rank-and-file support melted away. They were seized just after 1 a.m., with little more than a scuffle, in the midst of preparing a call for the armies to rescue them "in the name of the French people." (Hardman 1999: 201) Guillotined later that same day, the "Robespierrists" gave way to an avalanche of self-justification, genuine liberalization, partisanship, and (understandable) impulses to revenge that made up the complex "Thermidorian reaction." It was in this context that the past began to be labeled as a reign of terror, and its actors – especially those not of the educated elite – as "terrorists."

References

Andress, David (2004). *The French Revolution and the People.* London: Hambledon & London.

Andress, David (2005). *The Terror: Civil War in Revolutionary France.* London: Little, Brown.

Andress, David (2011). "Living the Revolutionary Melodrama: Robespierre's Sensibility and the Construction of Political Commitment in the French Revolution." *Representations,* 114: 103–128.

Baker, Keith Michael (ed.) (1987). *Readings in Western Civilization, 7: The Old Regime and the French Revolution.* Chicago: University of Chicago Press.

Baker, Keith Michael (1990). *Inventing the French Revolution: Essays on French Political Culture in the Eighteenth Century.* Cambridge: Cambridge University Press.

Biard, Michel (2002). *Missionnaires de la République: Les Représentants du peuple en mission (1793–1795).* Paris: CTHS.

Bienvenu, Richard (ed.) (1968). *The Ninth of Thermidor: The Fall of Robespierre.* Oxford: Oxford University Press.

Bosher, J.F. (1989). *The French Revolution.* London: Weidenfeld & Nicolson.

Brown, Gregory S. (2008). "Review Article: Am 'I' a 'Post-Revolutionary Self'? Historiography of the Self in the Age of Enlightenment and Revolution." *History and Theory,* 47: 229–248.

Brown, Howard G. (1995). *War, Revolution and the Bureaucratic State: Politics and Army Administration in France, 1791–1799.* Oxford: Oxford University Press.

Burstin, Haim (2005). *L'Invention du sans-culotte: Regard sur le Paris révolutionnaire.* Paris: Odile Jacob.

Campbell, Peter R., Thomas E. Kaiser, and Marisa Linton (eds.) (2007). *Conspiracy in the French Revolution.* Manchester: Manchester University Press.

Cobb, Richard (1987). *The People's Armies: The Armées Révolutionnaires, Instruments of the Terror in the Departments April 1793 to Floréal Year III,* trans. Marianne Elliott. New Haven, Conn.: Yale University Press.

Cowans, Jon (2001). *To Speak for the People: Public Opinion and the Problem of Legitimacy in the French Revolution.* London: Routledge.

Edelstein, Dan (2009). *The Terror of Natural Right: Republicanism, the Cult of Nature, and the French Revolution.* Chicago: University of Chicago Press.

Edmonds, W.D. (1990). *Jacobinism and the Revolt of Lyon 1789–1793.* Oxford: Clarendon Press.

Forrest, Alan (1990). *Soldiers of the French Revolution.* Durham, N.C.: Duke University Press.

Furet, François (1981). *Interpreting the French Revolution.* Cambridge: Cambridge University Press.

Gérard, Alain (1999). *"Par principe d'humanité": La Terreur et la Vendée.* Paris: Fayard.

Gough, Hugh (1987). "Genocide and the Bicentenary: The French Revolution and the Revenge of the Vendée." *HJ,* 30: 977–988.

Gross, Jean-Pierre (1997). *Fair Shares For All: Jacobin Egalitarianism in Practice.* Cambridge: Cambridge University Press.

Gueniffey, Patrice (2000). *La Politique de la Terreur: Essai sur la violence révolutionnaire, 1789–1794.* Paris: Fayard.

Hampson, Norman (1976). "François Chabot and his Plot." *Transactions of the Royal Historical Society*, 5th series, 26: 1–14.

Hanson, Paul R. (2003). *The Jacobin Republic under Fire: The Federalist Revolt in the French Revolution.* University Park: Pennsylvania State University Press.

Hardman, John (1999). *Robespierre.* London: Longman.

Haydon, Colin and William Doyle (eds.) (1999). *Robespierre.* Cambridge: Cambridge University Press.

Higonnet, Patrice (1985). "The Social and Cultural Antecedents of Revolutionary Discontinuity: Montagnards and Girondins." *EHR*, 100: 513–544.

Higonnet, Patrice (1998). *Goodness Beyond Virtue: Jacobins during the French Revolution.* Cambridge, Mass.: Harvard University Press.

Hufton, Olwen H. (1992). *Women and the Limits of Citizenship in the French Revolution.* Toronto: University of Toronto Press.

Hunt, Lynn (1984). *Politics, Culture and Class in the French Revolution.* Berkeley: University of California Press.

Hunt, Lynn (1992). *The Family Romance of the French Revolution.* London: Routledge.

Kelly, George A. (1980). "Conceptual Sources of the Terror." *Eighteenth Century Studies*, 14: 18–36.

Landes, Joan B. (1988). *Women and the Public Sphere in the Age of the French Revolution.* Ithaca, N.Y.: Cornell University Press.

Le Goff, T.J.A. and D.M.G. Sutherland (1983). "The Social Origins of Counter-Revolution in Western France." *P&P*, 99: 65–87.

Linton, Marisa (2010). "The Man of Virtue: The Role of Antiquity in the Political Trajectory of L.A. Saint-Just." *FH*, 24: 393–419.

Lucas, Colin (1973). *The Structure of the Terror: The Example of Javogues and the Loire.* Oxford: Oxford University Press.

McPhee, Peter (2012). *Robespierre: A Revolutionary Life.* London and New Haven: Yale University Press.

Martin, Jean-Clément (2001). *La Guerre de Vendée.* Paris: Éditions Geste.

Martin, Jean-Clément (2006). *Violence et Révolution: Essai sur la naissance d'un mythe national.* Paris: Seuil.

Offen, Karen (1990). "The New Sexual Politics of French Revolutionary Historiography." *FHS*, 22: 909–922.

Outram, Dorinda (1989). *The Body and the French Revolution: Sex, Class and Political Culture.* New Haven, Conn.: Yale University Press.

Ozouf, Mona (1988a). *Festivals and the French Revolution.* Cambridge, Mass.: Harvard University Press.

Ozouf Mona (1988b). "La Révolution française et l'idée de l'homme nouveau." In Colin Lucas (ed.). *The French Revolution and the Creation of Modern Political Culture*, vol. 2: *The Political Culture of the French Revolution.* Oxford: Pergamon Press. 213–232.

Palmer, R.R. (1941). *Twelve Who Ruled: The Year of the Terror in the French Revolution.* Princeton, N.J.: Princeton University Press.

Petitfrère, Claude (1988). "The Origins of the Civil War in the Vendée." *FH*, 2: 187–207.

Reddy, William M. (2000). "Sentimentalism and its Erasure: The Role of Emotions in the Era of the French Revolution." *JMH*, 72: 109–152.

Rose, R.B. (1965). *The Enragés: Socialists of the French Revolution?* Melbourne: Melbourne University Press.

Schama, Simon (1989). *Citizens: A Chronicle of the French Revolution.* New York: Viking Penguin.

Scott, William (1973). *Terror and Repression in Revolutionary Marseilles.* London: Macmillan.

Secher, Reynald (2003 [1986]). *A French Genocide: The Vendée.* Notre Dame, Ind.: University of Notre Dame Press.

Slavin, Morris (1986). *The Making of an Insurrection: Parisian Sections and the Gironde.* Cambridge, Mass.: Harvard University Press.

Slavin, Morris (1994). *The Hébertistes to the Guillotine: Anatomy of a "Conspiracy" in Revolutionary France.* Baton Rouge: Louisiana State University Press.

Wahnich, Sophie (2003). *La Liberté ou la mort: Essai sur la Terreur et le terrorisme.* Paris: La Fabrique.

Walter, Gérard (ed.) (1986). *Actes du tribunal révolutionnaire.* Paris: Mercure de France.

Walton, Charles (2009). *Policing Public Opinion in the French Revolution: The Culture of Calumny and the Problem of Free Speech.* Oxford: Oxford University Press.

Part VII

Searching for Stability, 1794–99

CHAPTER NINETEEN

The Thermidorian Reaction

LAURA MASON

In the final volume of his magisterial history of the French Revolution, Jules Michelet described Maximilien Robespierre's defeat on 9 Thermidor II (27 July 1794) and the agonizing death that followed. Then he came to a full stop. "Breathe," he counseled readers, "let us avert our eyes" (Mathiez 2010 [1929]: 7). Convinced that this fatal moment did not merely end the Terror but prepared a reversal of the Revolution's greatest achievements, he would go no further. His successors advanced to take fuller measure of the Thermidorian Reaction, the fifteen months that separated Robespierre's defeat from the Directory's inauguration, but they shared Michelet's conviction that here the Revolution doubled back on itself. So, for a century and more, historians confined themselves to debating the scope and merits of that reversal. Marxists like Albert Mathiez, Georges Lefebvre, and Albert Soboul agreed that the Reaction returned France to the liberal aspirations of 1789 and collectively regretted this repudiation of republican social revolution (Lefebvre 1964 [1957]; Mathiez 2010 [1929]; Soboul 1975 [1962]). The revisionist François Furet distinguished himself by extending the Reaction's reach, to argue with Tocquevillian ambition that it resumed a centuries-long consolidation of the administrative state, and by celebrating Thermidor as a liberation, claiming that it freed civil society from the ideological servitude of the Terror (Furet 1981; Furet and Richet 1970). So fixed was the notion of reversal that no one offered a fundamentally new diagnosis until the late twentieth century, when the Polish philosopher Bronislaw Baczko argued that the Thermidorian Reaction did not reverse the Revolution but posed the complex question of how to end it (Baczko 1989, 1994).

With *Ending the Terror*, Baczko joined Furet's refusal to demonize the Reaction with his own scrutiny of its legislative rhetoric to describe the uncertain means by which legislators groped their way forward in the wake of Robespierre's defeat. As

A Companion to the French Revolution, First Edition. Edited by Peter McPhee.

the same men who legislated the Terror, those taxed with ending it faced troubling dilemmas. They had first to shatter the "wooden language of the year II," which expressed compulsory unanimity, and recover a language of diversity and opposition. In so doing, however, they laid bare the "conflicts and hatred" accumulated beneath their superficial concord, immeasurably complicating the equally important task of allocating responsibility. For how were they to identify those guilty for the Terror's crimes without endorsing revenge? And how were they to repudiate the Terror without rejecting all of the Revolution? The National Convention saw the political pendulum swing wildly from radicalism to reaction and came to understand that the only way to prevent it from perpetually doing so was by ending the Revolution. Deputies accepted the "recoil of public opinion which demanded reparation for the [Terror's] evils" and preserved the republic by adopting a constitution that safeguarded against Robespierrism and royalism alike (Baczko 1994).

Baczko's work was ground-breaking. By jettisoning a notion of reversal that evacuated all political meaning from the years between Robespierre's defeat in 1794 and Napoleon's coup in 1799, he reintegrated the Reaction into the Revolution to illuminate the dynamism of the entire decade. Rightly insisting that the Thermidorian period (July 1794–October 1795) played a creative role in transforming radical Jacobin democracy into the conservative republic of the Directory, Baczko laid the foundation for a new generation of scholarship. Historians who follow in his footsteps have knitted together pre- and post-Thermidorian politics to explain how legislators and private citizens continued to rework the revolutionary heritage right up to the proclamation of Empire in 1802, founding modern French civil and political society (Dupuy and Morabito 1996; Gainot 2001; Jainchill 2008; Livesey 2001; Serna 1997, 2005; Vovelle 1997).

Even as Baczko opened new vistas, however, his narrow focus on the content of reactionary discourse occluded the social, political, and institutional interests of the men who formulated it. This absence of context gives the impression that the Revolution's Year III may be reduced to the single question of whether or not to dismantle the Terror. And it suggests that the only possible solution was either to accept a reaction that degenerated into purges and popular violence or sustain the system that banished civil liberties and rule of law from France in the Year II. Baczko's Reaction, rooted in a history of ideas and organized through binary opposition, appears coherent and inevitable. But when his Thermidorian rhetoric is restored to its broader context, the Reaction appears less an irresistible force than a contingent outcome, less a natural outpouring of feeling than the product of competing and often self-interested alliances that would deprive hundreds of thousands of citizens of rights, assistance, and personal safety.

As historians like Françoise Brunel, Sergio Luzzatto, Martyn Lyons, and Raymonde Monnier have made clear, Thermidor and the Reaction that followed were produced by a struggle among factions within and beyond the Convention (Brunel 1989; Luzzatto 2001; Lyons 1975; Monnier 1996, 1997). Those who emerged victorious did not simply discredit Jacobinism but advanced the Montagnard project of consolidating the republican state while, paradoxically, destroying the Mountain itself. By broadening Robespierre's assault on popular militants to take in Jacobinism, reactionaries would shatter the radicalizing forces that had propelled the Revolution onward since 1789, freeing the Assembly from its dependence on the Paris crowd. But they did not, in so doing, broaden the government's base of support. Replacing crowd with army as the Assembly's threatening guardian, the Thermidorians sustained revolutionary mistrust of the countryside. Their narrow settlement ended the Terror and founded the Directory even as it sowed the seeds of that government's defeat and suspension of the republican experiment for another half-century.

The Thermidorian Reaction may be divided roughly in half. The late summer and early autumn of 1794 were months of confusion as legislators, journalists, and private citizens scrambled to determine the nation's future. They had not only to debate whether to retreat from the Terror but, if so, how? Would the Convention simply trim extraordinary laws and institutions, or was the democracy promised in 1792 to be fully restored? And what of civil liberties like free speech and a free press that had been so brutally circumscribed? As these debates unfolded, competing political factions brokered alliances to appeal to a newly mobile opinion. It was not until late fall that the public mood began to coalesce around recognizably reactionary sentiment, empowering right-wing deputies to transform the Republic.

If the long-term implications of Robespierre's defeat were uncertain, it was immediately clear that this was the first political crisis a revolutionary Assembly had weathered without the crowd's intervention. Nine Thermidor was a legislative coup, engineered by a handful of deputies and realized by their colleagues on the floor of the National Convention. Although a few thousand citizens turned out when they heard of the challenge, the crowd milled about aimlessly while the vast majority of their peers stayed home. The Convention's deputies alone ushered in a new phase of the Revolution (Rudé 1959).

Inside the Convention, the coup left in place the uneasy alliance of deputies who engineered it: extremists who had challenged Robespierre because they feared he was retreating from the Terror, moderates determined to foster just such a retreat, and disgraced deputies who hoped to protect themselves from the Incorruptible's retribution. This incongruous coalition initially sustained its equilibrium by enacting cautious measures that restored power to the legislature but left the Terror's key institutions intact. The Convention limited the reach of the Committees of Public Safety and General Security but did not abolish them. It trimmed the powers of the Revolutionary Tribunal but acknowledged that its services might yet be needed. And it restored deputies' parliamentary immunity by repealing the draconian Prairial Laws. The implications of the last move reached beyond the Convention, because the Prairial Laws violated regular judicial procedure and narrowly limited free speech, but the legislature only attended directly to private demands for liberalization by agreeing to open the Terror's prisons. Even here, it preserved ascendency by making liberation dependent on specific legislative concessions rather than wholesale amnesty or abolition of the law on suspects. The Convention alone would continue to define what constituted legitimate political activity (Baczko 1994; Gendron 1993; Lefebvre 1964 [1957]; Mathiez 2010 [1929]).

In sum, the Convention initially sustained the Montagnard policy of isolating itself and jealously safeguarding political initiative. Had the deputies remained united, the Assembly might have continued to define single-handedly the nation's retreat from Terror. But the profound political differences that had been obscured by common opposition to Robespierre emerged in late summer, when corrupt legislators joined with moderate colleagues to push the pace of reform. The most outspoken of the opportunists were Jean-Lambert Tallien and Stanislas Fréron, deputies-on-mission recalled to Paris the preceding spring for excesses and misuse of funds. Having joined the cabal against Robespierre to escape prosecution, they continued to shroud their failings by challenging others' transgressions in ways that would prove singularly important in mobilizing reaction.

Fréron initiated the battle in late August by demanding that the Convention decree unlimited freedom of the press to reverse the Terror's devastating erosion of free speech. Although the deputy was clearly using the issue to empower himself, he made his case with the timely argument that a free press would prevent another tyranny like Robespierre's by "frightening, unmasking and halting the plots of the ambitious" (Fréron 1794a: 12). Colleagues applauded the sentiment but balked at the motion. That they were driven by reluctance to cede authority to the public was made explicit by Jacobin deputies who exploited the familiar fear that "counter-revolutionaries" might use a free press to subvert the Republic. Fréron's proposal was buried in committee (Baczko 1994).

Undaunted, moderate deputy Laurent Lecointre broadened the attack with his proposal that the Convention consolidate its victory over Robespierre by indicting those members of the Committees of Public Safety and General Security who had survived 9 Thermidor. He made his case by echoing a speech Tallien had given which raised the question of political responsibility in a wildly inflammatory way. Both men condemned the Terror as a "tyrannical abuse" that "paralyzed" the Convention and destroyed "the people's energy," and Lecointre added epithets heretofore reserved for the dead Robespierre, calling active deputies "tyrants" and "monsters" (Lecointre 1794; Tallien n.d. [1794]). Although Lecointre accused only seven members of the Convention, opponents understood that the indictments he proposed could generate a widening spiral of accusation and revenge. They reminded him that they had all freely authorized the committees' activity, so the Convention bore collective responsibility. Although they offered an equally unpalatable course of action, to simply forget the past, they kept the upper hand. They lambasted Lecointre as a "counter-revolutionary" and dismissed his motion as "slanderous" before the Convention rejected it (Baczko 1994; Gendron 1993; Wahnich 1997). The assembly was at deadlock.

Frustrated within the Convention, Fréron and Tallien challenged its isolation by rousing the public. Former Jacobins, they appreciated the power of the street and knew that allies were already mobilizing there. On the same day that Fréron addressed the Assembly, fellow reactionary Mehée de la Touche (1794) published a scathing satire that broadcast the deputy's demand for a free press and foreshadowed Lecointre's charges by accusing the committees of perpetuating Robespierre's tyranny. *La Queue de Robespierre* ("Robespierre's Tail") was a wild success: it sold 70,000 copies in a single week and generated a torrent of imitators, feeding the dazzling revival of the press unleashed by repeal of the Prairial Laws (Gough 1988). Fréron and Tallien exploited the new liberty directly by subsidizing the *Journal de la liberté de la presse* edited by democratic militant Camille Babeuf, and founding newspapers of their own. And yet, although Babeuf and Fréron, at the masthead of the *Orateur du peuple*, initially made common demands for press freedom and a purge of Robespierre's "acolytes," they soon parted company. Their different trajectories illuminate the defining political contests of the fall of 1794.

Camille Babeuf was a seasoned provincial militant who had witnessed the Parisian popular movement at its height during the spring and summer of 1793. Plucked from the ferment by arrest, he returned at the time of Thermidor to find the capital very much changed. In the interim, Jacobins determined to rein in the popular forces that brought them to power had exerted relentless pressure. The Montagnard Convention restricted sectional assembly meetings, closed women's clubs, hounded populist *enragés* into silence, and presided over the arrest and execution of radical journalist Jacques-René Hébert. Although 9 Thermidor struck down Robespierre, it continued his assault by sweeping away the Paris Commune, which had provided institutional expression of sans-culottes demands.

Babeuf was determined to renew popular democracy, which he believed to be the cornerstone of the republic. Declaring victory in the battle to free the press, he renamed himself Gracchus to honor the classical plebeian advocates and turned his readers' attention to Parisian militants' efforts to restore democracy. The democratic militants, organized through the newly created Electoral Club, demanded that the Commune be restored, the constitution activated, and municipal elections organized to restore power to the electorate. Babeuf advertised their efforts in the *Journal de la liberté de la presse*, publishing their petitions and echoing their argument that the Convention could not claim victory over tyranny until it restored popular sovereignty (Babeuf 1794; Tønnesson 1959, 1960).

All of this was, in Kare Tønnesson's words (1959: 57), the labor of leaders without troops. But it suggests another route the nation might have taken in the wake of Robespierre's defeat. Had the Convention activated the democratic constitution and organized prompt elections as the Electoral Club demanded, it would have given evidence of a genuine determination to dismantle the tyranny of the Year II. Had it realized the democratic republic promised by the Constitution of 1793, it would have bolstered its own legitimacy and been compelled to foster broad social and political alliances. But the deputies were not so inclined. Fatally conflating representative government with an ideology of direct democracy that authorized ongoing popular militancy, they refused all concessions.

Hardliners and reactionaries, who had been deadlocked over the nature of reform within the Convention, united against popular demands to resurrect democracy. Deputies and journalists with whom they were allied answered the Electoral Club's appeals with warnings that the preparation of elections or activating the constitution in wartime might empower the nation's enemies. They refused to hear Electoral Club addresses to the Convention, seized and gutted its meeting hall, and ordered the arrest of its principal spokesman. Fréron endorsed the repression and broke with Babeuf, withdrawing his subsidy from the *Journal* and telling his printer to seize its most recent issue (Babeuf 1794; Fréron 1794b; Rose 1978). Hounded by police and unable to rally sufficient popular force, the democratic movement melted away.

By refusing to accommodate the democrats, the Convention opened the door to reaction. For even as Fréron joined in the challenge to popular democratic activism, he was using the *Orateur du peuple* to rally a new kind of militancy. Turning his back on the working people who formed the bulk of the sans-culottes, he addressed politically moderate clerks, shopkeepers, petty bureaucrats, and men of letters. These men were displacing radicals from the sections and becoming an ever more visible presence in Parisian streets, theaters, and cafés, where they advertised their loathing of the Terror and challenged its social leveling. Known as "gilded youth," they would be galvanized by sympathetic journalists like Fréron and public debate surrounding the deputy Jean-Baptiste Carrier, accused of committing atrocities in the city of Nantes (Gendron 1993). When public fury against Carrier extended to his fellow Jacobins, the youth brawled with club members until the Convention, blaming the latter for the disorder, shut them down.

Closure of the Paris Jacobin Club rid the National Convention of a key rival for power whose alliance with the people had produced legislative purges, radical decrees, and the Mountain's victory in June 1793. Although hundreds of smaller Jacobin clubs remained scattered throughout the provinces, their days were numbered: prohibited from associating with one another or engaging further in local politics, they lost their purpose. Membership dwindled and clubs were shuttered until just a handful remained when the Convention formally dissolved them in the summer of 1795 (Kennedy 2000).

As the Jacobins declined, the gilded youth prospered. Their role in the Club's closure cemented their reputation as enemies of the old order, and public opinion tipped visibly in their favor. The youth ruled the streets, attacking anyone who looked like a radical and bullying café and theater owners to strip their establishments of emblems that recalled the old order. Fréron celebrated their activity in the *Orateur du peuple* as exemplary of a new political mood (Gendron 1993). Just as radical sans-culottes were once celebrated as exemplars of a widespread radicalism that served the Jacobins, so now the gilded youth buttressed reactionaries in the legislature. By late November, those deputies could overcome the Convention's political deadlock.

The Assembly's first order of business was to restore the seventy-three deputies expelled in June 1793 for protesting against the expulsion of the Girondins. Economic liberals, these men enhanced the changing climate of opinion within the legislature, where even old Montagnards had come to believe that freeing trade would foster growth. So the next steps were to close public arms workshops that employed hundreds in Paris, and abolish the general maximum, which guaranteed affordable food. Admittedly, working people were equally eager for repeal of the maximum because it restricted wages as well as prices (Dorigny 1996; Hincker 1997). But by undertaking dramatic reform whose costs fell disproportionately on the most vulnerable as winter arrived, the Convention set the stage for what came next. With the opening of 1795, the Thermidorian Reaction entered its second phase as it came fully into being. The repeal of the maximum provoked ferocious inflation, which would reignite popular militancy. When that militancy found expression through violent crowd actions, it intensified the Reaction. In the end, the Thermidorians would sweep away all promise of democracy to create a stronger republican state, but at terrible cost.

The opening months of 1795 were devastating. Repeal of the maximum triggered runaway inflation that was intensified by a terrible winter which froze the Seine and suspended grain transports. The disparity in suffering was shocking: working people starved as high society danced on the tomb of Jacobin austerity, flocking to theaters, balls, and gala dinners. Hunger intensified resentment at the sans-culottes' political marginalization and the widespread repudiation of republican egalitarianism (Tønnesson 1959). When Paris thawed, longing for the days when Robespierre guaranteed respect and affordable food revitalized popular militancy.

In early April (12–13 Germinal III), thousands marched on the Convention to demand bread. But, in a reversal of the democratic activism driven by leaders without troops in the summer and fall, Germinal was the work of troops without leaders. Lacking spokesmen or friendly deputies to channel its energy into legislation, the crowd only galvanized reaction. The Convention faced down the people by calling in National Guard and gilded youth to protect it, and declaring martial law. Then it purged its ranks. Falling back on terrorist practices, the Assembly violated its own parliamentary immunity to order deportation without trial of three of the committee members Lecointre had targeted, and arrested another sixteen former Montagnards (Lefebvre 1964 [1957]; Tønnesson 1959).

Without legislation to relieve inflation and scarcity, the famine intensified. Men were too weak to work, women collapsed in the streets, children died in scores. Despair sent suicide rates skyrocketing (Tønnesson 1959). In late May (1 Prairial III), Parisians marched on the Convention again, to demand bread and the Constitution of 1793, staging what would prove to be the last radical uprising of the Revolution. Leaderless still, they discredited themselves with undisciplined fury. The first insurgents to invade the Assembly's halls struck down a deputy who tried to block their way, cut off his head and paraded it among his colleagues on a pike. Others tapped barrels of wine in the courtyard upon which hungry, exhausted citizens became drunk before returning to insult debating legislators. Late in the day, a few deputies proposed to restore revolutionary government and improve provisioning shortly before the National Guard arrived.

Once liberated from the crowd, the deputies determined to be done with it for good. They sent armed forces into the rebellious faubourg Saint-Antoine and created a military commission that judged 149 presumed insurgents, sentencing thirty-six to summary execution (Tønnesson 1959). The Convention's efforts were seconded by moderates in the Paris sections eager to prove their loyalty and rid themselves of local radicals. Those men sent 1,500 suspected militants to prison to linger uncharged for months, and disarmed another 2,000, striking blows both practical and psychological at the popular movement by taking away the pikes that were the symbol *par excellence* of sans-culottes militancy (Burstin 1996).

Police repression found an echoing response in newspapers that repudiated celebrations of popular militancy stretching back to 1789 with jeremiads against the crowd. Raymonde Monnier describes 1 Prairial as the symbolic inverse of 14 July: newspapers evoked the September Massacres as they excoriated a monstrous people and championed as heroes the deputies who withstood them. Those papers even reimagined the capital's political geography, destroying the popular faubourg Saint-Antoine's reputation as the heart of revolutionary energy to restore its notoriety as a shady neighborhood of dangerous classes (Burstin 1996; Monnier 1996).

Within the Convention, Prairial became an excuse to complete the purge of ranks. Deputies ordered the arrest of forty former Montagnards, the most celebrated of whom would prove to be the six condemned for abetting the crowd in Prairial. Those six, who included Gilbert Romme and Sylvain Goujon, had proposed the restoration of revolutionary government and better provisioning, but none were notorious Robespierrists during the Terror nor outspoken hardliners against the Reaction. All defended their motions as efforts to protect the Assembly as much as to preserve the people, but the military commission condemned them anyway. When sentenced, they stabbed themselves like Roman heroes to win a place in the virtual pantheon of uncompromising radicalism. Nonetheless, their deaths advanced the vast chill of popular militancy that would endure for two generations (Brunel 1996; Brunel and Goujon 1992).

Having defeated the popular movement, the Convention turned its attention to the suspended democratic Constitution of 1793, whose restoration democrats had been demanding since Thermidor. Germinal and Prairial provoked decisive action here too. The Committee of Eleven, formed to enact the constitution, scrapped it for a new and far more conservative code. Speaking on its behalf, Boissy d'Anglas explained their guiding principles. The Constitution of 1793 institutionalized anarchy, he insisted, by authorizing insurgents, political clubs, and the Paris Commune to compete with the Assembly; it sowed the seeds of tyranny by shielding the Assembly from tutelage by an upper house or strong executive. The new constitution would correct all of this by creating a strong government whose powers were judiciously balanced and whose leaders were men of property. For, he concluded, "we should be governed by the best, by those with the greatest education and the greatest devotion to upholding the law ... you will only find such men among those who, as proprietors, are bound to the country that houses their property, the laws that protect it, and the peace that preserves it ..." (Boissy d'Anglas 1821 [1795]: 125).

The Constitution of 1795 abolished the threat of "anarchy" by limiting external opposition to the Assembly as much as was possible. Most pointedly, its drafters suppressed the right of insurrection, that "calamitous axiom of disorganization" guaranteed by the constitution of 1793 (Boissy d'Anglas 1821 [1795]: 151). More troubling were the limits they placed on rights of association and free speech. They forbade outright the organization of popular societies, like those that played such an important part in the sans-culottes movement of the Year II, and erected a barrier against the emergence of another power like that of the Jacobins by prohibiting individual political clubs from communicating with one another. They guaranteed a free press but took with one hand what they gave with the other, for the same article that made the promise permitted its breach should "circumstances require" (Hall 1951: article 355; Luchaire 1999).

So determined was the Convention to eradicate any constitutional language that might justify popular revolt that it abolished even the promise of "common good" (*bonheur commun*) and the affirmation of natural rights that graced the brilliant

Declaration of the Rights of Man and of the Citizen of 1789. Both principles, they feared, might generate disorder. As one deputy explained when condemning the assertion that "all men are born free and equal in rights," perhaps the most famous phrase of the Revolution's founding: preserving it would require the Convention to itemize each right and explain whether it existed prior to or was concomitant with society. To do otherwise would risk vague promises that malcontents might exploit to justify insurgency. Rather than brave such potentially troubled waters, it was better to ratify only temporally and culturally bounded rights (Jainchill 2008: 54–55).

The Convention agreed to shape a government of Boissy's "best" by replacing universal male suffrage with an indirect and narrowly defined electoral process. All resident men over the age of 21 who paid any tax whatsoever would be eligible to vote in the first round of elections, but only literate citizens would retain that privilege when a decade was up. That this was truly limiting is made clear by the absence of an accompanying provision guaranteeing free and universal education. Limits on suffrage became still more rigorous at the second round of elections. Here, only men who held property or had an income worth five to seven months' labor could participate, and all had to travel at their own expense to electoral assemblies. Each voice would be deemed to represent the wishes of 200 citizens, twice as many as those for whom electors were claimed to speak in 1791. In sum, a government responsible for some 27 million citizens was to be chosen by roughly 30,000 men. Once elected, the constitution's drafters expected that the government would not only speak for the people but inform them of their "true, if unknown, interest" (Jainchill 2008: 52; Lefebvre 1964 [1957]; Sydenham 1974).

Having claimed to fear tyranny as well as anarchy, Boissy and his colleagues limited the Assembly's power. They created upper and lower houses, dividing between them the functions of proposing and authorizing legislation, and they crafted an executive of five men, elaborating duties and limitations for a branch of government about which the Constitution of 1793 had been almost wholly silent (Le Bozec 1995, 2003). But, however important these innovations meant to balance power within the government, they were in no way so extensive as the barriers erected against external challenges. The Convention's final provision for the new government of the Directory made this abundantly clear. Expressing a profound mistrust of the electorate, the deputies decreed that two-thirds of the old legislature must be re-elected to the new. If an insufficient number of men were named at the polls, they would be co-opted by sitting deputies.

Having freed itself of popular forces and affirmed the state's role in guiding France, the Assembly confronted one last rival in Paris. The gilded youth had, in the wake of the sans-culottes' defeat, degenerated from "useful auxiliaries into … reckless, domineering hooligans" (Gendron 1993). The Convention struggled with them until mounting tensions came to a head over the two-thirds decree. When a national plebiscite accepted that decree in the fall of 1795, reactionaries condemned any effort to extend the tenure of deputies who had presided over the Terror and expressed fears that a mild thaw in official relations with former Jacobins signaled a desire to renew Robespierrist tyranny. Organizing through the same sectional assemblies that once served the sans-culottes, they attacked. The

Convention answered with troops that quickly retook the city. The ensuing repression in no way matched the spring assault on the sans-culottes – city gates were left open to allow insurgents to flee and the men condemned *in absentia* were never sought – but the gilded youth were finished as a political force (Gendron 1993; Lefebvre 1964 [1957]).

By the time the Directory was elected in October 1795, legislators believed they had not only ended the Terror but also the Revolution. They had completed the Montagnard project of reining in Parisian militancy by transforming Robespierre's political terror into an all-out assault that compounded the confiscation of vital institutions with mounting malice against working people and, finally, sheer starvation. For if the Assembly was surprised by the inflation that repeal of the maximum produced, its persistent refusal to provide assistance in its wake exhausted the people and drove them to desperate measures. Those measures elicited the death-blow of Prairial: far-reaching legal repression seconded by the scorn of an angry press. The people of Paris would not rouse themselves again until well into the nineteenth century. Freed from the rivalry of Jacobins and the Paris crowd, the Convention cemented its authority with a constitution that not only guarded against renewed popular militancy but circumscribed all political activity, excluding most of the nation from active citizenship and imposing new barriers on extra-electoral activism. And yet if the Assembly strengthened the republican state by eliminating its nearest rivals, it did so at terrible cost. For it allowed reactionaries and counter-revolutionaries to run riot in the provinces and continued the revolutionary assault on the notion of loyal opposition.

Absorbed by political battles in the capital, the Thermidorian Convention ceded critical advantages to counter-revolutionaries in the west and reactionaries in the south. In Brittany and the Vendée, it negotiated peace treaties of foolishly generous terms that privileged both regions over the rest of France by granting complete freedom of worship and exemption from military service. Most dangerously, by amnestying former combatants and allowing them to remain armed, ostensibly to police themselves, the Convention practically guaranteed renewed revolt and the widespread lawlessness that simmered for years (Brown 2006; Mathiez 2010 [1929]; Sydenham 1974).

Circumstances in the south were bleaker still. Prepared to accept an unofficial reaction, the Convention replaced Jacobins with men willing to accept a private settling of the Terror's scores. The consequences were disastrous: reaction fused with long-standing factional disputes and traditional notions of justice in the Midi to produce the White Terror. Throughout the spring and summer of 1795, Jacobins and Jacobin sympathizers fell victim to harassment, brutalization, and murder. Prison massacres dotted the region, and mutilated bodies were tossed in rivers or left festering on roadsides. Although this explicitly political violence receded during the Directory, it left marauding bands of uprooted men to prey on travelers and isolated farmhouses for years (Clay 1999; Cobb 1970, 1972; Lewis 1983; Lucas 1983).

The private costs of the violence in the west and the south were terrible. So too were the public costs. Howard Brown has argued that the persistent chaos first weakened the Directory by suggesting that it was incapable of imposing order, and then encouraged the government to rely on "undemocratic and illiberal ... methods of repression," which undermined its promise to respect the rule of law. This was the Directory's legacy to Napoleon, who ended the Revolution as much because of his willingness to increase repression as to negotiate compromise over religion, conscription, and warfare (Brown 2006).

Provincial chaos was not the only cost of the Year III. The nation's deadly see-sawing between left and right fostered a conviction that the only men capable of guaranteeing peace and stability were those who could rise above politics to contain both ends of the political spectrum. This had much to do with the self-serving activism of men like Fréron and Tallien, who fanned the flames of just anger against the Terror into a raging blaze and who helped to translate a legitimate search for justice into purges and vigilantism. The Reaction's vilification of the left fueled a spiraling revenge whose excesses came to be equated with counter-revolution. By the time the Directory was inaugurated, citizens at both ends of the political spectrum had been dismissed as opponents of the constitutional order. But those same citizens quite legitimately considered themselves victims of extremism as well. This widespread sense of victimization would jeopardize future efforts at rapprochement because each side panicked at the first sign of discord, convinced that they were about to be persecuted once more. At the same time, government centrists exploited their opponents' status as irreconcilables, dismissing the left as "anarchists" and the right as "royalists" to strengthen their own grip on the state. As Pierre Serna has argued, such centrists would elaborate a notion of "neutral" executive power to justify the coups that regularly rattled the Directory before bringing it down, once and for all, in 1799 (Serna 2005). In sum, rather than ending the Revolution, the Reaction initiated a stumbling search for order that ended only with the Napoleonic dictatorship.

The Thermidorian Reaction did far more than simply return France to the liberal aspirations of 1789–91, as the Marxists claimed. It produced a regime that was both less and more conservative than the one brought into being by the Revolution of 1789. On the one hand, the Thermidorians affirmed the abolition of the monarchy. On the other, Boissy and his colleagues expunged from the Constitution of 1795 the affirmations of natural rights and iron-clad guarantees of civil liberties that made the 1789 Declaration of the Rights of Man a beacon of humanitarianism.

What may be less clear is just how the Reaction described here departs from the long consolidation of state power described by Alexis de Tocqueville and François Furet. There is undeniable justice to that case, but the long view obscures as much as it reveals. For although the Thermidorians consolidated the state, they could not conjure away the memory of popular democracy, promised in 1792 and ratified by the Constitution of 1793. That memory would serve as a rallying point for working-class militancy through the nineteenth century.

Finally, there is the problem of contextualization. Restoring social, political, and institutional interests to the Thermidorian Reaction illuminates how the nation might have ended the Terror and the Revolution while affirming the rule of law. Had the Thermidorians been willing to share power by revising and enacting the democratic Constitution of 1793 and organizing new elections, they might have rallied the citizenry. Had they agreed to a searching examination of responsibility for political excesses and more quickly reformed exceptional laws and institutions, they might have saved the nation from the costs of demonizing whole categories of citizens and arbitrarily scapegoating a few high-profile figures. Had the Convention acted more decisively to feed working people during the terrible winter of 1795, it might have saved itself from Germinal and Prairial, and the violence that news of those insurrections excited in the Midi.

Such second-guessing is not meant to hint at a parallel history of the Thermidorian Reaction but to restore contingency to the event. It should as well suggest the value of amalgamating Bronislaw Baczko's framing of the Reaction with three generations of social history. Just as we need not believe that the Reaction folded the Revolution back on itself to advance the rise of the bourgeoisie, as Marxists like Lefebvre and Soboul suggested, neither must we accept that the Reaction could have been nothing but a violent paroxysm that swept France and laid waste the Revolution's democratic promise.

As a more capacious understanding of the events and possibilities of the Revolution's Year III refines what we know, it raises new questions. Above all, we still do not sufficiently understand how the Terror was reimagined beyond the confines of the National Convention. This is vital to explaining why the Reaction unfolded as it did and how its reification of the Terror proved so enduring. Some historians are broaching this subject by looking more closely at the great trials of the Reaction, to ask what role the prosecution of men like Jean-Baptiste Carrier and Joseph Lebon played in criminalizing the Terror and why those trials failed to resolve the post-Thermidorian search for justice (Brown 2010; Gomez-Le Chevanton 2006; Steinberg 2010). Closer examination of the anti-terrorist press would also explain how particular notions of Robespierrism and Terror were popularized. For although we know that periodicals and ephemera exploded after repeal of the Prairial Laws, we do not know much about their actual content beyond the copious scholarship devoted to Gracchus Babeuf and some very suggestive comments by Sergio Luzzatto (Chalmin 2011; Dommanget 1935; Luzzatto 2001; Rose 1978). Even Stanislas Fréron's *Orateur du peuple* which, taken as a whole, is one of the most important polemical texts of the period, has not received the sustained attention necessary to unpack the editor's complicated relationship with the Reaction. Finally, how did Jacobins explain the Terror for which they alone would be held responsible? Pierre Serna's exemplary work on P.-A. Antonelle's careful assumption of responsibility and Sophie Wahnich's thoughtful consideration of how Jacobins positioned themselves between past and future suggest possible approaches to the study of Thermidor's beleaguered left (Serna 1997; Wahnich 1997).

A fuller appreciation of reactionary culture must be complemented by a more thorough understanding of its audience. There is, at present, a persistent association of urban reaction with the well-to-do. Admittedly, gilded youth were the Reaction's stormtroopers and this same period saw the emergence of privileged "muscadins" and "merveilleuses," who flaunted their wealth as the poor starved. But we require more sustained study of ordinary Parisians through the fall and winter of 1794–95, for these were the people who not only refused to turn out for Robespierre on the night of 9–10 Thermidor but who also failed to mobilize behind democratic reformers in the Electoral Club. What were their political opinions and expectations? How did their political attitudes change through the winter of 1794–95? Did all working people endorse the riots of Germinal and Prairial or did some of them continue to support the Convention? Such work would help us better to understand the newly mobile opinion of the Thermidorian Reaction.

As scholarship on the Reaction continues to advance, it illuminates the importance of a period once considered a mere ellipsis in the Revolution and locates continuities in a republic we once believed irredeemably shattered by Thermidor.

References

Primary Sources

Babeuf, Gracchus (1794). *Journal de la liberté de la presse*, nos. 18, 27, 29. Paris: de l'Imprimerie de Guffroy.

Boissy d'Anglas, François Antoine de (1821 [1795]). "Discours préliminaire au projet de Constitution pour la république française, prononcé ... 5 messidor an III." In *Choix de rapports, opinions et discours prononcés à la Tribune Nationale depuis 1789 jusqu'à ce jour*, vol. 15: *Année 1794–95*. Paris: Alexis Eymery, Libraire.

Dommanget, Maurice (1935). *Pages choisies de Babeuf.* Paris: Armand Colin.

Fréron, Stanislas (1794a). *Opinion sur la liberté de la presse...* Paris: Imprimerie Nationale.

Fréron, Stanislas (1794b). *Orateur du peuple*, X, XIII. Paris: Imprimerie de Laurens Jr.

Hall, John Stewart (ed.) (1951). *A Documentary Survey of the French Revolution.* New York: Macmillan.

Lecointre, Laurent (1794). *Les Crimes de sept membres des Anciens Comités de Salut Public et de Sûreté Générale* ... Paris: Chez Maret.

Méhée de la Touche, Jean Claude Hippolyte (1794). *La Queue de Robespierre, ou les dangers de la liberté de la presse.* Paris: Imprimerie de Rougyff.

Tallien, Jean-Lambert (n.d. [1794]). *Discours prononcé à la Convention nationale, dans la séance du 11 fructidor, l'an II ... sur les principes du gouvernement révolutionnaire.* Paris: Imprimerie Nationale.

Secondary Sources

Baczko, Bronislaw (1989). "Thermidorians." In François Furet and Mona Ozouf (eds.). *A Critical Dictionary of the French Revolution*, trans. Arthur Goldhammer. Cambridge, Mass., and London: The Belknap Press of Harvard University Press. 400–413.

Baczko, Bronislaw (1994). *Ending the Terror: The French Revolution after Robespierre*, trans. Michel Petheram. Cambridge: Cambridge University Press.

Brown, Howard (2006). *Ending the French Revolution: Violence, Justice and Repression from the Terror to Napoleon.* Charlottesville and London: University of Virginia Press.

Brown, Howard (2010). "Robespierre's Tail: The Possibilities of Justice after the Terror." *Canadian Journal of History*, 55: 503–535.

Brunel, Françoise (1989). *Thermidor: La Chute de Robespierre.* Brussels: Éditions Complexe.

Brunel, Françoise (1996). "Pourquoi ces 'six' parmi les 'derniers Montagnards'?" *AHRF*, 304: 401–413.

Brunel, Françoise and Sylvain Goujon (1992). *Les martyrs de Prairial.* Geneva: Georg Éditeur S.A.

Burstin, Haim (1996). "Échos faubouriens des journées de Prairial." *AHRF*, 304: 373–385.
Chalmin, Ronan (2011). "La République populicide: Relire 'Du système de dépopulation' de G. Babeuf." *Dix-huitième siècle*, 43: 447–468.
Clay, Stephen (1999). "Réaction dans le Midi (1795–1800)." *Dictionnaire des usages socio-politiques (1770–1815). Fasc. 6: Notions pratiques.* Paris: Institut National de la Langue Française.
Cobb, Richard (1970). *The Police and the People. French Popular Protest, 1789–1820.* London: Oxford University Press.
Cobb, Richard (1972). *Reactions to the French Revolution.* London, New York, and Toronto: Oxford University Press.
Dorigny, Marcel (1996). "La Gironde sous Thermidor." In Roger Dupuy and Marcel Morabito (eds.). *1795: Pour une République sans Révolution.* Rennes: Presses Universitaires de Rennes. 230–242.
Dupuy, Roger and Marcel Morabito (eds.) (1996). *1795: Pour une République sans Révolution.* Rennes: Presses Universitaires de Rennes.
Furet, François (1981). *Interpreting the French Revolution*, trans. Elborg Forster. Cambridge and New York: Cambridge University Press.
Furet, François and Denis Richet (1970). *The French Revolution*, trans. Stephen Hardman. New York: Macmillan.
Gainot, Bernard (2001). *1799, un nouveau Jacobinisme?* Paris: CTHS.
Gendron, François (1993). *The Gilded Youth of Thermidor*, trans. James Cookson. Montreal and Kingston: McGill-Queen's University Press.
Gomez-Le Chevanton, Corinne (2006). "Le Procès Carrier: Enjeux politiques, pédagogie collective et construction mémorielle." *AHRF*, 343: 73–92.
Gough, Hugh (1988). *The Newspaper Press in the French Revolution.* London: Routledge.
Hincker, François (1997). "Comment sortir de la terreur économique?" In Michel Vovelle (ed.). *Le Tournant de l'an III: Réaction et Terreur blanche dans la France révolutionnaire.* Paris: CTHS. 149–158.
Jainchill, Andrew (2008). *Reimagining Politics after the Terror: The Republican Origins of French Liberalism.* Ithaca, N.Y. and London: Cornell University Press.
Kennedy, Michael (2000). *The Jacobin Clubs in the French Revolution, 1793–1795.* New York and Oxford: Berghahn Books.
Le Bozec, Christine (1995). *Boissy d'Anglas: Un grand notable libéral.* Privas: Fédération des Oeuvres Laiques de l'Ardèche.
Le Bozec, Christine (2003). "An III: Créer, inventer, réinventer le pouvoir exécutif." *AHRF*, 332: 71–79.
Lefebvre, Georges (1964 [1957]). *The French Revolution*, vol. 2: *From 1793 to 1799*, trans. John Hall Stewart and James Friguglietti. New York: Columbia University Press.
Lewis, Gwynne (1983). "Political Brigandage and Popular Disaffection in the South-East of France 1795–1804." In Gwynne Lewis and Colin Lucas (eds.). *Beyond the Terror: Essays in French Regional and Social History, 1794–1815.* Cambridge: Cambridge University Press. 195–231.
Livesey, James (2001). *Making Democracy in the French Revolution.* Cambridge, Mass., and London: Harvard University Press.
Lucas, Colin (1983). "Themes in Southern Violence after 9 Thermidor." In Gwynne Lewis and Colin Lucas (eds.) *Beyond the Terror: Essays in French Regional and Social History, 1794–1815.* Cambridge: Cambridge University Press. 152–194.
Luchaire, François (1999). "Boissy d'Anglas et la Constitution de l'an III." In Gérard Conac and Jean-Pierre Machelon (eds.). *La Constitution de l'an III: Boissy d'Anglas et la naissance du libéralisme constitutionnel.* Paris: PUF. 43–49.

Luzzatto, Sergio (2001). *L'Automne de la Révolution: Luttes et cultures politiques dans la France thermidorienne*, preface by Bronislaw Baczko, trans. Simon Carpentari Messina. Paris: Honoré Champion.

Lyons, Martyn (1975). "The 9 Thermidor: Motives and Effects." *European Studies Review*, 5(2): 123–146.

Mathiez, Albert (2010 [1929]). *La Réaction thermidorienne*, introd. Yannick Bosc and Florence Gauthier. Paris: La Fabrique.

Monnier, Raymonde (1996). "L'Étendue d'un désastre: Prairial et la révolution populaire." *AHRF*, 304: 387–400.

Monnier, Raymonde (1997). "Le Tournant de Brumaire: Dépopulariser la révolution parisienne." In Michel Vovelle (ed.). *Le Tournant de l'an III: Réaction et Terreur blanche dans la France révolutionnaire*. Paris: CTHS. 187–199.

Rose, R.B. (1978). *Gracchus Babeuf, the First Revolutionary Communist*. Stanford, Calif.: Stanford University Press.

Rudé, George (1959). *The Crowd in the French Revolution*. London, Oxford, and New York: Oxford University Press.

Serna, Pierre. (1997). *Antonelle: Aristocrate révolutionnaire, 1747–1817*. Paris: Éditions du Félin.

Serna, Pierre (2005). *La République des Girouettes*. Paris: Champ Vallon.

Soboul, Albert (1975). *The French Revolution, 1787–1799*, trans. Alan Forrest and Colin Jones. New York: Vintage Books.

Steinberg, Ronen (2010). "The Afterlives of the Terror: Dealing with the Legacies of Violence in Post-Revolutionary France, 1794–1830s." Ph.D dissertation. University of Chicago.

Sydenham, M.J. (1974). *The First French Republic, 1792–1804*. Berkeley and Los Angeles: University of California Press.

Tønnesson, Kare D. (1959). *La Défaite des sans-culottes: Mouvement populaire et réaction bourgeoise en l'an III*. Oslo: Presses Universitaires.

Tønnesson, Kare D. (1960). "L'An III dans la formation du babouvisme." *AHRF*, 32: 411–425.

Wahnich, Sophie (1997). "La Question de la responsibilité collective en l'an III." In Michel Vovelle (ed.). *Le Tournant de l'an III: Réaction et Terreur blanche dans la France révolutionnaire*. Paris: CTHS. 85–97.

Vovelle, Michel (ed.) (1997). *Le Tournant de l'an III: Réaction et Terreur blanche dans la France révolutionnaire*. Paris: CTHS.

Chapter Twenty

The Political Culture of the Directory

James Livesey

The duchesse d'Abrantes, in her 1838 history of the salons of Paris, wrote that the Directory, which she thoroughly disliked, was the period that exemplified republican social life, art and culture (d'Abrantes 1838: vol. 3, 231). In the 1820s the same observation had been made by one of the Directors, Louis-Marie Larévellière-Lépeaux. In his memoirs he also complained that the history of the period had been systematically falsified, "by a horde of writers who think of themselves as excellent liberals," who had once supported the republic but had then rallied to Bonaparte (Larévellière 1895: vol. 1, 365). In recent years the expanded body of work on the Directory has overcome the image of a moment of anti-political excess created by the Goncourts, but research is still developing a mature account of the republican political culture that contemporaries claimed that the period exemplified (Goncourt 1855). The Directory instituted a national education system, created the first national industrial exhibition, and experimented with electoral practices that would inform French politics in the following centuries; it provided the shaping context for a variety of important periodicals, notably the *Décade philosophique*, and inspired important work in political theory and political economy from figures such as Destutt de Tracey, Germaine de Staël, and Jean-Baptiste Say. The Directory was also a key moment in the elaboration of key cultural institutions such as the Institut and the Musée d'Histoire Naturelle, and was the period in which a new ideal for sustained work in natural philosophy, the professional scientific career, was defined (Gillispie 2004). The four years of the Directory were absolutely central to the articulation of a new zone of privacy and consumption that would form the kernel of bourgeois life, but they were also key moments in the shaping of public institutions and forms of politics (Spang 2002).

Isolating what is specific to the Directory from this confusion of creativity and calumny is difficult. It is even more difficult to identify the elements of its political

A Companion to the French Revolution, First Edition. Edited by Peter McPhee.

culture that retained sustained importance. The Directory, for instance, created the Bureau of Weights and Measures that defined the metre and the gram, and succeeded in embedding their use in the country. The new metric system was an important symbol of the goals of the Directory, eulogized in the *Bulletin décadaire* as an instrument of universal peace: "it will finally be the rallying point for all commercial peoples as it will regularize all conventions; sooner or later it will become the universal system of Europe" (2e décade Frimaire VII/October 1798). However, the aspiration for a uniform system of weights and measures was not a novel idea and long preceded 1789 (Alder 1995). Moreover, the law on the metric system of 18 Germinal III (7 April 1795) was not a law made under the Directory, but one of the last acts of the Convention, and the law of 19 Frimaire VIII (9 December 1799), making the system obligatory for all purposes in France, was passed a month after the coup of 18 Brumaire. Even then the law of 19 Frimaire proved temporary, repealed by Napoleon in 1812, and the old regional measures reintroduced; it was not until the 1840s, under Louis-Philippe, that the metric system became securely and definitively established. Accurate, textured accounts of the political culture of the Directory have to respect very complicated and even contradictory narratives. It is tempting, but ultimately unhelpful, to see the Directory as a stage on the apprenticeship to citizenship, a forerunner of the Third Republic; that teleology obscures too much of what was important to the period. A viable account of the political culture of the Directory has to recognize the fractures, inconsistencies, and contradictions it contained.

Louis-Marie Larévellière-Lépeaux offers a useful point from which to investigate the specificity of the Directory. Only Paul Barras served as a Director for longer than Larévellière, and Barras, unlike Larévellière, supported the coup of 18 Brumaire, if not the eventual dominance of Napoleon. Larévellière refused to rally to Napoleon and so did not subsequently falsify or even refashion the positions he had taken between 1795 and 1799. His refusal was not just pique or frustration at seeing another exercise the power that he had coveted. He thought that there was a difference of principle between the kind of authority the Directors aggregated to themselves and that seized by Napoleon Bonaparte. He took this seriously enough that he gave up public life, his membership of the Institut and the pension that went with it in the Year XI and so, as he explained to Chaptal, "I no longer find myself in the position of having to take the oath you asked of me yesterday" (Larévellière Commonplace Book, 9 Prairial IX/29 May 1801). Even after its fall he continued to articulate the ideals of the Directory.

Larévellière-Lépeaux, like so many of the leading figures of the Revolution, emerged from the provincial bourgeoisie: born in 1753, his father had been mayor of Montaigu in the Poitou for thirty years. The family's wealth had been based in the region's declining textile industry and was in the process of being transformed into land and the professions. He was trained as a lawyer, but failed to make a Parisian career. By 1782 he had settled into provincial obscurity as an improving farmer, at his wife's vineyard at Faye d'Anjou in what is now the department of the Maine-et-Loire, and as a natural historian, giving a yearly course in Linnean botany for the Société des Botanophiles in Angers. His local notoriety unexpectedly promoted him for election for the Third Estate of Anjou and later to the Convention, where he voted for the king's death but was proscribed after 31 May 1793. As a thinker, and as a public man, Larévellière-Lépeaux could be mediocre, self-deluding, and ineffectual, patronized by Thiers as "ce pauvre imbecile à principes" (Taine 1885: 598). Lazare Carnot, who was his colleague but was the object of the coup mounted by Larévellière, Reubell, and Barras in Fructidor V, gave a reasonably measured judgment of the man:

> Révellière offers to the world another example of the important truth, that rigorous private morals alone, if not allied to education, a strong character and some political sense, far from providing a solid basis for good government, can be the source of all the faction and disorder that ruin it. (Carnot, An VIII/1799–1800: 238)

Larévellière made the same point about himself in a fragmentary diary, "a man with a loving soul and a tender heart is not the right man to govern" (Larévellière Commonplace Book). Larévellière offers a useful point of entry to the political culture of the Directory not because he was endowed with some species of political genius that allowed him to understand and master the moment, but precisely because he reflected its confusions and ambivalences and so illustrates them for us.

A new, and surprising, consensus has emerged that holds that the central contribution of the Directory to the complex history of French political culture is the legacy it left to the nature and practice of the French state, and in particular the state's executive function. The work of Pierre Rosanvallon, Isser Woloch, and Pierre Serna has refocused our attention on the power and the exceptionality awarded to itself by the executive and the emergence of a "radical center" that claimed to represent the public interest above and beyond any representative institutions. The idea of some peculiar immobility at the heart of the French polity has a long history, stemming notably from Tocqueville. This new work gives a much more empirically and historically grounded account of the genesis of the anomalous French state. Serna's notion of the *girouette*, the turncoat, fleshes out and explains Woloch's finding that in great part the agents of the Brumaire coup were the *Directorials*, the supporters of the regime. These were the original *girouettes* (Anon. 1815). These political elites set the pattern for the *hauts fonctionnaires*, high state functionaries who, in France, would protect the state from opinion by representing and institutionalizing a practice of sovereign reason. In Serna's account the *girouette*, patterned on the one-time republican allies of Bonaparte, did not maintain the stability of the state by finding the compromise position between social interests. Instead he maintained a radical moderation, an ideological centrism between left and right, which insulated the executive from threats to its role generated by different ideas of legitimacy, democratic or constitutional. The *girouette* was described in the pages of the *Décade philosophique* by Pierre Jean George Cabanis in the immediate aftermath of the Brumaire coup: "thinkers allied to active men, attached to those noble principles which can no longer be obscured by the abuses of royalism or the crimes of anarchy, men philosophical by taste and temperament" (10 Nivôse VIII/31 December 1799). The research of recent years suggests that even if the historical moment in which this formulation appears is the Brumaire coup, it was incubated in the Directory.

The notion of an idiosyncratic executive, equipped with a corresponding public culture and political identity, illuminates and gives focus to the history of the Directory. Howard Brown's study (2006) of state repression after 1795 unites the empirical study of military courts and the use of exceptional state powers to a reading of the literature on executive power from Hobbes to Agamben in order to argue that the Directory founded a "security state" where the public interest was respected by providing order through the law rather than liberty under the law. Studies of the culture of state employees under the Directory reinforce the claim that it was the key moment in the development of a political culture of the state. Catherine Kawa's close analysis of the employees of the Ministry of the Interior and Ralph Kingston's study of the physical organization of ministerial offices both capture the social world that grew around this culture (Kawa 1996; Kingston 2006). The Directory and the Consulate created the template for the modern executive as an independent power in the French polity and generated its distinctive claim to guarantee, rather than threaten, the liberty and independence of the citizenry.

The twinned ideas of the security state and the radical center as the two defining concepts of the political culture of the Directory are not historians' neologisms. Both ideas were powerfully deployed in the period, even by the opponents of the regime. Contemporary commentators, such as Charles Théremin and Germaine de Staël, laid out the fundamentals of this analysis of the executive, arguing that its exaggerated role had historical roots. De Staël argued for a cultural continuity: Richelieu's innovations had destroyed the French political character and made governance impossible without a strong executive (de Staël 1983: 75). Théremin appealed to a different historical context, that of the ancient republics, to explain that the contradiction between the conditions of ancient citizenship and modern commercial life was the cause of "the lack of public spirit that is universally complained of" and opened the door to an overweening executive (An V/1797–98: 7). Bertrand Barère, a reliable weathervane and an oppositional Jacobin, warned in 1797 that "too much government has destroyed many empires" and that the Directory ran the danger of becoming a military government in fact even if it remain a civil government in law, so describing the phenomenon (An V/1797–98: 9; 1798). All of these observations concurred that the executive of the republic had acquired a preponderant role and was defining the space of citizenship.

The political crisis of the summer of 1797, and the coup in autumn, illuminated the dynamics of the political culture of the executive. In the elections of the Year V conservative and royalist critics of the Directory won the majority of the one-third of the seats contested in the Conseil des 500 and the Conseil des Anciens and, by the count of Jean-René Suratteau, held a plurality, though not a majority, of the seats in the legislature (1971: 303). The Directors, and Larévellière in particular, saw the electoral result not as a response to their governance but as a challenge to the legitimacy of the republic: "the constitution of the Year III unfortunately has not given the Directory any legal means of defending the constitution against attack ... Moreover, there was such a exaggerated fear of the executive power, as divided and temporarily held as it was, that we were left with the alternatives of allowing the constitution to fall with us, or to horribly offend constitutional principles in defending them" (Larévellière 1895: vol. 2, 63–64). He claimed that the weakness of the executive drove it to force; it was necessary to destroy the constitution to defend it. Confusion about the definition of legitimate power drove the Directors to scold the French people for having disappointed their government. In drawing a picture of the devotion to the Republic that should animate the population a government propagandist wagged his finger at the "French people, this is what you should be, and what you could be already if you had truly embraced the spirit of the constitution ..." (Directoire Exécutif, An V/1797: 5). Larévellière cited the idea of an unwitting alliance of the extremes against the reasonable center as justification for the coup: "citizens, the real danger of anarchy is that if it is victorious the crimes it commits and the calamities that will follow can only lead to the re-establishment of monarchy" (Lesage, An V/1797a: 3). The flexibility of the culture of the radical center meant that exactly the opposite claim could be and was made in defense of the executive. In the aftermath of the coup an anonymous pamphlet asserted that "royalism raises discontent and thus generates the resistance and struggles we have had to overcome" (Anon., An VI/1798: 1). Royalism generated faction and anarchy in this formulation rather than the other way around, but the function of the executive, to maintain and sustain a rational political community above faction, remained the same.

Emotions and imagination were integral elements of revolutionary political culture, and fear was a central component in the public culture of the Directory. The coup of Fructidor was animated by the same set of anxieties that Étienne Dumont noticed at work among the Gironde in 1792: "everyone unwittingly collaborated in destroying the monarchy, driven by fear and by the hope of freeing themselves from a kind of phantom that haunted them. One may mock, if one wishes, those imaginary terrors, but they made the second revolution" (1832: 391). The inability to imagine the executive as anything other than the unitary executor of sovereign power was a phantom that haunted all parties to the political crisis of the summer of 1797. As a pamphleteer put it, "yes my friend, fear governs the republic; fear of royalism drives the majority of the Directory to violent measures, and fear of anarchy leads the Council of 500 down its ill-considered pathway; fear puts them both in a state of war" (Lesage, An V/1797a: 1). Fear of civil war governed politics more effectively than anything else. Larévellière had cited that fear in his support for the two-thirds law guaranteeing the *conventionnels* control of the councils (*Bulletin de la Convention nationale*, 13 Fructidor III/30 August 1795). He was even more emphatic about the fear of civil war in private notes he made on the Fructidor coup. The royalists who imagined they could play the role of a General Monck ignored that the republic in France had altered the society as well as the state. To overturn it would demand a general civil war. Hobbes threw a significant shadow on the era.

While the idea of the radical center, integrated by fear of faction, did organize and direct the thinking of the majority in the Directory, it was not the only content to political life. The politics of the Directory was not a zero-sum game for control of the executive, and the option of integrating differing political ideals as a constituent element of republican stability was always entertained. Even the crisis of public finance created possibilities for compromise. In principle Larévellière was open to councils having ultimate control of public spending; in 1796 he had demanded a unified budget as a way in which the councils could maintain ultimate control of the state's finances while respecting the authority of the executive over its own agents. The problem in 1797 turned on the difference between annual budgets and votes on particular projects. The councils' control of the funds for particular projects allowed them to hamstring the efforts of the Directors without having to take the political risk of directly opposing particular initiatives. As a counter-revolutionary pamphleteer put it, "we openly admit it was because of public finance that the monarchy fell; and that is also how the republic must perish" (Anon., 1798: 21). The fiscal crisis of the regime, which included an almost totally depreciated currency and a tax strike, was recognized by the Genevan political economist and counter-revolutionary François d'Ivernois as the driver of political crisis. Faced with resistance to increases in funding from the council, the Directory "did not need to explain that it had no alternatives open to it other than a slow and ignominious default, or some desperate measure whose success would only prolong its precarious existence" (1798: 210). Underneath d'Ivernois' partisan position was an appreciation that public debt could, potentially, become the basis for integrating the country around the regime, the process that had stabilized the American Republic. The *Conservateur*, in the aftermath of the Fructidor coup, acknowledged that the coup created the opportunity to effectively default by paying of two-thirds of the debt in ***domaines nationaux***. That measure gave the regime some room for fiscal manoeuvre and the possibility to encourage "every kind of industry and huge strides in agriculture" to replace the fevered speculation that was destroying the economy. Yet it regretted the lost opportunity to rally the Republic around its credit. In the aftermath of default some foresaw it would create "an indifference among republicans for a republic which was no longer the repository of their wealth" (30 Fructidor V/16 September 1797). The fiscal difficulty of the regime created vulnerabilities but also opportunities to find new bases of support and a different relationship with French society.

Pierre Rosanvallon was at the forefront of the renewed attention to the state and the radical center, but was also among the first to attempt to confront the apparent paradox that, despite languages of politics that struggled to find representations of any politically or legally relevant entities between the citizen and the state, republican France has always enjoyed a strong associational culture and a mobilized citizenry. In his recent *Le Modèle politique français*, Rosanvallon pointed out that, despite its theoretical hostility to "intervening bodies," in practice republicanism had fostered, or at the very least tolerated, a thriving and complex associational life (2004). The political culture of the Directory is one of the sources of the set of languages that mediate what otherwise seem to be irreconcilable features of the polity. The imagined polarity between the executive and the people was clearly a central feature of the political culture of the Directory. However, alternative strong ideals of collective action first elaborated under the Directory, if less directly politically relevant at the time, latterly became absolutely central to French republicanism and continue to structure some of its core institutions.

The political culture of the Directory was not exhausted by the innovation of the radical center; indeed even theorists of executive power were clear that executive power was ultimately answerable to democratic norms and values. The culture of the "radical center" was only one of the four currents in the political culture of the Directory, all of which were efforts to respond to the democratic turn taken by the Revolution after 1792. Just how problematic that turn was needs re-emphasis. Clearly the Terror and revolutionary government bequeathed a difficult legacy to the Republic, but even without that trauma instituting, or even conceptualizing, a modern democracy would have posed a real challenge. John Dunn's work on the idea of democracy in the French Revolution, what he calls democracy's second coming, has done the great service of reminding us just how surprising it was that "democracy" should have emerged as a powerful idea at all (2005). For centuries democracy had been a word denoting an archaic form of direct popular rule, equivalent to popular anarchy, and had been rejected as a viable political model. The form of democratic mobilization that emerged in 1792 and was further developed in the constitution of 1793 and under the subsequent revolutionary government, promised forms of participation far beyond those developed in Paine's *Rights of Man* or in Mably's idealization of popular government in a "republic of laws." Popular societies, the military volunteers that brought down the monarchy on 10 August 1792 and significantly contributed to the victory at Valmy on 20 September, the local revolutionary sections: these all reflected the Athenian vision of direct popular participation, not the neo-Roman vision of mixed government that had dominated political thinking in the eighteenth century. This experience went well beyond even the most populist versions of republicanism that had offered a predominant role to the people, the many, in the early years of the Revolution. After 1792 the Republic became one institutional expression of democracy; before 1792 democracy had been a particularly unpopular version of a republic.

Intelligent royalists were particularly alive to the radical difference between democratic politics after 1792 and the republican politics that had preceded it. Mallet du Pan, writing in the *Mercure français*, explained that, "up to now republican competition has been restricted within the class of *propriétaires*," and warned that even though democracy was inherently unstable it would be unstoppable because it would electrify and unleash every popular passion and imagination. Democracy would be powerful because it would wash away all limitations, all countervailing forces, "public opinion ... Constitution ... state interest ... military power" (7 April 1792). Malouet explicitly pointed up the same transition. Popular government was tolerable when representative, but the mobilized people of Paris formed a "democracy more turbulent and more anarchic than that of Athens" (1792: 23). An anonymous royalist writing to William Eden, Baron Auckland, British ambassador at the Hague in late 1792, made the same point that democracy was uniquely powerful because unconstrained when "in its full flow" and so urged Eden to support a British declaration of war on France. French democracy would undermine the peace of Europe, "either we succeed in suffocating the French Democracy, or we can look forward to the overthrow of the greater part of Europe" (Anon. 1792).

Maximilien Robespierre exemplified this democratic revolution. After Thermidor he became a useful repository of responsibility for the Terror and a symbol of the despotism that the radical center held at bay. However, even after his fall his definition of a modern democracy held, and continued to frame the political culture of the Republic under the Directory. Robespierre's report to the Convention in the name of the Committee of Public Safety in February 1794 explained the challenge of defining the goals of a democratic revolution, in terms very close to those of its conservative critics. He understood and explained that one change the revolution had brought about was to make the Republic synonymous with democracy. He then enunciated the democratic principle of subsidiarity which transformed the meaning of the republican principle of representation: "democracy is not a state in which the people, continuously assembled, regulates by itself all public affairs ... Democracy is a state in which the sovereign people, guided by laws which are its own work, does by itself all it can do well, and through representation delegates all that it could not" (1965: 213). Representation, in this account, was not a substitute for direct engagement in public life, but a supplement to it. What Robespierre never satisfactorily defined was the space in which the people could "do by itself all it can do well"; his demand that virtue and equality characterize citizenship was never located in any specific institutional setting. The political culture of the Directory could reasonably be interpreted as an effort to succeed where Robespierre had failed. A series of experiments to locate and define the space for active citizenship made it a productive moment in the history of European democracy.

Contradictory as it may appear, the official culture of the Directory responded to Robespierre's problem of identifying how active citizenship could be exercised in a large commercial state. The dilemma was to locate and define the sphere of the modern polity that replicated the *agora*. Where did citizens act freely to give norms and values to themselves since all 26 million could not gather as one political assembly or law court? For Larévellière a civic religion provided that context. He was an enthusiastic supporter of both theophilanthropy and the *culte décadaire*, to the point that Carnot thought he had lost all perspective and become lost in anticlericism: "anyone who made fun of theophilanthropy was marked down by Révellière as a Pope-lover" (An VI/1798–99: 48). Larévellière did attract a lot of correspondence that urged him to institute theophilanthropy as an established religion to replace Catholicism, but he was impatient with such ideas and instead saw the various revolutionary cults as elements of a civil rather than religious order. As the founder of theophilanthropy, Jean-Baptiste Chemin-Despontès, explained, the goal of the organization was to "create a useful institution, which would heal the wounds of the revolution ... and unite the people in a genuine fraternity" (An X/1801–2: 9). Larévellière agreed that a fraternal cult was necessary to the Republic, but did not go far enough. A democratic republic needed three different sorts of moralizing institution: a religious cult, civil ceremonies, and national festivals. Civil ceremonies, he argued, should mark the transitional moments in the life, and even death, of the citizen. The role of the family as the school of the virtues and the frame for everyday life was made central to that cult. As the minister of the interior explained in his circular in the *Rédacteur* on the festival of marriage planned for Floréal VII, "the political connection of this festival is not its least important. These modest and domestic moral principles, of order, decency, frugality are essential supports of republican government" (5 Floréal VII/24 April 1798). The national festivals were planned to be spectacular in order to inspire the citizenry and Larévellière-Lépeaux wished to turn the Champ de Mars into a vast open arena for athletic contests, on the model of the Greek and Roman games. The festivals created by the minister of the interior, François de Neufchâteau, were in many ways more creative. Rather than mimicking the ancient games he synthesized the techniques of the *spectacles* of Paris with the political goals of the Republic. At the Festival of Agriculture, held in Messidor (late June) 1799 on the Champ de Mars, a commercial village was built around the agricultural show so that "both rural and urban dweller can find objects to delight their eyes, meet their needs and feed their desires [*fantaisies*]" (*Rédacteur*, An VII/1798). The most successful national festival was the Festival of the Foundation of the Republic, which, in the Year VI, was transformed into a five-day industrial exhibition. It was popular, so much so that it had to be extended for a further five days, and culturally important. The theme of the exhibition was that the real basis of the Republic was not the political violence that had attended its birth but "industry" because "the freest nations are necessarily the most industrious" (*Rédacteur*, 3e jour complementaire VI/19 September 1798). The booths of the exhibition were an entertainment, but also an illustration of how every French citizen participated in democratic politics through their work, and contributed to the common good through the products of that labor. The festivals were not a space of democratic politics, but illustrated what the Directors thought to be the real locus of democratic equality: a morally transformed everyday social life.

The relationship between these institutions and democratic politics was explicated in the first number of the *Bulletin décadaire*, a publication designed to knit together the civic services of the communities across the nation. The article reiterated the fundamental idea of democratic self-government: "every citizen is called to formation of the law, to its improvement and its reform and to fill all the public functions down to the most minor roles of the magistrature." Under modern conditions in large commercial societies it was impractical, and had proven dangerous, for the citizenry to assemble directly, so a representative system was necessary. This carried its own dangers because citizens could lose their sense of their role in the "the general system." Public institutions were necessary because the citizens' "souls must be nourished with elevated sentiments, because they must learn to put the public interest above their personal interest. Without this kind of civic education all the vital functions of representative government become paralyzed, and liberty has not been properly founded" (*Bulletin décadaire*, 1ère décade Vendémiaire VII/September 1798). The vision of an inclusive culture extended very far; even the democratic dead remained active in the Republic, remembered in garden or forest cemeteries that could form part of the social space of the republic (Larévellière, An VI/1797–98: 8).

The more innovative strand of the political culture of the Directory was commercial or modern republicanism. Commercial republicanism shared with the public culture of the Directory the intuition that democratic equality was experienced and exercised in society; what differentiated this strand of political culture was the centrality it gave to political economy in understanding that society. The languages of political economy allowed the thinkers and statesmen to conceptualize modern societies as arenas of active engagement by the citizenry, the core of the democratic republic, in creative ways. Charles Théremin, in his review of Jean-Baptiste Say's *Olbie* in the *Décade philosophique*, laid his finger on the possibility political economy offered of moving the locus of political identity away from the state. Political economy illuminated how:

> practical morality, based in institutions and in habits that acquire the force of law, has made more or less progress among different peoples. The civilized nations of Europe, in which every low act is under an anathema, all the more efficacious because the laws do not proscribe that kind of behavior, are the best example. One observes more good faith in commerce among them, and as they reap the benefits of their behavior, they are confirmed in the principles they have adopted, holding to them constantly without any legal coercion, just from the simple consideration of their personal interest. (20 Ventôse VIII/11 March 1800)

Government could be separated from citizenship in a rational way through the categories of political economy.

Modern republicanism was a capacious project under the Directory. Antoine Marbot, president of the Conseil des Anciens writing in the *Rédacteur*, put political economy at the heart of his explanation for the outbreak of the Revolution itself: "if, at last, the cry of liberty made itself heard, it was because of the great impulsion toward the objects of political economy" (30 Messidor VI/18 July 1798). Intensive modern commerce promised to provide the basis for independent citizens. Modern republicanism would break the connection between republican liberty and slavery; in the modern republic the citizens' work, rather than their voice, would be their central contribution to the common good. Improved agriculture was at the heart of this vision because by making peasants wealthy the country could provide the market for manufactures and so initiate a virtuous emulatory circle. The industrious republic, most vividly portrayed in Say's *Olbie*, would allow the republican state to avoid war with other states competing for control of long-distance trade (An VIII/1799). At a policy level commercial republicanism inspired a program of economic development based on the promotion of improved agriculture and internal communications (Livesey 2001: 88–166).

The project of "improvement" had a long genealogy reaching back to the sixteenth century, and agriculture had been singled out as the exemplary occupation for a free man as early as the "Christian agrarianism" of Fénelon; what marked out the modern republicanism of the Directory from these antecedents was the sustained commitment to democracy. Sophie de Grouchy's *Letters*, the preface to her translation of Adam Smith's *Theory of Moral Sentiments*, articulated the idea of commercial or modern citizenship with real clarity (Smith, An VI/1798–99). Reversing Rousseau's drama of alienation, she argued that as societies become more complex they amplify the capacity of individuals for empathetic understanding of one another. Their education through society in their dependence on one another allows citizens to glimpse universal rules of justice and equity. Only the rich and powerful, cocooned away from the common life of interdependence, would be insensitive to the education of a commercial society in compassion. The political consequences of inequality created the role for the state: "one of the primary goals of the laws ought to be to create and maintain an equality of wealth among the citizenry." Her argument was not for material but moral equality. Gross material need would "render them incapable of the degree of reflection necessary for the perfection of all natural sentiments, and particularly that of humanity." The same notion of a social democracy was developed in the work of Jean-Baptiste Salaville, who argued that pleasure and virtue were mutually reinforcing when embedded in political equality (An VII/1798–99). Society and democratic citizenship were harnessed together through the optic of political economy.

Modern republicanism fractured after Brumaire. Liberal republicanism, particularly in the writing of Benjamin Constant, emerged out of the wreckage as a separate strand. This line of thought would attempt to turn back to classical republican themes of divided government and marry them to a new vision of society comprised of private individuals rather than citizens (Jainchill 2008). This fracture eventually opened up a gap between the liberal and republican traditions in France. However, that divorce could not have been predicted under the Directory and was not a feature of its politics. While there were important variants of modern republicanism, it formed one culture. Germaine de Staël, who is one of the central figures in liberal republicanism, was a declared supporter of the Directory, even if a critic of many of its impolitic acts. In the aftermath of the Fructidor coup the *Conservateur*, edited by Garat, Daunou, and Chénier, all modern republicans themselves, argued that the defense of the Republic was also the defense of female genius, in the person of de Staël. "Everything she loves and everything that loves her would have disappeared in the general crisis, if the republic had fallen; and the furious rage expressed by the royalists in their insults against this celebrated woman, prove that in their triumph, had they triumphed, her sex would not have saved her from being one of their victims" (30 Fructidor V/16 September 1797). Reaction to the Napoleonic adventure, not the Revolution, would divide republicanism from liberalism in France.

The complexities of the political culture of the Directory also expressed themselves in the international sphere. The challenges of creating a democratic order for international society were even greater than those in the domestic arena. As Bernard Gainot explains, the Directory had two central, but conflicting, ideals that organized its thinking on the international state system, that of the "grande nation" and the idea of the European federation (Gainot: 2009). Of the two the idea of the "grande nation," the hegemon guaranteeing international order, is the more familiar. Hobbes, of course, asserted that in organized societies the real state of fear was found between sovereigns, in international relations. That was the real war of all against all. The pamphleteer who recognized how anxieties about power drove domestic politics was convinced that the same was true of the Directory's international behavior; in fact he thought that if anything at least in the international sphere that stance was justified, "it appears just as great and terrible outside the borders as it appears weak and miserable within them" (Lesage, An V/1797b: 4). Clearly there was a fairly close relationship between the activity of the Directory in the two spheres. While the causes of the Fructidor coup were structural, its occasion was a contingent moment in international negotiations. Reubell and Larévellière broke with Carnot over the question of the demand by Britain for compensation in the Dutch and Spanish colonies if she was to return the French colonies and recognize French conquests in Europe. Carnot thought this was a sacrifice of allies worth making. It was in the French interest and it would aid in a general peace. Larévellière's refusal to go along with this line of policy seems impolitic and also lends support to the contention that the French republic was inherently expansionist.

However, this entirely coherent picture of a newly dominant executive exercising *Machtpolitik* at home and abroad turns out not to reflect the reality of the Directory's foreign policy. In the aftermath of the coup of Fructidor the Directors made a genuine effort at instituting a European peace. They continued negotiations at Lille with Britain and sought, by a congress at Rastadt, a general settlement in Europe. Even when those efforts failed they continued to look for an accommodation that would allow the interests of the European powers to be resolved. In a memorandum written for the Directory on the international situation, Talleyrand even allowed himself some ironic commentary on the manner in which French policy respected international norms when everyone else ignored them (Talleyrand, 4 Brumaire VII)/25 October 1798). On the death of Catherine the Great they tried to approach Paul to re-establish diplomatic ties, "which was more in the interests of commerce than our political interests." Such an approach flew in the face of one hundred years of French policy to use Sweden as a counterweight to Russia in the Baltic. Talleyrand argued that the very effort to establish ties was quixotic since Russia was so obviously an expansionary power and uninterested in a general settlement. He went on in this memorandum to point out that France's decision unilaterally to abide by the letter of the laws of war and to respect neutral shipping had undermined its war effort. Effectively the armed neutrality was guaranteed by France while the neutrals (Denmark and Sweden) made ineffectual protests at British interdictions of trade to France. Talleyrand argued that the international settlement that the Directors hoped for was entirely unlikely: "through our military successes we have astonished the universe; but because of our political principles we have frightened every state base whose power is founded on principles contrary to our own. We find ourselves in a situation where everyone who ceases to be our enemy puts all their effort into making sure they do not become one again, but we have no friends." In consequence he recommended abandoning pursuit of the goal of reconciling Russia and building a European confederation of states and replacing it with a more realistic, and traditional, alliance with Prussia, and a guarantee to Britain by recreating the traditional buffer between France and the Batavian Republic. Talleyrand's critique of the foreign policy of the Directory was that it relied too much on the cosmopolitan idea of Europe, and that it was not adequately based on the logic of competing sovereigns.

Talleyrand's realist foreign policy proposal was contested and rejected for lacking perspective. France's interest, argued the *Rédacteur*, was to continue to support a cosmopolitan international order, because in the long run a regime of law and liberty would make France more economically efficient: "does not the example of England already illustrate, that industry develops among a people in parallel to liberty?" (1 Floréal V/20 April 1797). American diplomacy might favor English commerce in the Jay Treaty, but in the long run American interests would turn to republican France. As late as 1798 voices in the press still argued that the dual commitment of the French and British peoples to liberty made them natural allies: "the affinity of our principles with those which formerly made up the basis of the English constitution, makes us hope that these two nations, so long rivals, will soon become friends" (1 Germinal VI/21 March 1798). The Directory was genuinely shocked when the French plenipotentiaries to the peace negotiations at Rastadt were assassinated by Austrian troops when returning to France under diplomatic passports. The offense was not just to the prestige of France but to the "principles of humanity" that had been violated.

Cosmopolitanism was not restricted to Larévellière or to diplomacy. One of the most interesting experiments in education under the Directory was the Institution Nationale des Colonies, a multi-racial school for the "Americans" created in the buildings of the old Collège de la Marche (Calvin's old college) on the Montagne Sainte-Geneviève in the Year V (Gainot 2007: 158). The school was the project of Pierre-Louis Ginguené, director general of public instruction in the ministry of the interior, long-time abolitionist and member of the Société des Amis des Noirs. The goal of the school was to educate the future leaders of the Republic in the Caribbean, and it attracted students such as one of the sons of Toussaint-Louverture and Ferdinand Christophe, son of Henri Christophe, who would later be the first king of Haiti. Prize-giving at the school was one of the notable events in the life of the Republic, publicized in the republican press. The school was closed in 1802 and its pupils dispersed as part of the same conservative reaction under Bonaparte that saw the black troops in Guadeloupe and Saint-Domingue disarmed and slavery reinstated.

The political culture of the Directory was complex. The culture of the radical center, revolutionary civil religion, modern republicanism, and international cosmopolitanism did not amount to an internally coherent polity or a consistent set of ideas through which the Directory could organize its political life. Moreover that political culture was confronted with alternatives, de Maistre's radical conservatism and Babeuf's communism, that systematically rejected both the democratic and political projects of the modern republic. De Maistre embraced the authoritarian state, but rejected the idea of democratic legitimacy; Babeuf retained the aspiration to an equal society, but rejected political citizenship as a meaningful experience. Yet all of these projects, even those that were most hostile to one another, negotiated with the democratic turn of the Revolution. The political culture of the Directory was only the first of the long series of polities that were to struggle with that legacy.

References

Alder, Ken (1995). "A Revolution to Measure: The Political Economy of the Metric System in France." In M. Norton Wise (ed.). *The Values of Precision*. Princeton, N.J.: Princeton University Press. 39–71.

Anon. (1792). "Letter to Eden." British Library Add. MSS 34,448/313.

Anon. (An VI/1798). *Liberté, Égalité, Fraternité: Journée du dix-huit fructidor*. Paris.

Anon. (1798). *Le 18 Fructidor ou anniversaire des fêtes directoriales*. Hamburg.

Anon. [Société des Girouttes] (1815). *Dictionnaire de Girouettes, ou, nos contemporains peints d'après nous-mêmes*. Paris.

Barère, Bertrand (An V/1797–98). *De la pensée du gouvernement*. Paris.

Brown, Howard (2006). *Ending the French Revolution: Violence, Justice and Repression from the Terror to Napoleon*. Charlottesville: University of Virginia Press.

Bulletin Décadaire (1798–1800).

Bulletin de la Convention nationale (1792–95).

Carnot, Lazare (An VI/1798–99). *Réponse de L. M. N. Carnot, citoyen français*. Paris.

Carnot, Lazare (An VIII/1799–1800). *Histoire du Directoire constitutionnel, compare à celle du gouvernement qui lui a succédé*. Paris.

Chemin-Despontès Jean-Baptiste (An X/1801–2). *Qu'est-ce que la Théophilanthropie?* Paris.

Conservateur (1797–99).

d'Abrantes, Laure Junot (1838). *Histoire des Salons de Paris*, 6 vols. Paris: Ladvocat.

de Staël, Germaine (1983). *Considérations sur la Révolution française*, Paris: Tallandier.

Décade philosophique (1794–1807).

Directoire Exécutif (An V/1797). *Extrait des registres des déliberations du Directoire exécutif*. Paris.

d'Ivernois Francis (1798). *Tableau historique et politique de l'administration de la République française pendant l'année 1797 ...* London.

Dumont, Étienne (1832). *Souvenirs sur Mirabeau et sur les deux premières Assemblées législatives*. Paris: Charles Gosselin.

Dunn, John (2005). *Democracy: A History*. New York: Atlantic.

Gainot, Bernard (2007). *Les Officiers de couleur dans les armées de la République et de l'Empire (1792–1815): De l'esclavage à la condition militaire dans les Antilles françaises*. Paris: Karthala.

Gainot, Bernard (2009). "Vers une alternative à la 'Grande Nation': Le Projet d'une confédération des États-nations en 1799." In Pierre Serna (ed.). *Républiques soeurs: Le Directoire et la Révolution atlantique*. Rennes: Presses Universitaires de Rennes. 75–86.

Gillispie, Charles (2004). *Science and Polity in France: The Revolutionary and Napoleonic Years*. Princeton, N.J.: Princeton University Press.

Goncourt, Edmond and Jules Goncourt (1855). *Histoire de la société française pendant le Directoire*. Paris: Le Promeneur.

Harris, James (1844). *Diaries and Correspondence of James Harris, First Earl of Malmesbury*, 4 vols. London: R. Bentley.

Jainchill, Andrew (2008). *Reimagining Politics after the Terror: The Republican Origins of French Liberalism*. Ithaca, N.Y., and London: Cornell University Press.

Kawa Catherine (1996). *Les Ronds-de-cuir en Révolution: Les Employés du ministre de l'intérieur sous la première République*. Paris: CTHS.

Kingston Ralph (2006). "The Bricks and Mortar of Revolutionary Administration." *FH*, 20: 405–423.

Larévellière-Lépeaux, Louis-Marie (n.d.) Commonplace Book Beinecke Library Gen. MSS 549/3/68.

Larévellière-Lépeaux, Louis-Marie (An VI/1797–98). *Du Panthéon et d'un théâtre national*. Paris.

Larévellière-Lépeaux, Louis-Marie (9 Prairial XI/29 May 1801). Letter to Chaptal, Beinecke Library, Gen. MSS 549/1/2/4.

Larévellière-Lépeaux, Louis-Marie (1895). *Mémoires de Larévellière-Lépeaux, membre du Directoire exécutif de la République française*, 3 vols. Paris: Plon.

Lesage (An V/1797a). *J'ai peur! et je leur fais peur! Lettre d'un militaire à l'un de ses camarades de l'armée d'Italie, sur la cause des débats actuels entre les majorités du Conseil des Cinq-Cents et du Directoire exécutif*. Paris.

Lesage (An V/1797b). *J'ai tort et tu as tort, cède et je céderai*. Paris.

Livesey, James (2001). *Making Democracy in the French Revolution.* Cambridge, Mass.: Harvard University Press.

Malouet, Pierre-Victor (1792). *Lettre de M Malouet à M de Lally-Tollendal.* Paris.

Mercure français, politique, historique et littéraire (1791–99).

Ministre de l'intérieur (An VII/1798–99). *Aux administrations centrales et municipales: Fêtes commemoratives des 14 juillet, 10 août, 9 thermidor et 18 fructidor, 30 prairial.* Paris.

Rédacteur (1795–1800).

Robespierre, Maximilien (1965). *Discours et rapports à la Convention.* Paris: Union Générale des Éditions.

Rosanvallon, Pierre (1989). *L'État en France de 1789 à nos jours.* Paris: Seuil.

Rosanvallon, Pierre (2004). *Le Modèle politique français: La Société civile contre le jacobinisme de 1789 à nos jours.* Paris: Seuil.

Salaville, Jean-Baptiste (An VII/1798–99). *L'Homme et la société, ou, nouvelle théorie de la nature humaine et de l'état social.* Paris.

Say, Jean-Baptiste (An VIII/1799–1800). *Olbie, ou, essai sur les moyens de réformer les moeurs d'une nation.* Paris.

Serna, Pierre (2005). *La République des girouettes (1789–1815 et au delà), une anomalie politique: La France de l'extrême centre.* Paris: Champ Vallon.

Smith, Adam (An VI/1798). *Théorie des sentiments moraux, ou, Essai analytique, sur les principes des jugemens que portent naturellement les hommes, d'abord sur les actions des autres, et ensuite sur leurs propres actions: Suivi d'une Dissertation sur l'origine des langues; par Adam Smith; traduit de l'anglais, sur le septième et dernière édition, par S. de Grouchy Veuve Condorcet. Elle y a joint huit Lettres sur la sympathie.* Paris.

Spang, Rebecca (2002). "The Frivolous French: 'Liberty of Pleasure' and the End of Luxury." In Howard G. Brown and Judith M. Miller (eds.). *Taking Liberties: Problems of a new Order from the French Revolution to Napoleon*, Manchester: Manchester University Press. 110–125.

Suratteau, Jean-René (1971). *Les Élections de l'an VI et le "coup d'état du 22 floréal" (11 mai 1798).* Paris: Les Belles Lettres.

Talleyrand-Périgord, Charles Maurice de (4 Brumaire VII/25 October 1798). Letter to Emmanuel-Joseph Sieyès. Archives Nationales 284 AP 12/3.Taine, Hippolyte (1885). *Les Origines de la France contemporaine: La Révolution, le gouvernement révolutionnaire.* Paris: Hachette.

Thérémin, Charles-Guillaume (An V/1797–98). *De la situation intérieure de la république*, Paris: n.p.

Woloch, Isser (2002). *Napoleon and his Collaborators: The Making of a Dictatorship.* New York: W.W. Norton.

Chapter Twenty-One

The New Security State

Howard G. Brown

Many attempts have been made to express the essence of Napoleonic rule in a pithy phrase. These range from the greatest enlightened despotism (relatively favorable) to a form of modern Caesarism (deeply historical), from republican monarchy (oxymoronic) to military dictatorship (fundamentally wrong). Each of these crisp characterizations tries to combine the personal importance of Napoleon Bonaparte with the nature of his regime. It can be helpful, however, to distinguish between these two strands, even if they did become increasingly twisted together over time. The term "security state" stresses the apparatus of rule over the person as ruler. Looking beyond the figure of Bonaparte helps to reveal the trajectory of politics during the First Republic, one in which political legitimacy came increasingly from institutions that offered security, rather than those that embodied democracy. The security state was born out of raising a secular and militarized state above both partisan politics and constitutional constraints.

The French Revolution led to the emergence of a security state in France because the constitutional Republic (1795–1804) repeatedly resorted to emergency measures that contravened the constitution in order to parry threats, whether actual or overblown, to the Republic's survival. Counter-revolutionary insurgencies and conspiracies, especially those that received support from royalist *émigrés* and foreign powers, posed the gravest danger. Threats to the polity also came from more radical republicans whose provocative activities extended from plots against the government to purging the executive. Those in power contributed to political instability by serving a cocktail of paranoia and belligerence that helped to provoke opposition. Such attitudes made it harder to restore order in the countryside, where economic and social upheaval fostered the greatest crime spree in French history. Protecting the Republic at home and abroad, while also trying to stamp out widespread criminality, spawned the institutions of the security state. These

A Companion to the French Revolution, First Edition. Edited by Peter McPhee.

began as an enhanced role for the army in domestic policing, more frequent exceptions to due process, greater penal repression, and increased discretionary power for the executive. They grew to include replacing elected officials and magistrates with appointed ones, routine violation of *habeas corpus*, and permanent forms of exceptional justice. Such means served to restore public order after years of turmoil, thereby helping to consolidate the Consulate as a republican regime. However, these exceptional measures also paved the road for Bonaparte to turn an authoritarian republic into a personal dictatorship in 1802. Thereafter, going from Life Consulate to Empire was largely a matter of style: the Napoleonic security state had already become the substance.

Concepts

In a comparative analysis of the French, Russian, and Chinese revolutions, Theda Skocpol (1979) found that they shared common phases. In the early phase of these revolutions, politics focused on fundamental issues of sovereignty and how social power should shape political power. In the later phases, politics became a struggle over who controlled the emerging state structures and how they should be used. According to Skocpol's analysis, neither conflict between social groups nor Jacobin ideology did as much to shape state-building during the French Revolution as did the demands of waging war and coping with the domestic consequences. Such an approach reduces the significance of "the bourgeois revolution" and highlights the emergence of a "professional-bureaucratic state." This combination of class struggle, state-building, and international conflict is a more comprehensive explanation for the French Revolution's tortuous journey from liberty and equality to authority and empire. All the same, the Napoleonic outcome of the Revolution was not as inevitable as Skocpol claims. The greatly enhanced power of the state need not have been used to establish French hegemony in Europe; exceptional leadership could have turned more of the state's enhanced capacity toward domestic social purposes. However, republican leaders chose not to beat their swords into plowshares and instead opted for military expansion abroad and unconstitutional coercion at home as their preferred means to consolidate the Revolution. Such a choice brought a shift away from democratic republicanism and toward liberal authoritarianism, the ideological underpinning of the new security state that emerged in the years 1797–1802.

Each of these terms needs to be clarified in order to grasp the significance of the overall process. Lynn Hunt has provided a notably sophisticated understanding of democratic republicanism. Rather than seeing it as merely an ideology, she treats it as a complex mix of rhetorical claims, innovative symbols, and collective political practices. Hunt (1984) asserts that democratic republicanism was "the most important outcome of the Revolution" even though she later simply states that in 1799 it "crumbled from within." The legacy of democratic republicanism proved vital in the history of France, but more needs to be said about its failure to take root in the 1790s. The truth is that as welcome as the early Revolution had been for many people, the Republic that emerged in 1792 soon alienated much of the French population through fierce hostility to religion and costly intrusions into village life. Increasing factionalism at both local and national levels sparked widespread civil strife, followed by ad hoc methods of bloody repression dubbed the Reign of Terror. The messy process of dismantling the Jacobin dictatorship cleared the way for anti-republican vendettas and a resurgence of royalism. As a result, the syndicate of Thermidorian politicians who created and staffed the Directorial regime (1795–99) found it impossible to broaden the narrow political base of the new polity. Any challenges to their leadership from opponents on the royalist right or the Jacobin left were treated as threats to the regime itself. Despite holding annual elections, the Directory simply could not accept pluralistic politics. Under these conditions, saving the Republic seemed to require repeated violations of the constitution. These included annulling election results, eroding rights to a jury trial, and using the army to restore order in the countryside. Democratic republicanism steadily gave way to liberal authoritarianism.

Political leaders continued to use the rhetoric and symbols of republicanism even as they undermined and then eliminated democratic and parliamentary elements. The alternative form of politics that emerged is best termed liberal authoritarianism (Brown 2006). It developed as a set of *ad hoc* responses to domestic instability in the late 1790s and blossomed into a tacit philosophy underpinning the regime that emerged after 1799. The judicial and military practices that formed the initial building blocks of the security state will be discussed later. For now, it should be noted that the inherent messiness of these practices led to a growing consensus in favor of revising the Constitution of Year III in order to end political instability. The politicians who backed the *coup d'état* of 18–19 Brumaire VIII (November 1799) did so for practical, not ideological, reasons. Nonetheless, the main architect of the coup, Emmanuel Sieyès, had a political philosophy to justify the anti-democratic outcome. He thought that as long as the power of the state was limited by legal protections for individual rights, the political elite could be chosen with little involvement of the people. In other words, the core of modern liberalism – legal protections that give individuals the freedom to pursue their own ends – could be best assured through authoritarian rule – Thomas Hobbes' notion of a sovereign ruling by law. The Constitution of Year VIII adopted in late 1799 instantiated this liberal authoritarianism in the new institutions of the Consulate (Jainchill 2008). However, subsequent events proved the danger of basing a political system on Sieyès' ideas. By the summer of 1802, Bonaparte had exploited various opportunities to turn the regime into a personal dictatorship, the legitimacy of which depended heavily on the new security state.

The Brumaire coup brought Bonaparte to power, but it should not be treated as historical shorthand for the transition from democracy to dictatorship in France. The process took years to complete, extending from the coup of 18 Fructidor V (September 1797) to the Life Consulate (August 1802), which is when the Revolution truly ended (Brown 2006). Moreover, the transition interacted directly with the construction of a new security state. The term "security state" draws attention to the predominant source of legitimacy for the administrative and judicial structures of the Consulate that replaced the dubious democracy of the late Directory, namely, the ability to restore and maintain law and order. Napoleon Bonaparte was a military hero and political genius, but these personal traits have largely obscured the fact that the authoritarian regime constructed under his leadership was the product of a general consensus among active citizens. Such people had not withdrawn their support from the Directory because it was insufficiently democratic; they came to despise the regime because it failed to end factional politics, repair the economy, and restore public order. The Brumairians agreed with Bonaparte in combining a stronger executive with less partisan appointments. Depoliticization depended on a greater concentration of authority both in the person of the ruler and in the apparatus of rule.

The basic lineaments of the security state were in place by 1802. Bonaparte played a role in this, of course, but the nature of the new apparatus of rule was determined mainly by the social and political circumstances of ending the French Revolution. The creation of the new security state depended on several key developments: the emergence of a modern bureaucracy; choosing foreign war over domestic programs; using the army for both policing and justice; and incorporating exceptionalism into the new regime.

Modern Bureaucracy

France's revolutionary leaders strongly objected to the patrimonial administration of the *ancien régime*. Prior to 1789, all magistrates, even appointed ones such as secretaries of state and provincial *intendants*, owned offices as personal property. Venal offices by definition put private interests before public service; therefore, venal office holders were not really civil servants in the modern sense. They did not serve society so much as they advanced personal and family interests through owning and exploiting a slice of sovereignty. The revolutionary alternative was to turn those who performed administrative tasks on behalf of the monarchy into public functionaries. And yet revolutionaries objected to bureaucracy with almost equal vehemence. They believed that unelected officials were unresponsive to the people.

The earliest revolutionary leaders sought to establish democratic governance in which the people could elect officials at every level, from village justices of the peace to national legislators. Revolutionaries knew that effective government would also require a myriad of appointed and salaried administrators, but feared that bureaucrats with specialized expertise and privileged access to information would be able to thwart the intentions of the elected representatives of the people. Moreover, as the Revolution intensified from 1791 onwards, the inherent tensions between democracy and bureaucracy grew more fierce. The many demands of war, which included previously unimaginable interventions in the economy, required administration to expand exponentially. At the same time revolutionary factionalism increased suspicions about the loyalty of appointed officials.

The continuous struggle over gaining and retaining control of the government shaped everything from judicial practices to war aims, from selling national properties to requisitioning shoemakers. Political considerations therefore mixed with practical pressures to determine progress toward a more rational, that is more professional, state administration. A truly massive expansion of the central administration during the years 1792–94, then the replacement of ministries by executive commissions operating under committees of the National Convention during 1794–95, and finally a return to ministerial structures under the Directory, provided ample opportunity to think and rethink how best to organize various administrative functions. The result was increased specialization for different bureaus and the organization of employees into clear hierarchies with commensurate grades of pay and authority for each. Continuous political upheaval, including a dizzying turnover in government ministers, inspired rampant patronage and repeated purges on the basis of personal or factional loyalties. This continued for a decade. The seven ministries under the Directory were headed by thirty-four men over four years. This in turn led to scores of different division heads within each ministry, the War Ministry being the worst (perhaps because the most critical). Such instability at the top, however, was offset by growing stability of personnel as bureau chiefs and ordinary clerks. The resulting increase in expertise made it possible to apply more consistently and equitably the many new laws and generalized rules – or red tape – needed to run a highly complex organization.

The French central administration changed not only to become more efficient, but in order to concentrate power in the hands of the official representatives of the people – the new sovereign (Brown 1995). Those features of modern bureaucracy that made significant progress during the Republic – greater specialization of functions, clearer hierarchical structures, and generalized rules – all increased efficiency and made the bureaucracy more responsive to political leadership. On the other hand, less progress was made toward recruiting on the basis of objective qualifications and treating administrative service as a career because both would have made the bureaucracy more independent and, therefore, less responsive to political leadership. Finally, efforts to ensure that administrative duties were performed honestly and impartially reveal the difficulty of changing the cultural ethos associated with patrimonial administration. Redefining traditional perquisites as bribery and graft did not make them easy to eliminate. Moreover, signing large contracts with politically reliable companies could be seen by rivals as simple corruption.

The creation of this large and sophisticated bureaucracy gave the government unprecedented means to police society. Those who ran the state in the early 1800s possessed exponentially more information about the French populace than did the absolute monarchy of the 1780s. They also had an unprecedented ability to retrieve and use that information thanks to multiple registers, file indexes, and case codes. The nature of this information and the means to retrieve it clearly reflected the state's priorities. These included the pressing need to restore law and order, which led the Directory to create the Ministry of General Police in early 1796. The new ministry grew steadily in size even as other ministries were forced to fire large numbers of staff. The result was a far greater ability to track threats to the regime. For example, after a decade of struggles against organized rebellion in western France, the Ministry of Police was able to compile a veritable biographical dictionary of brigands and *chouans* contained in a set of hefty registers (Archives Nationales, F^7 2261–2270). Here, finally, were the usual suspects, even if rounding them up was not so easy. Nonetheless, it now happened far more often thanks to improved coordination between the many civilian and military agents charged with law enforcement (Brown 2007).

Choosing War

The bureaucratic capabilities developed by the revolutionary state could have been devoted to other purposes: the security state was not inevitable; it was a congenital deformity that emerged from foreign war and domestic strife. France's victory at Fleurus in June 1794 ended the threat of invasion and so made it possible to overthrow Robespierre and end the Terror. France's fourteen armies no longer fought in defense of an endangered fatherland, but in order to defeat its enemies abroad. With the country out of imminent danger, republican leaders could have demobilized many of these reluctant conscripts. Having made herculean efforts to mobilize for war, however, they could not resist the temptation to continue waging it. The ease with which French forces overran the Austrian Netherlands and the Dutch Republic in late 1794 seemed to justify the strategy. Henceforth, achieving peace through victory became central to republican politics. Peace treaties with Holland, Prussia, and Spain in 1795 greatly favored France and encouraged her leaders to continue waging war against Austria and Britain. Had the fate of the Directory depended on the campaign of 1796 in Germany, it may well have collapsed; only victories over Austria in Italy kept the republican hawks in power. And yet Bonaparte's genius had its own price: the Peace of Campo Formio in December 1797 did not resolve issues with Austria and encouraged the Republic to continue expanding its domination. Rather than consolidating its supposed "natural frontiers" (the Pyrenees, the Alps, and the Rhine), the French Republic opted for a provocative presence in northern Italy.

Talleyrand, France's foreign minister, believed in 1798 that Europe would happily come to terms with the French Republic so long as she abandoned her propagandistic expansionism (Waresquiel 2003: 219–220). The Directory took no notice. The string of satellite states, known as sister republics, eventually stretched from Amsterdam to Naples. This *cordon révolutionnaire* did less to protect republican France than it did to antagonize her opponents. Mounting an expedition to Egypt in an attempt to weaken Britain not only strengthened her ties to Austria, but provoked Russia into declaring war as well. When full-scale war broke out again, the catastrophic results of an ill-advised offensive on all fronts in early 1799 drained the French interior of troops needed to maintain order. The ensuing upheaval cost the regime its last vestiges of domestic authority. The Directory managed to stabilize the military situation in October, but not in time to avert domestic disaster and the advent of Bonaparte. With a brilliant general at the top and seasoned armies on hand, the campaigns of 1800, first into northern Italy and then southern Germany, knocked Austria out of the war by early 1801. Britain now stood alone, whereas France had the aid of Spain, Holland, and the Russian-led League of Armed Neutrality. Economic crisis and parliamentary politics forced Britain to sign the unpromising Peace of Amiens in March 1802. Thus, despite political opposition at home and major setbacks in the field, the drive to obtain peace through victory provided continuity across the regimes of the Convention, Directory, and Consulate.

Pursuing peace through victory had important domestic consequences. Regardless of its political rhetoric, most Frenchmen experienced the Republic as a regime that privileged war over social programs, domestic tranquility, and even representative democracy. Military crisis had given birth to the Republic and it was military success that largely sustained it. Bonaparte later claimed that the Directorial regime depended on it: "to exist it needed a state of war as other governments need a state of peace" (Woronoff 1984: 167). He said this without a hint of irony, even though he put his own imperial rule in a similar light. But military glory was not the only issue: waging aggressive war helped to justify domestic coercion, especially against opponents of the Republic. A forced march from patriotism to jingoism to imperialism was not inevitable, but it was not surprising either.

The two famous levies of February and August 1793 added more than half a million soldiers to the French armies, raising them to an unprecedented total of 750,000 men under arms. All the same, hundreds of thousands of young men also managed to dodge the draft. Moreover, once France's enemies had been driven from its soil, the armies began rapidly to shed soldiers. The horrific privations of 1795 prompted a swelling stream of deserters flowing back to their native villages. There they depended on kin, neighbors, and complicit officials to evade the gendarmerie. Already at odds with law enforcement, draft dodgers and deserters frequently joined roving groups of outlaws. Numbering scores of men at any one time, the most organized of these brigand bands conducted their own kind of war, attacking stagecoaches, republican officials, and purchasers of "national properties," often under the banner of God and king.

Lacking an actual conscription law, but unwilling to consider a compromise peace, the early Directory appointed a bevy of fierce recruiting agents to round up refractory soldiers. The armies briefly grew again, but so too did the animosity between villagers and the republican state. These exacerbated the grave tensions created by the revolutionaries' continuing refusal to tolerate public forms of Catholic worship as well as their insistence on collecting unpaid taxes despite the state of the economy. In October 1798, the Directory adopted national conscription. The new process once again provoked rural resistance, especially when multiple age cohorts were called up together in the summer of 1799. This touched off a massive rebellion around Toulouse and fueled a major recrudescence of guerrilla warfare in western France. During the first two years of the new conscription, over one-third of the young men called up either evaded recruitment or deserted en route to the front. The state responded by billeting soldiers with recalcitrant families and sending mobile columns into the hills and woods to round up refractories. As a result, the Republic's armies gained an additional 280,000 men by the summer of 1800 (calculations made from Hargenvilliers 1808). This nearly doubled the number of men under arms and gave the Consulate the forces it needed to achieve peace through victory. The whole process taught the government that local officials, no matter how primed by patriotic rhetoric, could not be relied upon to operate conscription effectively. When it came time to replenish the ranks in 1802, the government sharply reduced the role of community officials and concentrated the task in the state apparatus. A combination of military oversight and bureaucratic fine-tuning, as well as allowing the prosperous to pay for substitutes, gradually made the "blood tax" a more acceptable part of being French (Woloch 1994: 387–426).

Social Democracy

The Republic's unwillingness to accept peace on any other terms than French hegemony in western Europe led to severe neglect of other functions that would have improved conditions of life for most ordinary people. The years of Jacobin ascendancy generated much revolutionary rhetoric (and some important legislation) aimed at caring for those in need. However, the temptation to pursue military expansion, together with a shift toward social conservatism, turned these goals into empty promises. Two areas, education and poor relief, illustrate the road not taken. Prior to the Revolution, the church took responsibility for almost anything that today would be called social services. The revolutionaries' dismantling of the church left a vacuum that they planned to fill, but never did. Therefore, rather than constructing a social democracy, or even a modern welfare state, the French Republic developed the first security state instead.

Republicans believed that education provided the key to citizenship. However, the main scheme to provide secular education for the masses, the Lakanal law of October 1794, failed miserably due to a lack of teachers and a failure to pay them adequately in the face of runaway inflation. The Thermidorian Convention abandoned the principle of free primary education for all and replaced it with an emphasis on secondary education for a few. Rather than receiving government salaries, teachers in public primary schools relied on student fees, just as they did in private schools. Private schools, most of which had religious origins, easily won the resulting competition for parental support, both in fees and ideology. The new secondary schools created in each department also suffered from a lack of financial support for both teachers and scholarships. As a result, the number of secondary students dropped to about 10,000 in 1799, one-tenth the number enrolled before the Revolution. Other boys, and all girls, were left to obtain whatever basic instruction was available from virtually unregulated private schools (Palmer 1985).

The new secular state that emerged in the 1790s handled poor relief with a similar mismatch between the rhetoric of enlightened reform and the reality of inadequate support. Revolutionaries reimagined the solution to extreme poverty by rejecting religious charity as self-serving for the donors, humiliating for the recipients, and inefficient for everyone. In its place came an array of government-sponsored remedies dubbed *bienfaisance* (welfare). Under Jacobin influence, the Convention adopted an admirably expansive approach to *bienfaisance* by promising calibrated annual pensions to a wide variety of people in poverty. These ranged from orphans and unwed mothers to the aged and infirm. A major effort by local authorities generated extensive lists of eligible recipients. Despite having identified massive need, the government only authorized one major disbursement of funds. The unfulfilled program dashed so many hopes that one historian has concluded that it might have been better if the project had simply been recorded and forgotten (Woloch 1994: 250).

In lieu of its comprehensive public assistance program, the Jacobin Convention narrowed its focus to the human detritus created by the extreme hardships of rural life, namely decrepit artisans, aged farmhands, desolate widows, and unmarried mothers. State pensions for such people were registered in the *Grand Livre de*

Bienfaisance. However, likening such people to military veterans who deserved "patriotic assistance" soon proved more than a rhetorical device. As the size of the Republic's armies swelled, so too did the number of needy war widows and hospitalized soldiers. Nonetheless, in July 1794 the Convention expropriated all charitable property and endowments, notably those of hospitals, to pay for the war. The more scarce funds became, the more the regime favored veterans and their dependants over other categories of the needy. By 1795, the Commission of Public Assistance was spending one-third of its pension money on the dependants of soldiers and two-thirds of its medical funds on wounded soldiers back in France.

Soon after the government's promises of public assistance reached their peak, the revolutionary currency collapsed. By 1797 the Republic had revoked most of the generous laws governing public assistance, save pensions for army veterans and war widows. Reforms in 1799 and 1803 generally reduced entitlements for ordinary soldiers, while making eligibility more dependent on rank and seniority. Just as it had done with primary education, the Republic reneged on its self-proclaimed responsibility for poor relief. By the late 1790s, lawmakers no longer believed that the state could or should provide basic education or a social safety-net for the mass of its citizens. The Republic had other priorities – waging war abroad and ending resistance at home; these became its alternative sources of political legitimacy.

Republicans made a more sustained attempt to preserve representative democracy, but here too they ultimately relented. The Directorial regime offered an apprenticeship in democratic practices, albeit with income restrictions on voting. When given an opportunity, however, most Frenchmen voted against staunch republicans in 1795 and again in 1797. The Directorial coups of Fructidor V (September 1797) and Floréal VI (May 1798) left dozens of seats in the legislature empty until the following years' elections. But local offices could not be left vacant, which allowed the government to replace scores of elected officials (such as department administrators, public prosecutors, and court justices) with its own appointees. The Directory naturally named supporters who would be tough on crime, especially resistance to authority. Conviction rates jumped noticeably, as did house-to-house searches and arbitrary detentions. The elections of 1799 were not disrupted, but then only about one in nine eligible citizens voted that year (Crook 1996: 155). The resulting legislative counter-coup of Prairial VII (June 1799) not only purged the Directory, it also led to a massive turnover in the government's own agents at the local level. Once the Jacobin wave subsided, many of the former agents were restored to their posts (Gainot 2001). This constant game of musical chairs alienated the citizenry. The ease with which the Consulate brushed aside opposition from democratic republicans reveals just how little support they actually had by the end of the 1790s.

The coup of 18–19 Brumaire VIII was not planned as a personal seizure of power, but as a means to reduce the instability caused by elections as well as to strengthen government. The Constitution of 1799 contained no declaration of rights, eliminated most elected offices (except justices of the peace), and replaced them with appointed officials. The new administrative and judicial institutions, especially department prefects and village mayors, gave the government important new tools to overcome open hostility to taxation, conscription, and economic regulation. All the same, it took additional reforms in policing and criminal justice to get the upper hand. In the meantime, the army undertook heavy-handed repression, especially in areas where the Republic's authority had largely collapsed.

Military Repression

The Directory relied on the army for policing and domestic repression. The appalling state of France in 1795, together with widespread distrust of republicans after the Terror, made it impossible to establish a democratic republic without resorting to considerable coercive force. Though admirable in themselves, representative elections, a constitutional rule of law, and jury-based criminal courts could not end the continuing civil war in the west or the prolonged cycles of violence in the southeast. It took suspending the constitution and a brutal campaign of counter-insurgency before the Vendée was pacified in 1796. Elsewhere, district commanders were charged with repressing urban food riots and providing added muscle for law enforcement. Too often, however, they took sides in the partisan politics that plagued many districts. Some, such as the reactionary generals Willot and Ferrand, even got elected to the legislature in the spring of 1797. As a result, the Fructidor coup not only annulled the results of partial elections in half the departments of France, it led to a purge of more than twenty generals from interior commands. Thereafter, generals appointed to interior commands tended to be more staunchly republican and more responsive to government orders.

With more reliable generals in domestic posts, the Directorial regime entrusted them with greater powers of repression. This included billeting troops on villages that failed to pay taxes or deliver conscripts. It also meant being able to muster national guardsmen for arduous expeditions in pursuit of bandits, rebels, or refractory priests. Such outings could provoke their own troubles, especially in mountainous regions where villagers had long engaged in armed hostility to the state's demands. Such obvious lack of gratitude for the benefits of citizenship invited even more heavy-handed responses. These ran from the improvised and illicit – beatings, extortion, theft, and pillage – to the planned and licit – courts martial for armed rebels and martial law for whole municipalities.

Martial courts and martial law developed separately, but eventually became a package of coordinated responses (Brown 2006). A law introduced in June 1795, and in effect for decades thereafter, authorized the army to use military courts to judge rebels captured with arms in hand. At first such courts were hastily created whenever necessary, but in 1797 better-regulated and permanent courts martial took on the task. Sentencing options remained limited: firing squads for convicted rebels or a few months in prison for their accomplices. The scattered records of these military courts indicate a trend from exemplary severity toward procedural regularity. No such trend existed when it came to martial law. Rather than use local national guardsmen to impose martial law as required, the Republic preferred to use the regular army to clamp down on urban unrest and so resorted to declaring a troublesome municipality under "state of siege." The Directory made extensive use of this measure in the years after the Fructidor coup. By late 1799, over 200 communes had seen the police powers of civilian officials pass to army commanders.

Most of these were small towns or *bourgs*, but they included the major cities of Lyon and Marseille, the naval ports of Toulon and Brest, as well as cities in annexed territories, such as Nice, Geneva, Antwerp, and Ghent. None of these many places was in fact besieged by a foreign army; rather, this emergency measure was used as both punishment and prophylaxis in the struggle against civil strife. The Consulate greatly reduced the practice by 1801. A decade later, however, a Napoleonic law combined the "state of siege" with authority to put insurgents before military courts, thereby creating the basis for repressing urban uprisings throughout the nineteenth century.

Political Measures

The emergence of a security state depended also on a range of political measures that sapped the democratic and constitutional basis of the Republic. These included the coup of 18 Fructidor V and became increasingly prevalent thereafter. The Fructidor coup proscribed sixty-five individuals, including two Directors and fifty-three lawmakers. Most eluded the police, but those who could be arrested were deported without trial to Guyana, where they were expected to die from the harsh climate (hence the term "dry guillotine"). The coup also gave the Directory added powers to deal with returned *émigrés*, who were deemed a special threat to security, whether they had been deported priests or voluntary exiles. In 1792, emigration had been made an act of treason punishable by death. And yet those who fled France in the 1790s did so for many reasons, ranging from joining a counter-revolutionary army led by the prince de Condé to escaping persecution during the Reign of Terror. The difficulty of distinguishing between hapless victims and secret enemies provoked intense controversy from 1795 onwards. The government's official lists of *émigrés* were riddled with incomplete names, mistaken identities, and falsely accused absentees. The Thermidorians addressed the issue by authorizing the return of members of the lower social orders who had fled the repression of 1793–94, especially in the Midi and the Rhineland. Others who wished to return to France, or to emerge from their hiding places in barns and attics, had to apply for removal from the official lists. Despite having more than 100,000 names on the lists, processing applications on a case-by-case basis kept removals to a small trickle. At the same time, locally elected officials, moved by personal friendship, political sympathy, or simple bribery, turned a blind eye to the illegal return of many *émigrés*. Their presence in France swelled the tide of anti-republicanism, which crested in the summer of 1797. In response, the coup in September included reviving military commissions to judge and execute returned *émigrés*. The draconian policy drove thousands of *émigrés* into exile once again. Though intended to purge the Republic of dangerous enemies, the military commissions also put to death a number of women, teenage boys, and old men. Although the Directory soon narrowed their scope, during two years of operation the military commissions judged over a thousand individuals in some fifty towns and cities around the country. They publicly executed almost 300 *émigrés* (one-third of whom had been nobles or priests) and deported another 120 (Brown 2006: 151–171). This "Directorial Terror" reflected an inability to rely on regular judicial means to handle the challenge posed by *émigrés* dedicated to destroying the Republic.

The threat of invasion that faced the Republic in the summer of 1799 provoked another remarkable political measure designed to enhance its security: the law of hostages. Though adopted as a means of counter-insurgency, the law proved more ideological than practical by making the relatives of *émigrés* and nobles the primary targets. The law included families of known rebels as possible hostages, but explicitly gave them the lowest priority. In the event of an attack on an official, soldier, or purchaser of national property, the government could deport four persons already held as hostages. This required local officials to round up scores of people and intern them in local prisons wherever the legislature authorized application of the law. The inherent dangers of such a law were apparent to anyone interested in truly pacifying insurgent areas. Even the notorious minister of police, Joseph Fouché, worried that it would "become an instrument of vengeance, hatred or private interest" and wanted it used only against those who, on the basis of their past or current behavior, were "presumed to be an accomplice of our enemies" (Archives Nationales, F^7 3820). Locking people up on presumptions alone eroded confidence; therefore, the legislature limited the number of areas where the law of hostages could be implemented. All the same, this law also echoed aspects of the Terror and thus earned the Directory widespread opprobrium.

The Brumaire coup that ended the Directory was billed as a pre-emptive strike against a plot by Jacobin lawmakers, so it made perfect sense to discredit one of their signature laws. As soon as he became First Consul, General Bonaparte personally freed several dozen hostages from a Paris prison. Such a move had nothing to do with legal scruples or humanitarian impulses. Bonaparte had used some brutal and unsavory methods of repression in Italy and Egypt, including taking notables as hostages after a rebellion, and he was prepared to do likewise again. As First Consul, he suspended the constitution in the insurgent departments of Brittany, authorized military courts to continue judging rebels captured arms in hand, and ordered the local commander to burn some large villages in order to terrorize the inhabitants into submission. He also gave General Férino special powers to restore order in the Rhône Valley, including the authority to shoot armed brigands on site and without trial.

It is hardly surprising, therefore, that Bonaparte reacted to the attempt to blow him up on Christmas Eve 1800 with a completely arbitrary form of political repression. Despite the discovery of clear evidence that the perpetrators had been royalists, the First Consul ordered Fouché to compile a list of 130 republican radicals, then had the Senate order them all to be deported without trial as "a measure to preserve the constitution." Here was a mirror image of the Fructidor coup, although the Consulate's deportations led to many more deaths than had the Directory's. In either case, these political measures were short-term expedients intended to ward off immediate threats: long-term survival called for more regulated forms of exceptionalism. The failed assassination attempt persuaded most lawmakers that some people were too dangerous to be accorded due process: the issue was how to limit the travesties of justice that might ensue.

The Security State at Work

The political elite had long struggled with the contradiction of defending a constitutional republic by employing exceptional measures that violated the principles that gave it legitimacy. Special Tribunals reflect the ultimate resolution to this problem. They were created in February 1801 despite fierce opposition from liberal deputies in the Tribunate, who argued that they subverted the jury-based system of justice. In fact, they were a compromise between the uncertain justice of regular courts and the uncontrolled brutality of military commissions, one deemed necessary due to the continuing scourge of brigandage.

Three years earlier, a temporary law had required military courts to prosecute highway robbery and housebreaking committed by more than two people. Although these military trials included significant legal safeguards, the law ensnared more people than intended and so lawmakers allowed it to expire in early 1800. This left a major gap in the government's arsenal of repression, especially given that royalist banditry in the south, *chouannerie* in the west, and a host of armed robberies elsewhere continued to plague France. The First Consul initially tried to fill this gap with more primitive methods of repressing rampant lawlessness. In regions where the interweaving of politics and criminality had made violence especially intractable, Bonaparte created seven extraordinary military commissions, sometimes attached to "flying columns." These commissions lacked any jurisprudence and carried out sentences within 24 hours. Four such commissions were at work in the Midi in the early months of 1801. They pronounced verdicts on more than 400 individuals: half were executed, only one-fifth were exonerated, and the rest were sent to the army or locked away as "violently suspect." The public firing squads usually took place in the criminal's native community, especially where extortion, robbery, and arson had become commonplace means to resist the Republic. Executing accomplices had a deliberately terrifying aspect. In one case, four shopkeepers were shot in front of their neighbors for buying lace stolen in a hold-up. As one reported, "Arnavon left six children; Brunel's wife left seven. She was nursing; milk and blood flowed from her corpse. All of L'Isle closed its doors and moaning was heard throughout the town" (Archives de la Guerre, B^{13} 128). The southeast had not experienced summary justice like this since the Terror. However, giving the army such arbitrary power inevitably led to abuses, including pillaging, extortion, and shootings without trial. This risked reversing the cooperation that many villages had begun to show in the fight against politicized banditry.

Herein lay the inspiration for a more controlled form of expedited justice. Not until both royalism and Jacobinism had been dealt severe setbacks, and an increased use of military repression had crippled organized resistance, could republican legislators create a more stable balance between exceptional measures and the rule of law. Special Tribunals combined civilian judges and army officers whose proceedings were more regulated than those of military courts. They prosecuted a variety of crimes committed in rural areas: any armed robbery, housebreaking, or assault committed by three or more individuals, ambush killings, arson, sedition, vagabondage, counterfeiting, recruiting would-be soldiers, and aiding in prison escapes. Such crimes had little in common other than their links to brigandage and anti-republican insurgency. In other words, the writ of Special Tribunals was specially crafted for the circumstances of 1801.

The Consulate first created Special Tribunals in twenty-seven departments of the west and south, then added nine more by 1803 (or thirty-six of 102 departments). They began trials in May 1801 and quickly became an integral part of the machinery of justice. They issued one-third of all felony convictions and, through relatively harsh verdicts, greatly increased judicial repression. From 1801 to 1804, France's non-military courts sentenced on average over 800 individuals to death and 3,000 others to terms of hard labor per annum. The Consulate also continued to use a few military courts and military commissions wherever brigandage remained especially intractable, which added another 200 to 300 executions a year. As a result, the Consulate executed at least four times as many people per capita as the absolute monarchy had executed during the 1780s. The tide finally turned after 1804 when the number of executions dropped sharply to about 520 a year (Brown 2006: 326–330; Lentz 2007: 303). Although Special Tribunals were supposed to end operations when France secured international peace (that is, after the Peace of Amiens), this temporary expedient became a permanent feature of France under Napoleon. In short, Special Tribunals lay both functionally and emblematically at the heart of the new security state: they impinged on due process, but within clear limits, they gave the army a significant role in the civilian apparatus of justice, and they substantially raised the amount of penal repression meted out at the time.

Other important features of the new security state emerged alongside Special Tribunals. In order to increase the powers of prosecution, lawmakers approved the creation of so-called "security magistrates" charged with supervising police investigations and preparing felony indictments. In order to enhance its capacity for policing, the government expanded the gendarmerie for the third time in four years, taking it from 8,500 men in 1797 to 15,700 in the summer of 1801, four times the number of rural constables in service at the end of the *ancien régime*. A series of purges and structural reforms over these years had greatly improved the quality of gendarmes and made the corps more responsive to the central government. With a modern, national police force at its disposal, the Consulate abandoned earlier efforts to make the National Guard a vital part of local law enforcement. Henceforth, the sometimes irritating, but usually respected, gendarme became the real face of the regime in the countryside, even more than Bonaparte himself, at least according to one of his advisors (Roederer in Vandal, 1902–7: vol. 2, 499). The revolutionaries' hope for community policing had been replaced by the late Republic's preference for policing communities.

Bonaparte earned great admiration for solving some of the most intractable political problems raised by the Revolution. Few scholars have recognized, however, that the Consulate's solutions only became possible after years of building up the government's capacity to control repression and police society. This development is illustrated by the means used to solve the problem of *émigrés*. In early 1800, the Consulate closed the list of *émigrés* and created a special political commission to screen applications for removal from it. The process remained slow and was badly tainted by bribery and favoritism. Six months later, the government adopted a partial amnesty. This granted automatic readmission to whole categories of *émigrés*, while also continuing to screen others on an individual basis. The key to the operation lay in requiring every returned *émigré* to register with a departmental prefect or urban police commissioner, who then reported to the minister of police. This enabled the government either to deny admission outright or to order police surveillance of any individual *émigré* deemed dangerous. This massive operation occupied one-third of all employees in the Ministry of Police. The minister, Joseph Fouché, showed no qualms about having dozens of returned *émigrés* suspected of royalist activities arrested and locked away in state prisons without trial. The whole process violated the Consulate's constitution, which, like that of the Directory, explicitly barred the return of proven *émigrés*. All the same, combining an amnesty that irritated republicans with police measures that contradicted the basic principles of the early Revolution proved very successful politically. In April 1802 the Senate adopted an almost total amnesty for *émigrés*. This removed most of the discretionary categories, but none of the police surveillance. Fouché instructed provincial officials to repress "with inflexible severity" any subversive activity, including trying to get nationalized property back (Madelin 1903: vol. 1, 327–349). In the end, the magnanimity of allowing all but a few thousand *émigrés* to return would have been impossible, and certainly unimaginable, without a security apparatus that combined an elaborate bureaucracy with appointed officials such as was in place by 1802.

By this time, France was descending rapidly into dictatorship. The Concordat, enacted along with restrictive "organic laws" in April 1802, and the purge of liberal members from the Tribunate at much the same time, dismayed those who remained committed to a secular, democratic state. But their opposition was too little, too late. The many exceptional measures and institutions of repression they had previously approved now paved the road to Bonaparte's personal dictatorship. As well as making him First Consul for Life, the Constitution of Year X (August 1802) strengthened his hand in choosing lawmakers, authorized him alone to ratify treaties, gave him the power to grant pardons, to suspend the constitution, and even to suspend jury trials where he saw fit. The plebiscite that endorsed such changes confirmed that political legitimacy now rested in the person of Bonaparte and the apparatus of his rule, to the detriment of lawmakers and civil liberties alike. The new security state was as much a product of the French Revolution as Napoleon himself.

References

Archives de la Guerre

Archives Nationales

Brown, Howard G. (1995). *War, Revolution, and the Bureaucratic State: Politics and Army Administration in France 1791–1799*. Oxford: Clarendon Press.

Brown, Howard G. (2006). *Ending the French Revolution: Violence, Justice, and Repression from the Terror to Napoleon*. Charlottesville: University of Virginia Press.

Brown, Howard G. (2007). "Tips, Traps and Tropes: Catching Thieves in Post-Revolutionary Paris." In Clive Emsley and Haia Shpayer-Makov (eds.). *Police Detectives in History, 1750–1950*. Aldershot: Ashgate. 33–60.

Crook, Malcolm (1996). *Elections in the French Revolution*. Cambridge: Cambridge University Press.

Gainot, Bernard (2001). *1799, un nouveau jacobinisme?* Paris: CTHS.

Hargenvilliers, A.-A. d' (1808). *Compte général de la conscription depuis son établissement*. Paris: Imprimerie Nationale.

Hunt, Lynn (1984). *Politics, Culture, and Class in the French Revolution*. Berkeley: University of California Press.

Jainchill, Andrew (2008). *Reimagining Politics after the Terror: The Republican Origins of French Liberalism*. Ithaca, N.Y.: Cornell University Press.

Lentz, Thierry (2007). *Nouvelle histoire du Premier Empire*, vol. 3: *La France et l'Europe de Napoléon, 1804–1814*. Paris: Fayard.

Madelin, Louis (1903). *Fouché, 1759–1820*, 2 vols., 2nd edn. Paris: Plon.

Palmer, Robert R. (1985). *The Improvement of Humanity: Education in the French Revolution*. Princeton, N.J.: Princeton University Press.

Skocpol, Theda (1979). *States and Social Revolutions*. Cambridge, Mass.: Harvard University Press.

Vandal, Albert (1902–1907). *L'Avènement de Bonaparte*, 2 vols. Paris: Plon.

Waresquiel, Emmanuel de (2003). *Talleyrand: Le Prince immobile*. Paris: Fayard.

Woloch, Isser (1994). *The New Regime: Transformations of the French Civic Order, 1789–1820s*. New York: W.W. Norton.

Woronoff, Denis (1984). *The Thermidorean Regime and the Directory 1794–1799*. Cambridge: Cambridge University Press.

Chapter Twenty-Two

The White Terror: Factions, Reactions, and the Politics of Vengeance

Stephen Clay

Few terms have acquired such poignancy and prominence in the revolutionary lexicon as the word "reaction" in the months and years following the overthrow of Robespierre on 9 Thermidor. What many later historians, beginning in the 1820s, came to call the White Terror was known to contemporaries as the "Reaction" – an attack, violent and symbolic, on the personnel, institutions, and more generally those in any way sympathetic with the Terror of 1793 to 1794. While the Reaction did have its social and economic dimensions, the term as it was more widely used in the political discourse was a synonym for persecution and violence. In the months and years after July 1794, hundreds if not thousands of men, women, and children, their relatives, friends, and allies, became the targets of rage and revenge in a vast episode of account-settling at once ideological and personal. Individually, or in small groups or in crowds, many victims of the Terror, or those acting on their behalf, dramatically turned the tables, perpetrating in the name of justice countless acts of extrajudicial violence. The dagger and the hangman's noose more than the guillotine became the distinguishing emblems of this bloodstained history.[1]

Estimates of the number of victims killed, assaulted, mutilated, harassed, or compelled, in fear, to abandon their homes and towns have ranged widely: some contemporaries put this figure as high as 45,000; others calculated that the Reaction cost the lives of about 2,000 persons. And while some local administrations made efforts to draw up lists of those persecuted in different ways during the Reaction to record their sufferings and indemnify the victims and their families, the central government never systematically tabulated these often fragmentary and imprecise sources; hence, the exact number of victims must remain a matter of speculation. Yet these official lists, however incomplete, together with the seemingly endless recital of similar incidents in other judicial and administrative sources, left contemporaries and later historians with a picture of France torn apart by ceaseless

A Companion to the French Revolution, First Edition. Edited by Peter McPhee.

and uncontrollable violence, part of a mounting heritage of hate that had marked many aspects of the revolutionary experience since 1789.

The Reaction in the polarized and political language of the day was invariably characterized as "royalist." Indeed, the noun "Reaction" rarely appeared unaccompanied by the qualifying adjective "royalist" in the proclamations, addresses, newspapers, and official and unofficial correspondence in the second half of the 1790s. The celebrated and controversial *Mémoire historique sur la Réaction royale et sur les massacres du Midi*, by Stanislas Fréron, stands as perhaps the most well-known exemplar of this widespread practice.[2] Behind this language often lurked a persistent belief in the reality of a conspiracy, long-standing and indestructible, to destroy the Republic by destroying republicans. The prevalent inclination among revolutionaries to perceive politics in terms of conspiracies found in the Reaction more grounds for the darkest suspicion of an ever-present threat to what so many believed was a still fragile regime. Moreover, a political language that represented politics in stark Manichean opposites as either patriot or aristocrat, republican or royalist reinforced the tendency, particularly conspicuous among victims, to ascribe a purely royalist nature to the Reaction.

Some historians, too, in the republican tradition of F.A. Mignet, Louis Blanc, Ernest Hamel, and Edgar Quinet, spoke of the Reaction as fundamentally anti-republican, counter-revolutionary and royalist. It soon became a commonplace in the historiography of the nineteenth century to contrast the "Red Terror" with the " White Terror," as the title of Louis de Laincel's polemical book (1864), *Terreur rouge et Terreur blanche* attests. In addition, historians and writers as diverse as Marc-Antoine Baudot, Durand Maillane, Charles Nodier, Jules Michelet, Hippolyte Taine, and Albert Mathiez also remarked that the methods and nature of these two forms of terror were strikingly different. As Mathiez noted, "the Red Terror, almost always, had been carried out with a respect for formal procedures according to the law; the repression was done in the light of day in courts or in military commissions ... the White Terror, by contrast, violated all the rules, scoffed at the law – it was a succession of murders, purely and simply, often committed at night, in the houses of the victims, or in prisons whose doors had been broken open" (Mathiez 1929: 211). The regime of the Revolutionary Tribunal, in the picturesque prose of Louis Blanc, was replaced by the reign of assassins (Blanc 1862: vol. 12, 47).

Whatever degree of royalist sentiment figured in the violence of the Reaction, it remains undeniable that the chief motive inciting the widespread acts of violence, whether individual or collective, physical or verbal, was vengeance (Clay 2009). The term assumed a preponderant place in the writing about the Reaction by contemporaries no less than by later historians. Government officials in local and national administrations and criminal courts cited vengeance, frequently the *esprit de vengeance* and its corollary, "hatred," as the two ungovernable passions animating the violence raging in many parts of the country after the fall of Robespierre. "Vengeance, vengeance, this is the demand of all the republicans," the editor of the conservative newspaper the *Messager du Soir* wrote in late November 1794, before the full impact of the Reaction had made itself felt in the spring of the following year.[3]

The metaphor of "blood that cries out for vengeance" punctuated much of the correspondence of national and local authorities. Political discourse was permeated with the theme of vengeance – vengeance for the crimes of the Terror, for the victims of summary justice, false denunciations, arbitrary arrests, for properties confiscated or devastated and family fortunes destroyed, for lives ruined or ended. "How could the Convention not exact vengeance," Antoine-Claire Thibaudeau asked in his *Mémoires*, "in the name of the law after these abominable crimes?" (Thibaudeau 1824: vol. 1, 240). And more than one public official turned a blind eye to the escalating violence directed at the partisans of the Terror. Many might openly condemn incidents of violence perpetrated against former terrorists and their families yet admit that such enormities were largely explicable, almost excusable, after the bloodletting of the previous year. No less than the adjective "royalist," the word "vengeance" was forever associated with the Reaction, its essence and driving force.

The intensity of the Reaction corresponded almost exactly with the intensity of the Terror. Where the Terror had claimed most lives or recorded its greatest impact, it was there that the violence of the Reaction erupted most spectacularly, and could be the most prolonged. There was a geography of the Reaction, just as there had been a geography of the Terror (Clay 2006; Cobb 1970; Vovelle 1987). Certain parts of the country, however, like the department of the Pyrénées-Orientales, boasted almost no incidents of vengeance killing after Thermidor, their inhabitants proud to announce that their region had not been "disgraced" by either the Terror or the Reaction. "Since we have not had any terrorists," the commissioner attached to the departmental administration wrote, "we have had no form of Reaction."[4]

But the key to the violence was well understood by contemporaries: it lay in the violence of the Terror. Speaking of the small village of Velleron and its barely 900 inhabitants in the Vaucluse, a member of the local administration noted that "under the reign of Terror, several among them had been sent to the guillotine because of denunciations by their fellow citizens; after 9 Thermidor, and in the course of 1796–1797, the relatives and friends of these unfortunate victims exacted vengeance on their persecutors through arson and murder."[5] And a member of the band of Pastour, one of the local killer gangs operating in the Vaucluse in the following year, proclaimed that he "wanted to kill … all those who had tried to have [him] guillotined."[6] Reflecting on the Midi in general, the deputy Maximin Isnard, a former Girondin forced into hiding during the Terror, and sent on mission to the departments of Provence in the spring and summer of 1795 later remarked in a speech dated 20 March 1796: "I cannot deny that the horrible reign of the Terror has in this region produced a Reaction."[7] Not surprisingly, the phrase "I want to avenge the death of my father," or close variants thereof, was often intoned by those committing acts of violence against former terrorists.

The politics of the Reaction, then, was deeply rooted in the particular revolutionary histories of towns and regions (Clay 2006). This accounts for variations in killing patterns within the same department: why, for instance, in the perpetually troubled department of the Vaucluse, Avignon and Carpentras each experienced repeated acts of violence, while the small, relatively quiescent town of Apt in the foothills of the Luberon was spared any large-scale atrocities. Even though small towns could mobilize an impressive repertory of anti-terrorist invective, no less vehement than that of larger towns, the violence of the Reaction was chiefly an urban phenomenon. Cities like Lyon, Saint-Étienne, Montbrison, Marseille, Aix, Avignon, Orange, Béziers, Lons-le-Saunier, and Bourg were so many centers of the Reaction, places where political violence became a regular feature of daily life and a constant threat to public order.

But demography, if highly significant, was not all-determining. A small community of about 8,000 inhabitants like Aubagne was the scene of sustained violence between 1795 and 1797, much of it related to the local impact of the Terror and to the town's earlier history (Sutherland 2009). Continuity of conflict remained an almost inviolable rule serving to explain much of the history of the Terror as well as of the resulting Reaction (Clay 2006). Throughout much of the Midi and in those parts of France like the Rhône Valley where revolutionary conflict had been long, bitter, and bloody from the opening days of the Revolution, the violence of the Reaction, by no means predictable, did follow a certain logic of local rivalries between families, clans, and factions. In the department of the Bouches-du-Rhône, where the Revolutionary Tribunal and the Military Commission in Marseille claimed the lives of 412 persons, there was an clear correlation between the number of persons judged from a specific commune by this "exceptional justice" and the history of revolutionary tumult from earlier years: Aix, Arles, Aubagne, Marseille, and Tarascon, the five towns in the department with the largest number of persons judged *révolutionnairement*, each had a long past of bloody struggles between rival factions dividing their communities – a reality that would translate into a corresponding percentage of death sentences handed down by the Revolutionary Tribunal and the Military Commission in 1793 and 1794 (Clay 2009: 33–34). These same towns would each be the scene of a prison massacre during the Reaction, in the spring of 1795. Similarly, the department of the Loire, known for its long-standing communal conflicts and intense factional rivalries, a department where the Terror had left deep scars, was dominated after Thermidor, as so often before, by the politics of vengeance. In and around Montbrison alone, more than 258 persons, men, women, and children, reported incidents of violence to them or to others committed chiefly from April to June in 1795 (Lucas 1979, 1983). And in the department of the Gard, religious hatreds pre-dating the Revolution erupted with particular ferocity during the revolutionary decade, often making the Terror and the Reaction phases in a long history of conflict and reciprocal vengeance (Lewis 1978).

Such comparisons and statistics are suggestive, but not definitive. They demonstrate, however, the importance of locality and long-standing conflicts – political, ideological, religious, and, no less, personal – in the dynamics of the Revolution, especially in the period after Thermidor. The persistent struggle between local factions for control of revolutionary administrations and national government was the essence of political life in towns and villages across most of France. These rival groups emerged in most communities as early as 1789, often reflecting wide differences in wealth, ideology, and age. Drawn principally from members of the former Third Estate, the rival factions engaged in an unremitting conflict that intensified with each phase of the Revolution. Usually members of each faction were known by the name their enemies bestowed on them: patriots or aristocrats, and later republicans and royalists. The history of the Revolution was perceived – and lived – by most contemporaries as an alternating power struggle, often issuing in violence, between warring factions. Frequently members of these opposing factions occupied separate neighborhoods within their localities and could be identified by their own set of distinctive songs, symbols, and dress. The extent to which political rivalries masked economic competition and personal antagonisms is usually difficult, if not impossible, to determine. Rhetoric and ideology could cloak other motives or coexist with these, consciously or unconsciously, in varying degrees. While the political vocabulary of the revolutionary years showed a good deal of uniformity, the individual histories of different localities with long traditions of inter- and intra-urban strife, separate customs, and communal practices made for a rich mosaic of variety and contrast. The conflict between the factions, virtually omnipresent, intensified hatreds in many localities between persons who became easily identifiable as targets of recrimination and violence. The Reaction was a continuation in many ways and in many places of pre-existing tensions and bitter and bloody struggles (Clay 2006).

The focus of much dissension in local communities, especially those later affected by the Reaction, was the local *sociétés populaires* or Jacobin clubs. The developing network of these clubs within departments and across France exhibited wide variations in density and participation. Often the degree of politicization of a town or a region can be measured by the growth and activity of the different clubs. While providing civic education, engaging in many matters related to the social and economic welfare of their communities, overseeing and sometimes participating in local government, and generally promoting and defending the ideals of the Revolution as they interpreted them, these clubs could be as exclusive in their politics as they were aggressive in their rhetoric. Many identified themselves totally with the Revolution, practicing techniques of exclusion and exercising active surveillance over public life by denouncing enemies of the Revolution. Violence between clubbists – as they were most frequently called – and non-clubbists marred the politics of many localities. The appropriation of the term *patriote* normally applied to all partisans of the Revolution by many clubbists fostered partisanship and dissent. And while the membership of some among these local Jacobin clubs – and certain towns like Aix, Toulon, Nîmes, Bordeaux, Lyon had more than one – could vary over time and with political circumstance, the core militants remained largely the same throughout the successive phases of the Revolution.

The federalist revolts and the Terror were critical moments in the history of the clubs, and for the nation as a whole. The confrontation between what were essentially two groups of republicans with two contrasting views of the Republic embraced the major cities and most of the minor towns of provincial France, most notably Lyon, Bordeaux, and Marseille. These episodes were fundamentally contests of power and ideology between clubbists and their more moderate adversaries. The closing of the clubs, and the dispersal, imprisonment, and execution of some of their members at the hands of the federalists, intensified a desire for revenge once the tables had been turned. The active involvement of many members of the *sociétés populaires* in the management and administration of the Terror deepened divisions between the clubbists and their long-standing enemies while creating new ones, providing the immediate background and animus for the Reaction. Indeed, one contemporary, reflecting on the violence of the Reaction, noted that the terror had simply changed sides: "The Terror changes sides but the terror still continues; sometimes the role of the executioner is played by the victims and the victims rival their executioners in atrocities. Does vengeance know any limits?"[8] The terms *Terreur royale* or *Terreur réactionnaire* became loosely synonymous with the Reaction.

In the historiography of the Revolution, the Reaction or White Terror refers to those months mainly in the spring and summer of 1795 marked by episodes of violence against former terrorists and the institutions of the Terror. Yet many contemporaries did not restrict their use of the term to this period. In their view, the Reaction, long, terrifying, murderous, a continuous bloodbath waged against former terrorists and, more generally, loyal patriots, continued long after the end of the Convention, lasting until 18 Fructidor V (4 September 1797), two years later. Amid the jubilant addresses sent to the Directory and the Corps Législatif by different local administrations congratulating them on foiling the "vast royalist conspiracy" of 18 Fructidor, a number remarked, too optimistically in many instances, that this *journée* had brought to an end the Reaction of the previous years. In Marseille, the newly established newspaper the *Anti-Royaliste* added to this chorus of praise by expressing the hope, in March 1798, that the Republic, long weakened by "the frightful turmoil of the post-Thermidorian Reaction," would recover its strength and reaffirm itself.[9] Throughout France, even in those departments left comparatively untouched by its violence, administrations began to refer to the Reaction in the past tense, as a long sufferance patiently and heroically endured by patriots whose dedication to the Republic never wavered. "The Réaction Royale has for too long a time spilled the blood of patriots throughout the Republic," the municipality of Le Havre proclaimed on 16 January 1798.[10] This view was echoed across the country, in departments as far apart as the Ariège and the Manche – a tribute to a pervasive hope and a sign of how completely the reality and concept had become part of revolutionary discourse.

The term "Reaction" itself came to have a political sense essentially after 9 Thermidor; before the Revolution, the word, normally paired with the corresponding notion of action, had a predominantly scientific connotation. While the term had different meanings in the writings of Sièyes, Marat, and Robespierre, the "Reaction" as a political concept emerged largely from late July 1794 (Clay 1999; Monnier 1999). Invariably capitalized, it rapidly became a staple of Jacobin discourse before entering the more general political vocabulary in the weeks following Thermidor. More than one Jacobin group worried about a growing Reaction to the Terror and its agents. Jacobin groups, especially those members implicated in the repression of the previous months, grew apprehensive, with reason, that the recent change in political events and climate would provoke a Reaction: "Having been suppressed for so long," the Jacobin Club of Paris wrote as early as 18 Thermidor (5 August), only eight days after the execution of Robespierre, "one should expect a Reaction as strong as and proportional to the misfortunes that we had had to endure."[11] Over the following months, the word

"Reaction" was used in different ways to mean either a reaction against the Revolution itself, particularly the "Revolution of 9 Thermidor" and the reaction of justice against the Terror, its men and institutions. With the very word *terreur*, the concept of Reaction haunted Thermidorian discourse, fatally associated with violence and vengeance.

Some observers, however, identified not one Reaction but several Reactions shaping the political life of entire portions of the country after Thermidor. Increasingly, the dynamic of "actions and reactions" was imported as a concept into politics to describe the oscillating conflict of factions. In pamphlets, proclamations, newspapers, speeches, and administrative correspondence, "Reactions" in its plural form was more and more employed to describe something inherent in the dynamic of politics. Benjamin Constant, in his pamphlet *Des réactions politiques*, theorized this notion by pointing to reactions against ideas, and others against persons, concluding, "the reactions against men, the effects of a previous action, are the causes of future reactions. The oppressed group oppresses in its turn."[12] The catalyst of these reactions is vengeance; their enemy is moderation. In a region dramatically convulsed by different Reactions, the Marseille journalist Ferréol Beaugeard commented that the desire for vengeance was in the heart of all whose lives were compromised by the upheavals of the Reactions.[13] And members of the municipality of Aix-en-Provence, having endured at least two Reactions that had buffeted the town between 1795 and 1796, rightly observed that "in a region where the different Reactions have caused so much blood to be spilled, where so many families still mourn their fathers or their spouses, it is very difficult to stop the flood of vengeance that each party tries to justify."[14] With their long traditions of fratricidal conflict and political violence, the regions of Languedoc and Provence together with the Rhône Valley from Lyon to Marseille, would be the favored terrain of the politics of Reaction.

The National Convention's decision in October 1795 to send two deputies, Stanislas Fréron and Jacques Reverchon, both former Jacobins and former terrorists, on special missions to those departments deemed to be especially troubled by the anti-terrorist violence with the aim of ending this persecution and arresting the progress of royalism, gave substance to the notion of multiple reactions (Clay 2006; Gainot 2003; Lucas 1977: 231–260). The political actions of these *commissaires du gouvernement*, as they were called, involving controversial purges of administrative and judicial personnel and their replacement largely by former terrorists, and the pursuit, not always successful, of those responsible for the killing of the previous year, led some disgruntled contemporaries to speak of a new Reaction taking place after that of the spring and summer of 1795. Indeed, three years later, in 1798, the departmental administration of the Loire, one of the departments most affected by Reverchon's mission, specifically referred to "la Réaction sanglante de l'an III" to distinguish it from the one ushered in by Reverchon; in the Bouches-du-Rhône, the center of Fréron's operations, the departmental administration referred to the Reaction of 1795 by the name of the reactionary, anti-Jacobin representative-on-mission Paul Cadroy, thought to have inspired the murders – "la Réaction Cadroy" – in contrast to the "Reaction" provoked by Fréron during his mission. The departments of the southeast, those corresponding to the Eighth Military Division, would experience yet another Reaction soon after the end of Fréron's mission when General Amédée Willot was assigned to the region from mid-August 1796 to June 1797. Willot's palpable and vociferous anti-Jacobinism invited charges of partiality, abuse of power, open persecution of local patriots, and attempting to establish a military dictatorship in violation of the constitution; he was accused of introducing a third Reaction in Provence, one that local Jacobins came to call "la Réaction Willot."

These "reactions" of the First Directory from 1795 to 1797 would be facilitated by two highly contentious laws promulgated by the National Convention in the tense aftermath of the recent elections to the new Corps Législatif in September and October 1795 and the "royalist" uprising of 13 Vendémiaire IV (5 October 1795). In its last two parliamentary sessions, the National Convention introduced the law of 3 Brumaire IV (25 October 1795) and that of 4 Brumaire IV, the first a law of exclusion, the second a law on amnesty. Each law was to have far-reaching repercussions on local and national politics and fuel the politics of Reaction. With the law of 3 Brumaire IV, the government excluded from public office – including the national legislature – persons as well as their relatives whose names had not been definitively removed from the list of *émigrés*. In the hands of their adversaries, mostly former Jacobins, this was a potent weapon in the war between the factions. It permitted the removal from office of political opponents on legal grounds, and nullified many of the results of the recent elections, creating vacant posts throughout large portions of the country, above all those affected by large-scale emigration such as the centers of federalism. Overnight, newly elected officials were obliged to surrender their offices, a fact that disrupted many local judicial, municipal, and departmental administrations. The Directory lost no time in filling these posts with the beneficiaries of the law on amnesty. This law dismissed any formal accusations, arrest warrants, or legal actions arising from "facts" related to the Revolution (except for crimes defined by the Criminal Code), and ordered the immediate release of those imprisoned for such acts, unless these were linked to the recent "royalist" conspiracy of 13 Vendémiaire IV. Such legislation effectively freed hundreds of former terrorists incarcerated on charges of various abuses during the Terror and still awaiting judgment.

These two laws transformed local politics, activating feelings of resentment and revenge against local personalities no less than the national government. And they prompted vehement debates about the nature of exclusionary politics. What many called the Reaction of the Year IV had grown out of that of the Year III.

The anti-terrorist Reaction, corresponding to the last fifteen months of the National Convention from 10 Thermidor II (28 July 1794) to 4 Brumaire IV (26 October 1795), came to be known as the *Réaction thermidorienne* or the *Réaction post-thermidorienne*, in the political writings of the following year. In debates in the national legislature, in pamphlets by deputies, and most of all in the national and local press, the word signified the persecutions visited upon patriots by the passions of hatred and vengeance. The term gained currency during the Directorial years, then fully entered the historiography of the Revolution in the nineteenth and twentieth centuries. At first, the word mostly referred to the violence directed against former terrorists; later, it was employed more broadly to designate the period itself.

The first tremors of what would be the political earthquake known as the Reaction were felt shortly after the 9 Thermidor. In the days and weeks following the overthrow of Robespierre, confusion reigned in Jacobin circles as many began to feel a distinct change in the political climate. Congratulatory addresses from local administrations, *sociétés populaires*, and a multitude of other persons across France inundated the Convention with praises for having saved the Republic by deposing the "tyrant" Robespierre, now demonized as a "monster," a "tiger," "the new Catilina," "the modern Cromwell" (Baczko 1989, 2008). Anti-Jacobin pamphlets multiplied. The purge of local administrations by new representatives sent out after Thermidor; the release of hundreds of suspects languishing in the prisons of the Terror; the reduction in number of the local *comités de surveillance*, the very backbone of the local repression; the suppression of organs of revolutionary justice such as local revolutionary tribunals and military commissions; the revelation of "horrors" and atrocities committed during the previous year – all contributed to ending what was recently known as the "Reign of Terror" without effacing its terrifying memories. Throughout the country, survivors recounted their ordeals at the hands of revolutionary justice and remembered family members, friends and colleagues executed or like themselves forced into flight, dispossessed of their property, or weakened by months of fear and imprisonment. An increasingly audible cry for justice was heard, as petitions flowed into local and national administrations chronicling the experiences of lives damaged or destroyed. In the autumn Jacobin clubs were purged or closed, and moderates, including many former federalists, returned to positions of power in local administrations and courts. New waves of representatives-on-mission oversaw and orchestrated many of these "de-terrorization" measures that saw terrorist groups increasingly isolated within their communities.

Anti-terrorist invective soon became commonplace in the Thermidorian discourse. Former terrorists were stigmatized with epithets such as *buveurs de sang*, *monstres*, *cannibals*, *fripons*, *reptiles*, *tigres*, *vampires*, *anthropophages*, as *partisans du système de Robespierre*. They were depicted as assassins, naturally violent, corrupt, profiteering, cruel, lubricious, intriguing, as "ferocious enemies of the human race." And if there was one word that pervaded the anti-terrorist language of the day, it was blood: "the system of the Terror," a phrase increasingly used to describe the period of the Terror itself, was often labeled "the system of blood," and the invocation "innocent blood that cries out for vengeance" captured the anguish and, at times, encapsulated a program of the Terror's victims. Indeed, in the language of Thermidor, few words acquired such notoriety as "vengeance." Symbols, too, became the targets of anti-terrorist rage. Political vandalism was directed at emblems of Jacobin rule: monuments were demolished, streets bearing the names of revolutionary personages changed, liberty trees cut down and mutilated, and busts of Le Pelletier and Marat smashed in public ceremonies. It was frequently prohibited to shout the slogans, *Vive la Montagne, vivent les Jacobins*, though antithetical ones – *à bas la Montagne*, *à bas les Jacobins* or *les terroristes* or *buveurs de sang* – were often overheard in public places. The song *Réveil du Peuple* with lyrics condemning the Terror and terrorists was sung in theaters and in the streets, even in some of the recently purged Jacobin clubs, reflecting, as many proclaimed, that a new era had begun.

The eagerly awaited trial and execution in Paris on 16 December 1794 of the terrorist Jean-Baptiste Carrier, notorious for his role in the Terror in Nantes, nourished hopes of the possibility of justice for the victims of the Terror (Baczko 1989: 191–254; Dupâquier 1994; Gomez-Le Chevanton 2006). Other representatives-on-mission, such as Claude Javogues, Collot d'Herbois, and Étienne Maignet, were also denounced for their conduct while on mission during the Terror. The forceful and abundant demands for the judgment of former terrorists in Paris and the provinces for alleged acts of tyranny, arbitrary arrests, false denunciations, and abuses of power of all sorts led to a wider condemnation of revolutionary justice in general as arbitrary, unjust, summary. This condemnation would lead to the suppression of the Revolutionary Tribunal and the execution of its public prosecutor, Fouquier-Tinville, as well as other agents of revolutionary justice like the members of the Commission d'Orange and the president of the Revolutionary Tribunal of the Gard (Dunoyer 1912; Vaillandet 1929). The expression *Justice à l'ordre du jour*, so frequently used after Thermidor, signified for many that the rule of law had been restored as a guiding principle of French justice. And it meant that former terrorists would be held responsible for the crimes of the Terror.

Within weeks of the fall of Robespierre, and increasingly throughout the winter and spring of 1793 and 1794, former terrorists, and those suspected of having played a role in the Terror, men and women alike, were arrested often amid jeers, insults, and blows. Members of revolutionary administrations, tribunals, above all the *comités de surveillance*, equipped as these were with the powers of arrest, were prize catches; most of those arrested were familiar faces in their communities, identifiable even by name, accused of various misdeeds, from orchestrating the Terror to criminal offenses such as theft, profiteering, and false denunciation: some of these abuses, particularly the extortionist *contributions forcées*, pre-dated the Terror itself. At times, the task of identifying and finding former terrorists was facilitated by published lists of names such as the *Liste exacte et fidèle des terroristes de Moissac, district de Lauzerte* or the infamous *Liste générale des dénonciateurs et des dénoncés tant de la ville de Lyon que des communes voisines et de celles de divers Départemens*, published in the spring of 1795. The disarmament of former terrorists ordered by the decrees of 21 Germinal III (10 April 1795) and 1 Prairial III (20 May 1795) also rendered many among them doubly vulnerable to arrest and aggression. And the arrival in a department or region of a staunchly anti-terrorist representative-on-mission prone to making inflammatory proclamations and intent on eliminating vestiges of the Terrorist regime, could further inflame hatreds, embolden local belligerency, and incite more arrests: Paul Cadroy, whose name soon became inseparably linked to the Reaction, himself took the initiative to order the arrest in Marseille of at least seventy-seven former terrorists.[15] The number of those arrested mounted with the unfolding of national and local events: the insurrection of thousands of workers at the arsenal in Toulon from mid- to late May 1795, for instance, prompted waves of arrests throughout the departments in the south of France and as far north as Lyon (Poupé 1924: 283–312). That many of the arrests conducted during the period of the Reaction were the product of purely personal animosities emerges as a recurrent theme in the petitions of the incarcerated. In addition, more than one observer expressed concern that among those arrested figured a sizable number of former Jacobins in no way implicated in the Terror. Predictably, countless numbers of persons of varying degrees of complicity with the Terror – or not – sought safety in flight, just as thousands of *émigrés* had done the previous year.

But the distinguishing characteristic of the Reaction of the Thermidorian Convention of the Year III or of later Reaction was violence. If justice was proclaimed the order of the day, vengeance was its auxiliary and its nemesis. Hatred and resentment generated during the Terror – or before – exploded in one of the most destructive episodes of popular justice of the revolutionary decade. Beginning gradually in the autumn, then gathering momentum in the spring and summer of 1795, various acts of violence ranging from insults to beatings to mutilations to murders, individual and collective, were perpetrated in the name of outraged humanity against terrorist personnel and other victims of impassioned rage. Normally, the affair of small groups of armed men, the violence of the Reaction was at once spontaneous and premeditated; it erupted against isolated terrorists passing in the street or recognized in the marketplace, and at the same time it was the consequence of planning and careful contemplation. While each act of violence was unique, patterns remained much the same: individuals and groups killed other individuals and groups, categorized by labels and identified by factional alliance, in a murderous manifestation of pre-existing antipathies and violence, often accompanied by insults, humiliation, and mutilation. The violence of the Reaction was in its nature a continuation of other acts of popular justice known in France since 1789, and had much in common with the repertory of violence inherited from the *ancien régime*. Like other forms of popular justice, it was extra-legal: it was perpetrated in the name of justice, but in defiance of the law.

The role of local administrators and judicial personnel, not mention representatives-on-mission, as accomplices or foils to this violence is hard to establish. Again and again, in their proclamations and addresses, these authorities condemned wanton acts of individual violence: "The law alone has the right to punish the guilty," the municipality of Aix-en-Provence admonished its citizens in a proclamation against the mounting incidents of arbitrary violence in the vicinity.[16] Other authorities in the region, no less than in other parts of France, expressed this conviction to populations impatient for justice to be done. The injunction not to allow private passions to be substituted for the rule of law was a dominant refrain widespread in contemporary discourse: "banish all personal resentments; do not exercise private vengeance," the representative-on-mission Girot-Pouzel stated on 18 February 1795 as if in anticipation of the outbursts of violence that would overwhelm towns and villages later in the year.[17] His words would find a resonance with exhortations issued by other administrations besieged by seemingly uncontrollable violence. Yet this discourse, as abundant as it was repetitive, was often fraught with ambiguity. While lamenting the crimes of the Reaction, openly deploring that "passions and above all vengeance could sometimes prove more powerful than the law" – as the *procureur-syndic* of the department of the Bouches-du-Rhône put it on 11 May 1795 on the very day that a prison massacre in Aix-en-Provence cost of the lives of some thirty prisoners – authorities, whether local administrations or representatives-on-mission, made little effort to curtail their own invective leveled at former terrorists.[18] They regularly mobilized in proclamations and printed speeches an arsenal of insults and name-calling scarcely calculated to calm political temperatures often already beyond the boiling-point. The remark made by the representative Jean-Michel Chambon calling upon citizens, in his words, not to imitate their executioners, insisting that the law alone should deal with those he called "*scélérats* who still dare sully the land of liberty" is only a modest illustration of the kind of double message proffered throughout the period about former terrorists.[19]

The conservative Parisian and provincial press, a mirror and motor of public opinion, kept anti-terrorist sentiment at a high pitch during the Reaction of the Year III, as so often later, with similar language and similar objectives. Newspapers like the *Journal de Marseille*, the *Anti-Terroriste* of Toulouse, and the *Journal de Lyon* together with such conservative Parisian papers as the *Messager du Soir*, *Gazette française*, and *Courrier républicain*, informed their readers about the progress of the Reaction sparing no details, however gruesome, of anti-terrorist violence, depicting terrorists as a vanquished yet still dangerous faction of tyrants and assassins. Opposition papers, those like the *Sentinelle* or the *Journal des hommes libres*, defending the cause of embattled patriots, castigated the Reaction as royalist and anti-republican, and soon called for prompt and severe justice for those they called patriots with the same vehemence as the conservative press demanded justice for those it called terrorists. Both sides agreed: justice was long overdue.

If violence persisted with such intensity, even increasing across the spring and summer in many places like the Midi and the Rhône Valley, it was in no small measure, many argued, because of the time it took local criminal courts to deal with the mounting load of cases by adhering to the forms of regular justice. Not wishing to imitate what many believed to be the discredited system of revolutionary justice with its hasty and fraudulent practices, the courts of the Thermidorian Convention proclaimed a different style of justice marked by a respect for procedure and the accused. While these ideals were often compromised, the Thermidorian courts, even in those places like Lyon and Aix-en-Provence where the wounds of the Terror were freshest, and where violence posed an ever-present threat to public order, took time for the most part to follow codified regulations in the trial of former terrorists. It was not unusual for large trials against former terrorists to stretch over several days or weeks and involve scores of witnesses: the trial of those implicated in the "Affaire" of 5 Vendémiaire III (26 September 1794) in Marseille consumed eight days of deliberations and involved some fifty witnesses, and the vast affair of Salon about political abuses, some of them dating back to the summer of 1792, was judged over eighteen days, after twenty-seven sessions and 174 witnesses heard for and against the accused.[20] Some of these trials could be stormy affairs, like that against the former judges of the Commission d'Orange between 20 June and 25 June 1795 where the accused, once sentenced, were nearly murdered by crowds before being executed the next day (Vaillandet 1929). Many former terrorists, like the president of the Revolutionary Tribunal in Nîmes or one of Marseille's leading terrorists Isoard, were tried and executed, and several others sentenced to prison or deportation or acquitted.[21] Still, the presence of so many terrorists in the country's prisons constituted a provocation for those impatient with judicial formalities that might delay their judgment. "We cannot conceal," the district administration of Carpentras noted in late May 1795, "that the slowness of justice has been a source of exasperation; previously [during the Terror] one needed so little time to send the finest citizens to scaffold."[22] More than one local authority rightly worried about the safety of former terrorists in such an atmosphere.

Indeed, the large-scale prison massacres of the late spring and summer in Lyon, Aix-en-Provence, Tarascon, the Fort Saint-Jean, to name only the most spectacular, were planned and executed by crowds mainly composed of men eager to take justice into their own hands (Clay 1997; Fuoc 1957; Gaffarel 1909). In fact, two of these massacres – at Lyon and Aix – took place while trials against some among the terrorists were currently under way in the local courts. Other prisoners, murdered in transit to prisons or to courtrooms or in fields or dark back streets or in public squares, added to the number of victims of unbridled passion, passion that local administrations could not – or would not – control. Most incidents of popular violence committed during the different Reactions – or at other times during the Revolution, for that matter – attest to the inability of constituted authority to maintain order and impose the rule of law. The prompt judgment of imprisoned terrorists together with a lingering fear of renewed violence grew into major preoccupations concerning troubled regions of the country. And while some observers showed compassion at the plight of victims of such wholesale massacre, many in the National Convention and local administrations and representatives then on mission were inclined to minimize the carnage and blame the victims: such violence, it was stated, paled before the horrors of the Terror and was, in their view, brought on by the terrorists themselves, by their own violence and disregard for human life.

Yet it was one thing to rationalize the acts of private and collective vengeance raging in the country or to feign disapproval, or to exhibit indifference, or even to turn a blind eye to the killing in an act of tacit complicity; it was quite another to physically participate in murder and atrocities and other acts of brutality. Those implicated in the violence were men and women who for the most part belonged to the town or region where the violence was committed; they were members of their communities, though they rarely enjoyed any social prominence. To judge from surviving judicial records, police reports, and contemporary descriptions of all sorts, the vast majority of those eventually brought to trial for their offenses were men – the *jeunes gens* – mostly in their twenties, with ages usually ranging from their late teens to their mid-thirties, though there were exceptions at both ends of the spectrum. For the most part, they came from the artisanal professions, or were small shop-owners or workers. Some among them were marginalized within their communities, living on the fringes of common criminality; others were deserters or returned *émigrés*. Many were members or related to members of the political faction opposed to the Jacobins – federalists or moderates. And a significant number had been victims directly or indirectly of the Terror: they had suffered imprisonment, lost loved ones, been forced into hiding, or generally lived with the fear of the knock on the door from a man with an arrest warrant. Most of those who committed violence against former terrorists knew their victims, sometimes by name. Equally, their victims usually had no difficulty identifying their assailants.

Most violence was carried out by groups, consisting of at least three people, usually as many as ten or twenty. The largest of these groups went under the name of the Compagnie du Soleil, or Compagnie de Jésus, a large, semi-organized band chiefly operating in Lyon and its environs from the spring of 1795 to the summer of 1797 – though the name Compagnie du Soleil was also widely applied by the press as well as by government officials to other bands operating with varying degrees of organization throughout France, mainly in the Midi. Virtually all of them targeted former terrorists or known republicans; hence their reputation among Jacobins as royalist in purpose. But some of these groups, while attacking individuals marked by their political convictions, also indulged in acts of outright thuggery and criminality. Some companies were thought to be financed by English gold, or by local bourgeois or nobles eager to avenge themselves at a distance, without direct confrontation. Like other partisan groups, members of these companies often wore distinguishing emblems – ribbons, buttons, *gances blanches*, *cadenettes*, or distinctive hairstyles. The infamous Bande d'Aubagne or the much larger Compagnie de Jésus in Lyon kept their respective communities in paralyzed fear and murdered many former terrorists before they were brought to justice (Benoît 1995: 16–18, 1997: 497–507; Cobb 1972: 19–62; Lenotre 1931; Sutherland 2009).

For most contemporary Jacobins, the people behind the violence of the Reaction, whether organized or not, were resolute royalists, perpetrators of a vast conspiracy to overthrow the Republic by organizing a Saint-Barthélemy of the *patriotes*. In their view, their aggressors were not only seeking revenge, but were committed to an ideological program dedicated to restoring the monarchy. In his report to the National Convention on 6 Messidor III (24 June 1795), Marie-Joseph Chénier called for vigorous measures against the recalcitrant Compagnie de Jésus, then spreading panic and murder in Lyon, arguing that this band, though indisputably royalist, was nothing less than a collection of killers who under the pretext of avenging the crimes of the Terror dishonored by their murderous acts the very nature of justice, substituting one Terror for another.[23] Others, too, would rise up to denounce the crimes of the Reaction, though little beyond verbal condemnation was done to pursue these crimes over the summer of 1795 and bring the guilty to justice. In September, in the aftermath of the Parisian *journée* of 13 Vendémiaire, the deputy Pierre-Louis Bentabole implored the Convention to take measures to punish the perpetrators of the violence of the Reaction.[24] Chénier, again, spoke out against this violence, this time proposing still more measures making local officials legally responsible for pursuing these crimes.[25] The Convention's decision to halt the spread of the Reaction and prosecute its authors by sending on mission the deputies Jacques Reverchon and Stanislas Fréron to those departments particularly troubled by its violence would end up by creating another Reaction (Clay 2009; Lucas 1977).

Within months of their arrival in the regions of Lyon and Provence, respectively, Reverchon and Fréron had purged local administrations, dismissed judicial personnel, freed former terrorists still in prison awaiting judgment, implemented the legislation of 3 Brumaire expelling from office former *émigrés* and their relatives, pursued refractory priests allied to the Reaction, and launched judicial investigations against those held responsible for the violence against *patriotes*; in short, they had overturned the local politics in substantial portions of France. Their policies overtly favoring former terrorists and Jacobin cadres aroused fierce opposition in Paris and the provinces, and their vigorous application of the recent law of amnesty released into the population and public life men intent on wreaking vengeance on their political adversaries. The actions of these two men did much to advance and consolidate the notion of political Reaction as a substitution in power of one political group by another, often accompanied by violence. For while these deputies disapproved of violence of any form between the factions, their partiality implicitly promoted the politics of Reaction. In part of France, however, the Reaction begun during the Thermidorian Convention – the first Reaction, as some commentators said – continued unabated as a permanent feature of the political life of the Directory.

With the discovery of the Babeuf conspiracy, the violent elections of Thermidor IV in Marseille and Aix-en-Provence, and the abortive Camp de Grenelle, the politics of the Directorial regime moved again in the opposite direction in many respects. Among these was the appointment of the steadfastly anti-Jacobin General Amédée Willot to the Eighth Military Division, roughly corresponding to the departments of Provence where only months before Fréron had provoked a strong Reaction led by local Jacobins and ex-terrorists. The arrival in the region of Willot, with his undisguised, doctrinaire abhorrence of Jacobinism, would contribute to the establishment of yet another Reaction in the local politics in those departments under his military control. Indeed, his aggressive program of promoting the opponents of local Jacobins made his mission no less controversial than that of Fréron in a region persistently torn by factional rivalries. He was derisively dubbed the "Roi du Midi," charged with persecuting former Jacobins and their families, maligned as a tyrant, and accused of aspiring to impose military despotism and of committing other flagrant violations of the constitution. His inflammatory presence in the Midi, widely reported in the Parisian and local press, made Willot into something of a national personality, the symbol for his adversaries of counter-revolution and Reaction. Violence between the factions continued, even intensified, during his stay in Provence. Elsewhere, too, particularly in regions like the Midi and the Rhône Valley, the anti-Jacobin violence of the Reaction or Reactions occurred as local factions vied for political power or succumbed to a heritage of hate. In Provence, victims of the "Réaction Cadroy" were again persecuted during the "Réaction Willot," forced into exile and hiding, or made into victims of unappeased rage. For many embattled groups of former Jacobins whether in Provence or elsewhere the *Réaction royale* or *anarchie royale* appeared as one long Saint-Barthélemy of the *patriotes*. The Reactions sweeping over large parts of the country had contributed in no small way to fostering the seemingly uncontrollable lawlessness so characteristic of the Directorial years.

The *coup d'état* of 18 Fructidor V (4 September 1797) annulled the electoral results in forty-nine departments that had seen the ascension to public office of many conservatives and some outright royalists in the spring of 1797. This political turn-about again changed the political climate in many parts of the country. The law of 19 Fructidor V, creating as it did military commissions and other repressive measures, endowed the executive Directory with wide-ranging powers (Brown 2006). Not surprisingly, many observers saw in this dramatic reversal of local and national politics the germ of a new Reaction. The dismissal from public office of thousands of public officials and their replacement in many instances by former Jacobins, some of them ex-terrorists; the execution of refractory priests and *émigrés*, among so many others, at the hands of military commissions; the forced emigration of countless individuals of all ages; the enforcement of obligatory festivals and observance of the republican calendar – all conspired with other heavy-handed government practices to give substance to fears of a new Reaction. It became a conspicuous practice in the months following the Fructidor coup to speak of Reactions in the plural, occurring in response to a revolution whether the "revolution of 9 Thermidor" or that of Fructidor. But the repeated hope expressed in a multitude of addresses that the Royalist Reaction, understood as violence against *patriotes*, had finally subsided, proved more wish than reality in large parts of the country. Yet more than before local judicial and administrative authorities initiated legal proceedings against the "leaders of the Reaction." Indeed, apart from the trial of those charged with the violence of the massacre of the Fort Saint-Jean, virtually all the legal action taken against the killers of the Reaction from Thermidor to Fructidor was completed after the coup of Fructidor V (Clay 2007: 109–133; Jarre 2008; Lenotre 1931). These trials were disappointing if judged by the number of convictions, for very few of those implicated in the violence of the Reaction were ever tried or punished.

The phenomenon of Reaction persisted in political practice and in the political lexicon well beyond the end of the Revolution in Brumaire. Indeed, it acquired new intensity and renewed scope in the Reaction of 1815, often involving the same men, or their families and descendants, in another cycle of violence and revenge. By the 1820s the term "White Terror" was used interchangeably with "Reaction" to signify the violence of the revolutionary decade as well as that of 1815. During the early nineteenth century, the term "Reaction" came to be applied to any real or potential reversal of current politics, a change invariably associated with royalism and perceived as threatening to political stability. In dictionaries, political treatises, and political discourse, the phenomenon of the Reaction was viewed as an integral part of the revolutionary dynamic. And as attested in the voluminous works of nineteenth-century historians from Michelet to Quinet, the Reaction or White Terror had become a permanent chapter in the historiography of the French Revolution.

Notes

1 The documentation for this chapter is largely drawn from unpublished manuscripts in the National Archives (chiefly the series AFIII, DIII, F7, F9, F1bII, F1cIII, F7, F9, and BB18); the departmental archives of the l'Ain, Bouches-du-Rhône, Drôme, Gard, Gironde, Haute-Garonne, Haute-Loire, Hérault, Landes, Loire, Rhône, Var, and the Vaucluse; and the municipal archives of Aix-en-Provence, Arles, Avignon, Bordeaux, Carpentras, Lyon, Marseille, Montpellier, Orange, Tarascon, Toulon, and Toulouse. To avoid encumbering the text with lengthy archival references to this abundant documentation, I have kept such citation to a minimum, and would refer the interested reader to the footnotes to my articles mentioned in the notes.

2 Fréron, *Mémoire historique sur la Réaction royale et sur les massacres du Midi.* Paris: Baudouin, 1824.
3 *Le Messager du Soir* (3 Frimaire III)
4 Archives Nationales (hereafter AN) F7 7319.
5 Service Historique de la Défense B13 83.
6 Archives Départementales (hereafter AD) Vaucluse 15L 35.
7 AN AD XVIII A 39: Maximin Isnard, Discours sur la situation du Midi, 30 Ventôse IV.
8 AN F7 7254.
9 *L'Anti-Royaliste*, 13 Ventôse VI.
10 AN F7 3689 (2).
11 Aulard 1889–97: vol. 6, 325.
12 Constant 1988 [1796–97]: 96.
13 AN F7 7298.
14 AN F7 7170.
15 Archives Municipales de Marseille A. 29.
16 Archives Municipales d'Aix-en-Provence LL 81.
17 AD Hérault L 5750.
18 AD Bouches-du-Rhône L 242.
19 Archives Municipales d'Aix-en-Provence LL 244.
20 AN DIII 29; ADBR L 3020.
21 AD Gard L. 3057; AD Bouches-du-Rhône L 3020.
22 AD Vaucluse 1L 222.
23 Bibliothèque Nationale, Le3801507: Marie-Joseph Chénier, Rapport fait à la Convention nationale, 6 Messidor III.
24 *Le Moniteur*, no. 24, 24 Vendémiaire IV.
25 AN AD XVI 25: Marie-Joseph Chénier, Rapport fait a la Convention nationale, 29 Vendémiaire IV.

References

Aulard, Alphonse (ed.) (1889–97). *La Société des jacobins: Recueil des documents pour l'histoire du club des jacobins de Paris*, 6 vols. Paris.

Baczko, Bronislaw (1989). *Comment sortir de la Terreur? Thermidor et la Révolution.* Paris: Gallimard.

Baczko, Bronislaw (2008). *Politiques de la Révolution française.* Paris: Gallimard.

Benoît, Bruno (1994). "Analyse des violences urbaines à l'époque révolutionnaire: L'Exemple lyonnais." In Bruno Benoit (ed.). *Ville et Révolution française: Actes du colloque international de Lyon, mars 1993.* Lyon: Presses Universitaires de Lyon. 147–162.

Benoît, Bruno (1995). "Les Compagnons de Jéhu ont-ils existé?" *Histoire*, 185: 16–18.

Benoît, Bruno (1997). "Chasser le mathevon à Lyon en l'an III." In Michel Vovelle (ed.). *Le Tournant de l'an III: Réaction et Terreur blanche dans la France révolutionnaire.* Paris: CTHS. 497–507.

Blanc, Louis (1862). *Histoire de la Révolution française*, 12 vols. Paris: Pagnerre/Furne.

Bonnefoy, Marc (1892). *Les Suites du neuf Thermidor: Terreurs blanches 1795–1815.* Paris.

Brown, Howard G. (2006). *Ending the French Revolution: Violence, Justice, and Repression from the Terror to Napoleon.* Charlottesville and London: University Press of Virginia.

Clay, Stephen (1997). "Le Massacre du fort Saint-Jean, un épisode de la Terreur blanche à Marseille." In Michel Vovelle (ed.). *Le Tournant de l'an III: Réaction et Terreur blanche dans la France révolutionnaire.* Paris: CTHS. 569–583.

Clay, Stephen (1999). "Réaction dans le Midi: Le Vocable de la vengeance." In Jacques Guilhaumou and Raymonde Monnier (eds.). *Dictionnaire des usages socio-politiques (1770–1815)*, vol. 6. Paris: Klincksieck. 157–186.

Clay, Stephen (2006). "Les Réactions du Midi: Conflits, continuités et violence." *AHRF*, 345: 55–91.

Clay, Stephen (2007). "Justice, vengeance et passé révolutionnaire: Les Crimes de la Terreur Blanche." *AHRF*, 350: 109–133.

Clay, Stephen (2009). "Vengeance, Justice and the Reactions in the Revolutionary Midi." *FH*, 23: 22–46.

Cobb, Richard (1970). *The Police and the People: French Popular Protest 1789–1820.* Oxford: Clarendon Press.

Cobb, Richard (1972). *Reactions to the French Revolution.* London, New York and Toronto: Oxford University Press.

Constant, Benjamin (1988 [1796–97]). *De la force du gouvernement actuel de la France et de la nécessité de s'y rallier (1796). Des réactions politiques. Des effets de la Terreur (1797).* Preface and notes by Philippe Raynaud. Paris: Flammarion.

Dunoyer, Alphonse (1912). *Fouquier-Tinville, accusateur public du Tribunal révolutionnaire (1746–1795) d'après les documents des Archives nationales.* Paris: Perrin.

Dupâquier, Jacques (1994). *Carrier. Procès d'un missionnaire de la Terreur et du Comité révolutionnaire de Nantes (16 octobre–16 décembre 1794).* Paris: Éditions des Étannets.

Fuoc, Renée (1957). *La Réaction thermidorienne à Lyon (1795).* Lyon: Éditions de Lyon.

Gaffarel, Paul (1909). "Les Massacres royalistes dans le département des Bouches-du-Rhône aux premiers mois de 1795: Épisode de la Réaction thermidorienne." *Annales des Facultés de Droit et de Lettres d'Aix*, 1–66.

Gainot, Bernard (2003). "Aux origines du Directoire: Le 'Proconsulat' de Jacques Reverchon (Brumaire–Ventôse an IV)." *AHRF*, 332: 129–146.

Gomez-Le Chevanton, Corinne (2006). "Le Procès Carrier: Enjeux politiques, pédagogie collective et construction mémorielle." *AHRF*, 343: 273–292.

Jarre, Hélène (2008). *La Contre-Révolution en Haute-Loire, 1789–1799: La Compagnie des Ganses blanches, la Terreur blanche, le procès des Compagnons de Jésus.* Polignac: Éditions du Roure.

Laincel, Louis de (1864). *Terreur rouge et Terreur blanche.* Paris.

Lenotre, G. (1931). *La Compagnie de Jéhu: Épisodes de la réaction lyonnaise 1794–1800.* Paris: Perrin.

Lewis, Gwynne (1978). *The Second Vendée: The Continuity of Counter-Revolution in the Department of the Gard, 1789–1815.* Oxford: Clarendon Press.

Lucas, Colin (1977). "The First Directory and the Rule of Law." *FHS*, 10: 231–260.

Lucas, Colin (1979). "Violence thermidorienne et société traditionnelle: L'Exemple du Forez." *Cahiers d'histoire*, 24: 3–43.

Lucas, Colin (1983). "Themes in Southern Violence after 9 Thermidor." In Gwynne Lewis and Colin Lucas (eds.). *Beyond the Terror: Essays in French Regional and Social History, 1794–1815.* Cambridge: Cambridge University Press. 152–194.

Mathiez, Albert (1929). *La Réaction thermidorienne.* Paris: Armand Colin.

Monnier, Raymonde (1999). "Un mot nouveau en politique: Réaction sous Thermidor." In Jacques Guilhaumou and Raymonde Monnier (eds.). *Dictionnaire des usages socio-politiques (1770–1815)*, vol. 6. Paris: Klincksieck. 127–156.

Poupé, Edmond (1924). "La Répression de la révolte terroriste de Toulon fin Floréal an III." *Le Var Historique et Géographique*, 283–312.

Sutherland, Donald M.G. (2009). *Murder in Aubagne: Lynching, Law and Justice during the French Revolution.* Cambridge: Cambridge University Press.

Thibaudeau, Antoine-Claire (1824). *Mémoires sur la Convention et le Directoire*, 2 vols. Paris: Baudouin.

Vaillandet, Paul (1929). "Le Procès des juges de la Commission révolutionnaire d'Orange." *AHRF*, 6: 137–163.

Vovelle, Michel (1987). "Massacreurs et massacrés: Aspects sociaux de la contre-révolution en Provence, après Thermidor." In François Lebrun and Roger Dupuy (eds.). *Les Résistances à la Révolution: Actes du colloque de Rennes, 17–21 septembre 1985*. Paris. 141–150.

Part VIII

The Revolution in International Perspective

CHAPTER TWENTY-THREE

The International Repercussions of the French Revolution

MIKE RAPPORT

> May God cause the upheaval in France to spread like syphilis to the enemies of the Empire, hurl them into prolonged conflict with one another, and thus accomplish results beneficial to the Empire, amen.

Ahmed Efendi, the Turkish sultan Selim III's secretary, committed these less than charitable thoughts to his diary in January 1792 (Blanning 1986: 184). His prayer was certainly answered: for the rest of the decade the shockwaves from the French Revolution were felt across the world, shaking even the diarist's beloved Ottoman Empire. The repercussions were felt, firstly, through the ways in which its political culture resonated around the world; secondly, in the impact of the revolutionary war; and thirdly, in the conservative response to the first two factors. The reception of the Revolution outside France depended on pre-existing political and social tensions or regional conflicts – but the impact almost always radicalized or intensified them.

Historiography

Edmund Burke famously wrote in 1790: "It looks to me as if I were in a great crisis, not of the affairs of France alone, but of all Europe, perhaps of more than Europe" (Burke 1968: 92). Since then, the European impact has been studied in terms of the diplomatic fall-out (Sorel 1885–1905; Schroeder 1994); the response of radicals outside France and the spread of French ideas and institutions (Godechot 1983; Goodwin 1979; Jourdan 2008; Lesnodorski 1965; Robertson 2000; Schama 1992); the torment of the French revolutionary wars, including the experience of occupation and resistance (Blanning 1983, 1996; Broers 1997); forms of counter-revolution (Lebrun and Dupuy 1987) and the cultural repercussions,

A Companion to the French Revolution, First Edition. Edited by Peter McPhee.

including the rise of nationalism and shifts in attitudes towards the "other" (Broers 2005; Dann and Dinwiddy 1988; Woolf 1989, 1992). This work has nuanced older interpretations which either, on the political left, regarded the impact as the herald of a democratic or social-democratic order, or, on the right, stressed how conservative reactions to the French Revolution aroused popular patriotism and religious fervor.

Other historians have sailed in the brinier context of the Atlantic. Palmer and Godechot argued that the revolutionary movements of the late eighteenth-century Atlantic world were broadly similar in origins and aims, making this an age of "democratic," "Atlantic," or "western" revolution (Godechot 1971; Palmer 1959–64). In the ideologically charged atmosphere of the Cold War, this aroused considerable bile: Godechot (1983: 9) later claimed that some historians accused them of being paid by NATO or the CIA. Cooler heads among "Marxist" historians, such as Marcel Reinhard and George Rudé, argued that the "Atlantic" interpretation robbed the French Revolution of its radicalism, which was exceptional when compared to upheavals such as those in America and the Netherlands. The French Revolution was *the* bourgeois revolution, while the radicalism of the sans-culottes presaged the socialism of the modern proletariat (Amann 1963).

The "linguistic turn," which emphasizes the Revolution as a transformation in political culture, has reinvigorated the Atlantic thesis, since historians have looked again at the connections and common features amongst the revolutions in the Atlantic world. Pre-eminent among these is Jourdan (2004), whose study of the American, Dutch, and French revolutions underscores their essentially "republican" frames of political reference, the similarities in political mobilization, and the fears and aspirations of the revolutionaries. Where they differed was in the extent of violence, change, resistance, and circumstances. A recent explosion in interest in the Haitian Revolution of 1791 has demonstrated that the Atlantic revolution also enveloped the Caribbean and the African diaspora. Extending the chronology beyond 1800 allows historians to include the Latin American wars of independence (Klooster 2009). So what, if anything, was exceptional about the French Revolution?

Recent work on global history has also suggested that the French Revolution was merely one of many eruptions which amounted to a critical phase in the emergence of the modern world (Armitage and Subrahmanyam 2010). For Bayly (2004: 86–120), the epoch between 1780 and 1820 saw "converging revolutions," transformations arising in different societies which would eventually transform the global order. Darwin (2007: 160) suggests that a "Eurasian revolution" arose from a series of crises which erupted in South Asia and Europe (and North America), tipping the global equilibrium in Europe's favor. France was merely one epicenter among many, perhaps not even the most significant. If Atlantic interpretations once pushed the French Revolution into the water, the global perspective might well come along and steal its clothes. It is hard to deny that the collapse of the Mughal Empire in India, the transitions in the Ottoman Empire, as well as the revolutions in America, Haiti, and Latin America had global repercussions. Yet what distinguished the French Revolution *individually* from the others was the geographical scale and power of its impact.

The Ideological and Cultural Repercussions

In 1789, contemporaries were astounded by the spectacle of one of the most powerful monarchies in Europe humbled by its own subjects. In a world experiencing the emergence of "public opinion," there was a ready-made market which eagerly consumed the news from France: from 1789, journals in the United States gave between three and four times as much space to French affairs as previously. The Declaration of the Rights of Man and of the Citizen was translated and published in, for example, the *Magyar Kurir* in Budapest and the *Saint Petersburg Gazette*. In the age of the "Grand Tour" and the cosmopolitan Enlightenment, there was a market for eyewitness accounts, published as diaries, letters, or travel writing in all European languages. The Revolution was depicted in prints, cartoons, and caricatures, in poetry and on the stage: in London, a veritable "Bastille war" (Schürer 2005: 50–81) erupted between rival theater managers as they tried to outdo each other in presenting the drama of the great event.

Moderate British reformers saw 1789 as a French equivalent to their own revolution of 1688–89. The Whig parliamentary opposition warned the government to concede mild electoral reform, since France revealed the dangers of "preventative remedies ... not thought of in time" (Dickinson 1977: 237). German intellectuals looked on France benignly, believing that the Revolution was securing what Germans already enjoyed, or would soon enjoy, under their "enlightened" rulers. In the United States, even federalists, politically the more conservative wing of American politics, initially welcomed the French Revolution: as John Marshall later recalled, "I sincerely believed human liberty to depend ... on the success of the French Revolution" (Wood 2009: 174–175). For most moderately progressive people, "1789" was France catching up with other "enlightened" societies.

Yet the impact also worked on deeper conflicts. Where the emancipating ideals of the Rights of Man fused with pre-existing revolutionary movements, they produced a potentially explosive mix. The Dutch "Patriots," overrun by a Prussian army in 1787, the democrats from the Belgian struggle for independence from Austria in 1789–90; Swiss radicals; British and Irish proponents of a democratic reforms – all saw an ideological inspiration and, sometimes, an ally in the new France. While they show that the French Revolution was not the only upheaval, this should not obscure the fact that the French Revolution powerfully influenced them, especially because they had been defeated or frustrated prior to 1789. Many Dutch, Belgians, and Swiss were exiles in France, where they adopted much of the rhetoric, ideology, and symbolism of their French hosts. Called "patriots" or (not always accurately) "Jacobins," they and their compatriots back home would provide the hard core of collaborators for the French conquerors during the revolutionary war.

Across Europe and the Atlantic world, the Revolution raised the ideological stakes, laying greater emphasis on natural rights and popular sovereignty and encouraging the emergence of mass movements, where earlier campaigns for reform had been the work of elite and middle-class circles. These developments, in turn, encouraged radicals to be more ambitious in their demands, or led a minority to contemplate new possibilities, such as social as well as political change. British radicals, especially under American influence, had already argued that sovereignty lay with the people (and not Parliament), so everyone (or all men) should have equal political rights. Yet they based these arguments on the historic birthright of "freeborn Britons": Magna Carta, the "ancient" constitution and the Bill of Rights of 1689. During the French Revolution, British radicals were more likely to insist that all men shared the same political rights, simply because they were the inalienable rights of all men. Thomas Paine's *Rights of Man*, part 1, published in 1791, had a particularly dramatic impact: the tract offered a trenchant defense of the French Revolution and its emergent constitution, helping to persuade even such genteel organizations as the Manchester Constitutional Society to embrace universal male suffrage. More radical still, part 2, published in 1792, attacked monarchy and aristocracy and outlined a full program for social justice (Paine 1984: 247–248). This went too far for most British radicals, who insisted that they merely wanted a democratic reform of the House of Commons. None the less, they acknowledged the power of Paine's work so that, by 1793, *Rights of Man* had sold 200,000 copies. French inspiration galvanized British radical organizations, which expanded in numbers and broadened their social base. They spread their propaganda through a mass media of pamphlets, newspapers, and prints and created the earliest British political clubs for artisans and workers, the first being the Sheffield Society for Constitutional Information in November 1791, followed by the London Corresponding Society (LCS), founded in early 1792: with low membership fees, it grew to a membership of 10,000 at its peak. Inspired in some measure by the French Jacobin clubs, the LCS planned to correspond with the other British reform societies, in order to bring about a concerted campaign for parliamentary reform. In times of economic crisis, as in the winter of 1794–95, its open-air meetings may have drawn as many as 150,000 people.

In Scotland, Societies of the Friends of the People arose in almost every major town and city by the end of 1792. In December that year, the societies organized a convention in Edinburgh to combine their efforts in petitioning for parliamentary reform. Although such conventions had a venerable Scottish pedigree, in late 1792 it echoed its French namesake and adopted French forms: its first meeting closed with "the French oath of live free or die" (Meikle 1912: 110). The Irish reforms of 1782 granted Ireland its own parliament, but fell short of extending the suffrage and of enfranchising Catholics. Now Protestant radicals, particularly in Belfast and Dublin, were enthused by Paine and the French Revolution: in October 1791 a number of them, including Theobald Wolfe Tone, created the Society of the United Irishmen in Belfast, aiming to secure the vote for all Irishmen whatever their religion. The organization rapidly spread.

In countries tantalized by the promises of eighteenth-century enlightened absolutism, the Revolution was often welcomed by reformers disappointed with the slow pace or even reversal of change. In the Habsburg Empire, Emperor Francis II's former tutor, Andreas Riedel, called for the abolition of the nobility, while the Hungarian physics professor Ignácz Martinovics declared that "the contract binding members of society grants equal justice to all" (Wangermann 1959: 13–14). Enlightened Italian rulers had tried to reduce the power of the church, the nobility, and the guilds, changes that were not universally popular. In Tuscany in 1790, reformers were hammered by a riotous popular reaction. Yet while the most virulent opposition to change was conservative, some radicals argued that reform should involve popular representation and sensitivity to patriotic feeling. Ugo Foscolo in Venice and Vincenzo Cuoco in Naples adopted a "Jacobin" position in which democratic citizenship would bring about equality and fraternity amongst all Italians. In 1792, radical clubs were established clandestinely in Naples and in Genoa. In Poland, King Stanisław August Poniatowski had been busily overhauling the state to make it less vulnerable to foreign interference: the Constitution of 3 May 1791 gave Poland a hereditary monarchy (it had been elected), and abolished the *liberum veto*, which had given every individual nobleman the right to block legislation. Stanisław was adamant that this "Polish Revolution" was infinitely preferable to the French version "from below," but Warsaw's radical press saw the constitution merely as the foundation for further reform, declaring that, as in France, the "National Will" had to be the true basis for change (Lukowski 1999: 138–141).

The impact on the United States was no less profound. There were already bitter political divisions between conservative federalists and the more radical republicans, a searing hostility in which the French Revolution was deeply symbolic. After the general enthusiasm of 1789, many federalists began to distance themselves from the events in France. When Benjamin Franklin died in 1790, the National Assembly in Paris went into three days' mourning, but federalists balked, since the great sage was far too Francophile and democratic for their taste (Wood 2009: 176). In inverse proportion to growing federalist skepticism, Republicans noisily exulted in the French Revolution. They sang songs such as *Ça Ira!* and the *Marseillaise*, wore tricolor cockades, planted trees of liberty, and held festivals to celebrate such landmark events as the fall of the Bastille, the overthrow of the monarchy, the proclamation of the Republic, and the first French victory in the war at Valmy. As Newman (1997, 2011) has shown, American republicanism was being sculpted by trans-Atlantic currents in politics and culture.

Yet it was not only in the United States that the reverberations were felt. More dramatic still were the shockwaves in France's overseas empire: while the repercussions in Haiti were easily the most striking, the Revolution resonated in the furthest-flung of France's colonies. News of the Revolution did not arrive in the French trading posts (*comptoirs*) in India until late February 1790, but when it did it legitimized open resistance against royal authority among the French communities. The leading French citizens in Pondichéry gathered in a General Assembly from 25 February, calling for the formation of a civic guard and control of the arsenal. The upheaval was echoed in the other *comptoirs*, Chandernagore, Mahé, Karikal, and Yanam (Sen 1971). When the news of the fall of the monarchy arrived in March 1793, the citizens in Pondichéry planted a tree of liberty, held a banquet, and saluted each other with cries of *Vive la Nation!* and *Vive la République!* The elation was short-lived: within three months, the British had overrun all the *comptoirs*.

The ideological, cultural, and political impact of the French Revolution, particularly in Europe and America, shows that while "Jacobinism" emerged from localized roots, it was energized and sometimes radicalized by influences from France. This relationship would prove to be problematic, even downright dangerous, with the outbreak of the French revolutionary wars.

The Impact of the French Revolutionary Wars

Despite the Revolution's ideological challenges, most governments welcomed the debilitation of the once mighty French state: in September 1789 William Grenville, then British home secretary, hoped that France "for many years [would not be able] to molest the invaluable peace which we now enjoy" (Rudé 1964: 181). Emperor Joseph II, Marie-Antoinette's brother, remarked in August, "It is in my interest to be perfectly neutral in this business, no matter what may happen to the King and the Queen" (Blanning 1994: 203). These sanguine attitudes would change when the Revolution took a radical turn and France embarked on a war of military expansion.

In the first two years after July 1789, the French cautiously avoided giving any signals that they wanted to export the Revolution: they politely, but cautiously, received the applause of such foreign radicals as the "Orator of the Human Race," Anacharsis Cloots. On 22 May 1790, fearful of being dragged into a war against Britain over an incident in distant Nootka Sound, the National Assembly proclaimed that "the French nation renounces the undertaking of any war of conquest and will never use its forces against the liberty of any people" (Godechot 1983: 66). Yet the approach of conflict in western Europe from the autumn of 1791 radicalized the rhetoric: Jacques-Pierre Brissot proclaimed that the war which eventually broke out in April 1792 would be "a crusade for universal liberty" (Blanning 1986: 111). After the first French victories in the autumn, the "Edict of Fraternity" of 19 November offered "fraternity and help" to "all peoples who wish to recover their liberty" (Rudé 1964: 210). Yet harsh strategic realities soon bit: national self-determination for the Belgians and Rhinelanders was excellent in theory, but in practice left them vulnerable to Austrian or Prussian domination. France, Georges-Jacques Danton argued in January 1793, needed a defensible frontier: "The limits of France are marked out by nature, we will reach them in the four corners of the horizon: the Rhine, the Ocean and the Alps" (Godechot 1983: 72). These strategic objectives combined with the financial and material pressures of the war to produce the decree of 15 December 1792. It abolished the *ancien régime* in the occupied areas, but it also forced the local population to defray the costs of their "liberation" and ordered plebiscites which, held within earshot of the tramp of French boots, were foregone conclusions: Belgium, the Rhineland, Nice, and Savoy voted for annexation by France. This left the question as to what to do with those territories which might be conquered beyond France's "natural frontiers" and the Convention hit on "sister republics," satellite states allied to the French Republic, with constitutions and laws reflecting the French model, albeit with local variations. Although the tide of the war again turned against the French until their decisive victory at Fleurus on 26 June 1794, the pattern had already been set for expansion: first exploit the conquests, then either annex them or convert them into "sister republics."

Exploitation took place for three reasons: firstly, France itself had been devastated, with shortages of specie, manpower, cereals, livestock, tools, and horses. Asset-stripping the conquests would therefore replenish the skeletal French economy. Secondly, these resources would pay for the French war effort, as the

Committee of Public Safety declared, "one of the first principles of military administration is to feed war by war" (Blanning 1983: 76). Thirdly, the revolutionaries wanted to make sure that the territories could not be used to support another allied invasion of France. As the French reoccupied Belgium and western Germany after Fleurus, "Agencies of Commerce and Extraction" seized an extraordinary array of materials: in Belgium, the list ran to 202 products, including raw materials, finished goods, foodstuffs, livestock, fuel, and machinery, while in the Rhineland, the demands were even more exhaustive (Rapport 2002: 63). Later, with Napoleon Bonaparte's invasion of Italy in 1796, works of art were top of the list. Metal currency was taken through financial levies: between September 1794 and November 1798, the French repeatedly inflicted demands for millions of *livres* on the Rhineland, including a single demand for a gargantuan 50 million in December 1795. In Italy in 1796, Parma was told to disgorge 2 million *livres*, Genoa 2 million, and Milan an eye-watering 20 million – this last amounting to five times the annual taxation of the *ancien régime*. Ordinary people suffered the most, since official "extractions" came on top of the day-to-day requisitioning of supplies by French soldiers. All too often, this degenerated into violence against the civilian population: a junior French officer in Germany in the autumn of 1795 frankly admitted that "there was murder, rape, looting of every kind – everything possible was committed" (Blanning 1983: 98).

Yet there were still local "patriots" or "Jacobins" who were willing to collaborate with the French: they may always have been a minority (although they were probably more numerous in the Netherlands and Italy than in Belgium or Germany), but the French conquest seemed to offer a quick road to power and thus a means of bringing their plans to fruition. In reality, their freedom of action was restricted by French strategic and military needs. Above all, they would be forced to implement measures – requisitions, conscription, secularization – which would damn them amongst their compatriots. Except in Francophone Savoy and Nice, there was little popular enthusiasm for French annexation: petitions in favor of annexation in the Rhineland in the winter of 1797–98 returned the signatures of a mere 4.5 percent of the population. They went ahead anyway in Nice and Savoy (1792–93), Belgium (1795), the Rhineland, Geneva, and Mulhouse (1798), and Piedmont (1799). Annexation was, at least, a means of escaping the horrors of military rule, since it would bring a regular system of civilian administration, taxation, and law. Beyond these expanded frontiers, the French established "sister republics": the Batavian Republic (Netherlands, May 1795) was the first, followed, in Italy, by the Cispadane Republic (October 1796, later part of the larger Cisalpine Republic, June 1797), the Ligurian Republic (Genoa, June 1797), the Roman Republic (the Papal States, February 1798), and the Neapolitan Republic (January 1799); Switzerland became the Helvetic Republic in March 1798. These satellite states were very much younger siblings vulnerable to some very heavy-handed treatment by Republic senior. All sister republics were expected to raise their own armies, subordinate them to the French, and pay indemnities for protection. The Dutch had to support 25,000 French troops and pay 100 million florins; the Swiss were told to raise 18,000 men, and the Cisalpine Republic to pay for 25,000 French troops, while raising 22,000 men of its own. Since these states had legislatures, there was scope for legal resistance, which arose in the Batavian, Cisalpine, and Helvetic republics. Yet the French engineered or supported *coups d'état* to enforce changes in policy and make the republics more amenable.

Yet there were compensations. In the annexed territories, the entire French system of rights, law, and administration was introduced. Much of the population of the annexed departments and the sister republics engaged in political citizenship, often for the very first time, in elections, in political clubs, and through debates in the press. Seigneurial rights and dues, the tithe, and manorial justice were abolished, as were tolls, internal customs barriers, guilds, and corporations. Education was secularized and the freedom of religious minorities, especially Jews, was recognized. Little of this would have looked out of step with some of the more radical reforms of the former enlightened absolutists. Both types of regime also closed down convents and monasteries (although the republicans also nationalized *all* church property, as in France). None the less, these very reforms were among the reasons that the French-inspired regimes were deeply unpopular amongst a conservative population: opposition to what amounted to an attack on religion, old economic and social habits, and the loss of *ancien régime* patronage provided the ideological and material focus for popular resistance.

While the international impact was more fully felt in western Europe, the revolutionary war also had wider repercussions. In the east, Catherine the Great seized the opportunity to destroy the Polish Commonwealth. Although she claimed that she was fighting "Jacobinism" in Poland, her main goal was territorial expansion. On 18 May 1792, Russian troops streamed into Poland, which was stripped of much of its territory by both Russia and Prussia in the Second Partition of 1793. The Poles rose up against Russian military occupation in March 1794, an insurrection that owed some inspiration to the French Revolution: in place of "Liberty Equality, Fraternity," the uprising's motto was "Liberty, Integrity, Independence" (Davies 1981–82: vol. 1, 539). Tadeusz Kościuszko had visited Paris in January 1793 and had promised the French that he would abolish serfdom and grant rights to all Polish citizens. When he did so, in May 1794, the peasant masses were rallied in a Polish equivalent of the *levée en masse*, creating an army of 72,000 men. A Warsaw "Jacobin" club appeared and there was a faint echo of the Terror when four traitors were hanged and seven others slaughtered in prison by a mob, but that was the extent of "Polish Jacobinism." The Russians crushed the insurrection in November and Poland was erased from the political map in the Third Partition in January 1795 between Russia, Austria, and Prussia. At the other end of Europe, the war had equally serious repercussions in Ireland. In March 1798 an insurrection erupted against British rule. The long-term causes had little to do with the French Revolution, since it was rooted in rural poverty and Protestant–Catholic rivalries over access to land, yet since 1795 the United Irishmen, driven underground by the failure of political reform, had been developing a democratic ideology which was republican, nationalist, and anti-sectarian. The French managed to land 1,000 men in remote Connacht in August, but it was too late: the British arrived in force, having already crushed the insurrection, and the French surrendered in September. Ireland lost its parliament in a union forged with Britain in 1800, creating the United Kingdom.

The wars also had global repercussions. The United States clung tenaciously to its neutrality. In August 1793 President George Washington secured the recall to France of Edmond Genêt, the French ambassador who had been whipping up public enthusiasm for the French cause, and armed American privateers for attacks on British shipping. The harassment of American merchantmen by the Royal Navy brought Britain and the United States to the brink of war, but when the differences were resolved in the Jay Treaty of 1794, the French regarded this as the final rupture of the Franco-American alliance of 1778. When it was finally ratified by the Senate in April 1796, the Directory tried to influence the result of the November presidential elections. The French minister in the United States, Adet, issued the "Cockade Proclamation," which called on all French citizens in America to wear the tricolor as a public display of their loyalties, a call enthusiastically taken up by American republicans. Even so, the federalist John Adams won the presidency, and French privateers were soon descending on American shipping, provoking a naval war which, while never escalating into a full-blown conflict, culminated in the crisis of 1798. That year, the Directory's foreign minister, Talleyrand, tried to bribe the American peace delegation in Paris through three unknown French agents, "X, Y, and Z." When the evidence was published, the "XYZ Affair" caused a storm of protest in the United States, unleashing a political reaction against those sympathetic to the French Revolution.

Bonaparte's invasion of Egypt toppled the Mamluks who had governed the country in the Ottoman sultan's name and the reverberations were felt across his empire. It inadvertently consolidated the position of the semi-autonomous magnates – *ayans* – who ruled various provinces in the sultan's name, but who posed a significant threat to the integrity of the empire. In 1798, Sultan Selim III was engaged against one of these over-mighty subjects in the Balkans, Pasvanoğlu, pasha of Vidin. When the French struck in Egypt, Selim had to break off his campaign, leaving Pasvanoğlu free to support the rebellious janissaries, the corrupt military elite, in their power-struggle against the Ottoman governor in Belgrade. Selim allowed the local Serbian population to take up arms to defend themselves against their depredations, but Serb resistance developed into a full-blown war of independence in 1804. There were reverberations in Asia, too: the presence of French military contingents in the service of Indian princes (in Mysore, Hyderabad, and the Maratha polity) were always alarming to the British East India Company, which by 1789 was emerging as one of the predominant powers in South Asia. The French invasion of Egypt prompted fears of an onward thrust towards India, giving the British the excuse to reduce their Indian rivals. In Mysore, a French adventurer named Ripaud had established a "Jacobin" club in Seringapatam, while Tipu Sultan, the kingdom's ruler, had sent diplomats to the French governor on the Île de France (Mauritius), asking for an alliance against the British, and the governor publicly appealed for French recruits. The news from Egypt crystallized British anxieties and they launched their assault on Mysore between February and May 1799. Tipu was killed in the storming of Seringapatam, one of the defining moments in the British drive for empire in India.

The Conservative Backlash

France's military reach therefore provoked a countervailing reaction in parts of the world thousands of miles away. For conservatives, however, the danger lay also in the ideological challenge that the Revolution posed to the established order and the danger that it would undermine the cultural and moral foundations of the *ancien régime*. Amongst the earliest intellectual defenses of the old order was that of the Irish politician and philosopher Edmund Burke, *Reflections on the Revolution in France*. Against the French revolutionary order based on "abstract" rights, Burke presented a vision of a slowly evolving society based on custom and prescription. What liberties people had were very basic freedoms endowed by custom: they were not universal and natural. Change, when it took place, should do so with due deference to tradition: "All the reformations we [the British] have hitherto made, have proceeded upon the principle of reference to antiquity" (Burke 1968: 117). Burke's ideas gained wider currency as the French Revolution gathered pace. British Tories argued in support of an old system based on a social hierarchy ordained by God, the rule of law, a constitution in which the king and the lords were essential and British liberties defined by prescription and property. This was underpinned by a strong sense of "Britishness," defined by such features as a commitment to the "ancient" constitution, Protestantism, the profits from empire, and a commitment to the war against France (Colley 1992). German intellectuals, proud of the achievements of Germany's enlightened absolutists, saw no need for a revolution in Germany. Imbued with the ideas of the *Aufklärung*, they argued that freedom began with the education and morality of the individual, not with attempts to regenerate the state through constitutions (Blanning 1974: 329). Such ideas were not confined to the elites: just as radicals exploited the opportunities offered by an expanding civil society, so, too, did the conservatives, who distributed their propaganda with the help of government subsidies. In Britain, it took the form of newspapers, broadsides, chapbooks, sermons, and even children's stories. The Habsburg monarchy recognized the importance of popular attitudes: in February 1793, the government ordered that writers should be paid "to publish books setting forth the evil results of the French Revolution in a manner both lively and comprehensible to ordinary people" (Wangermann 1959: 126).

Alongside the ideological defense came repression. For almost all governments, the priorities included the censorship of "dangerous" ideas; the surveillance of suspects, and the prosecution of alleged "Jacobins." One of the earliest victims was the well-heeled Russian nobleman Alexander Radishchev, who enraged Catherine the Great with his innocuous-sounding *Journey from Saint Petersburg to Moscow* in 1790, since it rounded on the injustices of Russian society, including serfdom. The author, the tsarina wrote, was "sowing the French infection: an aversion towards authority." Radishchev was condemned to death, a sentence commuted to exile in Siberia (Alexander 1989: 282–285). In Austria censorship, already strict from 1789, became harsher with the outbreak of the war. Newspapers were banned from printing political discussions: they were only to report the bare facts. In September 1792 measures were taken to ensure that cheaper, more popular newspapers did not print anything "unsuitable." In Britain, a "proclamation against seditious writings" was issued in May 1792, declaring that "wicked and seditious" publications were inciting people to riot and revolt. Prosecutions began in earnest with the war: of the 200 cases for "seditious libel" (defined as writings which incited civil disobedience) in the 1790s, the majority fell in the first six months of 1793 (Emsley 1981). In the US in the crisis of 1798, the federalists castigated their republican opponents as traitors who were "*Frenchmen* in all their feelings and wishes" (Miller 1951: 11) and who wanted nothing less than mob rule. The Alien and Sedition Acts of June and July 1798 made "false, scandalous and malicious writing" against the government liable to a $2,000 fine or two years' imprisonment. In all, fifteen prosecutions were brought, with ten convictions, before the Act expired in 1801.

Meanwhile, governments watched for subversives. The US Alien Acts empowered the president to imprison or deport dangerous foreigners. Although Adams never used these powers, which expired in 1800, the targets of the law were made explicit in the original bill, which declared the French people and government to be enemies and imposed the death penalty on any citizen who gave them assistance. In late 1792 the Austrian police swooped on the French expatriates in Vienna, deporting half of them. In Britain, the Aliens Act of January 1793 confirmed royal authority to order any foreigner to leave the kingdom and empowered the government to arrest anyone who disobeyed. It also established an office for the registration of foreigners and an embryonic "secret service" to watch out for revolutionaries. After the execution of Louis XVI in January 1793, Russia and Spain ordered the expulsion of French citizens, unless (as the Russian edict declared) they publicly renounced the Revolution's "godless and subversive principles" (Rapport 2000: 342).

Governments also moved against domestic radicals and their organizations. The Austrian police put intense pressure on Masonic lodges (widely believed to be responsible for spreading revolutionary ideas) and kept close watch on coffee houses. The government struck first against the Viennese "Jacobins" in July 1794 and then against those in Hungary in August and September. In 1795, the Hungarian courts handed down sixteen prison terms and eighteen death sentences: Martinovics was put to death on 20 May 1795. In Vienna, two "Jacobins" were sentenced to hang, while ten were sentenced to long terms in prison. The government backlash in Britain accelerated with the approach of war against France. In December 1792, after boisterous public celebrations of the first French military victories, the government struck. The first blow fell in Scotland, where the Edinburgh convention was closed down. Undeterred, the Scots invited English delegates to a British convention in 1793, which was dispersed on its opening day. Its leaders, including Thomas Muir, were tried for treason and transported to Botany Bay. In April 1794 the leadership of the London Corresponding Society and the Society for Constitutional Information were arrested for treason. *Habeas corpus* was suspended in June. Yet the prosecution failed to prove any direct collusion with the French at the "treason trials" in the autumn, which finished with the acquittal of the accused. *Habeas corpus* was restored in June 1795, but after the London mob stoned King George III's coach at the opening of Parliament, the "Two Acts" were passed: one, on seditious meetings, banned all meetings of more than fifty people unless permitted by a magistrate, while the Seditious and Treasonable Practices Act defined as treason any verbal or written attack on the king and his ministers. *Habeas corpus* was again suspended in 1798, when there was a very real threat of French invasion: a hard core of radicals had formed a "revolutionary underground" organized in societies of United Scotsmen and United Englishmen, which forged ties with the United Irishmen. A United Irish agent, a priest named James O'Coigley, was arrested in February 1798 and hanged for treason. Finally, in 1799, the Corresponding Societies Act banned the London Corresponding Society and the United Irishmen by name.

Government repression certainly silenced and discouraged "Jacobinism," but what really overwhelmed it was the tide of popular conservatism, with its violence, intimidation, boycotts, and sheer weight of numbers. The British Association for the Preservation of Liberty and Property against Republicans and Levellers, founded in November 1792, disseminated loyalist propaganda through its pervasive if short-lived network. More impressive were the Volunteers, militias called up by the government from 1794 to defend Britain against both the French and British radicalism. By 1803 there were no fewer than 380,000 Volunteers, many of whom were expressing their loyalty to the established order and a conservative form of British nationalism. In French-occupied Europe, the boundaries between politically motivated opposition (counter-revolution proper), reactions to particular measures such as taxation and conscription, or a rejection of outside interference and forms of criminality (such as banditry) were often blurred. Resistance was not always aimed at restoring the old order, but rather at defending a way of life against all figures of authority and wealth, whether French or local (anti- rather than counter-revolution). The popularity of the "Sanfedist" insurrection led by Cardinal Fabrizio Ruffo against the Neapolitan Republic between February and March 1799 illustrates these complexities. Ruffo crossed from Sicily to Calabria with only four men, but soon he had gathered a large "Christian Army," by appealing to the Catholic faith of the peasantry, but also by abolishing seigneurial rights and dues (which the republicans had failed to deliver promptly). It certainly helped that their Jacobin targets included property-owning bourgeois and nobles. As the uprising gathered pace, the violence became more indiscriminate against all people of property. Similarly in Tuscany, in Arezzo and Siena, anti-Jacobinism combined with social protest: in the anti-French uprisings in both cities in 1799, the crowds attacked those rich bourgeois and nobles who were not only classed as "Jacobins" but who were also believed to be conspiring to starve the people (Mori 1947: 147).

Religion often encouraged or justified popular resistance against the "Godless" French. Across Catholic Europe, insurrections were often preceded by reports of blinking or weeping images of the Virgin Mary: on the eve of the popular uprising in Arezzo on 6 May 1799, a painting of the Madonna was reported to have miraculously changed color (Mori 1947: 137, 144–148). In the Tyrol, the campaign to mobilize the population in the war against France in the 1790s was accompanied by reports of all sorts of miracles, including sightings of the Virgin Mary and visions of saints. Passion plays became ever more popular, being staged with more frequency and drawing hundreds of people. There was a dark side to this piety, for the targets of popular counter-revolution were often religious minorities and, in particular, the Jews, who had been emancipated by the French regime. In the

Rhineland, a criminal gang led by Schinderhannes was popular with the locals because it not only targeted the French, but also the Jews. During the uprising in Italy in 1799, the Jewish population in Siena was slaughtered in a pogrom. In Britain, one of the more egregious acts of loyalist violence occurred in Birmingham in July 1791, where the scientist and Unitarian Joseph Priestley's home, library, and laboratory were destroyed by a "Church and King" mob.

Religion could often fuse with a sense of national or regional identity. In Austria, a not atypical 1796 pamphlet, entitled "War-cry against the French enemies, for the defense of religion and the fatherland," pulled out all the stops: the French were the sons of Satan who had copulated with whores on church altars, had shed Christian blood, and whose "liberty" was actually the enslavement of the soul by Hell (Blanning 1983: 323). In the Tyrol, the clergy mobilized the people behind the war against France, combining defense of the "Fatherland," meaning "our dear Tyrol," with the defense of Catholicism against "the unholy enemies of the state and religion" (Cole 2000: 487, 491). In Germany, Protestant and Catholic writers launched a noisy propaganda campaign against the Revolution, calling for a mighty alliance of "throne" and "altar," supported by the piety of the good German people against the atheistic French.

The violence of popular reactions was partly due to the horrors visited upon the population by the war, but here the boundaries between counter-revolution and criminality became blurred. In the Rhineland, bandits were motivated by a desire for plunder and a lifestyle characterized by heavy drinking, easy sex, and local status. Yet they enjoyed some popularity because, whatever their motivations, they were at least resisting the French. The boundaries between crime and political opposition were therefore continually crossed and recrossed. More alarming for the French were those insurrections which were explicitly counter-revolutionary: already seething with anger at the revolutionary assault on the church, the Belgian peasantry were pushed into revolt by the introduction of conscription in September 1798. After a desperate last stand at Hasselt on 5 December, the insurgents were crushed. A similar revolt erupted in Luxemburg, where it was called the Klöppelkrieg, the "cudgel war," after the peasants' weapon of choice. While no such uprising occurred in the Rhineland, there were myriad instances of "everyday resistance," replicated across French-occupied Europe. People refused to wear the tricolor cockade and to play republican anthems. People celebrated allied victories, hacked down liberty trees and raised crucifixes instead. Exploiting linguistic differences was common, since it allowed locals to shelter behind a wall of ignorance, real or feigned. Officials and judges in Belgium and the Rhineland refused to accept positions in the new administrations and law-courts, a veritable "administrative strike" as serious as that which arose in parts of France under the Directory. Much of this behavior came from genuine revulsion at the Revolution, but it was also driven by intimidation and violence against "collaborators." Where elections took place in the annexed territories – as they did for the first time in Belgium in the spring of 1797 – people voted for candidates who were hostile to the Republic, or at least lukewarm about it: Belgian deputies were among those purged in the Fructidor coup in September 1797. There is probably much truth in Doyle's statement (1989: 368) that if, by the late 1790s, the revolutionaries could still count on thousands of friends beyond France's borders, they were diminishing in number, while their enemies ran into the millions.

Conclusion

The worldwide surge of the French Revolution and the conservative backwash was of an intensity and geographical scale unmatched by any other single political upheaval of the eighteenth century. The repercussions of the French Revolution and the wars redrew the political map of the world in three crucial regions: in Europe, in the Americas, and in South Asia. In Europe, Poland was erased altogether, while the French annexation of the Rhineland marked the beginning of the end for the Holy Roman Empire, which was finally abolished in 1806. Venerable old states were obliterated, including Genoa, Geneva, and Venice (the victim of early Napoleonic wheeling and dealing). In the Americas, Haiti gained its independence by 1804, making the revolution there the only successful slave revolt in modern history. This would virtually guarantee that the abolition of slavery would be on the agenda when Spain's American colonies won their independence in 1810–30. In South Asia, the dangers, real or imagined, of a French descent on India spurred the British into a concerted drive for empire which by 1805 they had almost achieved. None of these developments stemmed entirely from the French Revolution itself: all flowed from longer-term geopolitical pressures, but the revolutionary shockwaves accelerated the trends. The French Revolution and its wars, in other words, drove forward the process by which the nineteenth-century international order emerged in Europe, the Americas, and Asia. The precise ways in which the ideological and military reverberations from France shaped this global process still need to be traced in detail.

Yet the Revolution also had a positive cultural and political impact: in proclaiming the sovereignty of the nation and experimenting with democratic practices, it left a stock of symbols, rhetoric, and ideals which could be adopted by nationalist movements around the world. So if in the 1790s the French Revolution was associated with conquest and exploitation, in the long term it was not forgotten that it also sowed some of the ideological seeds of resistance to empire. Sometimes, these ideologies, both conservative and liberal, were reactive and explicitly anti-French – and there is still room for work exploring the long-term development of nationalism as it passed across the watershed of 1789–99. Yet such nationalisms could equally have been encouraged by the French, particularly where their collaborators were fairly widespread. In Italy, the very act of forging sister republics from once separate states sparked public debates about the possibilities of national unity: "Why," asked a Jacobin journalist of his fellow Italians in 1796, "are they not uniting their wisdom and strength into one whole, so that all may work to the same end?" (Beales and Biagini 2002: 200). The symbols of the French Revolution proved to be easily adaptable to different contexts: the Italian tricolor, now Italy's national flag, was the banner of the Cispadane Republic. The Mainz Republic of 1793, the butt of hostility for contemporaries, is remembered in Germany as the first ever German republic. Such examples of the workings of historical memory are legion, but while much work has been done on Europe's revolutionary inheritance, its comprehensive history has yet to be written.

References

Alexander, John T. (1989). *Catherine the Great: Life and Legend*. Oxford: Oxford University Press.

Amman, Peter H. (ed.) (1963). *The Eighteenth-Century Revolution: French or Western?* Lexington: D.C. Heath.

Armitage, David and Sanjay Subrahmanyam (eds.) (2010). *The Age of Revolutions in Global Context, c.1760–1840*. Basingstoke: Palgrave.

Bayly, C.A. (2004). *The Birth of the Modern World, 1780–1914: Global Connections and Comparisons*. Oxford: Blackwell.

Beales, Derek and Eugenio F. Biagini (2002). *The Risorgimento and the Unification of Italy*. Harlow: Pearson Education.

Blanning, Timothy (1974). *Reform and Revolution in Mainz 1743–1803*. Cambridge: Cambridge University Press.

Blanning, Timothy (1983). *The French Revolution in Germany: Occupation and Resistance in the Rhineland, 1792–1802*. Oxford: Clarendon Press.

Blanning, Timothy (1986). *The Origins of the French Revolutionary Wars*. London: Longman.

Blanning, Timothy (1994). *Joseph II*. London: Longman.

Blanning, Timothy (1996). *The French Revolutionary Wars, 1787–1802*. London: Arnold.

Broers, Michael (1997). *Napoleonic Imperialism and the Savoyard Monarchy 1773–1821: State Building in Piedmont*. Lewiston: Edwin Mellen.

Broers, Michael (2005). *The Napoleonic Empire in Italy, 1796–1814: Cultural Imperialism in a European Context?* Basingstoke: Palgrave.

Burke, Edmund (1968). *Reflections on the Revolution in France*. London: Penguin.

Cole, Laurence (2000). "Nation, Anti-Enlightenment, and Religious Revival in Austria: Tyrol in the 1790s." *HJ*, 43: 475–497.

Colley, Linda (1992). *Britons: Forging the Nation, 1707–1837*. New Haven, Conn.: Yale University Press.

Darwin, John (2007). *After Tamerlane: The Global History of Empire since 1405*. London: Allen Lane.

Davies, Norman (1981–82). *God's Playground: A History of Poland*, 2 vols. Oxford: Clarendon Press.

Dickinson, Harry T. (1977). *Liberty and Property: Political Ideology in Eighteenth-Century Britain*. London: Methuen.

Dann, Otto and John Dinwiddy (1988). *Nationalism in the Age of the French Revolution*. London: Hambledon.

Doyle, William (1989). *The Oxford History of the French Revolution*. Oxford: Clarendon Press.

Emsley, Clive (1981). "An Aspect of Pitt's Terror: Prosecutions for Sedition during the 1790s." *Social History*, 6: 155–184.

Godechot, Jacques (1971). *France and the Atlantic Revolution of the Eighteenth Century, 1770–1799*. London: Collier Macmillan.

Godechot, Jacques (1983). *La Grande Nation: L'Expansion révolutionnaire de la France dans le monde de 1789 à 1799*, 2nd edn. Paris: Aubier Montaigne.

Goodwin, Albert (1979). *The Friends of Liberty: The English Democratic Movement in the Age of the French Revolution*. London: Hutchinson.

Jourdan, Annie (2004). *La Révolution, une exception française?* Paris: Flammarion.

Jourdan, Annie (2008). *La Révolution batave entre la France et l'Amérique (1795–1806)*. Rennes: Presses Universitaires de Rennes.

Klooster, Wim (2009). *Revolutions in the Atlantic World: A Comparative History.* New York: New York University Press.

Lebrun, François and Roger Dupuy (1987). *Les Résistances à la Révolution.* Paris: Imago.

Lesnodorski, Boguslaw (1965). *Les Jacobins Polonais.* Paris: SER.

Lukowski, Jerzy (1999). *The Partitions of Poland, 1772, 1793, 1795.* Harlow: Longman.

Meikle, Henry W. (1912). *Scotland and the French Revolution.* Edinburgh: James Maclehose.

Miller, John C. (1951). *Crisis in Freedom: The Alien and Sedition Acts.* Boston: Little, Brown.

Mori, Renato (1947). "Il popolo toscano durante la rivoluzione e l'occupazione francese." *Archivio Storico Italiano*, 105: 127–152.

Newman, Simon (1997). *Parades and the Politics of the Street: Festive Culture in the Early American Republic.* Philadelphia: University of Pennsylvania Press.

Newman, Simon (2011). "La Révolution française vue de loin: La Célébration de Valmy à Boston, en janvier 1793." *RHMC*, 58: 80–99.

Paine, Thomas (1984). *Rights of Man.* New York: Penguin.

Palmer, Robert R. (1959–64). *The Age of the Democratic Revolution: A Political History of Europe and America, 1760–1800*, 2 vols. Princeton, N.J.: Princeton University Press.

Rapport, Michael (2000). *Nationality and Citizenship in Revolutionary France: The Treatment of Foreigners, 1789–1799.* Oxford: Clarendon Press.

Rapport, Michael (2002). "Belgium under French Occupation: Between Collaboration and Resistance, July 1794 to October 1795." *FH*, 16: 53–82.

Robertson, John (2000). "Enlightenment and Revolution: Naples 1799." *Transactions of the Royal Historical Society*, 6th series, 10: 18–44.

Rudé, George (1964). *Revolutionary Europe, 1783–1815.* Glasgow: Fontana Collins.

Schama, Simon (1992). *Patriots and Liberators: Revolution in the Netherlands, 1780–1813.* London: Fontana.

Schroeder, Paul W. (1994). *The Transformation of European Politics 1763–1848.* Oxford: Clarendon Press.

Schürer, Norbert (2005). "The Storming of the Bastille in English Newspapers." *Eighteenth-Century Life*, 29: 50–81.

Sen, S.P. (1971). *The French in India, 1763–1816.* New Delhi: Munshiram Manoharlal.

Sorel, Albert (1885–1905). *L'Europe et la Révolution française.* Paris: Plon.

Wangermann, Ernst (1959). *From Joseph II to the Jacobin Trials: Government Policy and Public Opinion in the Habsburg Dominions in the Period of the French Revolution.* London: Oxford University Press.

Wood, Gordon S. (2009). *Empire of Liberty: A History of the Early Republic, 1789–1815.* Oxford History of the United States. Oxford: Oxford University Press.

Woolf, Stuart J. (1989). "French Civilization and Ethnicity in the Napoleonic Empire." *P&P*, 124: 96–120.

Woolf, Stuart J. (1992). "The Construction of a European World-View in the Revolutionary-Napoleonic Years." *P&P*, 137: 72–101.

Chapter Twenty-Four

Slavery and the Colonies

Frédéric Régent

In 1789 the king of France exercised authority over colonial settlements characterized essentially by the production of commodities by slaves. In order of size of population, these slave-based colonies were the French section of Saint-Domingue (today Haiti), Martinique, Guadeloupe and its dependencies (Marie-Galante, the French part of Saint-Martin, the Île de la Désirade, the Saintes), the Île Bourbon (Réunion), the Île de la France (Maurice) and its dependencies (the Île Rodrigue and the Seychelles), Guyane, Sainte-Lucie, and Tobago. All these settlements were characterized by the export to Europe of commodities (sugar, coffee, indigo, cotton, cocoa) produced by African slaves. This export trade was exclusively for France: the "Exclusif." French colonial territory also included bases for commercial fishing (Saint-Pierre-and-Miquelon), for the slave-trade (the islands of Gorée and Saint-Louis du Sénégal), and for trade with India (Pondichéry, Chandernagor, Mahé, Yanaon, and Karikal). The focus on Saint-Domingue in this chapter is due to its significance among the French colonies (it was responsible for about three-quarters of sugar production and about 500,000 of the 700,000 slaves in 1790). The French slave-trade reached its zenith, with more than 54,000 captives loaded onto French slave-ships, in 1790. In the period 1786–90, French merchants contributed about 40 percent of the European slave-trade, ahead of Portuguese and British ship-owners.[1] Colonial products and goods in the colonial trade (textiles, porcelain, and so on) represented 38 percent of the value of imports into the kingdom of France in 1787. The colonial products were for the most part re-exported, and made up 33 percent of the kingdom's exports, as much as manufactured goods. Moreover, the colonial trade was in a phase of rapid growth when the Revolution began. It was the focus of special attention for the monarchy, as is attested by the subsidies it received. The bonuses granted to the slave-trade were 2.4 million *livres* of the 3.8 million awarded to manufacturing and trade in the 1780s (Saint-Louis 2008: 234).

A Companion to the French Revolution, First Edition. Edited by Peter McPhee.

In essence, the colonial economies were based on the exploitation of African slaves and their descendants. Voices were heard denouncing slavery throughout the eighteenth century (Erhard 2008). On 19 February 1788 the Société des Amis des Noirs was founded. Its goal was the immediate cessation of the slave-trade, followed by the gradual abolition of slavery. For the first time a humanitarian society pleaded the cause of humans in distant places, far from sight, whose suffering was unknown to the majority of the French. The Société des Amis des Noirs was a model for the political societies which appeared in 1789. From 1788 some of the future great figures of the Revolution attended meetings: Lafayette, Sieyès, Mirabeau, the Lameth brothers, Duport, Brissot, Clavière, and Condorcet. The society was at the same time a meeting-place for these men and a "training camp" in thinking, argument, and oratory. Colonial questions such as slavery and the slave-trade were among the preoccupations of future revolutionary leaders well before the meeting of the Estates-General.

On 26 August 1789, the Estates, now the Constituent Assembly, adopted the Declaration of the Rights of Man and of the Citizen. This text affirmed the principles of equality and liberty among all people. However, this was not applied to the colonies. It was not until 28 March 1792 that "free men of color"[2] achieved equality with whites and not until 4 February 1794 that all people in the colonies were declared free. Questions must be asked about the reasons for this delay between the articulation of abolitionist principles and their application in the colonies. In this regard, too, the decree of 4 February 1794 was not applied in all the colonies. Where it was actually applied problems of work were created for former slaves. Debates occurred about the best way to utilize the colonial workforce. For some, a return to slavery was the only way through which there could be a return to colonial prosperity. Napoleon Bonaparte maintained slavery in colonies where it had not been abolished (Martinique, Mascareignes) and re-established it in Guadeloupe and Guyane in 1802. We need to ask the reasons for the return to slavery and for the delay between Napoleon's seizure of power (1799) and its re-establishment (1802). In Saint-Domingue, attempts to return to the previous system were thwarted, and the colony proclaimed its independence on 1 January 1804. We need to ask too why the re-establishment of slavery was not even attempted in the most prosperous of the colonies before the Revolution.

Colonial Society on the Eve of Revolution

Slavery and color prejudice were the twin pedestals of colonial societies: non-whites had fewer rights than those deemed to be white. My research has found that very many colonial whites were actually descended from a mixture of Europeans, Africans, and Amerindians (Régent 2007: 57–64). "Across a few generations, the color black disappears completely; I've seen quatroons whose skin-colour rivalled that of the most beautiful Creoles; and, even in Guadeloupe, how many have wealth and time enabled to pass from this class to that of the whites!"[3] A part of the racially mixed population was therefore relegated to the other side of the color barrier by those who saw themselves as white. "Free persons of color" did not have the same privileges as whites. In any case, membership of a category of color was more a socio-cultural convention than a biological reality. Free colored persons did not have the right to the title "Monsieur" or "Madame"; they were excluded from certain positions (membership of the Conseil Supérieur, positions in the armed forces) and from certain occupations (lawyer, doctor, pharmacist). They lived in a humiliating situation at the same time as their economic and demographic dynamism was becoming menacing for their white competitors. The totality of such discrimination constituted was then called color prejudice. It functioned like noble prejudice in *ancien régime* France.[4] Just as the nobility was mostly made up of ennobled people, so in the colonies the juridical group of whites was largely made up of mixed-race people, descended at the same time from Europeans and Amerindian, Indian, or African women. By the end of the eighteenth century, color prejudice was well developed in the colonies. Those who were reputedly white rejected those who had not broken through the color barrier. This phenomenon was accentuated by the large-scale arrival in the colonies of poor white immigrants with only one privilege, the color of their skin. The juridical segregation in which free colored people were placed became sharper, with new rules. In effect, every time a regulation was made, different modes of application were imposed for them.

With color prejudice, the principal characteristic of colonial society was slavery. A slave may be defined as someone whose freedom belongs to another. In fact, a slave-owner could at any moment give back liberty by means of granting freedom. Slavery enveloped Africans captured by the trade and their descendants within a totality of domination. Slaves as a group were marked by a hierarchy between those identified as slaves and Negro farmers, and between Africans and Creoles (born in the colonies). Slaves had no rights; their masters simply had a few obligations towards them. Some slaves tried to flee slavery, or to escape from work by slowing production, through flight, sabotage, poisoning their masters, or foot-dragging. But the slave regime was one of terror: the master and his lieutenants imposed a permanent terror on the slave. The inverse is that the master feared the slave. Fears of poisoning or of revolt were recurrent in the discourse of masters and colonial administrators. To make slaves obedient, the master used both the whip and the promise of freedom. "When he grants freedom to a slave, he gives hope to a thousand others. It's like a lottery," according to Vertus Saint-Louis, whose analysis I share.[5]

The Success of the Colonial Lobby over the Société des Amis des Noirs

No representation for the colonies was allowed for in the convocation of the Estates-General. However, the colonies and slavery were present from the outset of the Revolution, notably through the great white colonial landowners who requested representation and through the drafting of the *cahiers de doléances*, in about forty of which the question of slavery was raised. The Amis des Noirs launched a campaign to influence public opinion on the question of slavery. So Condorcet sent to all *bailliages* (districts) a manifesto entitled "Du corps électoral contre l'esclavage des Noirs."[6] In the kingdom as a whole, the main *bailliages* produced 482 *cahiers* (164 from the Third Estate, 155 from the clergy, 150 from the nobility, and thirteen from two or three orders together). Of these *cahiers*, twenty-three requested the abolition of the slave-trade and ten that of slavery, and nineteen denounced the practice or raised the question cautiously or imprecisely (Thibau 1989: 118–125). So a little less than 10 percent of the *cahiers* at *bailliage* level addressed slavery or the slave-trade.[7] While a minority, it demonstrated the growing influence of the Société des Amis des Noirs, of which a few members were elected to the Estates-General (including Lafayette, Mirabeau, and Condorcet).

There was therefore a significant abolitionist movement at the heart of the kingdom of France. However, it was confronted by another pressure group made up of slave-owners and slave-ship owners present in Paris and the great ports. In 1789, some of the rich plantation owners of Saint-Domingue lived in Paris. By their networks of birth, marriage, and wealth, by their relationships within the court and the colonial and naval administration, they played a predominant role in the management of colonial affairs. On 18 July 1788, fifty-six of these proprietors organized themselves as a Comité Colonial, at the head of which they placed nine *commissaries*, all wealthy nobles: the dukes de Cereste-Brancas and de Choiseul-Praslin, the counts Reynaud de Villevert, de Magallon and de Peyrac, the marquis de Paroy, de Gouy d'Arsy, and de Perrigny, and the chevalier de Dougé. Two-thirds of these *commissaires* had never set foot in the colonies (Saint-Louis 2008: 97–98). These men possessed plantations with a value often greater than 1 million *livres tournois.* The marquis de Gouy d'Arsy and his spouse were owners of four sugar factories and one coffee factory in Saint-Domingue. He was one of the queen's *protégés* and linked to the duke d'Orléans, himself a landowner in Saint-Domingue. He claimed that all of Saint-Domingue had a presence in the king's household (Saint-Louis 2008: 365–366). These rich landowners who resided in Paris wanted deputies in the Estates-General. However, the principle of colonial representation was rejected by the king, and the regulation of 24 January 1789 on the convocation of the deputies denied the colonies the right to send delegates.

However, following a battle for influence, the colonial landowners (a more accurate designation than "colonials") had their way. They were granted six deputies for Saint-Domingue plus twelve substitutes instead of the thirty-six requested. They first entered the Assembly on 3 July 1789. Immediately afterwards, Guadeloupe and Martinique each obtained two deputies and the trading-posts in India and the Îles Mascareignes had one deputy each. The real power of the Comité Colonial was revealed: among its nine *commissaries* two were deputies (Gouy d'Arsy and Perrigny) and three were substitutes (Magallon, Dougé, and Reynaud). While the Constituent Assembly prepared the Declaration of the Rights of Man and of the Citizen, the members of the Comité Colonial, the representatives of Atlantic trade and of the ministry of the navy and colonies founded the Club de Massiac on 20 August 1789, with the objective of opposing the Société des Amis des Noirs.

Structural reforms to the administration and organization of power made within the Constituent Assembly were thus elaborated in the presence of the colonial deputies. For continuity with the *ancien régime* and under the influence of the

Club de Massiac, the colonies were "preserved" from reforms adopted for metropolitan France. The principle of "special nature" was maintained until 1792, when a complete reversal led to the integration of the colonies in common statutes. For the whites in the colonies, these revolutionary troubles were the moment when complaints could be aired against representatives of the Crown who had remained in place until 1792. The colonial committee was established by the Constituent Assembly on 2 March 1790, principally composed of men from the Club de Massiac. Under the committee's influence the principle of "special nature" was continued (Charlin 2009: 19). Its partisans pushed its logic to the point of wanting to divest the Constituent Assembly of the power to elaborate a colonial constitution. François-Pierre Blin, a deputy from Nantes, neatly summarized this outlook:

> It would be a mistake as dangerous as it is unforgivable to envisage the colonies as provinces, and to want to subject them to the same regime ... a land so different from ours in every way, inhabited by different classes of people, distinguished from each other by characteristics unfamiliar to us, and for whom our social distinctions offer no analogy ... needs laws which might be called indigenous ... it belongs only to the inhabitants of our colonies, convened in the colonies themselves, to gather to elect the body of representatives to work in virtue of its powers and without leaving its territory, to create the constitution, that is to say the form of the internal regime and local administration which is most suited to assure colonials of the advantages of civil society.[8]

To the "centralizing tendency" of the *ancien régime*, the Constituent Assembly preferred to recognize autonomy at the heart of the nation, resulting in part from the refusal to apply to the colonies the principle of equality which was the foundation of metropolitan law (Charlin 2009: 20).

The Calling into Question of White Supremacy

The several hundred free coloreds who lived in Paris sought equality with whites. Their principal representatives were Vincent Ogé and Julien Raimond. Their contacts with the Club de Massiac were fruitless; they decided to take their demands to the National Assembly. The two major grievances of the free coloreds were equality before the law and the facilitation of grants of freedom even if slavery would be fully maintained. They demanded the freeing of all mixed-bloods so that the taint of slavery would disappear completely from this category of the population. Their demands seem to have found a favorable reception in enlightened circles. On 12 October 1789, Brissot, a member of the Société des Amis des Noirs, wrote in the *Patriote français*, "the admission of free Blacks into the National Assembly will prepare the way for the abolition of slavery in our colonies" (Bénot 1989: 71–72). On 22 October 1789, a deputation of free persons of color went to the bar of the National Assembly and presented its grievances.

The president of the Assembly welcomed their request but, on 22 October, a limited suffrage was introduced and from that an initial infraction was committed against the Declaration of the Rights of Man; a second one concerned free persons of color. The latter continued their battle by writing a letter to the Comité de

Vérification of the National Assembly on 23 November. This document revealed that the two main objections to representation for free coloreds were that they were already represented by the white colonial deputies and that the method of electing colored deputies would represent only a minority from Paris.[9] On 24 November the free coloreds went to the Société des Amis des Noirs, whose members were continuing their struggle in support of the abolition of the slave-trade and slavery. It is significant that the free coloreds had been to the planters before going to the society. Given their rebuff at the Club de Massiac, a turn to the society, powerless to abolish the slave-trade in the face of the support of the colonial lobby, changed the nature of the battle. The Amis des Noirs saw free coloreds as oppressed human beings rather than merely the property of slave-owners. Perhaps it thought it could open a breach in the slave system by obtaining equal rights for one sector of the colored population. The society welcomed their grievances and adopted a motion asking those of its members who were deputies in the National Assembly to support the coloreds' cause. The latter declared themselves in favor of a gradual abolition of slavery, as shown in the writing of Ogé and Raimond. In 1789 the former had declared: "this Liberty, the first and greatest of benefits, is it for all men? I believe so. Must it be given to all men? I believe that, too. But how must it be given? What should be the timing and conditions? That is for us, gentlemen, the first and most important of questions; it involves America, Africa, France, the whole of Europe."[10] The idea of gradual abolition was taken up again by Julien Raimond in 1793, when he declared that "slaves must be brought towards the status of liberty in such a way that they can reach it without trouble and by lawful means."[11] The joint steps taken by the free persons of color and the Société des Amis des Noirs ended in stalemate.

In June 1790 Vincent Ogé left for Saint-Domingue to continue the struggle there. He attempted an insurrection which ended in failure. On 25 February 1791 he was beaten to death in particularly atrocious circumstances. By March the news of Ogé's suffering was circulating in Paris. Free persons of color asked to be heard again by the National Assembly.[12] They again demanded the rights of active citizens in the colonies while remaining very cautious on the lot of slaves: "citizens of color can only look with distress on the sad plight of black slaves; but, like you, they feel it necessary not to initiate any change in this regard."[13] Their claims would henceforth be supported by some of the popular societies.

The colonial debate recommenced. On 11 May 1791 Robespierre intervened in support of equality of rights between white and colored citizens, suggesting that this would strengthen the power of masters over their slaves (Bénot 1989: 79). The next day, Julien Raimond, granted admission to address the Assembly, took up the argument.[14] On the 13th an important concession was granted to the colonials because it was decreed as a constitutional article that any law on the status of unfree persons (slaves) could only be passed in response to a formal and spontaneous request from the colonial assemblies.[15] On the 15th, free men born of free mothers and fathers were granted political rights, while the rights of freed slaves would be decided by colonial assemblies. The colonial deputies resolved to abstain from the Assembly's deliberations after the adoption of this law.[16] On 12 June the Jacobin Club in turn decided to expel from its membership those colonial deputies who had voted against the law of 15 May.

The colonial assemblies refused to implement the decree of 15 May 1791. In Saint-Domingue, free men of color were excluded from elections for the colonial assemblies in July. The following month, free men of color held a large-scale meeting at Mirebalais and created a council of forty members to voice their grievances. On 11 August this council sent a copy of its deliberations and demands to Governor Blanchelande. The latter declared their meeting illegal. The free men of color organized an army under the command of Louis-Jacques Bauvais and André Rigaud, recruiting slaves by promising them freedom. Early in September 1791 free men of color put to flight a troop of patriot *petits blancs* near La Croix-des-Bouquets. Their victory can be explained by the military experience they had acquired in the militia and during the American War of Independence. Each side armed slaves to defeat its adversaries, and the civil war spread during the summer with the more widespread arming of slaves. It was in this context that the great insurrection of slaves on the Plaine du Nord erupted during the night of 22–23 August 1791.

The Spreading of Revolts in Saint-Domingue

Another factor favoring the development of the insurrection was the absence of the great white landowners who dominated the north of Saint-Domingue in particular. The plantations were left in the hands of attorneys and managers who often allowed the property to fall into disrepair. The planters were often more concerned to return to France, to the center of politics which had become even more attractive with the Revolution. They mortgaged their dwellings to obtain cash from commercial houses: the private debt of planters with the firm of Rombert et Bapst went from 4,721,287 *livres* on 31 December 1788 to 9,380,771 *livres* in December 1791 (Thésée 1972).

The threat represented by the intensity of the revolt led to a rapprochement between the free coloreds and the white planters. On 11 September 1791 aristocrats from the west of Saint-Domingue reached an agreement with free coloreds at La Croix-des-Bouquets. Another convention was signed between free coloreds and the patriot *petits blancs* at Port-au-Prince on 23 October. The agreements anticipated the implementation of the decree of 15 May 1791 and the disappearance of color distinctions in public life (Dubois 2004: 119–120). At the same time slaves fighting for the various factions were disarmed.

Agreements between whites and free coloreds were reached almost everywhere in Saint-Domingue; in Paris, however, the colonial committee rode the reactionary wave of the summer of 1791 to abrogate the law of 15 May on 24 September. On the 25th, Adrien Duport, the Lameth brothers, and Barnave were expelled from the Jacobin Club for their role in the revocation of the decree of 15 May. In fact, the rules of the society required the expulsion of any member who acted or argued against the rights of man.[17] The free coloreds won meager consolation in the promulgation of a decree on 28 September on the liberty and citizenship of free persons of color in metropolitan France (Piquet 2002: 118). The day before, Jews had been accorded citizenship rights.

The abrogation of the law of 15 May reignited the conflict between the free coloreds and the whites. The agreements were broken. On 21 November 1791 clashes took place in Port-au-Prince: the town was set on fire and 800 houses were destroyed. *Petits blancs* and free coloreds accused each other of arson. The latter, furious with the *petits blancs*, would henceforth be at war with them in the south and west of Saint-Domingue. Each camp renewed their recruitment of slaves. The alliance between free coloreds and aristocrats was reinforced. In March 1792, radical *petits blancs* who had been recruiting among slaves attacked the camp of the free coloreds allied with the aristocrats, at La Croix-des-Bouquets. They were repulsed thanks to the intervention of an army of 10,000 to 15,000 slaves armed with batons and machetes. These clashes led to the extension of the slave insurrection in the southern and western provinces because of the recruitment of slaves as soldiers and the subsequent risks in their demobilization. In the south, from the summer of 1791, free men of color scoured the plantations belonging to their adversaries calling on slaves to join forces with them by promising them freedom. Agents of the free coloreds moved through plantations belonging to whites to recruit slave soldiers, sometimes by force. In response, whites freed their own slaves to recruit them as soldiers. At Les Cayes, a local regulation even ordered that one slave in ten be recruited by whites to fight against the free coloreds (Fick 1990: 133).

The Victory of the Free Coloreds

Towards the end of October 1791, news of the insurrection in Saint-Domingue gave Brissot a pretext to blame the troubles on the intransigence of the representatives of the white planters in Paris. He demanded the rearming of free coloreds to fight against the slaves in revolt.[18] On 7 December the Legislative Assembly adopted a decree ratifying the agreements between whites and free coloreds. The colonial assembly refused to apply it.

News of the spread of insurrection in Saint-Domingue reached Paris at the end of March 1792. Debates on the causes of the troubles began in the Legislative Assembly on 21 March. On the 28th a decree was passed granting citizenship to all free coloreds in the colonies. The timidity of the measure is astonishing given the strategic positions held by Brissot, influential in the Assembly, and the minister Clavière. The Brissotins chose to prioritize support for the free coloreds. The Constitution of 1791 outlawed the right to collective petitioning and association: it therefore became more difficult to launch a public campaign. For Brissot, the granting of citizenship to free coloreds would give slaves the hope of an improvement in their condition. In fact, the search for freedom was a constant element in a slave's life. The improvement of the lot of free coloreds therefore also represented progress on the distant horizon of freedom for the slave, always potentially a free person. So this was compatible with Brissot's project of the gradual abolition of slavery.

The Legislative Assembly responded to the slave insurrection by sending as civil commissioners Sonthonax and Polvérel, men with ideas close to those of the abolitionists, and troops. Their instructions were to reconcile whites and free coloreds by applying the decree of 28 March 1792, sanctioned by the king on 4 April.[19]

The commissioners arrived in Saint-Domingue in September 1792 with 6,000 soldiers. On the 24th they made an announcement supporting the institution of slavery, Sonthonax stating: "it has never been the intention of the [Legislative] Assembly to abolish slavery, and ... should this assembly be misled into announcing abolition, they [the commissioners] swear to oppose it with all their strength."[20] On 12 October, they dissolved the colonial assembly, the provincial assemblies, and the municipal councils. In the period leading up to new elections, a temporary commission composed of six whites and six coloreds was appointed.

The Long March Towards the Abolition of Slavery

Conflicts continued despite these measures. The royalist faction was henceforth led by the new governor, d'Esparbès, who had arrived with the commissioners. He could count on the support of Cambefort, the commander of the Cap regiment, and the mounted National Guard, made up of the sons of the richest families. The patriot camp was composed of dragoons of the 16th Orléans regiment under Étienne Laveaux's orders, a battalion from the Aisne and the National Guard infantry made up of *petits blancs* (Saint-Louis 2009: 241–242). In the first place, the civil commissioners made an alliance with the autonomist patriots. At the end of October 1792, d'Esparbès and the royalists, whose goal was to send the civil commissioners back, were themselves forced to flee. Autonomist patriots sought to obtain posts in the administration to improve their conditions. The continuation of these conflicts could only exacerbate revolts. Hence, by September 1792, 60,000 slaves would be in a state of insurrection in the north. It seems that none of the numerous bands of them had more than 3,000 men. In the west there were few insurgents; in the south there would be 12,000 (Saint-Louis 2009: 248). A witness described the plain around Port-au-Prince (in the west) during his stay in November 1792: "you no longer see workplaces functioning because of fear, and I have seen with my own eyes a great slackening among the slaves either in making their way to work or to undertake it."[21]

The monarchy was overthrown in Paris on 10 August 1792. The Brissotins dominated political life even more completely. However, on 16 August the National Assembly decreed that those trade subsidies which had not been abrogated would be paid for the period 1 January 1791 to 16 August 1792. The decree thus implied the payment of subsidies for the slave-trade. Merchants seized the advantage by claiming unpaid subsidies.[22] They made their claim under the cover of strengthening the patriotism of ship owners in the context of the war which had just been declared. On 2 and 13 February, two decrees reinforced that of 16 August by requesting payment of subsidies due to trade and implicitly to owners of slave-ships. At the same time, a National Convention, elected by universal suffrage, was convoked to replace the Legislative Assembly and to give France a new constitution. The decree of 22 August 1792 proclaimed for the first time: "the colonies are an integral part of the French Empire ... all citizens who inhabit them are, like those of metropolitan France, called to participate in the formation of the National Convention."[23]

If the question of the rights of free coloreds had been resolved in Paris, those of the slave-trade and slavery were left hanging. On 26 January 1793 Brissot wrote: "the immediate abolition of slavery would be a calamity, but gradual abolition is useful and necessary: any land cultivated by slaves must be done so even better by free labor."[24] On 5 March, however, a law was adopted on the motion of Camboulas (Raynal's nephew) giving the commissioners the power to reform the slave workshops. On 17 April, the Brissotin deputy Isnard submitted to the colonial committee a draft plan for the abolition of slavery. He envisaged freedom for all slaves. They would each have to pay 1,200 *livres* to their former owner, whether in the form of 6 *livres* weekly in cash or three days' work per week. Such a purchase of freedom would thus be complete in about four years.[25] The draft was stifled by the colonial committee. In the spring of 1793 the question of the war was at the heart of the preoccupations of the Brissotins wishing to secure the support of merchant groups. Slavery still preoccupied the Brissotins, but they did not throw their full political weight behind its abolition. What was the situation among their Montagnard adversaries?

On 24 April 1793, Robespierre used the example of the slave-trade to oppose the notion that property should be declared an imprescriptible human right while the National Convention was debating the draft of the new declaration of the rights of man in the preamble to the Constitution of 1793. Despite this speech, when the Montagnards overthrew the Brissotins on 2 June 1793 they did not make use of the chance this offered to abolish slavery. The day after the fall of the Brissotins, on 4 June, a delegation of sans-culottes and coloreds led by Chaumette demanded the abolition of slavery. According to the mulatto Julien Labuissonnière, first signatory of their petition, it was "received without being read, sent into the dust and gloom of a committee" despite the interventions of "the humane, virtuous Grégoire, Saint-André, Robespierre and the rest of the just men who thundered from the summit of the Mountain" (Piquet 2002: 259). The Convention instead sent it to the colonial committee (where Marat sat alongside Grégoire). However, the committee no longer had more than four members, the rest being *en mission*, and it could not usefully deliberate. Labuissonnière was imprisoned for forging documents a few days later. In a letter of 24 June, addressed to Jean Dalbarade, acting as minister for the navy and colonies, the deputies Cossigny and Broutin from the Île de France claimed that the petition was the work of the English government looking to destroy French trade and colonies. They emphasized the risk that the petition could provoke civil war in the colonies.

On 24 June the Convention adopted a new Declaration of the Rights of Man as the preamble to the new constitution. Its Article 18 stated that "Any man may commit his services or his time; but he may neither sell himself, nor be sold; his person is not alienable property. The law recognizes no domestic status [*domesticité*] whatsoever; only an agreement of care and recognition between the working man and the employer may exist." However, Article 3 of the constitution affirmed that the French people "is distributed, for administration and justice, among departments, districts and municipalities." The term colony did not appear in the constitution, thereby placing colonies outside its jurisdiction. The deputies from the Île de France (Maurice) intended to protest against this silence concerning the colonies but then thought better of it since it suited them to the extent that it comforted the colonies with the regime of special jurisdiction and hence slavery (Wanquet 1998: 31–33). Thus, if the declaration preceding the constitutional text of 1793 contained the germ of abolition of slavery, no aspect of the principle of special treatment for the colonies was called into question (Charlin 2009: 22). Moreover, the application of the constitution was suspended until peacetime. Even if a majority of deputies supported the abolition of slavery, as the deputies of the Île de France feared in July 1793 (Wanquet 1998: 33), slavery was not explicitly abolished. In France, the revolt of the slaves in Saint-Domingue was presented in the press like a second Vendée (Sieger 2010). Understanding the slave insurrection as a royalist revolt modified the approach of republicans towards slavery: some republicans did not want to reward rebellious slaves with its abolition.

The Club de Massiac was dissolved after 10 August; however, new support for the maintenance of slavery emerged in Paris. Pierre-François Page and Jean-Augustin Brulley were designated by the colonial assembly of Saint-Domingue on 15 May 1792 to advocate the indispensability of slavery in the colonies. Arriving in France in July 1792, they presented themselves strategically as colonial sans-culottes and Jacobins. They were received by the Jacobin Club in February 1793 and became close to Jacobins such as Amar. Page and Brulley led a campaign of defamation against Sonthonax, accusing him of being a Brissotin wanting to sell Saint-Domingue to the British. So, on 16 July 1793, at the instigation of Page and Brulley, Sonthonax and Polvérel were formally accused. In colonial matters, the Montagnards, now in power, simply condemned the Brissotins, the faction which Sonthonax was believed to support. However, on 27 July, Grégoire proposed and obtained the ending of subsidies for slave-ships. This measure was taken at a time when there were no longer many slave expeditions because of the war with Britain. The number of slaves disembarked in French colonies was about 3,000 in 1793, compared with eighteen times that number in 1790.

If the autonomist patriots had chosen to become Montagnards, the aristocratic planters took the opposite route of making an alliance with the British. De Curt, an *émigré* planter and former deputy in the Constituant from Guadeloupe, was joined in London in January 1793 by two representatives sent directly from the colony, Dubuc and Clairfontaine. They requested that Guadeloupe be placed under British protection. When France declared war on Britain on 1 February 1793, the proposition of the *émigré* planters was accepted. Guadeloupe was then delivered up to the British Crown on condition that it would be ceded back to the Bourbons as soon as they were restored, after payment of the costs of occupation (Geggus 1982: 83). Armed with this treaty, de Curt, Dubuc, and Clairfontaine exhorted those planters who had remained in the islands to rise up and facilitate future British military operations. On 25 February another treaty was made between representatives of the colonials of Saint-Domingue and Great Britain (Geggus 1982: 395–399). Autonomist patriots and royalist planters pursued two different paths to the maintenance of slavery.

The alliance of aristocratic planters whom we might henceforth designate as royalists with the British was rapidly put in place in the colonies. From March 1793 Saint-Domingue was placed under strict embargo. The Spanish supported the insurgent slaves in the north. This support came at the moment when the civil commissioners' troops were on the point of victory over the insurgents. Towards the end of 1792 the patriot autonomists began to draw closer to the royalists to oppose the civil commissioners and free coloreds. Each faction in its struggle to seize power had a vested interest in using the insurgent bands in the conflicts. The slave insurgents became true mercenaries for freedom. They sold their armed services to whoever offered the strongest guarantee of freedom. The soldiers of the civil commissioners were decimated by yellow fever, and the free men of color soon became the sole real military support for the civil commissioners. On 20 June 1793, Sonthonax and Polvérel were threatened by an offensive led by a heterogeneous coalition of sailors and whites from the town of Cap-Français. The commissioners only had as defenders 200 free men of color; to defend himself, Sonthonax armed slaves and rallied the bands of insurgents. On 21 June the civil commissioners freed all the slaves fighting for the Republic and gave them the rights of French citizens. This was a question of the first mass emancipation of 10,000 slaves from among which 1,000 were recruited and regimented into a battalion called the "Guard of the Mandatories of the National Convention." Strengthened by this support, Sonthonax and Polvérel retook control of the town of Cap-Français, which had burned down during the fighting. Sonthonax tried to win new supporters for the Republic but, while according liberty to the combatants, he did not offer anything beyond that offered by the royalists or the Spanish. It was for that reason that he decided to offer freedom also to the families of the Republic's soldiers. Given the balance of forces, more and more unfavorable to the republicans in Saint-Domingue because of the alliance between royalist colonials, insurgent slaves, the British and the Spanish, Sonthonax decided to go even further in his quest for support from insurgent slaves for the republican cause by abolishing slavery, on 29 August 1793. Sonthonox relied on the decree of 5 March 1793 which had given the commissioners the power the reform slave workshops. On 22 September Sonthonax and Polvérel, who had put in place the election of deputies (Dufay, Mills, Belley), sent them to Paris to have the Convention endorse the abolition of slavery.

News of abolition reached Paris on 25 September 1793. The Convention made no decision. It should be recalled that the Montagnards had strong reservations regarding Sonthonax et Polvérel, considered to be Brissotins. Besides, on 3 October Amar had presented his report against the Brissotins, who were accused of having wanted to deliver the colonies to the British "under the false guise of philanthropy" (Piquet 2002: 282). The actions of Page and Brulley, deputies of the Îles Mascareignes to the Convention, allowed it once more to avoid the question of slavery. When the Saint-Domingue deputies arrived in France, Page and Brulley used their contacts among the Montagnards to have them incarcerated on 29 January 1794; they spent four days in prison before being released on the orders of the Committee of Public Safety. They were admitted as deputies to the Convention on 3 February. The next day the debate took place on the situation in Saint-Domingue and the abolition of slavery. The deputy Dufay indicated that the only means to pacify the insurgents and keep Saint-Domingue within the Republic was a general emancipation. He stated to the Convention: "the Spanish and the English, whom a great number of counter-revolutionaries have already joined forces with, were fully anticipating that they [the insurgent slaves] would ask for assistance and were extending a helping hand to them." When the deputy Levasseur de la Sarthe proposed the decree of abolition someone interrupted, saying "It has already been decreed," to which Levasseur replied "Yes, for the continent but not the colonies." This illustrates once again the manoeuvres of the colonial lobby to avoid an explicit abolition of slavery in the colonies. The abolition was nevertheless adopted. About 180 deputies were present at the session, about average for the Convention (Piquet 2002: 337–338). Abolition was approved by acclamation.

Abolition was therefore enabled by a burst of enthusiasm in the Convention, a particular circumstance like many others the Revolution had seen. The Brissotins and Montagnards were slow to abolish slavery because of their reluctance to abandon the general scheme of gradual abolition and, moreover, their certainty that the immediate abolition of slavery would lead to the ruin of the colonies. War with Great Britain strengthened that view. Brissotins and Montagnards believed that the safety of colonial trade, and hence of French trade, depended on the short-term maintenance of slavery. The interests of French commerce and of the producers of colonial goods had to be protected by sacrificing the principle of general emancipation to interests of the state. Commercial interests had more voices in Paris than did slaves. Brissotins and Montagnards remained very influenced by the colonial and commercial middle classes. That influence was all the greater because the men of the Convention had very little knowledge of the colonies.

The decree of 4 February 1794 stated that "Negro slavery is abolished in all colonies: in consequence it is decreed that all men, without distinction of color, resident in the colonies, are French citizens, and will enjoy all the same rights guaranteed by the Constitution." On 12 April the Committee of Public Safety ordered the dispatch of the decree of 4 February to all the colonies. At the same time as the decree of emancipation was sent to Saint-Domingue a warrant arrived for Sonthonax and Polvérel. The two men agreed to return to France and left Saint-Domingue on 12 June. They arrived in Paris on 3 August. The Montagnards having been overthrown on 27 July, the warrant was suspended, and Sonthonax and Polvérel were provisionally declared free men (Saint-Louis 2008: 332–333).

The Difficult Application of Abolition

A military expedition under the command of Victor Hugues was charged with the abolition of slavery in the Îles du Vent (Guadeloupe, Martinique, Sainte-Lucie), then occupied by the British. On 7 June 1794, Hugues proclaimed the abolition of slavery on Guadeloupe. Between June and December he succeeded in reconquering Guadeloupe by the large-scale incorporation of former slaves into the army. Moreover, the Guadeloupe army took Sainte-Lucie, Grenade, Saint-Martin, Saint-Eustache, and Saint-Vincent in 1795. The same year, an expedition to retake Martinique failed. Recruitment took the total armed force to 11,000 men at the end of 1795, on eight islands: Guadeloupe, Marie-Galante, Désirade, Saint-Eustache, Saint-Martin, Grenade, Saint-Vincent, and Sainte-Lucie.[26] This was a considerable number in comparison with the 1,000 sans-culottes who had arrived with Hugues in June 1794. On 14 June 1794 the abolition of slavery was also proclaimed in Guyane, which had remained French.

The signing of the Treaty of Basle with Spain in 1795 put an end to the activities of the armies of Jean-François and Biassou. The latter, tempted for a moment to enter service with the British, finally refused because he would have been obliged to follow the orders of white generals. Jean-François and Biassou went into exile, the former in Spain and the latter in Florida. The decree of abolition and the skill of those sent from France (Sonthonax, Hugues) enabled a massive recruitment of slaves to repel the British. The expansion in the Caribbean of republican armies formed primarily of slaves would reach its peak in 1795.

On 18 June 1796, the two agents Baco and Burnel disembarked in the Îles Mascareignes, charged with the abolition of slavery. Three days later, they were forcibly re-embarked by planters who refused to accept their mission. A *cordon sanitaire* was put in place to prevent any diffusion of the news. The colonial assembly in Réunion took measures to prevent any indiscretion concerning general emancipation (Wanquet 1980–84). The decree of 4 February 1794 abolishing slavery was applied neither in the Îles Mascareignes, where the colonials were powerful enough to rebuff those sent by the Convention, nor in Martinique, which was under British occupation.

In the colonies where the abolition of slavery was proclaimed the question remained of work for the former slaves. Éric de Mara has illustrated the complexity of the situation at Saint-Domingue by analyzing notarial registers, showing that, through successive periods of domination, a particular neighborhood could experience general emancipation one moment then slavery a few months later, depending on the presence or not of republican forces.[27] In Saint-Domingue, the proclamation of abolition on 29 August 1793 was accompanied by a regulation of workplace cultivation. This subjected former slaves to residence on their respective plantations, and required them to undertake daily work for which they were paid a wage to an equivalent of one-third the total income from their labor. Domestic servants and workers remained in the service of their former masters, and were paid a salary negotiated from time to time. Those who worked in agriculture and domestic servants could not leave their commune without the permission of the municipality. As in Saint-Domingue, in Guadeloupe the work of agricultural laborers and domestic servants remained the property of their former masters or, by default, of the Republic. A man who worked on the land had no freedom of movement without authorization from his master. He had, however, a civic identity which would allow him access to property. In practice, few would become landowners and, when they did, they acquired only modest property (such as huts without ownership of the land). The mass of these regulations relating to farming demonstrates the embarrassment of colonial authorities regarding the question of the remuneration of the work of former slaves. In the colonies, only whites, persons of color already freed before the decree, and former slaves in the army or on warships really benefited from general emancipation.

Bonaparte's Colonial Reaction

In Paris, the *coup d'état* of Bonaparte in November 1799 ended the parliamentary republic. Colonial politics also changed. Article 6 of the Constitution of Year III (1795) made clear that "the colonies are an integral part of the Republic and are subject to the same constitutional law," and the first article of the Constitution of

Year VIII (1799) affirmed the unity and indivisibility of the French Republic, making clear that "its European territory is distributed into departments and communal *arrondissements*." But Article 91 declared that "the regime of the colonies is determined by special laws." It was a centralizing specificity, the colonies being excluded from the elaboration of regulations concerning them. This article at the same time adduced the principle of distinct legislation but also its formulation by national authorities (Charlin 2009: 23). Bonaparte justified himself by declaring that "this arrangement derives from the nature of circumstances and from the difference in climates. The inhabitants of colonies situated in America, in Asia, in Africa, cannot be governed by the same law. The difference in habits, in customs, in interests, the diversity of the land, cultivation, production require various modifications."[28] It was thus in the name of difference that the rupture occurred with juridical assimilation, also called "isonomie républicaine" by Bernard Gainot (Dorigny and Gainot 2010) or "identité législative" by Frédéric Charlin (2009). Bonaparte also called into question the principle of the uniform application of the abolition of slavery. The First Consul declared to the session of the Conseil d'État on 16 August 1800: "it is not a question of knowing whether it is good to abolish slavery ... I am convinced that [Saint-Domingue] would be English if the negroes were not attached to us through the self-interest of their freedom. They will make less sugar, perhaps, but they will make it for us and they will serve us, in case of need, as soldiers. If we have one less sugar factory, we will have another citadel occupied by friendly soldiers."[29] If in the name of pragmatism Brissotins and Montagnards, despite their principles, had delayed the abolition of slavery, Bonaparte acted from pragmatism. In spite of his lack of abolitionist principles, he maintained general emancipation where it had been proclaimed: Saint-Domingue and Guadeloupe. This situation was sanctioned by the law of 30 Floréal X (20 May 1802), which maintained slavery in the colonies returned by Great Britain in the Treaty of Amiens (Martinique, Sainte-Lucie, Tobago) and in the Îles Mascareignes where the colonials had refused general emancipation. Article 4 of the same law stated that, "notwithstanding all earlier laws, the colonial regime is subject for ten years to regulations which will be made by the Government." Three months later, the senatus-consultas or decree of 16 Thermidor X (4 August 1802) reorganizing executive power granted to the Senate the preparation of a colonial constitution, but the text would never see the light of day (Charlin 2009: 24). The colonies would thus henceforth be administered by a system of special decrees.

In Saint-Domingue and Guadeloupe, colored officers in the colonial army had authority over the metropolitan authorities. In 1797 the black general Toussaint Louverture was the veritable master of the north of Saint-Domingue, and the mulatto general André Rigaud that of the south. Their confrontation, in 1799–1800, was worthy of the struggle between Caesar and Pompey or Octavius and Mark Antony. The civil war between the two pro-consuls of the colonial army ended in the victory of Toussaint Louverture. In Guadeloupe, colored soldiers overthrew the metropolitan representative. The signing of peace preliminaries with Great Britain allowed Bonaparte to try to re-establish order in the colonies. An expedition commanded by Leclerc was sent to Saint-Domingue, and another under Richepance to Guadeloupe. According to Philippe Girard, whose view I share, the objective of these operations was first of all to allow Bonaparte to rid himself of his colonial rival, to punish colored officers who had disobeyed metropolitan agents, and to re-establish production. I do not agree that there were secret instructions detailing a pre-existing plan to re-establish slavery as certain historians have suggested (Girard 2011: 3–28). These expeditions had different outcomes. In Saint-Domingue, the expedition found expression first in the subjection of the colonial colored army and notably the deportation of Toussaint Louverture in June 1802. Richepance's expedition ended with the death or deportation of all colored soldiers in Guadeloupe. The repression led to 3,000 to 4,000 dead and as many deported between May and December 1802.

The very day of the death of Delgrès, the chief of the rebels in Guadeloupe, on 28 May 1802, Richepance issued a decree inviting the population to return to their places of domicile, in order to enjoy the "benefits of a paternal and conservative government," like that of Richepance on 16 Prairial (5 June). They were encouraged to return to agricultural activity, and owners of plantations where the workforce had left, as well as inhabitants who had in their personal service men of color, were encouraged to come and "reclaim" them so that they might be "returned."[30]

In July 1802, Bonaparte was informed of Richepance's successes in Guadeloupe. His minister of the navy and colonies, Decrès, wrote to Bonaparte on 24 July that Richepance "had prepared the way for your decree [of 16 July] on slavery." On 13 August the same man declared that Richepance, who "has done marvels, and achieved successes well in excess of what one hoped, has re-established slavery."[31] It was in this context that Napoleon Bonaparte issued a decree on 16 July re-establishing slavery in Guadeloupe, a text that has been closely analyzed by J.-F. Niort and J. Richard (2009),[32] extending to Guadeloupe the law of 30 Floréal X (20 May 1802). Two arguments were developed to support the re-establishment of slavery. The first found general emancipation responsible for the decline of production of export products and foodstuffs. The second denounced "the frightening use that the blacks of Guadeloupe have made of liberty," accusing them of laziness, roaming, license, and above all rebellion against metropolitan government. The re-establishment of slavery was presented as a punishment for the revolt of the coloreds.

In Guadeloupe, the politics of return to the old order continued. On 17 July 1802, Richepance annulled the citizenship of men of color and lowered the wages of plantation workers, while re-establishing the right of masters to discipline their workforce. In mid-July, the sale of slaves was reintroduced. These measures were repeated in Saint-Domingue and had a major influence on the revolt of the colored army against Leclerc in October 1802. He and his army succumbed to rebel attacks, but above all to yellow fever. On 1 January 1804, the French part of Saint-Domingue proclaimed its independence under the name of Haiti. The colony in which had been concentrated two-thirds of the slaves in French colonies at the start of the Revolution affirmed in its Constitution of 20 May 1805 that slavery was abolished forever. The balance-sheet of the Haitian Revolution was heavy: on the eve of the Revolution the population of the colony was about 550,000; by 1804 it had been reduced to 300,000. In Guyane, the authority of the consular government was upheld by Victor Hugues, who had arrived in 1800. He had put in place strict regulation of cultivation, and no popular uprising occurred. Napoleon Bonaparte decided the fate of the former slaves of Guyane in a decree of 7 December 1802, which put neighborhood conscription in place, with the effect of "attaching [slaves] irrevocably to the property or workshop," which could be ended only by the "hitherto used ways of granting freedom." A consular decree of November–December 1802 led to a dual system in French Guyane of total slavery for certain blacks and simple rural conscription for others.[33] Historians have so far not found any document which officially re-established slavery in Guyane. In our current state of knowledge, decisions taken concerning this seem to corroborate the idea that Bonaparte had no predetermined plan to re-establish slavery when he dispatched the expeditions of Leclerc and Richepance. In fact, in Guyane, where he was able to re-establish it easily, he did not re-establish it officially. It was by a local decree that Victor Hugues regulated the practices of slavery on 25 April 1803.

Several factors explain why reconquest by France and its corollary, the re-establishment of slavery, were able to be carried out in Guadeloupe but not in Saint-Domingue. In the latter, slaves and free coloreds fought continually for more than ten years, in the context of civil wars between different factions and the conflict with Great Britain and Spain. In Guadeloupe, armed conflict lasted only a few months in 1794. In Saint-Domingue there was a general arming of the population, which was not the case in Guadeloupe. Armed men in Guadeloupe had been conscripted into the army, which was not the case in Saint-Domingue where many of them were insurgents to begin with. There was no mass mobilization of cultivators against expeditionary forces. If Richepance was able to crush the rebellion in Guadeloupe before the arrival of the rainy season and yellow fever, Leclerc was only able to subject the colored army temporarily. In addition, if at the end of July 1802 Richepance deported the mass of coloreds who had borne arms during the revolutionary period, Leclerc was able to achieve this only for Toussaint Louverture and a few other men. The measures taken by Richepance in Guadeloupe reached Saint-Domingue and reinforced the conviction among non-whites that there was a threat of the re-establishment of slavery and of color prejudice. So colored men already freed before the decree and former slaves formed an alliance against Leclerc's expeditionary force.

Leclerc committed a serious political mistake. While the First Consul's directives enjoined him to attach mulattoes to his cause to neutralize the blacks, Leclerc did the opposite: he deported General Rigaud and several of his officers shortly after his arrival to avoid a clash with the blacks. In that way he deprived himself of his best allies. Leclerc died on 1 November 1802, to be succeeded by Rochambeau. The latter received reinforcements in December 1802 but, rather than using them to reinforce places which were still holding out, Rochambeau threw them into assaults on several lost positions. If the towns were retaken, these battalions were rapidly decimated by war and sickness, and Rochambeau was reduced to the same position as Leclerc: crowded into coastal towns while awaiting reinforcements. When the latter arrived in late March/early April 1803, Rochambeau committed the same error as at the outset of his rule and immediately engaged them in the south to retake Les Cayes. The war of ambush conducted by an armed population there decimated his troops. The resumption of war with England in May 1803 isolated the island still further from metropolitan France and from the reinforcements that the latter could send. Little by little, all the coastal strongholds held by the French were isolated and besieged. With the Royal Navy blocking by sea the last means of supplying these places, they fell one by one, generally into the hands of the British, to whom the French preferred to surrender rather than the indigenous army. On 18 November 1803, Rochambeau held only the Spanish part, Le Môle Saint-Nicolas and Le Cap was defeated near this town at Vertière. He negotiated his surrender: it was the end of French colonization in the west of Saint-Domingue.

Conclusion

Colonial issues were among the preoccupations of the principal actors of the French Revolution. Three subjects were of particular interest: the status of free persons of color, the question of slavery, and the application of the constitution to the colonies. How these three matters were addressed varied according to the political regime in place. Hence the Constituent Assembly turned to the colonial assemblies to deal with these questions, the Legislative Assembly gave rights to free coloreds, the Convention abolished slavery, and the Directory expanded the application of the constitution to the colonies. Reaction under the Consulate placed all this progress in question. Color prejudice and slavery were re-established, and the colonies were made subject to a special legislative regime. It must be noted that all the decisions were made in response to what was happening in the colonies themselves. Pressure, revolts, the expulsion of representatives of central authority: all of these influenced decisions made in Paris.

The revolutionary period seems to have ended with a return to how things had been at the outset. Laws from before 1789 were reintroduced deliberately; that in any case was the formula used to maintain or reintroduce slavery. Nevertheless, a return to the *status quo ante* did not happen in the most populous of the colonies: Saint-Domingue. This land, which had had two-thirds of the slaves in the French colonial empire, was no longer French. In the end, the re-establishment of slavery by Napoleon Bonaparte affected only a minority. By reintroducing slavery and color prejudice, Bonaparte's regime deprived itself of armed forces for the new war which broke out with Great Britain in 1803. The loss of the largest colony (Louisiana, sold to the United States) and of the colony most productive of wealth (Saint-Domingue) in 1803, anticipated the loss of the totality of French colonial possessions in 1808–10. France lost its colonies rapidly by not taking advantage of large-scale recruitment of colored soldiers which would have compensated for the inferiority of the French navy. Freed of its colonial rival, Great Britain was able to intervene more prominently and effectively in the war in Spain, described by contemporaries as the "tomb of the Grande Armée" of Napoleon. The latter's colonial failures anticipated his final defeat in 1814. It should be noted, moreover, that Great Britain, which had originally returned Mauritius in 1814, kept it definitively after the episode of the Hundred Days in 1815, as if to punish France for having accepted the ephemeral return of Napoleon Bonaparte.

France regained four slave colonies in 1815 (Guadeloupe, Guyane, Martinique, Réunion). The Revolution of 1830 would enable free persons of color to have equality with whites, that of 1848 would grant slaves freedom. The day after liberation, these four colonies would become "overseas departments" in 1946, as they had been under the Directory. The French Revolution was indeed a laboratory of modernity as far as the colonies were concerned.

Notes

1 http://www.slavevoyages.org, statistical base coordinated by David Eltis (accessed 10 Dec. 2011).
2 From the outset of colonization, masters freed certain slaves for the services they performed. It was a question above all of women and the childen they had had with them. This type of emancipation was common but not systematic. Any child whose mother was free at the moment of birth became free. Thus the juridical class of free persons of color was made up of freed persons and their descendants. They were the victims of color prejudice which placed them in a juridically inferior position to whites.
3 Longin 1848: 48.
4 In 1789 a work appeared in London entitled *Observations sur le préjugé de la noblesse héréditaire*. Its author, Nicolas Bergasse (1750–1832) was also a member of the Société des Amis des Noirs. He was a deputy at the Estates-General. In this pamphlet he demanded the destruction of noble privileges.
5 Interview with Vertus Saint-Louis, 9 Jan. 2010. http://www.frantzfanoninternational.org/spip.php?article211 (accessed 30 Dec. 2011).
6 Condorcet 1806: vol. 16, 147–157.
7 There were also *cahiers de doléances* at lower levels than *bailliages* (parishes, *communautés*, and so on).
8 *Archives parlementaires* (hereafter *AP*), vol. 12, 7–13, annex to the session of 2 Mar. 1790.
9 ANOM (Archives Nationales d'Outre-Mer), Bibliothèque Moreau de Saint-Méry, 1st series, vol. 20, pièce 16. "Lettre des citoyens de couleur des Isles et colonies Françoises; à MM. Les Membres du Comité de Vérification à l'Assemblée Nationale du 23 novembre 1789."
10 Speech of Vincent Ogé, 9 Sept. 1789 (Ogé, n.d.: 5).
11 Raimond 1793: 13.
12 ANOM Bibliothèque Moreau de Saint-Méry, 1st series, vol. 124, pièce 6. *Pétition nouvelle des citoyens de couleur des îles françoises à l'assemblée nationale*. Paris: Chez Desenne, Bailly et au Bureau du Patriote François, 18 Mar. 1791.
13 Ibid., 7.
14 ANOM Bibliothèque Moreau de Saint-Méry, 1st series, vol. 31, pièce 14. Julien Raimond, "Réponse aux considérations de M Moreau dit Saint-Méry député à l'assemblée nationale sur les colonies par M. Raymond, citoyen de couleur de Saint-Domingue," 12 May 1791.
15 ANOM Bibliothèque Moreau de Saint-Méry, 1st series, vol. 33, pièce 9. Extract from the decree of 13 May 1791.
16 *Le Moniteur*, no. 138, 18 May 1791. Paris: Plon, 2nd edn., 1858: 418.
17 Aulard 1889–97: vol. 3, 149.
18 Brissot 1791: 17.
19 Article 10 of the decree of 28 Mar. 1792 envisaged representation of colonies in the Legislative Assembly.
20 Archives Nationales (hereafter AN), DXXV 4, dossier 41.

21 Letter written by Guilhermy, secrétaire adjoint of the Commission Civile Déléguée at Saint-Domingue, dated Lorient, 23 Dec. 1792 (Benzaken 2011: 171).
22 On 25 Feb. 1791 a law forbade any subsidy to trade or manufacturing without the agreement of the National Assembly. A new law was therefore necessary to allow subsidies to be granted. From 1 Jan. 1791, no subsidy was given to the slave trade.
23 *AP*, 48: 621–622, session of 22 Aug. 1792.
24 *Le Patriote français*, no. 1264, 26 Jan. 1793.
25 AN, DXXV 79, dossier 778, pièce 44. Isnard, "Projet de décret pour rétablir l'ordre et la paix."
26 AN, C7A 48, folios 39–40. "Lettre des commissaires délégués au Comité de Salut Public de Port-de-la-Liberté, le 30 brumaire an IV."
27 Intervention at the colloquium "Les Colonies, la Révolution française, la Loi," held on 23 and 24 Sept. 2011 at the Université de Paris 1-Panthéon-Sorbonne.
28 "Lettre du Premier Consul Bonaparte aux citoyens de Saint-Domingue," dated Paris, 4 Nivôse VIII (25 Dec. 1799) (Bonaparte 1821: vol. 3).
29 Pierre-Louis Roederer, *Œuvres* (Paris, 1856), 334, cited in Brevet n.d.: 9.
30 Reproduced in Adélaïde-Merlande et al. 2002: 190, 215.
31 AN, AF IV 1190.
32 Niort and Richard found the minute of the decree dated 27 Messidor X (16 July 1802), together with a proposed decree concerning the re-establishment of slavery in Guadeloupe and its dependencies (AN, AF IV, no. 379).
33 ANOM C14/80, folio 53. "Arrêté des consuls tendant à établir à Cayenne et dans la Guyane française un esclavage total pour certains Noirs et une simple conscription rurale pour les autres (minute)," Frimaire XI (Nov./Dec. 1802).

References

Primary Sources

Adélaïde-Merlande, Jacques, René Bélénus, and Frédéric Régent (2002). *La Rébellion de la Guadeloupe, 1801–1802.* Gourbeyre: Archives Départementales de la Guadeloupe.

AP: Archives parlementaires de 1787 à 1860. Recueil complet des débats législatifs et politiques des chambres françaises, imprimé par ordre du corps législatif sous la direction de mm. J. Mavidal et E. Laurent. Première série, 1787–1799 (1867–1913), 82 vols. Paris: P. Dupont.

Aulard, Alphonse (1889–97). *La Société des Jacobins. Recueil des documents pour l'histoire du Club des Jacobins de Paris*, 6 vols. Paris: Librairies Jouaust, Noblet et Quantin.

Benzaken, Jean-Charles (2011). "Lettre inédite sur la situation à Saint-Domingue en novembre 1792." *AHRF*, 363: 171.

Bonaparte, Napoléon (1821). *Œuvres de Napoléon Bonaparte.* Paris: Panckoucke.

Brevet, Mathieu (n.d.). "Les Expéditions coloniales vers Saint-Domingue et les Antilles (1802–1810)," thesis, Université de Lyon 2.

Brissot, Jean-Pierre (1791). "Discours sur un projet de décret relatif à la révolte des noirs," National Assembly, 30 Oct.. Paris: Imprimerie Nationale. Reproduced in vol. 8 of *La Révolution française et l'abolition de l'esclavage* (1968), 12 vols. Paris: EDHIS.

Condorcet (1806). *Œuvres.* Brunswick.

Longin, Félix (1848). *Voyage à la Guadeloupe: Œuvre posthume (1818–1820).* Monnoyer.

Ogé, Vincent (n.d.). *Motion faite par M. Vincent Ogé jeune à l'Assemblée des colons, habitants de S.-Domingue, à l'Hôtel de Massiac, Place des Victoires.*

Pétition nouvelle des citoyens de couleur des îles françoises à l'assemblée nationale. Paris: Chez Desenne, Bailly et au Bureau du Patriote François, 18 Mar. 1791.

Raimond, Julien (1793). *Réflexions sur les véritables causes des troubles et des désastres de nos colonies, notamment sur ceux de Saint-Domingue: avec les moyens à employer pour préserver cette colonie d'une ruine totale; adressées à la Convention Nationale.* Paris: Imprimerie des Patriotes.

Secondary Sources

Bénot, Yves (1989). *La Révolution et la fin des colonies.* Paris: La Découverte.

Charlin, F. (2009). "Homo servilis: Contribution à l'étude de la condition juridique de l'esclave dans les colonies françaises (1635–1848)." Doctoral dissertation, University of Grenoble.

Dorigny, Marcel and Bernard Gainot (2010). "La Révolution et la 'question coloniale' (1789–1804)." In Michel Biard (ed.). *La Révolution française: Une histoire toujours vivante.* Paris: Tallandier. 269–285.

Dubois, Laurent (2004). *Avengers of the New World: The Story of the Haitian Revolution.* Cambridge, Mass.: Harvard University Press.

Erhard, Jean (2008). *Lumières et esclavages: L'Esclavage colonial et l'opinion publique au XVIIIe siècle.* Paris: André Versaille.

Fick, Carolyn (1990). *The Making of Haiti: The Saint-Domingue Revolution from Below.* Knoxville: University of Tennessee Press.

Geggus, David (1982). *Slavery, War and Revolution: the British Occupation of Saint-Domingue, 1793–1798.* Oxford: Clarendon Press.

Girard, P. (2011). "Napoléon voulait-il rétablir l'esclavage en Haiti?" *Bulletin de la Société d'histoire de la Guadeloupe*, 159: 3–28.

Niort, J.-F. and J. Richard (2009). "À propos de la découverte de l'arrêté consulaire du 16 juillet 1802 et du rétablissement de l'ancien ordre colonial (spécialement de l'esclavage) à la Guadeloupe." *Bulletin de la Société d'Histoire de la Guadeloupe*, 152: 31–59.

Piquet, J.-D. (2002). *L'Émancipation des Noirs dans la Révolution française (1789–1795).* Paris: Karthala.

Régent, Frédéric (2007). *La France et ses esclaves: De la colonisation aux abolitions (1620–1848).* Paris: Grasset.

Saint-Louis, Vertus (2008). *Mer et liberté: Haïti (1492–1794).* Port-au-Prince: Imprimeur II.

Sieger, D. (2010). "La Presse et l'insurrection des esclaves de Saint-Domingue, octobre 1791–avril 1792." Master's dissertation, Université de Paris 1-Panthéon-Sorbonne.

Thésée, F. (1972). *Négociants bordelais et colons de Saint-Domingue: La Maison Bapst et Cie 1788–1793.* Paris: Société Française d'Histoire d'Outre-mer.

Thibau, J. (1989). *Le Temps de Saint-Domingue: L'Esclavage et la Révolution française.* Paris: J.-C. Lattès.

Wanquet, C. (1980–84). *Histoire d'une Révolution, la Réunion (1789–1803).* Marseille: Éditions Jeanne Laffite.

Wanquet, C. (1998). *La France et la première abolition de l'esclavage 1794–1802.* Paris: Karthala.

Further Reading

1802 en Guadeloupe et à Saint-Domingue: Réalités et mémoire (2003). Gourbeyre: Société d'Histoire de la Guadeloupe/Archives Départementales de la Guadeloupe.

Bénot, Yves (1997). *La Guyane sous la Révolution.* Matoury, Guyane: Ibis Rouge.

Bénot, Yves and Marcel Dorigny (eds.) (2003). *1802, rétablissement de l'esclavage dans les colonies françaises.* Paris: Maisonneuve et Larose.

Cauna, J. de (ed.) (2004). *Toussaint Louverture et l'indépendance d'Haïti: Témoignages pour un bicentenaire*. Paris: Karthala and Société Française d'Histoire d'Outre-Mer.

Dorigny, Marcel and Bernard Gainot (1998). *La Société des Amis des Noirs (1788–1799): Contribution à l'histoire de l'abolition de l'esclavage*. Paris: UNESCO.

Garrigus, John (2006). *Before Haiti: Race and Citizenship in French Saint-Domingue*. New York: Palgrave Macmillan.

Geggus, David (1989). "The French and Haitian Revolutions, and Resistance to Slavery in the Americas: An Overview." *Revue Française d'Histoire d'Outre-Mer*, 282–283: 107–124.

Geggus, David (2002). *Haitian Revolutionary Studies*. Bloomington: Indiana University Press.

Geggus, David (2009). *The World of the Haitian Revolution*. Bloomington: Indiana University Press.

Popkin, Jeremy (2010). *You Are All Free: The Haitian Revolution and the Abolition of Slavery*. Cambridge: Cambridge University Press.

Régent, Frédéric (2004). *Esclavage, métissage, liberté: La Révolution française en Guadeloupe (1789–1802)*. Paris: Grasset.

CHAPTER TWENTY-FIVE

The Revolutionary Mediterranean

IAN COLLER

On the evening of 12 Floréal III (1 May 1795) a deputy from Marseille, Joseph Stanislas Rovère, climbed to the tribune of the National Convention to read out a letter addressed to the revolutionary representative Cadroy. The letter was written by a "Turk," a North African merchant named "Mohamed Dyghis":

> I swear to you by our holy prophet, Citizen Representative, that my expressions of affection toward you are not motivated by commercial interests. They are a homage for the good things I have witnessed you doing here. I love the justice that you love, I worship the principles of humanity that you consistently profess. Your good deeds have elevated my soul, and that alone makes us brothers in our hearts. No matter where I first drew breath, or the religion in which I was born, we are brothers. Indeed, we are more than brothers when every moral precept is shared by two thinking beings. (*Moniteur* 1795: 336)

This extraordinary expression of revolutionary sympathies from the further shore of the Mediterranean confronts us with the inadequacy of our present understanding of the experience of the French Revolution on a global scale. We know something of the conditions through which Dyghis may have come to be familiar with the events and ideas of the Revolution: the commercial relations with North Africa in which he was engaged, and the flow of staples necessary to the survival of the meridional regions of France in this period (Masson 1903); the diplomatic role of French consuls throughout the Ottoman Empire that both protected and policed French subjects (Windler 2002); and the political and military agreements between sovereigns long necessary both to the balance of power in Europe and to the safety of French and allied shipping (Groc 1997; Panzac 2005). But Dyghis' letter goes further. It presents us with questions that take us far beyond diplomacy, trade, and

A Companion to the French Revolution, First Edition. Edited by Peter McPhee.

military alliance, explicitly rejecting expediency or self-interest as the basis for his alignment with the Revolution. Dyghis invokes a series of dimensions for this relationship that throw it into a very different light. He expresses a deep, affective moral and intellectual connection with the universalism of values expressed by revolutionaries. But at the same time he grounds this adherence in his own North African society and culture, and plays gently on European misconceptions about "Barbary" – the eighteenth-century term for the littoral regions of the Maghreb. It is, he writes, "so much less barbarous than you may imagine." Lastly, and most strikingly, he makes this profession of revolutionary commitment under the sign of his own Muslim faith. Dyghis rejects the idea that religion might act as a fundamental division between the shores of the Mediterranean: an idea that has dominated, consciously or unconsciously, our understanding of Mediterranean dynamics in this period.

In the decade after 1789, and particularly after 1793, the Mediterranean became in many ways the great laboratory of the Revolution. Looked at from the Mediterranean, the "French Revolution" seems considerably less French, and much more global in its nature and impact. Revolutionaries on the borders of France helped to drag the Revolution onto the world stage: Dutch, Liégois, Brabançons, and others contributed their passion and their blood to the making and the survival of the French Revolution, even if they ultimately found themselves shut out of the "French" revolutionary legacy and folded back into multinational empires. But it was across the Mediterranean that the experiment of the revolutionary Republic would be expanded to its greatest extent, beyond the boundaries of Europe and its colonies, testing its universal claims in the crucible of difference. The first territorial extension of sovereignty by revolutionary France was the admission of Corsica on 30 November 1789, as a result of demands by Corsican revolutionaries. The revolutionary retaking of Toulon in 1793 unleashed a movement into the Mediterranean that reached its high-water mark in 1799, bringing Palestine and Upper Egypt, as well as Malta, Calabria, and Corfu, under the aegis of the new Republic. But it did more than this – it raised both hopes and dangers for people across the Mediterranean, in Spain, Italy and Greece, through North Africa and in the great Ottoman cities from Cairo to Istanbul. In complex and differential ways, men and women across the Mediterranean – Muslims, Christians, and Jews – responded to new challenges arriving in many different forms: from the sea, by land, through diplomatic channels, in books and newspapers.

If this Mediterranean was no stagnant backwater, nor was it a self-enclosed and unchanging "system." The Mediterranean was connected in multiple ways to the world beyond, to the Atlantic and the Americas: to Africa and the Arabian peninsula; through Tartary to the Black Sea; along the great caravan routes to Asia and India and beyond into the Pacific. The Mediterranean of the eighteenth century was not yet the global hub that the piercing of the isthmus of Suez would make it in the following century, but those explosive global forces were already detectable early in the century, and not only on its European shores.

Yet the Mediterranean remains the great unasked question of the Revolution. The legacy of assumptions passed down in our historiography have made it almost impossible to conceive of the "revolutionary moment" as something shared with the further shores of the Mediterranean, into the Muslim world beyond, and onward to Asia and Africa. In fact, a considerable scholarship exists that may form the basis for new answers to this question, much of it completed at the periphery of the major historical traditions, and hitherto valued only as exotic marginalia. It can point the way to a vast and untapped archive of documents that may shed new light on the meanings and processes of the Revolution itself, and its significance for today's plural world.

The Problem of the Mediterranean in the Eighteenth Century

More than half a century since the sun rose on the Atlantic thesis, the revolutionary Mediterranean has as yet received little more than a few rays, a footnote or a brief allusion here and there in the vast scholarship generated on this question. And yet there is no reason for us to believe that the Mediterranean, so lyrically painted by Fernand Braudel (1972), should somehow, in the interval between the age of Philip II and that of Louis XVI, have become a barrier rather than a bridge between Europe, Asia, and Africa. But if a curtain has fallen, it is more in the minds of scholars than in any of the actual conditions pertaining to the Revolution itself, or the consciousness of those who lived it. A challenge lies before a new generation of scholars, to think the Revolution as a global event, an event profoundly shaped both by local and by global factors. Thinking the revolutionary Mediterranean does not mean stretching the Atlantic thesis outward onto to a global canvas but rather fundamentally rethinking the global logic within which we have formed our enquiry. In this process we cannot sweep away events as mere fleck on the waves of the *longue durée*, nor substitute ethno-national determinisms with thalassic ones. We need to begin investigating the Mediterranean, not as a "liquid continent," but as a sea of complex and contradictory possibilities, criss-crossing vectors of conflict and commerce, of communication and conquest.

In the preface to the English translation of his work, Braudel reiterated his conviction that the Mediterranean constituted a unity, that "the Turkish Mediterranean lived and breathed with the same rhythms as the Christian, that the whole sea shared a common destiny" (Braudel 1972: 14). But the Mediterranean that Braudel evoked was nonetheless, even by his own account, one heavily weighted toward the northern peninsulas, from Spain to Greece – in itself a vast and complex geographical and historical zone. The physical contours of the eastern and southern Mediterranean, the Atlas Mountains and the Nile delta did help to frame the question, but the exploration of the Ottoman Mediterranean, and its connections to a world beyond, was constrained by linguistic challenges. Braudel's research was conducted for the most part in European archives and texts, and only skirted the edges of the great mass of Ottoman documents.

This was a very different Mediterranean therefore from that evoked by Marshall Hodgson, who approached world history very consciously from the perspective of Islam. Hodgson's Mediterranean was just one element in an "Afro-Euro-Asiatic ecumene" that united the Indian Ocean to the Sahara, the Caspian, and the central Asian plains (Hodgson 1974). For Hodgson, the late eighteenth century was precisely the moment at which the developing fault-line in the unity of agrarian economic and social life across the ecumene became suddenly apparent, not gradually but in the manner of an earthquake responding to pressure built up over time. In historical terms, Hodgson identifies this seismic shift directly with the moment of the French Revolution (Hodgson 1974: 205). This "transmutation" was based on the emancipation of citied elites from economic dependence on the agrarian base. If the shift emerged initially in Europe, along with the great tide of precious metals flowing across the Atlantic and the emergence of new forms of global commerce, this did not make it an innately "Western" process. "Muslim rulers of the generation of 1789," Hodgson noted, "were in fact attempting to meet a situation that had been developing throughout the eighteenth century" (1974: 207). But, despite the extraordinarily rich picture of the early modern Mediterranean developed by recent historians (Dakhlia 2008; Greene 2002; Husain and Fleming 2007), this trans-Mediterranean "generation of 1789" has been almost entirely neglected. The later part of the eighteenth century has remained a blank spot in Mediterranean history, just as the Mediterranean has remained largely outside the purview of revolutionary historiography.

For "classical" historians of the French Revolution, the further shore of the Mediterranean was separated by an irreducible distance, both geographical and cultural, from the key zone of revolutionary change. In the Marxian schema, the chief question arising out of the Revolution involved its ultimate *consequences* in world-historical terms, as the first point in a series of revolutions – 1830, 1848, and 1871 – culminating in 1917. Although Georges Lefebvre brought the vast rural space of France to bear in his finely tuned analysis of revolutionary dynamics, his interpretation drew up blank at the Mediterranean. Responding implicitly to the challenge posed by Braudel, he explained that the eighteenth-century Mediterranean had "ceased to be the dynamic centre it had once been, a change hastened by the fact that part of its shores belonged to Islam" (Lefebvre 1962: 5). Instead, revolutionary historians began to look toward what Belgian scholar Charles Verlinden called the "new Mediterranean of our time" – the Atlantic (Verlinden 1953: 378). Verlinden's project was to connect these "two Mediterraneans," building on Braudel. However, in 1955, Robert Palmer and Jacques Godechot seized the initiative, presenting a different thesis that framed the Atlantic as a world and a "civilization" distinct in itself, one "more liberal and more dynamic than that of the East of the old continent" (Godechot and Palmer 1955: 204), built on the idea of a shared revolution.

The connection of the American "Revolution" with the French raised eyebrows because of the flagrant differences in the nature of the two revolutions: one primarily a local war of independence against an external power, the other the overthrow of a regime by its own people and its replacement with a new form of government inflected by radical universal principles. Each of these "revolutions" had more often been used to point out the deficiencies in the other than to elaborate some larger common investigation. But in some ways the Atlantic thesis was as important for what it shut out as for what it included: rather than rendering the French Revolution more global, it corralled it back into what Palmer had already named "the World Revolution of the West" (Palmer 1954).

Where the Atlantic thesis was more radical, however, was in challenging the diffusionist models of the French Revolution, by reframing the French experience as part of a larger revolutionary phenomenon in Europe and the Americas. Palmer's great two-volume work on *The Age of the Democratic Revolution* sought to demonstrate the "democratic" continuities between European and American revolutions, finding in them a common transformation toward representational government, freedom of religion, and liberty of expression. He rejected the conventional terms of radiation, ripples, or "contagion," emphasizing instead the contemporaneous conditions that gave rise to revolutionary phenomena, and the dynamic and concatenating ways in which events could influence one another. Thus Palmer insisted that this was "not simply a question of the 'spread' or 'impact' or 'influence' of the French Revolution … There was one big revolutionary agitation, not simply a French Revolution due to purely French causes, and foolishly favored by irresponsible people in other countries" (Palmer 1959: 7). Godechot's *La Grande Nation* (1956) sustained a more tutelary role for France in a less clearly defined revolutionary ferment, out of which grew the national and imperial trajectories of the nineteenth century. What continued to underpin these Atlantic visions, however, was a common understanding of a world dominated by an East–West dichotomy The unity of what Palmer called a "World Revolution of the West" and Godechot an "Occidental Revolution" was assured by an "outside," albeit defined in a rather slippery fashion: at once the undemocratic "East" beyond the Iron Curtain, and a baggier "non-West" lagging two centuries behind.

Thus the revolutionary Atlantic took on a rather peculiar shape, stretching from Greece to Tennessee and Quito, but excising Morocco, Angola, and the Caribbean. In his seminal *Black Atlantic* (1993), Paul Gilroy challenged the occlusion of Africans from this history, and restored the "middle passages" of exchange and communication, which carried millions of Africans across Atlantic routes into the Americas, and connected West Africa into the American and the French revolutions. Gilroy did not simply argue for the reinsertion of African experience into the Atlantic interpretation of this period, but posited it instead as a distinctive "counterculture of modernity," thereby throwing into question the terms which had been used to constitute the Atlantic as a political space for the emergence of a unitary modernity. The inclusion of the "slave revolts" and the revolutionary struggles on the island of Saint-Domingue – which would ultimately result in the independence of a new state, Haiti – transformed the terms in which the Atlantic could be understood, not as an oceanic democratic unity, but as a complex space of contradictory and sometimes violent currents. These questions have very gradually been brought back to the metropole, and to the French Revolution itself, as the economic, cultural, and political implications of slavery, contestation, and abolition have gradually been recognized as fundamental to events in Europe. It is with considerably greater difficulty, however, that the African societies from which these slaves were taken have been able to enter into this scheme. The very conception of a history turned toward the Atlantic, and not to the Sahara or the great rivers flowing from the interior, closes them out of the story.

"Can we not try," Palmer and Godechot wrote in 1955, "to describe 'the Atlantic of history' just as Braudel set out to define 'the Mediterranean of history'?" But their "Atlantic" was not composed of the same long and patient historical rhythms, climatic and environmental constants, and gradual evolutions, it was instead constituted out of a rapid and accelerating destiny, out of the collapsing of distances and the erasure of physical barriers. What they set out to describe was really the "Atlanticization of history" and not the Atlantic itself. In this sense it was fundamentally opposed to Braudel's project. In a sense, returning to the Mediterranean is "de-Atlanticizing" this history, unpicking the hastily cobbled together "West" which no longer serves our global historical understanding. Yet in another way it involves "Atlanticizing" the Mediterranean, by restoring the complexity of events and historical transactions, the change and acceleration occurring in this region, which should no longer be considered a backwater or a barrier to the main action of revolution.

The Mediterranean of the early eighteenth century was still a series of shores along which multiethnic empires coexisted in spite of conflicts over piracy. A century later it would be an open arena of the struggle for imperial supremacy between France and Britain, a series of hot and cold wars that would be perpetuated by new belligerents into the twentieth century. For a brief period in the "revolutionary moment" of the late eighteenth century, new possibilities emerged that we can perhaps better comprehend today as another revolutionary movement sweeps those same shores. We can do little more here than sketch a few initial lines of that revolutionary simultaneity as they have emerged in the study of the French Revolution.

The Mediterranean and Revolutionary Universalism

On the evening of the 19 June 1790 a revolutionary journalist, Jean-Baptiste Cloots, led a deputation of thirty-six foreigners to the bar of the National Assembly. They presented a petition requesting permission to participate in the "Festival of the Federation," the forthcoming anniversary celebration of the fall of the Bastille. Although born in the Prussian town of Kleve to a noble family of Dutch extraction, Cloots would later be accorded full French citizenship, and even elected as deputy of the Oise, in part on the strength of the notoriety he gained on this day. According to the official account in the *procès verbal*, the deputation was composed of "Arabs, Chaldeans, Prussians, Poles, English, Swiss, Germans, Dutchmen, Swedes, Italians, Spaniards, Americans, Syrians, Indians, Brabançons, Liégois, Avignonnais, Genevans, Grisans." These people might appear to present eyes like a motley collection of rootless cosmopolitans, but they represented in quite calculated ways the coming vectors of revolutionary universalism. France's allies – Swedes and Poles – stood alongside the "Americans," men of color from France's Caribbean colonies; those from the new revolutionary republics in Liège and Brabant, and the insurgent Dutch; sympathetic English and Russians (but notably not Austrians); the Prussians and Swiss from France's borders, and even from its internal exclave of Papal Avignon, which would be annexed in 1792. Alongside the numerous representatives of the European Mediterranean – the Italian peninsula, Sicily, Spain – stood a small deputation from its further shores, from Turkey, Syria, Tunis, and Tripoli, their oriental clothing attracting more attention than any other aspect of the embassy.

Two of the "oriental" members of this deputation are well known through other sources – Dom Chawich, a Syrian orientalist who worked at the Bibliothèque

Royale, and Joseph Chammas, a merchant from Diyarbakir who had been living in Paris for many years (Cloots later described him as a "member of the oppressed sovereign of Mesopotamia"). Two other (less legible) signatures on the document indicate a "Manakmety de Tounisse" and "Si Hamed de Tripolie." There are no further details on the provenance of these individuals, but it is quite possible that the latter was the same Mohamed Dyghis who wrote of his deep connection to the Revolution in 1795. Dyghis, as we have noted, was from Tripoli, which maintained very close political and economic contacts with Tunis. That he should not mention the connection with Cloots in his later communication would seem surprising, although Cloots would later attract accusations of extremism that would lead him to the guillotine, so it would perhaps have been unwise for anyone to draw heavily on that association.

The response of the National Assembly was rapturous: the figures in turbans and Ottoman robes in particular dramatized the sense that the Revolution was a universal human achievement with the potential to bring world conflict to an end. The idea of the nation has most often been presented as the great winner of the French Revolution, but what this moment demonstrates is the complexity of that idea, and its distance from what we may later identify as "nationalism." Dubbing himself the "Orator of the Human Race," Cloots spoke not of the nation, but rather of the "oppressed sovereign" – an idea ready to be expanded to include other fraternal peoples under the French aegis: but in doing so it offered to modify the very meaning of "French," a position he would later articulate more fully. Cloots had begun his career with two major works – the *Wishes of a Gallophile* (1786), which articulated his powerful sense of belonging to French culture, and his *Certitudes and Proofs of Mahometism* (1780), a work attacking Christianity through the masquerade of Islam, but which contained a long and detailed series of notes developing a serious study of the Muslim world. In the same way, his deputation combined elements of reality and elements of theater in a manner quite typical of revolutionary events.

When Cloots had concluded his speech, Chawich, an Arab resident of Paris, addressed the Assembly – partly in French and partly in Arabic, according to the *Mercure de France* – to "express the sentiments of respect and admiration inspired in him by a Constitution destined to ensure the happiness of the Universe." His words were not recorded because his speech was largely unintelligible to those transcribing the session. But this linguistic difficulty seemed only to increase the enthusiasm of the participants, heightening the significance of this moment in which the Revolution seemed destined to unite the world, a United Nations in the making. The president of the session (the baron de Menou, who would notably convert to Islam in Egypt) replied that where Arabia had once given Europe lessons in philosophy, now France "wanting to repay Europe's debt, gives you lessons in liberty, and exhorts you to make them flourish in your own *patrie*" (*AP* 1795).

The emotion provoked by these "generous foreigners" led Alexandre de Lameth to propose the immediate removal, from monuments celebrating the victories of Louis XIV, of the ignominious depictions of the "tributary peoples" of the French provinces at the feet of the king. A moment after this motion was passed, another deputy, declaring "this day is the tomb of vanity," proposed the abolition of all noble titles. Against the furious opposition of the right, the proponents of the motion insisted that since one did not speak of "Marquis Franklin, Count Washington or Baron Fox," nor should it be necessary to carry any other title but the name of a citizen. The motion was passed, and aristocratic titles were rendered null in France until they were re-established by Napoleon in 1808. If the abolitions of 4 August 1789 were taken in the shadow of rural revolts, it is significant that this fundamental shift in French social structure should take place in such a global setting.

Some historians have used unsubstantiated rumors of charlatanry to make this moment emblematic of the "cheap and meretricious" radical pretensions of the Revolution, making a useful contrast to its more acceptable liberal ambitions (Doyle 2007: 290). In mocking or anathematizing Cloots, they have tended to misunderstand the universal aspirations of revolutionaries, shared across Europe and beyond through this period. As Adolphe Thiers wrote later, "these scenes, which appear ridiculous to those who were not there, profoundly moved those who witnessed them" (Thiers 1839: 235). Robert Darnton (1990) has written of the emotional power of revolutionary fraternity, a sentiment which may be understood in a more global context, reflecting the passionate avowals of Mohamed Dyghis with which we began. Italian historians have more easily recognized the radical implications of the deputation, which had its echoes in the universalizing conceptions of Italian revolutionaries such as Matteo Galdi and Filippo Buonarotti, as Anna Maria Rao has shown (2006). Italian revolutionaries looked across the Mediterranean in both directions, seeing a much larger vision of the French Revolution. But this "intellectual" apprehension of the revolutionary possibilities of the Mediterranean must be seen alongside another revolutionary movement "from below," whose traces are more difficult to recover.

The Many-Headed Hydra in the Mediterranean

In September 1792, the sister of the British consul in Tripoli, Miss Tully, wrote of witnessing "the effects of the Revolution in France" on the further shores of the Mediterranean:

> On the fourteenth of last July the crews of several French vessels came on shore to celebrate the anniversary of the destruction of the Bastille and of the general oath of allegiance taken in the Champ de Mars. They sung the horrid song of *ça ira* and danced the festive dance on the sea side but on discovering their intentions of planting the tree of liberty on shore the consuls applied in time to the Bashaw and easily persuaded him to prevent this from taking place. (Tully 1817: 300)

This was no isolated occurrence: Miss Tully's letters describe repeated revolutionary incidents – affrays between sailors of various nations, and contestation of the power of the local French consul and even of the Ottoman authorities. In April 1793 she wrote of the arrival of a new republican consul, which produced great unease among many in the town, fearing that the former consul and his family were in danger of their lives. In the event "a long speech was composed partly by the French and partly by the rest of the consuls here and was delivered with such success to the mob at the French house as to arrest and turn their intentions and after a short time a loud cry of *Vive la Nation*, *Vive la République*, and *Vivent les Citoyens*" (Tully 1817: 323). Atlantic historians have written of "the many-headed hydra" of revolution from below, made mobile by the ocean, set adrift by mutiny and pirate organizations, and mixing their own motley crews among maroon slaves and free people of color, dispossessed veterans, and outcasts, and "turbulent people of all Nations" as the governor of Jamaica put it (Linebaugh and Rediker 2000: 242). But, as Miss Tully shows, the revolutionary practice of these sailors, however shocking it was to her English sensibilities, was highly politically organized, focused in its use of language and symbols, and quite effectively channeled by the introduction of revolutionary institutions of justice and amnesty.

Such scenes were repeated across North Africa and through the Levant. Revolutionary festivals were celebrated in cities from Algiers to Baghdad. In Istanbul, the capital of the vast Ottoman Empire, Antoine Fonton, provisional first deputy of the French nation, wrote to the minister of foreign affairs on the day of the king's execution in January 1793:

> The tree of liberty was planted there in the middle of a large terrace overlooked by many houses of the Frankish suburb, by the palace of the Sultan's pages, by a number of Turkish houses and by a very busy street. There was an enormous crowd of spectators who squeezed into all the windows and the surrounding streets, and the tree was put up to the sound of a band of musicians, repeated cheers of Long Live Liberty, Equality and the Republic, and the thunder of a twenty-one-gun salute fired by the cannons of a French ship moored in the port for this purpose. ... we toasted the health of all our heroes, all the true Patriots, all the friends of Liberty, and the Turks who are the first nation to have allowed the French to make a public homage to ... their Revolution. (Fonton 1793)

In Cairo, the French residents formed their own National Guard, began training in the square, and requested permission from the authorities to build a Temple of Reason (Charles-Roux 1910: 246). Jacobin clubs were established in Smyrna, Aleppo, and Istanbul, and became a hot issue for discussion in the National Assembly and the newspapers at the height of the emergency in 1794. A famous cartoon by Gillray shows Horatio Nelson knee-deep in the Mediterranean, beating tricolored crocodiles with a club labeled "English Oak" as they vomit thousands of tiny red white and blue offspring into the vast watery expanse.

Human mobility is a key vector that must be developed in thinking the revolutionary Mediterranean. During the eighteenth century, accelerations in sail-driven transport made the seas into a battleground and a great global highway, a gap that continued to widen until the emergence of rail in the middle of the nineteenth century. Commerce was one crucial vector of such movement: where British trade interests expanded through the Atlantic to Asia via the Cape route, France intensified its commerce in the Mediterranean, not through the charter of trading companies, but through communities of "Franks" in what were known as the *Échelles du Levant et de Barbarie* (Coller 2010). These people formed a corporative component of Muslim society, governed through a complex set of agreements between the Ottoman Porte and European sovereigns (Van den Boogert 2005). Throughout the eighteenth century, the French state tightened its controls over these extraterritorial subjects, undermining their customary liberties, and usurping the role of Marseille as the "capital" of these extraterritorial entities (Masson 1911). These residents of Ottoman cities were closely aligned to the revolutionary events in France.

Most historians dealing with the revolutionary experience of these people have considered them as temporary consular residents, and have thus concluded that the events in France necessitated only a minor "adaptation to new institutional norms" (Faivre d'Arcier 2007: 2). But in a more detailed study of the interface between consuls and Muslim authorities in Tunis, Christian Windler (2002) concluded that the Revolution brought about a serious rupture in the diplomatic structure of relations between French and Muslim authorities. Far from continuing "business as usual," the new French regime rejected the diplomatic conventions inherited from its predecessor. Instead, it insisted upon the introduction of a series of new symbols representing the "system of liberty" and national sovereignty. A striking instance can be seen in the sudden shift to the familiar *tu* in official correspondence written to the Dey of Algiers in 1794 (Plantet 1889: 438). In this sense, North African rulers and their ministers were directly affected by key shifts in revolutionary culture. In response, they sought to gather information and explanation of these changes, rather than responding in arbitrary and hostile ways (Chenntouf 1989). Similarly, the large and more unwieldy imperial bureaucracy in Istanbul began to recognize the insufficiency of its networks of casual informants to provide accurate information on the social, diplomatic, and military changes occurring in Europe, and dispatched a series of envoys to Paris, Vienna, and London, to be followed by the first permanent Ottoman ambassador to France in 1797.

But the "Échelles" were more than simply consular posts – they were communities that included French subjects, other European "Franks," local Christians, and Jews who acted as agents and intermediaries, either independently or under the aegis of a *berat* or certificate of protection. Muslim subjects of the sultan could equally act as intermediaries, protectors, or hired janissary guards. Moreover, the official lists of the Échelles were notoriously inaccurate, and included only those Europeans who had official residence, and not those passing through unofficially for shorter sojourns. The authorities in France insisted that all those departing Marseille for the Échelles apply for a certificate, but they had no control over other forms of passage overland, through Italy or other parts of the Mediterranean: the "labor migrants, cunning entrepreneurs, travelers, shipwrecked sailors, missionaries, women in distress and a whole host of others" described recently by Julia Clancy Smith (2010: 7), and the considerable population of enslaved Europeans across North Africa, who provided motivations for revolutionary intervention (Weiss 2011).

As the events of the Revolution unfolded in France, they were translated very rapidly into these French communities, which were already organized in the form of a "nation" with its own assembly, albeit under the control of the consular authorities. The patriotic conception of nationhood was rapidly taken up by these communities, and they sought to mark their allegiance to and participation in the Revolution through the swearing of oaths, the raising of patriotic donations, and the institution of revolutionary dress, particularly the revolutionary cockade. But, as Miss Tully noted to her alarm, the sailors whose activity ensured the relationship between these communities and the metropole represented a key vector of radicalization. In Istanbul and Aleppo, as in Tripoli, the arrival of large numbers of sailors carrying news and ideas from France had an immediately polarizing effect. But it is also clear that these sailors sought to engage in revolutionary activity within the Échelles themselves, whether in confrontations with the sailors of hostile powers, by participating in the local struggles for power between factions, or in open rebellion against their captains. In this sense, the ports of the Levant and North Africa could also become radicalizing spaces, sending "sans-culotterie" back to France.

In 1795, the representative-on-mission to the army of the Mediterranean, Le Tourneur, told sailors that their *jour de gloire* had arrived:

> Let us set out bravely on the seas to punish the tyrants. The genius of Liberty will swell your sails, and guide you in the field of honor. What a great and sublime spectacle you will offer to the universe! Brave sailors, it is you who are called upon to seal the triumph of the Republic by punishing our proud enemies for their reckless audacity. It is you who can cauterize the wounds they have inflicted on the *patrie*. They strangle the channels of our maritime traffic. They deprive us of the riches of Africa and the Levant. They spread terror and corruption everywhere. Brave sailors, it is time to repair so many evils. Weigh anchor, unfurl the banner of freedom, and let us avenge with confidence the outrages they have dared to perpetrate against it. (Rouvier 1868: 549)

This winged "genius of Liberty" appears in many of the revolutionary documents and images of the new "sister republics" in Italy, created for French officials by Italian artists helping to visualize and shape the local meanings of the Revolution in which they were participating. One of them, designed for General Mathieu in Rome, shows that winged spirit, carrying both torch and spear, straddling the Mediterranean from Paris to Africa, Arabia, Persia, Bengal, and onward to China and Asia (Boppe 1911: 91). His foot hovers over the first step, the city of Cairo in Egypt. For a brief moment, in the closing years of the eighteenth century, this revolutionary Mediterranean seemed very near at hand.

Conflict and Conjuncture in the Mediterranean

> Egypt is so well known by the Infidels of the West that each wants to have it and it will be the object of their eternal discord. (Murad Bey, quoted by the Egyptian Legation, in Haddad 1970: 180)

In October 1801 a large number of Egyptians and Syrians boarded British ships to travel to France, neatly paralleling the journey that had brought the French army to Egypt a little over three years earlier. On board one of the English frigates, the *Pallas*, a small group designating themselves the "Egyptian Legation" entered into a series of discussions with the captain, Joseph Edmonds, to be communicated confidentially to the British admiralty. At the same time, they were in communication with the authorities in France, with the aim of appearing at the projected peace conference in Paris. Rather like the Paris Peace Conference of 1919, this projected meeting seemed to offer possibilities for a "new world order" that would meet the expectations of groups hoping for national independence from imperial sovereignty, which the legation believed was the best hope for stabilizing Egypt and restoring their society to prosperity. In their arguments they drew upon their own indigenous leaders such as Murad Bey, rather than the conventional European Enlightenment thinkers. Murad was one of the Mamluk leaders whose "despotic" rule the French had ostensibly come to punish. But the legation, composed of Muslims, Copts, Syrian Catholics, and Franks, cited his insight into the danger that Egypt posed, in its critical strategic position between Europe, Asia, and Africa, for the provocation of European struggles over global supremacy. Murad was proven correct in 1840, 1880, and 1956, as France and Britain found themselves drawn into damaging conflicts in which Egypt played a crucial role: and Egyptians themselves found their society riven by these superpower rivalries.

This ill-fated French involvement in Egypt has been framed in many ways: most often as an exotic adventure dictated by Bonaparte's personal lust for glory, but also as an attempt by the Directory to rid itself of this troublesome general, or as an attempt to block British commerce with India by seizing the overland route and making contact with Indian rebels. There are valid aspects to each of these explanations, but they all fail equally in disconnecting this episode from the larger history and dynamics of the Revolution, and from the history of Egypt itself. No other episode, from the landing in Ireland to the exile of Jacobins to Guyana, has been quite so exoticized as the "Egyptian expedition," and this distorting lens has limited our perspective on the revolutionary Mediterranean as a whole. I have argued elsewhere that the decision to take the Republic into Egypt must be understood in the light of the evolving politics of the *Républiques sœurs* in Europe, and most particularly in Italy, and the annexation of the Ionian islands. It is here, Henry Laurens has argued, that revolutionary politics made a significant shift away from republican expansion, or the constitution of a defensive ring of allied regimes, and toward the politics of the "Grande Nation" – association with or administration by France under the aegis of revolutionary values (Laurens 1988). He shows that a faction of local Muslims and Christians in the Aegean rapidly sought to co-opt the influence of revolutionary France against Ottoman power.

The much-debated "origins of the Egyptian expedition" must be sought both in the Revolution itself and in the indigenous conditions of Egypt. A combination of global geopolitical factors, metropolitan politics, and local attraction was involved in the final decision to dispatch the bulk of French forces, under its most talented general, across the Mediterranean. That decision would lead to the loss of the French fleet and the turning point of the European coalition against France. The retaking of Toulon had marked the beginning of the outward expansion of the Revolution (Groc 1997). The siege of Acre would mark its endpoint. It was in Acre that Bonaparte, hearing rumors of the weakening regime at home, made the decision to return to Paris by night, sneaking out of Alexandria past the cordon of British ships.

Egypt's relationship to the ending of the Revolution may appear to be purely aleatory, but it raises a series of important questions about the convergence and interaction of global trajectories during this period. The French failure in Egypt made possible the crushing of Tippoo Sultan's resistance against British imperialism.

It also restored the Ottoman Empire to its important position in the European balance of power, thereby helping to sustain the broad program of reform launched by Selim III. Most historians would now reject the proposition that 1798 was some kind of watershed in the Middle East, the putative "discovery" of a previously undreamt-of modernity. The rejection of such Eurocentric presumptions should not lead us to neglect the importance of this event, either for France or for Egypt. Despite the important contributions of recent scholars (Armitage and Subrahmanyam 2010) our tools for dealing with the incommensurability of these different historical paths remain relatively rudimentary.

Christopher Bayly has emphasized the need to begin thinking about multiple paths of revolutionary impact and counter-impact "in the context of much wider and longer-term transformations in the inland polities of the Middle East and Asia which also reflect revolutionary ideological and political changes in the broadest sense" (Bayly 2010: 23). While not suggesting that all insurrections during the eighteenth century should be considered on the same plane, Bayly insists on the importance of confronting "conjunctural revolutions" – and in particular the great millenarian revolutions of the eighteenth century, such as Wahhabism in Arabia, whose impact on the contemporary world have been so great. However, we must take care, in widening this lens, to preserve some sense of what was "revolutionary" about these transformations.

Karen Barkey has argued that insurrectionary events in the eighteenth century Ottoman Empire demonstrate the emergence of "new forms of dissent" and their role in reshaping state–society relations: their result was "a forceful broadening of the base of political power in the empire… a process of politicization that ratcheted up significantly the stakes in politics, spread to the provinces, ignited rebellions, and transformed the nature of factions and alliances in faraway regions of the empire" (Barkey 2008: 200). This was certainly the case in Egypt during the late eighteenth century. The conditions there cannot be said to be "revolutionary" in the sense of the events occurring in America and Europe, yet their impact would eventually draw France into the further reaches of the Mediterranean. In particular, the long-established French population of the Échelles of Cairo and Alexandria, which we noted earlier, played a key role in invoking the republican aegis for protection in 1798, like the "patriots" of other nations (Charles-Roux 1910). One result of the French occupation, along with violence and resistance, was the emergence of a nascent party of independence, organized in a national way, across the different religious and regional lines of traditional Egyptian society (Coller 2011).

The internal conflicts in Egypt may seem impenetrable to European historians, and incommensurable with the events occurring in Europe. But they would have a powerful effect on the course of the Revolution, helping to drag it onto the world stage, and eventually to demonstrate the failure of those universal ambitions. Egypt was the point at which the apparent weakening of central authority in the Ottoman imperium intersected with the resistance to strengthening British territorial control in India. Other intersections can be traced across the Muslim world, from the withdrawal of Spain out of North Africa to the shifts taking place in the Safavid Empire in Iran, and these conjunctions too played an important role both in the conditions of revolution in Europe and in the nature of Muslim responses. A much wider range of actors was involved in the revolutionary Mediterranean than we have previously imagined, and the nature and extent of that participation remains a rich and largely unexplored terrain. But elucidating these rich possibilities does not mean reducing the French Revolution to the tectonic shifts of a "world system" or splintering its significance in a kaleidoscope of fragmentary rebellions and resistances. Seen from the Mediterranean, the Revolution remains an exceptional and extraordinary transformation. Indeed, this "French exception" was all the more revolutionary for being less "French."

Conclusion: The Mediterranean Revolution

The Mediterranean is a sea without boundaries, a complex of seas, a collection of shorelines and physical features, a carrier of goods, people, and ideas, a zone extending deep into three continents. But above all, the Mediterranean is an *idea*, a way of seeing that pushes us to think globally, in the Atlantic, in the Indian Ocean, in the Pacific, each of which has been considered as a Mediterranean in its own right, or as containing other smaller Mediterraneans, from Melanesia to the Malay archipelago or the Caribbean. In thinking of the French Revolution as a Mediterranean revolution, we do not seek to close off its internal complexities, its European networks, its Atlantic or Pacific connections, but rather to open it onto all of these. The Mediterranean is a chameleon of human inventiveness, both in the spreading aspirations for liberty and equality and in the ambitions for power and domination. From the Mediterranean perspective, the French Revolution was not only a reorganization of French society but a fundamental transformation in the way human relationships were understood at a local, national, and international level. But more than this, it was the product of a vast range of actors, both conscious and unconscious of their role, who, in large or small ways, shaped this great human experience. In another "revolutionary moment" across the Mediterranean, when the impossible again seems possible, when people across the world watch with elation and anxiety the progress of other struggles for freedom, a new history of the revolutionary Mediterranean seems all the more pertinent.

References

AP: Archives parlementaires (1795). *Archives parlementaires de 1787 à 1860: Recueil complet des débats législatifs et politiques des chambres françaises. Première série, 1787–1799*, vol. 16: *Assemblée nationale constituante, 31 May 1790 – 8 July 1790*, 82 vols. Paris: P. Dupont.

Armitage, David and Sanjay Subrahmanyam (eds.) (2010). *The Age of Revolutions in Global Context, c.1760–1840*. London: Palgrave Macmillan

Barkey, Karen (2008). *Empire of Difference: The Ottomans in Comparative Perspective*. Cambridge: Cambridge University Press.

Bayly, Christopher A. (2010). "The 'Revolutionary Age' in the Wider World, c.1790–1830." In Richard Bessel, Nicholas Guyatt, and Jane Rendall (eds.). *War, Empire and Slavery, 1770–1830*. London: Palgrave Macmillan. 43–60.

Boppe, Auguste (1911). *Les Vignettes emblématiques sous la Révolution*. Paris: Berger-Levrault.

Braudel, Fernand (1972). *The Mediterranean and the Mediterranean World in the Age of Philip II*, trans. Siân Reynolds. London: Collins.

Charles-Roux, François (1910). *Les Origines de l'Expédition d'Egypte*. Paris: Plon-Nourrit.

Chenntouf, Taïeb (1989). "La Révolution française: L'Événement vu d'Algérie." In H. Khadhar (ed.). *La Révolution française et le monde arabo-musulman*. Tunis: Éditions de la Méditerranée. 61–63.

Clancy Smith, Julia (2010). *Mediterraneans: North Africa and Europe in an Age of Migration, c.1800–1900*. Berkeley: University of California Press.

Coller, Ian (2010). "East of Enlightenment: Regulating Cosmopolitanism between Istanbul and Paris in the Eighteenth Century." *Journal of World History*, 21: 447–470.

Coller, Ian (2011). *Arab France: Islam and the Making of Modern Europe 1798–1831*. Berkeley: University of California Press.

Dakhlia, Jocelyne (2008). *Lingua Franca: Histoire d'une langue métisse en méditerranée*. Arles: Actes Sud.

Darnton, Robert (1990). *The Kiss of Lamourette: Reflections in Cultural History* London: Norton.

Doyle, William (2007). "The French Revolution and the Abolition of Nobility." In B. Simms (ed.). *Cultures of Power in Europe during the Long Eighteenth Century*. Cambridge: Cambridge University Press. 289–303.

Faivre d'Arcier, Amaury (2007). *Les Oubliés de la liberté: Négociants, consuls et missionnaires français au Levant pendant la Révolution, 1784–1798*. Brussels: Peter Lang.

Fonton, Antoine (1793). "Letter to Minister Le Brun." *Archives du Ministère des Affaires Étrangères*, Paris: CP Turquie. 184.

Gilroy, Paul (1993). *The Black Atlantic: Modernity and Double Consciousness*. Cambridge, Mass.: Harvard University Press.

Godechot, Jacques (1956). *La Grande Nation: L'Expansion révolutionnaire de la France dans le monde de 1789 à 1799*. Paris: Aubier Montaigne.

Godechot, Jacques and R.R. Palmer (1955). "Le Problème de l'Atlantique du XVIIIe au XXe siècle." *Relazioni del Congresso Internazionale di Scienze Storiche*, 5: 175–239.

Greene, Molly (2002). *A Shared World: Christians and Muslims in the Early Modern Mediterranean*. Princeton, N.J.: Princeton University Press.

Groc, Gérard (1997). "La Mediterranée, une ouverture diplomatique de la Révolution française en orient." In C. Villain-Gandossi et al. (eds.). *Méditerranée: Mer ouverte*. Malta: International Foundation. 123–130.

Haddad, George (1970). "A Project for the Independence of Egypt, 1801." *Journal of the American Oriental Society*, 90: 169–183.

Hodgson, Marshall (1974). *The Venture of Islam*, vol. 3: *The Gunpowder Empires and Modern Times*. Chicago: University of Chicago Press.

Husain, Adnan and K.E. Fleming (2007). *A Faithful Sea: The Religious Cultures of the Mediterranean, 1200–1700*. London: Oneworld.

Laurens, Henry (1988). "Bonaparte, l'Orient et la 'Grande Nation'." *AHRF*, 273: 289–301.

Lefebvre, Georges (1962). *The French Revolution from its Origins to 1793*. New York: Columbia University Press.

Linebaugh, Peter and Marcus Rediker (2000). *The Many-Headed Hydra: The Hidden History of the Revolutionary Atlantic*. London: Verso.

Masson, Paul (1903). *Histoire des établissements et du commerce français dans l'Afrique barbaresque (1560–1793). (Algérie, Tunisie, Tripolitaine, Maroc)*. Paris: Hachette.

Masson, Paul (1911). *Histoire du commerce français dans le Levant au XVIIIe siècle*. Paris: Hachette.

Moniteur (1795). *Réimpression de l'ancien Moniteur, seule histoire authentique et inaltérée de la Révolution française depuis la réunion des États-généraux jusqu'au Consulat*, vol. 24.

Palmer, R.R. (1954). "The World Revolution of the West: 1763–1801." *Political Science Quarterly*, 69: 1–14.

Palmer, R.R. (1959–64). *The Age of the Democratic Revolution*, 2 vols. Princeton, N.J.: Princeton University Press.

Panzac, Daniel (2005). *Barbary Corsairs: The End of a Legend, 1800–1820*. Leiden: Brill.

Plantet, Eugène (1889). *Correspondance des Deys d'Alger avec la Cour de France (1571–1830)*, 2 vols. Paris: Félix Alcan.

Rao, Anna Maria (2006). "L'Espace méditerranéen dans la pensée et les projets politiques des patriotes italiens: Matteo Galdi et la 'république du genre humain'." In Marcel Dorigny and R. Tlili Sellaouati (eds.). *Droit des gens et relations entre les peuples dans l'espace méditerranéen de la Révolution française*. Paris: SÉR. 115–137.

Rouvier, Charles (1868). *Histoire des marins français sous la République, de 1789 à 1803*. Paris: Arthus Bertrand.

Thiers, Adolphe (1839). *Histoire de la Révolution française*, 10 vols. Paris: Furne.

Tully, Miss (1817). *Narrative of a Ten Years' Residence at Tripoli in Africa*. London: Henry Colburn.

Van den Boogert, Maurits (2005). *The Capitulations and the Ottoman Legal System: Qadis, Consuls, and Beraths in the 18th Century*. Leiden: Brill.

Verlinden, Charles (1953). "Les Origines coloniales de la civilisation Atlantique: Antécédents et types de structure." *Cahiers d'histoire mondiale / Journal of World History*, 1: 378–398.

Weiss, Gillian (2011). *Captives and Corsairs: France and Slavery in the Early Modern Mediterranean*. Stanford, Calif.: Stanford University Press.

Windler, Christian (2002). *La Diplomatie comme expérience de l'autre: Consuls français au Maghreb (1700–1840)*. Geneva: Droz.

Part IX

Change and Continuity in France

Chapter Twenty-Six

A Revolution in Political Culture

Isser Woloch

From its inception, the political culture of the French Revolution revolved around a triad of essentially new participatory institutions. The monarchy had introduced the first and most fundamental one, entirely new at least in living memory, when in January 1789 it called for elections to an Estates-General. In the wake of that unprecedented national mobilization inaugurated from above, two complementary modes of participation quickly arose from below: political newspapers and political clubs.

One could trace the history of revolutionary elections, of political newspapers, or of the clubs (as has been done in each case more than once) to capture a sense of the Revolution's arc, of what propelled it, fragmented it, and finally brought it to grief. But an overview of revolutionary political culture should not be an exercise in political science or cultural analysis; its social foundations and consequences should always be kept in view. Not to put too fine a point on it: can one discuss revolutionary political culture without exploring the term *sans-culotte*? We should also ask: a new political culture compared to what? To the political culture of the *ancien régime*, such as it was? To contemporaneous political cultures, as of the American revolutionary era, or the early American republic, or Britain during the reign of George III? To the political culture of Napoleonic or Restoration France?

Such comparisons will from time to time to help to illuminate particular points, starting with some observations about *ancien régime* political culture, where the rival factions at the court of Louis XV and XVI, and the abrupt changes of policy that could result from their comings and goings were the most obvious feature. Similarly, the low-intensity warfare between the Crown and the *parlements* (the thirteen regional high courts of France) periodically erupted into high-stakes conflict about the very "constitution" of the realm (unwritten, to be sure, but fundamental). Such disputes usually arose over fiscal policy, conflicts within the

A Companion to the French Revolution, First Edition. Edited by Peter McPhee.

body of the Catholic Church, police powers, or ministerial power grabs, and they aroused passionate interest among the public. In that sense, revolutionary political culture did not arise overnight. Its electoral, associational, and media structures had precursors of one sort or another in the *ancien régime* (see Baker 1987a: a path-breaking collection of essays). Of all such roots in the *ancien régime*, the rise of "public opinion" must head the list, if only for the dramatic turns it took in 1789 and after.

Public Opinion and Popular Opinion

In eighteenth-century western Europe, "public opinion" came to be recognized as a potentially powerful force as against the traditional or arbitrary exercise of established authority in various spheres. It was a force to be cultivated (or manipulated) and ultimately might stand as an arbiter of legitimacy. In parsing the term and making such claims, most writers distinguished between "public opinion" (taken as informed, reasoned, reliable) and mere "popular opinion" (uninformed, emotional, volatile). The contrast between public opinion and popular opinion in eighteenth-century thought comes across obliquely in Kant's *What is Enlightenment?* (1784), but more directly in writings by D'Alembert and Condorcet among others. Condorcet, for example, wrote in 1776: "When one speaks of opinion, three types must be distinguished: the opinion of enlightened people, which precedes public opinion and ends up by dictating to it; the type of opinion that is shaped by authority; and finally popular opinion, the domain of that segment of the people who are the stupidest and most impoverished." D'Alembert clearly distinguished between "the truly enlightened public" and "the blind and clamorous multitude" (Chartier 1991: ch 2; Ozouf 1987: 432–433n24).

This commonplace conceptual distinction reflected a fundamental social fault-line of that time: the chasm between people who worked with their hands for their living and those who did not. In central Europe the Prussian General Code, finally promulgated in 1791 but in gestation long before that, embodied it most strikingly. "The rights of a man arise from his birth, from his estate," it proclaimed, and went on to specify the extensive rights of nobles ("The nobleman has an especial right to places of honor in the state …") and the particular prerogatives of burghers (the urban middle class); peasants and workers were placed apart from these advantaged strata (Palmer 1959: 509–512). In England, a pervasive if informal social and cultural divide separated "the gentleman" of wealth, standing, or education (whether a peer or a commoner) from all others. And in France, notwithstanding numerous intra-elite rivalries and cleavages – between nobles new and old, nobles and non-noble elites, and within those two swathes of society – the basic divide between "gentlemen" and others was as manifest as the distinction drawn between public opinion and popular opinion.

The point is illustrated in a now famous document from 1768 entitled *État et déscription de la ville de Montpellier*, which sought "to give a true idea of that city." In effect the anonymous middle-class author provided three parallel descriptions, of which the third was by far the most meaningful to him: first an account of an official urban procession that evoked the formal corporate groups and hierarchies of the city; then an analysis of its nominal "estates" or broad social groups; and finally a description of the cultural markers that distinguished the most admirable kinds of citizens, in effect the gentlemen. The author's most evocative descriptor, which unifies the diverse components of this veritable elite, was "honnêtes hommes," whose taste in food, clothing, and the like, and whose urbanity, lifestyle, and dignified comportment distinguished them across the chasm in this society from what the writer here calls "the Third Estate," the artisans and laborers who worked with their hands (Darnton 1984: 107–140).

This prologue helps frame the emergence of a democratic political culture, which blurred or at least elided both of those classic eighteenth-century polarities: between gentlemen and the others, between public opinion and popular opinion. It could not of course negate or root them out altogether. (The nineteenth century would demonstrate their persistence even as qualified in France by durable legacies of the French Revolution such as legal civil equality and ostensible civic commitments to meritocracy and social mobility.) Indeed twice over – as they worked on their first constitution in 1790–91 and on their third in 1795 – the Revolution's legislators tried to circumscribe the democratic principle in various ways so that the commonweal could not be swamped by a volatile mass of citizens. But with all due qualification, revolutionary political culture in the 1790s was democratic. Contested from every direction, alternately expansive or restrictive, inclusive or violently exclusionary, but always in some meaningful sense democratic, at least relative to elite assumptions and behaviors of the Enlightenment era and to the decades after 1800.

Elections, Fulcrum of the New Political Culture

Based on "the sovereignty of the people" from its inception, revolutionary political culture was embryonically democratic, however unstable its parameters remained throughout the revolutionary decade. As the defining mechanism of the new regime, elections at all levels were intended to institute representative democracy and, as an implied corollary, to restrain tendencies toward direct democracy. To put it another way, elections were to be the fulcrum between popular sovereignty (the basic legitimating, if quasi-mythic, concept of French revolutionary ideology) and representation (the tangible means for giving voice to that sovereign people). An alternative if hazy notion of direct democracy (with a paternity of sorts in Rousseau's theoretical dismissal of representative government in *The Social Contract*) always lurked in the wings. But from the outset the National Assembly (taking its lead from the ideas of Sieyès) insisted that only its elected representatives could speak for the people, without constraint on their free deliberation by the imperative mandates or instructions that most deputies to the Estates-General had received from their electors, or by popular referenda on their legislation (Baker 1987b). Still, elections could be unpredictable, and in any case might not suffice to insulate new elected officials from outside pressures. Indeed the two other essential elements of the new political culture – the political press and the clubs – might easily invade the space of the new constituted authorities created by elections, and in the extreme challenge their very legitimacy.

The architects of the new political system in the National Assembly – perhaps drawing on distant and idealized memories of urban civic culture and rural parish assemblies – established an astonishingly wide array of elective offices. The list encompassed national legislators; departmental administrations; district administrations; mayors and municipal councils; judges at all levels (from the Tribunal de Cassation in the capital to the justice of the peace in every canton, with civil court judges in each district and criminal court judges and public prosecutors in each department); parish priests and diocesan bishops; and National Guard officers. In due course the list expanded to non-commissioned officers in the regular army and (at one moment in 1795) local primary school teachers.

Consensus on resort to elections at so many levels and in so many spheres was matched by sharp disagreement over certain modalities for this system. Agreement came easily on how elections should be organized. At the most local level – mayor and municipal council, justice of the peace – there would be direct election. But (drawing on the royal guidelines for the elections to the Estates-General) elections would be indirect for legislators and for most other administrators, judicial offices, and Catholic clergy. Thus "the elector" played a transitory but fundamental role as the intermediary in this political system where most elections were indirect. With a certain logic, indirect or two-tiered voting was conjoined with election of department-wide slates for both legislative and administrative posts rather than single-constituency voting. Here the French revolutionary system contrasted sharply with the American states and with England, which both featured direct elections by voters in single constituencies. The French thereby sacrificed the liveliness of elections in the Anglo-Saxon world, the demonstrations, venial bribery, and popular rituals of participation in "the theatre of the hustings," especially among citizens who were not themselves qualified to vote (Lawrence 2009: ch. 1).

The Declaration of the Rights of Man and of the Citizen promised representative government but did not enumerate voting as one of those natural rights. Prudently so, since the National Assembly intended to define voting as a civic function for qualified persons rather than an individual natural right. The Assembly, and successive revolutionary legislatures, wrestled over the formulae for qualifications to vote or to serve as an elector, and for eligibility for serving as a deputy. These proved to be among the most contentious of the franchise issues, more so than requirements of age (25 or 21) and residence (settled domicile of a year or six months). Religion, gender, race, and property qualifications aroused intense controversies, some settled quickly and by wide consensus, others dragging on with sharp alterations of course.

The National Assembly extended full civic and voting rights to Protestants, despite some initial objections from traditionalist Catholic clergy. But only in the Assembly's last hectic days in September 1791 did Jews in eastern France receive full civic rights despite a sustained clamor against their enfranchisement from some of their neighbors and legislators from that region. The Assembly excluded women from voting early on, but only after a debate that was itself utterly without precedent, and where Condorcet among others spoke on behalf of women's suffrage. Similarly after a brief but intense debate the Assembly excluded free men of color in the colonies from voting in favor of local autonomy on such issues, which was sure to bar them – all in the name of protecting black slavery, seen by most deputies as the foundation of France's lucrative colonial plantation economy. But the linked issues of racial exclusion and slavery would not disappear and the Assembly fine-tuned its exclusion several times, down to its last days in September 1791, by which time it was too late to matter much, since these issues would erupt on the ground in successive rebellions and uprisings (Hunt 1996).

For good reason the conflicts over religious, gender, and racial exclusions from the franchise and other civic rights now receive a great deal of attention. But at the time, property or tax qualifications for voting and for eligibility proved the most divisive question related to elections. In the American states (which set voting qualifications) and in the handful of historically democratic constituencies for elections to the House of Commons, voters were supposed to have a material stake of some sort in the disposition of political power, expressed in a certain level of property ownership or tax payment. The majority of the National Assembly accepted this as a given, and sought to distinguish the forthcoming reign of civil equality from its extension into political equality. Their initial move was ham-fisted in the extreme and would not stand the test of time, as the Assembly distinguished between "active" citizens with political rights and "passive" citizens (for example, unpropertied citizens and women) entitled to liberty and civil equality but not to vote.

Popular participation in the epochal *journée* of 14 July, which saved the National Assembly at the cost of martyrdom for some in the crowd, plausibly called that formulation into question right from the start: for who could be a more "active" and worthy citizen than one who had risked life and limb in the siege of the Bastille at the supreme moment of peril? Back and forth various revolutionary assemblies went on this issue of political equality and the right to vote. But except for the hiatus of 1792–93, the decision held that voting and serving as electors must be linked to property-holding or tax-paying, with the qualification for voting in primary assemblies being a significant but fairly low hurdle, and that for serving as an "elector" a more substantial and exclusionary one.

In the revolutionary political system, enfranchised citizens voted in assemblies rather than casting their ballots individually on a designated day. This pattern had been set in the voting procedures for the Estates-General and essentially held during all the variations of the revolutionary decade. Primary assemblies, which chose electors, and departmental electoral assemblies, which chose slates of legislators, departmental administrators, and judges, each could consume several days. This system required a substantial commitment of time, and two procedural requirements reinforced this. First, designation in either kind of assembly required a majority of votes on a first or second round of balloting, with a plurality sufficing only on a third and final round if necessary. Secondly, although voting occurred exclusively in these assemblies, each voter cast his ballot in each round of voting by depositing it individually in a voting urn in the course of a laborious roll call.

Such procedures ensured a high level of tedium whatever the stakes. True, one could come and go in these assemblies, voting on some ballots but not on others. In an electoral assembly, for example, an elector could stay to choose the department's legislators, but depart before the balloting for local offices. On the plus side, the French system entailed secret balloting, using an urn rather than the open poll-books of the Anglo-Saxon world. If a voter was illiterate or disabled, however, assistance from an officer chosen for that purpose earlier by the assembly would effectively nullify such secrecy. During the upheaval of 1792 and the election of a National Convention, when voting procedures were in flux, a vogue surfaced for open, voice voting in the electoral assemblies and as many as thirteen departments adopted that practice. But open voice voting did not become the norm for elections then or afterwards.[1]

Another and problematic feature of the electoral system derived from the National Assembly's beliefs that disinterested virtue and talent would somehow rise to the top in the voting assemblies; that individuals rather than groups constituted the proper molecules in this electoral chemistry; that groups manoeuvring to carry elections were at best unhealthy factions, and at worst corrupt and damnable cabals. Accordingly, the system allowed for no political parties, no open electoral campaigns, not even declared candidates. (Perhaps the British experience of parliamentary factions and corruption helped inoculate the French against party competition.) This insistence on an impossible transparency, this "refusal of politics" as critics have stigmatized it, prevailed for the entire revolutionary decade, with one brief exception in 1797. Lists of candidates were available for that election, but by using a separate "reduction and rejection ballot" voters could strike off names they opposed before going on to choose their designees – a perverse and cumbersome innovation that was dropped the next year (Woloch 1994: 99). In the end the prejudice against declared candidates, campaigning, and parties endured as a dysfunctional straitjacket for an ostensibly democratic political culture. We will consider this capital matter at the conclusion, by way of a comparison with the United States.

Newspapers and Clubs

The two other legs of France's democratic triad – the political press and the political clubs – contributed mightily to the formation of a new political culture and then to its fracturing. At the outset newspapers and clubs publicized and (in most cases) supported the National Assembly's work, allowing its bold claims against the Crown and the traditional social order to sink roots in the country.

Under its restrictive privileges and censorship procedures, the newspaper press of the *ancien régime* could not in itself be generative of revolutionary political culture. In Paris, only four sanctioned journals with royal privileges could freely circulate, only one of which (the *Gazette de France*) dealt with government policy, in effect a conduit for royal government by press release and official leaks. True, the privileged or official newspapers had competition from a few periodicals published over the border from France or in London; from well-informed *nouvelles à main* that circulated in manuscript among the well-connected and were perhaps comparable to the late Soviet-era *samizdat*; from an underground of illicit pamphleteers and *libellistes*, often hired guns for some point of view or individual; and from published but uncensored legal briefs that in the 1770s and 1780s offered dramatic tales of corruption in high places being pursued in law suits. When the floodgates of press freedom were thrown open in 1789, printers, typographers, booksellers, and aspiring writers from the pre-revolutionary worlds of licit and clandestine publishing were ready to ply their trade in new forms as well as old.

During the fierce confrontation between Crown and *parlements* in 1774 and during the bruising conflicts among Crown's ministers, the Assemblies of Notables, and the *parlements* in 1787–88, "public opinion" had been fed less by the newspapers (though the few journals from across the border had their say) than by floods of illicit pamphlets generated by the protagonists (Darnton 1995: ch.10; Gruder 2007: part II). The same thing happened, but this time lawfully, when the king in January 1789 called for an Estates-General to meet later that year and invited the public to offer its opinions about this momentous event. To accommodate the outpouring of responses in pamphlets it suspended the usual methods of censorship and policing for this occasion. Then, when the Estates-General convened, several individuals challenged existing restrictions on newspapers (royal privileges and censorship) by publishing newspapers to report on events regardless of the consequences. By the summer of 1789 all such restrictions had fallen by the wayside. The political press became a hotbed of entrepreneurial activity by writers, editors, and printers in a competitive marketplace thirsting for reliable information and insightful commentary. Daily and weekly news-sheets proliferated in the capital in various formats (from broadsheet to pamphlet size) and in styles ranging from sober to incendiary. Some were short-lived and quickly folded, but others established themselves, developing subscriber bases in Paris and the provinces and strategies for retaining them. In the provinces publishers converted their *affiches* or commercial advertisers (virtually the only lawful local periodicals under the monarchy) into local and even regional newspapers (Darnton and Roche 1989; Gough 1988; Popkin 1990: chs. 1–2).

This new, unshackled political press was essential in constituting the community of citizens. Until the creation of the *Bulletin des Lois* in 1793, the government had limited channels for publicizing its decrees and laws. The newspapers founded in 1789 and after circulated more widely and deeply than other forms of official information, propelled by the sheer novelty and high drama of the Revolution. Revolutionary ideology held that transparency (that is, publicity) was the necessary sentinel for liberty. At any point, however, a newspaper could turn into an instrument for pressure against the newly constituted authority rather than its prop. As the Revolution developed the press increasingly broadcast independent opinions, which could as easily be critical of the Assembly or the king as supportive of them. By the time several rounds of elections in 1790–91 installed new town governments, departmental administrations, judges, and (in September 1791) a new legislature, the clubs and the press had completely breached the insulation those institutions were supposed to enjoy, and increasingly presumed to mediate the relationship between the people and its elected *mandataires.*

Radical journalists on the left like Marat and royalist rejectionists on the right like Royou refused to exercise self-censorship. In tandem they eventually provoked a backlash against the exuberant press freedom of the Revolution's first months (Bertaud 1984; Censer 1976). Successive legislatures during the entire revolutionary decade tried but failed to reach a consensus on a press law that would strike a balance between liberty and license, between acceptable dissent and subversion.

Freedom of the press, the archetypal natural right of 1789, soon became a volatile public policy issue and a casualty to spasms of ad hoc repression in every phase of the Revolution, much as it did in Britain and in the early years of the United States as well (Popkin 1990: ch. 4; Walton 2009: part II).

Newspapers and pamphlets reached multiple readers when they were read aloud or passed from hand to hand. The new political clubs assured such wider dissemination for the revolutionary press. Among their many and evolving roles, clubs acted as amplifiers for the newspapers of their choice.

Just as the purveyors of print culture could recalibrate to the sudden press freedom of 1789, so too could the habits of *ancien régime* sociability find new outlets and forms in "the Year I of liberty." Associations formal and informal were hallmarks of *ancien régime* life: among the elites, with their Masonic lodges, academies, reading clubs, chambers of commerce, and correspondence circles; among artisans with their confraternities; and in the collective popular culture of recreation, religion, and neighborhood sociability. All this perhaps prepared the ground for the efflorescence of political clubs, but they arose and took form only in the specific circumstances of summer 1789 and after.

The first cohort of clubs in the larger towns was following the lead of the Society of the Friends of the Constitution in Paris (known as the Jacobin Society after the former convent in which it met), which had begun as a caucus of patriot deputies to the Estates-General/National Assembly but soon admitted selected non-deputy members as well. The clubs initially thought of themselves as groups promoting civic education and supporting the Assembly, but soon evolved into organizations for local and even national political action that could challenge constituted authorities if they strayed from sound principles. This evolution intensified as clubs began to affiliate with the Paris Jacobins or with each other. Their developing repertory of activities included the passing of circular letters from one club to another; surveillance and, if need be, denunciation of local authorities; and the submission of petitions to local and national governing bodies, all of which gained impulsion from the crisis of the king's flight in June 1791 (Tackett 2003: chs. 4–7). It is impossible to recapture the implications of putting a signature on a petition in those days, but that palpable act of commitment reflected an acculturation into a new world of politics that went beyond voting. Petitions are among the foremost surviving artifacts of the new political culture.

The moderate leadership of the Assembly looked askance on the expanding activism of the clubs, and in the Assembly's waning days its constitutional committee attempted to thwart it. The ensuing debate underscored the inherent tension between representative democracy and participatory activism from below. "Nothing must hinder the actions of the constituted authorities," said the rapporteur Le Chapelier:

> Deliberation and the power to act must be located where the constitution has placed them and nowhere else ... There are no authorities except those delegated by the People, and there can be no actions except those of its representatives who have been entrusted with public duties ... [Accordingly the constitution] henceforth recognizes only society as a whole, and individuals. A necessary consequence of this principle is the prohibition of any petition or poster issued in the name of a group.

Le Chapelier equated the new political clubs with the discredited privileged corporations of the *ancien régime*, arguing that in taking on a public life the clubs "foster divisions that every good citizen should seek to extinguish ... producing accusations against unaffiliated citizens ... They commit a grave crime when they seek to influence administrative or judicial acts." The new law (which proved unenforceable) sought to return the clubs to an exclusively educational role. It prohibited the affiliation of clubs, collective acts including petitions, or the reporting by newspapers of their deliberations. For otherwise, Le Chapelier concluded, "a few affiliated members would have a free hand to destroy public freedom" (Censer and Hunt 2001: 68–72).

The "Sans-Culottes"

As clubs proliferated beyond the large towns, and spread geographically across much of the country, they evolved politically and organizationally but also in social composition. As the Revolution became more embattled, moderates tended to drop out; the clubs' politics narrowed and hardened, but they became more inclusive socially. The popular societies, as they were known by 1793, effectively bridged the chasm between the gentlemanly elites who dominated the earliest clubs and men who worked in some fashion with their hands. In 1793–94, in the radicalized forty-eight sections (wards) of Paris and in the provincial clubs the sans-culottes made their indelible historical mark.

The huge Parisian crowds that propelled the Revolution in various *journées* are no doubt the most iconic image of the French Revolution, the symbol or embodiment of popular will and the power of aroused people. These interventions of the crowd were relatively spontaneous in the case of 14 July 1789 or the march to Versailles that October, and highly organized in the case of 10 August 1792, which drove Louis XVI from the throne; in 1 June 1793 when an armed Parisian crowd coerced the Convention into purging its leading Girondin deputies; and in September 1793, when an armed crowd clamored menacingly for the Convention to adopt terroristic measures (Rudé 1959: chs. 4–8). But the sans-culottes did not appear on the historical stage solely in this episodic role. In remarkable fashion they established a presence in public life in the neighborhood wards of Paris and in provincial towns across the country. The sans-culottes were a new kind of social amalgam – neither exclusively middle-class nor specifically artisanal. The amalgam incorporated local businessmen, master artisans, shopkeepers, journeymen, white-collar workers and, in the rural *bourgs*, peasants. They made their presence felt in sectional assemblies and neighborhood clubs in the capital, in revolutionary committees, paramilitary units, and in the popular societies in the provinces whose number reached over 3,000 in the Year II (1793–94) (Cobb 1970: 118–129, 172–211; Soboul 1964: 18–248).

This was far from a realization on earth of Rousseau's idealized direct democracy. Small and shifting cadres around rival local personalities inevitably dominated this ground-level popular politics. Paris, a city of around 600,000, had only 6,000 or so fully committed militants across its forty-eight sections. Their cadres have aptly been described as a "sans-culotte bourgeoisie" – not the oxymoron it might seem according to the classic Marxist categories (Andrews 1985; Sonenscher 1991). Many sans-culottes had their own shops or local businesses that employed other labor: tailors, carpenters, locksmiths, clerks, builders, wine-sellers, and jewelers were among the typical occupations. They were usually well-known figures in their neighborhood, with tough, sometimes domineering temperaments. Rooted in their communities, they advocated on behalf of their proletarian neighbors (especially on the supply and price of subsistence staples) and could mobilize them for action when necessary. They were ferociously anti-aristocratic and sentimentally egalitarian and populist. They tended to distrust the National Convention even while serving as its fiercest partisans. They backed the war effort to the hilt on the home front, and advocated redistributive Jacobin social policies, such as welfare entitlements for needy families with children, alongside repressive measures against noble and middle-class "aristocrats," and rural producers who seemed recalcitrant about supplying the towns with food.

While never as dominant or as well organized as in Paris, sans-culottes in other towns turned out for the local clubs, held seats on local revolutionary committees, and filled the ranks of the paramilitary battalions formed (alongside the those of the capital) in several dozen provincial towns to provide "force behind the laws" of the Terror. Like the Parisians, provincial sans-culottes were obsessed with requisitioning food supplies from the countryside and policing emergency price controls. They reveled in punitive "anti-aristocratic" rhetoric, and in some places supported radical dechristianization. The fervor, violent temperament, populist intolerance, and philistinism of many sans-culottes brought down severe retribution for their temerity once their ascendancy ended abruptly in the summer of 1794. Two centuries later we have little reason to demonize or romanticize them, but their imprint on the Revolution's political culture, however temporary, was of great historical significance, not least for the social amalgam in their activism. Their typical local leaders may have been men of some property rather than impoverished workmen, but they fraternized with working men, fulminated with them against "aristocrats" of all kinds, and ardently embraced egalitarian values.

The sans-culotte family has not been much studied, but it should be. Although disenfranchised, women asserted themselves politically in various ways, in effect exercising citizenship even without voting rights (Godineau 1998; Sewell 1988). Rousseau's metahistorical view of distinctive gender roles may have helped inspire exclusionary decisions on the suffrage or the subsequent touting of "republican motherhood." But it did not preclude the civic activism of women in pivotal Parisian dramas (the October Days of 1789, the Champ de Mars in 1791) or local demonstrations. The participation of women in market riots and the like was common in the eighteenth century, but the Revolution opened new possibilities such as packing the galleries of assemblies, courts, or clubs; participating in revolutionary festivals; or intervening bodily in disputes over parish churches and clergy. Some women wrote pamphlets, signed petitions, or joined auxiliaries of established clubs. At the extreme, female militants and street brawlers in Paris created their own Society of Revolutionary Republic Women in 1793, which the revolutionary government suppressed in October 1793 along with local male radicals whom the Committee of Public Safety stigmatized as *enragés* and excised from public life (Rose 1965: ch.5).

After 1795, and certainly after 1800, the sans-culottes effectively disappeared, as their unique socio-political mix disaggregated. After the Restoration of the Bourbons, the National Guard in Paris helped restore the traditional line between the journeyman or small shopkeeper who could not afford the uniform necessary for membership and the merchants, professionals, top master-artisans or larger shopkeepers who could. The fighting across the barricades of the June days of 1848 provided the final epitaph for the ephemeral solidarity of *sans-culottisme.*

The institutional triad of elections, political newspapers, and clubs remained, with occasional lapses, the matrix of political participation for the entire revolutionary decade until all three were eliminated by Bonaparte's Consulate. The press and the clubs, in turn, helped shape and spread the new rhetoric of revolution and (after 1792) its republicanism: the new tropes, slogans, rituals, and symbols (liberty trees; red, white, and blue *cocardes*; liberty caps); the renaming of streets and public places (from the Palais Royale to the Palais d'Égalité), and the changing of first names (from François-Noel to Gracchus). All this formed a "revolutionary pedagogy" with campaigns from the top down and from the bottom up that crystallized and conveyed the new values of the Revolution, embodying what historian Lynn Hunt has aptly called the "didacticism" of revolutionary political culture (Hunt 1984: part I). A crucial example was the mutation of the Revolution's first slogan, "the Nation, the Law, and the King," which reflected the preoccupations of the National Assembly in 1789, into "Liberty, Equality and Fraternity" and "the Republic One and Indivisible," which conveyed the preoccupations of 1792–94, and appeared almost everywhere in revolutionary material.

Failed Constitutions and Political Parties

Two problems intensified the strains on the political culture of the revolutionary decade. First, the new constitution never had a chance to take root. On the contrary, France bounced between a dismaying total of four different constitutions between 1791 and 1800. The new political culture therefore lacked the firm anchor of a stable constitutional framework that set the ground rules for contending political viewpoints.

In 1789 the National Assembly decided to draft a constitution for the nation on its own authority without participation or approval by the king. It also decided, almost by default, not to submit its work to ratification by the people, but instead simply to launch the new constitution when it was finished. As the process neared its end, the Assembly decreed that its own members would not be eligible to sit in the Legislative Assembly to be elected under the new constitution (Richet 1988). In its final days the Assembly hotly debated the final shape of certain constitutional provisions but the lack of a ratification process raised little to no objection inside or outside the Assembly.

The Constitution of 1791 deprived the king of any claim to sovereignty but maintained him as the head of state with the power to appoint ministers and to block laws temporarily with a suspensive veto. It also laid out an unlikely procedure for removing him only under the most extreme circumstances. When Louis XVI's anti-revolutionary actions paralyzed the Legislative Assembly and enraged much of patriot opinion, a clamor arose against both the king and the Assembly, and by implication against the whole constitutional edifice, which had never been ratified by the people. As its last major act after the upheaval of August 10, a rump of the Legislative Assembly called for the election of a National Convention with three tasks: to govern the country temporarily, to decide the fate of the dethroned king, and to write a new constitution for a republic to replace the constitutional monarchy.

The Convention finally completed this last task only after the purge of the Girondins and, with them, some of their constitutional ideas. The Constitution of 1793 is therefore known as the Jacobin Constitution, and its hallmarks included an expansion of the Rights of Man to include the right to subsistence, to work or to public assistance, and to basic education, and a provision for almost universal manhood suffrage. The Constitution of 1793 also stipulated that it should be ratified by the people meeting in their primary assemblies specifically for that task.

Whereas primary assemblies ordinarily convened only to vote and not to deliberate, the Convention asked each primary assembly in July 1793 to hear the constitutional draft read, discuss it, accept or reject it, and if it wished to propose changes, although how such suggestions would be dealt with was not stipulated. This direct exercise of sovereignty, designed in part to bridge a growing gap between Paris and the provinces, proved to be a unique moment of democratic experience in the French Revolution, although the outcome might make it seem like an orchestrated exercise in political conformity. The assemblies, however, were generally open and free of intimidation; even an oath of allegiance was rarely required from the participants. The turnout rebounded somewhat from the low levels of voting in 1792 to almost 30 percent, with around 2 million of approximately 7 million eligible voters turning out. In their zeal, perhaps two dozen assemblies even allowed women to vote. The results, on the other hand, were entirely one-sided. Over 1,850,000 citizens voted to approve the constitution and only about 13,000 to reject it; 4,713 primary assemblies accepted the constitution and only 38, mainly in Brittany, rejected it. But if the end result seems formulaic, many of the assemblies did actively discuss the charter and approve it with enthusiasm, while about 140,000 of the "yes" voters attached a wide variety of proposals for modification. The plebiscite of July 1793 did not simply impose a ritualistic expression of political unity on a passive citizenry (Crook 1996: 104–115; Woloch 1994: 88–91).

But shortly after a delegate from each primary assembly carried its vote to a grand ceremony in Paris, the Convention voted to lay aside the charter for the duration of the emergency. ("The government of the Republic will be revolutionary until the peace.") When the Convention reversed course and repudiated its own Jacobin dictatorship less than a year later, it proceeded to curb and then close the clubs, to scrap the Constitution of 1793, and to write a new, more self-consciously moderate constitution for the republic, since it could not resurrect the constitutional monarchy of the 1791 charter. Among other things, this constitution omitted the socio-economic rights of 1793, restored a two-tiered franchise requirement similar to that of 1791, set up a bicameral legislature, and provided for a collective five-man executive power known as the Directory. As it did in 1793, the

Convention submitted the Constitution of 1795 for ratification by the people. Again voters approved it, although by a lower turnout, a less overwhelming margin, and without latitude to discuss it or propose possible changes. Finally, to look ahead, when a group of disgruntled moderate politicians colluded with General Bonaparte to overthrow the Directory regime, they drafted yet another constitution which vested most power in a new executive (First Consul Bonaparte), and eliminated genuine elections and representative democracy. The plotters too submitted their constitution to an up or down plebiscite, whose results they falsified in order to make popular approval seem more impressive than it actually was (Langlois 1972).

Constitution-making in revolutionary France thus unfolded as a dreary saga of futility instead of being a defining and stabilizing episode in the national experience as it was in the United States. To be sure both the drafting of the U.S. Constitution (a second try after the failed Articles of Confederation) and its ratification were more contentious than in France. But the art of compromise finally prevailed in the drafting, while the ratification process began with a long, passionate, and at times brilliant debate in the press and elsewhere. (*The Federalist Papers* were initially responses to critics of the draft in New York State.) Ratification depended not on the direct voting of citizens across the country, but on the election of delegates to state ratifying conventions, which then debated the charter intensively, the outcome in several states being by no means certain. Opponents of the constitution generally pushed for acceptance conditional on certain changes, but supporters successfully fought this off as a fatal threat to the whole enterprise. A consensus took shape across the states, however, that amendments defining rights and liberties would be added at the first opportunity, and so they were (Maier 2010: chs. 1–3, epilogue).

The second large problem throughout the decade was the failure to normalize political partisanship. All shades of the political spectrum had surfaced during the constitutional monarchy. After most were temporarily suppressed under the Terror, they re-emerged during the Thermidorian Reaction and the Directory years. To be sure, by that time apathy, cynicism, and disengagement were far more prevalent, leaving the field of political battle to small activist minorities on the neo-Jacobin left, the royalist right, and the elusive center where moderates hoped to find a safe harbor. The annual elections prescribed by the Constitution of 1795 ensured that the battles among left, right, and center would not subside. But the Directory insistently thwarted the emergence of rival parties in the name of national unity. Again newspapers and clubs amplified the clashes, and in turn endured spasms of closures and persecution by the government as the political tides shifted. In 1797 the Directory purged newly elected "royalists" from the legislature and local administrations. In 1798, fearing a resurgence of neo-Jacobins, it fostered schisms or walkouts in the electoral assemblies of certain departments by its supporters, who could then present more palatable slates of deputies, and where that did not suffice, it purged objectionable choices once again (Crook 1996: ch. 6; Woloch 1970: chs. 9–11).

The Americans had started from similar attitudes about the corrosiveness of organized factions or political parties, but within a few years the logic of their political situation compelled an acceptance of competing parties. In 1792 the hardening divisions in Congress led James Madison to write a newspaper essay, "A Candid State of Parties," arguing that two parties were "natural to most political societies." The spirit of party then spread beyond the desks of Congress to the political arena at large, when "democrats" organized through clubs and other means to promote the presidential candidacy of Thomas Jefferson in 1796, who in the end lost out to John Adams. In his Farewell Address of 1796 President Washington reaffirmed the traditional condemnation of organized opposition with an attack on partisanship clearly directed against Jefferson and his supporters. For George Washington parties were not natural but artificial, "of fatal tendency," and wholly illegitimate. They would distract "the constituted authorities" from calmly producing "consistent and wholesome plans digested by common councils and modified by mutual interests." In sum, the Olympian American president was defending non-partisan representative government against the potential encroachments of participatory democracy just as his French counterparts were doing, but he did so in vain (Wilentz 2011: 26–27; Wood 2009: ch. 4, esp. p. 161).

The emergent Federalist and Jeffersonian parties each claimed that they spoke for the people and that only their opponents constituted an unhealthy faction. But Jefferson's narrow victory in 1801 brought a turn from the resistance to parties. Many Federalists adapted by embarking on party-building activities of their own (caucuses and committees alongside their newspapers) and adopting a majoritarian vocabulary of democratic politics. One result of this unforeseen shift in American political culture was the need to amend the federal constitution with a new procedure for electing the vice president: instead of being the man with the second highest total of electoral votes for the presidency (now likely to be the winner's opponent), the vice president would be the running mate of the victorious presidential candidate, chosen by the electoral college in a separate ballot.

During the French Revolution's second chance under the Directory, that same tendency toward party formation was evident in the legislature but especially on a local level among political activists: rival groups (their identity well understood to those with local knowledge) were vying for political power, and their elected deputies and administrators often behaved as if they were members of two or three rival parties. But the Directory consistently rejected that logic, as had the National Assembly and the Committee of Public Safety before them, albeit for different reasons. The Directory continued to stigmatize nascent parties as potentially subversive cabals, whether to the right or to the left of their elusive center. These republican centrists dominated the government and intended to continue in that position. Eventually wearying of the unending "factionalism," however, some finally joined forces with General Bonaparte to close down the arena of political liberty altogether, and with it press freedom, political clubs, and genuine elections.

Note

1 There are now three major scholarly works analyzing and assessing French revolutionary elections: Gueniffey 1993a; Crook 1996; Edelstein (forthcoming). Readers wishing to pursue this will find that Gueniffey holds a critically negative view of how revolutionary

elections unfolded, but some of his key arguments are challenged by Edelstein's research and conclusions. Crook's balanced book did not engage directly with Gueniffey's work. For introductions to their perspectives see the essays of Crook 1991, Edelstein 1993, and Gueniffey 1993b.

References

Andrews, Richard (1985). "Social Structures, Political Elites and Ideology in Revolutionary Paris, 1792–94: A Critical Evaluation of Albert Soboul's *Les Sans-Culottes Parisiens en l'an II.*" *JSH*, 19: 71–112.

Baker, Keith Michael (ed.) (1987). *The Political Culture of the Old Regime.* Oxford: Pergamon Press.

Baker, Keith Michael (1987). "Representation." In id. (ed.).*The Political Culture of the Old Regime.* Oxford: Pergamon Press. 469–492.

Bertaud, Jean-Paul (1984). *Les Amis du Roi: Journaux et journalistes royalistes en France de 1789 à 1792.* Paris: Perrin.

Boutier, J. and P. Boutry (1983). "Les Sociétés politiques en France de 1789 à l'an III: 'Une Machine'?" *RHMC*, 36: 29–67.

Censer, Jack (1976). *Prelude to Power: The Parisian Radical Press 1789–1791.* Baltimore, Md.: Johns Hopkins University Press

Censer, Jack and Lynn Hunt (eds.) (2001). *Liberty, Equality, Fraternity: Exploring the French Revolution.* University Park: Pennsylvania State University Press.

Chartier, Roger (1991). *The Cultural Origins of the French Revolution.* Durham N.C.: Duke University Press.

Cobb, Richard (1970). *The Police and the People: French Popular Protest 1789–1820.* Oxford: Oxford University Press.

Crook, Malcolm (1991). "Aux urnes, citoyens! Urban and Rural Electoral Behavior during the French Revolution." In Alan Forrest and Peter Jones (eds.). *Reshaping France: Town, Country and Region during the French Revolution.* Manchester: Manchester University Press. 152–167.

Crook, Malcolm (1996). *Elections in the French Revolution: An Apprenticeship in Democracy, 1789–1799.* Cambridge: Cambridge University Press.

Darnton, Robert (1984). "A Bourgeois Puts His World in Order." In Darnton, *The Great Cat Massacre and Other Essays in French Cultural History.* New York: Basic Books.

Darnton, Robert (1995). *The Forbidden Best-Sellers of Pre-Revolutionary France.* New York: W.W. Norton.

Darnton, Robert and Daniel Roche (eds.) (1989). *Revolution in Print: The Press in France 1775–1800.* Berkeley: University of California Press.

Edelstein, Melvin (1993). "Electoral Behavior during the Constitutional Monarchy (1790–1791): A 'Community' Interpretation." In Renée Waldinger, Philip Dawson, and Isser Woloch (eds.). *The French Revolution and the Meaning of Citizenship.* Westport, Conn.: Greenwood Press. 105–122.

Edelstein, Melvin (forthcoming). *The French Revolution and the Birth of Electoral Democracy.* Rennes: Presses Universitaires de Rennes.

Forrest, Alan and Peter Jones (eds.) (1991). *Reshaping France: Town, Country and Region during the French Revolution.* Manchester: Manchester University Press.

Godineau, Dominique (1998). *The Women of Paris and their French Revolution.* Berkeley: University of California Press.

Gough, Hugh (1988). *The Newspaper Press in the French Revolution.* London: Routledge.

Gruder, Vivian (2007). *The Notables and the Nation: The Political Schooling of the French 1787–1788*. Cambridge, Mass.: Harvard University Press.

Gueniffey, Patrice (1993a). *Le Nombre et la raison: La Révolution française et les élections*. Paris: ÉHÉSS.

Gueniffey, Patrice (1993b). "Revolutionary Democracy and the Elections." In Renée Waldinger, Philip Dawson, and Isser Woloch (eds.). *The French Revolution and the Meaning of Citizenship*. Westport, Conn.: Greenwood Press. 89–104.

Hunt, Lynn (1984). *Politics, Culture, and Class in the French Revolution*. Berkeley: University of California Press.

Hunt, Lynn (ed.) (1996). *The French Revolution and Human Rights: A Brief Documentary History*. Boston: Bedford/St. Martins.

Kennedy, Michael L. (1982, 1988). *The Jacobin Clubs in the French Revolution*: vol. 1: *The First Years*; vol. 2: *The Middle Years*. Princeton N.J.: Princeton University Press.

Langlois, Claude (1972). "Le Plébiscite de l'an VIII ou le coup d'état du 18 pluviôse an VIII." *AHRF*, 43–65, 231–246, 391–415.

Lawrence, Jon (2009). *Electing our Masters: The Hustings in British Politics from Hogarth to Blair*. Oxford: Oxford University Press.

Lucas, Colin (ed.) (1988a). *The Political Culture of the French Revolution*. Oxford: Pergamon Press.

Lucas, Colin (1988b). "The Crowd and Politics." In Lucas (ed.). *The Political Culture of the French Revolution*. Oxford: Pergamon Press. 259–293.

Maier, Pauline (2010). *Ratification: The People Debate the Constitution, 1787–1788*. New York: Simon & Schuster.

Ozouf, Mona (1987). "L'Opinion publique." In Keith Michael Baker (ed.). *The Political Culture of the Old Regime*. Oxford: Pergamon Press. 419–434.

Palmer, Robert R. (1959). *The Age of the Democratic Revolution: A Political History of Europe and America, 1760–1800*, vol. 1: *The Challenge*. Princeton, N.J.: Princeton University Press.

Popkin, Jeremy D. (1987). "The Prerevolutionary Origins of Political Journalism." In Keith Michael Baker (ed.). *The Political Culture of the Old Regime*. Oxford: Pergamon Press. 203–223.

Popkin, Jeremy D. (1990). *Revolutionary News: The Press in France 1789–1799*. Durham, N.C.: Duke University Press.

Richet, Denis (1988). "L'Esprit de la constitution, 1789–1791." In Colin Lucas (ed.). *The Political Culture of the French Revolution*. Oxford: Pergamon Press. 63–68.

Rose, R.B. (1965). *The Enragés: Socialists of the French Revolution?* Melbourne: Melbourne University Press.

Rudé, George (1959). *The Crowd in the French Revolution*. Oxford: Oxford University Press.

Sewell, William (1988). "Le Citoyen/La Citoyenne: Activity, Passivity and the Revolutionary Concept of Citizenship." In Colin Lucas (ed.). *The Political Culture of the French Revolution*. Oxford: Pergamon Press. 105–124.

Soboul, Albert (1964). *The Parisian Sans-Culottes and the French Revolution, 1793–94*. Oxford: Oxford University Press.

Sonenscher, Michael (1991). "Artisans, *Sans-Culottes* and the French Revolution." In Alan Forrest and Peter Jones (eds.). *Reshaping France: Town, Country and Region during the French Revolution*. Manchester: Manchester University Press. 105–121.

Tackett, Timothy (2003). *When the King Took Flight*. Cambridge, Mass.: Harvard University Press.

Waldinger, Renée, Philip Dawson, and Isser Woloch (eds.) (1993). *The French Revolution and the Meaning of Citizenship*. Westport, Conn.: Greenwood Press.

Walton, Charles (2009). *Policing Public Opinion in the French Revolution: The Culture of Calumny and the Problem of Free Speech.* New York: Oxford University Press.

Wilentz, Sean (2011). "The Mirage: The Long and Tragical History of Post-Partisanship." *The New Republic*, 17 Nov. 2011: 26–27.

Woloch, Isser (1970). *Jacobin Legacy: the Democratic Movement Under the Directory.* Princeton, N.J.: Princeton University Press.

Woloch, Isser (1994). *The New Regime: Transformations of the French Civic Order, 1789–1820s.* New York: W.W. Norton.

Wood, Gordon (2009). *Empire of Liberty: A History of the Early Republic, 1789–1815.* New York: Oxford University Press.

Chapter Twenty-Seven

The Economy, Society, and the Environment

Peter McPhee

The marquise de la Tour du Pin was born in 1770 as Henriette-Lucy Dillon, the descendant of English and Irish Jacobites who had been exiled to France after the defeat of James II in 1690. Her husband was an army officer from an eminent and wealthy family. Her liberal father-in-law was minister for war in 1789–90, but his support for Louis XVI during his trial would cost him his life. Lucy and her husband emigrated to Boston in 1793, returning in 1796. Reflecting in later life on the impact of the Revolution, she focused primarily on the decrees on feudalism of 4–11 August 1789, which "ruined my father-in-law, and our family fortunes never recovered from the effect of that night's session. It was a veritable orgy of iniquities." With the loss of exactions from four other estates, she estimated that the annual income of her husband's family had fallen from 80,000 to 22,000 *francs* (La Tour du Pin Gouvernet 1979: 93–94, 243–244).

Historians agree that the abolition of the vestiges of seigneurialism was a socio-economic consequence of the Revolution. They do not agree, however, on just how significant this was, nor on what other socio-economic changes the Revolution generated. Did Lucy return to France in 1796 much poorer, but otherwise to a land of familiar economic practices and social assumptions?

Materialist historians have long argued that the Revolution was a triumph for the bourgeoisie and for the landowning peasantry. While they have recognized that there were important continuities in French society, Albert Soboul (1976b: 133), Gwynne Lewis (1993) and others (for example Heller 2006) have insisted that that the Revolution was "the point of departure" of capitalist society in France. In contrast, it has been claimed that Soboul's identification of the Revolution with bourgeois triumph and capitalist transformation was no more than Marxist wishful thinking. In the words of François Furet (1981: 24), "it makes the revolutionary break a matter of economic and social change, whereas

A Companion to the French Revolution, First Edition. Edited by Peter McPhee.

nothing resembled French society under Louis XVI more than French society under Louis-Philippe [1830–1848]."

Did the Revolution break the shackles on economic growth erected by centuries of aristocratic monopolies, privileges, and values? Or did the protracted military and political crisis of 1792–95 shatter the economic surge already evident under Louis XVI (Bairoch and Poussou, in *Révolution de 1789*: 939–984)? Given that the relationship with socio-economic change is the cornerstone of long debates about the meaning of the Revolution in the *moyenne durée* of modern world history, it is surprising how little attention historians have paid to these questions. Indeed, when France's leading economic historians gathered to answer them in 1989 their conclusion was that it was "an impossible assessment" to make (Asselain, in *Révolution de 1789*: 927–938, 1137–1188).

The Urban Economy

Nevertheless, the general outlines are clear enough. There is abundant evidence of the ways in which the Revolution and protracted wars had a crippling effect on the economy of coastal cities, while providing a stimulus for certain branches of industry. The uncertainties caused by wars and blockades and the abolition of slavery in 1794 hit overseas trade hard. The Atlantic trade through Bordeaux had grown perhaps tenfold after 1715; between 1790 and 1806 the downturn in trade caused the population of Bordeaux to fall from 110,000 to 92,000. That of Marseille declined from 120,000 to 99,000; that of Nantes from perhaps 90,000 to 77,000. By 1815, French external trade was only half its 1789 volume and did not regain pre-revolutionary levels until 1830. Marseille and Le Havre would later adjust to the changed world of maritime commerce, but Bordeaux and La Rochelle would never quite recover from the loss of Saint-Domingue. The French colonial fleet declined from about 700 vessels in 1789 to 500 in the 1830s (Butel 1991). Banking systems, relatively stable and extensive before 1789, were buffeted by the revolutionary wars, rampant inflation, and the deep suspicion of the financial professions in 1792–94. Not all of the old banking houses survived, but there were stories of remarkable resilience alongside the new firms which emerged under the Directory (Plessis, in *Révolution de 1789*).

Hinterlands suffered, too. East of Bordeaux, the small town of Tonneins had had 1,000 rope-makers in 1789: there were just 200 in 1800; it had had 1,200 workers in the tobacco industry; there were fewer than 200 in 1800. In the textile towns of Troyes and Saint-Quentin the number of looms fell from 2,000 to 800 and from about 13,000 to 3,000 respectively. In Saint-Étienne, the increase in arms manufacture, from 12,000 pieces in 1789 to 34,000 in 1803, could not compensate for the collapse of ironmongery and textiles (Butel 1991; Crouzet 1959; Le Goff and Sutherland 1991; Poussou, in *Révolution de 1789*).

In other inland cities the effects were not always as dramatic, and it is estimated that industrial output was still about 60 percent of its 1789 levels a decade later. The cotton, iron, and coal industries were stimulated by France's role in the continental system and protection from British imports, although it was not until 1810 that Napoleon claimed the right of the state to grant below-surface mining concessions on private land (Lewis 1993; Woronoff 1984). Certain branches of the textile industry fared well. Paris became a major center of cotton manufacture and the chemicals industries. Bédarieux and Lodève were two small southern textile towns which survived and at times prospered through army contracts, despite the loss of trade with the Levant (Johnson 1995: 13–15).

Such was the short-term impact of the revolutionary wars on commerce that in some areas France became, if anything, more rural. There were many men like Claude Bonnet de Paillerets, in the southern Massif Central, much of whose fortune had come from the trade in wool and textiles, but who hankered after noble status and abandoned commerce for landowning during the Revolution. He succeeded in entering the world of the nineteenth-century notable (Castaing 1992). At the northern extremity of the country, in Montigny and its region of Cambrésis, the period saw the collapse of the distinctive rural textile economy. The free trade treaty with England in 1786 had been a body blow; now the revolutionary and imperial wars of 1792–1815, which swept back and forth across the region, would destroy the market for linen. When the vast church lands were sold as national property after 1790, the merchant-weavers rushed to buy them as a refuge from a collapsing industry. Consequently, by 1815 the countryside was again as rural as it had been a century earlier, and a reconstructed textile industry was centered in towns (Vardi 1993).

In the longer term, changes which were to facilitate capitalist practices were accelerated by the Revolution. From 1789 there was a series of institutional, legal, and social changes creating the environment within which capitalist industry and agriculture would thrive (Koubi 1990). The free enterprise and free trade (*laissez-faire, laissez-passer*) legislation of the Revolution guaranteed that manufacturers, farmers, and merchants could commit themselves to the market economy secure in the knowledge that they could trade without the impediments of internal customs and tolls, differing systems of measurement, and a multitude of law codes. For example, the department of the Lot-et-Garonne in the southwest covered an area where before 1789 there had been sixty-five different ways of measuring length and twenty-six measures of the weight of grain: now there was just one national way of measuring. These evident benefits to business and commerce were accentuated by the abolition of tolls paid to towns and nobles and of internal customs. The manufacturers of the small Norman textile town of Elbeuf had complained bluntly in their *cahier* of 1789 about the "impediments to commerce" created by internal customs barriers and the maze of different weights and measures, and the lack of attention paid by government to the views of people like themselves. This budding industrial bourgeoisie achieved its goals, including the recognition of their own importance: in the Year IX the advisory role of chambers of commerce was formally institutionalized (Kaplow 1964).

It could be argued that life for urban working people had changed little. Work continued to be concentrated in small workplaces, where masters worked side by side with three or four skilled journeymen and apprentices. The Allarde and Le Chapelier laws of 1791 abolishing guilds and corporations only completed Jacques Necker's radical reforms to the guilds in 1776, which had enabled greater competition and labor mobility in an urban world already marked by labor disputes and capitalist practices (Kaplan 2001; Sewell 1980; Sonenscher 1989). An enduring function of the guilds had been to inspect and approve apprenticeship contracts. After the final abolition of the guilds by the law of 2 May 1791, these contracts were simply registered by a notary: it was assumed that they were the result of negotiation. Apprenticeships certainly continued: there were, for example, 123 in Bourg in 1789–99, but the number fell from an annual average of sixteen in 1789–93 to just six in 1794–99. In certain trades – such as wig-making and, more surprisingly, the printing and building trades – their numbers declined sharply (Subreville 1982).

A major grievance in 1789, indirect taxation, had been reintroduced, and customs-houses ringing cities and towns had been re-erected. The position of employers was strengthened by the Le Chapelier law and by the reintroduction by Napoleon of the *livret*, an *ancien régime* practice requiring workers to carry a booklet detailing their employment record and conduct. Memories of 1792–94 were to be cold comfort for dashed expectations of real social change. The descendants of the sans-culottes of the 1790s had to wait many decades for the realization of such hopes: until 1848 for the implementation of manhood suffrage (and women until 1944); until 1864 for the right to strike and twenty years more for the right to form trade unions; until the 1880s for free, secular, and compulsory education; and until the early twentieth century for income tax and social welfare provisions for the sick, the elderly, and the unemployed.

Whatever the grand schemes and principles of the Jacobins, the destitute continued to constitute a major urban and rural underclass swollen in times of crisis by poorer laborers and workers. The realization by the National Assembly that poverty was not simply the result of the church's charity, and that local government could not provide adequate poor relief, had generated a series of work schemes and temporary relief measures which were always piecemeal and never adequately financed by governments preoccupied with war. The hungry years after 1794, when the collapse of economic regulation coincided with harvest failure and inflation, exposed the poor to a starvation against which the charity of parish clergy with fewer resources could never be adequate protection. Artisans could respond to threats posed by free enterprise by new organizations such as mutual aid societies, but the poor remained particularly vulnerable. Nevertheless, one socio-economic legacy of the Revolution was the nervous attention paid by the state and employers to the threat of popular unrest: memories of the sans-culottes were slow to fade. Just as administrators otherwise committed to policies of *laissez-faire* sought to control the grain trade and supply sufficiently to provision large cities, so employers were cautious about introducing large-scale machinery into long-established industries (Horn 2006; Miller 1998). The Revolution reinforced the state *dirigisme* which has distinguished French political economy.

Rural Change and Continuity

Historians have mostly agreed with Georges Lefebvre that the peasantry "destroyed the feudal régime, but consolidated the agrarian structure of France" (Lefebvre 1954: 257; see also Aftalion 1990: 192–193; Jones 1988: 255–259; Le Goff and Sutherland 1991; Sutherland 2002). Most French people in 1799 remained, like their parents, owners of small plots, tenants, and sharecroppers. Decisions taken by successive assemblies, under massive peasant pressure in 1792–93, to finally abolish compensation due to nobles for the end of feudal dues and to make *émigré* land available in small plots at low rates of repayment, encouraged small owners to stay on the land. The 1791 and 1793 partible inheritance laws, further codified by Napoleon, ensured that farms would be constantly threatened by subdivision (*morcellement*) (Cobban 1964: chs 7, 12, 14; Jones 1990). The sales of *émigré* land further aggravated this: in the district of Pont-Audemer (Eure), for example, the 109 hectares belonging to Grossin de Bouville were sold in 108 lots (Bodinier 2010).

The Revolution was a watershed in rural–urban relations, one of the most dramatic socio-economic changes that it wrought. In many ways the towns which were centers of *ancien régime* institutions had been parasitic on the countryside. In provincial centers such as Arras, Dijon, and Laon, the revenue from feudal dues and tithes was expended by cathedral chapters, religious orders, and resident nobles on the employment of domestic servants, purchases from skilled trades, especially in luxury goods, and in provision of charity. As a direct result of the Revolution, the countryside largely freed itself from such control by towns, leaving marketing and administration as the remaining links. It was this which made the lot of the destitute so desperate in such towns and which caused the impoverishment of those directly or indirectly dependent on clerical and noble elites. To give but one example, in the countryside around Angers, the Benedictine abbey of Ronceray had formerly owned five manors, twelve barns and wine-presses, six mills, forty-six farms, and six houses, bringing into the town 27,000 *livres* annually. Some of it employed and was collected by lawyers in the fifty-three courts and tribunals charged with ensuring that the countryside met its obligations; the rest supported servants, artisans, and the poor (Hufton 1967, 1971; McManners 1960: chs. 1, 6).

While most nobles were pragmatic enough to withdraw from public life and accept, however grudgingly, the institutional changes of the Revolution, their losses were massive. Robert Forster's judgment (1967, 1980), though based on scattered and contrasting case-studies, was that, in real terms, an average provincial noble family's income fell from 8,000 to 5,200 *francs*. Seigneurial dues had represented as little as 5 percent of noble income near Bordeaux, while immediately to the north, in Aunis and Saintonge, they had amounted to 63 percent. While many noble families survived with their lands intact, some 12,500 – up to one-half – lost some land, and a few virtually all. To an extent, the losses of lands and dues were compensated for by charging higher rents to tenants and sharecroppers but, whereas 5 percent at most of noble wealth was taken by state taxes before 1789, thereafter the uniform land tax was levied at approximately 16 percent.

Most nobles kept their lands intact (Forster estimated that about one-fifth of noble holdings were seized and sold), but their method of "surplus extraction" of necessity changed fundamentally. The final abolition of feudal dues in 1793 implied that nobles' income from property would henceforth be based on rents charged to tenants and sharecroppers or on direct exploitation of noble holdings by farm managers employing laborers. Efficient use of landed resources rather than control over persons was now the basis of rural wealth. Moreover, nothing could compensate for the loss of judicial rights and power – ranging from seigneurial courts to the *parlements* – or the incalculable loss of prestige and deference generated by the practice of legal equality. The *émigré* noble returned to a transformed world, of litigation by creditors and peasants, the collapse of mystique, and the exigencies of running an estate as a business.

The continued economic prominence of the old nobility is remarkable: despite the loss of seigneurial rights and, for *émigrés*, land, nobles remained at the pinnacle of landholding, and landholding remained the major source of wealth in France. France in 1799 remained a sharply inegalitarian, hierarchical society, one in which most *ancien régime* nobles continued to be eminent. Across half of the country, a majority of the wealthiest landowners surveyed in 1802 were nobles, and they dominated the wealthiest areas, such as the Paris basin, the valley of the Rhône, Burgundy, Picardy, and Normandy (Bergeron et al. 1971). But despite these continuities, the source of economic power, social eminence, and political legitimacy had changed radically. The wealthy survivors of the landholding elite of the *ancien régime* were now only part of a far broader elite which included all of the wealthy, whatever their social background, and embraced notables in agriculture, business, and administration drawing their wealth from a combination of state employment and business.

Those peasants who owned their own land were the direct and substantial beneficiaries of nobles' losses (Markoff 1996; McPhee 2006). About 40 percent of the land of France belonged to peasants who worked it directly: that land was now free of seigneurial charges and tithes. The weight of these exactions had varied enormously, but a total weight of 20–25 percent of the produce of peasant proprietors (not to mention the *corvée*, seigneurial monopolies, and irregular payments) was common outside the west of France. Producers retained an extra portion of their output which was often directly consumed by a better-fed population: in 1792, only one in seven of the army recruits from the impoverished mountain village of Pont-de-Montvert (Lozère) had been 1.63 meters (5′ 4″) or taller; by 1830, that was the average height of conscripts (Higonnet 1971: 97). As Arthur Young (1929: 351) commented at the start of 1792, "small proprietors, who farm their own lands, are in a very improved and easy situation."

Research on the extent and social incidence of land sales during the Revolution remains piecemeal, but it was significant in most areas. The most detailed estimate is that 8.5 percent of land changed hands as a result of the expropriation of the church (about 6.5 percent) and *émigrés*. In all, there were up to 700,000 purchasers: about one family in six bought some land (Bodinier and Teyssier 2000). Church land in particular was usually of prime quality, sold in large lots by auction, and purchased by urban and rural bourgeois – and more than a few nobles – with the capital to thus expand pre-existing holdings. Sales of church property varied enormously, from 0.3 percent of the total area of the district of Tartas (Landes) and 0.6 percent of Nyons (Drôme) to 25.5 percent of the district of Arles (Bouches-du-Rhône) and 40.1 percent of Cambrai (Nord) (Bodinier 2010; Jessenne 2005). Sometimes the sales were spectacular: the Bordeaux merchant Abraham Fornerot paid 750,000 *livres* for the property of the Chartreux religious order in the Dordogne (Forrest 1996: 260; Jollet 2000). Most were modest, but enabled the total of peasant holdings to increase from perhaps one-third to two-fifths of the total (Jones 1988: 7–9; 2003: 245–250).

Tenants and sharecroppers experienced limited material improvements from the Revolution. In regions like the Vannetais in Lower Brittany, the failure to reform the *domaine congéable* in favor of tenants soon soured the countryside against the Revolution (Le Goff 1981: 343–353). Like every other group in the rural community, however, tenants and sharecroppers had been affected by seigneurial *banalités* (monopolies of mills, ovens, wine, and oil presses) and, with rural laborers, had been those most vulnerable to the often arbitrary justice of the seigneur's court. Its replacement by a system of elected justices of the peace was one of most valued innovations of the revolutionary period, providing villagers and townspeople with a way of resolving minor grievances that was prompt, cheap, less partial, and accessible (Crubaugh 2001).

Whilst it is difficult to generalize about the impact of the Revolution on standards of living, the inflation aggravated by the decision to deal with the heritage of state indebtedness by the printing of *assignats* made the decade of revolution a time of chronic difficulty for wage-earners and those on fixed incomes (Aftalion 1990). Nevertheless, historians' estimates of the increase in the purchasing power of wages from 1790 to 1810 have ranged from 10 to 20 percent (Postel-Vinay, in *Révolution de 1789*: 1025). One class of people who were significantly better off were the elite of farmers – *laboureurs* and *fermiers* – who in the hyper-inflation under the Directory were able to pay off their rents or loans in *assignats* and sell their produce for hard currency. Charles-Joseph Trouvé, a highly intelligent man from an artisan family to whom the Revolution offered opportunities which would once have been unthinkable, became Baron Trouvé, prefect of the department of the Aude in 1803–16, and recognized the improvement in the peasants' standard of living:

> The suppression of feudal dues and the tithe, the high price of foodstuffs, the division of the large estates, the sale in small lots of nationalized lands, the ending of indebtedness by [the inflation in the value of] paper currency, gave a great impulse to the industry of the peasantry. ... Although the Revolution had an impact on the diet of the people of the countryside, this impact was even more marked on clothing. ... In the old days, rough woollen cloth, or homespun linen, was their finest apparel; they disdain that today, cotton and velveteen cloth are the fabrics they desire, and the large landholder is often confused with his sharecroppers because of the simplicity of his clothing. (Trouvé 1818: vol. 1, 452–453, 563)

The gains for the peasantry went beyond tangible economic benefits. The abolition of seigneurialism underpinned a revolutionary change in rural social relations, voiced in political behavior after 1789. The social authority many nobles retained in the rural community was now based on personal esteem and direct economic power over the dependent rather than on claims to deference due to a superior order of society. Even when a noble survived the Revolution with landholdings intact, social relations underwent a major change. In the Provençal village of Lourmarin, de Bruny, a former councilor in the Parlement of Aix, retained his extensive property but became the largest taxpayer. The estimated annual value of his *seigneurie* had been about 16,000 *livres*, but by 1791 the taxable revenue from his lands was estimated at only 4,696 *livres*, a fall of about 70 percent. Relations between him and the village were henceforth those of property, labor, and rent, suggested by the speed with which locals began litigation with "citizen Bruny" after 1789 (Sheppard 1971: 211, ch. 8).

Capitalism in the Countryside

Across much of the country, the polycultural and subsistence orientation of agriculture would persist well into the nineteenth century. With few exceptions, agricultural production remained at similar levels in 1800 or 1820 as in 1780. Farming techniques were unchanged by the Revolution, and the household basis of rural production would dominate French rural society for many decades to come. In particular areas, however, profit-oriented farm enterprise was facilitated by a series of legislative changes and the relative consistency with which successive regimes after 1789 upheld the primacy of private ownership and control over collective usages and community decisions. Only the strength of the attachment to communal lands by the poorer members of rural communities (although in some areas wealthier peasants also valued such lands for grazing animals) prevented a thoroughgoing change to total private control of rural land. More specialized agriculture became possible with the abolition of the collection of tithes and dues in kind, especially grains; now landowners were able to use their land for their own purposes. This was particularly the case in parts of Normandy and Languedoc. In the countryside around Bayeux, the heavy, damp soils were quickly converted to cattle-raising once the church ceased exacting a fixed tithe in grain. On the lowlands of Languedoc, in contrast, peasants started extending their vineyards into fields formerly used for growing grain (Hufton 1967; McPhee 1999; Plack 2009).

There are other examples, particularly in northern France, of the ways in which the political economy of successive revolutionary assemblies facilitated capitalist agriculture, based on large-scale ownership or renting of land and the employment of labor. For example, in 1786 the Thomassin family of Puiseux-Pontoise, just north of Paris, owned less than 4 hectares and rented 180 more from the seigneur, the marquis de Girardin. They then bought up large amounts of nationalized property from the abbey of Saint-Martin-de-Pontoise, the Sisters of Charity and eight other ecclesiastical landowners: by 1822 they owned more than 150 hectares, 27.5 percent of the land in the commune, including much of the marquis' estate. This land was used for commercial grain-growing and, finally, for sugar-beet and a sugar distillery (Moriceau and Postel-Vinay 1992; Soboul 1976a: ch. 11).

Elsewhere, in areas close to cities or good transport, the retention of a greater share of produce increased the safety margin for middling and larger peasant landholders and facilitated the contemplation of the risks of market specialization. This *voie paysanne* or "peasant route" may have speeded up the expansion of capitalism in the countryside, and has been supported by studies of particular communities and regions which have identified small and medium producers as the initiators of change (Ado 1996: 6, conclusion; Gauthier 1977; Hoffman 1996; Livesey 2004; McPhee 1989a, 1999: ch. 7; Plack 2009). Gilles Postel-Vinay (in *Révolution de 1789*), for example, has emphasized those factors which stimulated demand for wine, especially the incentive offered by supplying cheap wines to the army and by the abolition of indirect taxes on wine until 1804. He has estimated that winegrowers were producing one-third more wine by 1812 compared with the years before the Revolution.

In many areas, rural producers responded to instability and the shrinking of urban demand by a temporary retreat into *auto-consommation* but, where small peasants felt greater security about producing for the market, the results could be dramatic, particularly in winegrowing. In the Gard, more than 70 percent of the land which had been seized and cultivated in villages such as Tavel, Pujat, Orsan, and Saint-Victor-la-Coste was planted in vines (Plack 2009: ch. 6). Land sales in Balazuc (Ardèche) were dominated by smallholders who used their purchases to create a new economy based on wine and silk (Merriman 2002: 68–69). In the Aude, similarly, the ending of seigneurial and church exactions in grain, coupled with the collapse of the textile industry, encouraged peasants to turn to wine as a cash crop. Across the thirty years after 1789, the estimates provided by mayors for the area under vines in the Aude showed an increase of 75 percent, from 29,300 to 51,100 hectares.

Some of this winegrowing was on uncultivated land belonging to the commune as commons or to former seigneurs. Previously used for grazing livestock, these "wastelands" or *vacants* were placed under extreme pressure as the rural poor cleared them for cultivation. One reason why the land-clearers of Languedoc were desperate in their desire for an arable plot, particularly to plant grapevines, was because of the collapse of Carcassonne's textile trade with the Middle East after 1783 and especially after 1792 (Chassagne 1978; Marquié 1993; Vivier 1998). That is, the desperate pressure of the peasantry to clear new land was above all a response to the decline of the local pastoral economy. The mayor of Lagrasse (Aude) concluded in 1828 that a pastoral economy had largely been replaced by viticulture: "since 1789, this land has gone from being a place of a nomadic people to one of an agricultural people" (McPhee 1999: ch. 7).

This first viticultural revolution "from below" is important evidence for an ongoing debate about the extent and nature of economic change wrought by the Revolution. It had social and political consequences as well. James Livesey, for example, has discerned in the language of the market in land and produce across rural France in the years of the Directory a "commercial republicanism" which was fundamental to the shift towards a democratic public culture (Livesey 2001; cf. Shovlin 2006: ch.6, conclusion).

These were also years when administrators struggled to contain continuing conflicts over ownership of forests and commons and to end illegal felling and clearances (Corvol 1993; McPhee 2001; Woronoff 1988). The revolutionary years exacerbated long-term stress on the environment. Only after 1801 was more effective control reimposed over forests: by then, perhaps one-quarter of France's forests had been felled, and in many regions vast areas of commons had been cleared for agriculture.

The Revolution and Social Change

The Revolution had other sweeping social consequences. The names of the new departments, drawn from rivers, mountains, and other natural features, undercut claims to other provincial and ethnic loyalties: for example, the Basque country would be the "Basses-Pyrénées," not the "Pays Basque," nor would there be any institutional recognition whatsoever of regions such as Brittany or Languedoc. The Revolution was not only a turning-point towards the uniformity of state institutions but, for the first time, the state embodied a more emotional entity, "the nation," based on citizenship. Mixed with other young citizens within a French national military bureaucracy, young men were exposed to the language of France, *patrie*, and nation. Just as "patriot" was a political term of pride or denigration, so "patriotism" pointed to the tension between the *pays* or region and the *patrie* or nation.

The French Revolution was a critical period in the forging and contesting of collective identities among the linguistic and ethnic minorities who together made up a majority of French people. Since the Ordinance of Villers-Cotterêts in 1539 in particular, French rulers had sought to make their language that of public administration; now, however, the French language was assumed to be intrinsic to citizenship, even to be at the core of the Revolution itself (Certeau et al 1975; Forrest 2004; McPhee 1989b: ch. 6). From early in the Revolution political elites expressed the view that French was the language of liberty and equality. The national language bore the name of its nation. On 10 September 1791, Talleyrand expressed his surprise to the National Assembly that:

> the national language ... remains inaccessible to such a large number of inhabitants ... Elementary education will put an end to this strange inequality. In school all will be taught in the language of the Constitution and the Law and this mass of corrupt dialects, these last vestiges of feudalism, will be forced to disappear. (Brunot 1927: 13–14)

The legal status of women changed significantly in specific areas (Sledziewski 1993; Viallaneix and Ehrard 1980). In 1791 the law on inheritance guaranteed daughters equal inheritance rights to their brothers; only the addition in 1801 of a share of property set aside for parental discretion altered a law that is essentially in force to this day. In Normandy, its impact was explosive (Desan 2004). For Basque and Catalan peasants in the Pyrenees, in contrast, the principle of equal inheritance undermined the central element of the continuity of the extended family and its house. Here and in the southern Massif Central, inheritance patterns continued, whereby sons ultimately received the family holding, so that daughters must have either been cajoled into renouncing their share or were compensated in other ways (Assier-Andrieu 1984; Claverie and Lamaison 1982: ch. 4; Darrow 1989; Jones 1985: 101–104; Lehning 1980: ch. 8). Whatever the case, the social consequence of this legislation was to focus attention on children's rights as well as on the family estate.

The effects of the new inheritance law and the abolition of seigneurialism may well have meant that women were both better nourished and in a stronger position within the family. In countless households after 1791, the rights of daughters became a family issue, just as the divorce law empowered wives – this was the most significant shift in the status of women in these years. Even though in the Basque country, for example, parents sought ways to sidestep revolutionary legislation, "the wind of equality got up," in the words of Jacques Poumarède (1989: 177), "and would never die down."

The *légende noire* of the Revolution's attack on the family was particularly powerful among those for whom these years represented a protracted nightmare of violent assault on the Catholic Church. The church emerged from the Revolution without its extensive property, internally divided, and with several thousand of its clergy prematurely dead. It had lost its privileges and – because of its role in the emigration, counter-revolution, and wars – much of its authority and prestige. The decline in the social authority of the church was reflected in changes to the seasonality of marriages. During the eighteenth century, only about 3 percent of marriages occurred in the months of December (Advent) and March (Lent). There was a sharp increase during the Revolution (to 12.4 percent in 1793–99), and while pre-revolutionary patterns re-emerged thereafter, they were never so marked: in 1820–29, 7.5 percent of marriages occurred in these two months (in towns the figures were a few percent higher) (Houdaille 1978).

Added to the losses of life during the revolutionary decade – for which there are no reliable figures, but which were in the order of 1 million – the birth-rate plummeted towards the end of the decade and in the early years of the new century: the total number of births in 1804 (933,700) was the lowest since 1748. Nevertheless, it is estimated that the population had increased by about 2.5 million by 1814, the result of an increase in the marriage rate and a decline in the mortality rate. There was a decisive decline in mortality and an increase in life expectancy from the 1780s to the 1820s: for women from 28.1 to 39.3 years and for men from 27.5 to 38.3 years. Nationally the decline in the birth-rate was from 38.8 per thousand in 1789 to 32.9 in 1804; the average interval between births increased from 19–30 months to 31–48 months, a further indication of deliberate limitation of family size. In searching for an explanation of a phenomenon unique in Europe, Paul Spagnoli (1997) concludes that it was directly linked to the consequences of the Revolution in the countryside: land sales, fiscal equity, the removal of seigneurial dues and the tithe, higher wages for agricultural laborers, and greater incentives to increase production. The collapse or absence of clerical authority over birth control facilitated the response of the peasantry to the Revolution's inheritance laws of 1790 and 1793 requiring children to inherit equally. Given the desire and need to keep small family holdings intact, rural people responded by deliberately limiting family size, usually by *coitus interruptus*, but also by using knowledge of the fertility cycle, abortion, douching, abstinence, and occasionally infanticide (Dupâquier 1988: ch. 7; Gautier and Henry 1958: 119; Jones 1988: 252–253; Reinhard 1966; van de Walle 1980).

For virtually all the 169,500 priests, monks, and nuns the revolutionary decade was a turbulent, terrifying and, for many, a tragic experience. But the laity – especially women – had proved their religious commitment in large areas of the countryside; from women, too, would come a widening stream of recruits to religious orders. Cultural practices continued to express deeply engrained Catholic morality. Like revolutionaries before and since, moreover, Jacobins were to find that the attempt to forge a new, revolutionary culture that would replace the religious dimensions of the *ancien régime* as surely as the republic had replaced the monarchy would founder on popular attachment to the rituals of belief. Despite the richness of the revolutionary culture, it could not replace a Catholicism that seemed to many people deeper in substance and promise. This was to be a key cause of the violence of the revolutionary decade.

Conclusion

When the restored monarchy drafted its budget for 1815, there was an astonishing – perhaps deliberate – continuity with Brienne's draft budget of 1788. Revenues were projected to be 639 million *livres* in 1788 and expenditure 620 million; after all the tumult of the intervening period, the figures for 1815 were 620 and 638 million (Bruguière, in *Révolution de 1789*: 988–989). But the place of property taxes in state revenue was about one-third higher because the privileged were no longer exempt; direct taxes were now 58 percent of tax revenue rather than 38 percent, and indirect taxes 22 rather than 50 percent. The continuity disguised fundamental, durable changes to socio-economic structures which left none untouched and some shattered.

The image of short-term economic instability but long-term continuity disguises a fundamental shift in the dynamic sectors of the French economy. The almost total collapse of Atlantic commerce – what Paul Cheney (2010) has dubbed "primitive globalization" – and of the vulnerable Mediterranean cloth trade was the precursor to the reorientation of the French economy towards greater agricultural specialization and northeastern industrialization within Napoleon's Continental System. The Atlantic trade slowly recovered after 1800 but the place within it of the great colonial plantations of Saint-Domingue had gone and the slave-trade and slavery were abolished everywhere else by 1848. In the countryside, the contrast became sharper between regions specializing in cereals, cattle, or wine and those still mainly polycultural and subsistence.

Except in places where the rural economy had changed abruptly, for example, to more market-oriented winegrowing, or where a branch of urban work had collapsed, most people worked in 1799 as they had in 1789. The nature of their work – manual, skilled, repetitive – remained the same. The production of wine, wheat, and cloth involved the same techniques: only the scale of production had changed in particular areas. As in 1700, the countryside in 1800 was a busy, crowded landscape of manual labor. Even in areas where land use remained unchanged, however, the Revolution had gone to the heart of community and family life. Certainly, some of the changes may have been ephemeral: under the Directory, the practice of giving revolutionary names to one's children or to one's community largely disappeared. The Napoleonic Code sharply restricted grounds for divorce. A resurgent church was soon as present in the countryside as before 1789. In other ways, however, the practices of daily life were changed forever, as were the markers in the mental universe which gave meanings to people about who they were and how the world might be.

References

Ado, Anatolï (1996). *Paysans en Révolution: Terre, pouvoir et jacquerie 1789–1794*. Paris: SÉR.

Aftalion, Florent (1990). *The French Revolution: An Economic Interpretation*, trans. M. Thom. Cambridge: Cambridge University Press.

Assier-Andrieu, Louis (1984). "Custom and Law in the Social Order: Some Reflections upon French Catalan Peasant Communities." *Law and History Review*, 1: 86–94.

Bergeron, Louis, Guy Chaussinand-Nogaret, and Robert Forster (1971). "Les Notables du 'Grand Empire' en 1810." *Annales*, 26: 1052–1075.

Bodinier, Bernard (2010). "La Révolution française et la question agraire: Un bilan national en 2010." *Histoire et sociétés rurales*, 33: 7–47.

Bodinier, Bernard and Éric Teyssier (2000). *"L'Événement le plus important de la Révolution": La Vente des biens nationaux en France et dans les territoires annexés, 1789–1867*. Paris: SÉR.

Brunot, Ferdinand (1927). *Histoire de la langue française des origines à 1900*, vol. 9, part 1. Paris: Armand Colin.

Butel, Paul (1991). "The Revolution and the Urban Economy." In Alan Forrest and P.M. Jones (eds.). *Reshaping France: Town, Country and Region during the French Revolution*. Manchester: Manchester University Press.

Castaing, T. (1992). "Histoire d'un patrimoine en révolution: Claude Bonnet de Paillerets, robin de Marvejols en Lozère de 1766 à 1815." *AHRF*, 290: 517–537.

Certeau, Michel de, Dominique Julia, and Jacques Revel (1975). *Une politique de la langue: La Révolution française et les patois. L'enquête de Grégoire*. Paris: Gallimard.

Chassagne, Serge (1978). "L'Industrie lainière en France à l'époque révolutionnaire et impériale, 1790–1810." In *Voies nouvelles pour l'histoire de la Révolution française*. Paris: Bibliothèque Nationale. 143–167.

Cheney, Paul (2010). *Revolutionary Commerce: Globalization and the French Monarchy*. Cambridge, Mass.: Harvard University Press.

Claverie, Élisabeth and Pierre Lamaison (1982). *L'Impossible mariage: Violence et parenté en Gévaudan, XVIIe, XVIIIe et XIXe siècles*. Paris: Hachette.

Cobban, Alfred (1964). *The Social Interpretation of the French Revolution*. Cambridge: Cambridge University Press.

Corvol, Andrée (ed.) (1993). *La Nature en Révolution: Colloque Révolution, nature, paysage et environnement*. Paris: Harmattan.

Crouzet, François (1959). "Les Origines du sous-développement économique du sud-ouest." *Annales du Midi*, 71: 3–21.

Crubaugh, Anthony (2001). *Balancing the Scales of Justice: Local Courts and Rural Society in Southwest France, 1750–1800*. University Park: Pennsylvania State University Press.

Darrow, Margaret H. (1989). *Revolution in the House: Family, Class and Inheritance in Southern France, 1775–1825*. Princeton, N.J.: Princeton University Press.

Desan, Suzanne (2004). *The Family on Trial in Revolutionary France*. Berkeley, Los Angeles, and London: University of California Press.

Dupâquier, Jacques (1988). *Histoire de la population française*, vol. 3. Paris: PUF.

Forrest, Alan (1996). *The Revolution in Provincial France: Aquitaine 1789–1799*. Oxford and New York: Oxford University Press.

Forrest, Alan (2004). *Paris, the Provinces and the French Revolution*. London: Arnold.

Forster, Robert (1967). "The Survival of the Nobility during the French Revolution." *P&P*, 37: 71–86.

Forster, Robert (1980). "The French Revolution and the 'New' Elite, 1800–1850." In J. Pelenski (ed.). *The American and European Revolutions, 1776–1848*. Iowa City: University of Iowa Press. 182–207.

Furet, François (1981). *Interpreting the French Revolution*, trans. Elborg Forster. Cambridge: Cambridge University Press.

Gauthier, Florence (1977). *La Voie paysanne dans la Révolution française: L'Exemple picard*. Paris: François Maspero.

Gautier, É. and Louis Henry (1958). *La Population de Crulai, paroisse normande: Étude historique*. Paris: Cahiers de l'INED.

Heller, Henry (2006). *The Bourgeois Revolution in France 1789–1815*. New York and Oxford: Berghahn Books.

Higonnet, Patrice L.R. (1971). *Pont-de-Montvert: Social Structure and Politics in a French Village, 1700–1914*. Cambridge, Mass.: Harvard University Press.

Hoffman, Paul T. (1996). *Growth in a Traditional Society: The French Countryside, 1450–1815*. Princeton, N.J.: Princeton University Press.

Horn, Jeff (2006). *The Path Not Taken: French Industrialization and in the Age of Revolution*. Cambridge, Mass.: MIT Press.

Houdaille, Jacques (1978). "Un indicateur de pratique religieuse: La Célébration saisonnière des mariages avant, pendant et après la Révolution française." *Population*, 2: 367–380.

Hufton, Olwen (1967). *Bayeux in the Late Eighteenth Century: A Social Study*. Oxford: Oxford University Press.

Hufton, Olwen (1971). "Women in Revolution 1789–1796." *P&P*, 53: 90–108.

Jessenne, Jean-Pierre (2005). "L'Histoire sociale de la Révolution française entre doute et renouvellement." In Jean-Clément Martin (ed.). *La Révolution à l'oeuvre: Perspectives actuelles dans l'histoire de la Révolution française*. Rennes: Presses Universitaires de Rennes. 23–39.

Johnson, Christopher H. (1995). *The Life and Death of Industrial Languedoc, 1700–1920*. New York and Oxford: Oxford University Press.

Jollet, Annie (2000). *Terre et société en Révolution: Approche du lien social dans la région d'Amboise*. Paris: CTHS.

Jones, P.M. (1985). *Politics and Rural Society: The Southern Massif Central c.1750–1880*. Cambridge: Cambridge University Press.

Jones, P.M. (1988). *The Peasantry in the French Revolution*. Cambridge: Cambridge University Press.

Jones, P.M. (1990). "Agricultural Modernization and the French Revolution." *Journal of Historical Geography*, 16: 38–50.

Jones, P.M. (2003). *Liberty and Locality in Revolutionary France: Six Villages Compared, 1760–1820*. Cambridge: Cambridge University Press.

Kaplan, Steven L. (2001). *La Fin des corporations*. Paris: Fayard.

Kaplow, Jeffry (1964). *Elbeuf during the Revolutionary Period: History and Social Structure*. Baltimore, Md.: Johns Hopkins University Press.

Koubi, G. (ed.) (1990). *Propriété et Révolution: Actes du colloque de Toulouse, 1989*. Paris: CNRS.

La Tour du Pin Gouvernet, Henriette (1979). *Escape from the Terror: The Journal of Madame de la Tour du Pin*, trans. Frances Harcourt. London: Folio Society.

Le Goff, T.J.A. (1981). *Vannes and its Region: A Study of Town and Country in Eighteenth-Century France*. Oxford: Oxford University Press.

Le Goff, T.J.A. and D.M.G. Sutherland (1991). "The Revolution and the Rural Economy." In Alan Forrest and Peter Jones (eds.). *Reshaping France: Town, Country and Region during the French Revolution*. Manchester: Manchester University Press. 52–85.

Lefebvre, Georges (1954). "*La Révolution française et les paysans*." In *Études sur la Révolution française*, Paris: PUF.

Lehning, James R. (1980). *The Peasants of Marlhes: Economic Development and Family Organization in Nineteenth-Century France*. London: Macmillan.

Lewis, Gwynne (1993). *The Advent of Modern Capitalism in France 1770–1840: The Contribution of Pierre-François Tubeuf*. Oxford: Clarendon Press.

Livesey, James (2001). *Making Democracy in the French Revolution.* Cambridge, Mass., and London: Harvard University Press.

Livesey, James (2004). "Material Culture, Economic Institutions and Peasant Revolution in Lower Languedoc 1770–1840." *P&P*, 182: 143–173.

McManners, J.M. (1960). *French Ecclesiastical Society under the Ancien Régime.* Manchester: Manchester University Press.

McPhee, Peter (1989a). "The French Revolution, Peasants, and Capitalism." *AHR*, 94: 1265–1280.

McPhee, Peter (1989b). *Collioure et la Révolution française, 1789–1815.* Perpignan: Le Publicateur.

McPhee, Peter (1999). *Revolution and Environment in Southern France: Peasant, Lords, and Murder in the Corbières, 1780–1830.* Oxford: Clarendon Press.

McPhee, Peter (2001). "'The Misguided Greed of Peasants'? Popular Attitudes to the Environment in the Revolution of 1789." *FHS*, 24: 247–269.

McPhee, Peter (2006). *Living the French Revolution, 1789–99.* London and New York: Palgrave Macmillan.

Markoff, John (1996). *The Abolition of Feudalism: Peasants, Lords, and Legislators in the French Revolution.* University Park: Pennsylvania State University Press.

Marquié, Claude (1993). *L'Industrie textile carcassonnaise au XVIIIe siècle. Étude d'un groupe social: Les Marchands-fabricants.* Carcassonne: Société des Études Scientifiques et Agricoles.

Merriman, John M. (2002). *The Stones of Balazuc: A French Village in Time.* New York: W.W. Norton.

Miller, Judith (1998). *Mastering the Market: The State and the Grain Trade in Northern France, 1700–1860.* Cambridge and New York: Cambridge University Press.

Moriceau, J.-M. and Gilles Postel-Vinay (1992). *Ferme, entreprise et famille.* Paris: ÉHÉSS.

Plack, Noelle (2009). *Common Land, Wine and the French Revolution: Rural Society and Economy in Southern France, c.1789–1820.* Burlington, Vt.: Ashgate.

Poumarède, Jacques (1989). "La Législation successorale." In I. Théry and C. Biet (eds.). *La Famille, la loi, l'État: De la Révolution au Code Civil.* Paris: Imprimerie Nationale. 167–182.

Reinhard, Marcel (1966). "Demography, the Economy, and the French Revolution." In Evelyn M. Acomb and Marvin L. Brown (eds.). *French Society and Culture since the Old Régime.* New York: Holt, Rinehart & Winston. 20–42.

Révolution de 1789: Guerres et Croissance économique (1989). Special issue of *Revue économique*, 40.

Sewell, William H. (1980). *Work and Revolution in France: The Language of Labor from the Old Régime to 1848.* Cambridge: Cambridge University Press.

Sheppard, Thomas R. (1971). *Lourmarin in the Eighteenth Century: A Study of a French Village.* Baltimore, Md.: Johns Hopkins University Press.

Shovlin, John (2006). *The Political Economy of Virtue: Luxury, Patriotism, and the Origins of the French Revolution.* Ithaca, N.Y., and London: Cornell University Press.

Sledziewski, Élisabeth G. (1993). "The French Revolution as the Turning Point." In Geneviève Fraisse and Michelle Perrot (eds.). *A History of Women in the West: Emerging Feminism from Revolution to World War*, trans. Arthur Goldhammer. Cambridge, Mass.: Harvard University Press. 33–47.

Soboul, Albert (1976a). "Concentration agraire en pays de grande culture: Puiseux-Pontoise (Seine-et-Oise) et la propriété Thomassin." In *Problèmes paysans de la Révolution*, 1789–1848. Paris: François Maspero. Ch. 11.

Soboul, Albert (1976b). "La Reprise économique et la stabilisation sociale, 1797–1815." In Pierre Léon et al. *Histoire économique et sociale de la France*, vol. 3, part 2. Paris: PUF. 65-133.

Sonenscher, Michael (1989). *Work and Wages: Natural Law, Politics and the Eighteenth-Century French Trades.* Cambridge: Cambridge University Press.

Spagnoli, Paul (1997). "The Unique Decline of Mortality in Revolutionary France." *Journal of Family History*, 22: 425–461.

Subreville, G. (1982). "L'Apprentissage à Bourg sous la Révolution." *Les Nouvelles Annales de l'Ain*, 127–162.

Sutherland, D.M.G. (2002). "Peasants, Lords, and Leviathan: Winners and Losers from the Abolition of French Feudalism, 1780–1820." *Journal of Economic History*, 62: 1–24.

Trouvé, C.-J. (1818). *États de Languedoc et département de l'Aude, 2 vols.* Paris: Imprimerie Nationale.

van de Walle, Étienne (1980). "Motivations and Technology in the Decline of French Fertility." In R. Wheaton and T.K. Hareven (eds.), *Family and Sexuality in French History.* Philadelphia: University of Pennsylvania Press. 135–178.

Vardi, Liana (1993). *The Land and the Loom: Peasants and Profit in Northern France 1680–1800.* Durham, N.C., and London: Duke University Press.

Vivier, Nadine (1998). *Propriété collective et identité communale: Les Biens communaux en France, 1750–1914.* Paris: Publications de la Sorbonne.

Viallaneix, P. and J. Ehrard (eds.) (1980). *Aimer en France, 1760–1860: Actes du colloque international de Clermont-Ferrand.* Clermont-Ferrand: Faculté des Lettres et Sciences Humaines.

Woronoff, Denis (1984). *L'Industrie sidérurgique en France pendant la Révolution et l'Empire.* Paris: ÉHÉSS.

Woronoff, Denis (ed.) (1988) *Révolution et espaces forestiers.* Paris: Harmattan.

Young, Alfred (1929). *Travels in France during the Years 1787, 1788 and 1789.* Cambridge: Cambridge University Press.

CHAPTER TWENTY-EIGHT

The French Revolution and the Family

SUZANNE DESAN

"If we finally accept as an organizing principle that the strong will no longer impose laws on the weak in the great family of the State, why would we allow it in our own families?" demanded the *Remonstrances des mères et filles normandes de l'ordre du tiers* in 1789. These "Mothers and Daughters of Normandy" articulated a crucial question, echoed by many French revolutionaries. Did not the revolutionary transformation of politics and society also demand fundamentally different practices inside households? In the 1790s many citizens and lawmakers asked how to introduce revolutionary principles, such as liberty and equality, into the intimate world of the family.

The French Revolution radically redefined the family, its internal dynamics, and its relationship to the state. In pursuit of more egalitarian and affectionate families, revolutionary deputies sought to overturn patriarchal practices that seemed to parallel the "despotic" characteristics of the *ancien régime* monarchy. Family reforms grew more ambitious as the Revolution radicalized. By 1793–94, the legislatures had initiated controversial changes: they legalized divorce, mandated egalitarian inheritance, reduced paternal authority, granted civil rights to illegitimate children, secularized the *état civil*, allowed adoption in principle, and placed jurisdiction over family disputes into the hands of arbitration courts, known as family tribunals. All of these policies proved deeply contentious. Citizens took to the courts to negotiate new family practices and flooded the legislatures with petitions on family matters. At the same time, revolutionary culture encouraged French men and women to transform their homes into sites of patriotic regeneration and to educate their children in the principles of citizenship.

A much older historiography portrayed these revolutionary innovations as an attack on the integrity of the family or marriage (Olivier-Martin 1901; Thibault-Laurent 1938). Legal historians more recently have worked to nuance and deepen

A Companion to the French Revolution, First Edition. Edited by Peter McPhee.

our understanding of revolutionary family law in its political and juridical context (Garaud and Szramkiewicz 1978; Halpérin 1992; Théry and Biet 1989; *Révolution et l'ordre juridique privé* 1988). Moreover, in the 1970s and 1980s, growing interest in social history spurred scholars to assess more carefully how families in diverse regions reacted to reform policies, such as divorce (Dessertine 1981; Phillips 1980) or inheritance (Darrow 1989). For James Traer, revolutionary transformations encouraged the turn toward more "modern," affectionate families (Traer 1980); likewise, André Burguière (1993, 2011) situates the Revolution within a longer-term tendency of the French state to encourage the "formation of the couple." Anne Verjus (2004, 2010) ties this focus on the couple to the rights of citizenship and voting: she argues that the revolutionaries placed "conjugalism" at the heart of their family policy and, as a result, married men as heads of households ideally acted as political citizens who represented the joint interests of dependent women and children.

The emergence of gender history produced lively debate over the Revolution's impact on women within families. Some scholars have argued that the Revolution laid the foundations for domesticity by excluding women from public politics and mandating a "private" role for them, above all as republican mothers within households (Gutwirth 1992; Landes 1988). Lynn Hunt (1992) suggested that male revolutionaries favored female domesticity because the overthrow of the king and of patriarchal models in politics and family awakened male fears of social disorder and sexual dedifferentiation. Some historians have emphasized the long-term influence and appeal of Rousseau's ideology in forging the domestic ideal across the revolutionary decade (Popiel 2008). In contrast, others have contested the public–private model and contended that, rather than isolating women in a domestic sphere apart from politics, revolutionary family reforms and debates over citizenship and nationality opened up new political and legal means for certain women to assert their rights and gain access to property, power, or independence (Desan 2004; Heuer 2005). Women gained new civil rights and new political avenues to make demands on the state. Hunt has observed that revolutionary leaders granted women civil but not political rights because "women simply did not constitute a clearly separate and distinguishable *political* category before the Revolution"; given this context, the extent of debate about their rights was surprising (2007: 169).

In part, it is possible for historians to have such different interpretations of the family in the 1790s precisely because the revolutionaries aimed to change so much. Revolutionary lawmakers vibrantly debated each round of legal reforms, but by and large they embraced the opinion voiced by the Mothers and Daughters of Normandy. A new kind of state should be underpinned by a new form of family. As the elemental building block of society and nation, the family ideally should become an arena for fashioning patriotism and testing out the practices of equality, liberty, and regeneration on the ground. And since one's position in the family played such a fundamental role in defining each individual's legal status, the act of creating juridical, individual citizens equal before the law inevitably raised the question of family reform. (Guibert-Sledziewski 1989; Mulliez 1987). At the same time, the political context encouraged thousands of family members – fathers and mothers, brothers and sisters – to join in the debate with the jurists, deputies, pamphleteers, and moralists over the ideal marriage and family.

Revolutionary reformers drew in part on Enlightenment writings that advocated for more open and affectionate families and proposed numerous legal reforms. In the late *ancien régime*, novelists, moralists, and legal writers had excoriated tyrannical fathers, recounted the unjust plight of illegitimate children, lauded marriage for love over arranged marriage, and exposed parallels between private and public immorality as a means to critique politics (Goy 1988a; Hunt 1992; Maza 1993; Pasco 2009). Various *philosophes*, ranging from Montesquieu and Morelly to the less well-known Cerfvol, called for divorce. They fused theories of natural law and marriage-as-contract with arguments based on utility, liberty, sentiment, happiness, and population growth (Blum 2002; Halpérin 1992; Ronsin 1990; Traer 1980). Many jurists, natural law theorists, and proponents of religious toleration focused attention on the invalid and unclear status of Protestant or Jewish marriages (Adams 1991; Hertzberg 1968). Some *philosophes* were so intent on family reform that they used their own families as laboratories for testing out Enlightenment principles in the home (Roberts 2011).

In addition, during the *ancien régime* some jurists had promoted the idea that France should move toward a more unified law code. Civil law practices varied across France. The Midi followed Roman law, also known as "written law" in its early modern form. In this region, fathers commonly had the right to grant legacies as they wished, and they tended to favor one child, preferably a son. To the north, over 300 variations on customary law created complex regional differences. While many of these regions tended toward more egalitarian inheritance, some, most prominently Normandy, favored sons over daughters. Likewise, if communal marital property held sway in much of the north, in Normandy and the Midi the dotal systems endeavored to preserve goods within the family line. Numerous other regional differences peppered civil law and family practices (Le Roy Ladurie 1972; Ourliac and Gazzaniga 1985; Yver 1966). *Ancien régime* jurists Robert-Joseph Pothier and François Bourjon argued for unification, using the customs of Orléans or Paris, respectively, as models. As Jean-Louis Halpérin (1992) has noted, the revolutionaries would push this drive for legal codification and unification beyond what many more conservative *ancien régime* jurists envisioned. Likewise, the revolutionaries built on and beyond the long-standing struggle of the monarchy to wrest control over family law from the Catholic Church and responded to calls in the *cahiers de doléances* to simplify family law and render it more accessible.

With the outbreak of revolution, when the Constituent Assembly embarked on its ambitious program of remaking every aspect of French public life, the deputies turned to the intimate sphere as well. Drawing inspiration from Enlightenment criticism, early revolutionary reforms included the abolition of *lettres de cachet* and primogeniture and the establishment of a new judicial institution, the *tribunaux de famille*, that aimed to make family litigation more accessible, affordable, and democratic. These family tribunals were temporary, local arbitration courts: quarrelling family members each chose two representatives to arbitrate their disputes and rule on issues such as inheritance, divorce, or parent–child conflict. Until their suppression in 1796, these innovative family tribunals handled the flood of claims spawned by the revolutionaries' attempt to remake the family.

As the early revolutionaries attempted to redefine church–state relations and stake out the meaning of citizenship, they inevitably turned to the question of marriage. Marriage played a pivotal role in establishing each citizen's nationality, filiation, legitimacy, and right to inherit or control – or in women's case, not to control – property. The act of creating rights-bearing citizens demanded that the revolutionaries rethink the legal nature of marriage. Deputies addressed conjugal reform as part of their drive to enact natural law, guarantee juridical uniformity, regenerate citizens, and build a secular state disentangled from Catholicism and tolerant of multiple religions. They gradually moved toward defining marriage as a civil, secular contract made between two rights-bearing individuals.

Lobbying from below reinforced the deputies' interest in reforming marriage. Individuals who faced difficulty in marrying – such as actors (who were considered "immoral") or couples of different faiths – petitioned the National Assembly to deal with their individual situations (Traer 1980). The Revolution also unleashed a deluge of pamphlets and petitions demanding that the legislature legalize divorce and help individuals to achieve happiness through more companionate marriages. Lamenting the "irons" or "chains" that made them "slaves to Hymen," petitioners urged the legislators to grant them the freedom to divorce. In the words of one petitioner, divorce alone offered "the liberty of breaking these cruel chains and living forever free in the bosom of loving friendship and happiness, invaluable for the life of every good French patriot."[1]

In the Constitution of 1791, the National Assembly defined marriage as a "civil contract." In 1792, shortly after the overthrow of the monarchy, the Legislative Assembly legalized divorce, reduced paternal authority over marriage choices, lowered the age of majority, removed all nuptial matters from clerical control, and established a secular *état civil*. Priests would no longer record births, marriages, or deaths. As Jean Jaurès remarked, by putting an end to the church's authority over family matters and by rooting the family in the state, this secularization of the *état civil* "was one of the most profoundly revolutionary measures … It changed, if I may say so, the very basis of life" (Jaurès 1970: vol. 3, 348).

Marriage rates rose also during the Revolution, in part because young men sought to avoid conscription. Couples also experienced a "more open marriage market": they tended to wed younger, to choose spouses from a wider social milieu, and to marry widows or widowers more readily (Daumas 2003: 143; Reinhard et al. 1968). According to revolutionary moralists and jurists, greater freedom within marriage should increase personal happiness and encourage social order and patriotism. As Nicolas de Bonneville stated in *Le nouveau code conjugal* in 1792, "Marriage is the social bond that unites the citizen to the *patrie* and the *patrie* to the citizen."[2] In many towns, civil marriages enacted this principle in public and took on a festive, patriotic character. For example, in La Rochelle in the spring of 1794, the "people" provided a "civic dowry" to help one solder marry the *citoyenne* of his dreams. They pronounced their vows amidst a festival that also featured a young mother adopting an abandoned child and an older couple renewing their vows after fifty years of marriage.

If revolutionary marriage as a "civil contract" marked a bond between citizen and state as well as husband and wife, this contract could also be broken. In a bold move, the 20 September 1792 law replaced the *ancien régime* system of *séparation de corps et d'habitation* with a remarkably liberal form of divorce. Couples could petition for divorce based on incompatibility, mutual consent, or one of seven grounds: insanity; condemnation to infamous punishment; cruelty or mistreatment; notoriously immoral behavior; abandonment for two years; absence without news for five years; or emigration. In the spring of 1794, the Convention added an even easier form of divorce based on six months' *de facto* separation. In contrast to couples who separated under *ancien régime* laws, divorced spouses had the right to remarry after a one-year wait. Nowhere in Europe had divorce without fault been allowed previously. The strikingly modern provisions for divorce based on incompatibility or mutual consent awakened controversy, especially when the climate grew more socially conservative after Thermidor.

The 1792 divorce law was also unprecedented in granting women and men virtually equal access to all forms of divorce. (Wives faced the disadvantage of having to undertake proceedings in their husbands' place of residence.) Both women and men turned most often to "mutual consent," "incompatibility," or the various forms of "absence" or "abandonment" as grounds for divorce. Notably, in every region studied so far, women initiated 65–75 percent of unilateral divorces (that is, those not based on "mutual consent"). As one petitioner, *femme* Berlin, commented, divorce could "remind certain men (what they have forgotten) that woman is not their slave but rather their companion, and she should not be the victim of their tempers and bad treatment." In her denunciation of conjugal tyranny, *femme* Berlin points us toward a pattern discovered by multiple historians: because wives held less power within marriages and had fewer options, they not only initiated more divorces but also made fuller use of the whole panoply of motives. Only the motive of adultery, "notoriously immoral behavior," was invoked more often by husbands than wives. But the centrality of divorce for unhappy wives should not obscure the fact that the new law also offered men an unprecedented opportunity to remake their lives. While men requested perhaps only 2 percent of *ancien régime séparation de corps*, they initiated some 25–35 percent of unilateral divorces, and participated just as much as women did in developing the new model of marriage based on compatibility and liberty (Desan 2004: 101; Dessertine 1981; Kruse 1983; Phillips 1980; Ronsin 1990).

Overall, some 38,000 to 50,000 couples took advantage of the law between 1792 and 1803, when Napoleonic laws made divorce more difficult to obtain. Divorce was far more prevalent in cities than in the countryside. In urban areas, couples had greater access to legal expertise, more exposure to revolutionary laws and political culture, and they were most likely to benefit from supportive neighborhood networks and diversified economic opportunities that made divorce at least thinkable. Divorce also followed distinct class patterns. Peasants, the rich, and the very poor dissolved their marriages far less often than did couples from artisanal, commercial, or bourgeois backgrounds. Finally, couples with children divorced less frequently.

Opponents decried that divorce shredded marriage, but revolutionary deputies and moralists in fact envisioned access to divorce as part of a new form of marriage: liberty and affection would strengthen the conjugal bond and help husbands and wives to play their complementary roles as they transformed the home into a site of political regeneration and patriotic conversion. At times, revolutionary jurists defended women's rights within marriage: beyond offering women access to divorce, in October 1793 the legislature voted in principle to grant women equal control over communal marital property, although this change never became enacted in practice (Brisset 1967). Yet, most often, the revolutionaries emphasized the different personal and political duties of husbands and wives within marriage. Republican wives should use their pronounced moral sensitivity, their *sensibilité*, to encourage men's moral development, cultivate their humane and sensitive qualities, and also foster their military valor and loyalty to the Republic. Women should also seduce men on behalf of the *patrie*, rewarding patriots with their charms and withholding their caresses from traitors and counter-revolutionaries.

Likewise, as republican mothers, women had a particular responsibility to raise their children as patriots and teach them republican ideals. While revolutionary leaders urged mothers to suckle their babies with the "milk of liberty," women's clubs across France taught patriotic songs to their offspring or held ceremonies rewarding them for memorizing the words of the Declaration of the Rights of Man. Republican gender ideology built on Rousseau's vision of motherhood's moral power and infused it with revolutionary significance. Rosalie Ducrollay Jullien, wife of the Jacobin Marc-Antoine Jullien, took this role to heart as she fused maternal advice with republican politics. "My dear son, be virtuous in the name of a mother's love," she wrote to her 20-year-old son Jules in 1794. "Work as hard as you are strong, be as zealous as you are capable, and know, without being prideful, that your existence brings prosperity to the Republic and happiness to your tender parents" (Parker 2011: 151).

In some parts of France, the most zealous revolutionary parents chose to endow their newborns with revolutionary names rather than saints' names. This practice peaked with the radical revolution of the Year II. Parents named their children after revolutionary values or heroes, such as "Égalité" or "Lepeletier"; respected figures from antiquity or recent history, perhaps "Brutus" or "Franklin"; revolutionary events like "Jemappes"; or, most frequently, names borrowed from the republican calendar, such as "Amaranthe" or "Jonquille." Expressing ambiguity or hedging their bets, some parents combined the old with the new: "Jean Marie Marat" or "François Abricot" had a nice ring and left open options for the future (Daumas 2003; McPhee 2006). In the 1790s, even more marked than the explicit choice of revolutionary names was an overall diversification of naming, as parents strove perhaps to express the individual or unique identities of their offspring (Daumas 2003).

For their part, republican men, too, should embrace the project of patriotic fatherhood and affectionate marriage on the home front, even as they acted as the public, political representatives of the family. True patriots married and produced families. "Now is the time to make a baby!" proclaimed a slogan on painted republican pottery (Darnton 1990: 11). In many ways, the revolutionary emphasis on fraternity and fraternal institutions, such as male political clubs and the army, encouraged homosocial bonds among men, or even homoerotic bonds (Crow 1995; Hunt 1992). As part of lightening the penal code of 1791, the Constituent Assembly decriminalized sodomy (Sibalis 1996). But at the same time, the revolutionaries nonetheless continued to use homosexual imagery to depict the corruption, effeminacy, or degeneration of monks and aristocrats in particular. The Revolution reinforced a heterosexual, masculine ideal to be carried out within patriotic families. The Constitution of the Year III not only required that members of the Council of Ancients be either married or widowed, it also emphasized the full spectrum of men's familial duties by declaring that "no one is a good citizen if he is not a good son, good father, good brother, good friend, and good husband." Particularly by the Directorial era, the *fête des époux* demonstrated both the public centrality of marriage and also the husband's role as an honorable *père de famille.* So pivotal were marriage and fatherhood to male citizenship that priests faced enormous pressure to marry in order to prove both their manhood and their patriotism. Jacobin club members in Périgueux proclaimed, "The only good priest is the one who binds himself to the public good by the sweet ties of marriage and of fatherhood" (Cage 2011: 150; Verjus 2010).

As the revolutionaries struggled to redefine fatherhood, they built on the *ancien régime* trend toward valorizing affection and equality over paternal "tyranny." Emblematic of this shift, in the April 1791 debate over equal division of intestate legacies, Honoré de Mirabeau, former victim of a paternal *lettre de cachet*, inveighed against the power of fathers "not just to disinherit their children, but to sell them." "What a strange way to win children's love … to say to them: 'If you don't obey me, I will disinherit you'," commented Jérôme Pétion in the same debate.[3] With the *patria potestas* of the Midi as the icon of "despotic fathers," in 1792 the Legislative Assembly lowered the age of majority to 21 for both sons and daughters and asserted the right of adult offspring to gain access to their property and to choose their own marriage partners. Fathers' control over inheritance was gradually whittled away. After abolishing primogeniture in 1790 and mandating equal inheritance for intestate legacies in 1791, in 1793–94 the legislature extended this egalitarian principle to all forms of inheritance in both direct and collateral lines. While the law of 12 Brumaire II (2 November 1793) granted equal inheritance to illegitimate children recognized by their parents, the law of 17 Nivôse II (6 January 1794) pronounced that all offspring, regardless of sex or birth order, would divide family property evenly. The Convention even declared these practices retroactive to 1789.[4]

No aspect of family reform generated more contestation in court than the egalitarian inheritance law of 17 Nivôse II. The law challenged traditional agrarian and family practices by altering the basis of lineage strategies and property arrangements and by questioning the usual distribution of power and goods between the genders and generations. In areas such as the Midi and parts of the north, the new policy undercut the long-established prerogative of the father to direct family strategy by offering a preferential legacy to one or more of his offspring. Even in those northern and western regions that customarily practiced egalitarian inheritance, the prohibition of entailment (in 1792) limited the father's options in managing family goods for future generations. Beyond weakening paternal authority, the new law empowered daughters and younger sons and affected gender relations within households not only because many regions of France customarily favored sons over daughters, but also because marriage arrangements everywhere in France were bound up with the eventual partition of estates.

In Midi, Normandy, and pockets of the north, east, and center, the new laws demanded a renegotiation of family goods, including any legacies that had changed hands since 1789. While some families redivided property peacefully with the help of notaries, other sets of siblings took each other to court to implement the new policies. Still other families developed strategies to avoid dividing land, such as false sales, forced gifts between siblings, *légitimes* (lawful portions) paid in near-worthless *assignats*, or new forms of marriage contracts. In some agrarian regions deeply resistant to change, such as the Gévaudan, these ploys became a dry run for efforts to undercut the egalitarian mandates of the Civil Code of 1804. (The Code maintained the principle of egalitarian divisions, but increased the size of the disposable portion to one-half for parents with only one child, one-third for those with two, and one-quarter for those with three or more children) (Claverie and Lamaison 1982; Collomp 1983; Darrow 1989; Goy 1988b; Poumarède 1989).

These new inheritance practices improved the legal standing of many women in Normandy, the Midi, and some smaller customary areas, where daughters generally had no claim on parental legacies beyond their original dowry or *légitime*. Daughters, like younger sons, lobbied the legislatures to demand and defend these new rights. As one anonymous Norman woman reminded the Convention, the 17 Nivôse law "re-established the *natural and imprescriptible rights* of the [female] sex ... The legislative assembly decreed all men equal in rights in 1789, and women and girls were included in this generis expression" (her emphasis). In these same regions, sisters and younger brothers repeatedly took their brothers to court to increase the size of their legacies, *légitimes*, or dowries. In the district of Caen in the Calvados, for example, sisters won 78 percent of their inheritance cases against brothers and negotiated compromises in another 7 percent of cases between 1791 and 1796. In Burgundy, daughters likewise were successful in increasing the size of their portions already allotted; here the revolutionary laws augmented a prerevolutionary trend toward more liberal dowering of daughters, and families frequently made mutual concessions without extensive conflict. Even before the new laws were passed, one son was inspired in 1793 to renounce his role as universal heir and make his sister an equal heir to his parents. In his words, he acted "as much because of [his] friendship with her as because of [his] love of justice and equality." The Midi, bastion of inegalitarian inheritance, also witnessed an upsurge of court cases in the Year II: younger siblings in the Pyrénées, for example, repeatedly challenged the embedded custom of privileging the eldest son (Bart 1968: 77; Collomp 1994; Desan 2004: 167; Fortunet 1988; Poumarède 1989).

In their drive to create more egalitarian families, lawmakers also decided that even illegitimate children, *if recognized by their parents*, could claim an equal share in their parents' legacies. The law of 12 Brumaire II (2 November 1793) also implicitly outlawed the customary right of unwed mothers to pursue paternity suits for lying-in expenses and child support. This bold but problematic law grew out of a complex combination of motives and factors (Bellivier and Boudouard 1989; Brinton 1936; Fortunet 1987; Gerber 2012; Mulliez 2000). Inspired by natural law ideology, the deputies hoped to restore the rights of natural children, who had long been stigmatized and legally disadvantaged. "Nature ... has not made it a crime to be born," declared Cambacérès.[5] The lawmakers also hoped to deal with the problem of rising rates of illegitimacy and child abandonment. They imagined that the new law would work in tandem with secular welfare. The 28 June 1793 poor relief law planned to offer aid to natural mothers who nursed their offspring, to pay their lying-in expenses, and even set up state-run homes for these women to raise their children as young patriots. At the same time, revolutionary jurists intended to free putative fathers from paternity suits and enable them to voluntarily embrace fatherhood.

As they attempted to fulfill all of these goals, revolutionary lawmakers curtailed their equality principle and wrote an unclear and tentative law. Only illegitimate children with ample proof of paternity would receive these new civil rights. In addition, to fully benefit from the law, natural children had to be born of unmarried parents who fully recognized them and whose estates had entered probate after 14 July 1789. Uneasy about encouraging illicit unions, the deputies limited children born of adultery to one-third of their full share of legacies. When cases entered the courts, they proved to be very difficult to win. Natural children had the greatest chance of success in 1794–95, but overall they faced an uphill battle in establishing a father's "voluntary" paternity. For those whose father had died between 14 July 1789 and the new law, only his public or private written acknowledgment of paternity or evidence of his ongoing care could work. For those cases opened after October 1793, the law did not clarify what evidence was needed. Furthermore, natural children confronted intense opposition from siblings or collateral relatives. Finally, in the increasingly conservative atmosphere of the Directory, the Tribunal de Cassation interpreted the law ever more narrowly, undercutting the intentions of its authors and overturning all but the most secure cases (Brinton 1936; Desan 2004).

Paradoxically, the new policies inadvertently did more to harm illegitimate children than to help them. While a few of them did indeed win parental legacies, far more natural children were deeply disadvantaged because their unwed mothers increasingly lost the right to press putative fathers for child support. The state promised these women only a small annual pension of 80 *livres*. Although the revolutionaries had hoped to create a more reliable system of state-run welfare and homes for natural mothers and their children, the state could not meet its poor relief goals (Forrest 1981).

Legal reforms, political and economic disruptions, a new political culture – from multiple angles the Revolution created opportunities, and also pressure, for families to reinvent themselves. Revolutionary changes seem to have encouraged families in certain regions and classes to adopt new practices that weakened their attachment to the family line and to focus their energy more intently on conjugal unity and the nuclear family. This "invention of the couple," to use Burguière's phrase, had roots in the *ancien régime* and had immense regional variations. Certain parts of the Midi especially seem to have clung to old lineage family models and developed strategies to prolong them in the face of revolutionary and Napoleonic transformations. Even in the Midi, however, distinct shifts occurred. In Haute-Provence in the early nineteenth century, for example, stem families declined in frequency. And while fathers continued to protect the lineage by privileging one heir, younger daughters and sons used the law to limit that share. In Normandy, a region once dominated by lineage mentality and by dotal systems that separated and protected lineage goods, couples turned more and more often to communal marital property arrangements that arguably gave the couple more autonomy from kin networks and increased their joint interest in marital ventures. While it is difficult to assess whether sentimental bonds between spouses grew stronger, in many regions husbands and wives in the 1790s took advantage of new laws allowing mutual gifts between spouses. These formal *donations entre vifs* often included expressions of reciprocal affection or friendship. In letters exchanged between bourgeois couples in the Lyonnais, the historians Davidson and Verjus uncovered the couples' joint emotional and managerial labor on behalf of the conjugal household. In Paris, artisanal families relied less on local lineage connections and expanded their commercial and marital networks to further the wealth, status, and opportunities of their immediate families (Boudjaaba 2008; Burguière 1993; Chaline 1982; Collomp 1994; Daumas 2003; Davidson and Verjus 2011; Garrioch 1996; Poncet-Crétin 1973; Poumarède 1989).

If the Revolution enabled or compelled families to reinvent themselves across mainland France, slave revolt and the attempt to build a post-emancipation republic in the Caribbean colonies had a tremendous impact on families both slave and free. Slave revolt and civil war sent white plantation-owning families into exile across the Atlantic world. "I was completely ruined, without home, without money, without clothes … Ignorant of the fate of my family … I believed them among the victims," lamented the white Creole author of *My Odyssey*, shipboard en route to the United States (Popkin 2010: 292). If the Haitian Revolution splintered some white families, for former slaves the family, especially marriage, became a site "in which the meanings of freedom were delimited, debated, and above all, negotiated" (Colwill 2010: 72). In Saint-Domingue, both French republican officials and Toussaint Louverture hoped to encourage marriage among former slaves: as an institution, marriage seemed to offer stability and set the post-emancipation state apart from the royalist plantation society that had torn families apart through slavery. In the eyes of republican officials, beyond sanctifying the state, marriage and conjugal families should also underpin the coerced labor regimes that replaced plantation slavery. Former slaves, however, chose to invent families as they wished. Marriage rates rose abruptly in 1793 when the French commissioners promised emancipation to enslaved women who married free men. (The route to freedom was gendered: initially, male slaves could liberate themselves by becoming soldiers.) But freedmen and women were far more likely to use the new civil records to register the births of their children than to transform their relationships into legal marriages. To register a birth cemented liberty, citizenship, and possibly even access to inheritance for a child of former slaves, while the benefits of marriage were far less clear. Freed women more often defended the integrity and needs of their families by refusing to act within the constraints of the post-emancipation labor regime. They expanded their garden plots into additional sectors, demanded equal pay with men, and claimed a second free day each week to cultivate family plots (Colwill 2009, 2010; Dubois 2004, 2010).

Although in a very different position than former slaves, *émigrés*, nobles, and foreigners back in France likewise experienced the need to invent their families anew in this turbulent time. Given their precarious political position, some wives of *émigrés* or nobles divorced in order to protect themselves and their familial property. At the height of radical revolution, in April 1794 the Convention expelled ex-nobles and enemy foreigners from Paris, military cities, and port towns. Many wives and widows petitioned for exception based on some circumstance that proved their loyalty to the "Great Family" of the nation, such as divorce from an *émigré*, forced marriage to a noble, "adoption" by the new nation as a natural child, etc. As Jennifer Heuer has shown, because revolutionaries believed that individuals could develop a stronger allegiance to the nation than to their own families, officials proved warily open to such arguments in 1794. But the Directorial period witnessed a shift in family–state relations. For women in particular, the bond to the family was now believed to surpass the tie to the state, and officials placed renewed emphasis on wives' subordination to their husbands, a shift that would be deepened by the Civil Code. So, for example, wives who had emigrated to follow their husbands were granted amnesty by a special clause of the law of 28 Vendémiaire IX (20 October 1800). And the Civil Code famously decreed that women who married foreigners had renounced their French citizenship through this freely chosen contract (Heuer 2005).

When Napoleon and his Council of State produced the Civil Code of 1804, they envisioned many family innovations of the 1790s as deeply disruptive of the gender order and social stability. The Code was both heir to the Revolution and reaction against it (Halpérin 1992). The Code fulfilled revolutionary goals in creating unified law, establishing private property and freedom of contracts, cementing the end of feudalism and privilege, and codifying the secularization of marriage and the *état civil.* Some of its family laws grew out of the 1790s: the Code maintained certain aspects of egalitarian inheritance for legitimate offspring and it allowed a much-curtailed version of divorce. But more often than not, the authors of the Code reacted against revolutionary innovations in family law. Above all, they reasserted the patriarchal authority of fathers over children and husbands over wives, and attempted to secure the boundaries of legitimate families.

While the revolutionaries had struggled – with mixed success – to recognize the rights of wives, adult offspring, siblings, natural children, and their parents, the Code opted for a more clear-cut definition of the juridical individual: the male head of household. Weaving together aspects of customary, revolutionary, and Roman law, the drafters of the Code worked to replace the revolutionary ideal of a more egalitarian and affectionate family with an honor-based, patriarchal family, rooted in male authority and the defense of family property. Although fathers had to share out one-half to three-quarters of their legacies equally between their offspring, they regained the right to imprison wayward offspring and control their sons' marriages until age 25. Likewise, the Code sought to protect fathers and family property from illegitimate children or unwed mothers: it definitively abolished paternity suits and inheritance rights for natural children. The Code allowed childless couples over the age of 50 to adopt an adult child to inherit their goods. (Although the revolutionaries legalized adoption "in principle" in 1792 and sporadic adoptions occurred, the process was not formalized until the Code.)

In the name of conjugal unity, the Code also crafted a model of marriage in which the wife was much more clearly subordinate to her husband. Legally, she must follow him to his place of residence, her nationality derived from his, and she lost various forms of access to state courts that had been available in the 1790s. Tellingly, while the Code reinstated *ancien régime séparation de corps* and made divorce very hard to get, it made it doubly difficult for wives. While a man could imprison and divorce his wife for adultery, a woman could file for divorce against an unfaithful husband only if he maintained his mistress within the conjugal household.

Much work remains to be done to untangle the long-term impact of the Revolution on families, especially given the lack of adequate research on early nineteenth-century family practices and given the complicated relationship between the Civil Code and the Revolution. But certain patterns stand out. In bringing about a social revolution within households, the Revolution made it both necessary and possible for families to reinvent their collective family strategies as well as the internal dynamics of gender and generation. In many regions, lineage families seem to have lost power, as couples placed greater focus on the conjugal family. Women in certain positions in the family used revolutionary laws to win independence or property. In fact, this era made the family into a crucial space for negotiating women's rights and identity and left a contradictory legacy. Revolutionary rhetoric praised women's moral power within families and highlighted their domestic potential. At the same time, rather than simply enclosing women within a domestic sphere, the Revolution had given women new civil rights and access to the state and generated languages and practices for attacking gender inequality. In the nineteenth century, domesticity grew stronger largely as a reaction *against* revolutionary gender instability and women's greater political and legal power. The Civil Code, rather than revolutionary family law, provided the legal architecture for domestic ideology.

Finally, the Revolution highlighted the political centrality of the family and fundamentally altered the frame for thinking about the relationship among the individual, family, and state. The revolutionaries simultaneously attacked the traditional conception of the family as an organic whole, did away with the corporate model of society, and undercut the political sacrality of the church. As they attempted to build a newly secular state and nation, the revolutionaries emphasized the individual liberty of citizens within households, but also fervently envisioned the family as a unifying political and social glue. In short, the Revolution promoted the family as a central locus for inventing modern politics, yet also left unresolved the relationship between the individual, the family, and society as a whole. Little wonder that over the next century political thinkers and activists – republicans and liberals, utopian socialists and conservatives – all argued heatedly over the role of the family in creating social and political cohesion for France.

Notes

1 Archives Nationales, DIII 33.

2 Bonneville, *Nouveau code conjugal, établi sur les bases de la Constitution, et d'après les principes et les considérations de la loi déjà faite et sanctionée, qui a préparé et ordonné ce nouveau code.* Paris: Cercle Social, 1792.

3 *Archives parlementaires de 1787 à 1860. Recueil complet des débats législatifs et politiques des chambres françaises, imprimé par ordre du corps législatif sous la direction de mm.*

J. Mavidal et E. Laurent. Première série, 1787–1799 (1867–1913), 82 vols. Paris: P. Dupont. *AP* 24: 511–515, 506–508, 2 April 1791. Talleyrand read the speech immediately after Mirabeau's death.

4 Those with children could freely dispose of one-tenth of their property; those without children had one-sixth disposable property according to the law of 17 Nivôse II (6 January 1794).

5 *AP* 66: 34–37, 4 June 1793. The 12 Brumaire law stipulated that children born of adultery could receive only one-third of an equal share of their inheritance.

References

Adams, Geoffrey (1991). *The Huguenots and French Opinion, 1685–1787: The Enlightenment Debate on Toleration.* Waterloo, Ont.: Wilfrid Laurier University Press.

Bart, Jean (1968). "L'Égalité entre héritiers dans la région dijonnaise à la fin de l'ancien régime et sous la Révolution." *Mémoires de la Société pour l'histoire du droit et des institutions des anciens pays bourguignons, comtois et romands*, 29: 65–78.

Bellivier, Florence and Laurence Boudouard (1989). "Des droits pour les bâtards: L'Enfant naturel dans les débats révolutionnaire." In Irène Théry and Christian Biet (eds.). *La Famille, la loi, l'État de la Révolution au Code civil.* Paris: Imprimerie Nationale. 122–144.

Blum, Carol (2002). *Strength in Numbers: Population, Reproduction, and Power in Eighteenth-Century France.* Baltimore, Md.: Johns Hopkins University Press.

Boudjaaba, Fabrice (2008). *Des paysans attachés à la terre? Familles, marchés et patrimoines dans la région de Vernon (1750–1830).* Paris: Presses de l'Université Paris-Sorbonne.

Brinton, Crane (1936). *French Revolutionary Legislation on Illegitimacy.* Cambridge, Mass.: Harvard University Press.

Brisset, Jacqueline (1967). *L'Adoption de la communauté comme régime légal dans le Code civil.* Paris: PUF.

Burguière, André (1993). "Les Fondements d'une culture familiale." In André Burguière and Jacques Revel (eds.). *Histoire de la France*, 4 vols. Paris: Seuil. Vol. 4: 25–118.

Burguière, André (2011). *Le Mariage et l'amour en France: De la Renaissance à la Révolution.* Paris: Seuil.

Cage, Claire (2011). "Unnatural Frenchmen: Priestly Celibacy in Enlightenment and Revolutionary France." Ph.D. dissertation, Johns Hopkins University.

Chaline, Jean-Pierre (1982). *Les Bourgeois de Rouen: Une élite urbaine au XIXe siècle.* Paris: Presses de la Fondation Nationale des Sciences Politiques.

Claverie, Élisabeth and Pierre Lamaison (1982). *L'Impossible mariage: Violence et parenté en Gévaudan, XVIIe, XVIIIe, XIXe siècles.* Paris: Hachette.

Collomp, Alain (1983). *La Maison du père: Famille et village en Haute-Provence aux XVIIe et XVIIIe siècles.* Paris: PUF.

Collomp, Alain (1994). "Le Statut des cadets en Haute-Provence avant et après le Code civil." In Georges Ravis-Giordani and Martine Segalen (eds.). *Les Cadets.* Paris: CNRS. 181–194.

Colwill, Elizabeth (2009). "'Fêtes de l'hymen, fêtes de la liberté': Marriage, Manhood, and Emanicipation in Revolutionary Saint-Domingue." In David Patrick Geggus and Norman Fiering (eds.). *The World of the Haitian Revolution.* Bloomington: Indiana University Press. 125–155.

Colwill, Elizabeth (2010). "Freedwomen's Familial Politics: Marriage, War and Rites of Registry in Post-Emancipation Saint-Domingue." In *Gender, War and Politics: Transatlantic Perspectives, 1775–1830.* Basingstoke: Palgrave Macmillan. 71–89.

Crow, Thomas (1995). *Emulation: David, Drouais, and Girodet in the Art of Revolutionary France.* New Haven: Yale University Press.

Darnton, Robert (1990). *What was Revolutionary about the French Revolution?* Waco, Tex.: Baylor University Press.

Darrow, Margaret (1989). *Revolution in the House: Family, Class, and Inheritance in Southern France, 1775–1825.* Princeton, N.J.: Princeton University Press.

Daumas, Philippe (2003). *Familles en Révolution: Vie et relations familiales en Ile-de-France, changements et continuités (1775–1825).* Rennes: Presses Universitaires de Rennes.

Davidson, Denise and Anne Verjus (2011). *Le Roman conjugal: Chroniques de la vie familiale à l'époque de la Révolution et de l'Empire.* Seyssel: Champ Vallon.

Desan, Suzanne (2004). *The Family on Trial in Revolutionary France.* Berkeley: University of California Press.

Dessertine, Dominique (1981). *Divorcer à Lyon sous la Révolution et l'Empire.* Lyon: Presses Universitaires de Lyon.

Dubois, Laurent (2004). *A Colony of Citizens: Revolution and Slave Emancipation in the French Caribbean, 1787–1804.* Chapel Hill: University of North Carolina Press.

Dubois, Laurent (2010). "Gendered Freedom: *Citoyennes* and War in the Revolutionary French Caribbean." In *Gender, War and Politics: Transatlantic Perspectives, 1775–1830.* Basingstoke: Palgrave Macmillan. 58–70.

Forrest, Alan (1981). *The French Revolution and the Poor.* New York: St. Martin's Press.

Fortunet, Françoise (1987). "Sexualité hors mariage à l'époque révolutionnaire: Les Mères et les enfants de la nature." In Jacques Poumarède and Jean-Pierre Royer (eds.). *Droit, histoire, et sexualité.* Lille: Espace Juridique. 187–198.

Fortunet, Françoise (1988). "Connaissance et conscience juridique à l'époque révolutionnaire en pays de droit coutumier: La Législation successorale." *In La Révolution et l'ordre juridique privé.* Orléans: PUF. Vol. 1, 359–371.

Garaud, Marcel and Romuald Szramkiewicz (1978). *La Révolution française et la famille.* Paris: PUF.

Garrioch, David (1996). *The Formation of the Parisian Bourgeoisie, 1690–1830.* Cambridge, Mass.: Harvard University Press.

Gerber, Matthew (2012). *Bastards: Politics, Family, and Law in Early Modern France.* New York: Oxford University Press.

Goy, Joseph (1988a). "La Révolution française et la famille." In Jacques Dupâquier (ed.). *Histoire de la population française.* 4 vols. Paris, PUF. Vol. 3, 84–115.

Goy, Joseph (1988b). "Transmission successorale et paysannerie pendant la Révolution française: Un grand malentendu." *Études rurales*, 110–112: 45–56.

Guibert-Sledziewski, Élisabeth (1989). *Révolutions du sujet.* Paris: Méridiens Klincksieck.

Gutwirth, Madelyn (1992). *The Twilight of the Goddesses: Women and Representation in the French Revolutionary Era.* New Brunswick, N.J.: Rutgers University Press.

Halpérin, Jean-Louis (1992). *L'Impossible Code civil.* Paris: PUF.

Hertzberg, Arthur (1968). *The French Enlightenment and the Jews.* New York: Columbia University Press.

Heuer, Jennifer Ngaire (2005). *The Family and the Nation: Gender and Citizenship in Revolutionary France, 1789–1830.* Ithaca, N.Y.: Cornell University Press.

Hunt, Lynn (1992). *The Family Romance of the French Revolution.* Berkeley: University of California Press.

Hunt, Lynn (2007). *Inventing Human Rights: A History.* New York: W.W. Norton.

Jaurès, Jean (1970). *Histoire socialiste de la Révolution française*, 7 vols. Paris: Éditions Sociales.

Kruse, Elaine Marie (1983). "Divorce in Paris, 1792–1804: Window on a Society in Crisis." Ph.D. dissertation, University of Iowa.

Landes, Joan (1988). *Women and the Public Sphere in the Age of the French Revolution.* Ithaca, N.Y.: Cornell University Press.

Le Roy Ladurie, Emmanuel (1972). "Système de la coutume: Structures familiales et coutumes d'héritage en France au XVIe siècle." *Annales*, 27: 825–846.

Maza, Sarah (1993). *Private Lives and Public Affairs: The* Causes Célèbres *of Prerevolutionary France.* Berkeley: University of California Press.

McPhee, Peter (2006). *Living the Revolution, 1789–1799.* Basingstoke: Palgrave Macmillan.

Mulliez, Jacques (1987). "Droit et morale conjugale: Essai sur l'histoire des relations personelles entre époux." *Revue historique*, 278: 35–106.

Mulliez, Jacques (2000). "La Volonté d'un homme." In Jean Delumeau and Daniel Roche (eds.). *Histoire des pères et de la paternité.* Paris: Larousse, 279–305.

Olivier-Martin, François (1901). *La Crise du mariage dans la législation intermédiaire, 1789–1804.* Paris: Librairie Nouvelle de Droit et de Jurisprudence.

Ourliac, Paul, and Jean-Louis Gazzaniga (1985). *Histoire du droit privé français de l'an mil au Code civil.* Paris: Albin Michel.

Parker, Lindsay Holowach (2011). "'In Silence and in Shadow': A Biography of Rosalie Ducrolly Jullien (1745–1824)." Ph.D. dissertation, University of California at Irvine.

Pasco, Allan H. (2009). *Revolutionary Love in Eighteenth- and Early Nineteenth-Century France.* Farham and Burlington: Ashgate.

Phillips, Roderick (1980). *Family Breakdown in Late Eighteenth-Century France: Divorces in Rouen, 1792–1803.* Oxford: Oxford University Press.

Poncet-Crétin, Paulette (1973). "La Pratique testamentaire en Bourgogne et en Franche-Comté de 1770 à 1815." Thèse de droit, Université de Dijon.

Popiel, Jennifer (2008). *Rousseau's Daughters: Domesticity, Education, and Autonomy in Modern France.* Durham: University of New Hampshire Press.

Popkin, Jeremy (2010). *You Are All Free: The Haitian Revolution and the Abolition of Slavery.* New York: Cambridge University Press.

Poumarède, Jacques (1989). "La Législation successorale de la Révolution entre l'idéologie et la pratique." In Irène Théry and Christian Biet (eds.). *La Famille, la loi, l'État de la Révolution au Code civil.* Paris: Imprimerie Nationale. 167–179.

Reinhard, Marcel, André Armengaud, and Jacques Dupâquier (1968). *Histoire générale de la population mondiale.* Paris: Montchrestien.

Remonstrances des mères et filles normandes de l'ordre du tiers. Rouen, 1789.

La Révolution et l'ordre juridique privé: Rationalité ou scandale? Actes du colloque d'Orléans. 11–13 septembre 1986 (1988), 2 vols. Orléans: PUF.

Roberts, Meghan Kelly (2011). "Cradle of Enlightenment: Family Life and Knowledge Making in Eighteenth-Century France." Ph.D. dissertation, Northwestern University.

Ronsin, Francis (1990). *Le Contrat sentimental: Débats sur le mariage, l'amour, le divorce, de l'Ancien Régime à la Restauration.* Paris: Aubier.

Sibalis, Michael (1996). "The Regulation of Male Homosexuality in Revolutionary and Napoleonic France, 1789–1815." In Jeffrey Merrick and Bryant T. Ragan Jr. (eds.). *Homosexuality in Modern France.* New York: Oxford University Press. 80–101.

Théry, Irène and Christian Biet (eds.) (1989). *La Famille, la loi, l'État de la Révolution au Code civil.* Paris: Imprimerie Nationale.

Thibault-Laurent, Gérard (1938). *La Première introduction du divorce en France sous la Révolution et l'Empire (1792–1816).* Clermont-Ferrand: Imprimerie Moderne.

Traer, James F. (1980). *Marriage and the Family in Eighteenth-Century France.* Ithaca, N.Y.: Cornell University Press.

Verjus, Anne (2004). *Le Cens de la famille: Les Femmes et le vote, 1789–1848.* Paris: Belin.

Verjus, Anne (2010). *Le Bon mari: Une histoire politique des hommes et des femmes à l'époque révolutionnaire.* Paris: Fayard.

Yver, Jean (1966). *Égalité entre héritiers et exclusion des enfants dotés: Essai de géographie coutumière.* Paris: Sirey.

CHAPTER TWENTY-NINE

The Revolution in History, Commemoration, and Memory

PASCAL DUPUY

The French Revolution was fought with an intensity that has enabled it to extend well beyond the chronological limits of its particular history. Because of the social and political realities it called into question, the revolutionary "event" has been the subject of debates that have facilitated the renewal and extension of its heritage in France, and beyond its boundaries as well. Few historical events past or present can boast a presence which is so dynamic that it has endured ever since, thus revealing its continuing relevance. The historiography that seized upon the Revolution from its beginnings was one of the vectors of this perpetual memorialization, assisted by many other conduits. Thus the various commemorations that, from the first centenary in 1889, celebrated the event in 1939 and 1989 also gave rise to polemics and controversies that encouraged reflection on its character as heritage. Finally, memory of the Revolution from 1789 to the present day has similarly distinguished itself by the fervent opposition between admirers and detractors of its achievements in a symbolic effervescence expressed in media ranging from literature to still or moving images, as well as songs and speeches. For all these reasons, far from being a cold and lifeless entity, the French Revolution is a historical "moment" whose traces surround us still today and the memory of which is perpetuated through the contestation of issues that are forever being renewed.

A Changing Historiography

Writings on the French Revolution appeared contemporaneously with the events. Edmund Burke in Britain launched the inflammatory, polemical, international approach to it in 1790. From London, too, many authors, of whom the most famous was Thomas Paine, were to answer Burke by taking up the defense of the Revolution. In France, the imprisoned Antoine Barnave, probably from December

A Companion to the French Revolution, First Edition. Edited by Peter McPhee.

1792, was to reflect on the causes, long-term but also contemporary, of the Revolution "in a first sketch of economic materialism" according to Jean Jaurès. In Germany, Emmanuel Kant followed by Johann Gottlieb Fichte praised the Revolution, which they regarded as the culmination of the Enlightenment and from which they hoped the German people would be able to draw inspiration. Nevertheless, during the early years it was the writings of conservatives and counter-revolutionaries that resonated loudest because they used theological arguments or the theory of a "plot" (Masonic or Protestant) to lend greater weight and depth to what were above all political diatribes. The first genuinely historical steps, that is, those founded on a study of the sources, would not appear until the early nineteenth century with various histories of the French Revolution, some not completed, but which aimed nonetheless at a greater objectivity through use of original sources and less partial accounts.

Under the Empire, a time when historians and thinkers were under strict surveillance, the Revolution was still a time of lived experience, whether of enthusiasm or rejection, but of which memory was still alive. And then, from 1815, the Revolution became a significant field of research and historical scholarship. At the beginning, narrative, memorial history – sometimes erudite, sometimes fanciful – was the mode for expressing the story of the French Revolution. However, gradually, the work of detailing and presenting the Revolution became the province of specialists in the discipline. This change dates from the period after 1860 when the triumph of positivism fostered the "historical method," exposing earlier approaches to the Revolution to the critical demands of historical science.

The way in which the French Revolution was written about, in other words its historiography, thus transformed itself across the two subsequent centuries. For all the obvious diversity, three currents were apparent from the beginning of the Restoration. First of all, the face of rejection, that of the counter-revolution, can be seen. Despairing, overtly unfavorable to the new realities against which it fought, the counter-revolutionary and fatalistic view rejected the essential contributions of the Revolution: the principle of national or popular sovereignty which it regarded as illegitimate; civil equality, which would destroy society, the natural family, and filial hierarchies that run counter to individualism; Promethean rationalism; the rejection of sacredness that comes from tradition in favor of the sanctification of the search for progress and happiness. At the other extreme stood the democratic republicans, united by their celebration of the Revolution of 1789, but also, sometimes, their ardor for the Year II of the Republic, the advent of popular sovereignty as the best expression of a sovereign nation, and even, at times, the *coup d'état* of Brumaire; for them, the French Revolution was the essential and strategic moment in the history of the nation and of humanity, of the march towards social progress, equality among citizens, and the quest for individual happiness. The 1793 Constitution was most often their guide and credo. Between these two camps was "liberal" acceptance of the Revolution as a "necessity" inherent in the inability of the *ancien régime* to reform itself. The liberals considered the Revolution as an absolute good, as far as the demands of natural law that established the rights of man in society and the right of all peoples to choose their constitution are concerned. But this acceptance was accompanied by blunt rejection of state despotism, even if imposed by "circumstances." As a result, together with Germaine de Staël and François Guizot, the liberals rejected both the revolutionary government and the personal power of Napoleon Bonaparte. They simultaneously refused to regard the demands of the people as legitimate if they claimed to impose restrictions on the sale of property and submit economic regulation and business initiatives to the law of a so-called "democratic" Republic. This historiographical division continued throughout the nineteenth century, yet it was seriously modified by new thematic interests, deeper scholarship, and the discovery of new sources interpreted in the light of new methodologies.

Although the twentieth century broadly followed this tripartite division, it remained the century in which respect for nuance and documentary precision became more important in relation to the still contested and bitterly debated French Revolution. If Hippolyte Taine in his *Origines de la France contemporaine* (1875–94) anticipated the twentieth century by analyzing the Revolution from sources found in departmental and even local archives, popular action played the decisive role in his account. Writing in the light of his traumatic experience of the Paris Commune of 1871, Taine expressed his contempt for the people and, above all, the revolutionary crowd. In his revulsion for the Commune, Taine might also have seen reverberations of the Revolution as the Commune, amongst other measures, resurrected the Committee of Public Safety of 1793–94 (Shafer 2005). Gustave Lebon (*La Révolution et la psychologie des révolutions*, 1912) took his inspiration from this in scenes in which he transformed the people into wild animals which had reverted to a state of nature. Jean Jaurès, philosophy teacher, then deputy, on the contrary, published a *Histoire socialiste de la Révolution française*, initially in booklet form (1900) then in volumes, in which he strove to understand the causes of the Revolution through its social and economic characteristics, as well as its political development, with particular emphasis on those who represented the "socialist" or "communist" wings of the revolutionary movement. And although the French Revolution was not socialist, Jaurès believed it had produced the best vehicles for advancing socialism. In addition to his work as a historian, he also spoke in support of the vote in the Chamber of Deputies on 27 November 1903 for "the funding necessary to begin classification and publication of archival documents relating to economic life during the French Revolution." This led to the establishment of the Commission de Recherche et de Publication des Documents Relatifs à la Vie Économique de la Révolution. Its field of investigation has grown from 1903 to encompass the entire history of the Revolution, while at the same time its current name has been simplified to the "Jaurès Commission," a commission which has long been attached to the Comité des Travaux Historiques et Scientifiques (CTHS), a state organization within which it continues to function by publishing theses, collections, and monographs more than a century after it was founded.

The motives of Alphonse Aulard were not so different, but his career was more narrowly academic. He was moreover the first person to be appointed, in 1890, to a chair at the Sorbonne dedicated to the study of the French Revolution, which he held until his death. In his lectures, his books, and the journal he edited (*La Révolution française*) he was an indefatigable defender of the Revolution, vigorously opposing the writing of Taine and his followers, such as Augustin Cochin. Finally, in an act combining memory and erudition, he took advantage of the commemoration of the centenary of the Revolution to instigate an immense effort to make sources public. Albert Mathiez and Georges Lefebvre, both academics, succeeded him only indirectly (when Aulard died, the Sorbonne chair was awarded to Philippe Sagnac and not to Mathiez) and should be regarded, because of their commitment to socialism and their interest in Marxism and the economic and social aspects of the revolutionary period, as the "heirs" of Jaurès. For many they came to incarnate the "Jacobin" camp of historians of the Revolution, that is to say defenders of the Revolution and believers in social and cultural history based on economics. Around Georges Lefebvre, who was appointed to the Chair of French Revolution History at the Sorbonne in 1939 and held it until 1955, clustered a group of scholars from France (such as Jacques Godechot, Albert Soboul, Marc Bouloiseau, and Jean-René Suratteau) and overseas (among them George Rudé, Richard Cobb, Kare Tønnesson, and Franco Venturi). Following in the footsteps, and with the blessing, of the man who at the time was the uncontested master of revolutionary studies, these scholars strove to ensure the triumph of research broadly defined by the linking of social relations to economic activity. The person who best represented this tradition was undoubtedly Albert Soboul, who was appointed to the Sorbonne Chair in 1968, a post he held until his sudden death in 1982, just as the organizational premises of the celebration of the bicentenary of the Revolution were being set out. Soboul devoted his thesis to the Parisian sans-culottes (*Les sans-culottes parisiens en l'an II*, 1958), a masterly piece of political and social history, and from the Sorbonne as well as from the presidency of the Société des Études Robespierristes, he taught, inspired many avenues of research, organized, and took part in innumerable conferences, while at the same time he declared himself heir to what he called "the classic historiography of the French Revolution" (Soboul 1974). Although Soboul was a less orthodox descendant than his adversaries wanted to make him out to be, his membership of the French Communist Party from 1939, which he did not conceal, engendered suspicion at the time of the Cold War. It was, moreover, after the Second World War that the most pronounced of the serious criticisms of this historiography, soon defined as a simple "vulgate" (Furet 1989), began to appear, first in the English-speaking world during the 1950s, then during the 1960s in France. The fuse was lit by Alfred Cobban in 1955 (*The Myth of the French Revolution*) and a little later with his *Social Interpretation of the French Revolution* (1964) in which he challenged the thesis of social causes of the Revolution, arguing that it was above all a political confrontation, divorced from any social factors. At the same time, but from a totally different perspective, Robert Palmer (*The Age of the Democratic Revolution*, 1959) provided a global interpretation of the different conflicts that had erupted on both sides of the Atlantic in the second half of the eighteenth century, denying that the French Revolution represented an "exception." The idea of "Atlantic revolution" or "western revolution" that Palmer elaborated was widely contested by historians, who accused it of an artificial unity; but it became part of a wider historical development, favoring the triumph of the Annales school, which tended to give preference to a vision of history founded on the *longue durée*, the ten years or so of the French Revolution characterized as an epiphenomenon in relation to the slow and deep movements of western history. François Furet and Denis Richet, in a book written for the general public (*La Révolution française*, 1965), also inspired a historical polemic which would unsettle revolutionary studies for several decades. In this work the two young authors put forward a vision of a revolution divided into two separate periods, the first, from 1789 to 1790, calm and confident, inspired by reformist convictions, and the second, with the intervention of the people and "skidding" (*dérapage*), when a revolution which had become violent and ungovernable was radicalized. This interpretation held political decisions to be largely responsible for triggering the Revolution and equally responsible for its later evolution. Moreover, the authors rejected the chronology that had been generally accepted in France and that deemed the period from 1792 to 1794, with its ambiguities and complexities, to be the key event of the revolutionary decade, favoring instead the very beginning of the Revolution. A riposte was not long in coming, with Claude Mazauric taking up the cudgels in a long and densely argued essay in *Annales historiques de la Révolution française*, swiftly followed by a rejoinder from François Furet. Originally an article, later reprinted as *Penser la Révolution française* (1978), a book which was very widely read, Furet denounced the "revolutionary catechism," whether the classical, "Jacobin" or "Marxist" interpretation of the French Revolution, and discerned within it a "totalitarian" essence that prefigured the revolutionary upheavals of the following centuries. The book had a considerable impact and Furet became a media personality, famous in France and throughout the English-speaking world.

The classical school appeared, in the 1980s, to have retreated. Michel Vovelle, who succeeded Albert Soboul at the Sorbonne in 1980, seemed a less public person. His previous areas of interest focused less on the history of the revolutionary period, rendering his appointment a pale rival to the "Furet galaxy," with its media links and overseas renown. Contrary to expectations, however, Vovelle revealed himself to be a pugnacious fighter, attracting many students, supervising dozens of doctoral theses, establishing many cultural history projects, traveling the world, and criss-crossing France at the time of the celebrations linked to the bicentenary.

With the dawn of the second millennium, the historiography of the French Revolution changed significantly. It became prolix, regionalized, diversified in terms of sources, its epistemological anchorage was refashioned, and it did not perhaps respond as schematically as it had in the past to the idea of "opposing schools." Moreover, the history of the Revolution became truly international, as Eric Hobsbawm presciently commented in 2007, in the afterword to the French translation of his book on revolutionary historiography published in English in 1990 (Hobsbawm 2007).[1] For Hobsbawm the "Furet Revolution is now over," but it had nonetheless left a "regrettable heritage" which he discerned in the "lessening" of French interest in research on the Revolution. This assertion might surprise us in view of the number of universities in France which teach the Revolution and the increased number of recent books from French historians dealing with subjects that had previously been neglected (the Directory, the neo-Jacobins, the colonies, visual representations, and so on). In the end, as Vovelle observed, challenging the Furet interpretation enabled a school that was perhaps inclined to get bogged down in repetitive history to take on new subjects, to refine new problems, and to include new fields in its research (Vovelle 2007).

Less agitated but still vibrant, the historiography of the French Revolution continues to paint its subject anew in the form of a picture that French and international scholars redraw with care and precision. And, as Marc Bloch demanded when he evoked the disfigured portraits of Robespierre ("Robespierristes, anti-Robespierristes, we beg for mercy; for goodness sake just tell us, what was Robespierre like?" (Bloch 1949), the French Revolution becomes a little closer and more familiar to us every day, while the actual event recedes inexorably into the past.

From Celebrations to Commemorations

Continuing the public demonstrations of collective sensibility hoped for by Jean-Jacques Rousseau, festivals and celebrations became indispensable occasions for revolutionary, and later republican, communities: they invaded the public space in France, and especially Paris, as early as 1790. Later, throughout the nineteenth and twentieth centuries, these practices both spread and were transformed.

From 1789 to 1804, the commemoration of 14 July 1789 provided a striking example of how the search for symbolic legitimacy was constantly subjected to the contradictions and evolution of national politics. The Festival of Federation that brought tens of thousands of men and women to the Champs de Mars on 14 July 1790 had been organized because of pressure from the "federalizing" movement coming from provincial towns and villages, which for once had made the capital follow their example by turning their movement into a national one. But by presenting a picture of a nation united around the king and the constitution to come, the Festival of Federation artificially concealed the insurrection of an angry crowd which, the year before, had seized the Bastille, bringing down with it one of the symbols of a despotic regime. The following year, under the pretense of "binding citizens to the fatherland or of uniting them through bonds of happy fraternity," Mirabeau also envisaged, in his report on festivals, establishing eight civil and military festivals, especially a "great national festival, called the Festival of Federation or of the Oath of Fraternity, which binds all citizens to each other." His premature death on 1 April 1791, however, prevented the presentation of the report, and the celebration of 14 July, having been left without an established format, would be directly affected by the political context of a revolution in search of its own memory.

Although the celebration of 14 July could, on occasion, assume a republican tone (as in 1798), during the revolutionary decade it was mainly regarded by the authorities with circumspection and suspicion. These reservations were due either to the fact that it was in competition with alternative political events or because it carried within itself the memory of popular spontaneity that did not suit the intentions of the authorities (under the Directory and the Consulate). From 1805, 14 July was officially ignored in France and was celebrated or evoked only by exiles or opponents of monarchy or the empire. Even under the Second Republic, 14 July was muted, despite the wish of the *quarante-huitards* to resurrect the heritage of 1789 in the minds, vocabulary, and symbols of the French. Divided between workers, socialists, and neo-Babouvistes who wanted a great festival on 14 July and the bourgeois republican liberals who, on the contrary, were quick to select particular parts of the revolutionary heritage, the celebration was once again spurned, and it was 4 May, the day of the opening of the Estates-General, that was retained and became the national day of the Second Republic. Though memory of the event was not completely erased, the idea of an official celebration on 14 July seemed to have been definitively put to rest. It reappeared again, however, at the end of the 1870s, when the Third Republic, at Gambetta's suggestion, was looking for a national history, heritage, and holiday. The conservative/authoritarian camp (Bonapartists, Orléanists, legitimists) certainly did not want that date. Republicans were divided. Some, like Louis Blanc, proposed 21 September in commemoration of the First Republic but were not opposed to 24 February in commemoration of the Second: others suggested 4 August and some, the neo-Robespierristes (smaller in number), were in favor of 21 January! In any case conservatives and republicans were united on one point: 14 July was a date that marked a cleavage, with a before and an after, with an accent on the mobilization of the people. The date was finally hastily adopted on 6 July 1880, just a few days before its first celebration. The choice of 14 July as the national day revealed a definite wish to break with the past. At a moment when the Third Republic was still being challenged, 14 July was retained in the interests of embedding in the national psyche a new republican regime. The date, however, had another advantage: it permitted a two-dimensional memorial, since almost a century later 14 July evoked both the taking of the Bastille in 1789 in a popular uprising, and also the Festival of the Federation in 1790 which, according to the republican historian and senator Henri Martin, "saw not a drop of blood spilled and was the consecration of the union of the whole of France" (Bois 1991: 151). Through its choice of the date of 14 July, France was thus taking on and justifying a pluralist heritage which allowed the simultaneous evocation of the liberty of 1789 and the artificial unity and fraternity of 1790, while at the same time ignoring most of the chronology of the Revolution and skirting round the years of war and Terror. But the date also carried within itself a stronger meaning, particularly according to Victor Hugo when he called for clemency and amnesty for the Communards, declaring in the Senate that 14 July was also "the festival of all nations" and that it marked the end "of all the Bastilles" and was an event that concerned "all humankind," invoking once more the universal reach of the revolutionary message of 1789.

Although Victor Hugo invoked the universal and did not conceal his attachment to the heritage of the "Great Revolution," most of the founders of the Third Republic were more embarrassed than enthused by the commemoration (1889) that they nonetheless accepted and were obliged to organize. This same unease among the authorities towards popular activism and mobilization would be found later, at the time of the commemorations of 1889, 1939, and 1989, whether it was a matter of celebrating or in fact opposing celebration. The first steps taken by the Third Republic were symbolic, but not completely insignificant. The choice of 14 July occurred at the same time as the enshrining of the *Marseillaise* as the national song (1879) and finally the reopening of the Panthéon (a monument firmly associated with the Revolution) as a shrine to receive, in 1885, the remains of one of those great men to whom the fatherland, in accordance with its 1791 dedication, owed its gratitude: Victor Hugo, poet, novelist, and man of politics, who embodied this republican and revolutionary memory. Despite these obvious appeals, the republican government dithered, waiting until 1886 before finalizing the official plans for a Universal Exhibition devoid of "all obviously commemorative content" (Ory 1992: 31) in Paris in 1889. A decree establishing the dates of festivals and ceremonies to mark the centenary of the Revolution and accompany the Universal Exhibition was not proclaimed until 16 March 1889. The Republic was still young; it still inspired a great many reservations domestically, and externally it was almost (and uniquely) encircled by more or less conservative monarchies. The first commemoration was therefore partly symbolic and above all intellectual, marked by the establishment of town-hall lectures on the French Revolution and the publication of archival texts. It was also a time of monuments, with statues erected in Paris glorifying Rousseau, Condorcet, and Danton, as well as in provincial towns, such as the statue of Barnave in Saillans, in the department of the Drôme. Finally, young people, the future citizens, were targeted through pedagogical circulars addressed to schoolteachers, inviting them to "inspire in the hearts of students feelings of profound admiration and gratitude for that France of 1789, that had so powerfully striven for progress." Overall, however, these initiatives were rarely due to the state, which, unsure of itself and undermined by the rise in Boulangism, was more inclined to leave any proposals up to municipalities or private enterprise. Although it was deeply republican, the government was nevertheless reluctant to celebrate and did not want to encourage debate by confronting the monarchists and Boulangists outright. Despite the Eiffel Tower, no significant monument was erected in 1889 in celebration the centenary of the Revolution. The tower, which constituted the "keystone" of the Universal Exhibition of 1889, and was, according to its originator, under the high patronage "of the men of science who have honored France since 1789," and the top of which is reached by climbing up 1792 steps, remains the symbol of the Universal Exposition of 1889 and was more representative of technical progress than the memory and heritage of the French Revolution.

Although the state thus refused to launch any expansive commemorative gesture, some semi-official propaganda was nevertheless produced thanks to republican intellectuals who filled the public commemorative space through a network of learned societies, university and mainstream publications, patriotic festivals, and the unveiling of statues and monuments. In 1889 it was the Republic itself that was commemorated rather than the Revolution (though the latter invoked it). This piece of self-promotion was made all the more significant by the fact that the regime still faced, as the Boulangist crisis had shown, stiff opposition (which may nevertheless have been more apparent than real).

The context was very different in 1939. If the Republic seemed strong, France appeared fragile. The government chose to place the celebration of the sesquicentenary under the aegis of a few great principles that in effect disguised the revolutionary character of the event being commemorated. The radical president Édouard Herriot, himself a historian, denied the egalitarian nature of the decade from 1789 to 1799 and opted for liberty and justice rather than equality.

Although the official ceremonies had nonetheless been envisaged as combining the celebrations of 1789 and 1792, commemoration was compromised, mainly because of the international environment. Nevertheless, even discounting the external crisis and conflict that were about to explode, the indecision of the authorities was palpable, and caused the republican Jean Guéhenno to write, in an unpublished piece printed later, that "France is celebrating the 150th anniversary of the Revolution. But it is all being done in a rather shame-faced fashion."[2] In the face of the looming conflict with Hitler's Germany, ideological and political reservations became clear and the manufactured or assumed desire of many deputies to concentrate on the present rather than celebrate the anniversary of a past event effaced the patriotic meaning of the commemoration. From the official and Parisian point of view, the commemoration of the sesquicentenary was thus incomplete and notably cautious. Outside Paris, however, plans and their realization were more numerous, even if they revealed a map of France in which the activities still mirrored the antagonisms produced by the Revolution. It was in the end among the opposition that the memory of the Revolution was liveliest in 1939, with the Communist Party taking an active part in the commemoration and opposing the fascists, who wanted to be rid of the revolutionary and republican heritage. The extreme right published increasing numbers of counter-revolutionary books, denounced the religious policies of the French Revolution (the emancipation of the Jews), attacked the "populace" or revolutionary "rabble," and turned Charlotte Corday into a new Joan of Arc from whom one should draw inspiration: for Drieu de la Rochelle, she was "a fascist before her time" (Mazeau 2009). In the other camp, in the Communist Party, commemoration was a political duty, historians and militants were mobilized, and demonstrations proliferated, notably in the municipalities of the "red suburbs" of Paris.

The state commemoration of the sesquicentenary demonstrated a lessening of revolutionary fervor compared to 1889. With the state in retreat, part of the population undecided, and spirits preoccupied with the impending war, official celebration of the sesquicentenary of 1789 remained marginal to "official" history, despite the efforts of the Communist Party and its supporters, who derived a slight political benefit from it within the Resistance.

In 1989 the Republic, a political regime accepted almost unanimously by the French, seemed incapable of being questioned. But it had to face other challenges. Although the socialist François Mitterrand was elected President of the Republic in 1981, he lost his parliamentary majority in 1986. "Cohabitation" existed until his re-election in 1988, when, in the same year, he once more gained a majority in the National Assembly. The commemoration which had been envisaged from 1981 by the first leftist government of the Fifth Republic could thus take place under the aegis of a body created for the purpose, the Mission for the Bicentenary of the French Revolution. Its first president, in 1986, was Michel Baroin, chosen by the Gaullist prime minister during the period of cohabitation. He was killed in an accident in February 1987 and replaced by an originally radical centrist republican, Edgar Faure, who himself died in March 1988 after a long illness. Mitterrand then named a socialist historian, Jean-Noël Jeanneney, to head the Mission. It was he who took on the organization of the commemoration.

As a result of the cohabitation of the past and the premature death of his two predecessors, Jeanneney found, on taking office, many disparate plans. Commemoration, moreover, was still a sensitive issue which some on the right (with nuances and exceptions) regarded with circumspection and others with hostility. Jeanneney's great achievement lay in perseverance, "and in rather spectacularly revealing the political resonance between certain revolutionary values and certain contemporary problems" (Kaplan 1995). Some of the events organized by his Mission enjoyed great, though often ambiguous, success. This was the case of the parade along the Champs-Élysées on 14 July 1989 organized by the publicist Jean-Paul Goude which, under the banner of "brotherhood among men," attracted millions of television viewers and was almost unanimously applauded by the press. But the Mission also enabled the realization of many regional events through a process of endorsing projects. The "21 March 36,000 trees for liberty" project certainly echoed the old revolutionary, later republican, tradition of planting a "liberty tree" and was a great success. But commemoration was not just a matter for Paris, and the whole of France, through the regional councils, took part in the celebration. Two other bodies played an equally "federating" role: the CLEF (Committees for Liberty Equality Fraternity) and the association Vive 89. The CLEF resulted from the union of two associations that had already participated in the two earlier commemorations: the League for the Rights of Man and the Citizen and the League of Education, whereas Vive 89 was created following a decision of the National Committee of the French Communist Party in April 1987. Local CLEF committees relied heavily on the school networks of the two associations at their head in developing commemorative activities ranging from publishing to organizing pedagogical addresses or theatrical productions all over the country. Vive 89 was inspired by a commemorative tradition that situated the French Revolution within a process of placing "progressive" values at the center of republican, socialist, and communist thought. To achieve this, Vive 89 relied on a dense network of historians, supporters, and unionists, in order to inspire, by functioning as a kind of coordinating unit, the organization of events and projects which would make the voice of the communists themselves heard as well as those of the most radical republicans within the general chorus of commemoration. According to Steven Kaplan, considering "how little funding and time it had at its disposal" the results achieved by Vive 89 were "more than honorable," particularly with a traveling exhibition and hundreds of festive gatherings. Altogether, just like the two earlier acts of commemoration, the bicentenary was a great popular success: according to one poll, almost one-third of all French people personally took part in a commemorative event in 1989. Despite all the indecisiveness of the politicians in power at the time, always embarrassed by the heritage of the Revolution and its contemporary meaning, the commemoration was the occasion of a real celebration.

In the end commemoration of the French Revolution, with its successes and failures, has always come up against the high stakes that have divided French public opinion since the Revolution itself. A shared memory, whose opposing tendencies run along a dividing line that will not fade, has formed, for good or bad, a French collective unconscious which was originally forged by the revolutionary event.

Memories and Histories

The history and memory of the Revolution of 1789 were omnipresent in nineteenth-century France. Artists derived inspiration from it and song-writers devoted couplets to it, because to sing of the revolutionary events of 1789 was "always to sing of a glory: that of the Nation, that of the people, that of the army, or that of a party" (Darriulat 2010). It is the reason that the Restoration and the July Monarchy long refused to admit its presence in schools. A different revolution, that of 1848, set it as a subject for study in senior classes. Later, having been once more purged from the curriculum under the Second Empire, the history of the Revolution underwent governmental attack on moral grounds from 1873 to 1877, before being definitively placed in the school framework under the Third Republic. If the study of the Revolution was set as a teaching subject under republican regimes, this was because it accorded with efforts in education and the political and cultural integration of the future citizen. The event itself, as much as its constructed story, encouraged civic appropriation in republican memory. To evoke the memory of the French Revolution meant inevitably to be made to retrace a divided history, made up of a feeling of repugnance towards its adversaries and admiration for the republicans, but the origin of this lay in the Revolution itself. According to historians, the term "counter-revolution" appeared in autumn 1789 or at the beginning of 1790, but its roots go back further and took hold within the ideological current of the anti-Enlightenment from the 1770s (McMahon 2001). This rejection took on a political dimension at the time of the "aristocratic revolution" in 1787 to 1788 and above all in the spring and summer of 1789. The counter-revolution certainly developed a doctrine and practice along republican-revolutionary lines in its discourse, but it also played a determining role, without ever admitting it, in the process of revolutionary radicalization as early as 1791. Outside France, its thinkers drew a dark and generally unequivocal picture of revolutionary events. Casting opprobrium on the Revolution, reducing it to conspiracy or to mere factional intrigue, could not, however, succeed in dismissing an event of such importance. With its actors transformed into martyrs (Louis XVI, Marie-Antoinette, the Vendée) the counter-revolution gave itself a tragic history and memory, which by playing on emotion and tradition nonetheless allowed it to acquire a stable social basis from 1815 to the final years of the nineteenth century. The Restoration played the card of condemnation regarding the Revolution through the use of a vocabulary founded on the notion of crime ("forfeit," "perversion") and the image of blood and cruelty ("barbarity," "inhumanity") in a biblical evocation of revolutionary "sin." Rejection of the "Men of the Revolution" among the country's senior bureaucrats was ultimately limited, but from the ideological, moral, and above all symbolic point of view, the Restoration monarchy determinedly rejected the heritage of the revolutionary decade, establishing a day of mourning on 21 January, setting up a revolutionary counter-calendar, forbidding the wearing of the cockade and Phrygian bonnet, and destroying or burning tricolor flags as a sign of repudiation of the Revolution and the Empire. At the same time, what Emmanuel Fureix called an "official iconoclasm" between 1814 and 1816 involved both publicly visible establishments (such as town halls, public monuments, churches, and shop signs) and also private dwellings. The objective was to eliminate all symbols likely to evoke the disgraced regimes of the past as much as to "destroy their possible triumph, now or in the future" (Fureix 2009). This destructive, counter-revolutionary, and anti-republican agenda can be seen from 1850, and again under the Second Empire, with liberty trees torn down, Phrygian bonnets destroyed, and the republican motto erased from public buildings. For all its work, the counter-revolution never managed to "restore" the prestige of the pre-revolutionary regime, to achieve a "de-revolution," to unravel the essentials of the institutions born of the Revolution and the Empire. The Restoration did not call into question the social transformations resulting from the decade of revolution and consolidated by the Empire, and accepted in severely modified form (only 15,000 qualified to be elected to the Chamber of Deputies under the Restoration, and only 50,000 had the right to vote) many of the political changes linked to the dawn of what Guizot described as "representative government". The French people rejected outright a return to the situation before 1789 with its so-called "absolute" monarchy, its privileges, and its control over the public mind.

For the next 200 years, evocation of the Revolution attracted the hatred of those wanting to attack the Republic, popular sovereignty, or the idea of social progress. In this context, the Vendée as a "region of memory" (Martin 1989) in some ways embodied the revitalization of the counter-revolutionary spirit. This "hodge-podge of memories" (Martin 1989), which was constantly renewed thanks to historians, graphic artists, and politicians, nourished the rejection of the secular and republican model inspired by the Revolution. The "War of the Vendée" (1793–96) gave rise to a virtual territory and place of memory on which a totally different history of France was constructed, that of "Vendéan memory." The Vendéan cause, regularly evoked thanks to the political disputes of the nineteenth and twentieth centuries, made a return to the historiographical and political stage, notably at the time of the bicentenary in 1989. The same traditional themes, vehemently though inaccurately reactivated, were aimed at encouraging a general condemnation of the spirit of the Revolution and discrediting the republican model. On the opposite side, the Republic was able to use memory of the anti-Vendéans in its own celebrations, especially through a patriotic perspective following the defeat in 1870 and the birth of the theme of "revenge." This is how the story of Bara, a young drummer killed in the Vendée by "white" gunfire in 1793, was used. The Third Republic, in school textbooks by Ernest Lavisse, turned him into a symbol of courageous, patriotic heroism (Forrest 2009).

In cases when the memory (or counter-memory) of the Revolution was not directly used, we can still see its influence on public discourse. Nineteenth-century literature thus generally looked to the revolutionary decade as a source of legend and romance. The publication of many works, described as "memoirs," drawing on the recollections of revolutionary or counter-revolutionary figures, provided the material for a lived history of the Revolution. The nineteenth-century historians of the revolutionary movement (Lamartine, Michelet, Quinet) made hay from these subjective sources and the genre itself became a "market" with "makers" of *Memoirs* becoming an actual professional category in France during the 1820s (Luzzatto 1991). Alongside this fashion was a literature which tapped into a memory of the

French Revolution that had attached itself in a very particular way to the dramatic years of 1793 and 1794. In the works of several of the great nineteenth-century writers (François-René de Chateaubriand, Victor Hugo, George Sand, Stendhal, Gustave Flaubert, Alexandre Dumas *père*, Honoré de Balzac, Jules Barbey d'Aurevilly, Erckmann-Chatrian, Eugène Le Roy, and Jules Vallès, down to Romain Roland and Anatole France) the debates and issues of the century were revisited: the Republic, friction between the state and religion, patriotism, notions of "popular" or "national" sovereignty, democracy, public education, and so on. As Victor Hugo summed it up in his *William Shakespeare* (1864): "The Revolution, the whole Revolution, there is the source of literature in the nineteenth century ... Democracy is in this literature. The Revolution forged the bugle; the nineteenth century sounds it."

Artists were convinced that an exceptional phenomenon that occurred at the end of the eighteenth century had carried their generation along in an irreversible movement of which they were both the heirs and the spokesmen. Thanks to the new technique of lithography, the word also profited from images that, depending on the tenor of the works of which they were part, functioned as either secular and republican or royalist and counter-revolutionary illustrations. Both the historical novel, which was very popular during the nineteenth century, and history books benefited from these illustrative additions. Apart from Tocqueville (too "philosophical") and Michelet, whose writing already called on the imagination of the reader, all nineteenth-century historians had their works illustrated, notably by the Johannot brothers or Raffet, while the publisher Furne played a dominant role in these various undertakings. When the Musée de l'Histoire de France, established in 1833 at Versailles by Louis-Philippe, was showing the national story as a great book of history, books themselves contained illustrations that claimed "to restore a kind of 'film' of history regarded as a series of strong images that the reader was expected to run through while turning the pages" (Le Men 1999).The iconographic story was taken up again in the twentieth century when cinematographers fell in love with the French Revolution. *Napoléon* by Abel Gance, a film that, despite its title, was dedicated to exalting the events of the revolutionary decade, made free use of illustrations found by the director in his extensive reading in preparation for his masterpiece. The French Revolution is an event frequently represented on film. Researchers have compiled a list of almost 300 made after 1897, a figure one might almost double given the large number of those from the silent era that were made (notably in Italy) but have disappeared. Cinema thus greatly contributed to the writing and memory of the Revolution, taking its inspiration in the early years from nineteenth-century historians and novelists (for example, Dickens and *A Tale of Two Cities* in the English-speaking world), and later by producing films that put forward a more personal view of revolutionary events, while at the same time carrying the imprint of the historical and political context of the times in which they were made. Thus *Orphans of the Storm* by D.W. Griffith (1921) reacted to the Russian Revolution of 1917. Jean Renoir's *La Marseillaise* (1938) should be viewed in the context of the political situation of the Popular Front when the threat of war with Nazi Germany became clear. In 1949 *Reign of Terror* by Anthony Mann referred back to the Cold War and Andrzej Wajda's *Danton* (1983) to the state of Poland during the 1980s as the socialist bloc was disintegrating. Although in some of these works the French Revolution was no more than a pretext for reflecting on the circumstances of the day, it still provided, because of its impact on the collective memory and its expressive force, an essential means of indirectly defending a cause and arousing debate.

Today the memory of the Revolution is less important than in 1848 or at the start of the Third Republic or even in the 1980s. While French politicians continue to refer to it, it survives, as it did in the nineteenth century, as an object of either admiration or rejection, and even though it is often only vaguely or confusedly evoked, it continues, as recently shown (Biard forthcoming), to allow people, through quotation or metaphor, to stigmatize and thus highlight tenaciously held public opinion of the right or left.

After more than two centuries the Revolution has left many memorial symbols: from the national motto on the facade of town halls, to the three colors of the national flag (according to Maurice Agulhon (1981) "the republican trinity"), a national anthem (*La Marseillaise*), a national holiday (14 July), and many other symbols, emblematic of a rich presence that will live forever. But apart from this symbolic material that could be the object of various celebrations or iconoclastic rejection, the memory of the Revolution, established with greater or lesser success by the republican state on the occasion of three official commemorations, is translated these days into a more or less intangible patrimonial legacy, which is still the foundation of public institutions, of individual freedoms, and of a form of egalitarian democracy that lives not only in France, but also in those countries (such as Italy) that partly inherited it when they became republics.

The Revolution thus appears as an act of choice, inscribed in parliamentary life and the democratic and political procedures at the heart of which freedom of expression and opinion are promoted. The revolutionary event restored and subdivided again France's national territory to allow the state to intervene more effectively and rationally across the whole country, contributing to the generation of a revolution in customs and in minds (Vovelle 2007). It abolished the threefold division of society into those who command, those who pray, and those who work: a radical and fundamental social change. The "revolutionized France" of the centuries following 1789 would be marked for all time by this period. In the same way the insurrections that occurred in the French colonies during the revolutionary decade contained within themselves other revolutions that accompanied the great international changes of the nineteenth and twentieth centuries.

Notes

1 It is not possible to establish an exhaustive list of the historians who, outside France, have greatly contributed to the revitalization of the study of the problems of the French Revolution over more than twenty years, but we can cite, in addition to the historians represented in this collection: David Bell, Ralf Blaufarb, Haïm Burstin, Malcolm Crook, David Hopkin, Melvin Edelstein, David Garrioch, Jeff Horn, Lynn Hunt, Colin Jones, Darrin McMahon, Ted Mardagant, Anna-Maria Rao, Rolf Reichardt, Jay Smith, and Timothy Tackett.

2 *Le Monde*, 16–17 July 1989.

References

Agulhon, Maurice (1981). *Marianne into Battle: Republican Imagery and Symbolism in France, 1789–1880.* Cambridge: Cambridge University Press.

Biard, Michel (forthcoming). "Les Références à la Révolution dans les débats parlementaires français des années 2000." In Martial Poirson (ed.). *Mythologies révolutionnaires.*

Bloch, Marc (1949). "Apologie pour l'histoire ou métier d'historien." *Cahiers des Annales*, 3.

Bois, Jean-Pierre (1991). *Histoire des 14 Juillet, 1789–1919.* Rennes: Ouest-France.

Darriulat, Philippe (2010). *La Muse du peuple: Chansons politiques et sociales en France 1815–1871.* Rennes: Presses Universitaires de Rennes.

Dupuy, Pascal and Claude Mazauric (2005). *La Révolution française: Regard d'auteurs.* Paris: Vuibert.

Forrest, Alan (2009). *The Legacy of the French Revolutionary Wars: The Nation-in-Arms in French Republican Memory.* Cambridge: Cambridge University Press.

Fureix, Emmanuel (2009). "L'Iconoclasme politique: Un combat pour la souveraineté (1814–1816)." In Annie Duprat (ed.). *Révolution et mythes identitaires: Mots, violences, mémoire.* Paris: Nouveau Monde. 173–195.

Furet, François (ed.) (1989). *L'Héritage de la Révolution française.* Paris: Hachette.

Hobsbawm, Eric J. (2007). *Aux armes historiens: Deux siècles d'histoire de la Révolution française.* Paris: La Découverte.

Kaplan Steven L. (1995). *Farewell Revolution: The Historians' Feud, France 1789/1989.* Ithaca, N.Y.: Cornell University Press.

Le Men, Ségolène (1999). "Raffet illustrateur de la Révolution." In *Raffet 1804–1860.* Paris: Éditions Herscher.

Luzzatto, Sergio (1991). *Mémoire de la Terreur.* Lyon: Presses Universitaires de Lyon.

McMahon, Darrin (2001). *Enemies of the Enlightenment: The French Counter-Enlightenment and the Making of Modernity.* Oxford: Oxford University Press.

Martin, Jean-Clément (1989). *La Vendée de la mémoire (1800–1980).* Paris: Seuil.

Mazeau, Guillaume (2009). *Le Bain de l'Histoire: Charlotte Corday et l'attentat contre Marat 1793–2009.* Seyssel: Champ Vallon.

Ory, Pascal (1992). *Une nation pour mémoire: 1889, 1939, 1989, trois jubilés révolutionnaires.* Paris: Fondation Nationale des Sciences Politiques.

Shafer, David A. (2005). *The Paris Commune: French Politics, Culture, and Society at the Crossroads of the Revolutionary Tradition and Revolutionary Socialism.* London: Palgrave Macmillan.

Soboul, Albert (1974). "Historiographie révolutionnaire classique et tentatives révisionnistes". *La Pensée* (177), 40–58.

Vovelle, Michel (2007). *1789: L'héritage et la mémoire.* Toulouse: Privat.

Further Reading

Aubry, Dominique (1988). *Quatre-Vingt-Treize et les Jacobins: Regards du 19e siècle.* Lyon: Presses Universitaires de Lyon.

Caron, Pierre (1946). "Le Cent-Cinquantenaire de la Révolution française." *AHRF*, 18: 97–114.

Collectif (1992). *Le XIXe siècle et la Révolution française.* Paris: Créaphis.

Garcia, Patrick (2000). *Le Bicentenaire de la Révolution française: Pratiques sociales d'une commémoration.* Paris: CNRS.

Gérard, Alice (1970). *La Révolution française: Mythes et interprétations.* Paris: Flammarion.

Gildea, Robert (1994). *The Past in French History.* New Haven and London: Yale University Press.

Huard, Raymond (1988). "La Révolution française, événement fondateur: Le Travail de l'histoire sur l'héritage et la tradition." *Cahiers d'histoire de l'Institut de recherches marxistes,* 32: 54–71.

Mazauric, Claude (2009). *Histoire de la Révolution française et la pensée marxiste.* Paris: PUF.

Mellon, Stanley (1958). *The Political Uses of History: A Study of Historians in the French Restoration.* Stanford, Calif.: Stanford University Press.

Nora, Pierre (ed.) (1984–92). *Les Lieux de mémoire.* Paris: Gallimard.

Orr, Linda (1990). *Headless History: Nineteenth-Century French Historiography of the Revolution.* Ithaca, N.Y., and London: Cornell University Press.

Peyrard, Christine and Michel Vovelle (eds.) (2002). *Héritage de la Révolution française à la lumière de Jaurès.* Aix-en-Provence: Presses Universitaires de Provence.

Index

A Companion to the French Revolution, First Edition. Edited by Peter McPhee.

CPSIA information can be obtained
at www.ICGtesting.com
Printed in the USA
BVHW082118271219
567911BV00005B/28/P

9 781118 977521